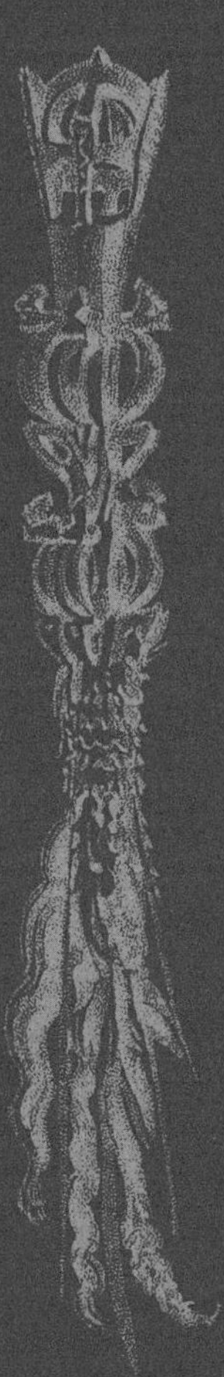

FOOD FOR THE FLAMES

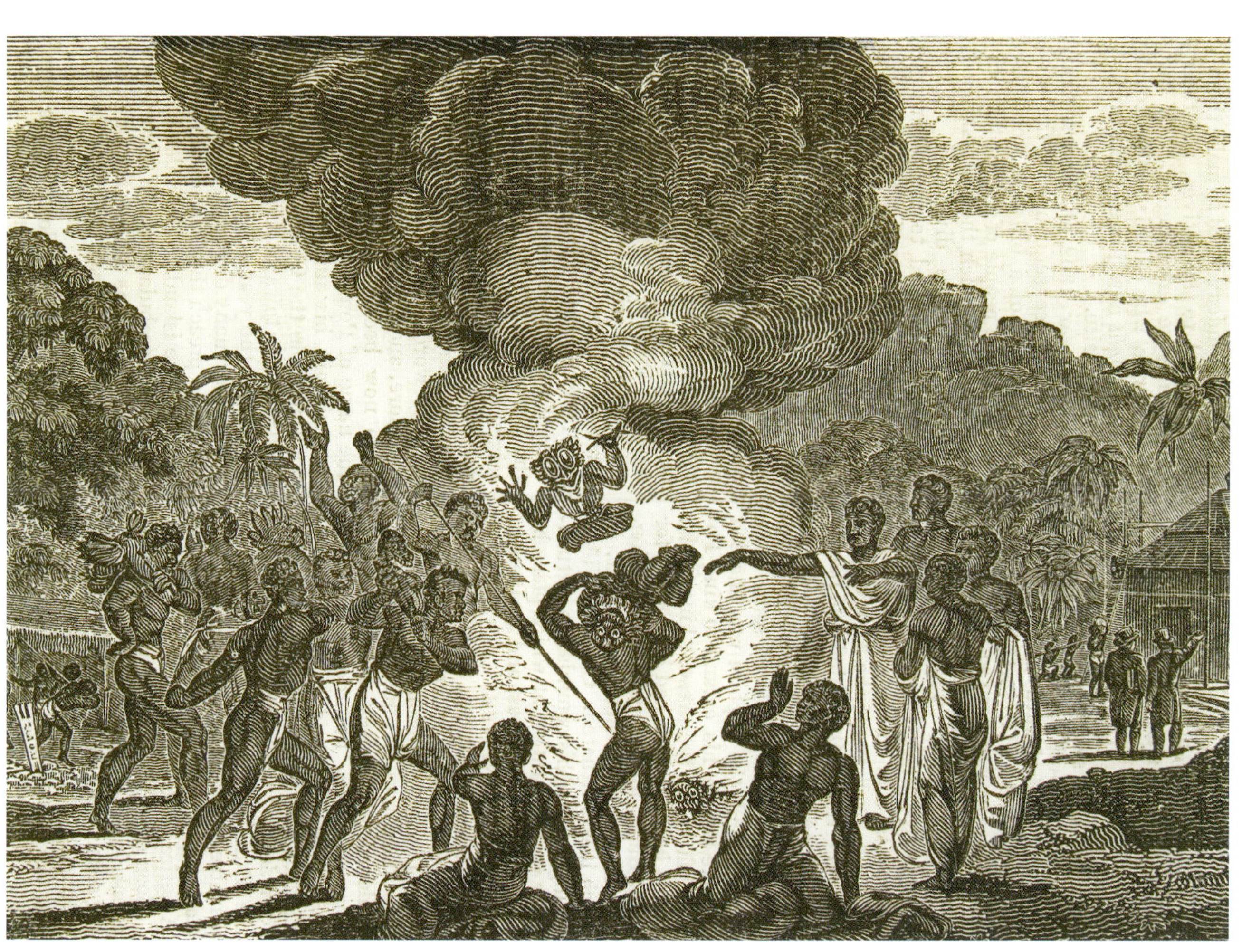

Food for the Flames

Idols and Missionaries in Central Polynesia

David Shaw King

Photography by Brian Carlson
Foreword by David Attenborough

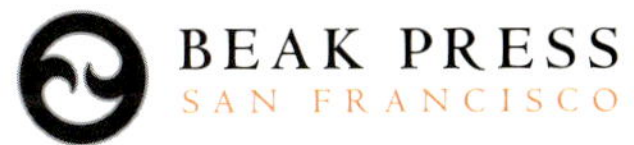
BEAK PRESS
SAN FRANCISCO

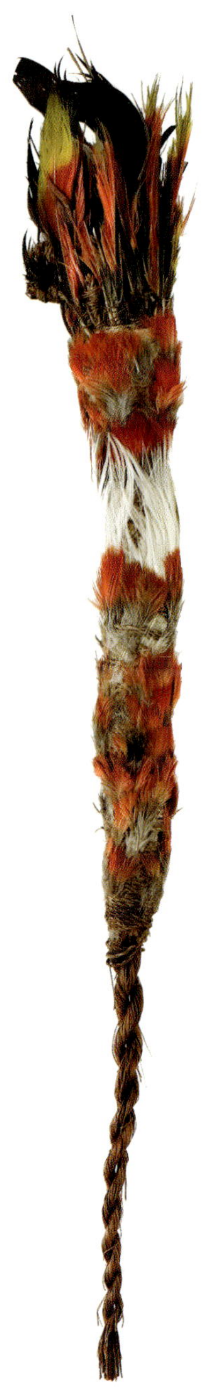

Contents

Acknowledgements

For innumerable helpful comments during the preparation of this book, I wish to thank Niel Gunson—also David Attenborough, Alison Twells, Rolf Du Rietz. For superb photographic and computer duty throughout, Brian Carlson. For expert help in producing this book, Chris Hall. For invaluable assistance at the British Museum, Jill Hasell, Jonathan King, James Hamill, Jenny Newell, Dorota Starzecka; at the LMS archives, Council for World Mission, School of Oriental and African Studies, University of London, Joanne Ichimura, Rosemary Seton; at Museum of Anthropology and Archaeology, University of Cambridge, Rachel Hand, Anita Herle; at Auckland Museum, Roger Neich, Fuli Pereira, Kryzstoff Pfeiffer; at The Bishop Museum, Betty Kam, BJ Short; at the Mitchell Library, Tracy Bradford; at the Hancock Museum, Leslie Jessop, Andrew Parkin, Gillian Robinson, Kelly Brown, Rachael Metcalfe; at the National Library of Australia, Sylvia Carr, Linda McInnes; at the Natural History Museum, London, Judith Magee; at the Congregational Library and Dr Williams's Library, Alice Ford-Smith; at the National Gallery of Australia, Michael Gunn; at the Field Museum, Christopher Philipp; at the Sutro Library, Martha Whittaker; at Otago Museum, Moira White. Thanks also to the staff of the Alexander Turnbull Library, Wellington; the Peabody Essex Museum, Salem; the Bancroft Library, University of California, Berkeley. I am grateful as well to Adelaide de Menil, Edmund Carpenter, Robert Paterson, Tim Teuten, Julian Harding, KJ Hewett, Irene Fletcher, Susan Attenborough, George Ortiz, Nelson Graburn, Ira Schrank, Valerie Reichert, Greg Dening, Patricia Curtan, Hermione Waterfield, Ordle, Sharleen Zhou, Steven Ruzin, Denise Schichnes, Adrienne Kaeppler, Arnold Falick, David Abel, Murray Frum, Steven Hooper, and Lewis Feldman. Finally, I especially thank Niloufer Ichaporia King for her unstinting tolerance and advice, and for her consummately succinct review of the initial manuscript—'unreadable'.

David Shaw King

Foreword

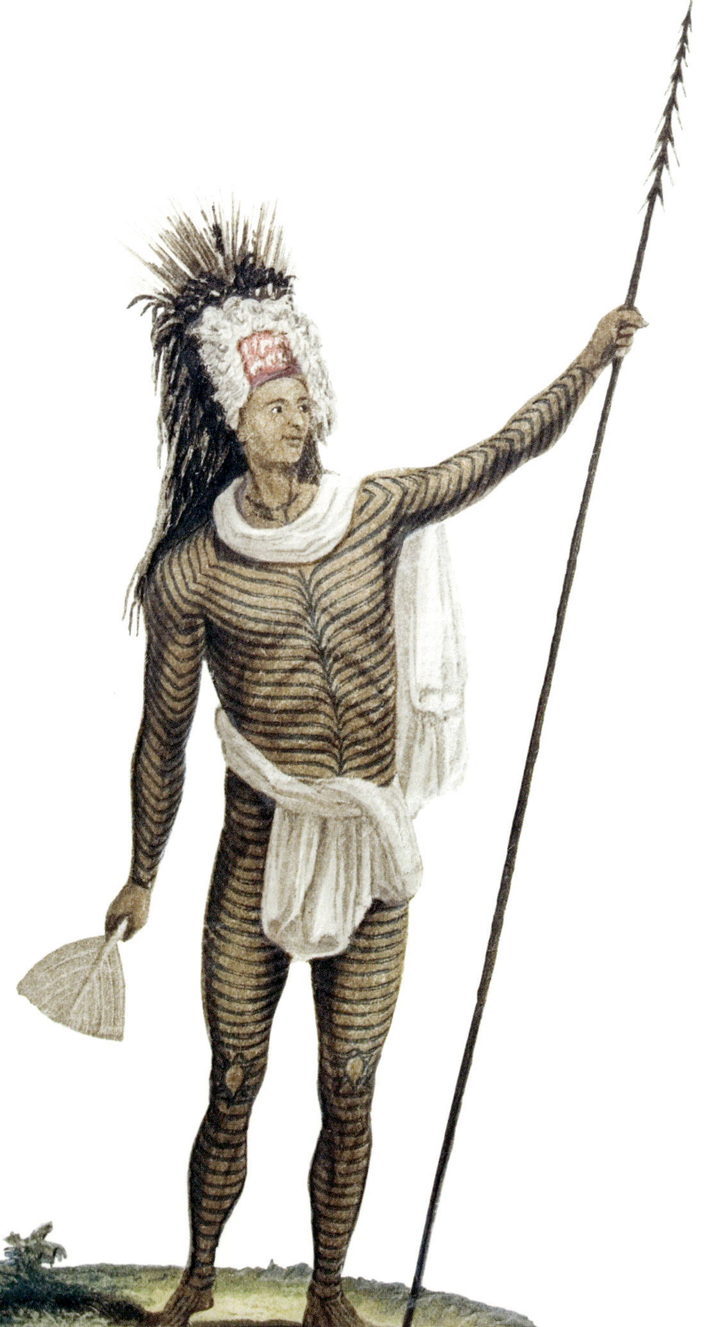

ANTHROPOLOGISTS AND MISSIONARIES are often supposed to be in conflict. The first, after all, are concerned with understanding, recording, even preserving the customs and beliefs of the people they study. The second do quite the opposite. They seek to destroy such traditions and replace them with beliefs of their own. Such generalisations may or may not be true. But one thing is quite certain. The missionaries generally got there first.

That was undoubtedly the case, as far as the Polynesian people of the Pacific are concerned. The European explorers of the last quarter of the eighteenth century who followed Magellan into the Pacific found in Polynesia islands of extravagant beauty, inhabited by people who had achieved an astonishingly sophisticated level of civilisation. Missionaries were quick to follow in the explorers' wake. Thirty, from the London Missionary Society, landed on Tahiti in 1797. Their aim, in the words of one of them, was to convert what they saw as 'a moral desert' into 'the garden of the Lord'. So it was missionaries and not anthropologists—who in any case did not then exist as such—who first recorded Polynesian traditions, beliefs and customs.

They were appalled by what they found—human sacrifice, loose sexual morals, infanticide, and idolatry. That being so, you might imagine that they would have done their best to eliminate all memory and material trace of the beliefs that they so abominated. And they attempted to do so—at least ostensibly. Indeed, they proclaimed their success on an island, symbolically, by persuading the people to make bonfires of their 'idols'. Paradoxically, however, some of the missionaries

(left) Te po, a Chief of Rarotonga. *Baxter colour print, 1837 (detail of fig. 101).*

recorded a great deal about Polynesian cultures. One of them, Rev John Williams, even gave instructions that what he described as 'the best' of the idols should be saved and sent back to their London headquarters so that the Society's supporters could visualise the magnitude of their victory over paganism. What he meant by 'the best' we can only guess. Maybe he meant the most finely worked and the most spectacular or the ones that the Polynesians themselves considered the most powerful. In one instance, he also asked that full details of the idols' names, use and symbolism should accompany them.

The objects themselves were very strange and varied. Many were carved from wood, others from stone. Some were hung with feathers, decorated with shells or swathed with bark cloth and bound with coconut fibre. A few were several feet long, others only a few inches. Initially they were kept in the Society's headquarters but eventually they were loaned and finally sold to the British Museum where most of them now reside, long ago separated from the meagre ethnological information that had originally been associated with them.

The author of this book, by profession, is neither an anthropologist nor a missionary. He is a molecular biochemist concerned with analysing the structure of protein molecules and synthesising new ones. But he is also a dedicated student of the material culture of the Pacific islands who uses his scientific mind and eye to detect tiny details—the weave and entwinings of cordage, the sharpness of edge in a wooden carving, the precise subspecies of a decorative molluscan shell—and uses them to determine the age and provenance of objects from the Pacific. His focus here is on central Polynesia—the Society, the Austral and the Cook Islands—and on the first Europeans who actually lived there and learned the local language, the missionaries. Curiously, this subject has remained largely neglected until now.

This book does much to fill the gap. The author has mined a large number of varied sources—journals from Spaniards from Peru, from Bougainville and from Bligh; missionaries' hand-written letters, lists, reports and journals; dictionaries and glossaries of the time; in addition to their published writings that many today would find unreadably dull. In doing so he has unearthed a great deal of new information. He examines, for example, a large group of enigmatic feather-decorated objects that have resided in the British Museum for the last 120 years for the most part unpublished and un-exhibited. They are identified as 'family gods' on the basis of an unpublished manuscript from the Society's archive which lists the idols and carefully describes their functions, names and attributes. In several cases he has been able to match these with particular objects in the British Museum.

These discoveries are set out in the pages that follow. They are fascinating and revelatory. And sometimes they are very surprising indeed for they shed new and intriguing light not only on the beliefs and attitudes of the Polynesians, but on the extraordinary Europeans who devoted their lives to trying to destroy those beliefs and yet enabled this book to resurrect them.

David Attenborough

(opposite) Missionary emblem from William Carey's An Enquiry into the Obligations of Christians to Use Means for the Conversion of the Heathens, 1792. The emblem incorporates Christian symbols of the gospel (centre) and eternity (snake); the fish net and crossed sickles are for harvesting souls. Carey's book provided a principal armature for the formation of the LMS and included a job description for missionaries. Courtesy British Library.

Food for the Flames

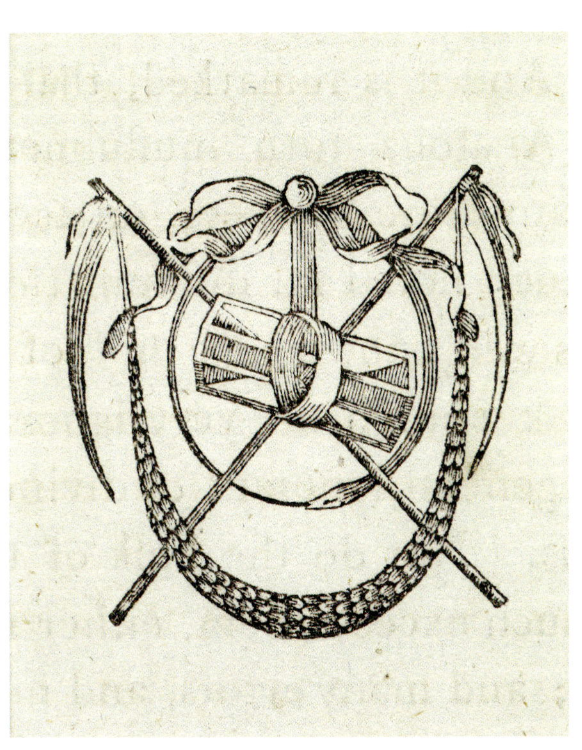

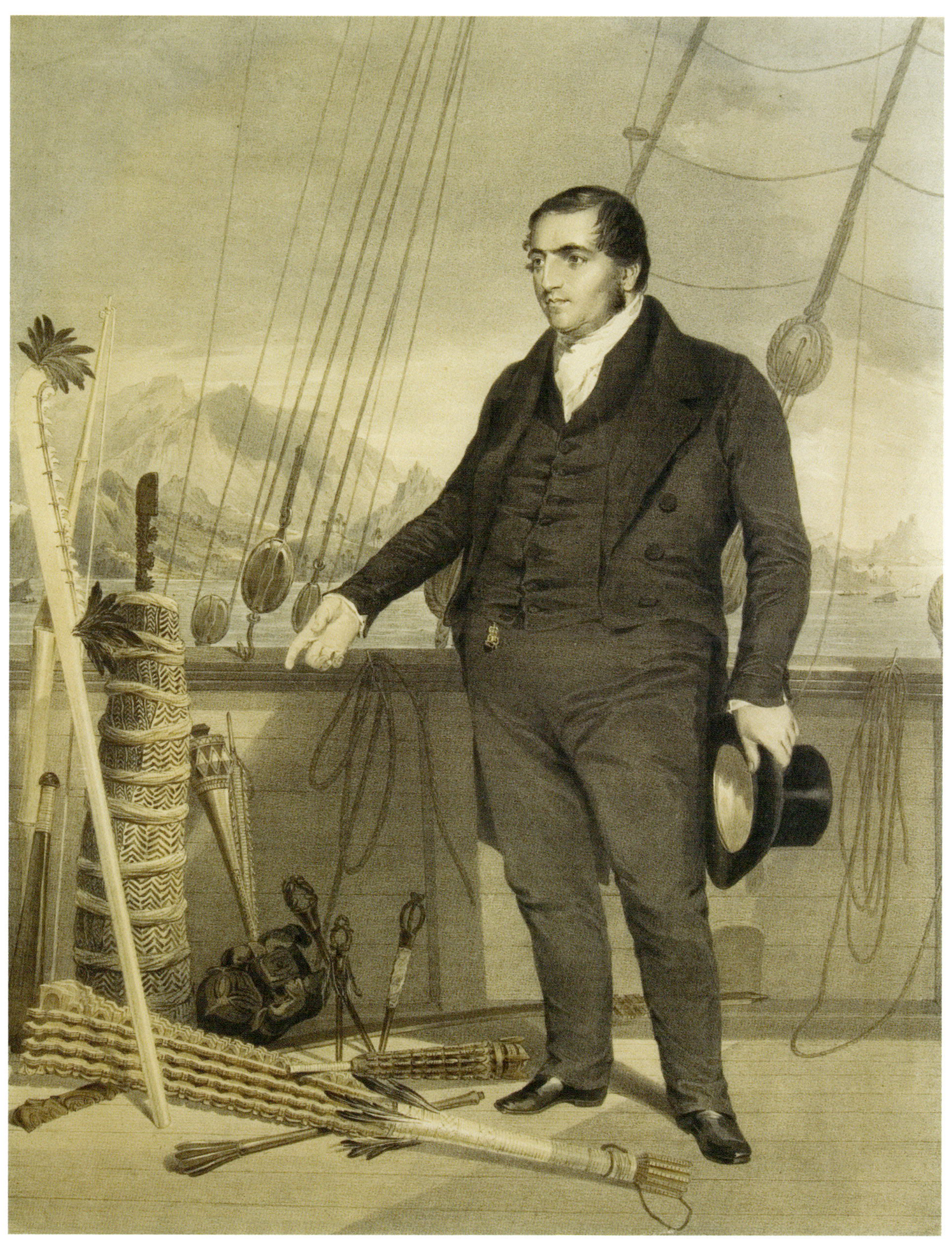

1 *Colour lithograph of English missionary Rev John Williams on the deck of a ship, with Polynesian idols lying about his feet; a faithful rendering of the Henry Anelay watercolour in the Rex Nan Kivell collection (NLA, Canberra). Artist unknown—perhaps Anelay himself; ca 1838–1840. LMS archives, SOAS. 35 x 44.5cm.*

FROM TITLE PAGE, *MISSIONARY CHRONICLE*, JUNE 1822.

Introduction

IN THE REX NAN KIVELL COLLECTION of Pacificana at the National Library of Australia is an unusual watercolour by a little-known artist named Henry Anelay (1817–83).[1] This small painting records a particular moment when the lives of the people of central Polynesia—the Society, Austral, and Cook Islands—intersected with the lives of the first Europeans to settle there, who were English missionaries. It is a portrait of one of them, the Reverend John Williams, born Tottenham High Cross, London, 29 June 1796, and killed at Erromango, Vanuatu (New Hebrides), 20 November 1839. John Williams was one of the earlier missionaries in the South Sea. Williams was ambitious; he became the best known of all of them, and was generally well-regarded.

The Anelay portrait depicts Williams, dressed in proper Sunday attire, on the deck of a ship. In the background is a lush high island—perhaps Ra'iatea, perhaps Rarotonga.[2] What is unusual about this portrait is what Williams is doing: he is gesturing towards an array of 14 objects, all Polynesian, strewn about the deck at his feet and leaning against the gunwales. Some of these objects are weapons, but most of them are idols—the very objects the missionaries found so offensive, and travelled 20,000 miles to eradicate.[3]

The Anelay watercolour provides a vivid image of the unlikely association of Polynesian idols with an

[1] National Library of Australia (NLA); 34 x 43cm; no date; probably 1838–1840. An accurate colour lithograph(?) version of this, also undated, perhaps by Anelay himself, is in the LMS archive at SOAS (fig. 1). Hardly anything is known about Anelay, except that he worked in England as a landscape watercolourist and book illustrator; he was born in Hull and worked at Sydenham from 1848. He illustrated *London Magazine, Illustrated London News, The British Workman, Uncle Tom's Cabin, The Mother's Picture Alphabet*, 1843–1861.

[2] The painting was first reproduced in the second edition of Bernard Smith's *European Vision and the South Pacific*; B Smith 1985,322 fig. 203.

[3] One other depiction of Williams with an idol is in the SOAS CWM LMS archives: a photograph of a lithograph (location of original unknown) showing Williams at desk, quill in hand, in front of him a breadfruit the size of an orange, and a 14-foot Rarotongan staff god, depicted in as many inches, on which is draped a shell necklace—all objects obviously copied from Baxter's wood engraving in Williams 1837,118. The name D Pasmore is inscribed; SOAS LMS SSP box2 folio5.

English missionary and raises a number of questions. For instance, what exactly are all these Polynesian objects, and why are they lying on the deck of a ship? Are the drawings of actual objects? If so, where are they now? Why is Williams gesturing towards them? Who made them, why, when, where? Using this picture as a nucleus, this book aims to provide some background and some details about the missionaries, the idols, and the people who made them.

John Williams started out as a worker at an iron-mongery, underwent a sudden conversion at age 18, and joined what soon became known as the London Missionary Society (LMS). The Society began as a non-denominational Evangelical Christian organization, founded in 1795, whose purpose Williams describes thus:

> The Missionary enterprise regards the whole globe as its sphere of operation. It is founded upon the grand principles of Christian benevolence, made imperative by the command of the ascending Saviour, and has for its primary object to roll away from six hundred millions of the race of Adam the heavy curse which rests upon them;—to secure their elevation to the dignity of intelligent creatures and children of God;— to engage their thoughts in the contemplation, and to gladden their hearts with the prospects of immortality;— . . . in a word, 'to fill the whole earth with the glory of the Lord.'[4]

At age 20, Williams set out from London to spread the word of the Christian God to the people of the South Sea, whom he perceived as idol-worshipping heathens, groaning under the reign of superstition and ignorance: 'It so outrages all decency, that the heart is hurried away in horror and disgust from the contemplation of the deep moral degradation into which our race is sunk.'[5] Williams and the South Sea Mission intended to rectify this situation. 'That great and glorious object, which is dearer to me than life—[is] the diffusion of the Gospel in the Islands of the South Seas . . . still sitting in the

region of the shadow of death.'[6] He sailed in 1816, with his 19-year-old wife, Mary Chauner, in the fourth wave of LMS missionaries,[7] was based at the central LMS station on Ra'iatea, travelled throughout central Polynesia for 17 years, oversaw the 'conversion' of more than ten islands, and is perhaps best known for his 'discovery' in July 1823 of the spectacular island of Rarotonga.[8]

Anelay's image of Williams was evidently copied from one of the five well-known portraits of Williams (see figs. 22, 23, 25).[9] These portraits are all prints, done by George Baxter (1804–1867), a popular book illustrator, who worked in collaboration with the official publisher to the LMS from 1838 to 1847, John Snow, 26, Paternoster Row, London. Baxter had patented an elaborate multi-woodblock, oil-based ink colour printing process; his aim was to bring colour pictures into the lives of those who could not afford oil paintings.[10] Williams and Baxter became friends. Other than the backgrounds, the portraits are all similar. They depict a rather portly man somewhere in his forties. Williams' features, expression, and dress are alike in all five. They were most likely done when Williams came back

---

4 From John Williams, *A Narrative of Missionary Enterprises in the South Sea Islands*, 1837, page x.

5 Williams 1837,102.

6 Williams in Campbell, 1838,vi.

7 See below, 'The early days of the LMS'.

8 Regarding the discovery of the other Cook Islands: Cook passed by the atoll Manuae (which he had sighted and named Hervey's Island in 1773 [second voyage]; he also sighted Palmerston and Suwarrow), and 'discovered' Atiu, Mangaia and Takutea in 1777 (third voyage) but was unaware of the other principal islands in the group. He originally named the group Sandwich Islands but changed the name to the Hervey Group; Hon Capt AJ Hervey was one of the Lords of the Admiralty and Earl of Bristol. The group was renamed Cook Islands in 1824. Aitutaki was 'discovered' by Lieutenant Bligh 11 April 1789, about a fortnight before the mutiny. Rarotonga: unrecorded 'discovery' in 1789 by the *Bounty* mutineers, who did not land; visited by the trading ships *Seringapatam* and *Cumberland* in 1814, prior to Williams and Bourne in 1823 (see Findlay 1877; Gosset 1940; Sharp 1960). Mitiaro and Mauke: Williams and Bourne 1823.

9 The portraits appear in a number of London Missionary Society publications; some were published as separates; all are catalogued in CTC Lewis 1908. Miniature portraits of Williams and his wife, not by Baxter, are in the LMS archives (SOAS SSP box 2 folio5; fig. 26). All but one (fig. 28) of Baxter's original watercolour sketches seem to be lost.

10 Baxter's 'oil pictures' were laborious productions. Some were said to involve over 100 blocks, in 22 colours, printed in perfect register. They became extremely popular in England—reaching the point of 'Baxtermania'. Testimony to this is a Christie's catalogue for Summer 1924: Canaletto £52; Constable £39; Guardi £242; Gainsborough £68; Goya £17; two Baxters, £250 and £900.

to England for nearly four years[11] prior to his return to the South Sea for the second and last time. The Anelay portrait is clearly based on the Baxter portraits and is undated; it was probably done about 1838–1840. No connection between Baxter and Anelay has come to light.

Regarding the 14 artefacts depicted in Anelay's painting, however, the situation is different. Four of them were clearly copied from wood engravings—again by Baxter—published in Williams' book, *Narrative of Missionary Enterprises in the South Sea Islands*, 1837. But regarding the rest of the objects, illustrations were not available during Anelay's lifetime, and his renderings of them appear in sufficient detail that they can be identified as actual objects in various LMS collections; evidently Anelay had seen these objects firsthand. Bernard Smith, in discussing the Anelay painting, quotes an LMS sermon delivered in Glasgow in 1818: '[W]hat sort of deities must they be, . . . images so ridiculously fantastic, so monstrously uncouth, so frightfully distorted'[12] and goes on to make the point that artists of the early nineteenth century 'not infrequently resorted to distortions of their own to further enhance the repulsive appearance of the idols.'[13] This is sometimes true; a number of nineteenth century renderings of South Sea idols are distorted beyond recognition; a good exam-

ple is in the woodcut 'The Destruction of the Idols at Tahiti' shown in figure 6.[14] Fortunately, in the case of the Anelay watercolour, this is not the case. Five of the 14 objects in the watercolour are weapons; with one exception, the rest are idols.

The aim of this book has been to fill in some background about the first English missionaries to come to Polynesia, and to present as much information as possible about central Polynesian idols, garnered from the accounts of the explorers and visitors to the Pacific in the late eighteenth century and from the London Missionary Society archives, publications, and collections. These are the earliest sources available. The period discussed spans from 1767 into the 1830s.

Much of what is presented here concerns the gods and idols of the Cook Islands. Every scholar of Polynesian cultural history points out that our knowledge of the amazingly isolated yet culturally linked islands of Polynesia is scant, especially regarding the Cook Islands. As Polynesian scholar Peter Buck put it, 'Unfortunately, no artist such as Webber [on Cook's third voyage] had the opportunity of depicting the native temples when religious ritual was being conducted, hence material for study is meager in comparison with that for the Society Islands and Hawaii.'[15] In the course of this investigation, a number of objects, catalogues, manuscript journals, lists, letters, and published writings have surfaced which shed light on this neglected landscape and which have up to this time not been considered. The outcome of this search is the subject of the following text and images. Throughout, the primary sources are allowed to speak for themselves.

---

[11] June 1834–April 1838, age 37–41; he returned to England and gave lectures in order to stir up interest in the South Sea Mission for fundraising reasons. He spoke in Glasgow, Bristol, Manchester, Leeds, Liverpool, Birmingham. Audiences were sympathetic and generous; the City of London gave £500. He returned to the South Sea with Captain Morgan on the *Camden*, purchased by the directors; 'The Departure of the Camden, Missionary Ship, April 11, 1838' was the first Baxter print that was produced as a separate; see fig. 14.

[12] B Smith 1985 footnote 3; sermon by Scottish Congregationalist Dr Ralph Wardlaw, published in *Missionary Sketches* 3, October 1818, in an article entitled 'The contemplation of heathen idolatry an excitement to missionary zeal'.

[13] B Smith 1985,322.

[14] *Missionary Sketches* 6, July 1819.

[15] Buck 1944,308. Sir Peter Buck, or Te Rangi Hiroa, a Maori physician turned anthropologist, was director of the BP Bishop Museum in Honolulu, 1936–1951.

aha-mata-tini. s. Sennet of various hues, fastened as external decorations to the god.

Te bure bure o te aha ra, e te rahi o te avei o te matatini ia e o to te atua ra una-una, o te ura ra te mea maitai roa.

The different colours of the Sennet, in the numerous strands, are the multiplied, faces, the decorations of the God, but scarlet feathers are best of all.

2 *Entry for* aha-mata-tini, *coloured sennit used on god images; from the only surviving volume (vol 6) of LMS missionary John Orsmond's 16–volume manuscript Tahitian dictionary. Inscribed dates 1850, 1851; possibly a copy. Mitchell Library MSS A2609.*

ONE

Sources

THE VERY FIRST SOURCES regarding the people and cultures of central Polynesia are the unedited journals of the first Europeans to contact the islands, the explorers of the late eighteenth century: Samuel Wallis, Louis Antoine de Bougainville, James Cook, and Spaniards from Peru, José Andía y Varela and Domingo Boenechea. They touched at a number of Pacific islands, but usually only to provision their ships with fruits, greens, wood, water, hogs and the like, or to ascertain that there was none to be had, and then to move on. At best, they stayed a few weeks, long enough to learn a few dozen words of the language. Cook, by far the most objective and inquiring of them, understood the limitations imposed by these brief contacts with other cultures, and how much he was missing; for instance, speaking of Tahiti: 'Their Religion . . . is a thing I have learnt so little of that I hardly dare touch upon it, and should have pass'd it over in silence. . . .'[1] Bougainville, also on the subject of Tahitian religion, performed an experiment; the result was inconclusive: 'Do they have a religion? Or not? I saw no temple. . . . In the leaders' houses one finds two large wooden figures, one for each gender. In order to find out whether these were idols, we knelt before them, then spat on them, stepped on them, these actions, each so different, attracted in equal the laughter of the watching Indians.'[2] It is quite remarkable in light of how brief their contact was, and how little they knew of the Polynesian dialects, that the earliest European visitors learned as much as they did.[3]

Essayist James Boswell found out firsthand that Cook was fully aware of the problems attendant to not knowing the language. Boswell dined with some

---

[1] Cook's *Journal*, July 1769; Beaglehole 1968 1,134.

[2] Dunmore 2002,73. CFP Fesche, a young volunteer on the *Boudeuse*, records the same incident (ibid.,260). See Neich 2007 re the remarkable indifference shown by Tongans towards what were supposedly figures of divinity, which were (quoting Forster) 'frequently trod upon and kicked about' when they were not inhabited by gods.

[3] See for example Wallis, Robertson, Cook, Banks, Parkinson, Ellis 1782, and especially Forster, re Tahiti. Boenechea as well mentions 'the many realistically carved figures they have in all their domains in the Island' (Cornet 1913 1,333).

members of the Royal Society, at the Mitre, 18 April 1776, two months before the third voyage:

> I placed myself next to Captain Cook and had a great deal of conversation with him. . . . Only I must observe that he candidly confessed to me that he and his companions who visited the South Sea Islands could not be certain of any information they got, or supposed they got, except as to objects falling under the observation of the senses; their knowledge of the language was so imperfect they required the aid of their senses, and anything they learnt about religion, government, or traditions might be quite erroneous.[4]

The most important primary sources regarding Polynesian culture are the accounts of the first Europeans who actually settled in Polynesia and stayed long enough to learn the language. The first of these was Máximo Rodríguez. Rodríguez was a young, friendly, enthusiastic Spanish marine from Peru who was assistant to the two inept, contemptuous and singularly unsuccessful Franciscan priests brought to Tahiti from Peru by captains Don Domingo de Boenechea and Don José Andía y Varela in 1774—between Cook's first and second visits. They came in order to Christianize the island, but failed to make even a beginning. The Spanish were in fact the first to send missionaries to Polynesia, 22 years before the LMS.[5] The Spanish called Tahiti Isla de Amat, after Don Manuel Amat, viceroy of Peru. Their ships were the *Águila* and the *Júpiter*. They brought a frame house, cattle, and provisions. Rodríguez, age 20, learned to speak Tahitian. Unlike the priests, he was deeply appreciative and respectful of Tahitians and their culture, befriending commoners and chiefs alike. His journal of the year he spent at Tautira is the first account of Polynesia and Polynesians that was written by someone who spoke the language. It is a major loss to the world that his *Extracto*—a detailed description of Tahitian culture and less of a daily narrative—has been 'lost' in Lima.[6]

The next Europeans to live in Polynesia long enough to learn the language fluently were the 19 'mutineers' from the *Bounty* who chose not to flee to Pitcairn Island with Fletcher Christian. They lived on Tahiti, and briefly on Tubua'i (in the Australs) in close contact with the islanders for a total of 29 months, from 1789 until Captain Edwards of the *Pandora* came to arrest them in 1791. Three of them kept journals: one was midshipman George Stewart (age 23–25); one was midshipman Peter Heywood (age 17–19); a probable third was boatswain's mate James Morrison (age 27–29). Heywood's journal contained 80 drawings. None of their journals survived the wreck of the *Pandora* on the Great Barrier Reef,[7] where Stewart died in an accident. Fortunately, Morrison reconstructed his own account back in Portsmouth, in 1792, aboard the *Hector*, while the mutineers awaited trial, sentencing, and execution or pardon. It is the earliest detailed account of Tahitian ethnography that exists.[8]

Another valuable source, now vanished, with the exception of a single entry, was a 'one hundred full-written folio page' vocabulary of Tahitian compiled by Peter Heywood. The first mention of its existence is in a letter written by Peter to his sister Nessy

---

4   Boswell's *Journal*, in Ryskamp and Pottle 1963,341. Banks, 1770: 'I shall give myself liberty of conjecturing and drawing conclusions from what I have observd, in which I may doubtless often be mistaken...' (Beaglehole 1963 2,1).

5   Voyages of the Spanish in Peru to Easter Island and to Tahiti—there were four of them between 1770 and 1775—have been largely ignored by historians, despite their having resulted in the 'discovery' of several islands including Ra'ivavae. Carlos III's October 1771 instructions relayed by Amat to Boenechea bear a striking resemblance to those issued by the directors of the Missionary Society to the English missionaries: 'The King directs that, in the Isle of San Carlos [Easter Island] his royal and Catholic zeal being kindled for the rescue of the natives from their miserable Idolatry, they may be converted by discreet and gentle means to a knowledge of the true God and the profession of our religion; [by establishing] a small settlement under the shadow of whose protection the Missionaries may make a beginning for implanting the seeds of the Gospel' (Corney 1913 1,265). Their second target was 'George' (Tahiti). Cook describes finding the abandoned settlement at Tautira and a large inscribed Spanish cross, which he reinscribed 'Georgias tertias rex' and replaced.

6   Tewsley's translation of coxswain Heinrich Zimmerman's account of Cook's third voyage mentions, 'In the interior of the [abandoned Spanish missionary] house [at Tautira] we found a barrel of Spanish writings.' This is not mentioned in Cook's journal; one wonders whether the barrel contained manuscripts; Tewsley and Anderson 1926.

7   Short extracts from the journals of Heywood and Stewart made by Captain Edwards of the *Pandora* are in the Ministry of Defense Library in London; see Rennie 1995,152.

8   Two versions survive in the Mitchell Library (ML), Sydney; the longer of them (MS2, 384 pages; ML MSS safe 1/42) was transcribed (omitting the numerous edits by Peter Heywood) and published by Owen Rutter; it is referred to here as Morrison 1935; see Du Rietz 1986. Both Morrison and Heywood were given death sentences and then pardoned. Neither actually took part in the mutiny; the term 'mutineer' is used here for identification only.

16 October 1792, a month after Peter received his death sentence: 'I am employing my leisure Hours in making a Vocabulary of the Otaheitian language.'[9] This vocabulary, like Morrison's account, was also written aboard the *Hector*, and was given to a clergyman from Suffolk by the name of William Howell, of Portsea, who attended the mutineers. Howell passed it on, along with Morrison's account, to LMS director Rev Dr Thomas Haweis (pronounced *haws*), who accompanied the first missionaries on the *Duff* at Spithead while they awaited for five weeks their departure to Tahiti.[10] A note in the 'Religious Intelligence' section of *Evangelical Magazine*, 1796, provides more details:

> Important information respecting Otaheite [Tahiti] . . . has been kindly communicated by the clergyman at Portsmouth, who attended the mutineers belonging to the *Bounty*, highly confirmative of every step the Directors have taken; and a vocabulary, or dictionary of the language, so complete, that the Missionaries will be able to learn enough of it on their voyage to converse with the natives as soon as they land on the Island.[11]

The missionaries copied Morrison's account and Heywood's vocabulary and made good use of both of these documents on the voyage. Forty-three years later, Rev John Campbell saw it as a sign: 'In connexion with the future evangelization of the islands of the South Sea . . . , the mutiny of the Bounty was one of those events in Providence, which plainly indicate the finger of God.'[12]

The first missionaries to arrive in Tahiti at the turn of the nineteenth century are also primary sources. They lived in Polynesia for years—Williams' first stint was close to 18 years, Henry Nott and William Henry were there 42 years, and John Davies 54 years—and they did, eventually, learn the language. Williams learned to speak both Tahitian and Rarotongan dialects with reasonable fluency. The early missionaries found Tahitian extremely difficult. *Duff* missionary John Jefferson commented, after two years on Tahiti, 'Our growth in the knowledge of the language still slow'; as fellow missionary Thomas Lewis put it, 'The more we acquire of it the more copious it appears to be.'[13] The eighteenth century explorers considered it a simple language of few words, and quickly learned a vocabulary sufficient for trading. Based on this view, the directors of the LMS figured that Tahitian could be mastered in three months. But Tahitian is in fact a rich language—one not easy to learn. It is replete with suffixes, prefixes, and infixes; words contain large numbers of vowels; subtle differences in pronunciation can impart different meanings to a single word. Arbitrary alterations were introduced from time to time on account of some words or syllables becoming sacred. Tahitians spoke rapidly and abbreviated words in conversation. Few missionaries became fluent, but of course some of their children did and later helped to translate and to revise the gospels published by the missionary presses.

The most proficient of the early missionaries at learning Tahitian was John Davies. Davies was an austere Welsh schoolmaster who arrived on the East Indiaman *Royal Admiral*, the second successful missionary voyage, in 1801; he was stationed on Tahiti, Huahine, and Mo'orea, until his death in 1855. Davies was bilingual (English and Welsh), and was a systematic linguist. By 1806, he had compiled a list of 2400 Tahitian words. He taught Tahitian to the later missionaries, including John Williams, John Orsmond and William Ellis. He published the first Tahitian grammars, starting in 1823, and a 12,000-word dictionary, which was printed by the LMS press in Papeete. It was ready for publication by 1838 but was not printed until 1851 because the missionaries could not agree on the orthography and because they had run out of type. Although he is named as author, other missionaries contributed to it: '9 April 1807. In the afternoon had a meeting to read our Taheitean English vocabulary . . . , commenced March 1805. From that time we have met twice a week … [and] paid a native to assure proper pronunciation.'[14]

9 Newbury Library; see Du Rietz 1986. The vocabulary was amongst Heywood's papers when he died in 1831, but has not been seen since.

10 Campbell 1840,156; Du Rietz 1986; Rennie 1995,156 and 160.

11 *Evangelical Magazine* October 1796,430. The O at the beginning of the word Tahiti was 'an article prefixed to proper names' and also could mean 'of, belonging to' (Davies 1851).

12 Campbell 1840,156.

13 Jefferson: *Trans Miss Soc* 1818,117. Diary of Lewis, 16 August 1798: *Haweis Papers Supplement*, Mitchell Library 4190X. See also Brown 1816,305.

14 *Trans Miss Soc* 1809 3,179.

The definitions in Davies' *Tahitian and English Dictionary*, assembled over a period of 38 years, take priority.

Although they learned the language, requisite of course for gaining knowledge about a culture, the English missionaries did not arrive in Tahiti until 1797—more than two decades after Wallis, Cook, Bougainville, and the Spaniards from Peru. Tahiti had changed in the meantime.

Captain George Vancouver saw these changes firsthand. He was on Tahiti for four weeks, beginning 27 December 1791. But he had been on Tahiti twice before, as a young gentleman on the *Resolution*, and as a midshipman on the *Discovery*—Cook's second and third voyages. He noticed, for example, the influence that European iron tools had wrought during those intervening 19 years:

> Their former tools and manufactures . . . are now growing fast out of use, and, I may add, equally out of remembrance. Of this we had convincing proof in the few of their bone, or stone tools, or utensils, that were seen amongst them; those offered for sale were of rude workmanship, and of an inferior kind, solely intended for our market, to be purchased by way of curiosity.[15]

Between 1792 and 1797, over a dozen European traders and whalers called at Tahiti. They carried with them European goods for the purpose of exchange, including an abundant supply of muskets and ammunition, and alcohol. They brought disease as well. Through these powerful agents, the population of Tahiti dropped from over 100,000 to 7,000.[16] Profound cultural and political change was inevitable.

The most enlightened of the early missionaries had ethnographic tendencies, and set out to learn about and to record the rapidly disappearing culture of 'old Tahiti'. John Davies has already been mentioned. Four years before him were John Jefferson, and William Henry, who arrived on the first missionary ship, the *Duff*. Next came John Orsmond and William Ellis. These five were sound missionary ethnographers. Missionary Charles Barff was an assiduous collector of traditions but unfortunately most of his papers were lost in a shipwreck. Most of Jefferson's journals are in the LMS archives at SOAS; many were published accurately in the LMS publication, *Transactions of the Missionary Society*. John Jefferson was a keen observer. His journals contain excellent, detailed accounts of missionary life during the difficult early years of the Tahitian Mission and offer many insights into Tahitian culture. They are a rich but generally neglected resource. One of his narratives especially relevant to this book is reproduced in Appendix 2.

Missionary John Orsmond arrived in 1817, the same year as Williams and Ellis. Orsmond was stationed on Mo'orea, Huahine, Ra'iatea, Borabora, and Tahiti. Over the course of 30 years, he compiled a detailed account of Tahitian legends, genealogies, and cultural history which he started writing in 1828 and presented to the French Ministère des Colonies in 1848. Unfortunately, this account was lost. His granddaughter, Miss Teuira Henry, who was also granddaughter of William Henry of the *Duff* voyage, devoted her life to restoring this work using what she possessed of her grandfather's original notes and manuscripts. She died in 1915, but fortunately her relatives and friends saw to its publication by the Bishop Museum in 1928. Orsmond's sources were Cook (through Hawkesworth), James Morrison, 'Pomare II and the priests generally' (he specifically credits Tamera, Pati'i, and Anani; Tahiti), as well as fellow missionaries and their wives. Orsmond also compiled what Niel Gunson refers to as an 'expanded dictionary', consisting of about 16 manuscript volumes, with detailed descriptions in English and in Tahitian accompanying each entry. Apparently only one of the 16 volumes still exists; it is a valuable resource, particularly regarding *aha* (sennit; see below).[17] With luck other volumes will some day come to light. Orsmond was dismissed from the LMS in 1845 for appearing to be too friendly with the French.

---

[15] Vancouver 1984 1,436; one year later, Lieutenant George Tobin, accompanying Bligh on the *Providence*, said the same thing about the same subject: '[N]ine tenths of those [adzes] brought home in the Providence were purposely made for sale. Though very profitable for them, the natives laughed at the avidity with which we coveted all their household and other goods' (Mackaness 1931,343).

[16] These numbers are of course very rough estimates; see Ellis 1844.

[17] Papers of Rev JM Orsmond, *Part of Tahitian Dictionary*; Mitchell MSS A2609; this volume, N°6, is inscribed with the dates 1850 and 1851; it may be a copy; see Gunson 1992,599.

Rev Dr Thomas Haweis, an LMS director in London and the principal proponent of the Tahitian Mission, compiled and edited, anonymously, the papers of Chief Officer William Wilson, Captain James Wilson, and the missionaries into an account of the first missionary voyage of the *Duff*; 12,600 copies were published in 1799, as an elegant illustrated quarto.[18] William Smith, age 21, a linen draper who went to Tahiti as a missionary, was the official chronicler of the voyage. The preliminary discourse on South Sea history was written by the other major proponent of the Tahitian Mission, the well-read Rev Samuel Greatheed. Rev John Campbell tells us what is clear on reading, that the source of the first appendix, about Tahiti, and a portion of the preliminary discourse, was the manuscript written by *Bounty* mutineer James Morrison aboard the *Hector*: '[Morrison's] description of [Tahiti] was extracted by Dr. Haweis, with little alteration but what he judged proper, in order to adapt it to this publication.'[19] This version of Morrison also appears anonymously in *The Universal Navigator and Modern Tourist*, 1805, as well as in William Smith's publication of 1813.

The most systematic missionary ethnographer was William Ellis.[20] Stationed at the LMS Tahitian missions on Eimeo (Mo'orea) and Huahine in 1817–22, Ellis was a careful, perceptive, and remarkably objective observer and historian. It was evident to him, as Vancouver had witnessed 26 years before, that extensive changes had taken place in Tahiti since Wallis' first visit in 1767: 'All their uses of antiquity have been entirely superceded by the new order of things . . . while the rising generation is growing up in total ignorance of all that distinguished their ancestors from themselves.'

Ellis wrote his detailed and oft-quoted two volume *Polynesian Researches*, published in 1829, 'to furnish . . . an authentic record . . . illustrating the essential characteristics of idolatry.'

He arrived in Tahiti after Christian conversion, so he only occasionally was an actual eyewitness to 'old Tahiti'.

Duff missionaries John Jefferson and William Henry were his primary sources; also John Davies, Charles Barff, John Orsmond and of course, James Morrison. It is a pity Ellis was stationed only in the Society Islands and in the Sandwich Islands (Hawai'i), and briefly so (four years and two years); although a secondary source, his *Polynesian Researches* is very valuable one.

Another useful source is the journal of Rev Daniel Tyerman and George Bennet Esq. In 1820, the directors of the LMS engaged Tyerman and Bennet to pay a visit to the missions in the South Sea. It had been over 20 years and several thousand pounds of expenses since the *Duff* had departed with the first load of missionaries; progress had been slow in coming, and the society wished an independent report, and advice. Bennet was a philanthropist from Yorkshire, Tyerman a minister on the Isle of Wight; he was also a naturalist, and could draw. They were both reluctant to go. 'The Deputation', as it was called, left on a whaler, the *Tuscan*, in 1821. Their journey took them throughout Polynesia, and to Java, Canton, Calcutta, Mauritius, and Madagascar, where Tyerman died: Bennet inadvertently hastened his death by letting 16 ounces of blood when Tyerman was ill and severely weak. Bennet returned to England in 1829. Their journal was assembled by a friend of Bennet's, a Sheffield publisher, poet, and composer of 400 hymns named James Montgomery, and was published in 1831—a vivid and informative account of an extraordinary journey covering 90,000 miles over eight years. Three of those years were spent in Polynesia; Tyerman and Bennet were pleased with the progress of the Tahitian Mission.[21]

All of the sources mentioned above, both explorer and missionary, pertain mostly to Tahiti. Far less is known about the other two principal island groups in central Polynesia, the Austral and the Cook Islands. The eighteenth-century explorers barely touched at these islands. Morrison provides a brief but informative account of Tubua'i in the Australs, where the mutineers attempted, unsuccessfully, to settle, in 1789.[22] The first Europeans to spend time in the Cook Islands were missionaries. They arrived in time to witness firsthand what they referred to as 'the idolatrous state', but compared with Tahiti, there were two important differences.

<hr>

18 This book is usually attributed to William Wilson, but Missionary Society papers, and Haweis' diary and letters, leave no doubt that the LMS delegated Haweis as editor; see Wood 1957,218; Du Rietz 1986,30. Nonsubscribers paid two guineas; subscribers paid £1 11s 6d; further details are in *Evangelical Magazine* 1799,209 and 242, and an advertisement therein.

19 Campbell 1840,156; Campbell credits this information to ms notes of Samuel Greatheed.

20 Ellis' biography was written by his son, John Eimeo Ellis, 1873.

21 See Twells 2009 for more on Bennet, Montgomery, and Sheffield.

22 Morrison 1935,64–73.

First, the earliest missionaries to settle both in the Australs and the Cooks were not English, but were converted Tahitian 'teachers' who were already familiar with the culture and therefore had little reason to document it; they were bent on conversion. Second, the few English missionaries who eventually did spend time on these islands in the early years, mainly on the Cooks, happened to be ones who were less interested in recording the 'old' culture than were the likes of Jefferson, Davies, Henry, Orsmond and Ellis.

The most valuable source for the Cook Islands would have been the unedited journal of the primary missionary to spend time there, John Williams. A line in Williams' biography by Ebenezer Prout indicates that it contained drawings: Prout mentions 'a pair of portraits from the pencil of Mr Williams sketched from life upon his journal.'[23] With the exception of some passages which appeared in various LMS publications, and two manuscript versions of a month-long voyage in 1823 from Ra'iatea to the central Cooks on the chartered schooner *Endeavour*, Williams' journal, from the time of his arrival in Tahiti in 1817 until his return visit to England in 1834, is evidently lost. So is 'a very long account of the island [Rarotonga], gods, introduction to Christianity, &c' (see Appendix 1, Anelay N°1). Fortunately, his journal was sent to England, and turned into a 590-page book. Entitled *A Narrative of Missionary Enterprises in the South Sea Islands*, it was published in April 1837. Most of it focuses on the Cook Islands and on Samoa, the scenes of Williams' most conspicuous missionary conquests. Williams wanted the *Narrative* to be 'at once cheap and elegant', and it was. The sewn octavo version sold for 2s 6d, and was illustrated with an oil print and several wood engravings by Baxter. It is not clear which parts are Williams' own work and which were written by others.

Information on how Williams' *Narrative* came about is contained in a letter written by Williams on Ra'iatea to LMS foreign secretary William Orme, 18 November 1830:

A homeward bound whaler having unexpectedly called at Raiatea we have thought well to send home our journal in the rough to you as it will in all probability be twelve months after the arrival of this vessel before we shall be in England. Mr Barff & I have thought it will make an interesting volume provided you will kindly correct our rough style & prepare it for the press [many illegible and missing lines] You will put it in any form you please we originally intended to supply a short description of each island at the end of the account.

It goes on to say

[B]ut we have no time now . . . the second edition may be enlarged and improved . . . all profits go to the teachers, . . . [and] please supply the men [teachers] with a cheap light suit of black and the females with a gown.[24]

Another letter, to LMS treasurer William Hankey, written the same day: '[O]ur journal . . . is entirely in the rough we think it will make an interesting volume if some gentleman would kindly undertake to correct our barbarisms & present the work in a style that would please the English ear.'[25] *A Narrative of Missionary Enterprises in the South Sea Islands* was an enormously popular book. Over 4000 copies were printed in 1837; by 1840 it was into the twentieth thousand, by 1845 the fortieth thousand. It is said that it was the second most popular account of exploration after Cook's *Voyages*.

It is a fortunate paradox that there were missionaries who wanted to record Polynesian antiquity after coming all the way from England to extirpate it. By documenting Polynesian culture as they did, the LMS missionaries showed that despite their Evangelical convictions, they could in a way be considered members of the Enlightenment.[26]

---

[23] Prout 1843,325. Williams' first son, John Chauner Williams (b 17 January 1818, d 1874), was also good at drawing; he became a South Sea merchant.

[24] SOAS LMS SS incom corresp box7 folio7 jacketC.

[25] Ibid.

[26] For more on this controversial subject, see Stanley 2001, and Gunson 1994.

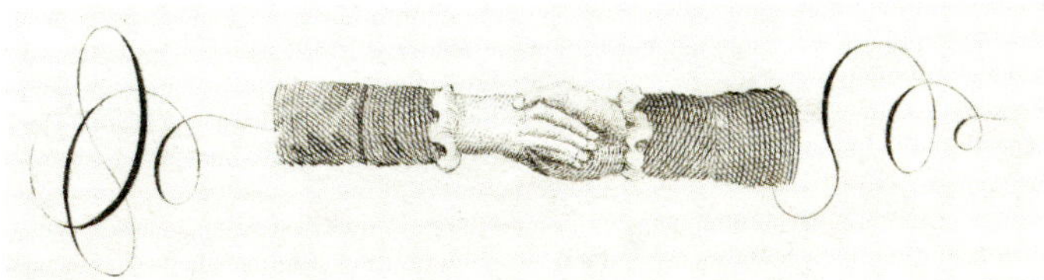

TWO

The Early Years of the LMS

'The revelation of the South Seas to eighteenth-century Europe, like the opening of the New World some three hundred years earlier, inspired Christian concern for societies at the periphery of the map. The coincidence of geographical discovery and evangelical revival was too striking to be anything less than a divine summons to convert the latest known corner of the earth.'

So begins historian Colin Newbury's introduction to John Davies' *History of the Tahitian Mission, 1799–1830*. It is a succinct statement of the circumstances in England during the late eighteenth century that led to the formation of a number of vigorous Protestant missionary movements. They gained momentum rapidly and became extraordinarily popular.

The missionary movement had its origins in the Evangelical religious revival which swept through Britain in the 1780s and 1790s.[1] Inspired by Methodism, which began in the 1730s and 1740s as a movement to regenerate the Church of England from within, Evangelicalism aimed to revitalize the nation through a commitment to a 'religion of the heart'. Its supporters emphasized the need to take the Good News of the Bible to the non-believer, stressing the capacity of all peoples, rather than a pre-chosen 'elect', to receive God's grace and salvation. By the 1790s, Evangelicalism had made a significant impact on the main Protestant denominations: the Baptists and Congregationalists and, via the Clapham Sect, the Established Church. All developed domestic missions during this period, which sought to evangelize society at home, including Catholics and Jews, with a particular focus—in the face of the revolutionary threat from France—on the poor. During the 1790s, while continuing to work with the heathen at home, they broadened their focus to include the campaign against the slave trade and the exciting field of heathenism overseas.

One important factor that galvanized the missionary enterprise was the publication, in 1792, of a small book entitled *An Enquiry into the Obligations of Christians to*

---

[1] Gunson 1978; Twells 2009.

Use Means for the Conversion of the Heathens. It was written by William Carey, a Baptist minister and former cobbler from Northamptonshire. In it is a 23-page table assessing the state of every part of the world, accounting for 731 million people, 420 million of whom were pagans. Carey lays out the problem:

> It must undoubtedly strike every considerate mind, what a vast proportion of the sons of Adam there are, who yet remain in the most deplorable state of heathen darkness, without any means of knowing the true God. Many of these . . . are cannibals, feeding on the flesh of the slain enemies, with the greatest eagerness . . . , poor, barbarous, naked pagans, as destitute of civilization, as they are of true religion.[2]

And he lays out a solution: 'Nay, in general the heathen have shewed a willingness to hear the word . . . ; all of these things are loud calls to Christians.'[3] That they were. Carey's book contains a job description for missionaries. Several missionary organizations soon took form and went to work. The aim of all of them was the same: 'to illume a dark and sinful world.' Each of these organizations of course considered itself uniquely able to save the heathen.

Carey was a founder of one of these organizations, the Baptist Missionary Society, and became a missionary himself. Originally interested in going to Tahiti, he went instead to Bengal, in 1793, to become an indigo planter, and to start a Baptist mission and college in a Danish settlement north of Calcutta called Serampore. He also founded a botanical garden there, and a museum. Carey's letters home met with enormous enthusiasm amongst Evangelical Christians. He wrote to urge the formation of a proper missionary society, in lieu of the lone missionary ventures in North America, the West Indies, Greenland and Sierra Leone, that had come before him.

Carey's book became one of the impelling forces behind the formation of a new Evangelical Christian organization, the London Missionary Society (until 1818 called simply The Missionary Society). The idea for the LMS germinated at a meeting in London, at Baker's Coffee-house on 'Change Alley, 4 November 1794.

More meetings followed the next year, at the Castle & Falcon Inn on Aldersgate Street; the Society was officially founded on 24 September 1795. Its design: 'We meet under the conduct of the Prince of Peace, and, unfurling the banner of his cross, desire to carry the glad tidings of his salvation to the distant lands, deep sunk in Heathen darkness, and covered with the shadow of death.'[4] The founders of the LMS saw it as ecumenical and nondenominational, envisioning what they viewed as 'the church universal'. 'Our church is formed upon independent principles.'[5] 'We desire to be neither exclusively Church men or dissenters, we contain a considerable number of Both, and on either Side of the Tweed. We form no parties in religion or politics; our Design rises from a broader basis.'[6] Their aim was to establish a spiritual dominion, not a territorial or economic one.

The founders of the LMS were mostly the editors of *The Evangelical Magazine*, which was started in 1793 by Rev John Eyre. Among the group were Rev David Bogue, a Scottish Presbyterian and author of a key address urging 'Let us all rise up to the work of God'; Revs Samuel Greatheed, Rowland Hill, Matthew Wilks, George Burder; and the learned scholar, preacher, and historian Rev Dr Thomas Haweis.[7] Haweis was impressed also by another book, Melville Horne's *Letters on Missions*, published early in 1794, and wrote an enthusiastic review of it for *The Evangelical Magazine*. Horne was one of two Evangelical Anglican missionaries who spent 14 months in Sierra Leone. That particular mission failed, but the book describes in detail the many lessons learned. Horne offered the blueprint for Haweis; Carey's mission in India was the example.

Rev Dr Thomas Haweis was unquestionably the father of the Tahitian Mission: 'Of all the dark places on earth, the South Sea Islands presented the fewest difficulties, and the fairest prospect of success.'[8] Tahiti was 'the country where the bread grows upon the trees'. He cited the salubrious climate, enchanting scenery,

2 Carey 1792,62.
3 Ibid., 73.

4 Haweis' first Missionary Society sermon, Spa Fields Chapel, 22 September 1795, in T Haweis *Sermons* 1795,5; Spa Fields Chapel was the Countess of Huntingdon's chapel in London.
5 Williams in Prout 1843,131.
6 Letter Thomas Haweis to Joseph Banks 12 September 1798; Sutro Library, San Francisco, Banks Correspondence LMS 1:39.
7 Gunson 1995; Morison 1814.
8 Williams' summary of Haweis' views in Williams 1837,2.

peculiar inhabitants, 'no persecuting government, no Brahmanic castes to oppose, a language of little difficulty to attain'.[9] Haweis inherited a portion of the estate of Selina Hastings, Countess of Huntingdon, and used the money generously to support his favoured project, called the South Sea Mission. Before the Missionary Society was born, Haweis tried to launch this project on his own. In 1791, he persuaded the Admiralty, with the influence of Joseph Banks and William Wilberforce, to have Captain William Bligh carry missionaries to Tahiti on the *Providence*, the second breadfruit voyage, after the ill-fated *Bounty* voyage, but the two painstakingly trained missionary volunteers, Michael Waugh and John Price, refused to sail unless they were ordained, which did not happen.[10]

Three years after Haweis' initial attempt, the South Sea Mission did go ahead, at a rapid pace. Four days after the Missionary Society was formed, the 34 directors engaged the services of a retired and extremely competent and experienced East India Company ship captain, James Wilson. In April the next year they purchased a ship, the *Duff*, for £5000, and hastily assembled an assortment of 30 men, mostly in their early twenties, to send to Tahiti as missionaries. They received next to no training. Only four were ordained ministers. Six had wives. There were three children. Most were of the artisan class; typical occupations were wheelwright, buckle and harness maker, shoemaker, carpenter, bricklayer, hatter, cooper—what the directors referred to as 'the honest arts'. LMS historian Richard Lovett referred to the group as 'this strange company'.[11] The *Duff* sailed down the Thames 10 August 1796, but had to wait at Spithead for a convoy.

It was towards the end of the five-week wait at Spithead that James Morrison's narrative of Tahiti and Peter Heywood's 100-page Tahitian vocabulary fell providentially into the hands of Haweis and the missionaries. As Campbell put it, referring to the mutineers, 'These poor misguided mariners were honoured to promote, in no ordinary measure, the cause of the first mission to the South Seas.'[12] The intelligence provided by the mutineers was extremely valuable, and also timely. Haweis had met considerable opposition from his fellow directors to the idea of establishing a mission on Tahiti. Morrison's views of Tahiti were far more positive and morally salubrious than those expressed by Wallis, Bougainville, and Cook—especially Wallis and Cook as rendered through Hawkesworth. In the eyes of his fellow directors, the mutineers exonerated Haweis.

The *Duff* left Spithead 24 September. They made record time and arrived at Matavai Bay, Cook's landing place, on 17 March 1797. Wilson distributed the boatload of missionaries to Tahiti (18), Tonga (10), and the Marquesas (2), and picked up a cargo of tea in Canton on the way back to help pay for the voyage.

Thus began the first wave of English missionaries to the South Sea. None of them spoke Tahitian. They were completely ill-prepared. The result was a disaster. They met with myriad difficulties, the chief ones being conflict and civil war amongst the Tahitians and hostility, or at best lack of sympathy, towards the missionaries. A year after landing they largely withdrew to Port Jackson (Sydney), which they referred to as 'the Colony'. The mission station there was at Parramatta, under Rev Samuel Marsden, who later became an invaluable aid to the mission. Haweis had severely underestimated the difficulties of his South Sea endeavour.

A second *Duff* voyage with 30 missionary reinforcements was a disaster in another way: the ship was captured first by a French privateer and then by the Portuguese off Brazil in 1798. The French ended up befriending the missionaries; the Portuguese returned the group to Lisbon.[13] By 1799, warfare in Tahiti had subsided and most of the Parramatta missionary refugees returned to Tahiti. A third missionary voyage from England, this time Captain William Wilson on the *Royal Admiral*, was successful. It brought 12 more missionaries, including John Davies, in 1801.

Progress in Tahiti remained slow. The missionaries' supplies for trading had dwindled; lack of fluency in Tahitian continued to be a problem, as did renewed

---

9   T Haweis *Sermons* 1795,13.

10 Banks was sympathetic to missionaries as agents to extend the British empire, and in general, to acquire knowledge. Haweis obtained much useful information about the Pacific from Banks, Bligh, and Vancouver. See Gunson 1965; Gascoigne in Lincoln 1998,39.

11 Lovett 1899 1,127.

12 Campbell 1840,156.

13 Howell 1809. Rev William Howell of Knaresborough was superintendent of the missionaries on the second *Duff* voyage; this was not the Rev William Howell of Portsea who attended the mutineers on the *Hector*.

warfare, disease, alcoholism, rivalry, discord, defection, 'indecent behaviour', and even murder. Some of the earliest Tahitian converts were selected for sacrifice to placate Tahitian gods. One of the missionaries married a Tahitian woman, and attempted to teach the Tahitians Hebrew. The missionaries isolated themselves. They were treated with indifference by the islanders.

But the missionaries were persistent, and they learned from experience. Eventually, after 15 long years, their success became coupled with the religious/political ascendancy of the paramount chief of Tahiti, Pomare II, who renounced idolatry, albeit to gain muskets and power, by 1806, and was baptized in July 1812.[14] Pomare was hardly a perfect specimen of Christianity, but Pomare and the missionaries needed each other; his conversion was the turning point for the Tahitian Mission. The missionaries proclaimed the event to the directors as *one of the greatest miracles of Grace ever exhibited on the stage of this world.*[15] The Tahitian station finally became firmly established with the aid of a fourth influx of missionaries, in 1817, which brought William Ellis, Robert Darling, John Orsmond, George Platt, Lancelot Threlkeld, Charles Barff, Robert Bourne, and John Williams. A landslide of baptisms and conversions ensued; churches and schools were constructed; Sundays were observed; houses were built in the European style; dress changed.

Mission stations were soon established on other islands in the Tahitian group—Mo'orea, Huahine, Borabora, Taha'a and, significantly, Ra'iatea. Ra'iatea (known then as Ulietea) was at the time the most important religious centre in the Society Islands, functioning as the Olympus of central Polynesia. The missionaries saw it as 'the grand emporium of idolatry', 'the Kingdom of Satan'. For Williams, 'Here was the citadel of evil!'[16] It was on Ra'iatea that the all-important god 'Oro was born and the cult of 'Oro originated. The primary marae (ceremonial centre) for 'Oro was Taputapuatea, originally called Vaiotaha, Feoro, or Teoro (accounts differ), at Opoa.[17] 'Oro, son of Ta'aroa, was a focus of fear and worship, offerings and human sacrifices, and occasionally grounds for violent interdistrict rivalry. He is often referred to as 'the god of war', but one must keep in mind that bloody and frequent war in Polynesia was, in Ellis' words, 'an object of the highest ambition, the road to most envied distinction, and the source of most ardent delight.'[18] Naturally, it was important for the LMS to establish a conspicuous foothold on Ra'iatea.

Ra'iatea was also a place for the new missionary arrivals to get away from the original missionaries on Tahiti, whom they regarded as peculiar, mentally or morally wrong, even 'barbarized'. In fact there was a complete division in the mission between the Windward (Tahiti, Mo'orea) and Leeward Islands (Ra'iatea, Taha'a, Borabora, Huahine). Each had its own missionary societies, presses, and native evangelists. At one stage they even celebrated the Sabbath on different days; in connection with this, the missionaries were mortified on discovering in 1822 that they had been a day off in their reckoning for 25 years—since their arrival in 1797.

In addition to the problems they faced on the islands, the missionaries also ran into problems with the LMS directors in London. The directors did not show a high regard for the missionaries, and after dispatching them, offered very little, and only occasional, support. They believed the missionaries could live off the land and off the people. This was true at first, but there soon came limits. Many letters in the LMS archives record the pleas of missionaries for more abundant and dependable financing than London was providing them. Williams wrote to his parents, only 11 months after arriving in Ra'iatea:

> I am sorry to say the directors of the missionary society have not no do not use us very well . . . their expressions are very kind and their professions are very encouraging but we cannot be clothed by expressions

---

[14] As early as January 1807, Pomare wrote the LMS directors about his intent to 'banish Oro, and send him to Raeatea', signing the letter 'May Jehovah save us all' (*Trans Miss Soc* 1807,176). Tahitians bore several names. Known also as Tu (by Cook) and Taina (by Bligh), Pomare I named himself. The name derives from po, night; mare, cough—the disease by which Pomare I's eldest daughter died. See Adams 1901,28, 106.

[15] Letter William Henry to LMS Parramatta, 17 June 1813; *Trans Miss Soc* 1814,12.

[16] Williams 1837,58; Williams at Sea to Brethren, 6 July 1823; Hayes 1922,20.

[17] More on marae and Taputapuatea in figs. 29–50. The meaning of the word Taputapuatea is not clear; Davies' entry for taputapu reads 'a sacrifice to the god Oro'; Taputapuatea was the name used for marae dedicated to 'Oro.

[18] Ellis 1853 1,275. For further discussion of the complicated subject of 'Oro, see Ellis 1829, Orsmond (T Henry 1928), Kooijman 1964, and Oliver 1974.

or fed with professions . . . those who come to Tahiti thousands of miles from civilized Society must be left to die on a Dunghill . . . the Directors say all our necessary wants may be supplied but the distance is so great [—] the natives call such talk as that Vaha-pape—water mouth.[19]

An 1825 letter from missionary George Platt, on Borabora, to the directors, takes them to task for sending no funds or correspondence for three years: '[Is it] really the wish of the directors to prosecute the work in which they had engaged or to blow up a bubble and leave it to its fate to burst or be borne away in the air . . . and then to blow up another and another like the amusement of children. . . . What God is doing in the islands is astonishing to us and amounts to a miracle', and so on.[20]

The missionaries relied on trading English goods for food and labour, but 'as their stock of European articles decreases, they must proportionally lose their influence over the natives'.[21] They were not nearly as self-sufficient as they wished: 'We cannot climb up breadfruit trees climb up Steep Mountains for mountain plantains—fetch water firewood etc ourselves. . . . We cannot buy a Pig under 2½ & 3 fathoms of cloth. . . . A native will not stick up a stick without being paid for it.'[22] The directors did not send anywhere near the required number of books or slates for the schools; the missionaries had to use 'sandboards'; sea urchin spines served as pencils for both. For the most part, the missionaries were on their own.

At the point when they most needed one, the Tahitian mission acquired an advocate whom the directors did respect. Extremely important in the organization and sustenance of the South Sea Mission but not always acknowledged was the generous and timely support of Rev Samuel Marsden, an Anglican, senior chaplain and magistrate to the convict settlement at Parramatta. Marsden is well known for his establishment in 1814 of the first missions in New Zealand, under the auspices of the Church Missionary Society. In 1804, he became official LMS correspondent and agent for the Tahitian Mission; he provided the directors with sage advice. He maintained a farm of 4000 acres and sent flour, rice, tea, sugar, cash, and encouragement to feed the infant mission. Williams was grateful: 'Mr Marsden's letter [of support] ought to be printed in gold.'[23] With his own money, Marsden purchased the 100-ton brig *Active* for the New Zealand and Tahitian missions. To address mission funding problems, Williams, aided by Marsden, attempted a number of business ventures in sugar, arrowroot, sennit cordage, cotton, salt pork, and tobacco. In 1821, for instance, 60 tons of coconut oil, collected as contributions from districts, in units called 'bamboos', were sent to England and sold for £1700. Indeed at one point Williams was reprimanded by the LMS Directors for appearing to be more merchant than missionary. The pragmatic Haweis sided with Williams and Marsden on this issue. They also agreed with the Raiatean teachers regarding contributions from the Tahitians: '[A] little property given, with the heart, becomes big property in the sight of God.'[24] The Tahitian Mission had somehow to be sustained.

The success of the Tahitian Mission was mixed. Ebenezer Prout was Williams' biographer; his rose-tinted, 20,000-mile-distant view of the early years of the LMS was much the same as that of the LMS directors: 'The current of prosperity flowed on with constantly accelerating force through ever-widening and deepening channels, and abundantly refreshed the eye and the heart of the devoted Missionary.'[25] Lines such as these often appeared in such publications as *The Evangelical Magazine* but of course were wishful thinking. The missionaries' private views of their accomplishments during this period, expressed in letters to their families, were more realistic and truthful. The 'complete' adoption of Christianity on this or that island, accomplished in a matter of months, days, or even hours, trumpeted by the missionaries in their letters to the London directors, turned out to be not quite so complete. Williams saw this straight away: 'But the spirit appears not to

19 Williams to parents 4 September 1819 SOAS LMS SSP box2 folder1.

20 Letter Platt to directors; SOAS LMS SS incom corresp box5A folder2 jacketA.

21 Turnbull 3,18 in Brown 1820 2,310. John Turnbull was master of the trader *Margaret*; he spent several months on Tahiti in 1802–3.

22 Williams to parents 4 September 1819. SOAS LMS SSP box2 folder1.

23 Ibid., referring to a letter of support from Marsden; see also Marsden 1858.

24 Prout 1843,116.

25 Ibid.,220.

have operated on many hearts—they don't seem to be convinced of the sinfulness of sin—the necessity of a Saviour—the love of Christ—the very fundamental principles of Christianity seem not to be felt by them.'[26] Missionary Charles Pitman wrote in 1827, after his first few months on Rarotonga: 'It is a pleasing thing to see and hear of nations "casting away their idols"—but we wish to see and hear something more than this.'[27] Pitman's wife, Elizabeth: 'I am far from considering the generality of them true Christians.'[28] The missionaries, naturally, did not mention this troublesome subject to the LMS directors.

As this book concerns the idols gathered by the missionaries, and as most of the idols were evidently acquired (or destroyed) during the period from 1816 to 1825, the decade following Pomare II's baptism, this brief account of LMS history is restricted to these early years. The history of the LMS in the South Pacific is complex; there were eventually dozens of missionaries, abbreviated 'misss' in their letters; they were disorganized, and they came and went and travelled about the islands and to Sydney like ants in an anthill. For further details, see the most complete LMS histories, those of William Ellis, 1844, and Richard Lovett, 1899; the firsthand accounts of John Jefferson and John Davies mentioned above; and the works listed below.[29] Subsequent periods of missionary history in the Cook Islands, fraught with problems, are covered by Ernest Beaglehole.[30] The social and religious fabric of the missionaries, and their interface with the islanders, is well covered by Niel Gunson.[31] LMS missions continued in Polynesia, particularly Samoa, spread to Micronesia, Vanuatu, and Papua in the 1840s, as well as to Africa, China, and more. The LMS merged with the Council for World Mission (CWM) in the 1970s, and continues its work to this day.

---

[26] Williams to parents 4 September 1819, after 11 months on Ra'iatea, SOAS LMS SSP box2 folder1.
[27] E Beaglehole 1957;31.
[28] Ibid.

[29] Full runs of LMS publications such as *Transactions of the Missionary Society, Missionary Chronicle, Missionary Sketches,* and *The Evangelical Magazine,* as well as missionary and home correspondence, are housed in the LMS CWM (Council for World Mission) archives at SOAS, and at the Mitchell Library. Subsequent LMS history resources are Morison 1814, Brown 1820, T Smith 1824, Smith and Choules 1832, Orsmond (T Henry 1928), Campbell 1840, King 1895.
[30] Beaglehole 1957; concerns Rarotonga and Aitutaki.
[31] Gunson 1978.

The Early Years of the LMS

3 The Cession of the District of Matavai *[Tahiti] to the Missionaries, 16 March 1797. Large (~2 x 3m), dark, highly romanticized painting by RA Smirke presented by the LMS directors to Captain James Wilson of the Duff on his return to England after delivering the first missionaries to Polynesia. It shows Wilson, his nephew, and well-attired missionaries witnessing the cession to the missionaries of a large plot of land along with a house built for Captain Bligh. Pomare II (borne on men's shoulders, with wife Idia) and his priest Haamanemane (crouching) are surrendering the land, even though it was not theirs to cede. More details can be found in Missionary Sketches 66, July 1829. SOAS. Photograph courtesy SOAS.*

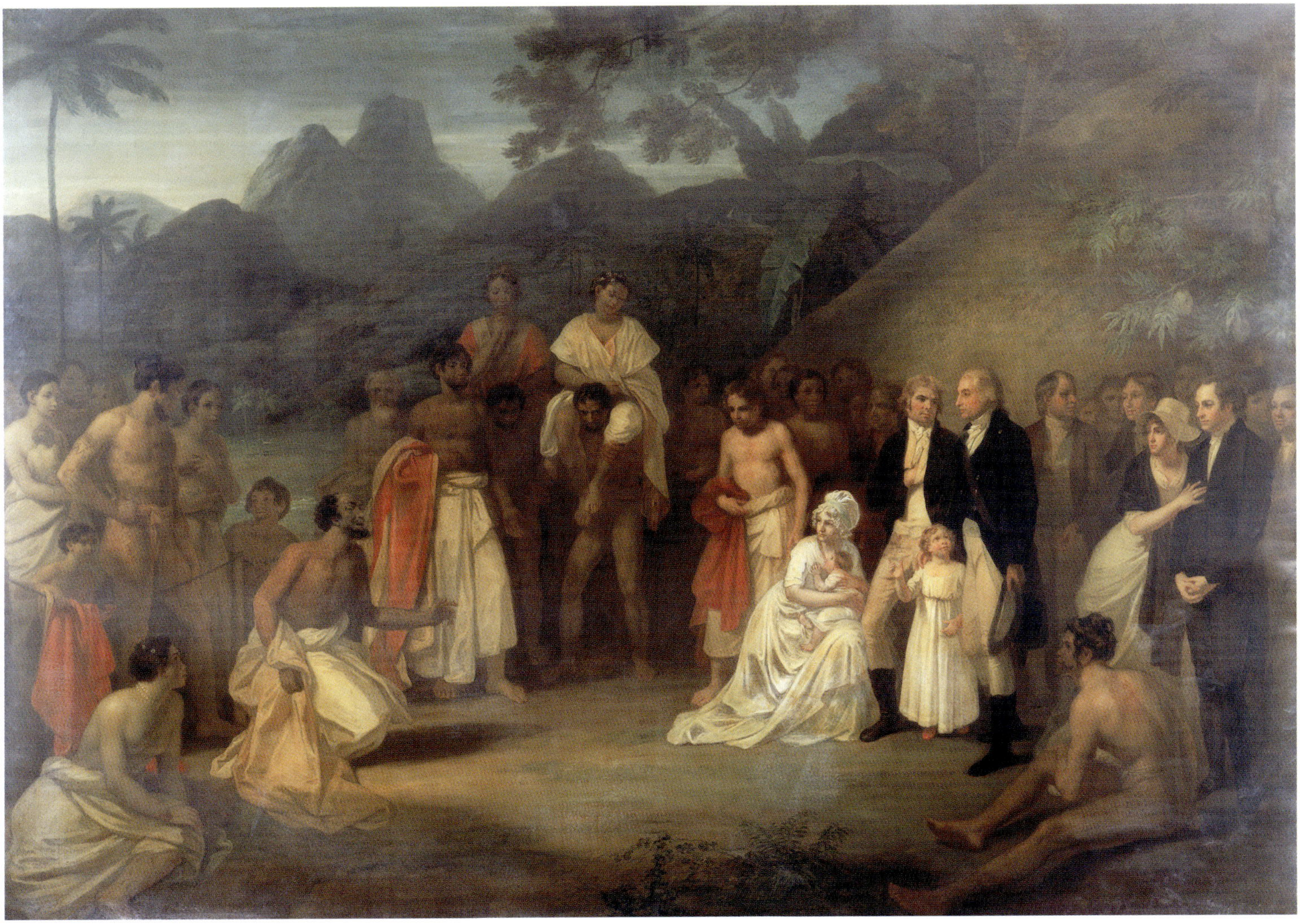

3

4

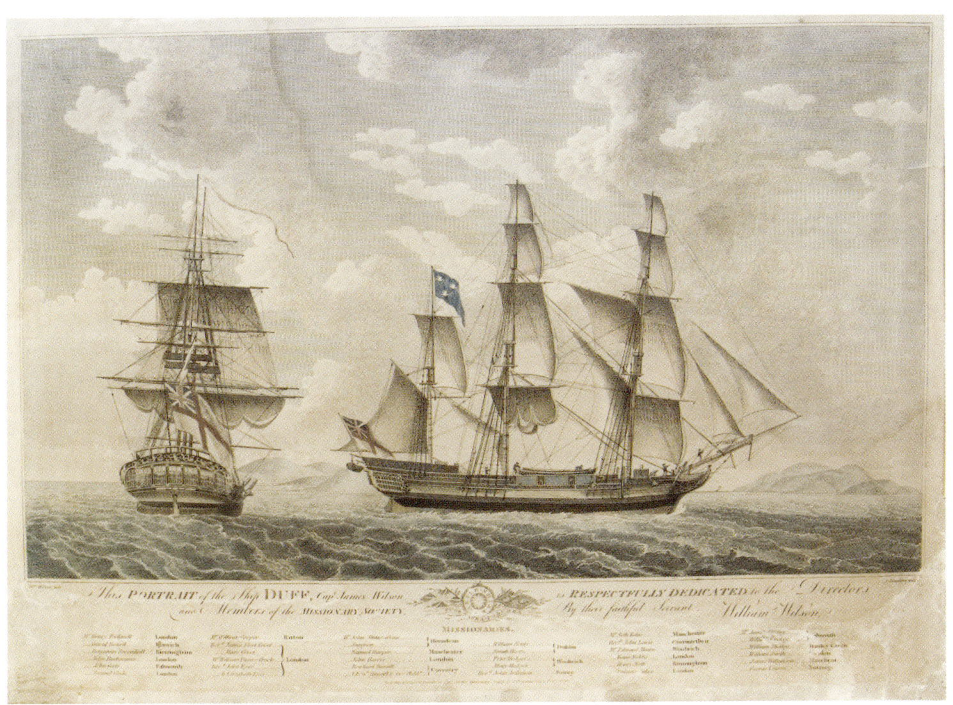

4 Portrait of the Ship Duff *engraved by J Saunders, printed by Chapman; from a drawing by William Wilson, which was presented to Thomas Haweis for engraving: 'The Directors will, no doubt, every one of them, wished to be possessed of it, and every friend of the Institution will look at it a thousand times with pleasure, and send up many a fervent prayer for the success of the Voyage.' It lists all 30 missionaries. William Wilson was Captain James Wilson's nephew, and Chief Officer on the Duff. Commissioned before their departure, it was published in March 1797, when the Duff had just reached Tahiti. For more details, see* Evangelical Magazine *1796,472.* SOAS. 52 x 37.5cm.

13

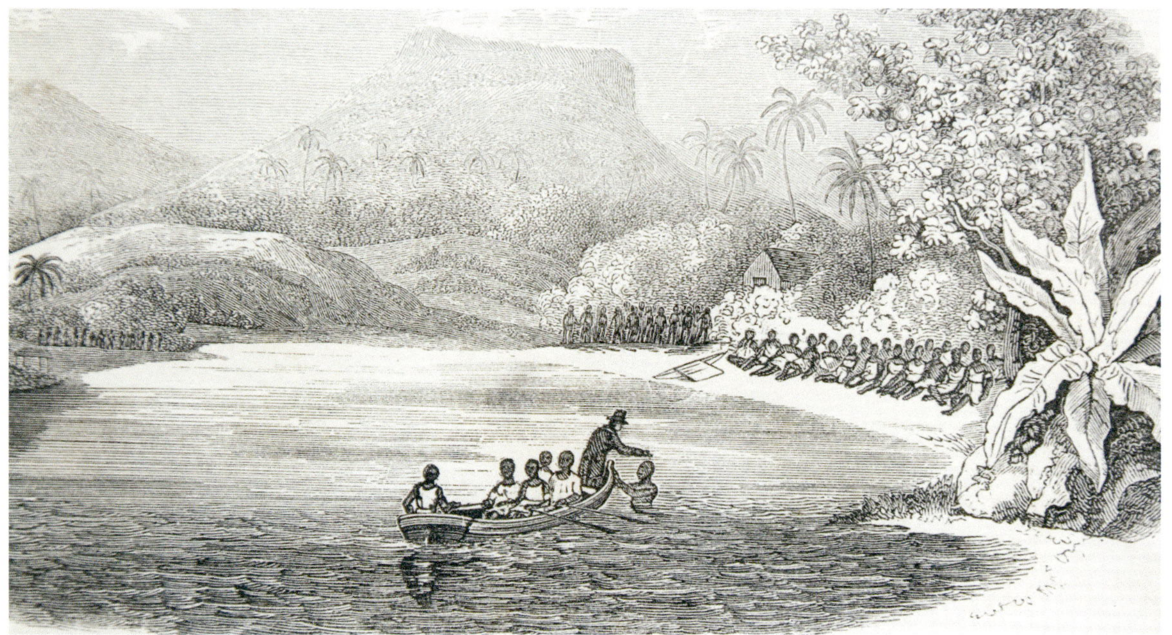

5

5 The interview at Leone Bay, Tutuila. *Baxter wood engraving from* Missionary Enterprises, *1837. Williams, in top hat and tails, is meeting Chief Amoano for the first time. Leone Bay (Samoa) had become Christianized by Raiatean teachers 20 months before. Group on beach at left are naked heathens; on the right, Christians, dressed, wearing white tapa armbands.*

6 Destruction of the Idols at Otaheite; pulling down a Pagan Altar, and building a Christian Church, *from the magazine* Missionary Sketches 6, *July 1819. SOAS.*

6

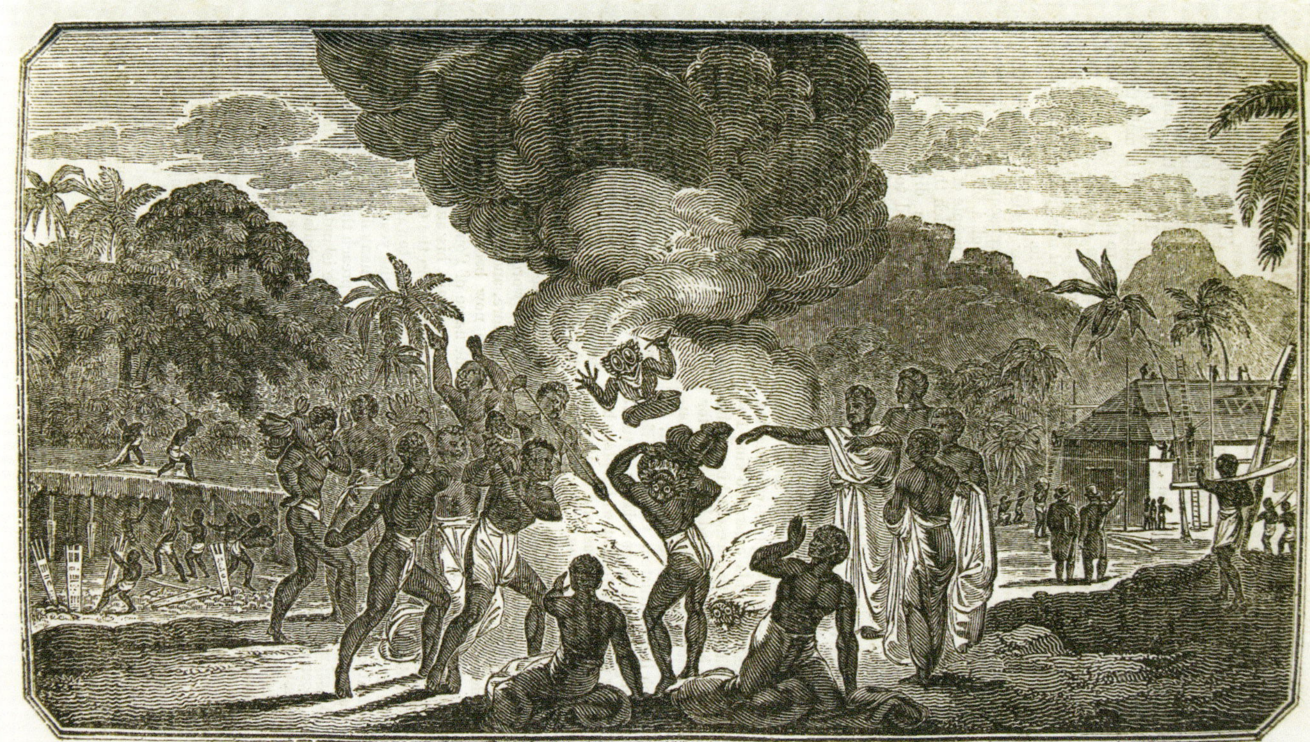

Destruction of the Idols at Otaheite; pulling down a Pagan Altar, and building a Christian Church.

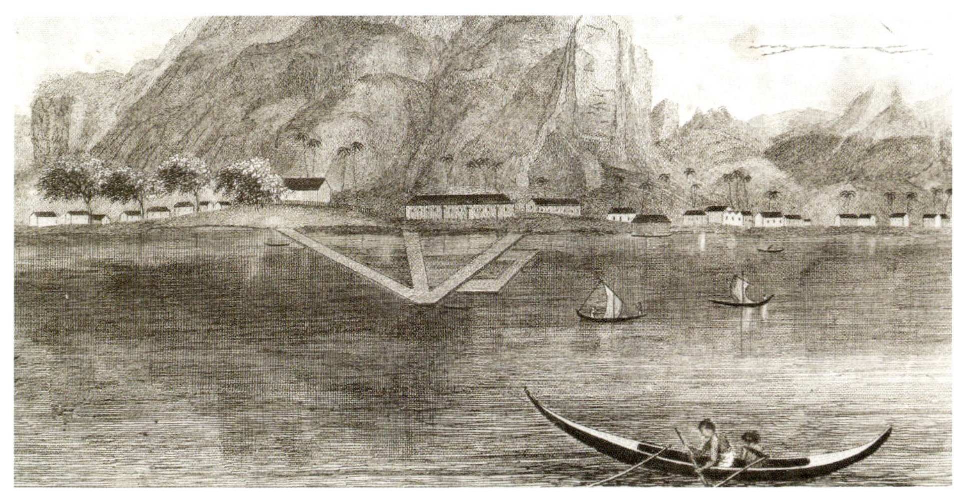

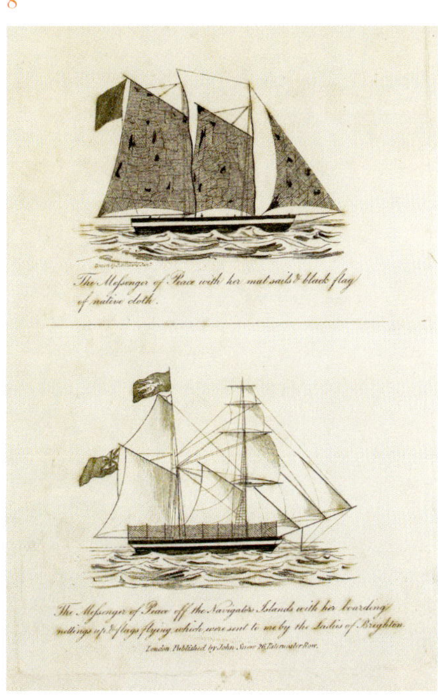

7 Missionary Settlement, Island of BoraBora. *Shows chapel, missionary residences, school, teachers' residences, and 365-foot-long coral pier. John Orsmond was the residing missionary. Engraving by J Dennis from a sketch by D Tyerman. From Montgomery 1832 1,232.*

8 The Messenger of Peace, *which Williams had built on Rarotonga in 1827 in order to get back to Ra'iatea. Top inage is the boat as built, with black tapa flag and pandanus mat sails. Bottom view is the boat after refitting in Ra'iatea, with canvas sails. After drawing by John Williams Jr who was 9 years old at the time. Engraving; unpublished? SOAS. Another version of top image is in Williams'* Missionary Enterprises,*164.*

9 Conveying the idols to the boat, Aitutaki. *Harvesting the trophies of victory. Baxter wood engraving in* Missionary Enterprises, *1837.*

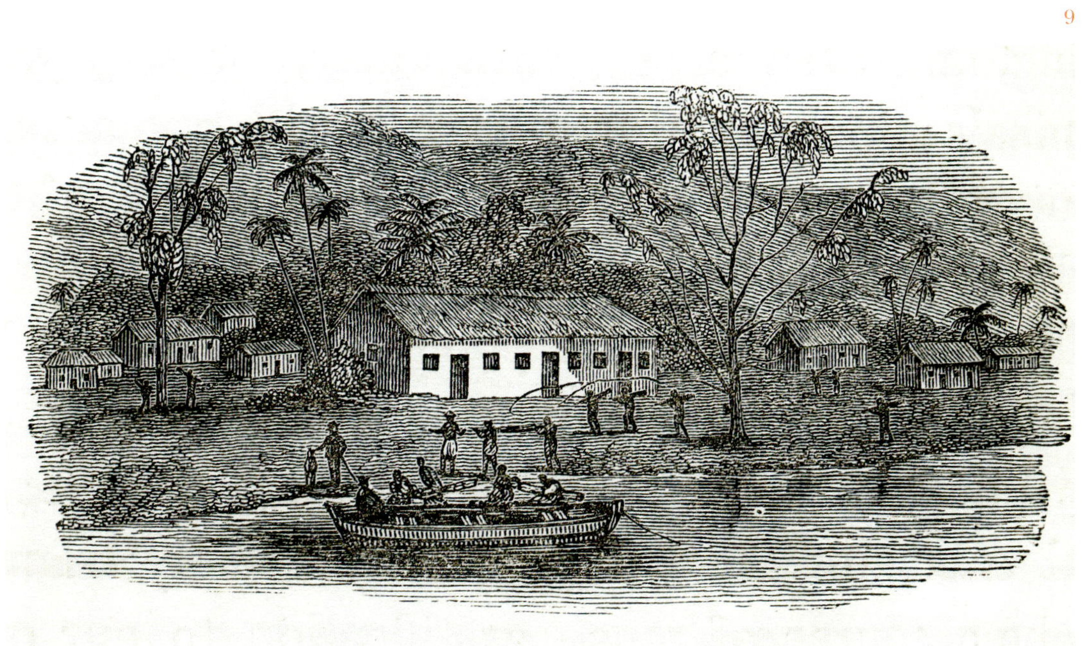

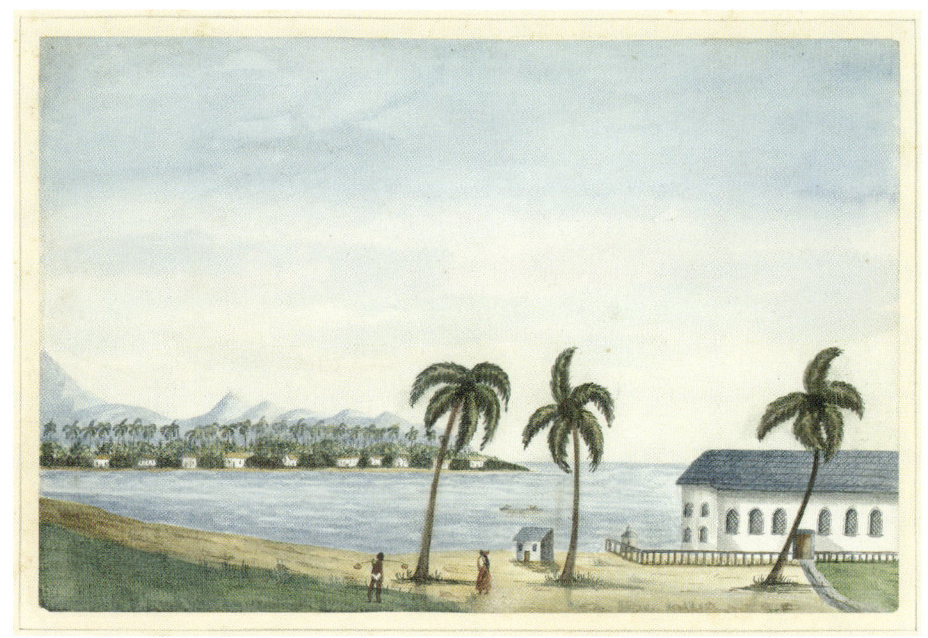

10

10 *Watercolour of mission station, Raʻiatea, painter unknown, nd, Rex Nan Kivell collection. Courtesy NLA, Canberra.*

11 *Watercolour of a church built on the ahu of a marae; artist unknown, nd, no title; Rex Nan Kivell collection. Courtesy NLA, Canberra. A 21 May 1822 letter (SOAS) from missionary William Henry contains poetry: 'Lines composed on the building of a Christian Church in the district of Papetoai, Island of Eimeo [Moʻorea], upon the ruins of the Royal Marae in that District.' Perhaps this is the church mentioned.*

11

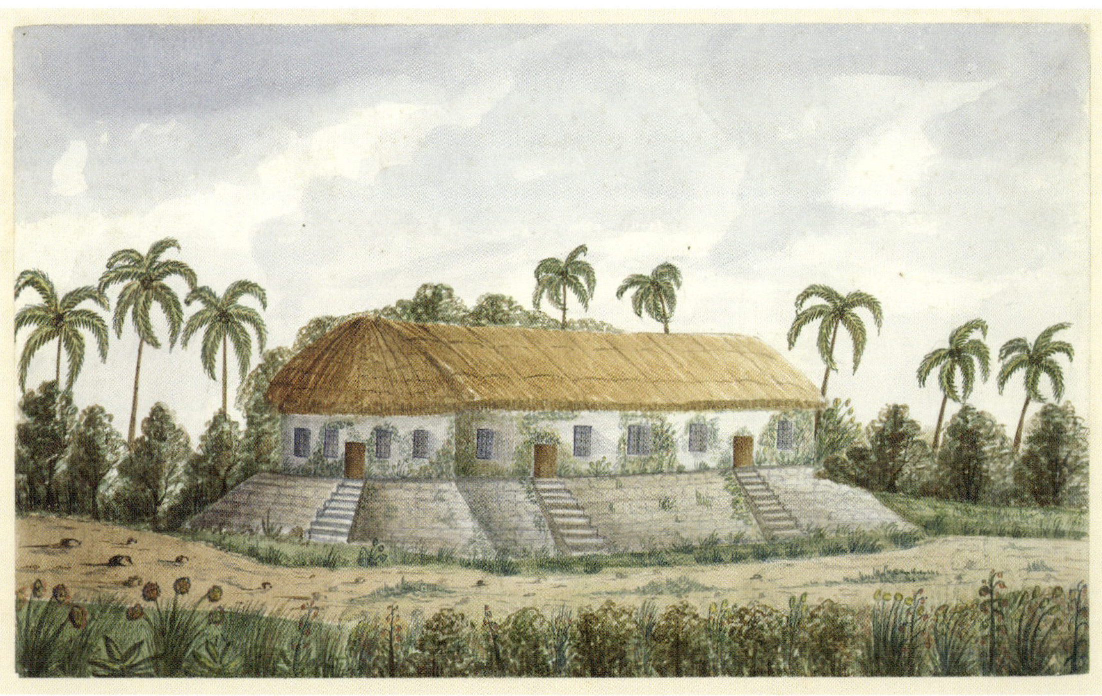

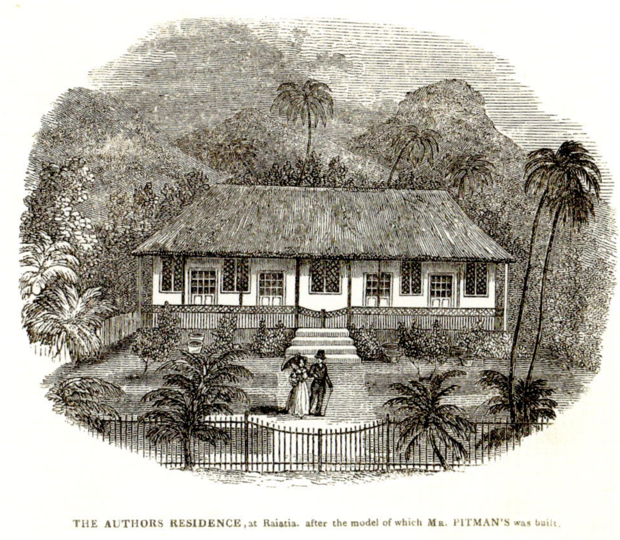

12

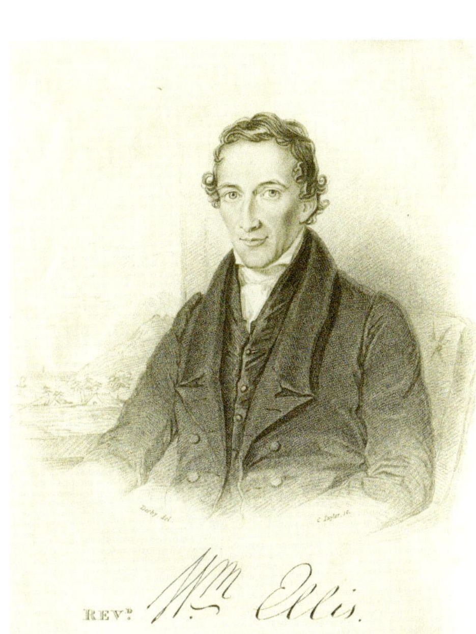

13

12   The Authors Residence, *Ra'iatea; Baxter wood engraving from Williams's* Missionary Enterprises, *1837; thatched roof, white coral plaster walls, glazed windows, garden and picket fence. This house set the standards for all residences on the island.*

13   *William Ellis; frontispiece of his* Narrative of a Tour through Hawaii or Owhyhee, *1827.*

14   *Detail of George Baxter's* The Departure of the Camden, Missionary Ship, April 11, 1838. *This was the first Baxter 'oil picture' issued as a separate. The* Camden, *with Captain Robert Morgan, left London 42 years after the* Duff. *It carried the fourth wave of LMS missionaries to Tahiti, along with Rev John Williams, who was returning after a four-year tour of England. Rex Nan Kivell Collection, NLA, Canberra.*

14

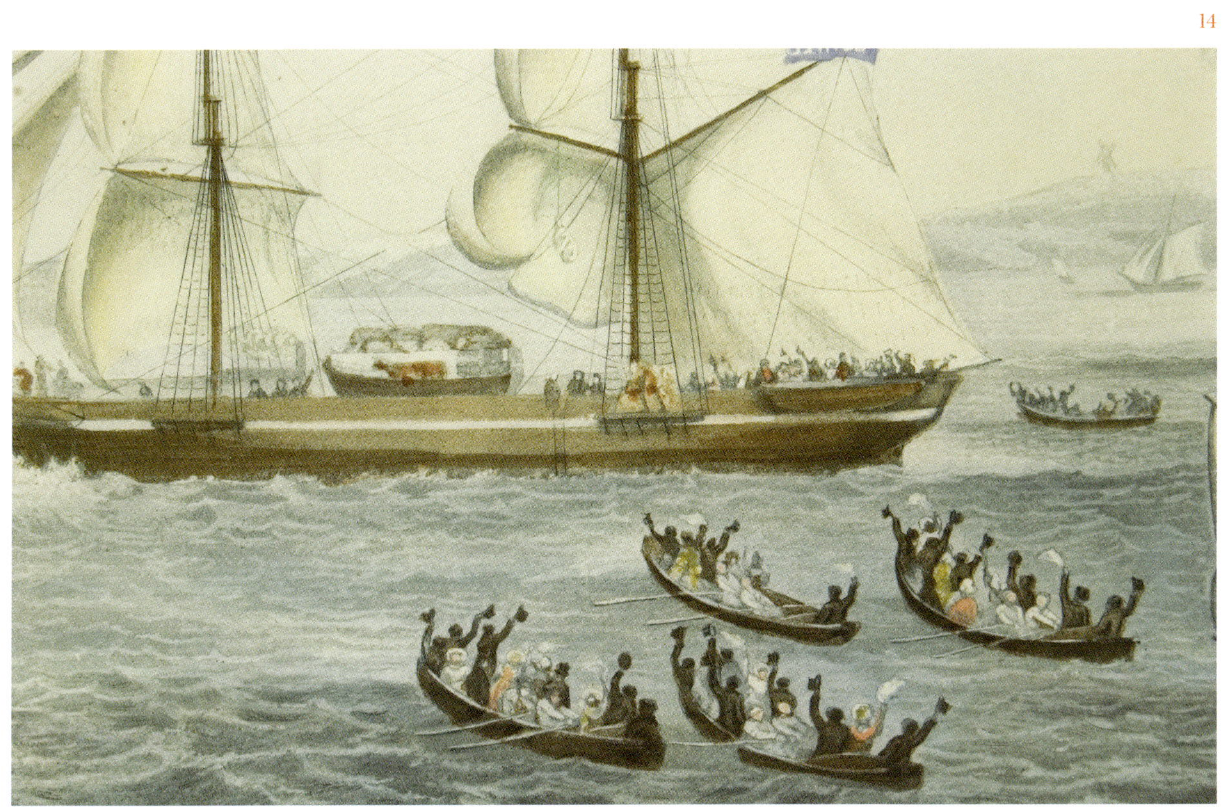

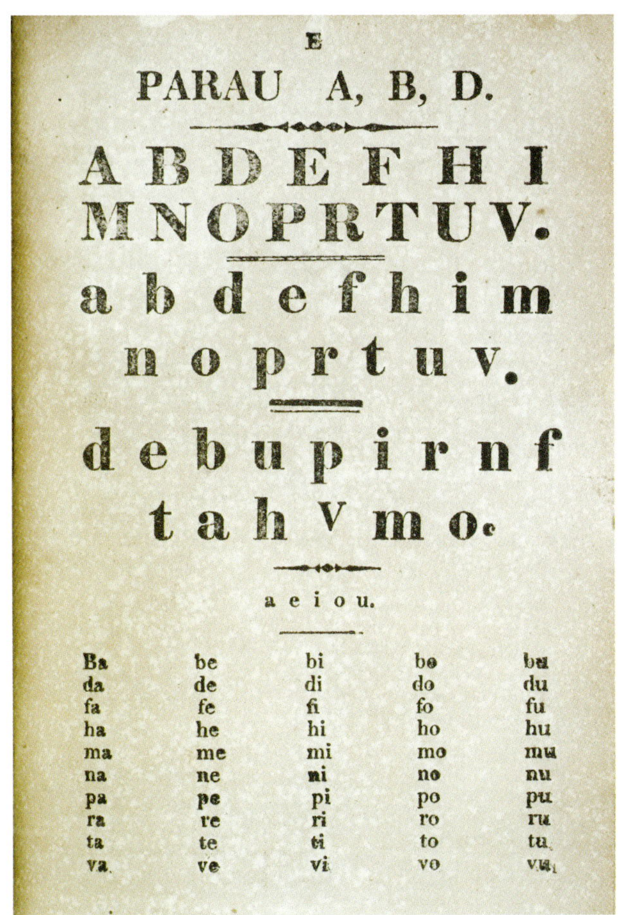

15

16

17

15 *Tahitian spelling book printed by the LMS Mission Press, Burder's Point, Punaauia, Tahiti, 1829. Courtesy BPBM. The concept of the written word, and books themselves, were enormously popular in Tahiti, and were important agents of Christianization.*

16 *Marquesan spelling book printed by the LMS in Tahiti, 1834; SOAS, CWML F.196. Polynesian alphabets typically had 15 letters, supplemented with about 6 more for foreign words. The missionaries transformed Polynesian dialects into written languages.*

17 *Letter written by Pomare II on Tahiti to the missionaries on Mo'orea, 1818; SOAS. Pomare was their first disciple. 'P.R.' is Pomare Rex.*

18

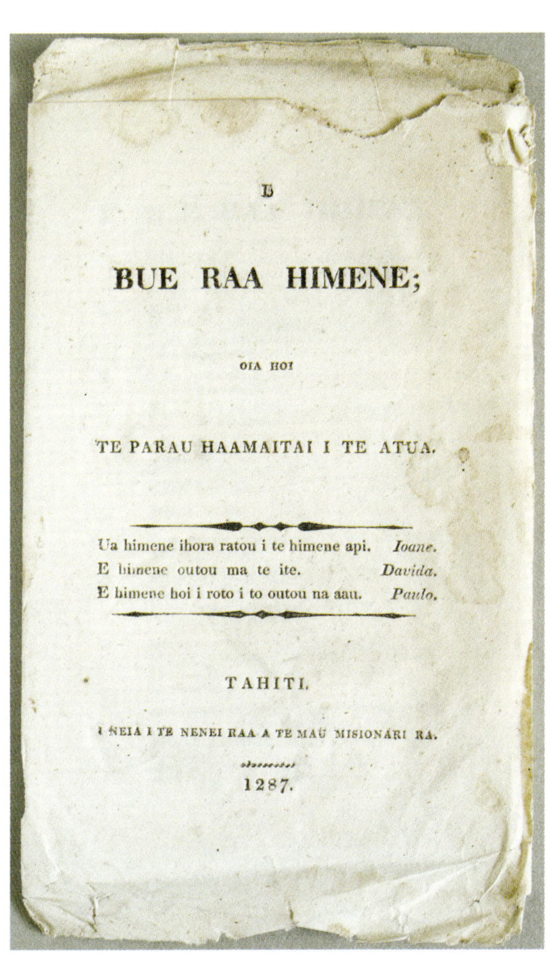

18

18 *Book of hymns, in Tahitian, printed by Robert Darling at Burder's Point, Tahiti, 1827. Called the Windward Mission Press, it was the most important one in central Polynesia.*

19 *The first Tahitian grammar, prepared by John Davies, printed at Burder's Point, Tahiti, 1823. Imprints averaged ~11 x 19cm.*

20 Epistles of Paul to the Galatians, *printed by Charles Barff in Huahine, 1828; translation by Williams and Pitman. This is the first book printed in Rarotongan. Courtesy Bancroft Library.*

19

20

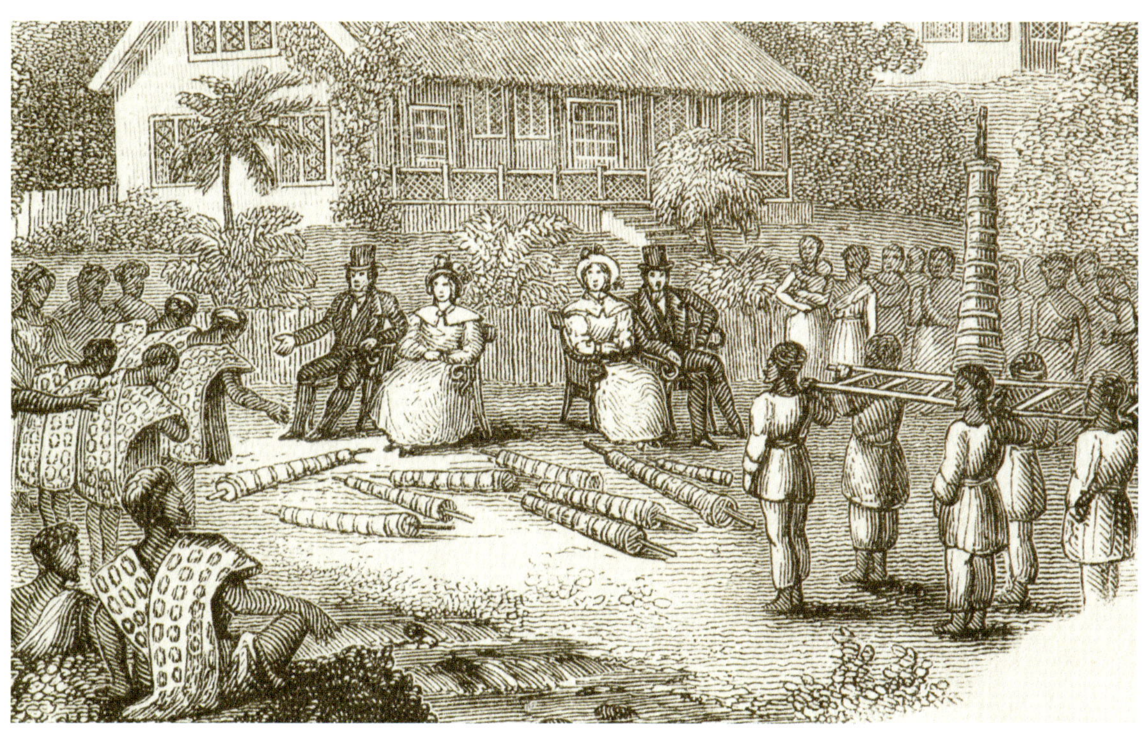

21 *Detail of Baxter wood engraving and legend, title page of Williams'* Missionary Enterprises, *showing Williams and fellow missionary Charles Pitman seated in front of a missionary residence with their wives, on Rarotonga. Ten tapa-wrapped staff gods are being brought to them to be decapitated and immolated, or perhaps to be spared and sent to the Missionary Museum in London.*

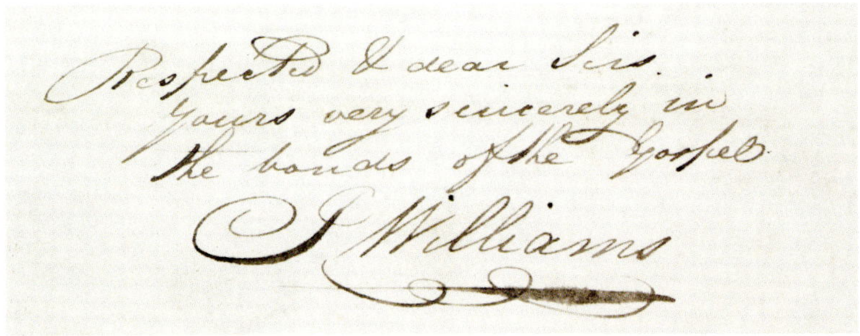

WILLIAMS’ SIGNATURE, LETTER TO DIRECTORS, 1825. SOAS.

THREE

Viriamu

JOHN WILLIAMS’ LIFE started out much like that of other missionaries but turned into perhaps the most remarkable one of all. Because he is central to much that is discussed in this book, a brief account of his life is presented here. Polynesians called him Viriamu (also spelled Wiliamu). His missionary years are well-documented in *Missionary Enterprises*. His earlier years are covered in two biographies, and in Williams’ address printed in *The Missionary’s Farewell*.[1]

Both his grandparents and his parents were ‘servants of God’. He received little in the way of formal education: ‘Of the classics he learned but little, and to still rarer attainments he was an entire stranger. His destination was commercial.’ Indeed, nearly all the missionaries of this early period were of the ‘mechanic’ class.[2] He had an active mind, and was called ‘a handy lad’. At age 14 he went to work as an apprentice at Mr Enoch Tonkin’s ‘furnishing ironmongery’, a workshop that made window hardware. Bored with desk work, he clearly preferred the apron and tool basket, and the forge, and soon became a better smith than the workers who had been there for years. But ‘his heart was not right with God’; he disregarded the Sabbath and

---

[1] All quotes in this section unless otherwise indicated are the words of Ebenezer Prout, author of Williams’ primary biography, 1843. Prout quotes from many of Williams’ letters. An interesting but more of a tract-type biography is Rev James J Ellis, *John Williams, The Martyr Missionary of Erromanga*, 1889; a biography written for children is Hayes’ *Wiliamu, Mariner-Missionary*, 1922. Williams’ address in Campbell, 1838, offers biographical insights found nowhere else. Niel Gunson’s 1978 *Messengers of Grace* is an excellent study of the background and motivation of Evangelical Christian missionaries. Rev John Campbell’s *The Martyr of Erromanga, or the Philosophy of Missions* is more about the philosophy than about the martyr. His prose is extravagant. He speaks of idolatry as a ‘crime and calamity . . . spread as a covering over the face of the Pacific Ocean, dyed in colours of the deepest hue, and traced in all possible and imaginable forms of wretchedness . . . the most heinous enormity conceivable or practicable by man . . . incomparably the greatest disaster this side of eternity’ (Campbell 1842,15).

[2] T Haweis had outlined the qualifications he envisioned of the ideal missionary: ‘A plain man, with a good natural understanding, well read in the Bible, full of faith and of the Holy Ghost, though he comes from the forge, or the shop, would, I own in my view, as a missionary to the heathen, be infinitely preferable to all the learning of the schools, and would possess, in the skill and labour of his hands, advantages which barren science could never compensate’; ‘a common man of ardent piety’ (*Sermons*, 14,15; 1795). This is a perfect profile of Williams—in Gunson’s words, ‘a godly mechanic’.

the sanctuary; 'His attendance there was only a heartless compliance with an irksome custom.' In Williams' own words, 'My course, though not outwardly immoral, was very wicked.'[3] He associated with several irreligious young men. 'His position now was most perilous.'

That all changed on Sunday evening 30 January 1814, when Williams was 18. He had arranged to go to a tavern with his irreligious friends, but 'his giddy companions did not keep their time.' Instead, Mrs Tonkin happened by, and took him to the Tabernacle, at Moorfields. The Rev Timothy East[4] spoke on the text 'What is a man profited if he shall gain the whole world, and lose his own soul?' The word came with power: 'From that hour, my blind eyes were opened.' Thereafter, '[h]e grew in grace. . . . While receiving instruction, he became anxious to impart it.' Williams taught an evening Sabbath school class, instructed the poor and the sick, and distributed religious tracts. He composed prayers and hymns. In the autumn of 1815, he heard the 'eccentric' Rev Matthew Wilks speak at the Tabernacle Auxiliary of the Missionary Society on the success of the African and South Sea Missions. Wilks spoke of Pomare's conversion and the need for helpers in Tahiti. Williams was interested, and Wilks became his mentor. In July 1816 Williams applied to the directors of the Missionary Society. They were impressed by his seriousness and zeal, and he was ordained 3 September 1816. He married Mary Chauner on 29 October. On 17 November, Rev George Burder gave him a Bible and told him, 'Go my young brother.' Williams and his young bride left for Tahiti on the merchantman *Harriet*, via Rio and Sydney. The voyage took one year. John was 20. Mary was 19.

Williams is customarily regarded as the most talented and resourceful of all the South Sea Missionaries. He learned Tahitian in ten months: 'I can tell the perishing heathens around me of the love of Christ in their own tongue' he announced to his parents in 1819.[5] Finding himself unexpectedly stranded on Rarotonga, he constructed (with much help, of course) a 50-ton schooner, *The Messenger of Peace*, solely out of native materials; over the years, he built five other boats. He constructed forges and devised a new type of bellows after rats ate the goatskin membrane off his original one. He built lathes for turning bedposts and chandeliers, made furniture, glazed windows, and made doors equipped with louvres—referred to as 'Venetian blinds'. Bridges, roads, gardens, plantations. He burned coral washed up on the beaches to manufacture lime plaster of three colours—white, French grey, and salmon. He made a cane press with turned wood rollers and taught the crystallization of sugar, a process he picked up in Australia. He constructed devices to make rope out of sennit. Some of the churches he built, or rather supervised, were elaborate and immense. One opened in May 1819 at Papaoa (Tahiti), called Hankey Town or Hankey City by the missionaries (the missionary stations were named),[6] measured 54 by 712 feet. Three pulpits were fixed equidistantly so that three missionaries could address three congregations at once; it could accommodate 6,000 people. William Ellis admired Williams' practical abilities, and his adaptability.

Williams was often a good observer. He thought that Polynesia had been peopled from Malaysia, which is, in general, the current view. He had an interest in natural history, especially snakes, which he kept as pets. Always keen on new plant introductions, Williams brought along with him on his return to Polynesia in 1838 rootstock of the well-known 'dwarf Cavendish' banana cultivar, originally from China, which he obtained from the Duke of Devonshire at Chatsworth.[7] Sound theories

3   Prout 1843,15.

4   In the William Oldman collection (N°413) is a large (66cm) wood figure from Ra'ivavae which Williams gave to Rev Timothy East 'for the purpose of illustrating his lectures to procure funds on behalf of the Mission to the islands'.

5   Letter Williams Ra'iatea to parents 4 Sept 1819 SOAS LMS SSP box2 folder1; no doubt an exaggerated claim.

6   The Tahiti and Eimeo (Mo'orea) mission stations were all named after various prominent personnel of the LMS in London. For example (letter missionary Robert Darling to William Alens Hankey Esq, LMS treasurer, 1 February 1825): 'You will perceive in our report that I have added your name to our station. It was purely from a feeling of attachment to you, ever since I had the pleasure of meeting you at our Bible meetings in Hackney. Be pleased therefore to allow it to be Hankey Town, as a token of my respect to you.' (SOAS LMS SS incom corresp box5A folder1 jacketB). Other stations were called Waugh Town, Wilks Harbour, Haweis Town, Griffin Town, Burder's Point, Roby's Place, Bogue Town, Bunnell Place. See map in Davies 1961, fig. 2.

7   'His son has a turn for botany, and they took out many plants that we thought would answer in the region to which they were bound'; 22 August 1837 entry in the Duke's *Handbook of Chatsworth and Hardwick*, 1845 (Colquhoun 2006,68). Other varieties of bananas, along with for instance chili, sweet potato, and bottle gourd, had already been brought to Polynesia from South America before the arrival of the first European explorers (see Langdon 2009).

regarding the formation of coral reefs and makatea (ancient uplifted coral formations on islands such as Atiu, Mauke, Mangaia) are discussed sensibly and in detail in a chapter in *Missionary Enterprises*, complete with references to Lyell's *Principles of Geology*, but then the theories are cast aside: 'After all . . . I have seen and thought, and read upon the subject, my impression is, that the islands remain much in the same state as when the deluge left them.'[8] Williams' mind, in his words, was 'unchilled by skepticism or infidelity.'[9]

'Light and shadows chased each other over the scene of his labours.' The light came from satisfying the inexorable, if incomprehensible, missionary drive to raise what he viewed as polluted and degraded people to a state of moral rectitude and Christian piety. He clung to this aim with tenacity, never questioned it, and was successful in realizing it: 'Williams was possessed of a peculiar talent which at once *won* upon the natives, whether chief or common people.'[10] Although 'willing to furnish facts and specimens which might gratify the curious or assist the Society, his main design was immeasurably superior.' He did not want to stop 'until all the islands that spot the bosom of the ocean shall be enlightened by the truth, and pervaded by the principles of the Gospel of the grace of God.'[11] Williams probably witnessed the introduction of Christianity into a greater number of islands than any other missionary.

The shadows were severe: the missionaries faced decades of extraordinary hardships in Polynesia. In Rarotonga, for example, the Christmas hurricane of 1831 brought down the churches and nearly a thousand houses in a matter of hours, and destroyed the food crops as well. The *Messenger of Peace* was carried hundreds of yards inland. An ensuing famine lasted for months afterwards,[12] and facilitated yet another epidemic.

Many perished. A number of Rarotongans blamed the disasters on the Pretane God,[13] and renounced Christianity; idolatry revived. There even followed a plot to bring back tattooing, which the missionaries viewed as a heathen practice. Other problems arose. There was antipathy towards the missionaries. Nearly every conversion caused unrest, anxiety, and power struggles, often leading to warfare.[14] Fighting was often accompanied by vengeful and thorough destruction of coconut and breadfruit trees, and plantations. Sometimes their houses and churches were burned down. All the missionaries faced periods of bad health; some died. Mary Williams bore three boys[15] and had seven stillborns. Williams could not swim, and nearly drowned seven times. The islands were overrun by rats: 'When kneeling down for family prayer they would run over us in all directions; and we found much difficulty in keeping them out of our beds.'[16]

Mail from England took a minimum of six months. Communication and support from the LMS directors was sparse and sporadic. Williams did not get along with Orsmond. Whalers and traders brought liquor and stills—and guns. Life was almost never easy.[17] Williams' 'disappointments' were indeed 'far more than sufficient to sicken the heart and subdue the energy of ordinary men.' But his courage and stamina were unrelenting. It is hard to fathom the degree of passion that at the turn of the nineteenth century could propel several dozen working men, largely in their twenties, to abandon their lives in London and take their young wives on a voyage that took close to a year, enduring danger, disease and discomfort in the extreme, and then be faced, completely on their own, with the harshness of life as the first European settlers in Polynesia. Despite their intolerances, and their unremitting drive

---

8   Williams 1837,37. Williams met with Charles Darwin, and supplied him with much information about the islands of the Pacific; he is cited numerous times in Darwin's *The Structure and Distribution of Coral Reefs*, published in 1842. Darwin went to Cambridge to become an Anglican clergyman; he was, and remained, sympathetic to missionaries. His first publication after the return of the *Beagle*, coauthored with Captain FitzRoy, was a defense of missionaries (FitzRoy and Darwin, 1836).

9   Williams 1837,25.

10   Fellow missionary Charles Pitman in James Ellis 1889–1890,18.

11   W Ellis in Campbell 1838,12.

12   Williams to Parents 1819 SOAS LMS SSP box2 folder1: 'The people were obliged to eat the Gigantic Fearn—one meal of which would kill a Director.'

13   The Polynesian term for the British god; also spelled *Beretani*.

14   Williams 1837,185.

15   John Chauner 1818–1874, Samuel Tamatoa 1826–1904, William Aaron Barff 1833–1904.

16   Williams 1837,152.

17   Williams expresses his irritation that other missionaries did not offer help for new missionaries: 'I have felt disappointed when reading the writings of Missionaries, at not finding a more full account of the difficulties that they have had to contend with, and the measures by which these were met. [They write] what might be written by one who had never left his native country.' Williams 1837,137.

to win converts to Christianity, there are aspects of the missionaries at which one can only marvel.

John Williams was killed in the line of duty on 20 November 1839 at the age of 43. After extending his missionary enterprise to Samoa, with ease and great success, he set his sights on the New Hebrides, New Caledonia, and New Guinea. He started with the New Hebrides. This was Melanesia, an area whose cultures and languages he did not know. He was apprehensive, but a warm reception at Tanna encouraged him. His next landing was on the beach at Dillon's Bay, Erromango. Things seemed to go smoothly at first, but then suddenly went very wrong: Williams and young missionary-to-be Mr Harris were clubbed to death and devoured. Williams' skull and a few bones were retrieved the next year by Captain Croker of *HMS Favourite*, and buried in Apia. Some years later, Scottish traveller and watercolourist Constance Gordon-Cumming learned that the Erromangans were under the impression Croker just wished to buy bones, and the skull and bones acquired were actually just taken at random from a native burial cave.[18] It turned out that Williams' and Harris' deaths were not a consequence of anything they did. Instead, they were killed in retribution for a prior, outrageously

brutal raid carried out by sandalwood collectors, who plundered yams and fruit, stole 300 pigs, and shot down and suffocated Erromangans without mercy.[19]

News of John Williams' death reached London on 6 April 1840 by overland mail from India, in a passage extracted from a Sydney into a Bengal paper. Williams' funeral service in London was held 20 May 1840, at the Tabernacle, and was conducted by Rev Timothy East.

Williams believed, as he himself put it, '[T]he Missionary enterprise is . . . the most effective machinery that has ever been brought to operate upon the social, the civil, and the commercial, as well as the moral and spiritual interests of mankind.'[20] The rich events of his life, and the timing of them, provided perfect fodder for the hagiographer. To his Evangelical audiences in England, Williams was a missionary hero, and after his violent death, a martyr; some Baxter portraits of Williams are inscribed 'The Martyr of Erromanga'. His life story gave credibility to the Evangelicals' cause. The tremendously popular *Missionary Enterprises* solidified it all.

Not surprisingly, another story coexists with this one, well dealt with by Gunson.[21]

---

18 Cumming 1882,142. Gordon-Cumming was companion to Lady Gordon, wife of Sir Arthur Hamilton-Gordon, the first British Governor of Fiji, 1875–1880.

19 It is alleged this raid was carried out by none other than Captain Samuel P Henry, son of missionary William Henry, with a crew of Tongans, in 1826; Captain Henry often helped the missionaries, and was converted in 1836; see Gunson 1978,118 and 170.
20 Williams 1837,582.
21 Gunson 1972.

22 *Baxter portrait of Williams on deck of ship, with chickens in cages; frontispiece, Williams' biography by Ebenezer Prout, 1843.*

23 *Baxter portrait of Williams, engraved by R Easton; frontispiece, first edition of* Missionary Enterprises, *April 1837.*

24 *George Baxter's stand at the Crystal Palace, London, 1851–1854. From Courtney Lewis, 1908.*

25 *Portrait of Williams, in 'oil colours', by Baxter, nd. Evidently produced as a separate; they sold for 10s 6d. SOAS.*

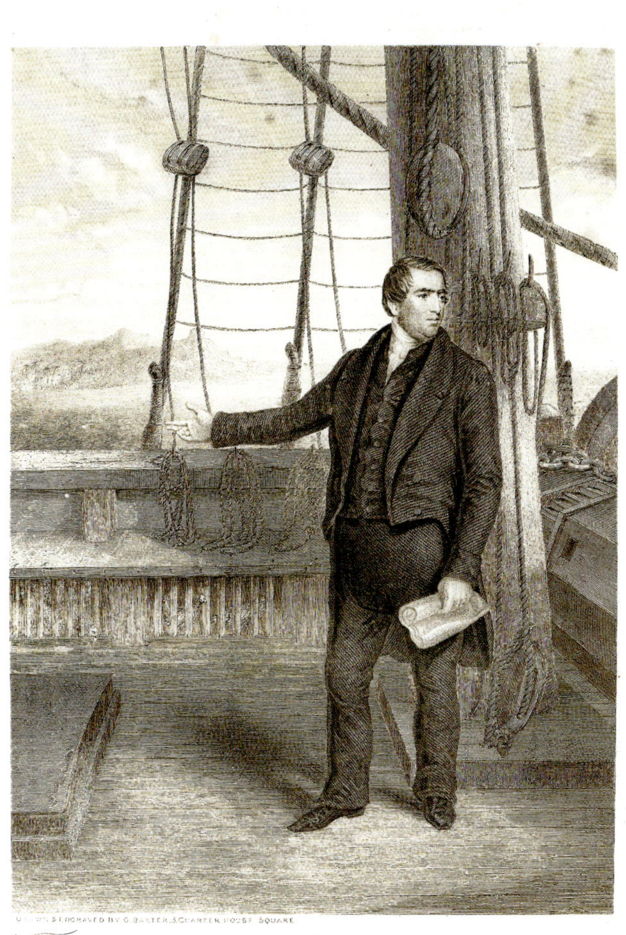

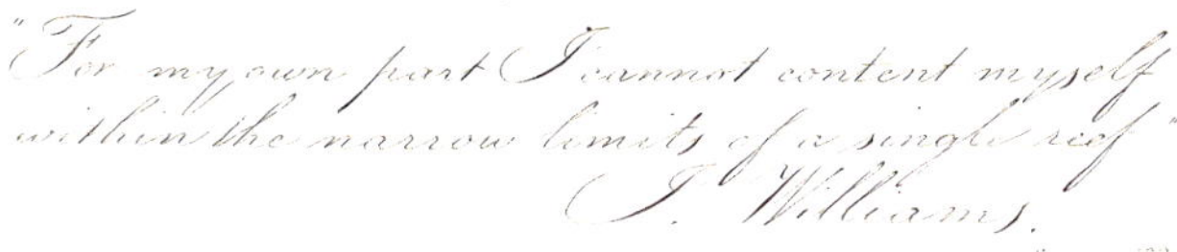

22

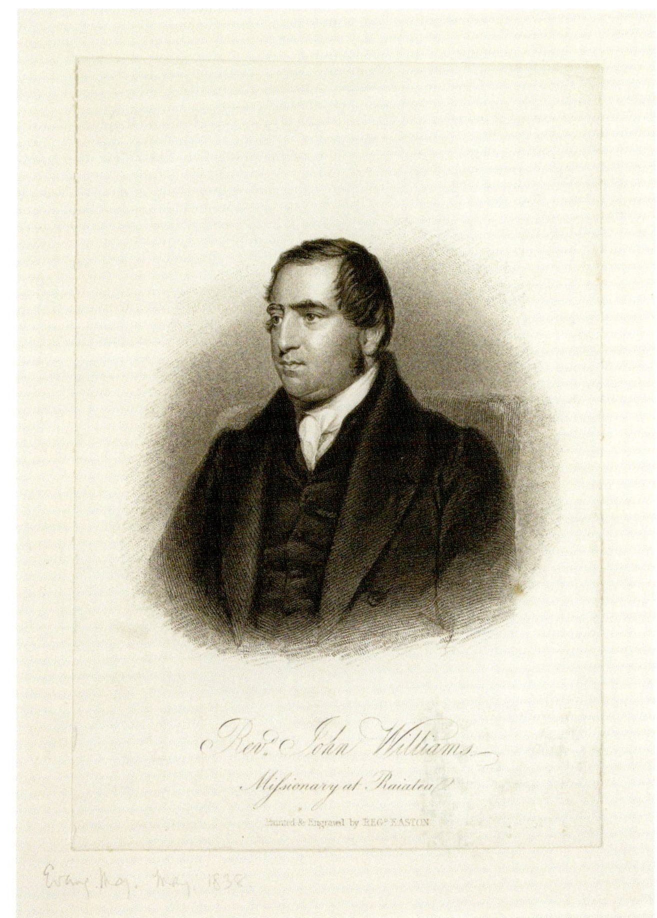

23

25

24

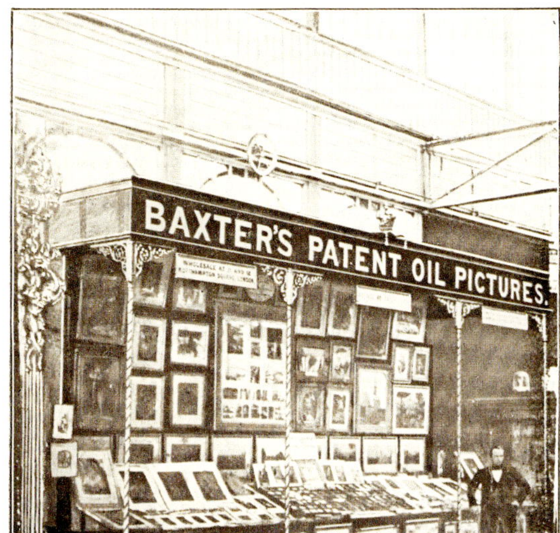

BAXTER'S STAND AT THE CRYSTAL PALACE.

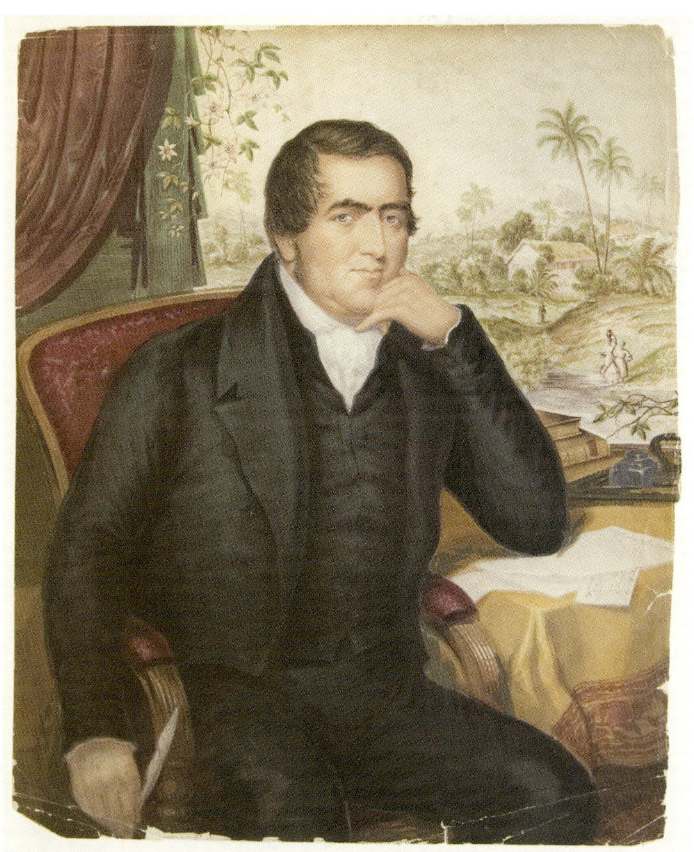

26 *John Williams on the eve of his departure to Tahiti, age 20. The LMS employed a miniaturist who bound together two series of portraits, each of about a dozen miniatures, accordion-style. The miniatures, made for identification purposes, were returned to the missionaries if they were dismissed. SOAS.*

27 *Example of missionary correspondence from the South Sea. 'Ship letter', Williams' second letter from Ra'iatea to his parents in London, 29 June 1821. Paper was scarce; letters wasted no space. SOAS.*

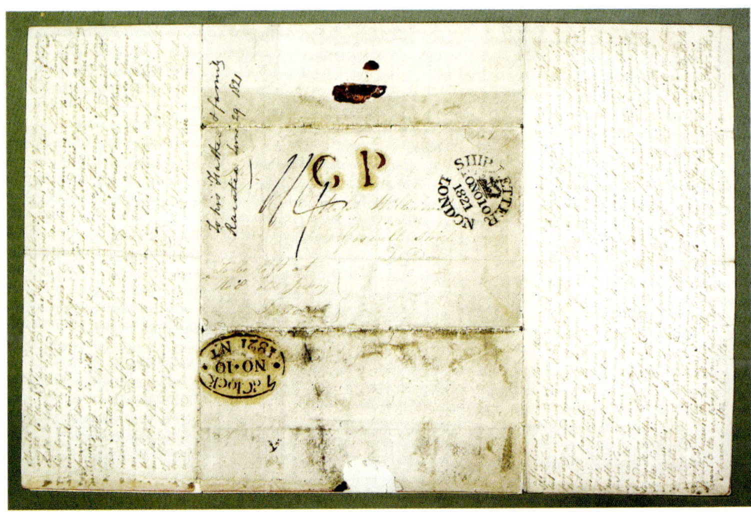

27

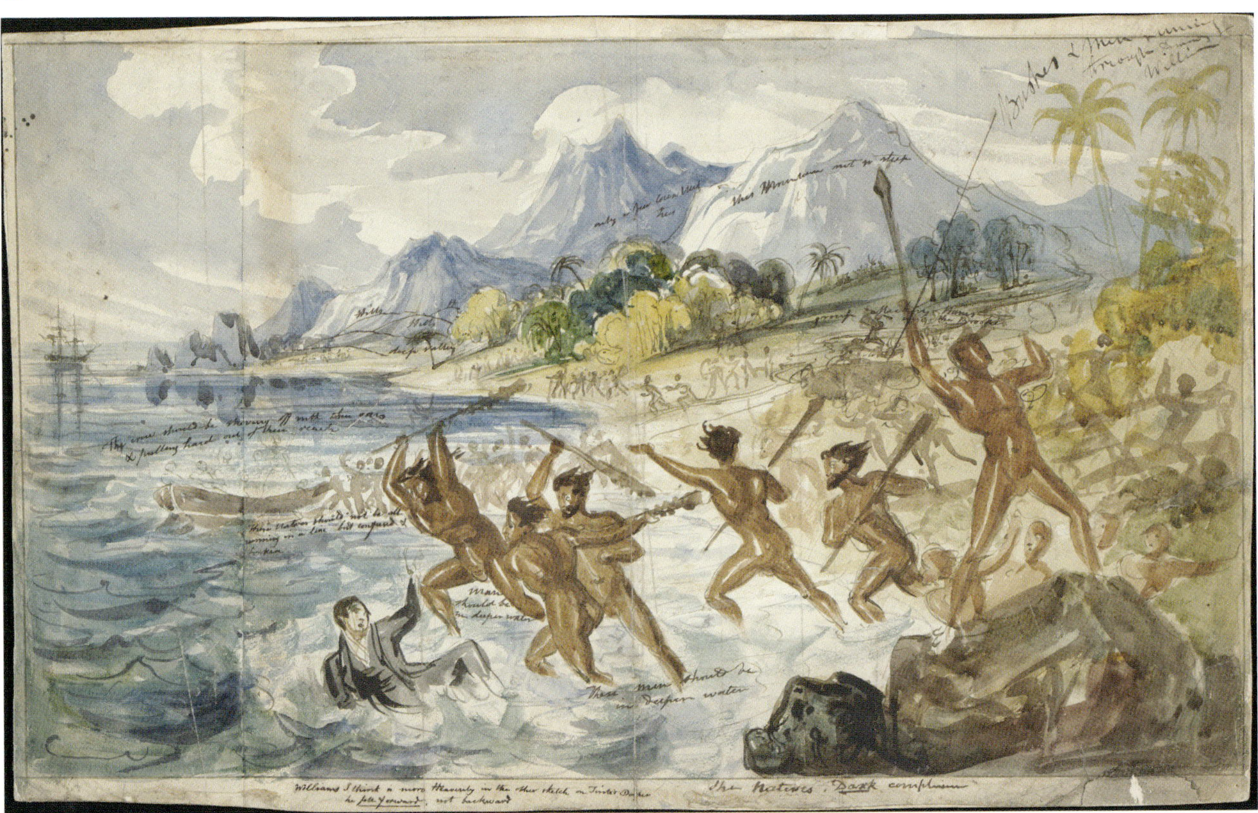

26

John WILLIAMS
Appt. 1816 –   –Died 1839
Register No. 173

28 *Baxter's watercolour sketch for the well-known 'oil colour' print,* The Massacre of the Lamented Missionary, The Rev. J. Williams, and Mr. Harris, 1841, *depicting the slaying of Williams at Dillon's Bay on Erromongo, New Hebrides, 20 November 1839. Rex Nan Kivell Collection. Courtesy NLA, Canberra.*

28

WILLIAM ELLIS, *POLYNESIAN RESEARCHES*, 1829 2,198.

FOUR

The Missionaries versus the Temples and the Idols

THE MISSION OF THE MISSIONARIES

BY AND LARGE, the missionaries had interests in Polynesia and Polynesians other than recording the culture: they came in order to convert the inhabitants to Christianity. They regarded Polynesians as a people who existed in a 'most degraded and wretched state of barbarism';[1] 'the blackest ink that ever stained paper is none too dark to describe them.'[2] Yet the missionaries had also read Cook and William Carey, who both considered that despite these shortcomings, such peoples 'appear to be as capable of knowledge as we are.' The missionaries' notion of their task is well expressed in a Biblical metaphor that they used often in their writings: 'Here is a fine field, ripe in the fullest sense of the word—"white to the harvest."'[3] The meaning of this is made clear at the onset of an LMS series entitled *The Harvest Field*: 'The harvest field brings before the mind a pleasant picture. A rich autumnal corn field of Europe or America, ripe, and ready for the sickle.'[4]

The missionaries' goal was 'transforming [the heathens'] barbarous, indolent, and idolatrous lives into a comparatively civilized, industrious, and Christian People.'[5] Polynesia was one of those enticing fields awaiting spiritual husbandry. '[The] Tahitian Mission [is] a fountain from whence the streams of salvation are to flow to the numerous islands.'[6] Williams put it vividly: 'I cannot content myself within the narrow limits of a single reef . . . while thousands around . . . and but a few miles off, are eating each other's flesh and drinking each other's blood, living and dying without

---

[1] Williams 1837,7.
[2] Carey 1792.
[3] Letter Williams Ra'iatea to his mentor Rev Matthew Wilks London 29 January 1825, in Prout 1843,219; this letter contains an excellent description of the missionaries' daily lives. The phrase 'white to the harvest' is from John 4:35.

[4] This is the first line in vol 1 N°1 of *The Harvest Field*, July 1880, re India and Ceylon.
[5] Williams 1837,6.
[6] Ibid.,9.

the Gospel.'[7] The missionaries frequently likened their endeavour to 'a bloodless war';[8] 'Of the islands we have visited, Rurutu, Aitutaki, Rarotonga &c, it may almost be said "we came we saw we conquered."'[9]

In accord with their aim to cast down Satan's Kingdom was the missionaries' well-known proclivity to see to the physical destruction of the emblems of Satan's Kingdom, the material symbols of Polynesian religion. Most important of these were (1) the sacred 'temples', the *marae*, where the idols were kept and ceremonies held, and (2) the sacred idols themselves. When the ruin of these was accomplished, the missionaries felt they had obtained palpable proof of successful conversion. The missionaries often flaunted their victory by engaging in the age-old gesture of erecting churches of Jehovah on the very sites, including the ahu (the 'altars'), of demolished marae. This was common practice; Bennet reports: 'Recently destroyed idol temples . . . abound, and we find almost every where a temple erected to Jehovah on the ruins thereof' (see fig. 9).[10] A good example is the church at the original LMS station on the west side of Ra'iatea, built on a marae platform; the ahu of the marae, at harbour's edge, is just 50 feet from the church. Well constructed, higher and larger than any other ahu in the Societies including Taputapuatea at Opoa, it probably proved too massive to tear down. This is Marae Ta'inuu in what is now the town of Ta'inuu, district of Teva'itoa. Both ahu and church, which was recently rebuilt on its original foundation, survive today.

Marae took many forms. Very little is known about Cook Island marae, but a good deal is known about Tahitian ones.[11] They were usually located on level ground near the coasts, or up the valleys on hills or ridges. They ranged from modest low rectangular platforms delineated with a row of stones and paved with basalt or coral, with a raised rectangular *ahu* ('altar') at one end, to enormous platforms with magnificent ahu that were stepped pyramids of dressed stone and coral over 200 feet long and 40 feet high; see figures 36, 40. Sacrificial victims were placed on the ahu. Offerings were placed on wooden platforms. Skulls were abundant; it was at marae that bones of ancestors were kept. The idols were housed nearby, in elevated god houses. Marae belonged to families of rank;[12] they were the palaces visited by the gods and were considered superlatively holy. The missionaries couldn't stand them. Tyerman and Bennet refer to them as 'the worst work of man', 'Satan's throne', 'the abomination of Huahine'.[13] Regarding the ceremonies that took place at marae, 'the bloody rites, the detestable profligacy—the worst words in our language would be abused in describing.'[14]

Despite their disapproval of everything connected with marae, the missionaries occasionally thought otherwise; Williams, for example, describes a Ha'apai (Tonga) god house as 'a most beautiful little temple [which] surpassed any structures I have seen in the Pacific.'[15]

One of the earliest and most informative eyewitness accounts of a marae ceremony is that of a missionary, John Jefferson, in 1798.[16] This neglected account is reproduced in Appendix 2.

On marae were stone uprights called *pou*, which Davies defines simply as 'post or pillar.' Small ones were perhaps a foot high; large ones extended more than ten feet above the ground. Some were of dressed limestone, others of natural prismatic basalt (see figs. 35–38, 48). Bligh, on the *Providence* voyage, describes

---

7   Prout 1843,189; this is probably a misquote (but a good one) from Williams' 30 September 1823 letter to Hankey: 'A missionary was never designed by Jesus to get a congregation of a hundred or two Natives & sit down at his ease as contented as if every sinner was converted while thousands around & a few miles from him are eating each others flesh & drinking each others blood with a savage delight living & dying without the knowledge of that gospel by which life & immortality are brought to light. . . . [F]or my own part I cannot content myself within the narrow limits of a single reef & if means is not afforded a continent to me would be infinitely preferable for there if you cannot ride you can walk but to these isolated Islands a ship must carry you.' Many of Williams' phrases echo those of William Carey and Thomas Haweis.

8   The enemy of course was Satan, adversary of God and man; letter Threlkeld 2 July 1820, SOAS LMS SS letters box3 folder6; Montgomery 1832 2,108.

9   August 1826 letter Williams to LMS directors, in Prout 1843,233.

10 Letter Bennet on Huahine to Edward McCoy (his nephew) 22 January 1822.

11 For more detailed accounts, see Banks, Jefferson, Morrison, Bligh, Tobin, Orsmond (Henry 1928), Ellis, Montgomery (1841,33), Bellwood, and especially Emory (1933, 1934) and Green and Green (1968).

12 Adams 1901,15.

13 Montgomery 1832 1,175 and 197.

14 Ibid., 1,178.

15 Williams 1837,320.

16 *Trans Miss Soc* 1804,98.

marae Taputapuatea at Utuhaihai, Pare, Tahiti, 1792: '[A] Pavement was in the front [of the ahu] where the Priests Sat & leaned their backs against Stone Posts [pou] for that Purpose.'[17] Jefferson, also at a marae in Pare, 1798, adds a bit more detail: 'Priests . . . sit cross-legged upon the pavement, and support their backs against the stones [pou]: and in this mode of adoration, with their faces towards the pile of stones [ahu] and boards [unu], they make their prayers.'[18] Emory suggests that pou were backrests for the gods. Tyerman and Bennet wrote: 'To these dumb blocks divine honors were accustomed to be paid, and prayers offered, by the fanatic priests and the deluded multitude.'[19]

Also on marae were sacred trees; Morrison describes marae on Tahiti 'planted thick with trees';[20] Tobin depicts this (fig. 26). Parkinson observed the platforms were 'planted with various sorts of flowering shrubs.'[21] All was enclosed by a wall or fence. A deep pit—*pafata*, according to Orsmond (T Henry)—gathered everything that was discarded; marae refuse was sacred.[22] Orsmond states that sometimes even the gods themselves were cast off if they were ineffectual in preventing illness or death.

There are a number of descriptions of what Morrison and Bligh refer to as 'travelling marae', a special double-hulled canoe used to transport the portable god house containing the god images.[23] An elaborate roofed superstructure housed the 'Oro image, placed in an ark-like *fare atua*, or god house.[24] Unu (discussed in next paragraph) were attached to the stern and to the god house; sacrificed hogs and dogs were placed on the prow. Jefferson describes a god house on a travelling marae in Pare, 1798: 'a box four or five feet long, and one foot square: the end towards the stem of the canoe open, and by which the divinity was said to enter.'[25]

Captain Bligh depicts in an annotated watercolour a travelling marae in remarkable detail (see figs. 45–47).

Adorning ahu of marae, sometimes in front of ahu or on marae platforms, were *unu*. These were large, complex, flat openwork carvings of wood, 'planks set upon their ends and carvd their whole length.'[26] Eighteenth-century drawings and watercolours often show them topped with figures of birds or humans. Boenechea describes them as having 'something the appearance of an organ, their upper extremity being surmounted by the crudely carved figure of a bird.'[27] Davies' definition of unu: 'piece of carved wood put up in the marae on offering up a man'; he lists the word *râ* as a synonym. Ellis describes unu as 'curiously carved pieces of wood [at marae], marking the sacred places of interment, and emblematical of their tii's or spirits.'[28] Tahitian unu were depicted numerous times by the artists on Cook's voyages, and also by Bligh, Tobin, and William Wilson (in Haweis 1799). There is mention in Williams' *Narrative* of unu on Rarotonga and on Aitutaki.[29] It is likely they were also in the Austral Islands. Jefferson, at Pare, comments about a group of five small unu: '[T]he tops are slit into five parts, to represent a hand with the fingers a little open . . . and these were called the hands of God.'[30] Sometimes they were painted with red earth. On occasions pou as well as unu were decorated with tapa and matting.[31] A number of renderings of unu are reproduced on figures 29–33, 38, 40. Not a single unu has survived.

Marae attendants—Orsmond (T Henry) calls them 'opu-nui (meaning large bellies)—were men who were the keepers of the gods. They lived in the god houses on marae grounds, kept the grounds clean, kept the rats and insects away from the images, and were allowed to partake of the food offerings and of the fruit from the sacred trees; they wore and slept in sacred brown tapa. They maintained the sacred marae drums, and they made tapa themselves.

Morrison provides us with a good description of marae on Tubua'i, in the Australs: 'The Morai's . . .

---

17 Oliver 1988,125. Utuhaihai was Cook's 'morai point' at the southwestern end of Matavai Bay; see Green & Green 1968.
18 *Trans Miss Soc* 1804,99.
19 Montgomery 1832 1,179.
20 Morrison 1935,179. Morrison (ibid.,147) and Davies mention specifically *miro* or *amae*; the leaves of this tree, *rau ava*, were used to make an intoxicating beverage, generally known as kava.
21 Parkinson 1773,70.
22 Henry 1928,178. Davies defines pafata as box.
23 See for instance Henry 1928,136; Dening 1992.
24 For more on god houses, see Hooper 2005, 2007; Kaeppler 2007.
25 *Trans Miss Soc* 1804,102..

26 Banks in Beaglehole 1963 1,318.
27 Corney 1913 1,337.
28 Ellis 1829 2,214.
29 See Buck 1944,308.
30 *Trans Miss Soc* 1804,102. The 'legs of god' supported the god houses on 'travelling marae'.
31 Henry 1928,159.

differ from those of the Society Islands, being all Flat pavements and having a number of large Flag Stones placed on end in tiers or rows in the Center, they are planted with the Tee or Sweet Root . . . a little house on on[e] side.' And he also provides information on Tubua'i pou: '[The sacrificial victim's body is cut up,] the Head, bones & Bowels are Interd in the Morai, and a Stone put up, not to perpetuate the Memory of the Man but as a mark of the Number that have been Offered there.'[32] Morrison also describes indoor marae, where men were buried, 'fenced by a teir of Flat Stones set up [on] end four or five feet high . . . [and where] they keep the Images of their Fore fathers or Tutelar deitys, as they believe that their Souls are fond of see-ing respect paid to their remains, and that they always hover about the place of these representatives.'[33]

Only one reasonably detailed LMS account of a Cook Islands marae seems to exist. WW Gill describes, from hearsay, an ancient marae on Mangaia: a raised rectangle 25 by 100 feet, filled with human heads 'cut off for the purpose, covered with earth, and topped with a layer of snow-white coral pebbles.'[34] For more on Cook Islands marae, see Trotter 1974, and Bellwood 1978. Marae, pou, and unu are of great importance in central Polynesian religion, but receive very little attention; a number of renderings of them are shown in figures 29–50 following this chapter.

THE PROCESS OF 'CONVERSION'

At the core (more accurately, at the surface) of the actual conversion process was a conspicuous, public display of sacrilege committed towards marae and towards idols. The method the missionaries and their 'teachers' used to prove that the idols had no power—and to expose 'the folly of idolatry'[35]—was to employ a clever and the-atrical test, or demonstration, in public, consisting of two steps: (1) persuading a primary convert, preferably a person of the highest rank, to lay waste to his marae and burn his idols; and (2) demonstrating that there followed no disastrous consequences, that no venge-ance of the gods poured forth upon the sacrilegious.

It was an open defiance of the tapu system. In the words of Tyerman and Bennet, this was 'the perilous experi-ment, which should prove whether the objects of wor-ship were gods or not'.[36]

One 'experiment' is described in striking detail in Appendix 6; another good example of this process: Williams, based on the accounts of Papeiha and Tibe-rio, two Raiatean Christian teachers, tells of the burn-ing of the first idol in Rarotonga:

> A cumbrous god . . . he threw at the feet of his teach-ers, one of whom fetched a saw to cut it up; but as soon as the people observed the saw applied to the head of the god, they all took fright and ran away. After a short time they returned; and in the presence of an immense crowd, the first rejected idol of Rarotonga was com-mitted to the flames. In order to convince the people of the utter futility of their fears, when the idol was reduced to ashes, the teachers roasted some bananas upon them, of which they ate themselves, and invited others to partake. No one, however, had the courage to admit so dangerous a morsel into their mouths, and waited, with no small anxiety, to witness the result.

But no harm came. Within the next ten days, four-teen idols were burned, then four more.

> [They took] a fire-brand, and set fire to the temple, the atarau, or altar, and the unus, or sacred pieces of carved wood, by which the marae was decorated. Four great idols were then brought and laid at the teachers' feet, who, having read a portion of the tenth chapter of the gospel of St Luke, which was peculiarly appropriate, disrobed them of the cloth in which they were enveloped, distributed it among the people, and threw the wood to the flames. Thus were the inhabitants of this district delivered from the reign of superstition and ignorance under which they had so long groaned.[37]

Tyerman and Bennet describe an earlier instance of public sacrilege, on Mo'orea; they speak of a chief,

---

[32] Morrison 1935,70.
[33] Ibid., 67.
[34] WW Gill 1880,27.
[35] Montgomery 1832 1,64.

[36] Ibid., 1,133.
[37] Williams 1837,177.

the first in Eimeo publicly to confess by throwing his idols into the flames. This he did in the presence of his countrymen, who stood shuddering at his hardihood, and expecting that the evil spirits, to whom the senseless stocks were dedicated, would strike him dead upon the spot for his profanation. He remained unharmed, however, and it was not long before other chiefs followed his example and the people joining in with them, the temples, the altars, the images of Satan were universally overthrown.[38]

Another occasion, also on Eimeo:

Papi brought his idols, three in number, upon his back, to the place of execution. There, throwing the lumber down upon the ground, he took an axe, hewed away the wicker-work that encased them, and split the uncouth shapes, to see what might be within, when bones of fishes and men, that had been sacrificed were found in the cavities. The dumb logs and stocks were then cast into the flames of a large fire, and presently consumed to ashes.

Again nothing dire happened as a consequence, and the spectators, witnessing the 'total impotence' of their gods, 'felt the faith of their ancestors not a little shaken.' Tyerman and Bennet called it a 'memorable conflagration.'[39]

Fire was evidently not the only method employed to destroy idols. Tyerman and Bennet mention another process, even more dramatic, employed at Punaauia (Tahiti): '[T]he house pulled down . . . wooden inhabitants shot through and through, and then consumed to ashes.'[40]

Although it would seem of prime importance that the Polynesians themselves destroyed their own marae and idols, at least on one occasion, English visitors took matters into their own hands. Tyerman and Bennet describe an incident on the north side of Oahu: 'In every instance, when we were strong enough, we tumbled these idols [stone uprights] over the edge of the cliffs into the sea, and scattered the votive offerings to the wind. Upwards of three score of these images . . . we hurled from their seats down the precipices.'[41]

Conversion was often aided by external circumstances such as death, disease, hurricanes, famine—times when the gods seemed to have deserted the people in their hour of need; in Williams' words, 'The downfall of idolatry was accelerated by ordinary occurrences, in which, however, a Divine agency was too conspicuous to avoid observation.'[42]

The diligent efforts of the missionary wives were also important agents in acclimating Polynesians to European culture and to Christianity. Both Mary Williams and Mary Mercy Ellis, for example, visited the elderly and the sick, held Sunday school sessions for children, and taught morning classes, including hymns, scripture, English domestic arts, and offered 'directions and encouragements' to as many as 30 women at a time. The missionary women were much in demand as family counsellors; as Ellis expressed it, 'the wives of the missionaries were as oracles to the native females.'[43] '[N]othing presented the religion of the Bible [better] than affectionate sympathy and kindness . . . rendered . . . towards those who were in circumstances of distress.'[44] Haweis believed from the start regarding missionary wives, 'I think they will greatly enhance [the mission].'[45] They were missionaries as well.

The first conversions were not easy. The early missionaries in Tahiti travelled about giving sermons, but their audiences were, of course, completely perplexed. The missionaries rapidly discovered that communicating the intricate fabric of Christianity without having a full command the Tahitian language was not possible. There were two instruments that established the missionaries' first inroads towards the Polynesians. Neither was anticipated, but both soon became apparent: one was music, and the other was the concept of putting language into writing.

It pleased the missionaries that Tahitians took to singing Christian hymns (*himene*) rapidly, and with enormous enthusiasm and proficiency—a talent that lasts to this day. They found Tahitian lent itself to song:

38 Montgomery 1832 1,71.
39 Ibid., 1,133.
40 Ibid., 2,193.
41 Ibid., 2,72.
42 Williams 1837,73.
43 Ellis 1836,97.
44 Ibid.
45 T Haweis 1795,173.

'[T]he Otaheitan language, which from its construction being chiefly of vowels, gives a peculiarly agreeable effect to versification.'[46] Tyerman and Bennet found Tahitian singing harmonious to the extent that they regarded it the 'Italian of Barbarians'.[47] Missionaries translated nearly 300 hymns into the Tahitian and Rarotongan dialects. They also composed their own. Song was eagerly received; prayers and sermons fell flat.

Books and printing presses were the other instruments. The interest that Tahitians showed in the concept of communicating by means of the written word was instant and intense, and unexpected. Hymnals, along with spelling books and scriptures, all prepared by the missionaries, were the first books printed in the Tahitian language (see figs. 15–20). A spelling and syllable book by Davies was the very first. It was printed in London in 1810 in an edition of 700 copies. The entire process took three years; it arrived in Tahiti unproofread and full of errors. The next seven books in Tahitian—again, spelling books, hymnals, and scriptures—were printed under the direction of Rev Samuel Marsden in Parramatta, 1813 to 1816. Printing in Australia was faster and resulted in fewer errors.

Finally, after repeated requests from the Tahitian Mission, the LMS in London sent the missionaries their own press, type, ink and paper, on the brig *Queen Charlotte*. The new press arrived at Eimeo (Mo'orea} 13 February 1817 along with William Ellis, who had been trained in printing. The press was set up in Afareaitu, in a fine printing studio with glass windows and a floor of basalt blocks—from a marae. Pomare II was fascinated and delighted by the idea of printing, both as technical process and theatre. So were other islanders; canoes lined the beach, throngs encamped. Pomare himself pulled the first pages of the 15 letter Tahitian alphabet on 30 June 1817. The day was declared a national holiday. Over the next three years Ellis printed several spelling books, hymnals, and gospels—a total of 9000 copies. Additional presses were established and named: The Windward Mission Press at Burder's Point (Punaauia, Tahiti), The Leeward Mission Press at Huahine, and finally one at Rarotonga, in 1834, under the direction of Rev Aaron Buzacott. The presses, like the missionaries, moved from island to island, accompanied by much rivalry and bickering. Polynesian grammars fixed the dialects. Demand for books was strong; they became valued gifts; islanders memorized and recited them. In these ways, books in Tahitian became important agents in Christianization.

Ten years later, the missionaries employed a third and even more powerful agent for effecting conversion, which was to use Polynesian missionaries to do the work instead of English ones. This idea came initially from the directors, who had instructed the missionaries via Captain Robson on the ill-fated second voyage of the *Duff*, 1798, to 'take with them a well disposed Chief to facilitate their introduction and establishment' if they went on to evangelize other islands.[48] The missionaries carried these instructions a step farther. They trained Tahitian converts, called 'native teachers', who were sent ahead, usually in pairs and frequently with their wives, to accomplish the initial conversions on their own. Williams explained the advantage of this strategy to Tyerman, with respect to the Aitutaki mission: 'You have no conception of what great advantage it is to have the previous labour of native teachers to enter upon.... Beside native teachers know how to [go] about clearing away the rubbish of idolatry & superstition better than newly arrived or even Old Missionaries.'[49] Williams' idea of how this worked: '[W]e listened with joy that we had so able an advocate . . . as he [a native teacher] was likely to be heard with much less prejudice than we should be.'[50]

The teachers' methods were not always wholesome, or approved, but they were effective. For instance, on Rarotonga: '[T]he teachers proposed . . . as he [an inspired heathen priest] entered the house, to take out their knives, and demand that they should be allowed to make an incision and search for the great god Tangaroa, who, he said, was within him.'[51] Missionary Charles Pitman describes a teacher in action: 'On

---

46 *Sydney Gazette* 19 February 1814, cited in *Evangelical Magazine* 1814,491.

47 Montgomery 1832 1,223.

48 *Evangelical Magazine* 1799,13. After his conversion, Pomare II, on his own, sent teachers to several other islands on missions of conversion.

49 Letter 21 August 1823 Williams (Ra'iatea) to Tyerman (Tahiti) SOAS LMS SS incom corresp box4 jacketB folderl.

50 Williams ms *Journal of a Voyage*; Pacific Manuscripts Bureau, Australian National University, PMB35; 44 pages.

51 Williams 1837,180.

the Wednesday after our arrival we attended service at the chapel, which was completely crowded. Tiberio, the native teacher, preached. To me, it was a pleasing sight. To witness so large a building, crowded with people who were but recently pagans, now listening to the word of God from the lips of a native teacher of another island, produced feelings not easily described.'[52]

MISSIONARY VIEWS OF POLYNESIANS AND THEIR RELIGION

The attitude of Williams and the other missionaries towards Polynesians was, of course, mixed, and contradictory. On the one hand, they described Polynesians as polluted, barbarous, 'veterans in Satan's service',[53] and so on; their descriptions are laden with disapproval. On the other hand, the missionaries profoundly respected the Polynesians. They found them good-natured and generous. They admired their wit, ingenuity, quickness of perception, humour, tenacious memory, thirst for knowledge, discernment, mathematical ability, and the great precision and force in the expression of their thoughts: 'In these, the South Sea islander does not rank below the European.'[54] Ellis saw Tahitians as happy, amiable, intelligent, and benevolent, with an 'air of romance', and 'no inferior powers of imagination'.[55] Even Tyerman and Bennet found them 'graceful and good-humoured', their oratory 'often exceedingly beautiful and appropriate'. Some missionaries would travel considerable distances just to listen to Polynesian oratory. It was as if the missionaries, and Tyerman and Bennet, admired everything about Polynesians except their religion.

Similarly, the missionaries considered Polynesian gods 'malignant',[56] and the god images 'disgusting', but not always. Williams makes some distinctions: 'Some were large, and some were small; some were beautiful,

while others were exceedingly hideous.'[57] Regarding Polynesian taste and technical skills, the missionaries, like the explorers before them, expressed enthusiasm and admiration: 'The ingenuity of all their works is wonderful, considering the tools they possess.'[58] Williams and Ellis: 'We were amazed at the patience and skill of the native artificers';[59]

> [M]ost worthy of notice in this island [Mangaia] is the ingenuity of the inhabitants; this is displayed in the fabrication and patterns of their cloth, in the construction of their spears, bowls, and other articles; but more especially in the exquisite carving of the handles of their stone axes. This they effect with a regularity, taste, and beauty which is surprising, when it is recollected that the only tools they formerly possessed were sharks' teeth and shells.[60]

They admired the mats, 'many of them exquisitely ornamented';[61] the king's *maro* (cincture), a 'splendid train';[62] and Austral bowls *(umete)*, 'neither inelegant nor rude'.[63] They even admired 'the ingenuity of the tattoos . . . , with a regularity and beauty that cannot but excite the imagination'. This quote is from Tyerman and Bennet, although ten pages later they refer to tattooing as 'this barbarous art';[64] tattooing was rapidly outlawed by the missionaries. There is no question the missionaries thought highly of the aesthetics and the ingenious craftsmanship of Polynesians. The objects they brought back to England attest to this.

Remarkably, missionaries at times permitted the incorporation of heathen elements into some of their newly-constructed South Sea Christian churches. Even Rarotongan staff gods: 'Some of these idols were torn to pieces before our eyes; others were reserved to decorate the rafters of the chapel we proposed to

---

[52] Prout 1843,245.
[53] Williams 1837,259.
[54] Ibid.,516.
[55] Ellis 1829 2,197.
[56] Ellis 1853 1,354; it is worth noting that the Evangelicals objected as much to idols as they did to the pomp and corruption of the Church of England: 'the eternal majesty is affronted by the abominable idols of the heathen, and the beastly image of a corrupt Christianity' (M Horne [Boston edition] 1834,26).

[57] Williams 1837,546.
[58] T Haweis 1799,330/William Smith 1813,55.
[59] Williams 1837,279.
[60] Williams 1837,263, commenting on the Mangaian adze he illustrates on p. 264.
[61] Montgomery 1832 1,229; Huahine.
[62] Ibid.,2,125. Maro is a long waistband—a sacred cincture of rank; Cook referred to these as girdles; see below, and figs. 219 & 220. Another term for maro is *tatua* (Davies 1851; Savage 1962).
[63] Ellis 1853 1,192.
[64] Montgomery 1832 1,93.

erect',[65]—presumably the 'rude imitation of the human head' portion, with the 'obscene figure at the other end' removed. Williams mentions a chapel built in 1827 in Ngantangiia (a district of southeast Rarotonga) under Papeiha's supervision: 'One of its most striking peculiarities was the presence of many indelicate heathen figures carved on the centre posts; . . . the builders thought that the figures with which they decorated the marae would be equally ornamental in the main pillars of a Christian sanctuary. The building was 250 feet in length, and 40 feet wide.'[66] Sometimes it was not the wooden carvings of the staff gods but their tapa wrappings that were incorporated: 'While we were fixing the rafters, the chiefs expressed a wish that two of their *varua kinos* (evil spirits) might be stripped of their cloth to wrap around, or ornament them. To this we agreed.'[67] When Williams returned to a completely converted Rarotonga, in 1831, things had improved: 'We were gratified at perceiving that the interior of the chapel . . . was fitted up more in the English style than any hitherto erected.'[68]

Thus the missionaries were of two minds about the people they came to convert. But there was one quality the missionaries found universally appealing about Polynesians: their 'religiousness'. 'Religious rites were connected with almost every aspect of their lives. An ubu or prayer was offered before they ate their food, when they tilled their ground, planted their gardens, built their houses, launched their canoes, cast their nets, and commenced or concluded a journey.'[69] Ellis could not have put it better: 'It is impossible not to feel interested in a people who were accustomed to consider themselves surrounded by invisible intelligences.'[70] Rev William Gill made a similar appraisal: 'These heathen tribes were, in their heathenism, a religious people. They had ideas concerning God, and right and wrong, their convictions of sin were pungent, and led to a practical concern about something they called salvation. But alas, poor distressed creatures! They were left to grope in the dark.'[71] All the missionaries had to do was to realign all this misdirected religious energy towards the Pretane god.

---

65 Williams 1837,117. William Gill (1856,47) gives us a slightly more detailed version of this: 'The roof was exposed; and at the request of the people, some of their former au tiki, or carved gods, were stripped of their sacred bark cloth, and hung by their necks at the rafters, as an emblem of their degradation and death'. The hanging of idols in Tonga has been well documented and discussed by Neich, 2007.
66 Williams 1837,123.
67 Charles Pitman in Prout 1843,246. Posts in Papeiha's Aitutaki chapel were 'covered with painted cloth'; Williams ms *Journal of a Voyage*,6; PMB35.

68 Williams 1837,380. Portions of stone images were incorporated as well (WW Gill 1880,193; Mangaia): 'Many years ago, when these people embraced Christianity, this huge stone idol was utterly defaced, and the fragments form part of the stonework of the church at the principal village.'
69 Ellis 1853 1,350.
70 Ellis 1829 2,198.
71 William Gill 1856,33.

Marae, Pou, Unu

29 Pulling down a Pagan Altar. *Detail from a wood engraving in the magazine* Missionary Sketches 6, *July 1819. SOAS. The missionaries engaged Tahitians to tear out and burn all the objects on their marae. The engraving is reproduced in full in fig. 6.*

30 *Openwork wood carvings called unu, and skulls, beneath altar with sacrifices, Tahiti; Ellis, 1829. J Jefferson, visiting a marae at Pare, Tahiti, in 1797, remarks about unu: 'the tops are slit into five parts, to represent a hand with the fingers a little open . . . and these were called the hands of God' (Trans Miss Soc 1804 1,99).*

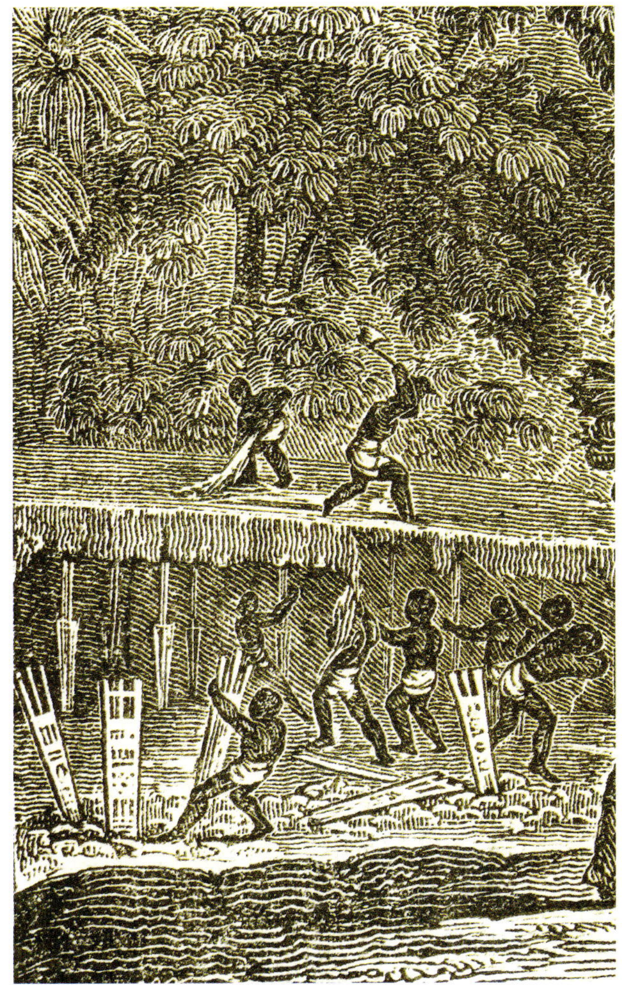

29

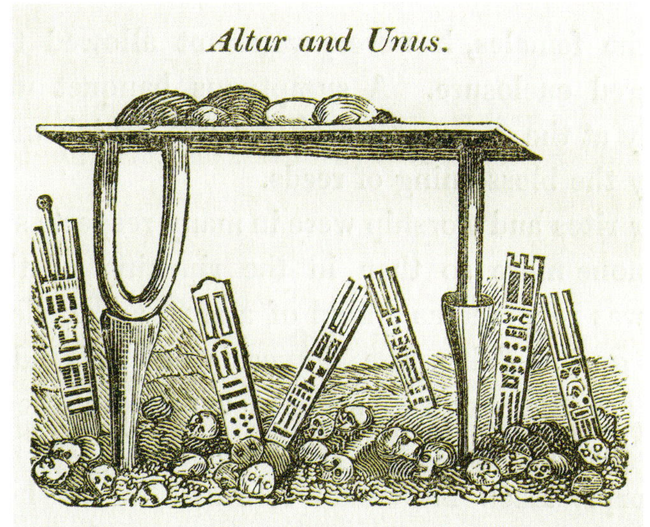

30

31 *Detail,* Morai & Altar at Attahooro with the Eatooa [gods]
and trees, *1797, after sketch by William Wilson, Chief Officer on
the* Duff; *from Haweis 1799, 208. Probably Marae Taata, Paea,
Tahiti, where Cook witnessed a human sacrifice in 1777; also depicted
by Webber. Here, the gods are unu, visible in the foreground. None
survives. There are no depictions of unu from the Australs or the
Cooks—only from the Societies.*

31

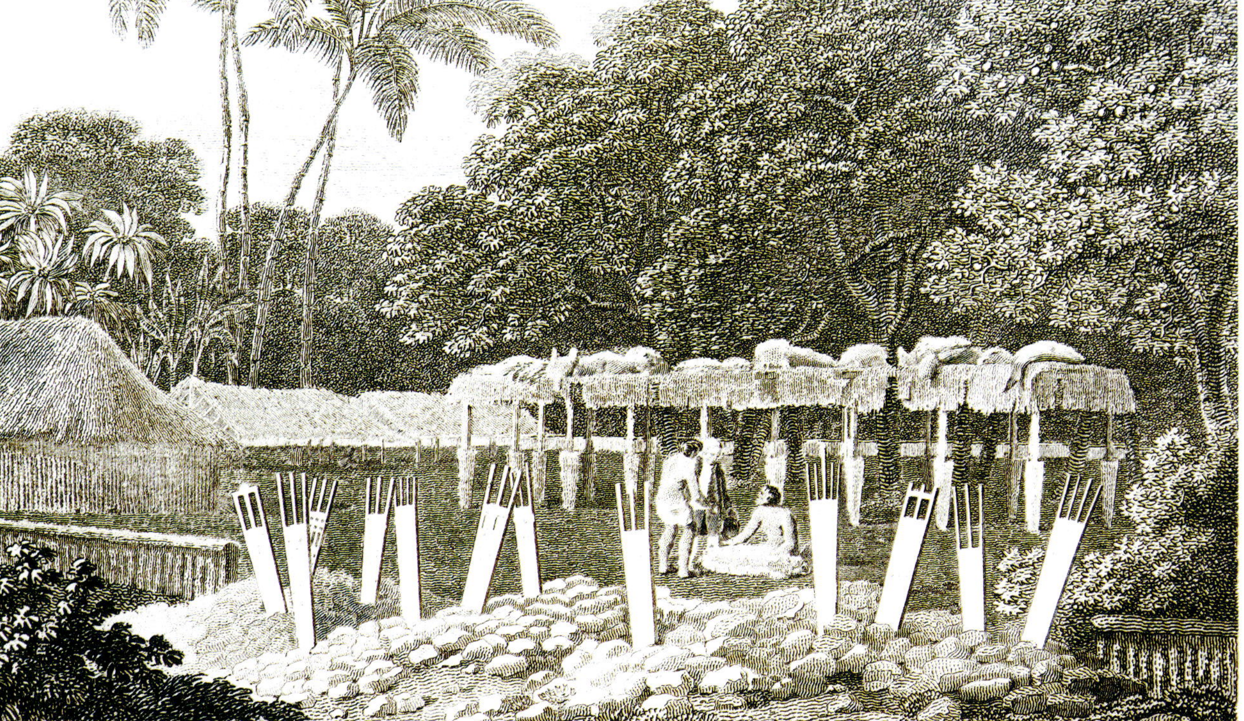

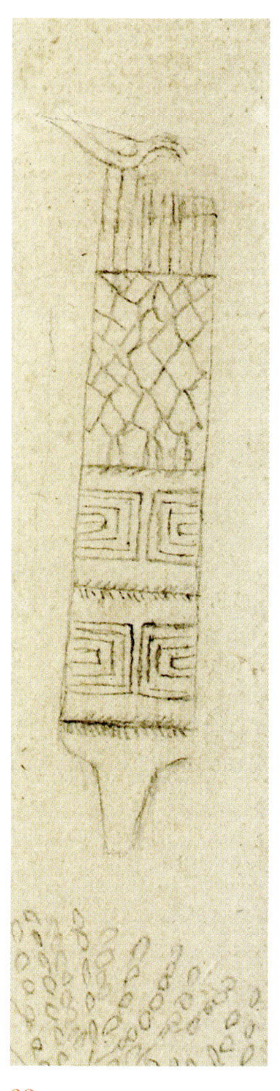

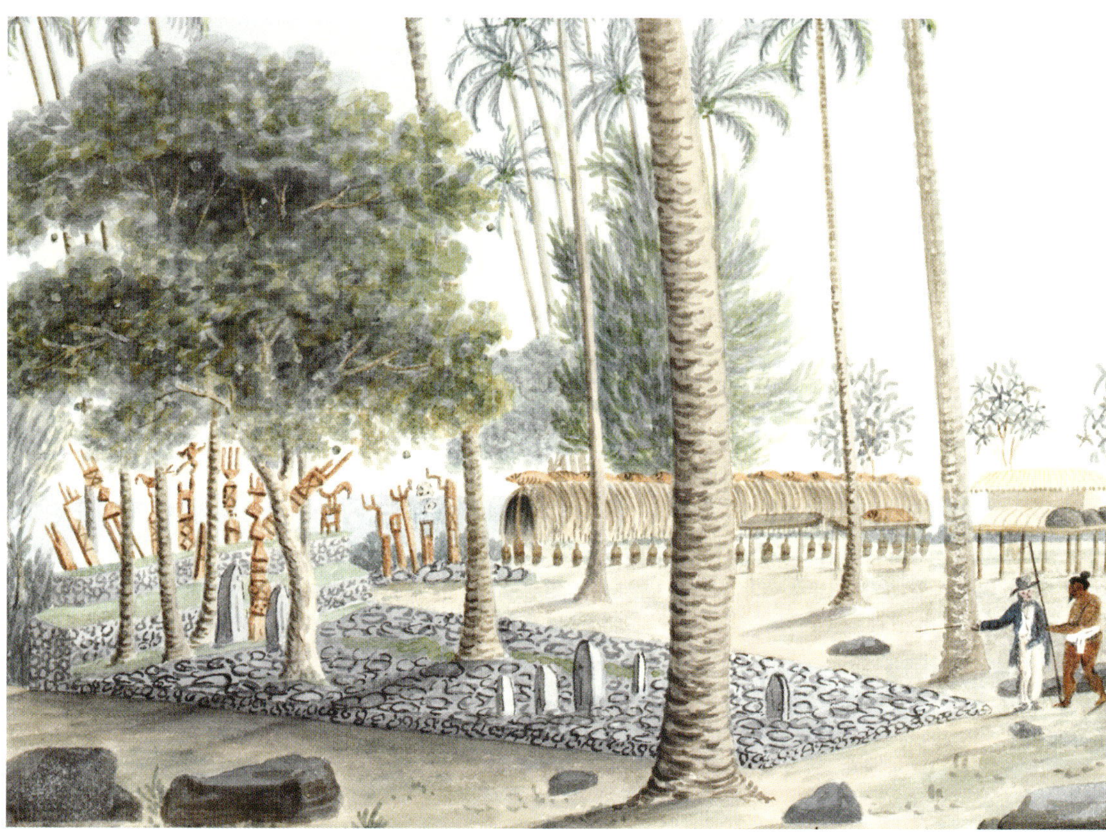

32   33

34

32   *Detailed pencil sketch of unu, drawn by Raiatean chief Tupaia, 1769; it appears in the margin of the rendering of marae shown in fig. 42. Courtesy British Library, Add. ms 15508,18.*

33   *Detail, watercolour of Marae Taputapuatea at Utuhaihai, Pare, Tahiti, showing unu; note abundance of trees growing on the marae platform. From George Tobin's* Providence *journal, 1792. Courtesy Mitchell Library. Unu were painted with red ochre, evident here; some had human, bird, or lizard figures on top. On occasions unu were decorated with tapa and matting (Henry 1928,159).*

34   Marae Unurau, Raivavae; *from S & K Routledge, 1921. Courtesy BPBM.*

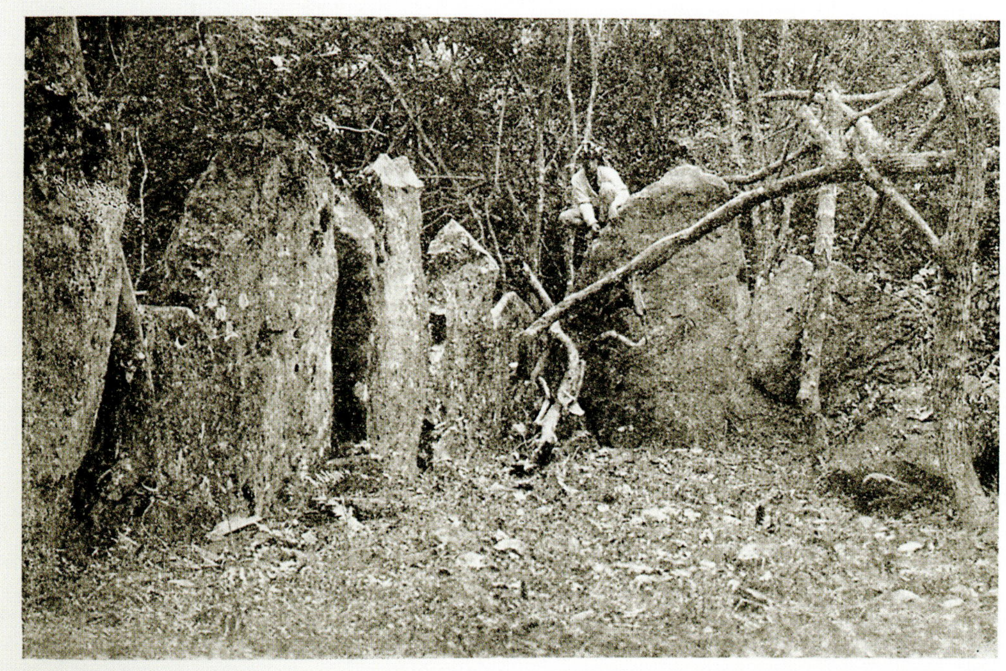

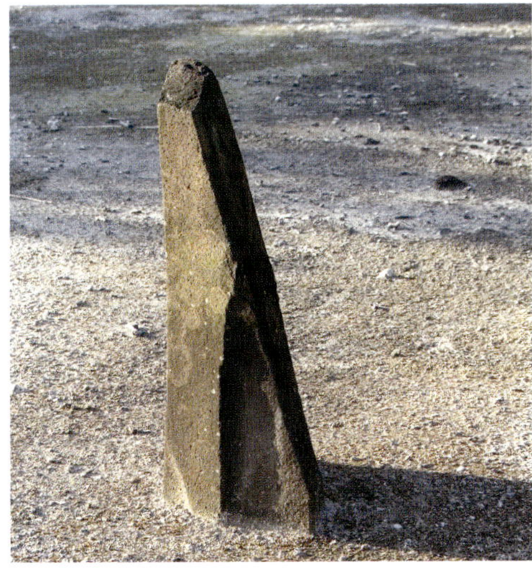

35

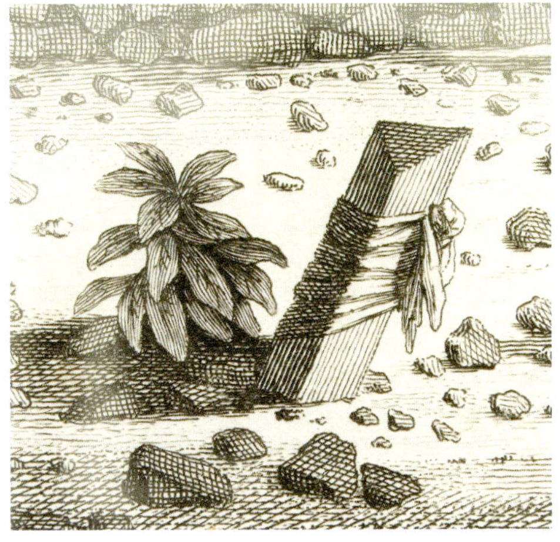

36

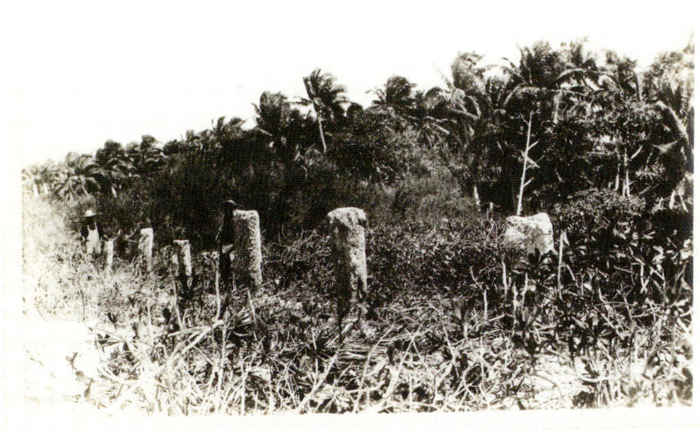

37

35 *Small prismatic basalt pou 40cm high, on a very small marae adjacent to Marae Taputapuatea, Ra'iatea. 2007. Pou, stone uprights rising 30 to 300cm above ground level, were located on and near marae, elsewhere as well, and were on occasions adorned with white tapa.*

36 *Small prismatic basalt pou, wrapped with undecorated tapa, on marae at Waimea, Kauai. Cook's 3rd voyage engraving after Webber, 1784.*

37 *Marae Nukurea, Vaiari, Tongareva (Penrhyn, Northern Cooks), 1924. Photo KP Emory. Courtesy BPBM.*

38 *Marae Taputapuatea at Utuhaihai, Pare, north Tahiti; watercolour by William Bligh, second breadfruit voyage, on the* Providence, *April 1792. Mitchell Library. Note numerous elaborate unu and six pou on the marae platform. This is the main portion of the watercolour; two more small marae with unu are depicted in the background in the entire image. These marae no longer exist.*

38

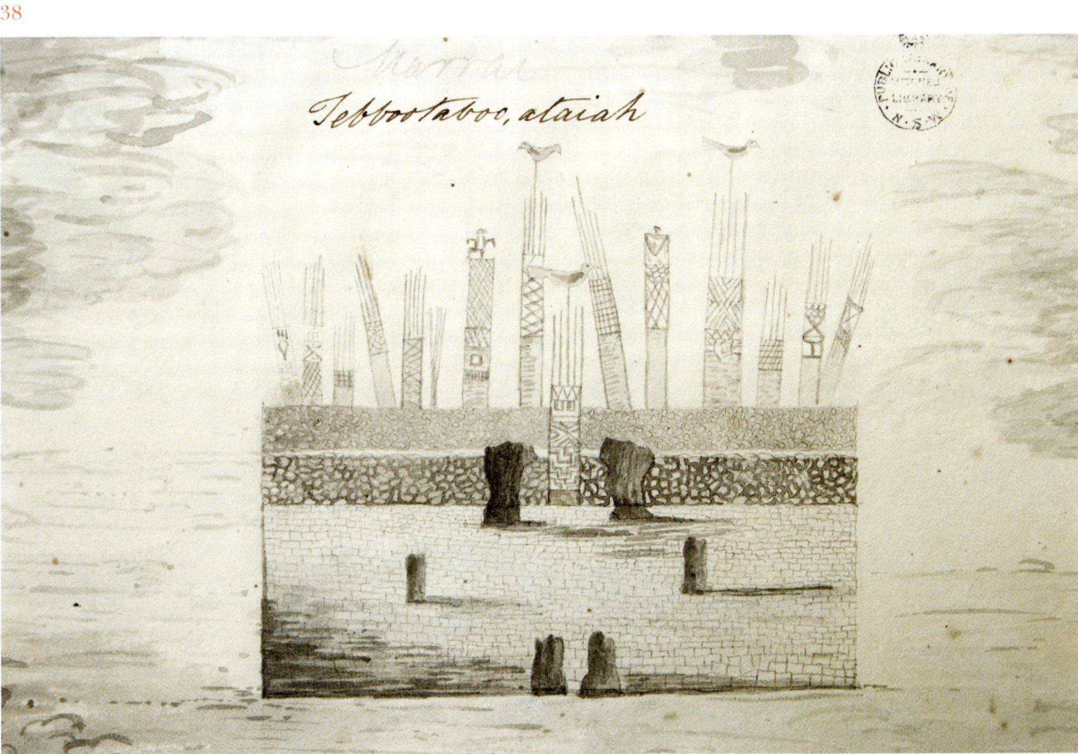

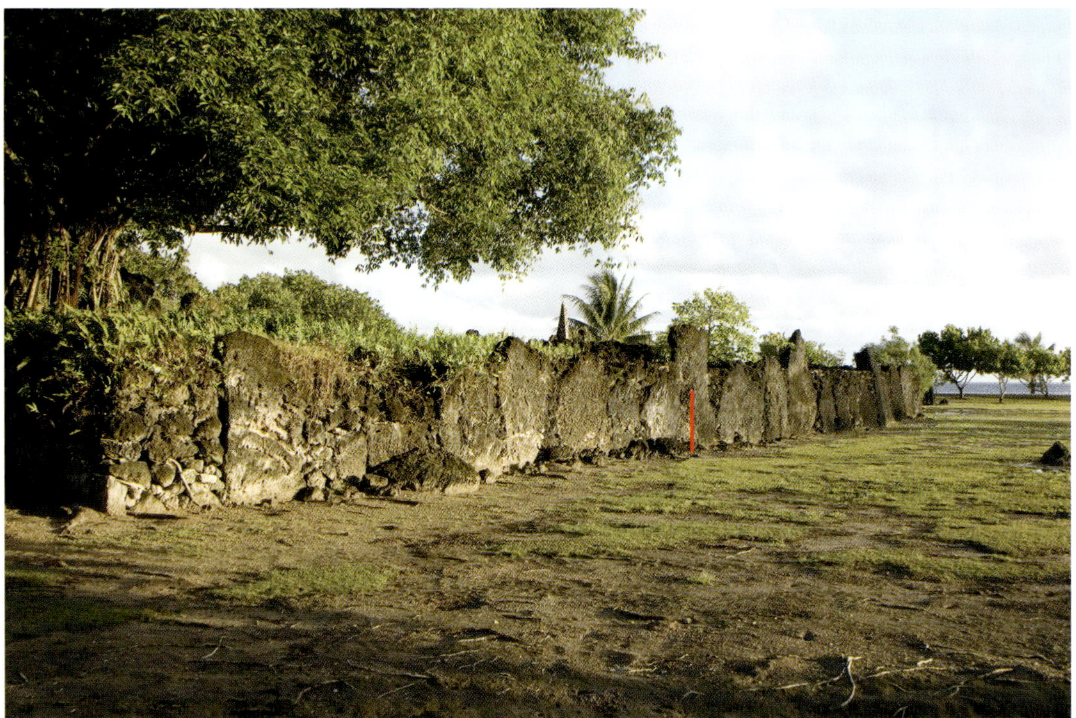

40

39   *Back side of ahu of the Great Marae Taputapuatea at Opoa, Ra'iatea; northeast corner. It dates to the 17th century (Sinoto 1966) or perhaps early 18th century (see Sharp et al. 2010). The ahu is 43m long, and is faced with massive dressed coral slabs extending up to 4m above the ground. Partially restored by Y Sinoto. In the foreground are burrow entrances of the large land crabs (Cardisoma carnifex) that formerly consumed much of the marae offerings, including the sacrificial victims. Red bar is approximately 2m high. Photo August 2007.*

40   *Detail of a wash by Sydney Parkinson, showing what appears to be the southeast corner of the ahu of the Great Marae Taputapuatea at Opoa, Ra'iatea, July 1769. A number of large unu are set on the top of the ahu. Opoa was the birthplace of the cult of 'Oro; Taputapuatea at Opoa was the most important marae in central Polynesia. Courtesy British Library, Add. ms 23921,28.*

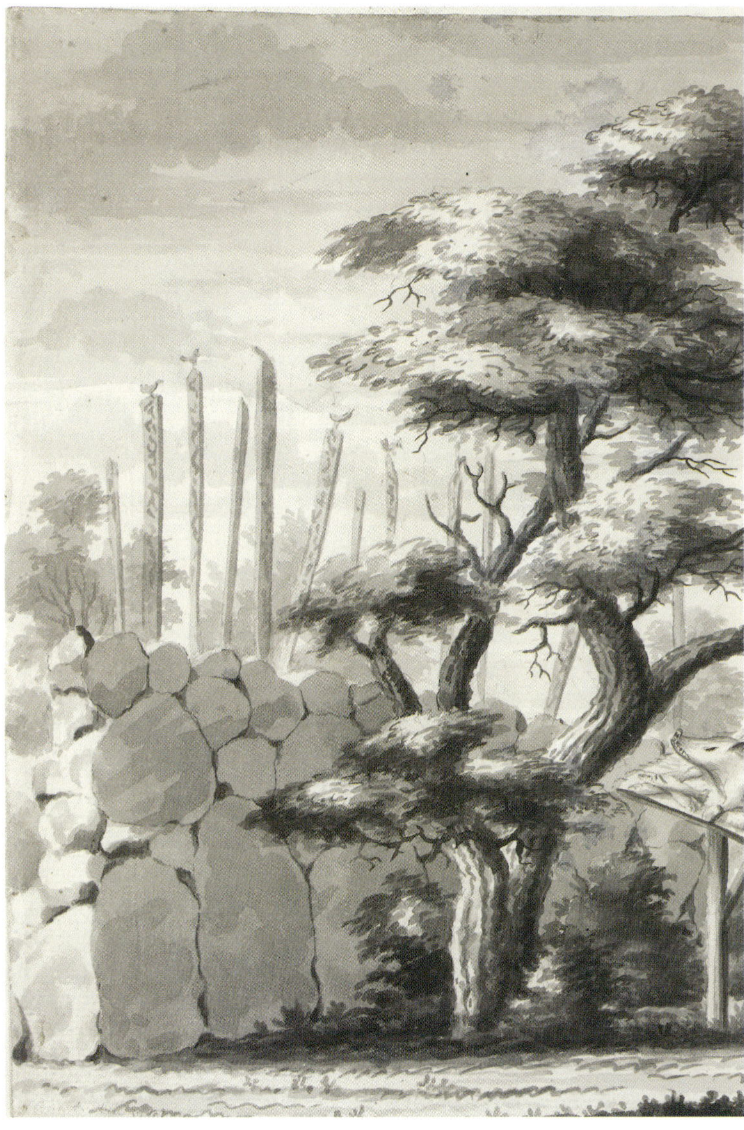

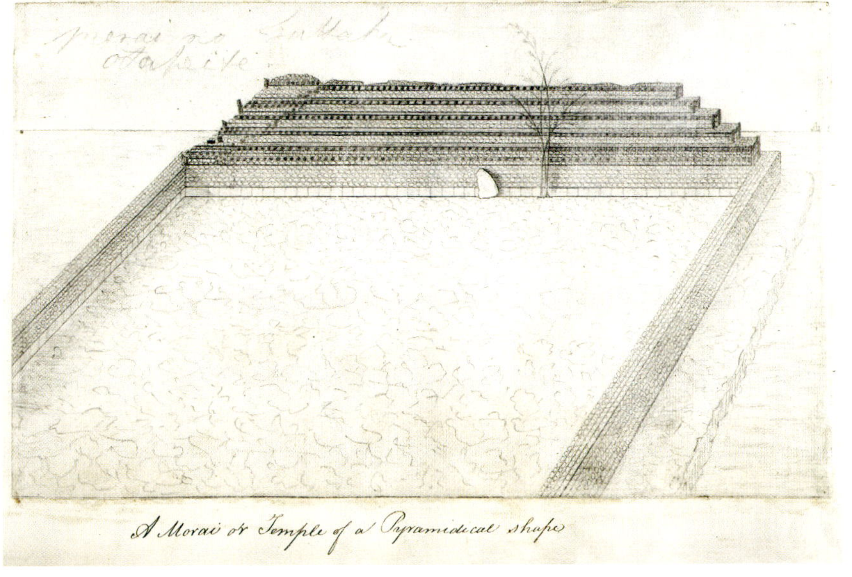

A Morai or Temple of a Pyramidical shape

41

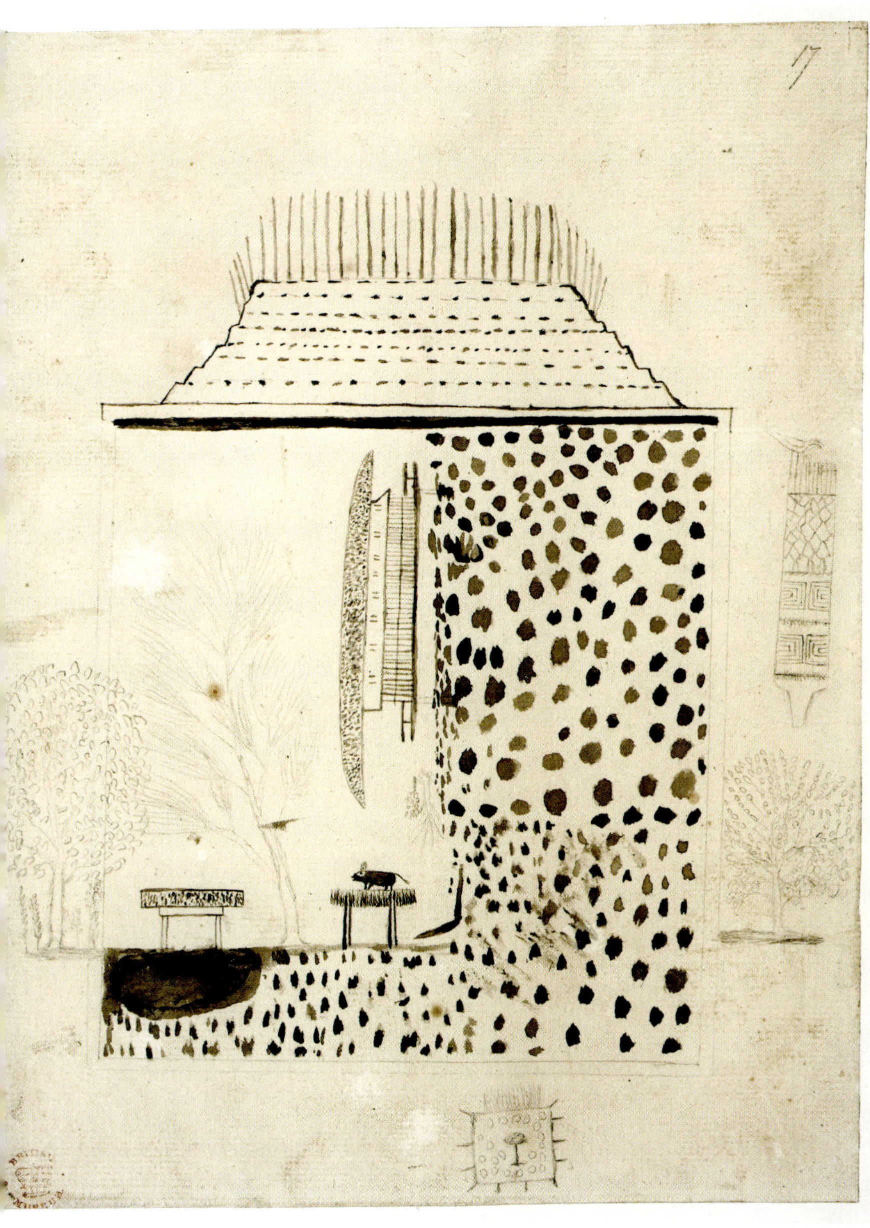

42

41 Morai no Tuttaha Otaheite. *Pencil drawing by Banks' secretary, and naturalist, Herman Spöring, 1769, Cook's 1st voyage; probably one of the marae at Utuhaihai, Cook's 'morai point', Pare, Tahiti. Shows walled marae platform, and pyramidal ahu of five steps. Courtesy British Library, Add. ms 23921,27(c).*

42 *Pencil and wash rendering of a marae, showing all the essential elements, each from a different vantage point. Drawn by 'The Artist of the Chief Mourner', identified as Tupaia (Carter in Lincoln,126), June 1769. Tupaia was a Raiatean priest and chief taken on board the* Endeavour *at Tahiti by Cook and Banks, to act as navigator and interpreter. He was evidently taught how to draw by Parkinson and Spöring. Shown are a multi-stepped ahu with numerous unu (top), a stone-paved marae platform, trees, a god house, a pig offering on a wood platform. It is unclear which marae is depicted. The stepped ahu is coastal Tahitian in type; the god house (fare atua; centre) is much like those depicted on Huahine. Courtesy British Library, Add. ms 15508,18.*

43 *Petroglyph depicting headdress, fau, near Marae Ta'inuu, Teva'itoa, Ra'iatea. Petroglyph height 70cm. Marae stones were only occasionally incised, usually with turtle figures or concentric circles. Photograph KP Emory. Courtesy BPBM.*

44 *Marae were constructed with basalt as well as with dressed coral, shown in this close-up, with embedded* Tridacna *still in place. Marae Hauviri, Opoa, Ra'atea, 2007.*

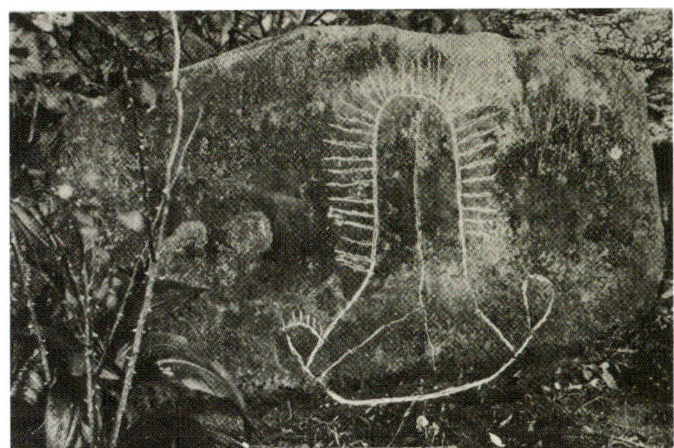

43

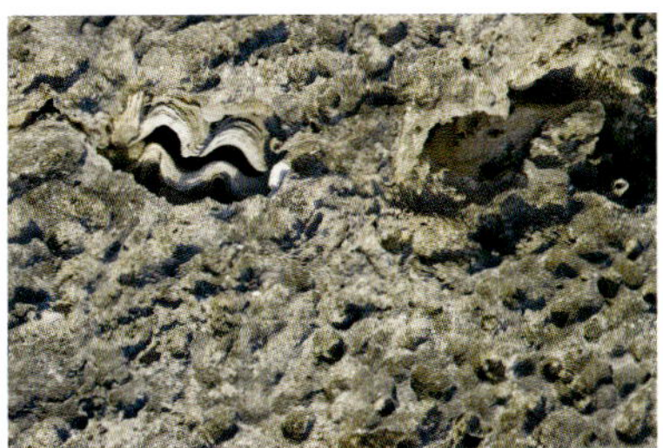

44

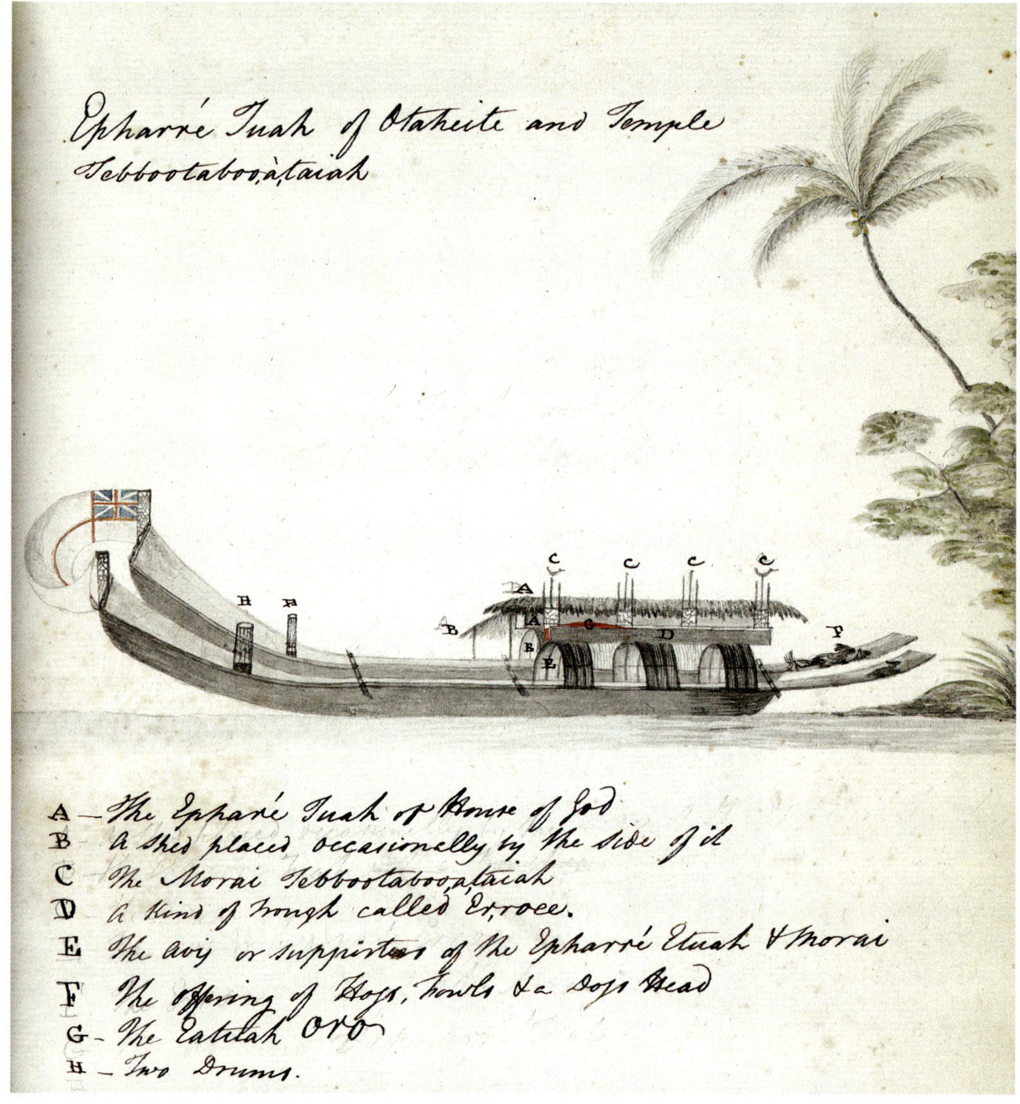

45

45 Epharré Tuah *[fare atua; god house]* of Otaheite and Temple Tebbootabooàtaiah, *annotated watercolour by Lt William Bligh of a travelling or portable marae, on a large double canoe. Tahiti. Mitchell Library. Bligh colours prominently the ensign, left by Cook, and the red trade cloth covering of 'Oro, either from Cook or from Watts.*

Both the land marae and the canoe marae were called Taputapuatea, located at Utuhaihai in the district of Pare, north Tahiti—not to be confused with marae of the same name at Punaauia, or at Tautira— or at Opoa on Ra'iatea. Bligh's watercolours in many cases contain more information than Tobin's.

Bligh's Journal, second breadfruit voyage, on the Providence:
Thursday, April 26th [1792]: At daylight this morning I walked with Tynah and Tootaha to see the great temple. I found it on a double canoe about a mile from Point Venus in the harbour of Taipippee near the small island of Mowdoow. It was hauled up on the beach—on the prow of the canoe was a baked hog, the head of a dog, a fowl, and a piece of sugar cane. After being seated in the canoe, Tootaha began a prayer in favour of King George and of myself . . . the purport of which was that we might never . . . be overcome by our enemies. His chanting was accompanied by two drums: one was beat by a native, the other by one of my people who came with me, so that it cannot be supposed that there was much harmony in it. There was an interval in prayer when the priest took off all his clothes and lifted a bundle like an Egyptian mummy covered with red cloth from out of its vault into a kind of trough on top of it. It contained, he said, the Etuah, the Marro Oorah, and other sacred things. I requested to have it opened, but he assured me that I should see it tomorrow at Oparre at a ceremony—this senseless lump and the canoe have been spoken of with much wonder and respect . . . they call the temple the Ephare Tuah or House of God. It is about 6 feet 4 inches long and 5½ feet high. (Lee 1920,88.)

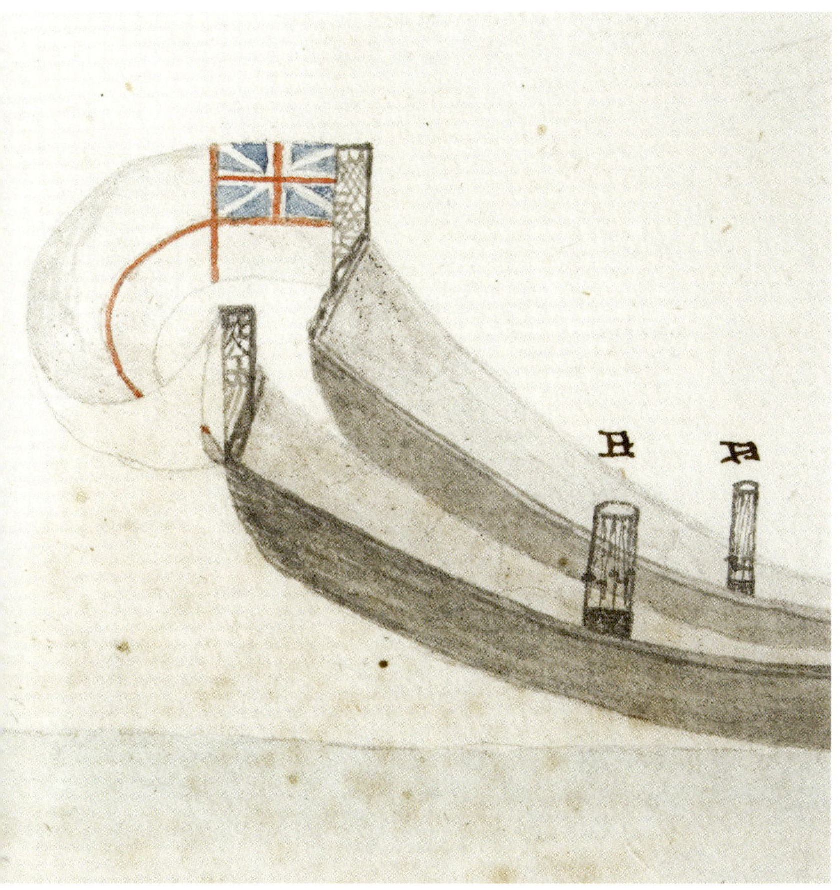

46 *Detail of stern, showing British ensign, left by Cook, flown from what appear to be two unu. Two drums (H) are also shown.*

47 *Detail of god house (A) atop travelling marae, bearing four unu (C), and conspicuously showing red trade cloth which covered bundle containing 'The Eatuah Oro', marked G, lying in a 'trough', marked D.*

46

47

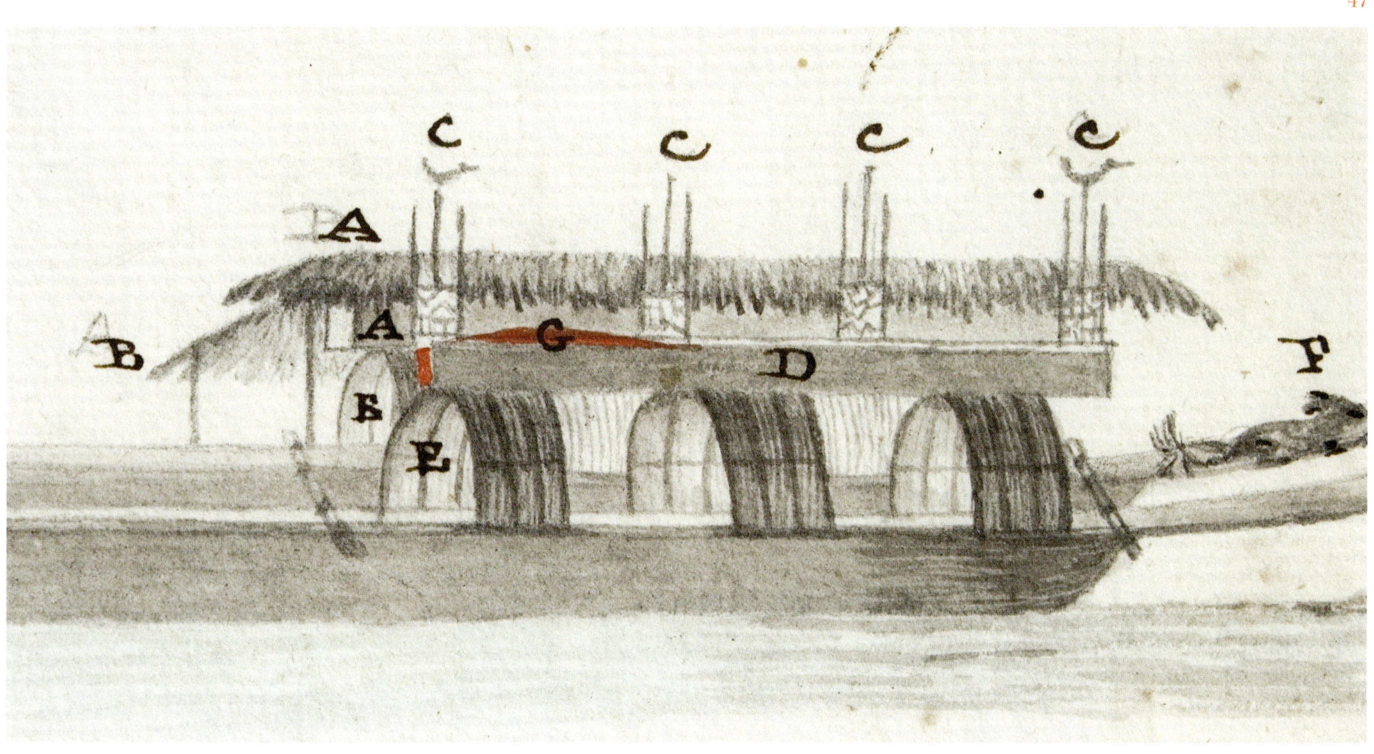

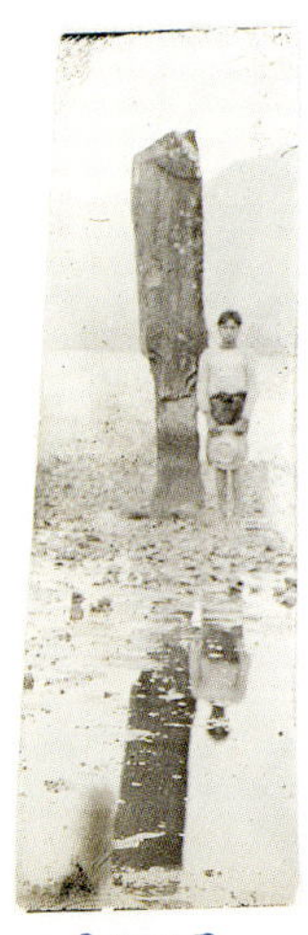
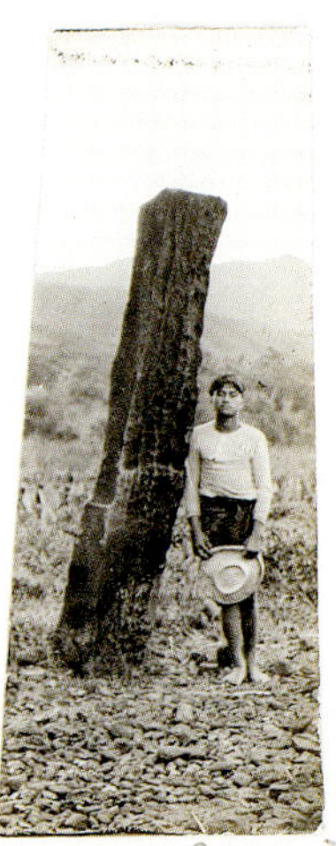
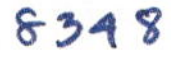

48 *Large pou on Rapa. KP Emory field photographs, 1934. Courtesy BPBM. J Jefferson observed (at a marae in Pare, Tahiti, 1797) 'Priests . . . sit crosslegged upon the pavement, and support their backs against the stones' (Trans Miss Soc 1804 1,99).*

49 *The Great Marae Taputapuatea at Opoa, Ra'iatea; from Arthur Baessler,* Neue Südsee-Bilder, *1900. This is probably the earliest published photograph of a central Polynesian marae.*

50 *Engraving,* Great Morai of Temarre at Papara in Otaheite, *after sketch by William Wilson, on the* Duff; *Haweis 1799. This was Marae Maha'iatea, the largest on Tahiti, with an ahu of 10 steps, 267 feet long, rising 44 feet (Banks) or 51 feet (Wilson), built 1766-1768. Banks (1769) described it with a large wooden bird and stone fish on the top. Wilson (1797) described it as going to ruins. It was dismantled by the French government in 1865 in order to build a bridge, which was promptly washed away.*

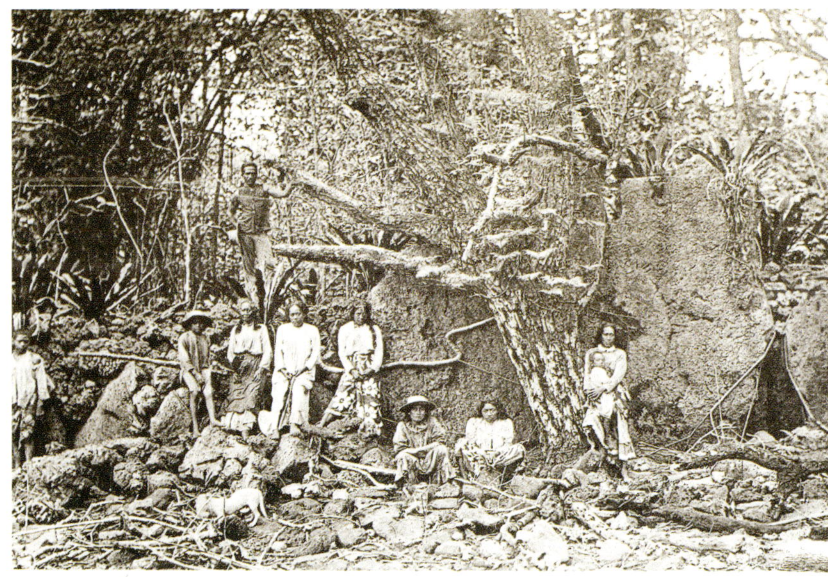

49

50

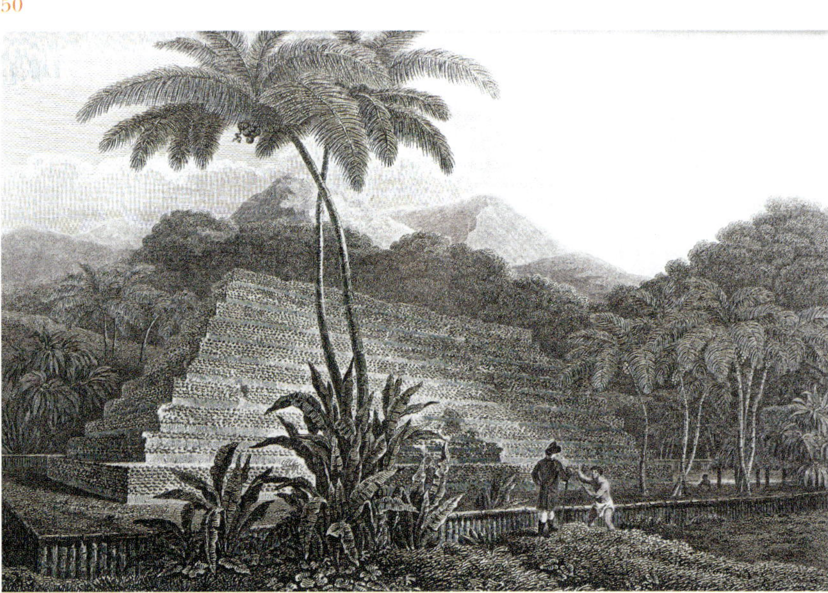

FIVE

Idol Materials: Feathers, Tapa, and Sennit

BIRDS AND FEATHERS

WHAT MADE Polynesian idols sacred? Two quotes from Papeiha, speaking on Rarotonga in 1823, convey the essential elements. 'We asked them [Rarotongans] what is your God—they replied—it is wood worked with our hands. We told them that ours was the same . . . [F]ormerly we cut down wood & decorated it [with] platted Sinnet & lashed red feathers to it . . . made cloth for it . . . placed it in the Marae & called it a powerful God, it killed our children & sacrifices were taken to it.'[1] A second quote is similar: 'What you worship is not god it is nothing but wood feathers and cocoanut husk that your own hands have made. . . . [T]hey are worthless things & will all be cast away and become food for the flames.'[2] Thus, according to Papeiha, the important elements were wood, sennit, feathers, and 'cloth'—meaning tapa. As Papeiha was from Ra'iatea,

he probably had in mind images of 'Oro. Evidently the same sacred materials were employed on Rarotongan god images as well.

Birds and feathers were of supreme significance in Polynesian religion. Ellis describes this well: 'A bird is a frequent emblem of deity; and in the body of a bird they supposed the god often approached the marae, where it left the bird, and entered the too, or image, through which it was supposed to communicate with the priest.'[3] 'Among the animate objects of their worship, they included a number of birds as well as fishes, especially a species of heron, a kingfisher, and one or two kinds of woodpecker, accustomed to frequent the trees growing in the precincts of the temple. These birds were considered sacred, and usually fed upon the sacrifices. The natives imagined the god was imbodied in

---

1   Williams ms *Journal of a Voyage*,41; PMB35.
2   Williams' translation of a letter from Papeiha, in letter 2 February 1825 Williams to Burder (SOAS LMS SS incom corresp box7 folder5 jacketC).

3   Ellis 1829 2,191; this recalls exactly the earlier narrative of Morrison (1935,181): 'the Deity . . . always makes use of Birds when he descends on earth'; also T Haweis 1799,337 and 358; *Missionary Records* 1839,57.

the bird, when it approached the temple to feast upon the offering. . . . The cries of the birds were regarded as the responses of the gods to the prayers of the priests.'[4]

Many on Cook's first voyage, landing on Tahiti, were quick to notice the close connection of birds and feathers with things sacred—red feathers especially; red was a sacred colour. Regarding birds, Sydney Parkinson, the young artist employed by Joseph Banks, mentions 'the birds sacred to Ethooa [which he defines as "a god"] of which there are two that fly about the morais, the grey heron and a blue and brown kingfisher.'[5] Regarding bird images, Banks describes near marae the unu, '[M]any carved boards set upright, on the tops of which were various figures of birds and men; on one particularly a figure of a cock painted red and yellow in imitation of the feathers of that bird.'[6] These are clearly depicted in Parkinson's wash of Marae Taputapuatea, Ra'iatea (fig. 40). François Vivès, surgeon on Bougainville's *Étoile*, landing on the east coast of Tahiti a year before Cook: 'Every evening on [the sun's] setting, they retire to their huts to adore some fetishes. They are broken shells, cut and sewn together in the shape of a bird with a long tail. . . . They also have some of these fetishes in all their boats.'[7] Haweis narrates a report from one of the brethren on the first missionary voyage: 'A priest, who pretended to great power in witchcraft, produced a rush wrapped up in the form of a bird and shewed me how they worshipped their god by this instrument, and intimated that it gave the divine response as our Bible. To a curious person it would have been a feast to examine, but my bowels yearned over their ignorance and idolatry.'[8] None of these bird images survives.

Regarding feathers: a simple long thin staff with large dark feathers attached to the terminus appears in several Cook first voyage renderings of priests in Tahitian mourning outfits, such as the detailed pencil drawing by Herman Spöring;[9] the priests themselves wore feathers of several types. And feathers were attached to canoe stern pieces, capes, maro, gorgets, headdresses, and idols—such as the images of 'Oro,

which were adorned and sometimes completely covered with red feathers, known as *ura* in Tahiti, *kura* in the Cooks.[10] 'Oro feathers, and ones contained in hollow gods, were replenished, along with their sacred wrappings, in the grandest of all religious rites, the *pa'iatua* festivals held every three moons, when all the idols were removed from the god houses, unwrapped, sunned, and re-wrapped in new, scented tapa.[11] Coconut oil scented with tiare ('mountain gardenia') and sandalwood provided the fragrance. Ellis reports that the god images were also anointed with fragrant oil on these occasions; Orsmond (T Henry) specifies that only the magician's images (ti'i) were oiled. Orsmond refers to these as 'fetchers', either neatly or roughly hewn out of wood, stone, or coral, 'in caricature form of human beings, which were dressed as little men and women in various kinds of tapa fastened on with fine sennit.'[12] Kaeppler stresses the importance of prayers, chanting, and music in imparting sacredness to the god images in the pa'iatua ceremony.[13] A few ura from 'Oro plus a stone from 'Oro's marae constituted a temporary marae—a symbol of the presence of the gods—on a canoe, at the outset of an Arioi voyage; Arioi was a sect of privileged, wandering, infanticide-practicing, 'Oro-worshipping players.[14] And conversely, gods taken in war were stripped of their feathers.[15]

Forster, on Cook's second voyage, tells us: 'After the burial of the bones the relations now and then renew some funeral ceremonies with the priest, who takes a bunch of the red feathers of a parroquet called oòra, and twisted together with coco-nut filaments, and fixes them on a small pointed stick in the ground; (these feathers are in high estimation with these people and

---

[4] Ellis 1829 2,202.

[5] Parkinson 1773,73 and fig. 40; Marae Taputapuatea, Ra'iatea.

[6] Banks in Beaglehole 1963 1,297; at Tautira, Tahiti.

[7] Dunmore 2002,231.

[8] Tahiti; T Haweis 1799,163.

[9] Joppien and Smith 1985 1,111, plate 1.48.

[10] Ellis 1829 2,203. The word ura (oòra) sometimes refers to the parrot itself.

[11] Ellis 1829 2,205; see also Henry 1928; Oliver 1974 1,112.

[12] Henry 1928,203. BM J 63, figured in Hooper 2006 fig. 123, is no doubt one of these. Perhaps human figures such as Saffron Walden 1835.185(E144) (Pole 1987 fig. 66) are fetchers as well.

[13] Kaeppler 2007,122.

[14] Ellis 1853 1,234. Arioi defies simple definition; see Oliver 1974 2,913. Cook called them 'male libertines', like freemasons; Morrison called them 'young men of wild, active and lively, amorous and volatile, devoted to roving, pleasure, and debauchery'; T Haweis 'the sink of lewdness and cruelty'; Ellis 'strolling players, infamous and licentious'; Orsmond 'the most obsessed and wicked creatures imaginable'; Tyerman and Bennet 'harpies; loathsome, earthly, sensual, devilish combined.'

[15] Henry 1928,167.

become the emblem of the divinity, and serve to fix their attention to the ceremony). . . . '[16] And Ellis: 'Throughout Polynesia, the ordinary medium of communicating or extending supernatural powers, was the red feather of a small bird found in many of the islands, and the beautiful long tail-feathers of the tropic [bird],[17] or the man-of-war bird. For these feathers, the gods were supposed to have a strong predilection; they were the most valuable offerings that could be presented; to them, the power or influence of the god was imparted, and through them transferred to the objects to which they might be attached.'[18]

Feathers generally from three types of bird were used. Tropic birds, *tavake* in the Cook Islands, *mauroa* in Tahiti, provided the very long filamentous red or white feathers, of which there are only two per bird. Large black feathers came from the frigate bird, called the man-of-war bird by mariners, and known as *kota'a* in the Cook Islands, *otaha* in Tahiti. The small red, green, and yellow feathers adorning Cook Islands feather gods came from a diminutive and spectacular nectar-eating lorikeet, *Vini kuhlii*. This species was formerly widespread in the Cooks and Australs. It was particularly abundant, and was harvested, on Manuae,[19] and on Rimatara, the westernmost of the Australs, the only island where it still survives. Another species of small parrot, *Vini peruviana* and two larger species, *Cyanorhamphus ulietanus* and *zealandicus*, lived in the Societies. Known as *a'a* or *vini* in Tahitian, most parrot species became extinct in the nineteenth century.

Missionary James Fleet Cover, in 1802, mentions doves: 'The most remarkable bird of Otaheite is the dove, which has a mournful note: this bird is held in high veneration by the natives, who give it the appellation of *Mannoo no te' Atooa*, that is, the Bird of God; by the medium of which they say, that the Supreme Being occasionally communicates his wish to the *Towwa*, or priest.'[20] Cover was one of the four ordained ministers who came to Tahiti on the *Duff*; he resigned from the mission in 1798, after just one year, on seeing the

'inefficiency for the accomplishment of its object'—a pity because he was an unusually astute observer.

The eighteenth-century explorers very rapidly realized the extraordinary value of anything red as objects for trade. Particularly red feathers. By Cook's second voyage, for instance, Forster was astonished to find that a two-inch square of a Tongan 'apron'—a woven sennit backing with many small red lorikeet feathers attached—could purchase in Tahiti an entire hog, or even a mourning outfit—which could not be secured for any amount of nails, hatchets or calico on the first voyage.[21] Cook laid in a good store of red feathers at Tonga; Anders Sparrman, botanist on Cook's second voyage, tells us they also brought feathers which had been dyed red in England.[22] Bligh brought red feathers on the *Bounty*. Morrison states that frigate bird feathers 'are held in Such Esteem that the Natives will give a hog of 100 Weight for one of them for Making their War & Heiva [dance] dresses &c.'[23] As William Ellis—the William Ellis on Cook's third voyage—put it: 'red feathers . . . are with these people the *summum bonum* and extent of all their wishes.'[24]

Spaniards from Peru, visiting Easter Island in 1771, after Roggeveen and before Cook, noticed immediately regarding the islanders that 'everything of a bright red colour pleases them greatly.'[25] Máximo Rodríguez found the same was true in Tahiti in 1774: '[A] red handkerchief . . . is what they most hanker after.'[26] And Bougainville: 'What I believe to be their most valuable manufacture is a red dye that seemed to us to be superior to that of the Gobelins.'[27] This was a scarlet dye derived from berries of the mati tree; the Gobelins were a family of Parisian dye makers famous for their scarlet. When Vancouver encountered the young Pomare II, he was being 'carried on the shoulders of a man and was clothed in a piece of English red cloth.'[28]

---

16 Forster in Thomas et al., 1996,335.
17 Parkinson and Bligh watercolours of some of these birds are reproduced in figs. 221–223. See Steadman 2006.
18 Ellis 1829 2,204.
19 WW Gill, 1880,177; see Steadman 2006.
20 Gunson 1980,219.

21 Forster 1778 in Kaeppler 1978.
22 Sparrman 1953,55.
23 Morrison 1935,218.
24 Ellis 1782 1,127.
25 Anonymous journal of voyage of Gonzalez and Domonte to San Carlos (Easter Island), translated by Corney 1903,98.
26 Corney 1918 3,111.
27 14 April 1768 entry in Bougainville's *Journal*, translated and edited by Dunmore 2002,74.
28 Vancouver 1984 1,395.

Wilson brought along on the *Duff* red cloth from England, and cochineal from Rio, for trading purposes.[29]

Specific details regarding the incorporation of red feathers into an idol appear in a letter written by Pomare II, 19 February 1816, which accompanied the presentation of his family gods to the missionaries on Eimeo. Pomare's gift included several 'Oro images: 'That principal idol, that has the red feathers . . . is Temeharo—that is his name— . . . that was Vairaatoa's own god, and those feathers were from the ship of lieutenant Watts; it was Vairaatoa that set them himself about the idol.'[30] Vairaatoa was Pomare I, Pomare II's father; Lt John Watts was midshipman on the *Resolution*, Cook's third voyage, who later accompanied Admiral Arthur Phillip transporting the first contingent of English convicts to Australia; Watts' ship in this case was *Lady Penrhyn* of the First Fleet, under the command of Captain William Sever. They continued on to Tahiti, and landed 10 July 1788. Temeharo is Nº3 in the engraving *The family gods of Pomare*, which appears on the cover of *Missionary Sketches Nº3*, October 1818 (see fig. 51); Temeharo is in the British Museum collection, LMS Oc1981,Q.1552 (fig. 199).[31] Of particular interest here is that the red feathers which adorned Temeharo were brought by Europeans as trade currency.

Feather gifts went in both directions. Wallis, on 24 June 1767, his fourth day at Tahiti: 'At last a man sitting on a canopy, fixed up in a large [double] Canoe, came near the ship, and gave a bunch of Red and Yellow feathers to one of our men, and pushed off again.'[32] This was, in fact, the very first recorded non-trade gesture of a Polynesian to a European. Wallis again, on 23 July: 'The Queen . . . made us sit down, and taking off my hat, she tied to it a bunch or tuft of feathers of various colours, such as I had seen no person on shore wear but herself.'[33] Two years later, Cook, on his first voyage, described an incident on Huahine: '[T]wo Chiefs

spoke . . . and presented us with some young Plantain Plants and two small bunches of feathers.'[34] Perhaps it would be more accurate to refer to these gestures as offerings rather than gifts; feathers and plantain leaves were presented to gods.

Morrison gives a remarkable account of the lengths to which Tahitians went to obtain feathers:

As they are very fond of the Tail feathers of the Tropic Birds which they esteem for dressing their Parais or Mourning dress they go two together to Hunt for them and as the birds are build in the Face of the highest Cliffs they are at Much trouble to get them. Their method is this—the Bird catchers are provided each with 10 or 12 fathoms of Rope of sufficient strength to bear His own weight, & having fixd their place of abode near the Clift, where provisions are in the greatest plenty. . . . they proceed together to the top of the Cliff, where bending their ropes together they make fast a stick of 18 or 20 inches long by the Middle and lower it over the face of the Cliff having a Stake fixd to Make it fast to on the top; if a Tree is Not Convenient, one hand then stays by the rope to haul up or lower down as the other shall order who goes down & seating himself on the Cross stick, swings from hole to hole in search of the Birds, holding on by the points of the stones which project or the Shrubbs which grow among the fissures of the Cliff—when he catches a Bird, he hauls out the Tail feathers which he secures in a Bamboo which he carrys for the purpose, and lets the Bird fly—having examined all the holes within his reach or is tired in the search he goes up and either shifts the rope to another part or attends it for his partner to take a spell.

This tho it may appear Dangerous to us is no more to them than Amusement, and seldom attended with any Accident tho they hang some hours in this manner, sometimes 20, 30 or 40 fathoms from the top & often four times that from the Bottom and perhaps do not get a single feather in a whole days search.[35]

---

29 Campbell 1840,230.

30 *Missionary Sketches Nº3*, October 1818; Griffin 1822,180; see fig. 200. 'Tamaharro' is one of the nine important named gods listed in T Haweis 1799,333.

31 Watts found that Tahitian esteem of red feathers had diminished substantially by 1788: 'they would accept them as presents indeed, but would not barter any one article for them' (Watts' narrative in Phillip 1789,ch20). The most acceptable items of trade rapidly became liquor and the musket (Tobin in Oliver 1988,171; *Trans Miss Soc* 1804,171).

32 *Extracts from Captain Wallis's Journal*, nd, ms, British Library, p. 17.

33 Ibid.,25.

34 Beaglehole 1968 1,141. The plantain was the 'Emblem of Peace' (Morrison 1935,238).

35 Morrison 1935,217. A comparable account regarding the collection of tropic bird feathers is in T Haweis 1799,364/William Smith 1813,83.

Another important emblem of deity was tapa—a strong cloth made by felting wet inner bark fibre with a grooved mallet.[36] Superior tapa, watermarked, white, extremely thin and supple, called *hopuu* in Tahiti,[37] was made from the inner bark of the paper mulberry tree. There were many types of tapa, made from many kinds of bark, as thick as leather or as thin as lace, dyed decorated glazed and waterproofed in numerous ways; many Polynesian terms apply. The word *tapa* is a European one. It was adapted by American and English sailors in the early nineteenth century from the Samoan term *tapa*, meaning uncoloured border, and the Hawaiian term *kapa*, meaning bark cloth or border. Use of the word spread throughout Polynesia. *Tapa* in the Cook Islands is a general word for cloth, as opposed to the bark cloth–specific Tahitian word *ahu*, although Davies defines *ahu* 'cloth and garments of all descriptions.' The missionaries often refer to tapa as 'native cloth'. Cook marveled at the properties of Polynesian tapa, and brought back a considerable number of samples; the missionaries (with the exception of William Ellis) regarded it as heathen, brought back very little of it, and imported English broadcloth as soon as they were able.

Tapa was used for the adornment or wrapping of objects considered sacred. The god images that Tyerman and Bennet toppled into the sea at Oahu were large, unworked, sacred rocks, placed upright in a bed of smaller stones, 'their tops . . . wrapped round with native cloth.'[38] Similar unworked basalt rocks 'clothed or ornamented with native cloth' were also held in high estimation in Tahiti.[39] Highly regarded ancestral skulls—*oromatua*—were wrapped in tapa.[40] Later on, so were Bibles. Sections, rolls or bales of beautifully made

tapa were significant offerings.[41] White tapa in particular. Normal tapa for daily use was made by women, during the day. But the coarse white tapa, often scented, which was wrapped around every god image and bound with sennit, was made by men, at night: 'The *'opu-nui* [marae attendants; "large belly" in Davies] planted *'aute* [paper mulberry] upon the sacred grounds, and from it they made the *'apa'a* [thick cloth scented with aromatic juices of plants] by moonlight, so as to be viewed by the goddess, Hina in the moon, their patroness. Thus the cloth was rendered most sacred, as covering only for the gods, for whom they also braided mats.'[42] White tapa on Cook Islands images was called *tikoru*; Savage defines it as 'white native cloth of fair thickness . . . for the robes of the priests . . . and for the purpose of decorating the ancient gods.'[43]

Unwrapping of the images, anointing them with oil, and rewrapping them in fresh tapa was central to maintaining the power of the god images, and was accomplished in the all-important pa'iatua ceremony. Pa'iatua is defined by Davies as 'an idolatrous ceremony on the new decoration of the too or image of a god.' Orsmond (T Henry) describes 'pa'iatua as 'the greatest of all marae ceremonies . . . , [the] assembling and uncovering of the gods.' Music, dance, and chant were involved; drums were important, and could be eight feet high. Orsmond (T Henry) provides a detailed description of the ceremony.[44] Ellis on the subject: '[M]en were appointed constantly to attend them [the gods], and to keep them wrapped in the choicest kinds of cloth, to take them out whenever there was a pae atua, or general exhibition of the gods; to anoint them frequently with fragrant oil; and to sleep in the house with them at night. All this was done, to keep them pacified.'[45]

Not surprisingly, wraps that were ancient were highly regarded. Pomare II, in 1816, told the missionaries 'The cloth in which the gods are wrapped is also old, and was accounted very sacred, being made not by women but by men, neither was it made by day, but by night.'[46]

---

[36] See Morrison 1935,160 (T Haweis 1799,369/William Smith 1813,87) for excellent accounts of the manufacture of tapa in Tahiti. See also Buck 1944, Kooijman 1962, Neich & Pendergrast 1997; ahu also refers to the raised 'altar' of a marae.

[37] Davies 1851.

[38] Montgomery 1832 2,74. Simple wood carvings and large stones adorned with tapa, on Kauai marae (marae are called heiau in Hawai'i), were figured by Webber; see Joppien and Smith 1985 vol 3 plates 3.172 and 3.176.

[39] Ellis 1829 2,204: 'rude, uncarved, angular columns of basalt, various in size, and destitute of carving or polish'; see figs. 35, 36.

[40] Oromatua referred to the skulls themselves as well as to a class of inferior, malevolent gods; see Davies 1851 and Appendix 8.

[41] Buck (1944,366) mentions a tapa fishing charm in Mangaia: 'It consisted of bark cloth (*autea*) folded into cones termed *poani* (plug) of which four were placed in different parts of the fishing canoe to plug up the four quarters from which the wind blew.'

[42] Henry 1928,151; see also Davies 1851.

[43] Savage 1962,382.

[44] Henry 1928,156.

[45] Ellis 1829 2,202.

[46] *Trans Miss Soc* 1818,170.

Tyerman and Bennet remarked on the importance—the sacredness—of outer wraps on their own: 'Tati, the chief [of Papara, Tahiti] . . . made us several presents of native manufacture; but those . . . most valued were parts of the dress of 'Oro, including his bonnet and two tawdry coverings which were cast over [the] idol on grand occasions; also a remnant of the maro, or sacred mantle, with which Pomare had been invested . . . by a ceremonial too detestable to be described.'[47] Davies describes 'a deputy idol prepared from some cloth and red feathers taken from the person of Oro at Opoa in Raiatea.'[48]

The first European to document wraps around a god image ('Oro in this case) was Joseph Banks:

> In the neighbourhood of [marae Taputapuatea on Ra'iatea we encountered] 4 or 5 Ewharre no Eatua or god houses which were made to be carried on poles. One of these I examind by putting my hand into it: within was a parsel about 5 feet long and one thick wrappd up in matts, these I tore with my fingers till I came to a covering of mat made of platted Cocoa nut fibres which it was impossible to get through so I was obligd to desist, especialy as what I had already done gave much offence to our new freinds. [49]

A single example of idols found with their original wrappings intact has been well recorded. Very fortunate was the astonishing discovery by a young Tahitian pig hunter, in 1925, of three feather-adorned 'Oro images in a cave in the Orofere Valley, in the Paea district of Tahiti. Each image was carefully bundled in successive layers of palm or palmetto leaf, finely stitched palm leaf strips, and finally, white tapa; the three were enclosed together in a final layer of white tapa, and bound with sennit. They were found undamaged. Kenneth Emory, a young archaeologist from the Bishop Museum, was on Tahiti at the time, and documented the layers of wrapping in a remarkable series of photographs, which have only recently been published.[50] Through the courtesy of the Bishop Museum, some of Emory's photographs

are reproduced here (figs. 214–217).[51] They provide vivid illustration of the elaborate wrappings of a Tahitian god image.

Tapa wrappings, as well as feathers, were important elements of god images in the Cook Islands as well, as Buck discusses. WW Gill speaks of god images on Mangaia: 'Occasionally the idols were sunned, to prevent their fine wrappings from getting mouldy. New white cloth was put on them from time to time.'[52]

By far the most conspicuous examples of tapa wrappings are those on the enormous Rarotongan staff gods, which had tapa wrappings of so many layers they were over three feet in diameter.[53] Tapa-wrapped staff gods are depicted in Williams' *Narrative*[54] and in the Anelay watercolour, Nº1 (see fig. 1). Ellis writes: 'Mr Bourne in 1825, saw fourteen about twenty feet long and six feet wide.'[55] It is entirely possible the dimension 'six feet wide' is not an exaggeration or a misprint, because there is evidence that yet more wrapping was involved with these staff gods. A letter from Williams to W Orme, secretary of the LMS, 18 November 1830:

> I am happy to inform you [part of letter missing] at last an opportunity of forwarding one of the idols from Rarotogna[56]. . . Capt[n] Hammer of the Sir Andrew Hammond has kindly taken it . . . you will perhaps have to pay freight for it . . . I did not think well to ask him to take it for nothing it being so large . . . I also have given Capt[n] Hammer permission to open it and shew to his owner Mr Mellish [?] if he wishes it. It is wrapped up in a matt and a covering of white cloth when these *two* coverings are taken off you come to the real idol—which is a large quantity of cloth wrapped round a long stick which is carved at top & bottom

47 Montgomery 2,193.
48 Davies 1961,137.
49 Beaglehole 1963 1,318.
50 Kaeppler 2007.

51 The location of this finding, site 26, is specified in Emory 1933,70.
52 WW Gill 1894,333.
53 Buck 1944,317.
54 Baxter wood engraving in Williams 1837,118; see fig. 192.
55 Quoted by Buck 1944,319, his ref Ellis 1830 2,221, a London edition. See anonymous, *Adventures in the South Pacific*,165: 'Tomara's . . . gods . . . were bigger than any we had ever met with. One was fourteen and another—if I recollect right—sixteen feet high. . . . They rose above the fence which enclosed them.' The source here is Robert Bourne's youngest son.
56 See fig. 192; evidently both of the large staff gods brought by Williams to Ra'iatea on the *Messenger of Peace* in May 1828 reached England, the first one with Captain Hammer, and the second one with Williams on the whaler *Sir Andrew Hammond*, Captain Cuthell, in 1834. Only one survives intact.

the outer covering being spotted cloth white & black bound round with white bandages about a foot apart so when you have taken off the Matt and white cloth covering you cease undoing any further.[57]

Tapa wrappings on people were also of major importance. Wallis describes Tahitian dress, with long sections of white tapa 'like a Mantle . . . five yards long and one broad' wrapped around the *tiputa*, which was in effect a tapa poncho.[58] People of high rank adorned themselves with vast amounts of tapa wrappings. Likewise, they also adorned their high ranking visitors—men such as Wallis, Cook, and Banks. Papeiha describes a major ceremony which he refers to as 'bure Arii', on Aitutaki, involving tapa dress: '[T]hey cover themselves completely with cloth except a small part of their faces . . . they remain for a month sometimes longer before the Marae . . . they go to the Marae & cover the Kings with Cloth in great abundance.'[59] Tapa on its own was an important gift, almost always the first one presented. Wallis found that the Tahitians at Matavai Bay would not accept the nails and hatchets offered in exchange for hogs until Wallis had accepted the tapa that was presented to him along with the hogs.[60]

An especially significant form of wrapping was the *maro 'ura*, a long narrow girdle (maro) adorned with red feathers ('ura), and the *maro te'a*, adorned with yellow feathers. Both were reserved for Society Islanders of the highest rank, the sovereigns, who were considered to be descendants of gods. Feather maro were sacraments of authority and emblems of extreme importance, worn only on occasions of great consequence, such as investitures. Like god images, they were kept at marae, carefully wrapped. They were constructed of tough and flexible fibre mesh with special tapa backings. Enormous numbers of feathers were attached, arranged in square patterns. Tyerman and Bennet describe a maro 'ura on Ra'iatea:

> [A] new king . . . was invested with a maro, or hereditary robe of royalty, of net-work [made of sennit[61]] covered with red feathers, and to which an additional lappet is annexed at the accession of each sovereign. This splendid train, which was wont to be wound about the body, and flowed upon the ground, is twenty-one feet in length, and six inches broad. The needle [of human bone] by which the fabric was wrought is still attached, [and the maro] has never been completed . . . ; this robe might be regarded as an hieroglyphic tablet of the annals of Raiatea. Tamatoa has cast off this relic of idolatry, and sent it, as another trophy of the gospel victories here, to the Museum of the London Missionary Society.[62]

Orsmond (T Henry) describes the same maro in detail, and maintains that the network backing was not of sennit but of roa—stronger and more supple than sennit, and far more likely—backed with 'choice ora (banyan cloth), closely perforated'.[63] Henry's editor notes that '[w]hen the collection of the LMS was recently turned over to the British Museum, this famous maro was missing.'[64] Covered with feathers, it no doubt became a memorable insects' banquet. In fact, no maro 'ura survive, but fortunately, a careful watercolour of one of Pomare II's maro, by Captain Bligh, is in the Mitchell Library (see fig. 224). Maro are thoroughly discussed by Roger Rose.[65]

Williams narrates 'A few years ago I sent to England a very sacred relic called *Maro ura*, or the red sash.' It measured six feet long by seven inches wide; a new section of about 18 inches was attached at the inauguration of every sovereign. Human sacrifices were required on each addition: one for stretching the maro on pegs, one for attaching the new section, one for removing the pegs.[66]

---

57 SOAS LMS SS incom corresp box7 folio7 jacketC, written Ra'iatea 18 November 1830, marked 'received London 11 March 1831'; '*two*' is Williams' own emphasis. This is an interesting letter. This staff god was sent to England accompanied by Williams' manuscript journal, which was rewritten to become Williams' *Narrative*, as discussed above.

58 Wallis ms nd,36.

59 Williams and Papeiha ms *More Joy for Christians*,5; SOAS LMS SSJ box4 folder59.

60 Wallis ms nd,21.

61 Montgomery 1832 2,193.

62 Ibid.,2,125.

63 Henry 1928,189; see ch 7, fn49 on roa/oronga.

64 Ibid., footnote 46.

65 Rose 1978.

66 Williams 1837,551; probably Ra'iatea, although Williams does not specify.

Sacred maro were also used in the Cook Islands. Savage names 13 types of maro, among which is maro kura, 'ornamented with red and yellow feathers…worn by the ariki [chief] or members of the ariki family.' The entry for N°21 on Papeiha's list mentions 'the one [garment] with feathers is a girdle in which the King blows a conch shell at some of their large Feasts'. Savage also tells us 'sometimes [maro kura] consisted of a long strip of red-coloured tapa cloth, the red colour denoting sacredness.' No maro kura survive either. However, a few examples of an unusual and highly labour-intensive type of maro, made of finely plaited bichrome pandanus leaf, do still exist. One of these in the British Museum, collected by WW Gill on Rarotonga, is 28 feet long (see fig. 225).[67]

Maro evidently also existed in Samoa. Williams describes Papo, which he refers to as 'god of war', on Savaii: 'nothing more than a piece of old rotten matting, about three yards long, and four inches wide.'[68] Following conversion, Papo's time for the fire arrived, but 'as drowning was a less horrible fate than burning, this should be his fate.' As it turned out, Papo suffered neither fate, thanks to the teachers, but instead was given to Williams, who placed it in the Missionary Museum. Papo was the *aitu* or spirit residing in an heirloom girdle. Papo cannot be located in the LMS collections.

SENNIT

The importance of sennit (*aha* in Tahitian[69], *ka'a* in the Cooks; the missionaries spelled it *senet, cinet, sinnit, sinnet*) in everyday life in Polynesia cannot be overemphasized, and it is no surprise that it occupied a central place in Polynesian religion. Sennit is a strong cordage of soaked, beaten, and carefully groomed coconut husk fibre, usually fashioned by twisting and braiding. The result was circular or sometimes flat in cross section (called *rapa* in the Cooks); it could be large scale and coarse, like rope, or extremely fine and precise. Sennit was used in fishing, canoe rigging, adze lashing, body ornaments; it took the place of nails and bolts in house and canoe construction. Sacrificial victims in Tahiti were hung from the trees with sennit rope passed through their heads. 'The first enemy slain in battle was called *aha*, because, when obtained, a piece of aha was tied to him, he was then taken to a marae [for] prayers and ceremonies'; *aha* also referred to 'the ceremony of presenting at the marae a piece of aha by a fleet of canoes after their landing as an acknowledgment of the protection of the gods.'[70] Specific sennit terms sometimes referred to acts connected with the gods with which the sennit was used as well as to the particular type of sennit itself.

Sennit was also an important ingredient of idols. 'Oro images were constructed in part or even entirely of sennit—likewise with some Cook Island god images. Sennit that was used on god images was regarded as sacred; and like sacred tapa, it was made by the marae attendants, priests, and chiefs. It was stored in the god houses. Orsmond (T Henry) repeatedly uses the phrase 'sacred sennit'.[71]

Orsmond devotes 37 out of the 110 pages in volume six of his Tahitian dictionary to descriptions of 15 types of sennit. Quoted below are four pertinent entries:

'aha-mata-tini   senet of various hues, fastened as external decorations of the god. The different colours of the senet in the numerous strands, are the multifolic faces, the decorations of the God, but scarlet feathers are the best of all.

'aha-vai   senet dyed black in the mire of a taro bog. It is said by that means to be more strong.

'aha-ura   red-coloured senet made from husks baked in the oven in the midst of the banana stalk.

'aha–pahu   senet used to draw the shark skin tight over the head of a drum.[72]

Bands of coloured sennit are suggested on some of the 'Oro figures in the wood engraving of Pomare II's family idols on the cover of *Missionary Sketches* for

---

67 BM 9963; Buck 1944 pl 6C; common maro were made of thick white or brown tapa, others of oronga network incorporating hibiscus flowers or ti leaves.
68 Williams 1837,438.
69 Another Tahitian term was *nape* (Davies 1851).

70 Entry for *aha*; Davies 1851.
71 Henry 1928,153.
72 Papers of Rev JM Orsmond, *Part of Tahitian Dictionary*; Mitchell MSS A2609.

October 1818 and August 1820, and are faintly visible today on the actual objects in the British Museum. Coloured patterns are clearly evident on the Tyerman and Bennet 'Oro image at Leeds depicted by AW Franks; the figure legend states the patterns are painted, but they were more likely made with dyed sennit (see fig. 212).

The subject of birds, feathers, tapa, maro, and gods is well brought together by Morrison in a passage about portable marae:

> In one of these Morais, which is their grand and principal one, and Is in the district of Oparre they keep a Moveable one something similar to the ark of the Jews, and which is the occasion of as many quarrels as it formerly was. This Morai is calld Tabbootebooa taya' thus translated 'Sacrafice the White hog', and is the place to which every Chief on the Island, and those who are subject to them on Other Islands, must repair to offer their sacrafices, as they think it the only residence of the Deity on Earth. This moveable Morai is a Box about 3 feet long 2 feet wide and one deep in which is kept the Three Deitys or rather the Images to represent them, as they are only for the purpose of remembrancers and are not Worshipd. Nevertheless they bear the Names of the Deitys. On the top of this Box is raised several pieces of rude Carved work on the tops of which are represented Birds with extended Wings, as the Deity is fond of Birds and makes use of them to come to Earth in—and the whole is decorated with bunches of Red & Yellow feathers, which to them are as Valuable as Gold. This, with a Moveable House which is part of the Morai and Fix'ed on a stand together, is Calld (Effarre attooa) 'the house of God'; they are Screend in and kept Covered with the best Cloth the Island produces, painted in different Collours and Here also is kept the Royal Marro &c. and none must approach, but the Priests on pain of Death, and even they are obliged to divest themselves of their Cloaths to the Waist, whenever they enter a Morai, and when they enter the Farre Etooa they strip Naked leaving their own Cloaths outside, and while there they cover their Nakedness with Cloathing belonging to the sacred place, which they pull off at their return leaving them there, and resume their own.[73]

[73] Morrison 1935,179; Tahiti.

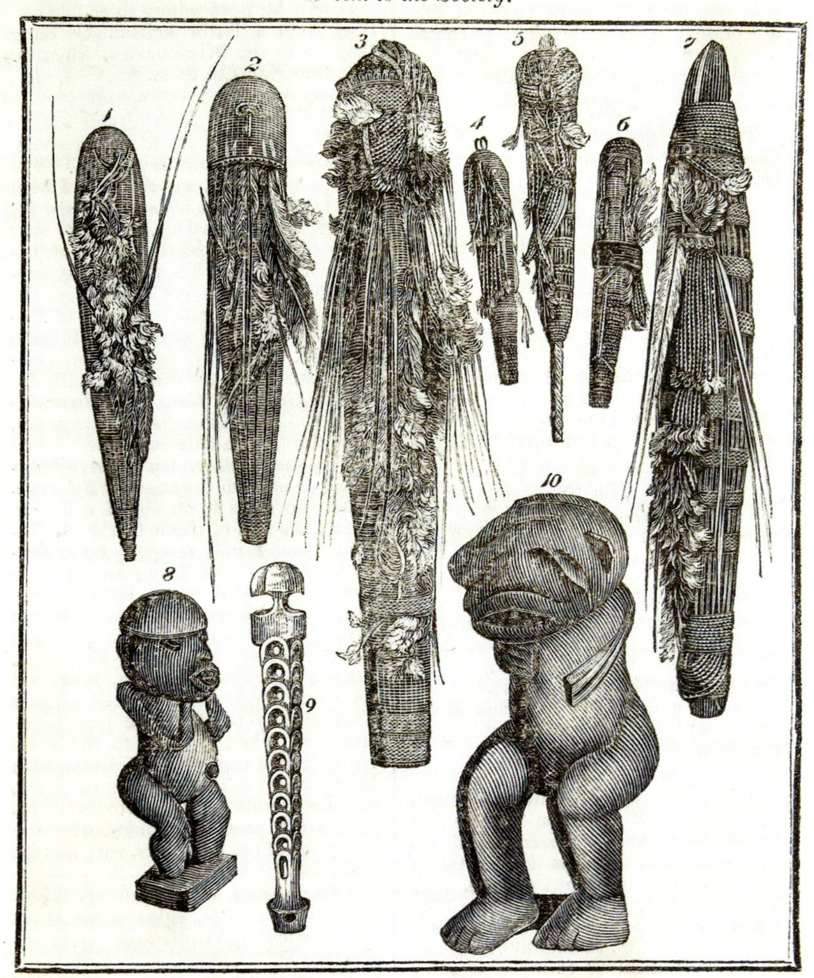

51 *Cover of* Missionary Sketches N°3, *October 1818, second edition printed August 1820. Engraving depicts ten of the idols which Pomare II of Tahiti presented to the LMS missionaries on Mo'orea in 1816, about ten years after his renunciation of idolatry. Pomare asked the missionaries to send the idols to London so that Europeans could see for themselves 'Tahiti's foolish gods'. Several of the idols in this plate still exist in the LMS collection in the British Museum. See figs. 120, 199, 210.*

SIX

Idol-Trophies and the LMS Collections

MISSIONARY COLLECTING POLICY

THE MISSIONARIES CAME to Polynesia with the idea of destroying the idols, but paradoxically, they ended up acquiring and preserving a good number of them. They did this in order to exhibit them at the missionary station in Ra'iatea, and eventually back at the Missionary Museum at the LMS headquarters in London, as trophies, attesting to the triumph of their evangelizing efforts in the South Sea. This chapter deals with how this change in policy came about, and how the various LMS collections took form.

Surprisingly, the person who was most influential in instigating the practice of idol collecting was not a missionary but a Polynesian, Pomare II, the paramount chief on Tahiti. He was the first Polynesian of high rank to renounce idolatry, which he did around 1806. About ten years afterwards, he presented his family idols to the missionaries on Eimeo (Mo'orea). He requested that the idols be dispatched to the LMS office in London: 'I wish you to send those idols to Britane . . . for the inspection of the people of Europe, that they may satisfy their curiosity, and know Tahiti's foolish gods!'[1] Pomare's family idols are the first god images in the LMS Polynesian collection that are documented (figs. 121, 199, 201, 209).

An astonishingly clear, candid, and shrewd document that describes the subsequent idol collection policy and philosophy of the missionaries is Williams' English translation (dated 6 July 1823) of his own 1821 letter of instruction (written in Tahitian) to two Raiatean teachers, Papeiha and Vahapata, on the eve of their dispatch to 'the land to which God will lead you', which was in this case Aitutaki. Williams advises to them: '[P]ay good regard to your own hearts; do not slacken.' Regarding outward appearances:

> [Y]ou have become like a city erected on a hill . . . you have more especially to regard those of the Heathen among whom you reside. They will watch you with *Rats Eyes* to find little cracked places in your conduct . . . beware of envy and evil thinking one of

[1] Pomare II to the missionaries 19 February 1816, in LMS *Catalogue* 1826,18; *Trans Miss Soc* 1818,10; *Missionary Sketches* 3, October 1818.

another . . . all their lesser evil customs[2] . . . you will cast down going in a state of nudity or nearly so . . . cutting and scratching themselves in seasons of grief . . . tattooing their bodies . . . eating raw fish[3] . . . their lewd dances . . . do not be in haste to propose laws; everything is good in its season; children are not fed with hard food . . . do not be lazy; a lazy missionary is both an ugly and a useless being . . . do not let the whole of your discourses be directed against the Evil Spirit [defined in a footnote as 'the whole system of idolatry'] that alone but exalt our Lord Jesus Christ. If you obtain idols burn some (but not the best) before their faces that they may see the consuming of them lest they should think in case of being overtaken with sickness or any other evil that their gods, who are still in existence, have inflicted it. Leave the greatest part and send to Raiatea as an encouragement to us and we will send them to England as a rejoicing to them. . . . J Williams. P.S. The translation is nearly literal which will account for the apparent oddity of some of the expressions.[4]

The policy spelled out in this letter worked. Certainly most of the idols in LMS collections were 'collected' by Polynesians. Details regarding idol harvests on several island groups are dealt with in the latter section of this chapter, considering first where the shipments were sent.

THE MISSIONARY MUSEUM AND OTHER LMS COLLECTIONS

Luckily, over 500 Polynesian objects acquired by various members of the LMS avoided the flames and still survive. The Missionary Museum, as it was called, was established promptly in London to house the 'Trophies of Christianity'. The October 1814 issue of *Evangelical Magazine* announces: 'The directors . . . have taken a set of Rooms in the Old Jewry, near Cheapside . . . nine in number [to accommodate] large Committees, . . . the Secretaries, . . . a library &c., [and] some for the reception of those curiosities which have been transmitted from Otaheite, China, South America, and particularly from South Africa. These will be prepared for public inspection as soon as possible.' By April 1815, it was 'open for inspection'—on Tuesdays and Thursdays, from eleven until three. Admission was free; a box for contributions was placed at the door.[5] On display were a stuffed giraffe, a rhinoceros head, dried scorpions and centipedes, and idols from the South Sea, Africa, the Ultra Ganges, and India—including a 'popish idol', a statue of the Virgin Mary sent in by two former Catholics from Mysore. By 1823 the museum had removed to Austin Friars, where, for £500, an additional room was added to house it; the directors had noticed that '[the museum] tends to promote amongst the numerous persons who visit it . . . a zeal for the Missionary cause.'[6] A descriptive catalogue was published in 1826. The Austin Friars building turned out to be dilapidated and damp, and the objects on display became disfigured by moths, spiders, and dust. In 1836 the collection was installed in a building at 14, Blomfield Street, Finsbury, that the Directors erected at a cost of £3080.[7] The LMS museum was mentioned in London guidebooks, and was featured in *Lady's Newspaper* and *Illustrated London News*.[8] Another catalogue was issued, probably in the early 1840s (reproduced in Appendix 7). An early description of the museum, referred to as 'an awful yet glorious place', was published in 1843 by Campbell;[9] it is reproduced in figure 284. The collection was acquired as a loan in 1890, and was purchased twenty years later, for £1000, by the British Museum; the curators responsible were Augustus Franks and his eventual successor, Charles Hercules Read.[10] The present British Museum LMS collection includes about 350 Polynesian objects.

---

2   'Infanticide, the most revolting and unnatural crime that prevails' (Ellis 1853 1,248} was perhaps the most objectionable custom; human sacrifice, idolatry, and the unspeakable and undescribed acts that took place, even publicly, during dances and ceremonies, were also high on the list. Warfare could also be a problem, but sometimes it wasn't: 'This shaking of the nation may be only plowing up the fallow ground for the better sowing the seed of eternal life' (*Trans Miss Soc* 1804,76).

3   Tyerman and Bennet refer to 'the loathsome practice of eating raw fish' (Montgomery 1832 2,150).

4   Williams; SOAS LMS SS incom corresp box4 folderl folioA; an edited version of this letter appears in Prout 1843,172.

5   *Evangelical Magazine* 1814,405; Seton 2010.

6   *Missionary Chronicle*, April 1823; see fig. 285.

7   See *Missionary Sketches*, October 1835.

8   1853 and 1859 respectively; Rosemary Seton pers. comm.; illustrations accompanying the two articles reproduced in Sivasundaram 2005 and Hooper 2006; see fig. 194.

9   Campbell 1843,133.

10 A full account of this transaction was written by Jill Hasell, Department of Africa, Oceania, and the Americas, British Museum, 'Trophies of Christianity: The Polynesian collections of the London Missionary Society in the British Museum'; unpublished typescript.

LMS objects were acquired by the missionaries, and by Tyerman and Bennet, as 'donations' and by exchange.[11] Many went directly to the Missionary Museum; others ended up in different locations, were subsequently distributed by gift, descent, or sale, and survive in various museum and private collections; still others are evidently lost. In 1823, for example, Williams sent 'an Idol from Aitutake to the *American Brethren*' in Hawai'i.[12] In 1837, he gave objects to the sixth Duke of Devonshire, whom he visited at Chiswick and at Chatsworth House. The gifts included a framed piece of Rarotongan tapa, described by the Duke as 'paper, but unlike paper, paint, but unlike paint, the work of savages'.[13] Williams also gave objects to his biographer Ebenezer Prout, and to Rev Timothy East,[14] and kept some himself to show during the lectures he made from 1834 to 1838 to raise interest and funds for the LMS in England. During these years his family lived at Bedford Square in London. Prout describes social gatherings held in Williams' parlour there, when

the curiosities which he had brought from the islands were drawn from their hiding places, and the various contents of several cases covered the table or the floor. A singular medley of idols, dresses, ornaments, domestic utensils, implements of industry, and weapons of war formed so many subjects of remark. Mr Williams arrayed his own portly person in the native tiputa [tapa poncho] and mat, fixed a spear by his side, and adorned his head with the towering cap of many colours, worn on high days by the chiefs; and, as he marched up and down his parlour, he was as happy as any one of the guests whose cheerful mirth he had thus excited.[15]

His Polynesian objects were evidently kept by his family after his death and displayed in 'The John Williams Room' at their house in Earlsmead, Essex. Four of these objects, including a Tongan club (Anelay N°3) and a Rurutu flywhisk handle, were donated in 2006 to the Anthropology Museum, University of British Columbia, by one of his descendants.[16]

George Bennet gave objects to the Leeds Philosophical and Literary Society (via independent churchman John Clapham), Whitby Literary and Philosophical Society (via LMS secretary John Arundel), and to the Saffron Walden Museum (connection unknown). Several are in the Cuming Museum. About 30 of Tyerman and Bennet's objects in Leeds, including an image of 'Oro, were sketched by AW Franks in his 'Leeds Notebook' (see fig. 212).[17] The Leeds collection was dispersed through Kenneth Webster in 1952; a number of Leeds objects went to the James Hooper and William Oldman collections. Many of Tyerman and Bennet's objects went to the Sheffield Literary and Philosophical Society during the period 1824 to 1829, while Bennet was still travelling, via James Montgomery—second president of the Society, missionary enthusiast, poet, publisher of *Sheffield Iris*, and a good friend of Bennet's. Bennet had originally intended objects go to friends and to the museum of Rotheram College, a training college for Independent Ministry, as the Sheffield Literary and Philosophical Society did not exist until 1822, well after the deputation had already left for Polynesia. Bennet continued donations after his return, at least until 1835. A number of his Sheffield objects are now in the Cambridge University Museum of Anthropology and Archaeology; others are in the William Oldman Collection and in the British Museum. A few remain in the Sheffield City Museum. Tyerman and Bennet gave a Mitiaro staff god to William Carey at the Baptist Missionary Museum in Serampore, on their way back to England in May of 1826 (see fig. 156).

In addition to god images, Bennet brought back other objects from Tahiti, the Cooks, and the Australs, such as nose flutes, tapa, breadfruit splitters, ray skin rasps, coconut drinking cups, necklaces, wood pillows, weapons (see figs. 239–249), as well as geological and

[11] Tyerman and Bennet record interesting details of a trading session on Mo'orea, 29 October 1821 (Montgomery 1832 1,97). The trading session had been instigated by Pomare (ibid. 90); see figs. 233, 234.

[12] Letter Williams (Ra'iatea) to Ellis (Oahu) 1 October 1823; SOAS LMS SS incom corresp box4 folder 2.

[13] *Handbook of Chatsworth and Hardwick* (1845) mentions the gift of 'breadfruit & cloth', 22 August 1837. During this year, according to Joseph Paxton, the Duke had come under the influence of an Evangelical clergyman, Rev Henry Beamish, of Trinity Chapel, London, who probably introduced the Duke to Williams (Colquhoun 2006,76).

[14] Oldman N°s 381, 392, 425 and Oldman N°417 respectively.

[15] Prout 1843,479.

[16] Mayer and Shelton 2009.

[17] Entitled *Eth. Notes. Leeds.* British Museum Anthropology Library, LS6.

natural history specimens. It is likely that many 'Bennet' objects were actually acquired by Tyerman, the more 'scientific' of the two.[18]

The idea of acquiring objects from Polynesia was in the air even before the missionaries had begun their work: objects were brought back on the *Duff*—including at least one idol. A letter in the Sutro Library from Thomas Haweis to Joseph Banks reads 'I don't know whether an Image in Toa wood of a female, whether Goddess or native, but sufficiently ugly would be acceptable to you, if you will please to tell me, I shall convey it to you.'[19] The letter was written 4 July 1799; the *Duff* had returned to England 11 July 1798. This letter provides the first documentation of an idol collected in the Pacific by the LMS and brought back to England; the relevant portion of the letter is reproduced in figure 287. Unfortunately, we do not know what or where the 'Image' is.

Two items unequivocally brought back on the *Duff* have been located by Leslie Jessop. The annual report of the Literary and Philosophical Society of Newcastle upon Tyne for 14 May 1800 mentions that in May 1799, 'a very valuable present of various articles from the South Sea Islands was delivered by Mr. John Langlands, from Captain Wilson, of London, late of the Duff'. The 'various articles' were not specified, but two large white tapa cloths in the Hancock Museum in Newcastle, C701 and 1998.H234, bear the inscription 'Literary Society, Newcastle, Care of M^r. John Langland' (see fig. 52).[20] Both tapa cloths appear to be Tahitian. John Langland was a well known Newcastle silversmith, and Wilson was well-to-do; the connection makes sense.

In the entry for 2 August 1797 of the *Duff* account is the mention that 'Iddeah [Pomare II's wife] presented the captain [Wilson] with a complete mourning dress'; the October 1814 issue of *The Evangelical Magazine* refers to 'curiosities which have been transmitted from Otaheite' that were about to be put on view at the Missionary Museum. Clearly a number of objects had been brought back on the *Duff* and were already on display in London roughly three years before Pomare's idols arrived. These objects remain unidentified.

The idea of bringing idols back from the South Sea was suggested by the directors at the outset. In a sermon delivered in 1795, at the founding of the Missionary Society, Haweis proposed that the Tahitian Mission should have a small ship at its disposal, 'solely employed in the service of the mission . . . to be employed in no traffic whatever . . . except the natural curiosities of the countries, and added to them, (a noble idea suggested by one of our brethren) their idols, now cast to the moles, and to the bats.'[21] One wonders which 'one of our brethren' Haweis had in mind. The phrase 'cast his idols . . . to the moles and to the bats' comes from Isaiah 2:20 and means to consign idols to dark and dirty places of desolation and ruin; it refers to mole-rats, and to bats, which were lumped together with birds, and considered unclean.

It is possible that even the idea of a missionary museum was in the minds of the directors from the start. At least two of them enjoyed museums. Rev Rowland Hill was one of the Missionary Society founders and directors, and constructed Surrey Chapel in Southwark, where the annual LMS meetings were held the second Wednesday in May; Hill wanted the chapel to be round, so the devil could not hide in the corners. His biographer, Edwin Sidney, wrote: 'Another of Mr. Hill's favourite places of resort, was the museum of the London Missionary Society. I have often gone there with him, where we used to meet his old fellow-labourer in the same cause, Matthew Wilks. . . . Mr. Wilks would say, "these are the signs of the great work, and it does our old hearts good to see them. . . . "'[22]

Indeed, awareness of the potential use of idols as agents for promoting the cause of Evangelicalism was evident eight years before the Missionary Society was formed. An issue of the Evangelical monthly called *Theological Miscellany* published in July 1787 contains an article sent in by a contributor with the nom de plume 'A———S', entitled 'THOUGHTS IN THE MUSEUM':

---

18 For details re Bennet objects, see Woroncow 1981 (Sheffield and Leeds), and Pole 1981 (Saffron Walden); see also Porter 1922, Twells 1999.

19 Sutro Library, San Francisco, Banks Correspondence LMS 1:33; see fig. 287. *Toa* is synonymous with *aito*, meaning *casuarina*.

20 *Seventh years report of the Literary and Philosophical Society of Newcastle upon Tyne*, 1800, entry for 14 May 1799; a likely third *Duff* object is a gorget of wood from the Masquesas; see Jessop 2003,114.

21 T Haweis 1795,173.

22 Sidney 1834,276. Octagonal chapels with circular interiors, a not uncommon Methodist design, were also constructed in Polynesia; see for example lithograph "The native church at the island of Mo'orea' (Lucett 1851 vol 1).

'I remember the last time I was walking through the British Museum . . . viewing some of the curiosities brought back from the South Seas, when this reflection struck me. Alas! What a miserable, revolted world is this!'[23] The writer viewed the 'IDOLS [as] evincing the fatal influence of that depravity that has infected the race.' Presumably A———S was referring to the 'goblin images' brought back by Captain Cook. The passage appears to presage the exhibition of idols at the Missionary Museum.

Regarding the idols in the LMS collection, as mentioned above, a number of 'idol-trophies' were presented to or acquired by the English missionaries or by Tyerman and Bennet, but the majority were collected by Raiatean Christian teachers. The English missionaries were initially appalled and repelled by these objects. But starting with Pomare II's gift, they rapidly learned to value, and even take pride in the idols; they were palpable evidence of moral victory, proof of the triumph of the gospel. The trophies were generally sent to the LMS station on Ra'iatea, then on to England. The majority arrived in London between 1817 (the first of Pomare's family idols) and 1829 (when Bennet returned). Documentation exists for several shipments.

THE FIRST SHIPMENTS: TAHITI

Following the *Duff* objects, the first known shipment to arrive in London from the Society Islands, as mentioned above, consisted of the family idols of Pomare II—about ten of them—presented to the Tahitian Mission in Eimeo. Pomare's gift, accompanied by a descriptive letter dated 19 February 1816, included several images of 'Oro. A letter from missionary William Henry on Eimeo to Samuel Marsden in Parramatta, 12 August 1816, tells us more details:

> I would send you a couple of idols I have in my possession, but that there are 5 or 6 to be sent to the Directors, which will of course go through your hands, and afford an opportunity of gratifying your curiosity in that particular. I shall therefore, I think, send the above two to his Excellency the Governor [Lachlan Macquarie] in whose possession you can have ready access to them should your curiosity lead you to desire a sight of them also. They are to be considered as only representatives of the gods who were supposed by the priests and more knowing of the people to be spirits in the Po [night] or invisible world.[24]

The brig *Queen Charlotte* had arrived in Eimeo the day before this letter was written, with a cargo of sandalwood, and the captain was eager to depart to the Leeward Islands for salted pork, and onwards to Parramatta. In a letter to the LMS directors, 31 October 1816, Marsden writes:

> Since I wrote last, the Queen Charlotte has arrived from Otaheite. . . . I have now the unspeakable satisfaction of forwarding to you some of THE IDOL GODS OF OTAHEITE, as the glorious spoils of Idolatry; no event could have given me more pleasure. They are now lying prostrate on the table before me, and were we not certain of the fact, we could not believe that any human beings could place their salvation in these wretched images, and offer up human sacrifices to avert their anger.[25]

The idols were sent onwards to London on a South Sea whaler, 'nailed up in a case, directed to Mr. Hardcastle. These are the king's family gods, and are a good specimen of the whole. The great national ones, which were of the same kind, only much larger, have been sometime ago entirely destroyed.'[26] The idols reached London in early 1817. The Missionary Museum had already been open nearly three years. Ten of Pomare's idols were illustrated in a woodcut entitled 'The Family Idols of Pomare', which appeared on the cover of the magazine

---

[23] *The Theological Miscellany; and Review of Books on Religious Subjects* 1787,373; Gunson 1995. Published from 1784 to 1789, this was the precursor of *Evangelical Magazine*.

[24] Original in Hocken Library, Dunedin; a copy made in 1915 for Joseph King (LMS organizing agent for Australasia) is bound in Letters Haweis to Marsden ML MSS A404,106.

[25] *Trans Miss Soc* 1818,161.

[26] Letter signed by eight missionaries, transcribed in *Trans Miss Soc* 1818,427, as well as in Griffin 1822,179; Joseph Hardcastle was the first treasurer of the LMS. Luckily one of the 'much larger' 'Oro images was presented by Pomare to Tyerman & Bennet, brought to England, and survives; this is LMS 101 (Edge-Partington 1895, Additional Notes; see also registration slip for LMS 101). The same provenance probably also applies to the other large British Museum 'Oro image, LMS 100. See figs. 205–208.

Missionary Sketches N°3 the following year.[27] Several of them can be identified in the British Museum LMS collection; (see figs.120, 199, 209).[28]

This shipment came at a critical moment in the history of the Tahitian Mission. The first conversions had taken an agonizing 15 years and the directors, referring to this period as 'the night of toil', were ready to abandon the Mission. Haweis and Wilks argued against it; Haweis contributed £200 more; a 'benevolent lady' contributed £1000. 'Letters of encouragement were written to the missionaries; and while the vessel which carried the letters was on her passage to Tahiti, another ship was conveying to England not only the news of the entire overthrow of idolatry, but also the rejected idols of the people.'[29] Williams knew the timing was not a coincidence; he saw in it 'the finger of God'.

A couple of years later, Pomare II sent Haweis another letter, in Tahitian, dated 3 October 1818, received in London 1 January 1820. Accompanying it was a translation by missionary William Crook. They were published together as a separate by LMS secretary George Burder immediately on receipt.[30] In the letter, Pomare tells Haweis that he is sending a 'little Idol [named] Taroa. . . . This is only a little one that remains. . . . I also send you two little fans.' Haweis was delighted at the idea of receiving a second batch of idols; in a letter written in Bath, 20 January 1820, no doubt to George Burder, he wrote:

> My dear friend, As I presume the Fans & the Idol came with the Letter you will not wonder I am very desirous to receive these tokens of Pomarre's regard and trust you to forward them to me without delay. . . . God be praised for all that he hath done at Otaheite. . . . When all the King's ministers, Mr. J. Banks, the Bishops of England & Ireland have read Pomarre's letter I hope it will make an impression which will forward our views.[31]

Haweis wrote this letter five weeks before he died; it is the last letter he wrote to the Society.

Evidently these 'two little fans' remained in the Haweis family for some time: in 1896, Rev Hugh Reginald Haweis, grandson of Thomas Haweis and an accomplished musician, described several of his grandfather's articles, 'now in my possession.' Included was '[a well-] preserved idol, made of beautiful yellow, green, and red feathers and woven with cocoa-nut fibre' and 'the sacred fan handles made out of carved human bones, which were laid up in the temples at Tahiti', as well as 'letters from King Pomare, written to Dr. Haweis, with tomato juice, in European characters, but in the Tahitian language.'[32] The identity of Taroa is unknown,[33] but it seems likely that the 'two little fans' are the two flywhisk handles (the missionaries used the terms *fan* and *flywhisk* interchangeably) constructed of intricately carved sperm whale tooth and wood segments fastened together with finely braided sennit, presently in the collections of Raymond and Laura Wielgus (65–271; now at Indiana University; see fig. 289) and the Metropolitan Museum in New York (65.80). Both passed through the hands of London dealer KJ Hewett, and both were associated with the name Haweis.

Haweis' enthusiasm for obtaining idols must have been important for the Missionary Museum. Early on, in 1801, he instructed Captain William Wilson of the *Royal Admiral* to bring back 'any curiosities'.[34] Haweis awaited the arrival of idols eagerly: 'The idols more welcome than the spoils of the Acropolis . . . are packed up and on the sea, & we wait with some impatience their arrival. . . . '[35] Soon after the first of Pomare's idols arrived from Tahiti, he was looking forward to receiving a second batch: '[T]he other islands in their vicinity [here speaking of the Leeward Islands of the Societies] . . . will furnish we trust fresh Trophies of the redeemer's Power.'[36] LMS director Burder also viewed the idols favourably: 'Blessed trophies! More valuable

27 *Missionary Sketches* N°3, October 1818 and a second edition August 1820; reproduced as frontispiece of *The South Sea Islander*, 1820; Montgomery 1841,24; also Davies 1961,199, Hooper 2006,63.

28 For instance N°2 is BM Oc1981,Q.1551; N°3 is Temeharo; see fig. 51. BM Oc1981,Q.1552 (both illustrated in Babadzan 1981,17 and 14); N°7 is LMS 102; see figs. 199, 209; see also Buck 1944 pl 16e.

29 Williams 1837,15; also in the vessel bound for England was the first cargo of native produce—£1800 worth of Tahitian coconut oil. A draft of Haweis' letter of encouragement and advice is in Dr Haweis papers supplement, ML MSS 4190X, 4⅞.

30 In Letters to Rev T Haweis, ML MSS A302¾ 165(301).

31 Ibid., 161(297).

32 HR Haweis 1896 2,224.

33 Taroa was likely a small 'Oro image. In a letter dated February 1837, Williams asked Haweis' widow Elizabeth if he could add to his *Narrative* a 'coloured engraving' of this idol; he had seen the idol in Bath (HR Haweis 2,326). Unfortunately this never happened.

34 Dr Haweis papers supplement, ML MSS 4190X,4 7/8.

35 June 1818 entry in Autobiography T Haweis 2,232; ML MSS Z/B1177. It is not clear which batch of idols he was referring to here.

36 Ibid.

than those at Waterloo.'[37] He praised Haweis: 'I cannot but congratulate you dear sir on having lived to see the desires of your heart gratified by the success of that mission of which *doubtless you are the Father.*'[38] The idols were seen as material proof—what Williams called 'ocular demonstration'—of the success of the South Sea Mission.

There is mention of another shipment of objects, presumably from the Society Islands, in a 2 July 1821 letter from Williams (on Ra'iatea) to the LMS directors, ending: 'PS: I have directed a box of curiosities for my friends to be left at the missionary rooms not knowing exactly their direction.'[39] Unfortunately, no details of these curiosities are given.

RURUTU

About five years after the dispatch of Pomare's family idols to London, a third notable shipment of idols occurred. This shipment was sent to the LMS station on Ra'iatea from the island of Rurutu, one of the Australs. A Rurutuan chief-turned-convert named Auura, in company with two Raiatean teachers, Mahamene and Puna, brought the gospel to Rurutu on their own, achieving 'success' in just over one month. 'The chief of Rurutu promised the brethren that he would send his gods to England.' Auura came through on his promise: 'In a few weeks, the Raiateans returned in triumph, bearing with them 'the gods many' of Rurutu—'the prisoners'[40]—'the trophies of Victory, the gods of the heathen taken in this bloodless war, and won by the power of the Prince of Peace.'[41] They returned 9 August 1821. This group of rejected idols included the well-known figure known as

A'a,[42] 'a rude figure made of platted sinnet, in the shape of a man, with an opening down the front, through which it was filled with little gods, or the family gods of the old chiefs, the points of spears, old slings &c., of ancient warriors', and 'all the family gods'.[43] Mentioned two months later was a Rurutu idol that was 'merely a small piece of wood covered with cloth in all about the size of a mans leg & thigh'[44]—a description that could well apply to a Tahitian image of 'Oro.

On a Sunday evening following their arrival in Ra'iatea, the trophies were exhibited in the chapel, illuminated with the light from ten chandeliers of turned wood, the central chandelier with double tiers of 18 coconut lamps. The Raiateans were excited by the event,[45] and by the idea that 'the rugged world is made smooth by the word of God'.[46] Not surprisingly, the missionaries were 'powerfully awakened to the great importance of extending the benefits and blessings of the Gospel';[47] 'They surveyed the rejected idols of Rurutu as sure pledges of future triumphs.'[48] This third group of idols, sent up from Rurutu by the Raiatean teachers, was quickly dispatched to London, and arrived mid-1823.[49] Tyerman and Bennet reported to the LMS directors: 'Until 15 months before our visit, this island had remained in the hand of the *enemy*, and in the slavery of idolatry. . . . The people abandoned their idols, which have probably reached you.' A footnote on the same page: 'The idols alluded to by the deputation have been received, and will be placed in the Society Museum.'[50]

---

37 Burder (Camberwell) to Haweis (Bath) 20 January 1818 ML MSS A302¾ 130(23).

38 Ibid.

39 SOAS LMS SS incom corresp box3 folder6.

40 Prout 1843,128. Details of the conversion of Rurutu by Auura, Mahamene and Puna are told in a letter within a report, Williams and Threlkeld 18 October 1821 to G Burder, 'An account of the renunciation of Idolatry & of the reception of Christianity by the natives of the Island of Rurutu an Island in the South Seas—150,51 East Long, 22,29 S. Lat called in Charts Ohetiroa' (SOAS LMS SS incom corresp box3b folder6). Extracts from this letter were published by Smith 1824 (2,90) and Montgomery 1832 (2,108). As this report contains much interesting information that has not been published, a transcription of it in its entirety appears in Appendix 3.

41 Williams 1837,44.

42 LMS 19; first published *Missionary Sketches* 24, January 1824. See Harding 1994, Sivasundaram 2005, Hooper 2007, 2008.

43 Threlkeld and Williams letter in Montgomery 1832 2,112. Exactly which trophies were in this group is unfortunately not known. It is likely that included in 'all the family gods' were a number of Rurutuan flywhisks, referred to in the LMS catalogues as 'various whips'; see fig. 112.

44 Captain John Grimes of the New Zealand and London-based sealer *Hope*, in letter Williams and Threlkeld to G Burder 18 October 1821; SOAS LMS SS incom corresp box3b folder6, transcribed in Appendix 3.

45 Uaeva's speech this evening: 'Look at the chandeliers! 'Oro never taught us any thing like this! Look at our wives, in their gowns and their bonnets . . . ' and so on (Williams 1837,46).

46 Tamatoa's speech (ibid.,45); Tamatoa was 'king' of Ra'iatea.

47 Ibid.,51.

48 Prout 1843,128.

49 'The Rurutu idols arrived a few weeks ago on the ship Westmorland.' *Missionary Sketches* July 1823.

50 Letter Tyerman and Bennet (in Ra'iatea) to directors, 14 November 1822, quoted in *Evangelical Magazine* September 1823,384.

Far more is known about a fourth group of 'idol-trophies', collected during a remarkable voyage of the schooner *Endeavour* from Ra'iatea to the central Cook Islands in 1823. The missionaries had already begun their labours in the central Cook Islands two years earlier. As Williams put it, 'The year 1821 was fraught with important events.'[51] The first native missionary society in Polynesia was formed, on Ra'iatea. Tahiti had become prosperous, warless, and Christian. Ra'ivavae, in the Australs, had become Christianized; in October the previous year, 'Pomare wishing to promote the instruction of the people, engaged Para, a person from Taheiti, acquainted with reading & writing, who was then with him, to stay on the island [Ra'ivavae] and undertake the work'.[52]

On 3 February 1821, Captain Samuel P Henry (son of missionary William Henry) of the brig *Governor Macquarie* was impressed to find on visiting Ra'ivavae that 'the whole of their gods are mutilated removed from their Morais and were converted into stools [these were probably cut-down drums] at the entrance of the church. . . . This surprising & happy change has taken place within the short space of only four months.'[53] Rurutu had fallen in 1821 as well; by the end of September, 'not a vestige of idolatry was to be seen, not a god was to be found in the island.'[54]

The second phase of the missionary conquest of the Pacific (Ra'ivavae and Rurutu) had occurred far faster (four months and one month, respectively) than the first phase (Tahiti; 15 years). The effective agency of native teachers in accomplishing conversion—'clearing away

the rubbish of idolatry'—was now apparent. Williams was ignited to move on. He decided to leave Ra'iatea: 'duty demanded the sacrifice.' His next target was Aitutaki, only 600 miles away. In 1811, missionaries Henry Bicknell and William Scott had called there on a voyage from Port Jackson back to Eimeo (Mo'orea). They found the island friendly, and thought it a convenient place to start a mission.[55] There was an easy boat landing. Williams had heard about it as well from Auura. But neither he nor his wife was well.[56] Williams wanted to regain health in Sydney. He also wanted to open a market there to sell island produce (coconut oil, arrowroot, sugar, salt, tobacco, sennit rope, indigo) in order to augment the meagre finances of the Mission; he wanted to purchase a ship; and he wanted to drop off two Raiatean teachers at Aitutaki on the way, to get things started. In October 1821, they embarked on the *Westmoreland* with two Raiatean teachers, Papeiha and Vahapata. On the arrival of the vessel at Aitutaki [26 October],

> we were very soon surrounded by canoes; the natives were exceedingly noisy, and as wild as possible both in their appearance and manners, and presented in their persons and manners all the wild features of savage life. Some were tatooed from head to foot; some were painted most fantastically with pipe-clay and yellow and red ochre; others were smeared all over with charcoal, dancing, shouting, and exhibiting the most frantic gestures.[57]

The chief of Aitutaki was named Tamatoa, age 15.[58] The teachers informed Tamatoa of the overthrow of idolatry in Tahiti and the Society Islands. They told

---

51 Williams 1837,53.

52 Announcement 'New Station in Raivaivai' in the December 1821 issue of *Evangelical Magazine*,529.

53 Letter from Captain SP Henry to the Tahitian Mission 3 February 1821, printed in the December 1821 issue of *Evangelical Magazine*. Reporting about the trip: 'My knowledge and observations are of a nature truly gratifying.' He found 'delightful' the sight of 800 quiet and devout natives assembled on an early Sunday morning. 'Each individual on entering the chapel kneeled down & uttered a prayer.' Pare performed the service. He and Tahuhu, the Chief of the island, implored the LMS in Ra'iatea to send a missionary to instruct in order to 'enlighten in the knowledge of our saviour [and] provide the road to happiness and eternal life.'

54 Rurutu visit of Tyerman and Bennet as reported by Williams (Williams 1837,51); in Tyerman and Bennet's words, 'All submitting to the scepter of the Prince of Peace . . . have cast away their cruelty with their idols' (Montgomery 1832 2,102).

55 Davies 1961,317.

56 'Our more directly missionary work is also prospering. Our congregations are large and attentive, and everything that can afford satisfaction to a missionary's heart is enjoyed by us, except health. Had we but that blessing, our cup would runneth over. . . . Oh! for health and strength—not to give to the vanities of the world—not to amass the riches of the East—but to spend and be spent among the perishing heathen' (letter Williams to Directors 13 November 1822, in Prout 1843,167).

57 Williams 1837,51.

58 Recall that Tamatoa was also the name of the 'king' of Ra'iatea. Chiefs abdicated as soon as they had a son, the son having higher rank than the father and often assuming chieftainship at an age that astonished Europeans; Pomare III, for example, became chief at age 18 months.

him that the idols there, including Tangaroa and 'Oro, had all been consumed with fire, and suggested the same course for Aitutaki. Tamatoa 'paid little attention' and proceeded to take them to visit the marae; 'we told him it was both useless and wicked to take us before the marae.'[59]

At Aitutaki, Williams learned more of the other islands in the Hervey group, 'numerously inhabited'—especially Rarotonga. 'This information increased in my estimation the value of the Aitutaki Mission.' He left Papeiha and Vahapata on Aitutaki and went on to New South Wales, where the Williams' health improved over the next several months. At Parramatta, he saw a message from Aitutaki that said 'tell Viriamu [Williams] if he will visit us, we will burn our idols, destroy our maraes, and receive the word of the true God.'[60] He also heard yet more about Rarotonga, 'large and beautiful, with a population so great, that it was divided up into nine-and-twenty districts.' This sounded like an ideal 'field [for] future labours, so evidently and delightfully white to the harvest. . . . '[61]

Williams returned to Ra'iatea,[62] and soon set out for Aitutaki with his wife Mary, their four-year-old son John, Mr and Mrs Robert Bourne (missionaries on Taha'a), and four more Raiatean teachers, 'to cast down Satan's kingdom.'[63] His sights were also on Rarotonga.

They sailed 4 July 1823, on a chartered British schooner named *Endeavour*, master John Dibbs.[64] In five days they arrived at Aitutaki, less than two years after they had dropped off Papeiha and Vahapata:

On the 9th early in the Morning we made the land . . . to our astonishment we found that the great Work was done before we arrived—We had a grateful salutation from every Canoe that passed us. . . . Some cried out Good is the word of God—& It is now well at Aitu-

take. Some pointed to their hats,[65] others held up a spelling book to convince us of the truth of what they said . . . we learnt from Te Bati one of the first who embraced the gospel that all the Maraes were destroyed & burned not one remained whole—that the profession of Christianity was general—so much so that not an Idolator remained. That a large chapel was erected nearly 200 feet long plastered & waiting my arrival to open it—we rejoiced at hearing this good & unexpected News.[66]

They also learned that all the idols that had escaped the general conflagration had been brought to Papeiha and Vahapata, and were in their possession: 'The whole population then came in procession, district after district, the chief and priest leading the way, and the people following them, bearing their rejected idols, which they laid at the teachers' feet, and then received from them in return a few copies of the gospels and elementary books.'[67] The idols were loaded onto the *Endeavour*.

Wishing a few quiet hours to consult respecting our future proceedings we determined to spend the evening on board the ship. The gods and bundles of gods, which had escaped destruction, thirty-one in number, were carried in triumph to the boat, and we came off to the vessel with the trophies of our bloodless conquest, 'rejoicing as one that findeth great spoil'.[68]

[59] Williams and Papeiha ms *More Joy for Christians*,1; SOAS LMS SSJ box4 folder59.
[60] Williams 1837,56.
[61] Ellis 1844 1,284.
[62] While in Sydney, the Williamses stocked up on shoes, stockings, teakettles, cups and saucers.
[63] Prout 1843,171.
[64] Sharp 1960,203. Interestingly, Dibbs' route is traced on Duperrey's 'Carte des Iles situées au Sud et a l'Ouest des Iles de la Société', dated 1823, in the atlas of his account of the voyage of *La Coquille*; see fig. 268.
[65] European style hats and bonnets signaled 'ocular demonstration of the beneficial effects of Christianity' (Williams 1837,62). Before the later missionaries brought English cloth, 'females dressed in white native cloth, their heads with white flowers, and cocoa nut leaves plaited in the shape of the front of a cottage bonnet' (Tahiti, 1817; letter Williams to Directors, in Prout 1843,51). Later, the missionary wives taught how to sew bonnets: 'the wives . . . actively employed in teaching the young girls and women of the islands . . . the use of the needle' (Ellis 1844 1,244). 'The European shaped hat was worn only by the Christian party, the idolaters retaining their heathen head-dresses, war caps, &c' (Williams 1837,59 footnote). There were residence standards as well: 'The house must [be] plastered in and out, have doors and windows, bed rooms with doors and shutters, and a garden encircling the house' (Orsmond 4 December 1825 SOAS LMS SSJ N°71; see fig. 12). Floors of planks, bedsteads with white tapa decorations, sofas of turned wood; windows with 'Venetian blinds' (adjustable louvres) were not uncommon.
[66] Williams ms *More Joy for Christians*,32.
[67] Williams 1837,74 and 59.
[68] Ibid.,63. Williams specifies 'the great idols are all burned the little ones all on board the ship' (Williams ms *Journal of a Voyage*,23; PMB35).

Williams and Bourne returned to Ra'iatea on 7 August 1823. 'We entered the harbour early in the morning with our vessel decorated with the trophies of victory.'[69] 'And as other warriors feel pride in displaying trophies of the victories they win, we hung the rejected idols of Aitutaki to the yard-arms and other parts of the vessel, entered the harbour in triumph, sailed down to the settlement, and dropped anchor amidst the shouts and congratulations of our people.'[70] Tyerman and Bennet mention on these occasions 'a general desire prevailed to see these objects of adoration' in order to celebrate their moral victory.[71] 'On the Friday evening following there was a public exhibition of all the Idols in our large chapel. It was lighted up and presented a brilliant appearance. I gave . . . part of the account of our interesting journey. The numerous idols were hung in various parts of the chapel but especially about the pulpit desk.'[72] The hymn was the Jubilee Hymn, 'Blow Ye the Trumpet, Blow'.[73] The teachers spoke as well:

Pointing to the idols he said the teeth of these monsters are blunted by the word of Jesus. They will devour no more men or children in the island of Aitutaki. . . . True indeed is the word that says all the gods that did shall be destroyed. Behold them hanging here this evening; poisons of the sea hanging here are the poisons of the land for both body and soul are poisoned by them. . . . Gods of wood or form are food for the fire but the god without form his head cannot be reached. . . . These idols are not obtained by means of spears clotted with human blood as formerly; no guns no spears no spikes no other weapon but the powerful gospel of our Lord Jesus Christ. . . . Behold these great these powerful gods once adored by us how foolish how contemptible in our sight they now appear.[74]

Clearly Aitutaki had been 'freed from the fetters of a foul and sanguinary idolatry.'[75]

THE CENTRAL COOK ISLANDS: AITUTAKI

Exactly what were all these idols brought back from Aitutaki? In this case, Williams attempted to find out. He tells us in *Missionary Enterprises*: 'I obtained from the chief of Aitutaki a short account of the relics of idolatry. Twenty-five of these I numbered and transmitted, with their names and history, to the deputation [Tyerman and Bennet] then at Tahiti; six others were sent to England, and many of them are now in the Missionary Museum.'[76] He includes partial descriptions of five of them.[77] Williams refers to these idols in a letter written from Ra'iatea to Rev G Burder at the LMS in London, 31 September 1823, mentioning shipment of 25 idols via Tyerman and Bennet to London: 'Dear Sir, All the idols in this case that are not directed are for the Society. The greater part from N°1 to N°25 are in the possession of the deputation as they were pleased to express a wish to take them round with them on their journey, please to forward the various parcels to the friends to whom they are directed.' Signed 'Wms.'[78] The remaining six were dispatched to England via the Colony on the *Active*, 6 October 1823.[79]

There is no question that the idols reached England. It is a pity the exact identities of almost all of them are lost, but it turns out that the descriptions are not lost, and there were more than 31 of them. In the LMS archives at the School of Oriental and African Studies (SOAS) at the University of London is a stitched-together 47-page manuscript in Williams' hand, written in pencil, in Ra'iatea, entitled: *More joy for Christians—or the power of Christ displayed in effecting mighty things by weak*

<hr>

69 Williams and Papeiha ms *More Joy for Christians*,36; SOAS LMS SSJ box4 folder59.

70 Williams 1837,107.

71 Montgomery 1832 2,111.

72 Williams and Papeiha ms *More Joy for Christians*,36; SOAS LMS SSJ box4 folder59.

73 The missionaries brought with them Rev John Campbell's *The Comprehensive Hymn Book; One Thousand Hymns, Original and Selected*, J Snow, Paternoster Row, nd (ca 1816); price 3s6d.

74 These quotes are all from Williams and Papeiha ms *More Joy for Christians*, SOAS LMS SSJ box4 folder59.

75 Campbell 1842,23.

76 Williams 1837,109.

77 Ibid.,109. These five descriptions are quoted and corrected by Buck 1944,330.

78 SOAS LMS SS incom corresp box4 folder2, letter reproduced in Appendix 6 (see figs. 266, 267); George Burder was Secretary of the LMS for 24 years and corresponded with the missionaries, 'aiming to cement them, by a tender bond, to the Directors and the Society' (Morison 1844,286); useful and energetic, he succeeded Eyre as editor of *Evangelical Magazine*.

79 Letter Threlkeld (Ra'iatea) to Burder, 26 Sep 1823: 'Another host of Gods are now forwarded from the Island of Vaitutake who have embraced the Gospel . . . The Active sails on Monday next to the colony.' SOAS LMS SS incom corresp box4 folder1.

instruments, in the complete overthrow of Idolatry in the Island of Aitutaki written by Mr Williams from the mouth of Papeiha one of the Native Teachers sent to that Island by the Church of Christ at Raiatea.[80] This manuscript describes events on Aitutaki from 1821 to 1823. Papeiha narrated the account to Williams on Rarotonga, and probably also on the *Endeavour* on their way back to Ra'iatea in July–August 1823.[81] Parts formed the basis for the Aitutaki sections in Williams' *Narrative*. It was prepared as a pamphlet or report for the LMS directors, and for the deputation. As this report has not been published, a transcription of it in its entirety, along with some notes, appears in Appendix 6.

Of particular interest here are the last nine pages of the manuscript; see Appendix 6. On them is an annotated list of the 31 idols that Williams mentions, 25 of them marked 'Descriptions of the Aitutaki Idols in possession of the Rev D Tyerman & G Bennet Esq—Deputation from MS [Missionary Society]', the remainder simply 'Sent to England'. The entries are brief, but informative. Most of them give the names and describe specific uses of the idols. Several of the objects are in fact 'bundles' of objects; evidently there were a good deal more than 31 items in the group. Many of them are described as 'sacred' fans and, more often, fan handles.[82] Some had tapa, sennit, or bird feathers attached. Papeiha tells of inferior gods, regard for the natural world, divination. Even an island as small as Aitutaki had districts, each with its own regional god, and versions of the same god within the same district. As Buck surmised, there is no doubt that many of these Aitutaki objects have ended up in the LMS collection in the British Museum. With five exceptions discussed below (p. 71), it is not possible without further information to connect every individual object on the list with specific objects in LMS collections.

THE CENTRAL COOK ISLANDS:
ATIU, MAUKE, MITIARO

Not all the objects Williams and Bourne brought back to Ra'iatea came from Aitutaki. In mid-July 1823 the *Endeavour* called at six other islands in the Hervey Group, and even succeeded in rediscovering Rarotonga.

Their first stop was the island of Mangaia. Four teachers and their wives went ashore, but were treated rudely. They were seized, pillaged, and stripped; their hats and bonnets were torn from their heads and dragged through the mud. They gave the Mangaians 'two pigs, animals they had never seen before. These were taken by a chief, who, casting off his own garments, decorated the pigs in the insignia of chieftainship, and sent them into the presence of their majesties, the gods.'[83] The missionaries gave up, and steered for Atiu.

At Atiu, a remarkable series of events ensued. They were met by a large double canoe, in the centre of which, on an elevated stage, was seated Roma-tane, the principal chief, tall slender and commanding. As soon as the Atiu chief came aboard, Tamatoa,[84] en route to visit Ra'iatea, took him aside and 'commenced his work by informing him that the maraes of Aitutaki were demolished, the great idols burnt, and the smaller ones were on board the ship.' As proof, 'he led the astonished chieftain into the hold of the vessel, and exhibited to his view their once dreaded, and, as they imagined, powerful gods, which were lying there in degradation.' Tamatoa worked on Roma-tane all night. The pivotal argument, the one that won over the Atiu chief, was a good one. In Williams' words:

> The natives have two words not very much unlike, but expressive of opposite ideas,—*moa* and *noa*, the *moa* meaning sacred and *noa* the very reverse of sacred. All that pertains to the gods is the superlative of *moa*; and all that pertains to food, and the cooking of food, is the superlative of *noa*. The idea now, for the first time, darted with irresistible force, into the mind of Roma-tane; and he perceived at once the excessive folly of making a god and cooking food with one and the same tree.[85]

---

80 Williams and Papeiha ms *More Joy for Christians*, SOAS LMS SSJ box4 folder59.
81 Williams 1837,170.
82 Sacred fans are discussed below, p. 73.
83 Williams 1837,80.
84 Probably the enthusiastic, younger Tamatoa; both the young 'king' of Aitutaki and his grandfather were named Tamatoa, and both joined the *Endeavour* at Aitutaki. Williams figured 'We had the impression that they might be of great service at the various heathen islands which we intended to visit.' He was right (Williams 1837,63).
85 Ibid.,86; see Kirch & Green 2001,239 for a recent appraisal of the concepts of mana, tapu, noa.

It worked. By morning, Tamatoa had proven himself an effective teacher: Roma-tane was keen to demolish his marae, burn his idols, and build a house for the worship of Jehovah. He was presented with an axe to accomplish the job and was eager to get started. But Williams heard that Roma-tane was also chief and sovereign of two nearby islands, Mitiaro and Mauke, neither of which had ever before been visited by Europeans.[86] He persuaded the chief to come along and pay a quick visit to both islands in order to ask his subjects to be kind to the two pairs of Raiatean teachers Williams wanted to drop off.[87] Roma-tane did just that, and he also went a step further. On landing, on both islands, he immediately sent for the chiefs, and explained his object to them:

> I am come to advise you to receive the word of Jehovah, the true God, and to leave you with a teacher, and his wife, who will remain with you and instruct you. Let us burn all our maraes, and all our evil spirits, with fire. Never let us worship them again. They are wood, that we have carved and decorated, and called gods. . . . The true God is Jehovah, and the true sacrifice is his Son Jesus Christ.[88]

Another account has Roma-tane advising ' . . . that they must burn all the Maraes—bundle up all the Idols and let them remain.'[89] The people on Mitiaro were—for a moment—astonished: 'Shall we not all be strangled? . . . Must we destroy Taria Nui?'[90] 'No replied he . . . it is out of the power of wood that we have ornamented & decorated & called a god to kill us.'[91]

The people of Mauke were evidently even more tractable, and simply said: 'We will do it.' It was indeed a remarkable voyage. Williams was elated: 'Were three islands ever converted from idolatry in so short a time! So unexpectedly!—islands almost unknown, and two never before visited by any European vessel!'[92] *Evangelical Magazine*, at the close of 1823, described the fruits of the *Endeavour* tour modestly: 'This triumph of the cross must be regarded as one of the most signal ever achieved since the world began. Glory to God in the highest. It is truly marvelous.'[93]

It is likely that all LMS objects from the central Cook Islands were collected during the 17–22 July 1823 portion of the *Endeavour* voyage: Papeiha went along on the trip and was a very good collector, and idolatry on every island generally ended abruptly as soon as Christianity took hold. So did the idols. Ellis, Williams, and Orsmond, for example, all state that 'every trace' of idolatry on Huahine, Taha'a, and Ra'iatea was gone before they arrived in 1818. Tyerman and Bennet, on Tahiti in October 1823 convey the same message, with an example: 'Mr. Bennet obtained a fare na atua, or house of a god [LMS 120], the only relic of the kind that we have seen in these islands; so utter was the demolition of such things, even when the idols themselves were preserved for transportation to England as trophies of the triumph of the gospel.'[94] Subsequent visitors to the central Cooks mention the remarkable victory of Christianity there; none mention the gathering of idols.[95]

The 1826 LMS *Catalogue* lists idols from Aitutake (Aitutaki), and from Maute (Mauke) and Rarotonga as well. Williams and Bourne offered most of the Aitutaki idols to Tyerman and Bennet. A week after the *Endeavour* returned, Bourne and Williams wrote them a letter:

<hr>

86 These were not densely-populated islands. Williams' population estimates were Mitiaro 100, Mauke 300, as opposed to Atiu and Mangaia (Auau) 2000 each, Rarotonga 6000–7000.

87 Maratai and Taua on Mitiaro, and Haavi and Faraire on Mauke, according to Williams.

88 *Missionary Chronicle* March 1825,119 re Mitiaro.

89 Williams ms *Journal of a Voyage*,27; PMB35.

90 The quote continues: '(or Great Ears*)[* the name of the god of which the king himself was the priest]'. The entry for British Museum LMS ms nd catalogue 35(circled number)[94][691] reads: 'TARINGA-NUE—great-ears the chief deity of Atiu, Mitiaro & Mauke.' See Buck 1944,346 for discussion of the confusion regarding Tarianui, Taringa-nui, Tangiia-nui, Tarignarue, and 'Great Ears'. The LMS ms catalogue, which appears to be in Edge-Partington's hand, is in the British Museum Anthropology Library.

91 Williams ms *Journal of a Voyage*,27; PMB35.

92 Williams 1837,90; Williams himself emphasizes that the conversion of all six islands was accomplished by native teachers—no European missionaries at all (Williams 1837,291).

93 *Evangelical Magazine* 1823,515.

94 Montgomery 1832 2,195. By the time of Marsden's death in 1838 '[I]dolatry had fallen; [the] idols were utterly abolished; they had found their way to the most ignoble uses, or to the museums of the curious, or those of the various Missionary Societies in Great Britain. So complete was their destruction that natives of Tahiti have actually visited the museum of the London Missionary Society within the last few years, and there seen, for the first time in their lives, a Tahitian idol' (JB Marsden 1858,311).

95 This would include the deputation in June 1824, Lord Byron on the *Blonde* in August 1825, and Williams and Bourne in October 1825; the next missionary visits were not until May 1827.

We have in our possession all the idols from Aitu-take—a great company of them—an excellent lot. Should you wish to take them with you to India, &c. we will not send them to England by Captain Charleton. If it were possible for you to see them, and propose questions to Tamatoa of Aitutake upon them, and get information yourselves from him respecting them, previously to his return to his own island, it would add much to the interest with which you would show them to your different friends in your journey, and at England.[96]

Tyerman and Bennet did take their allotment of 26 on the list, but they did not report finding out anything further about them. The other six on Williams' list were indeed sent to England by Captain Charlton, as some are specifically listed in the 1826 LMS *Catalogue*, and Bennet did not return to England until 1829; Tyerman died the year before, in Madagascar.[97] The 1826 LMS *Catalogue* states (p22): 'It is probable that we shall be able to give a more particular description of the South Sea Idols, and other articles, on the return of the Deputation. Additional specimens may also be expected.' Additional specimens did arrive, but the particulars did not.

The exact island origins of the numerous types of Cook Island god images brought back from the *Endeavour* voyage are not always certain. On an occasional British Museum LMS collection slip or specimen label is written the name of a specific island—Atiu, Metiaro,

Maute. Sometimes accurate, sometimes not, these notes are often all the locality information that exists. No mention of Atiu or Mauke objects can be found in any LMS documents,[98] but there is mention of idol collecting at Mitiaro; Romatane and Borabora teacher Maratai's instructions to the chief of Mitiaro were as follows: '[I]nstruct . . . the people . . . that they must burn all the Maraes—bundle up all the Idols and let them remain—that they must cast off all their customs relative to the Maraes.'[99] Both printed editions of the *Catalogue of the Missionary Museum*[100] are of limited help. They are full of erroneous information, or vague locality entries such as 'Hervey Group', and worse, 'Tahitian Group' or 'Otaheite'.[101] Or blank spaces. It does not help that there seem to be more than three sets of LMS catalogue numbers. There is a Hawaiian object in the LMS collection from Cook's third voyage.[102] Ascertaining the island of origin is further complicated by the fact that there was extensive communication and exchange amongst the central Cook Islands (see p. 78); they are not so distant from one another. Some of Buck's comments on the subject: 'Anything connected with Bennet carries the proof of age but not of accuracy regarding locality', and 'It is irritating that details such as their names and functions were not preserved.'[103]

Surely there has never occurred an easier or faster instance of heathens seeing the light than what the missionaries and the teachers achieved on the *Endeavour* voyage: three islands in three days. Few details are known about this whirlwind trip, probably because Williams and Bourne never actually landed; business appears to have been conducted from the boat—and not by Williams and Bourne, or even Papeiha, but by Tamatoa and Roma-tane. For the English missionaries, it was an armchair conversion. Because this was such an important trip, and because the story of it in

96 Letter Bourne and Williams to Tyerman and Bennet 11 August 1823, transcribed accurately in *Missionary Chronicle* October 1824,455; see facsimile, Appendix 4.

97 There is evidence that Tyerman and Bennet also sent objects from the South Sea back to England prior to their own departure from Tahiti, which was in June 1824. A 3 October 1823 letter Tyerman to the LMS directors ends: 'NB If there be anything acceptable to the Society in the two packages which Captn E____[probably Emment] is kind enough to bring home bearing my name—I [thought?] that you will appropriate it to the museum & let the remainder be unpacked in the same boxes until my return. [Several of these?] packages containing my best curiosities the captain was unable to take on board. Perhaps an application to government to be allowed to land our packages of such articles duty free would be successful. Many other packages will follow them when convenient & opportunity offers' (SOAS LMS SS home odds box10 folder2 jacketA). The cases arrived: a letter from McCoy to Montgomery, 10 May 1824, mentions 'two boxes of curiosities from Otaheite, consisting of War instruments, Dresses, Musical Instruments' received by the Sheffield Literary and Philosophical Society in 1824. See Twells 1999,60; Woroncow 1981.

98 An important reference here is a drawing of a fan acquired on Atiu, Cook's third voyage, discussed on page 74.

99 Williams ms *Journal of a Voyage*,27; PMB35.

100 The two LMS catalogues are listed in the bibliography as anonymous 1826, and anonymous nd.

101 The word 'Otaheite' could mean Tahiti, but it could also mean 'South Sea'; Buck re Cook collection labels in European museums: 'Thus, when in doubt they used the magic locality of Otaheite' (letter to Ngata 19 July 1933; Condliffe 1971,182).

102 LMS *Catalogue* nd p. 14, N°1: 'An idol representing a huge helmeted head, covered with red feathers, from the Sandwich Islands. Formerly in the Leverian Museum.' This is LMS 221.

103 Buck 1944,121.

Missionary Enterprises is jumbled and sketchy,[104] three of the four most detailed accounts of the *Endeavour* trip are reproduced here. The best source for this trip would be Williams' and Bourne's original journal, which was the basis of the *Missionary Enterprises* narrative, but it has not been located; it may no longer exist. Williams' and Papeiha's 47-page account appears in Appendix 6. Another version of a portion of their journal entitled *Journal of a Voyage*, in Williams' hand, is in the possession of Williams' family; it is available electronically.[105] A description of the Atiu-Mitiaro-Mauke portion of the trip was printed in *Missionary Chronicle* of March 1825 and appears in Appendix 5. 'An outline' of the voyage is a letter from Bourne and Williams (in Ra'iatea) to Tyerman and Bennet (in Tahiti) written 11 August 1823, four days after their return. This was accurately transcribed in *Missionary Chronicle* and appears in Appendix 4. The four accounts complement one another.

The *Endeavour* voyage of 1823 was a missionary's dream, and it wasn't over: Rarotonga was next.

RAROTONGA

Williams and Bourne spent six to eight days searching for Rarotonga, had no luck, returned to the central Cook Islands for three days, and then spent another five days searching. One evening, Friday 25 July 1823, a half hour before giving up, success came. An account of this part of the trip appears in *Missionary Enterprises*,[106] but detailed information about objects and collections from Rarotonga is almost nonexistent. Williams and Bourne left two teachers on Rarotonga after their initial brief visit which was, again, just one day long, and again, the English never left the ship. The teachers were first Papeiha, along with six Christianized Rarotongans they found on Aitutaki, joined four months later by fellow teacher Tiberio—also from Ra'iatea. Williams was not to return for four years. In the meantime, the teachers went to work. Conversion was not easily won, but was nearly complete by the time Tyerman and Bennet's deputation visited Rarotonga in June 1824, and was

entirely complete by the time Williams returned, with missionary Charles Pitman, in May 1827. Tyerman and Bennet reported: '[T]he gospel has been planted. But a twelve-month ago, these [people] were in the state in which we saw the Manaians—gross, fierce, crafty barbarians; now gentle, upright, and well behaved, attending with diligence to the Means of grace, and daily making progress in the arts of civilised life.'[107]

There are a number of tantalizing references to various caches of unincinerated idols, and shipments of idols, from the Cook Islands to Ra'iatea and London, in the period 1823 to 1827—between Williams' first and second visits to Rarotonga. Starting immediately after the burning of the first idol in Rarotonga in 1823, there is mention that Papeiha spared some of the idols from the flames; here speaking of the idols of Tinomana Ariki of Arorangi district: 'In the course of a few days all the idols in the district were brought to the teachers; some of these were destroyed, but the others they determined to send to Raiatea.'[108] Then in January 1825, Williams announced: 'From Rarotonga our men have brought us the most pleasing news, with ocular demonstration of the triumphs of the "mighty gospel". All idolatry is abolished in this populous island. They have erected a chapel 106 fathoms in length! The messengers brought with them a few idols; but they say a house nearly full is waiting my arrival.'[109] The ocular demonstration was sent to London without delay. In a letter of 2 February 1825 to Rev George Burder in London, Williams writes:

> I have sent a few of the idols from Rarotonga—indeed all they brought up & will be obliged if you will forward to the Revd Tyerman those directed for him. This is only as the drop of a bucket the greater part are still at Raratoa. . . . I shall make a selection & send,

---

[104] One should bear in mind that Williams' *Narrative* was written more than ten years after this voyage, and was not written entirely by Williams.

[105] Williams ms *Journal of a Voyage*, PMB35.

[106] Williams 1837,99; see also Williams ms *Journal of a Voyage*,33; PMB35; Gosset 1940.

[107] Montgomery 1832 2,241.

[108] Papeiha's account (to Williams) of his first weeks in Rarotonga; Williams 1837,179.

[109] Williams Ra'iatea letter to his mentor Rev Mathew Wilks, LMS, London 29 January 1825, in Prout 1843,219. This chapel was Papeiha's doing. Its size was measured by the missionaries. Note: 106 fathoms is 636 feet; Winchester Cathedral, the largest in England, is 550 feet. Called the Royal Mission chapel, it was the largest ever built in Polynesia; it had 133 windows with sliding shutters; 280 pillars supported the roof edge; the rafters were wrapped in fine matting (Smith and Choules 1832,360). The ends of the chapels were often semicircular.

of course not send all as the expense of freight etc would be great.[110]

On their way back to England via Sydney in 1824, on the *Endeavour*, Tyerman and Bennet stopped briefly at Mangaia 15 June, Atiu 17 June, and Rarotonga 19 June. They made no mention of collecting objects on this trip, but accompanying them was missionary Lancelot Threlkeld, who did; on Rarotonga, Threlkeld asked the resident teacher Tiberio to get for him two or three idols. Tiberio brought him three. Two were given to the deputation to present to Carey in Serampore. Threlkeld wanted to take the third back to England, but never returned; while in Australia, he arranged with Governor Brisbane to start an aboriginal mission at Lake Macquarie. What became of any of these three Rarotongan idols is not known.[111]

In autumn 1825, 'The Rarotongans had sent him [Williams, back in Ra'iatea] a special invitation to visit their island, accompanied by the promise that on his arrival, they would cast all their rejected idols at his feet',[112] an invitation not to disregard. Williams arrived at Rarotonga, his second visit, 5 May 1827.[113] He expected it to be a brief one, but month after month went by with no ships visiting and hence no passage back to Ra'iatea possible. To return, he had to build his own ship. With hardly any tools, no screws or nails, rudder pintles forged of a pickaxe and a hoe, caulking of breadfruit latex, rope of sennit, sails of woven pandanus, the project took three months. 'She is built entirely of tamanu, and about fifty or sixty tons, quite

sharp. I call her The messenger of Peace.'[114] (See fig. 8.) Williams returned to Ra'iatea, along with Makea Ariki of Rarotonga and 'two immense idols'[115] a year to the day after he set out. Again, there was a trophy exhibition at the May meeting; 'This was the third time we had enjoyed the privilege of exhibiting to the Raiateans the abandoned idols of other islands.'[116]

MANGAIA

Mangaia was the last of the Cook Islands to be Christianized; Williams had heard that Mangaia was still 'hostile to the Gospel' in 1828, and reported that idolatry did not fall until after his visit in 1830. The story, based mainly on oral tradition, is told by LMS missionary William Wyatt Gill, who came to Mangaia in 1852.[117] Gill lists with confusing specifics 13 gods presented to the resident teachers Davida and Tiere,[118] and describes the manufacture of these images by a skilled carver named Rori.[119] No doubt WW Gill's list includes the three large, intricate, well-known openwork-carved staff gods in the British Museum LMS collection (see fig. 197) as well as the one in the Oldman collection (N°432), although which is which cannot be determined.[120] WW Gill states that the staff gods were adorned with red feathers brought to Mangaia from other islands.

---

[114] This astounding feat of resourcefulness, accomplished of course with the aid of much island labour, made immediate news in England and was recounted in missionary publications for the next hundred years; see accounts in Williams 1837 and in letter Williams to Ellis in Prout 1843,254; tamanu, *Callophyllum inophyllum*, is a native lowlands hardwood resembling mahogany.

[115] Letter Williams (Ra'iatea) to directors 26 April 1828, in Prout 1843,270.

[116] Quote from an 1839 London edition of Williams 1837, in Buck 1944,317.

[117] WW Gill 1894,323. See also Buck 1993 and references therein.

[118] WW Gill 1894,331; see also Appendix 1 re Anelay N°8. Davida and Tiere, both from Taha'a, were dropped off on Mangaia by the deputation in June 1824 (Montgomery 1832 2,237).

[119] WW Gill 1880,ch28.

[120] Illustrated in Buck 1944 pl 14 F,G,H,I.

[110] SOAS LMS SS incom corresp box7 folder5 jacketC (out of order); he adds 'Some of the idols were sent up . . . a large house full of them awaiting my arrival.' Raratoa is the Tahitian spelling of Rarotonga.

[111] LE Threlkeld, 'Reminiscences', 1853–1855,140; typescript from Sydney newspaper articles in possession of N Gunson.

[112] Prout 1843,223.

[113] The ship was *The Haweis*.

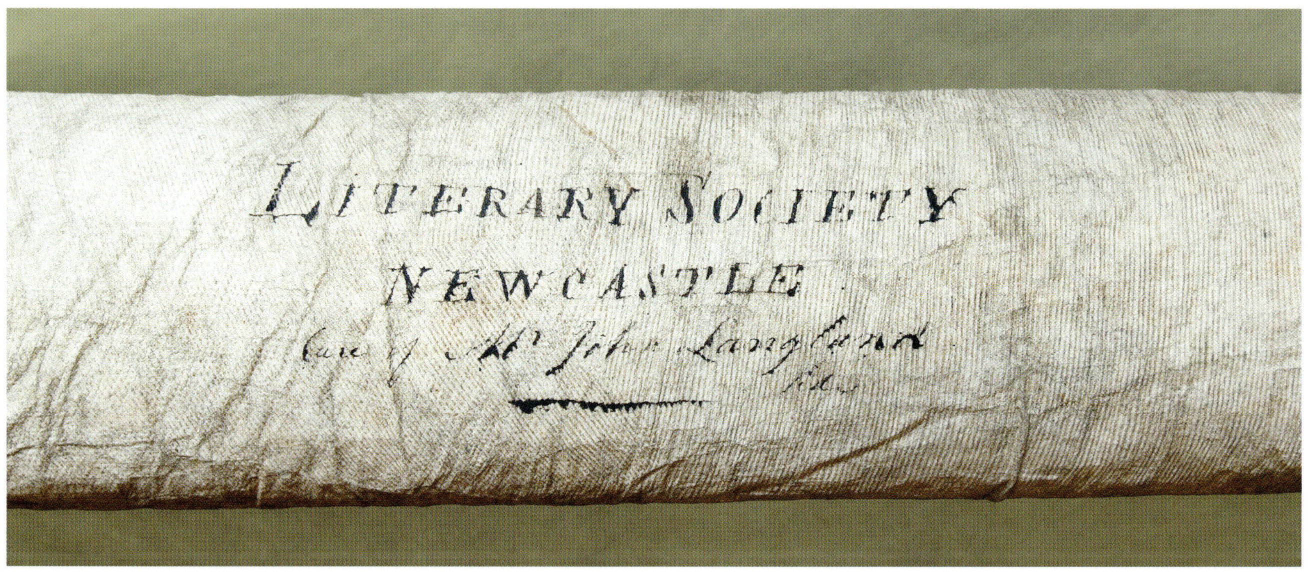

52

—At the same meeting, a very valuable present of various articles from the South Sea Islands was delivered by Mr John Langlands, from Captain Wilson, of London, late of the Duff.

53

52 *Inscription [*LITERARY SOCIETY, NEWCASTLE, *care of Mr John Langland] on a large roll of well-made white tapa, probably Tahitian; approximately 2 x 4 m. Hancock Museum, Newcastle upon Tyne, C701. This and one other similar tapa are the only objects unequivocally documented as having been brought back by Captain James Wilson on the* Duff. *They were presented to the Literary and Philosophical Society of Newcastle upon Tyne in May 1799 (discussed on p. 56; see Jessop 2003). John Langland was a well-known Newcastle silversmith. '[Wilson's] father was commander of a ship in the Newcastle trade, and brought him up from his earliest years in the sea service' (Griffin 1822,11).*

53 *Donation entry for 14 May 1800 on p. 6,* Seventh Year's Report of the Literary and Philosophical Society of Newcastle upon Tyne.

SEVEN

Findings

GODS AND GOD IMAGES

OBJECTS RELATED TO THE ONES depicted at Williams' feet in the Anelay watercolour—the ones that are not weapons—have been referred to in this text as idols or god images, and sometimes loosely as gods. What gods and god images (idols) really meant to eighteenth-century Polynesians is of course an intricate subject, and one that cannot be dealt with accurately at this point because all unequivocal sources are long gone. A number of Polynesian words are connected with gods and god images. They are not often used consistently. Probably the most productive approach that remains is to examine the earliest definitions of these terms as recorded by Europeans who spoke Tahitian; for more on this subject, see Appendix 8. The only term about which there is general agreement is the word *atua*.

The earliest surviving definitions of atua written by Europeans who spoke Tahitian are those of two *Bounty* mutineers; both James Morrison and Peter Heywood associate atua with *deity*. Morrison's discussion of *atua*

(he spells it *Eatooa*) appears in the 'Relegion' section of his manuscript *Account of the Island of Tahiti*. Owen Rutter's transcription of Morrison's *Account*, omitting Heywood's edits, is available.[1] Complementary to this is the definition of Eatooa taken from Peter Heywood's 100-manuscript page *Vocabulary of the Otaheitien Language*. As mentioned above, the *Vocabulary* has vanished, but fortunately the entry for Eatooa was transcribed by Thomas Haweis and published in 1797 as a letter in *Evangelical Magazine*.[2] As this reference is not readily available, the letter is reproduced, along with excerpts from Morrison's discussion of Eatooa, in Appendix 8.

John Davies is the third primary source for definitions on this subject. As noted above, Davies arrived in 1801, lived on Tahiti for 50 years, was a linguist, compiled the first Tahitian dictionary, and taught Tahitian

1   Morrison 1935,176.
2   *Evangelical Magazine* 1797,23; see also Du Rietz 1986,29

to later missionaries including William Ellis. Ellis arrived in 1817 and was on Tahiti only three years, but he was a diligent researcher and recorder, and fills in many details. Davies' *Dictionary*: 'Atua, God, the general name for a Diety; see Aitu'; 'Aitu, a god or goddess; see Atua.'

Morrison points out the distinction between the 'Deitys' and 'the Images to represent them [which] are only for the purpose of remembrancers and are not Worshipd';[3] in Buck's words, '[god images] were not worshipped in themselves. Hence the term idolatry applied to Polynesian religion by rival theologians is not quite accurate.'[4] Ellis explains: 'The general name by which these objects of worship were designated was atua, which is perhaps most appropriately translated god.'[5]

> They supposed their gods were powerful spiritual beings, in some degree acquainted with the events of this world, and generally governing its affairs; never exercising any thing like benevolence towards even their most devoted followers, but requiring homage and obedience, with constant offerings; denouncing their anger, and dispensing destruction on all who either refused or hesitated to comply.[6] But while the people supposed they were spiritual beings, they manufactured images either as representations of their form, and emblems of their character, or as the vehicle or instrument through which their communications might be made to the god, and his will revealed to them.[7]

There were family or household gods, local or district gods, and national gods, and there were many of them: 'The deities of Otaheite are nearly as numerous as . . . the inhabitants.'[8] 'Idolatry was interwoven with their naval architecture as well as every other pursuit';[9] there were gods of fishnet makers, valleys, mountains, precipices, dells, ravines, games, husbandry, healing, carpentry, ghosts, thatchers, thieves. There were gods who protected those in danger of falling from rocks or trees. Numerous gods were connected with fishing; Ellis states there were 14 principal marine divinities.[10] The 'malignant deities . . . were worshipped with enslaving fear.'[11] 'They prayed to the good gods to keep away the bad ones.'[12] 'These objects of fear and worship were exceedingly numerous . . . an enumeration would be tedious and useless.'[13]

God images took many forms, as is evident in the Anelay watercolour. Moreover, the god images reflected considerable regional differences, even within an island as small as Aitutaki. According to Williams,

> Idols: These were different in almost every island and district. I do not recollect to have seen two precisely similar representations of the same deity. Some were large and some were small; some were beautiful, while others were exceedingly hideous. The god-makers do not appear to have followed any pattern but were left to display their folly according to their own fancy. . . .[14]

Ellis, stationed on Mo'orea and Huahine, gives more details: 'Gods of some of the adjacent islands exhibit a greater variety of form and structure.'[15]

> The idols were either rough unpolished logs of the aito, or casuarina tree, wrapped in numerous folds of sacred cloth; rudely carved wooden images; or shapeless pieces covered with curiously netted cinet, of finely-braided cocoa nut husk, and ornamented with red feathers. They varied in size, some being six or eight feet long, others not more than as many inches. Those representing the spirits, they called tii; and those representing the national or family gods, toos. Into these they supposed the god entered at certain seasons, or in answer to the prayers of the priests. During this indwelling of the gods, they imagined even the images were very powerful: but when the

---

3   Morrison 1935,179.
4   Buck 1939,18.
5   Ellis 1829 2,200.
6   T Haweis 1799,174: 'A native coming into our apartments . . . owned the Otaheitean gods were enow, bad, for they ate men, hogs, bread-fruit, &c. which the Prētane God did not, and was a "good fellow."'
7   Ellis 1829 2,203.
8   T Haweis 1799,332/William Smith 1813,57.
9   Ellis 1853 1,164.
10   Ellis 1829 2,195.
11   Ellis 1853 1,381; William Gill (1856,31): 'They had painful anxieties and dreadful apprehensions . . . on approaching their gods.'
12   T Haweis 1799,164.
13   Ellis 1829 2,194; see Buck 1939 for more on Polynesian religion.
14   Williams 1837,456.
15   Ellis 1853 1,354.

spirit had departed, though they were among the most sacred things, their extraordinary powers were gone.[16]

Jefferson, also Tahiti: 'The image of their great god Oóro is nothing more than a piece of hard wood, called Eito, about six feet long, without any carving, wrapped up in sundry cloths, and decorated with red feathers &c. Into this log of wood the natives confidently affirm Oóro enters at certain times.'[17]

NATIONAL AND DISTRICT GODS

Major gods such as Tangaroa, Tane, Rongo, and others (Cook Islands spelling) were generally recognized on all the island groups as 'national' gods, but at the same time there were considerable differences amongst the islands, and at different times; the cult of 'Oro, for example, replaced the cult of Ta'aroa in Ra'iatea and spread to other islands of the Society group around 1750. Surprisingly, with the exception of images of 'Oro, no reliable information is available to allow connecting other central Polynesian god images with the particular gods represented. The large, spectacular, and more figural god images of Rarotonga, namely the staff gods (see figs. 192–195) and discussion of Anelay N°1 in Appendix 1) and the human figures, are customarily assumed, apparently on the basis of their size, to represent the 'national' gods. Rarotongan figures and staff gods have been abundantly illustrated and discussed over the years. Considered here are god images of the central Cook Islands, which have received less attention, but about which more is known. Starting with national and district gods, and keeping in mind that these terms are arbitrary, five specific, and conspicuous, examples brought back from Aitutaki can be identified on Papeiha's list with reasonable certainty, on the basis of multiple cross-references. Four of the gods are named.

The first is the remarkable 58cm-high human figure constructed of entirely of sennit and decorated abundantly with parrot, tropic bird, and frigate bird feathers, LMS 170, N°1 on Papeiha's list 'Sent to England'

(see fig. 280). It is figured in Edge-Partington, with the note 'Ronga? A rude human figure formed of cords of plaited sennit covered with feathers from Orutanga a district of Aitutaki.'[18] This note also matches the LMS slip, as well as LMS *Catalogue* nd entry N°34: 'RONGA, a rude human figure, covered with feathers, belonging to Orutanga, a district of Aitutaki', as well as an entry on the last page of the manuscript 'List of Curios proposed to be transferred to the British Museum': '1 Bundle in form of figure (Ronga: a rude human figure covered with feathers belonging to Orutanga a dist' of Aitutaki).' The entry for N°1 on Papeiha's list reads: 'Representation of Te Rongo belonging to Orutanga a district in Aitutaki[19]—Every district has an idol of the God to which it belongs.' According to WW Gill, 'Ro[ng]o' in the Cook Islands was a brother of Ta[ng] aroa, and was the same as 'O Rō' ['Oro] of Ra'iatea.[20] This view is debatable, but in any event, a lone description in Orsmond (T Henry) may be pertinent here: 'The image of 'Oro in this marae [Taputapuatea at Opoa, Ra'iatea] was woven with fine sennit into the shape of a man, two or three feet long, and covered with red and yellow plumage. It wore a girdle of red feathers.'[21]

The second identifiable god image brought back from Aitutaki is, surprisingly, the spectacular 74cm wooden openwork staff god, with a sennit attachment around the handle, LMS 168 (figs. 178–182), N°4 on Papeiha's list. This image is well known and has been often figured, generally attributed to the Society or Austral Islands. It is N°3 in the frontispiece of Ellis, 1829. It was also figured by Stolpe in 1891,[22] Read in 1892,[23] and subsequently by Buck,[24] Dodd,[25] Archey,[26] and Hooper.[27] Edge-Partington identifies it as 'The idol "Taaroa" the supreme deity of Polynesia Ellis Pol Res p. 220 and frontispiece no3 LMS Loan Coll.'[28] In 'Additional notes—1892' in

16 Ellis 1829 2,203.
17 *Journal*, 21 December 1797, in *Trans Miss Soc* 1804,221. For more on Tahitian 'Oro images, see Kooijman 1964, Babadzan 1981, Kaeppler 2007, and figs. xxx–xxx.

18 Edge-Partington 1890 1,22 N°1; Buck 1944,348 and fig. 218 (Atiu); also in Hooper 2006,230 fig. 203.
19 Arutanga, west Aitutaki; see map in Buck 1927.
20 WW Gill 1876,14; see Tregear 1891.
21 Henry 1928,121.
22 Stolpe 1891.
23 Read 1892, pl XIII fig. A.
24 Buck 1944,116 fig. A.
25 Dodd 1967,225.
26 Archey 1965 fig. 8 and pl. 8D.
27 Hooper 2006,202 fig. 165.
28 Edge-Partington 1890 1,22 N°4; colour figure in Hooper 2006.

the same volume, he adds: 'N°4. Taaroa in his symbolic form, left as his representative at the great Marae Natipaki.' This entry matches LMS *Catalogue* nd p. 7 N°23: 'Another form of TAAROA, left as his representative at the great marae, in the distr of Natipaki see Ellis fig 3', as well as LMS *Catalogue* 1826 p. 20 N°4: 'The district of NATIPAKI's IDOL of Taaroa, and left at the great Marae as its representative.' These descriptions in turn match Aitutaki idol N°4 on Papeiha's list 'Sent to England': 'The District of Natipaki's Idol of Tangaroa left at the great Marae as its representative.'[29]

A third is in the Oldman collection, pl 4, N°437: 'Deity; four figures one above the other; forked base; illustrated in Ellis 1829 frontispiece N°5 and described on p. 220 as "Terongo, one of the principal gods, and his three sons"' No locality. 88cm. In the British Museum LMS manuscript catalogue this matches 42[93]435[690] 'TE-RONGO and his three sons from Rarotonga' and in LMS *Catalogue* 1826 p. 20, 'TE BUA KINA: three sons of the great god Rongo. Tukarere is the name of the second; Tino Kura is the third; they are gods of the sea, to whom prayers are offered for the safety of canoes.' Papeiha's list, N°11 reads: 'Te Rongo & his three sons the name of the first is Te bua Kina—the second tu Ka rere—the third Tino Kura. They are gods of the Sea to them prayers are offered for the Safety of Canoes—at sea.'

The fourth is N°6 on Papeiha's list 'Sent to England', a large (1.28m) human figure in wood 'purchased with a fishhook', discussed and figured in *Missionary Enterprises*, and shown in figure 235; this is LMS 38. Although very large, it is identified on Papeiha's list as 'most likely a household or family God'.

A possible fifth is also in the Oldman collection, a 'slab god', pl 5, N°430; 66cm. Oldman's description states that it has two heads, and is 'believed to have been brought home by Rev. John Williams. Hervey Group.' The entry for LMS *Catalogue* nd N°29 reads: 'A ditto of RUATABU, with two heads and two cinnet appendages. Nukunoni was the distr to which it belonged, and it was placed at the marae, to superintend their affairs

and make them victorious in war.'[30] This entry is almost verbatim that of N°5 on Papeiha's list, 'sent to England': 'Nukunoni an idol of the great god Ruatabu—Nukunoni is the district to which it belongs . . . it is placed at the great Marae as their representative to superintend their affairs & make them victorious in their wars . . . . I can get no explanation of the two figures upon this or others of a Similar description.' The word *ditto* in the LMS *Catalogue* nd entry refers to the three previous entries: N°26: 'A carved flat club-formed idol, with an appendage of plaited cocoa-nut fibre' and N°s27,28: 'Two, resembling the last, with feather appendages.' Oldman 430 actually has one head with two faces, front and back. The one figured by Ellis 1829 (frontispiece vol 2 N°2; see fig. 171) cannot be located; it has two figures. There is no doubt that Papeiha's list N°5 is a 'slab god', but one cannot be sure exactly which one it is. These cross-references provide good evidence that the flat wood 'slab gods', noted 'Hervey Islands' on the LMS slips and usually ascribed to Aitutaki, do indeed come from Aitutaki.

GOD TAILS OF SENNIT

Oldman notes that the slab gods, with carved raised zigzags and serrated edges, 'resemble the "*Unus*," or burial-posts, described by Ellis, [1829 v2] p. 214, but the bases show no signs whatever of being inserted in the ground.'[31] This statement is true on both counts. They do resemble unu, the large flat vertical wood carvings on marae, discussed above. And it is not likely slab gods were inserted into the ground. None of the bases show abrasion, and importantly, there is evidence that long tufted sennit and/or feather appendages were attached to their bases, like tails. Intact tails still exist on several slab gods, in the Fuller collection (Field Museum 111709), Musée d'Histoire Naturelle, Lille (2105, 2100a, 2094), and British Museum LMS collection (LMS 44, 46). These tail appendages were intricate and carefully made; transverse sennit tufts were fashioned by insertion into two-ply or three-ply twisted sennit cord, or by adding into the sennit on alternating sides as it was being braided (see Buck's fig. 226, techniques a,

---

29 The next entry in the LMS Catalogue nd, N°24 'like the last', probably refers to the other very similar staff god LMS Oc 1982,Q.119 70cm, fig. 183.

30 Savage 1962,318 identifies Ruatapu as 'one of the famous ancestors of the Polynesian race'; see also Tregear 1891,482.

31 Oldman 1953,4.

b, c; reproduced in fig. 151). Techniques *a* and *b* were used on Aitutaki and Mitiaro god tails (see below); c on Austral flywhisks as well.

Tails were evidently integral to a number of Aitutaki gods; they are mentioned three times in Papeiha's list. Papeiha's list N°12, 'Family god called Vei with a tail which the priests take off & decorate themselves with when they wish to be inspired', may refer to slab god LMS 46, which is depicted on its LMS slip with a sizeable and apparently detachable tail of sennit and feathers, now separated (figs. 152, 155). Clearly, tails were important elements of certain Aitutaki god images.

Entry N°10 on Papeiha's list tells us that short segments of plaited sennit (perhaps temporarily attached to fan handles) could be instruments of divination:

[B]y the [platted] Cocoanutt husk the priest prognosticates the fate of Canoes & when gone whether they have arrived at the place to which they were going. . . . the Priest places the Cocoa nut husk in a certain position in the house of the god [—] if it remains a certain time in that position he assures the friends that the Canoe has arrived . . . if it be moved in the least—it is lost.

This entry is very close to the entry concerning a specific type of sennit in Orsmond's Tahitian dictionary:

Aha-moe[:]   priest performs a ceremony for person about to take a voyage, for the safety of their canoe against all disasters of the sea, & their safe arrival at their port. A piece of senet of a foot long was conveyed by the voyage[r]s to the Priest of the Marae. This he took and after repeating a certain form of prayer addressed to the army of gods of the sea, he placed it in a straight position under a flat stone and there left. All departed & under the assurances of safety from the Priest all set off, fearless of storms. After a long time, if an anxiety took possession of the friends who remained behind they applied to the priest who had performed the ceremony to know if the canoe had really reached her destined port. On examining the senet under the stone, if the senet remained unmoved, & flat, he pronounced safety on the canoe, if by any unknown cause the senet became displaced, he pronounced his doubt, if twisted, he saw the canoe is lost at sea, & you are the excuse for ye have not obeyed all

that I enjoined on to you in te oroa I te aha moe the ceremony of making sacred the solitary senet. All sat too to their weeping & howling.

Long tails of tufted sennit were also attached to the lower spatulate ends of the intricate openwork staff gods of Mitiaro. Three fragmentary LMS objects in Cambridge (CUM Z6045, Z6045A, Z6046) bear this out: they are clearly the bottom portions of Mitiaro staff gods, the thin and fragile carved wood top parts largely but not entirely missing, and with long bushy sennit tails still attached by means of sennit or strips of thin white tapa (fig. 161). The tails appear largely undamaged, and are several times longer than the wooden portions originally would have been if complete. The overall aspect of the fully intact Mitiaro staff god resembles that of a god in the British Museum attributed to 'Atiu(?)', with a 150cm feather and sennit tail (LMS 50) attached to a 39cm intricate wood carving (LMS 49), subsequently rendered into two pieces by rats—hence the two LMS numbers (see figs. 173–175). Mitiaro staff gods were also originally adorned with numerous feathers, which were attached with fine sennit to the 16 to 22 arched cleats arranged in rows running up the middle sections below the dome-shaped 'heads'. Remnants of feather attachments can still be seen on several of the existing examples. The feather cleats seem to be abstracted human figures, as suggested by the series shown on figures 166–169.

FAMILY GODS: FANS AND FLY-FLAPS

The frontispiece of certain editions of Williams' *Narrative* depicts a Rarotongan Chief named Te Po holding a fan (fig. 101).[32] A number of fans with triangular blades of coconut palm leaflets plaited with astonishing precision, fixed to wood tangs with carefully carved and finished handles, are known from Rarotonga[33] (figs. 102–104).

[32] 'Tepo, of Rarotonga . . . had himself tatooed . . . in consequence of the death of his ninth child'; Tepo was a minor chief, and an early convert; Williams 1837,540.

[33] Fans from the neighbouring island of Mangaia were unusual in design and construction, as well as size; see figs. 100 & 105. WW Gill writes: '[M]en daily carried about with them, in symbol of peace, an outrageously large fan, now obsolete. This fan was sufficiently large to protect the upper part of the body from sun or rain. It was found necessary to forbid its use in church, as the person of the owner was nearly hidden behind it' (WW Gill 1876,301).

Fans are the most abundant items on Papeiha's list of 'Idols'; he refers to them as 'sacred fans'.[34] Fans were of major significance to Cook Islanders. The association of fans with people of high rank was noticed within an hour after the very first landing of Europeans in the Cook Islands—on Atiu—Cook's third voyage. Anderson's journal entry for 3 April 1777 reads:

> [Shortly after arriving,] we were then led up an Avenue of Cocoa Palms, and soon came to a number of men arrang'd in two rows arm'd with clubs which they held on their shoulders much in the manner we rest a musket. After walking a little way amongst these we found a person who seem'd a chief sitting on the ground cross legg'd, cooling himself with a sort of triangular fan made from a leaf of the cocoa palm with a polished handle of black wood fix'd to one point. In his ears were large bunches of beautifull red feathers which pointed forward but he had no other mark or ornament to distinguish him from the rest of the people, though they all obey'd him with the greatest alacrity.[35]

Cook's party were presented with fans, as towards evening, 'The croud now robbed them without any Ceremony especially when they were not in the Company of a Chief. A fan which had been given to one of the Gent[nl] [Burney] by Oterrow [Atarau; the name of the 'king'] they attempted to snatch from him, but failing in that one of them wrenched it out of his Hands by force.'[36]

A fan from Atiu managed to find its way on board the *Discovery* that day. Fortunately, it was carefully depicted in a detailed pencil drawing by William Ellis, artist and surgeon's mate on Cook's third voyage—no relation to William Ellis of the LMS. The fan has evidently not survived, but courtesy of the Alexander Turnbull

Library in Wellington, the drawing of it is reproduced in figure 142. 'Whatdue?' (Atiu) is inscribed in black ink; on the reverse is a drawing of an outrigger canoe. The triangular blade appears to be made of precisely plaited pandanus or coconut palm leaf; it is similar to ones collected on Rarotonga by the missionaries, but is narrower. The handle appears to be of carved wood and terminates in an abstract Janus figure, much like LMS 131, and also resembling the more realistic Janus figures of LMS 51 (Anelay N°4), and (LMS) TAH.139 (Anelay N°5). The Ellis drawing is an important reference; it is the very earliest known depiction of a Cook Islands artefact, and portrays a type of fan and Janus figure handle manifestly characteristic of the central Cook Islands—perhaps Atiu itself.

The importance of fans in the Cook Islands stands in sharp contrast to the apparent unimportance or possibly even nonexistence of fans in the Societies and the Australs. Cook does not mention or depict fans from the Tahitian group or Rurutu, nor are there any Tahitian or Rurutuan fans known in Cook voyage collections.[37] We have not run across a single mention of fans in the Societies or Australs in LMS documents; and no unequivocally documented fans in early collections from either of these island groups are known. The word for *fan* in the Cook Islands is *ta'iri*—cognate with *tahiri* in Tahiti. It is interesting that this word appears only once in Orsmond (T Henry; Tahiti), but luckily, with a description:[38] 'a tahiri (fan), which was a waving cluster of tail feathers of the frigate bird and the tropic bird, attached to a long pole like a great duster, and resembling the royal kahili of Hawai'i.'[39] This description fits the feather-tipped Tahitian funerary staff mentioned on page 44 and drawn by Spöring. Scaled down, these staves resemble objects such as the one depicted in Parkinson's journal of Cook's first voyage, N°11 on plate 13, reproduced here in figure 116; Parkinson calls it a 'fly flap'.

Sennit or feather fly flaps with carefully carved and finished handles of wood—sometimes sperm whale tooth ivory, whale jawbone, or plain polished bird wing bones—are well-known objects in the Societies and

---

34 *More Joy for Christians*; for instance 'N°19 Bundle of fans—Sacred Fans.'

35 Anderson in Beaglehole 1967 3(part 2),834; also 'a second chief sitting fanning himself, and ornamented as the first' (ibid.,835). De Quirós in 1595, 175 years before Cook, comments on fans in the Marquesas (in Dalrymple 1767,19).

36 Samwell's account in Beaglehole 1967 3(part 2), 1007; this was not a case of common thievery: 'Omai said we were wrong in taking up any thing, for it was not the custom here to admit freedoms of that kind till they had in some measure naturaliz'd strangers to the country by entertaining them with festivity for two or three days' (ibid.,838).

37 Kaeppler 1978.

38 Henry 1928,13.

39 Henry 1928,193.

Australs.[40] Ones with very finely-carved wood handles terminating in Janus figures have been documented by Roger Rose as coming from Rurutu.[41] They were encountered by the *Bounty* mutineers on Tubua'i as well:

> The old men have Walking Staves & handles of Fly flaps made of [casuarina], highly finishd, on the Top . . . they generally have Carved a double figure of a man representing a figure with one Body & two Heads & some of two, standing back to back, their Fly flaps are made of the Fibers of the Cocoa Nut twisted & platted very Curiously.[42]

Fly flaps served, in part, a utilitarian purpose: Tahitians were 'much incommoded with a species of flies with which the island swarms; insomuch that at dinner time it was one person's employ to beat them off with a feather fly-flap, the handle of which is made of a hard brown wood, rudely carved, and somewhat resembles a human figure.'[43] The botanist Philibert Commerson, who was with Bougainville on Tahiti, speaks of the dead laid out on a 'mortuary display bed. . . . I believe these good people consider death simply as a long sleep . . . even stationing men around them [the dead] with fly-whisks to keep insects away.'[44] Haweis on

the subject of flywhisks: 'They all carry fly-flaps, which are usually made of feathers, and fixed to a handle of wood ten or twelve inches long, sometimes carved, sometimes plain. The wing-bones of the largest fowls, when cleaned, are used for handles . . . When you enter a house, or place where provisions are cooking, this is the first thing they offer you.'[45]

Fly flaps were also emblems signifying high rank, and sacredness; they are thoroughly discussed by Rose.[46] A number of them are shown on figures 112–127. It seems that the importance of flywhisks in the Societies and Australs stands in sharp contrast to the unimportance or possibly even nonexistence of flywhisks in the Cooks.

It should be emphasized that missionaries used the terms *fan* and *fly-flap* interchangeably. In Davies' dictionary, the noun *tahiri* is defined as 'a fan'; the verb *tahiri*, 'to fan, to shake a fly-flap.' Object N°9 in the woodcut 'The Family Idols of Pomare', *Missionary Sketches* 3, October 1818, depicts an intricately carved flywhisk handle of whale jaw bone; the figure legend refers to it as 'TAHIVI ANUNAEHAU, the handle of the sacred fan with which the priest drove off the flies, while about his prayers and sacrifices' (see figs. 119, 120). Ellis, stationed in Mo'orea and Huahine, refers to Austral flywhisks as fans.[47] Tyerman and Bennet (on the subject of Arioi): '[I]n the one hand they waved at arm's length a fan, made of the white hairs of a dog's tail, to drive away the mosquitoes; and in the other held a nasal flute. . . . '[48]

FAMILY GODS: FEATHER GODS

There is another category of sacred objects, clearly from the central Cooks, that has come up several times already, which might best be described as 'none of the above'. Most of these objects are small, 20 to 40cm long, and most have backbones, either of wood (often recycled fan handles), or of folded sennit fibre or sennit cordage, to which are attached sacred elements—namely feathers and small fibre-tied clusters of feathers. They are referred to here as feather gods. Sometimes other elements are incorporated as well, such as cloth-like coconut palm leaf base fibre, human

---

40 Fly flaps were also made on Tonga and Samoa; see Rose 1979, Hooper 2001. Polynesian wood carving was much admired by Cook: 'When one considers the tools these people have to work with one cannot help but admire their workmanship, these are Adzes and small hatchets made of a hard stone, Chisels or gouges made of human bones, generally the bone of the fore arm . . . ; to plane or polish their work they rub upon it with a smooth stone, Coral beat small and mixt with water, this is sometimes done by scraping it with shells and which alone they perform most of their small woodwork' (Cook in Beaglehole 1968 1,131). Banks: 'they polish everything . . . with Coral sand rubbd on in the outher husk of a Cocoa nut & rays skin.'

41 Rose 1979. Rose points out that Janus figures are a general tradition in figural sculpture of the Austral, Society, and Cook Islands.

42 Morrison 1935,69.

43 Parkinson 1773,18. 'Flies, indeed, may be said to be an abomination with these savages' (Montgomery 1832 2,84; Hawai'i). Flies were sometimes numerous; Rangiroa (Tuamotus) was named 'Fly Island' by LeMaire (Dalrymple 1767,34). 'Our residence on shore would by no means have been disagreeable if we had not been incessantly tormented with flies, which, among other mischief, made it almost impossible for Mr Parkinson, Mr Bank's natural history painter, to work; for they not only covered his subjects so that no part of its surface could be seen, but even ate the colour off the paper as fast as he could lay it on' (Hawkesworth 1773; Tahiti).

44 Dunmore 2002,299.

45 T Haweis 1799,344/William Smith 1813,66.

46 Rose 1979.

47 Ellis 1829, fig. op 181; see fig. 115.

48 Montgomery 1832 2,187.

hair, or in one instance, red trade cloth. These objects are composites, generally bound together into bundles, by means of sennit, white tapa, or *oronga*.[49] Two entries on Papeiha's list, N[os] 10 and 14, suggest that some may have had additional attachments, of sennit or coconut leaf, which, when detached, could serve functions on their own. Three fanless fanhandles appear in the Anelay watercolour decorated with tapa and feathers—now missing from all three (figs. 259–261). Feather gods were most probably wrapped in layers of white tapa when not in use, as were the major gods, such as Tahitian 'Oro images and Rarotongan staff gods.

It is an enigmatic and rarely mentioned group, perhaps because the objects are not large, and appeared strange, or trivial, to Europeans. Also, they seldom incorporate human images. In this respect they resemble 'Oro images. James Edge-Partington largely ignored them in his *Album*. Curiously, so did Peter Buck.[50]

There is no question that Edge-Partington actually saw all the feather gods, as he wrote and illustrated the acquisition slips for the British Museum LMS collection; although the listing of LMS objects on the slips is not complete, it includes most—about 30—of the feather gods.[51] But included amongst the numerous LMS objects illustrated in the first part of his *Album* are only two of them.

Buck spent six weeks at the British Museum in 1933, took photographs, and made careful notes and numerous sketches for an index card catalogue of objects from all the major island groups of Polynesia. From 1936 to 1939, Emory assisted with the cards; they are now in the Bishop Museum archives. A number of them are shown in the Artefacts section of this book. Many of Buck's sketches were redrawn for his comprehensive Bishop Museum publication, *Arts and Crafts of the Cook Islands*, 1944. But strangely, very few feather gods appear either in his cards or in his otherwise thorough monograph; perhaps he took literally the 'Tahitian Group' attribution for most of them on the slips. Or perhaps he never saw all of them; the fact that they are all still in remarkably good condition would testify that they have been packed up carefully for years. The LMS tried to divest them to the British Museum in their initial offer of 1889–1890, but the museum rejected them.[52] Yet, in numbers, they constitute the largest single group of related objects in the LMS Polynesian collection.[53]

Testimony to the last two points is a four-page handwritten manuscript in the Anthropology Library of the British Museum. 'London Missionary Society; 14, Blomfield Street; November 1890' is written across the top, followed by 'List of Curios proposed to be transferred to the British Museum'. Only a photostat has been located; a relevant portion of it is reproduced in figure 59.[54] It is an itemized list of ethnographic objects, almost all from Polynesia. There are 71 line entries of 'curios', itemizing such things as one large drum, one club wrapped in cinet, two Mangaian necklaces, one carved staff shaped idol Rarotonga, one gourd basket Sandwich Islands, one breadfruit splitter axe shaped, and more. A striking thing about this list is the number of specimens indicated for each line item: for 57 items: one specimen only. Twelve items: two specimens. One item: five. For one other single line item: 35 specimens. The pertinent entries for these 35 specimens are as follows:

<hr>

49 *Oronga*—Cook Islands term—is an extraordinarily fine, strong, supple fibre derived from the bark of the nettle tree, *Urtica argentea* (Savage 1962,210), usually twisted against the thigh into two-ply string; it was used to make fishlines and fine fishnets, and the mesh backings for feather girdles and capes. Called *roa* in Tahiti, accounts of its manufacture by soaking and scraping are in Morrison 1935, and WW Gill 1880,9. '[Fishlines of] Roaa are Equal if not superior to any in the World' (Morrison 1935,164). The cognate *olonā* fibre in Hawai'i is derived from the bark of another urticaean species, *Touchardia latifolia*. Oronga is one of the strongest plant fibres known; for an excellent treatment of Polynesian cordage, see Summers 1990.

50 Sivasundaram (2005,187) found mention of 'other matters of worship which are only bunches of feathers' in an article on the LMS museum in the *Illustrated London News*, 25 June 1859, indicating that the feather gods were on display at the time.

51 For an excellent biography of Edge-Partington, see Neich 2009.

52 In 1890, before the final British Museum purchase of the LMS collection, Rev Ralph Wardlaw Thompson, an LMS director and foreign secretary for over 25 years, had offered the British Museum only a selection of LMS museum objects, for 'permanent loan', but Franks and Read were disappointed that it did not include 'the most important idols'; they held out for the entire LMS museum, and finally got it.

53 Additional references to them are in the two LMS museum catalogues, for instance *Catalogue* nd p. 8 N°63–66: 'Numerous bunches of feathers, probably portions of broken idols or propitiatory offerings'; see p. 198.

54 This manuscript is likely the list of LMS museum objects originally proposed by Wardlaw Thompson to be transferred to the British Museum as a permanent loan; it appears to be in Thompson's handwriting; his name and the date 'Nov 1890' are written, in a different hand, across the top left corner of the first page.

—35 Household gods—handles &c

    Nº52 Han [presumably abbreviation of Handle].
From Maute. Several clusters of feathers attached
to pieces of wood & fibre.

    Nº61 Propitiatory offering to Rongo and Tagnaroa
to appease them when moved to new habitations.
Hervey Islands. [55]

    Nº63, Nº66 Bunches of feathers probably por-
tions of broken idols or propitiatory offerings.

—5 bundles ornamented with feathers. Included in 35.

—1 handle; 1 dº ?god.

Thus, conspicuously, half the items on this LMS
manuscript list are bundles of feathers, or fan handles
with feathers attached; all are referred to as 'Household
gods, handles &c.' Not much is known about household
or family gods. They are mentioned in Haweis 1799:
'Their deities are numerous. . . . [E]very district has its
own deity; and each family of note has one, whom they
consider as their peculiar patron.'[56] Ellis tells us, 'Every
family of any antiquity or rank had its tutelary idol.'[57]
Williams: 'in [their] heathen state . . . every man had
his god and his little heap of stones for his marae, we
never heard but of one man who was without a god.'[58]
Andía: 'Every person has several different gods.'[59] And
Morrison: 'Besides these [Eatooa], they have a number
of inferior Deitys evry Man & Woman having guardian
Angels who they supposed to be the souls of Departed
relatives who have been Deifyd for their good works

and whose business is to watch and protect them, While
on earth. . . . '[60]

Household gods, or family gods, including 'feather
amulets', were evidently kept at family marae, which
were described by Orsmond (T Henry):

> The Family or Ancestral temple, called *marae tupuna*,
> the god of which was always a family secret. . . . The
> form of the simplest family marae was a paving set upon
> the ground and walled in with stone slabs three or four
> feet high, each slab to the left and the right represent-
> ing a member of the household, against which he or
> she knelt to pray. . . . If a marae was built in pyrami-
> dal form, the leaning slabs were placed . . . upon its
> summit. The sacred family fetishes, in the shape of
> images, ancestral skulls, jawbones, and feather amulets,
> were secreted in flagstone cavities in the front part of
> the marae. The tutelar god or goddess was not made
> known by the family to any outsider for fear of being
> betrayed by enemies or supplanted by them in the good
> graces of the deity. Moreover, each individual had a
> sacred patron spirit . . . such as a tree, snail, lizard, or
> stone, to which invocations were made at any time.[61]

In 1892, a well-illustrated 24 page article appeared in
*Journal of the Anthropological Institute of Great Britain and
Ireland* entitled 'On the Origin and Sacred Character of
Certain Ornaments of the S.E. Pacific'. The author was
Charles Hercules Read, at the time in charge of the eth-
nographic collections at the British Museum.[62] In it, Read
pays attention to a subset of the very group of 'minor'

---

[55] This matches the British Museum Anthropology Library LMS
ms catalogue entry, in Edge-Partington's hand, 4th from last
page: numbered '63 113 447–8 702–3. Propitiatory offerings
presented to Rongo & Tangaroa when removed to a new habitation'; unfortunately it is still not known which object this refers
to, despite there being six reference numbers.

[56] T Haweis 1799,271.

[57] Ellis 1829 2,200. George Tobin: 'they worship through the medium
of images, scarcely a house being without them, and when taking
a journey, being sufficiently portable, they are never left behind'
(Schreiber 2007,130). De Bovis discusses the gathering of people
at the marae for ceremonies or prayers: 'Everyone had his idol
under his arm or in his pocket. . . . While the high priest unveiled
the idol, the people around the outside of the marae pulled theirs
out of their cases and respectfully placed them on the ground
or on a stone during the duration of the prayers.' (De Bovis is
relatively late, and sometimes of questionable accuracy; RD
Craig translation 1976,50); 'Temples to the gods of the water
were erected on every point of land, and family maraes in almost
every grove' (Ellis 1829 2,189).

[58] Williams, Rarotonga, 27 September 1832 letter to directors.

[59] Corney 1915 2,259.

[60] Morrison 1935,176.

[61] Henry 1928,141. Banks mentions rows of mens' jawbones, war
trophies in this case, attached to a model canoe and to the
lower part of a god house at Marae Taputapuatea on Ra'iatea
(Beaglehole 1963 1,318).

[62] *J Anthro Inst* 1892 21,139–159. In 1865, Augustus Franks, keeper of
the British Museum department which included the ethnographic
collections, known until 1921 as 'British and Medieval Antiquities', hired a 17-year-old named Charles Hercules Read to be in
charge of the newly acquired Christy ethnographic collection.
At this time, ethnographic objects in the British Museum were
second in popularity only to Egyptian mummies. Read rapidly
acquired a knowledge of ethnographic material that was both
remarkably unprejudiced and encyclopedic; he saw to more than
doubling the size of the ethnographic collection, and eventually
(1896) succeeded Franks. Together they effected the transfer of
the LMS collection to the British Museum—in 1890. (Braunholtz
1953; Miller 1974,318; see also chapters by Caygill and by King
in Caygill & Cherry 1997); J Hasell unpublished ts referred to in
Chapter 6, fn 10.

gods under discussion here. His plate XII depicts ten 'handles of fans, chiefly wanting the fan, the absence of which I will explain later.' The plate is reproduced in figure 91. 'This series is drawn from actual examples from the Missionary Museum, and illustrates in a very complete manner the degradation of an ornamental [pair] of human figures into a mere conventional symbol.' His first point is a case for an evolutionary continuum progressing from realistic to abstract; it is entirely plausible. His second point: 'It will be observed that nearly all of the fan handles have a binding of sinnit or tapa round the shaft, and that into this binding, feathers, human hair, or rough cocoanut fibre are interwoven.' He then evokes Ellis on the subject of the connection of feathers with things sacred, and concludes: 'It is evident therefore that all these objects have a sacred character, due to the addition of the feathers and other trappings, and apart from their form and special use as fans.' Figure 2 of Read's plate 12 is the Janus figure feather-adorned fan handle, perhaps from Atiu, depicted in the Anelay watercolour—N°4. Thus Read identifies these adorned fanless fanhandles as sacred objects—in 1892.

Fanless fan handle and feather bundle family gods are well-represented in the British Museum LMS collection; there are over 35 of them. Sometimes ascribed to 'Tahitian Group', sometimes to 'Hervey Group' on the British Museum LMS slips, most documentation points towards the latter. It seems reasonable to conclude that the '35 household gods' in the LMS manuscript 'List of Curios' and the numerous 'handles and fans' on Papeiha's list both refer to the same group of objects. Read's fanhandle continuum presents convincing evidence that the triangular fans with simple polished lanceolate handles,[63] usually attributed to Tahiti, belong here as well. All of these family gods were most likely brought back together from the Williams-Bourne-Papeiha round trip to Aitutaki-Atiu-Mitiaro-Mauke on the *Endeavour* in July 1823. No record of any subsequent trip to these islands mentioning idol collecting has been found. At least one of the idols from this trip, N°52 on the curio list, annotated 'Maute', does not come from Aitutaki. The 1777 Ellis fan drawing provides evidence that fan handles with arched-back Janus figures were

at least found on, and were likely made on, Atiu.[64] The complex openwork scaffolds for feathers such as Anelay N°7 are attributed on the LMS slips and in one of the LMS catalogues to Mitiaro.[65] Because the fanhandle/ feather bundle family gods are so rarely illustrated or even mentioned, most of them—about 35—are reproduced in the plates, the majority for the first time; see figures 56–90.

INTER-ISLAND CONNECTIONS

There are some noticeable similarities among god images and among carved wood (and stone) objects in general throughout central Polynesia. The widespread appearance of Janus figures and of notched or serrated edges are two good examples. This is not surprising because contact and concomitant cultural exchange amongst the islands, despite their being so widely dispersed, was longstanding and sometimes remarkably frequent.

Polynesians of every island group were generally well aware of neighbouring and even formidably distant islands well before Wallis' arrival. Cook and Banks on the first voyage, in 1770, took on an intelligent Raiatean chief, priest, and skilled navigator named Tupaia, who served as translator. Tupaia 'and several others' gave an account of 74 islands, and sketched a chart indicating their direction and distance from Tahiti. About half of the islands were unknown to Europeans at the time; the islands are positioned on the map according to several different directional criteria. The map includes several of the Australs (Ra'ivavae, Tubua'i, Rurutu, Rimatara), and the Cooks (Rarotonga [Orarathoa], Mangaia [Oahooahoo], Manuae), and even Samoa and Tonga—1500 miles west. The original map is apparently lost, but a copy of it, in Cook's hand, is in the British Library (see fig. 263). Tupaia died in Batavia, on the return trip. Harold Carter has identified Tupaia as Joppien and Smith's 'artist of the chief mourner'.[66]

There was longstanding exchange amongst the islands of central Polynesia as well. Bligh mentions

---

[63] Read 1892 pl XII N°11; see fig. 91.

[64] Compare the figures on LMS 49—also labelled 'Atiu'.

[65] LMS Catalogue nd N°49 entry reads 'Idols from Metiaro: one resembles the last'—implying they are all similar.

[66] Carter in Lincoln 1998,133. See also Beaglehole 1968 1,291; Turnbull in Lincoln 1998,126; Salmond 2003,110; K Smith 2005; D Lewis 1972 and references therein.

clubs from Tubua'i seen on Tahiti, 1792.[67] Kaeppler points out the depiction of Austral drums on Tahiti 15 years earlier.[68] By the time English missionaries arrived, connections between Tahiti and the Australs were even closer: an 1821 article in *Evangelical Magazine* tells us that 'Pomare had visited this island [Ra'ivavae] about two years before, and having procured peace between two contending parties, then at war, was requested to take upon himself the sovereignty of the island': Pomare was the sovereign of Ra'ivavae.[69]

Voyages between islands occurred both intentionally and unintentionally. The navigational skills of the Polynesians are legendary, but there were also accidental voyages that established inter-island contact inadvertently.

One of these unintended voyages established links between Tahiti and the Cook Islands in the mid-eighteenth century, and is documented in entries from 29 March to 6 April 1777 in the journals of Cook, Anderson, Samwell and Ellis, Cook's third voyage. They record encountering the Cook Islands for the first time, 44 years before the arrival of the LMS, and report the following history. Five islands of the Hervey Group were approached by Cook's ships over the course of eight days. As the islands were encircled with unbroken rings of shallow reef and violent surf, beyond which the depth dropped off so suddenly 'there was no such thing as anchoring', the ships could only stand off and on. Cook was anxious 'to procure some grass for our livestock which seem'd to droop from continually being fed on dry food.'[70] At Mangaia (Mangeea) and Manuae (Hervey's Island), the ships were approached by canoes and engaged in limited trading for food. Cook found the people there disorderly and clamorous, and moved on. At Atiu (Whatdu, Watee'oo, Wautieu), after three days, still unable to anchor, first Gore and Ma'i (Omai), then Anderson and Burney, were taken over the reef in canoes, and spent ten hours ashore 'surrounded by a great multitude . . . who flocked with a most eager curiosity.' Ma'i was startled to find 'the manners of these islanders, their method of treating strangers, and other circumstances are much like those of Otaheite &

its neighbouring isles. Their religious ceremonys and opinions are also nearly the same.'[71]

The reason that Atiu had so much in common with Tahiti became immediately apparent. Cook's company were astonished to learn of a mishap that connected the two islands and were quick to figure out its significance.[72] Anderson narrates that shortly after landing,

> Omaee [Ma'i] was deeply engag'd in conversation with some of his country men, who had been driven to this island by a strong wind, . . . near two hundred leagues distant, a circumstance which may easily explain the method by which many of these places are peopled. They suffer'd much in that time, several of them dying and of the whole number four only arriv'd at this place one of whom is since dead. The natives of Watee'oo [Atiu] have treated them kindly. . . . It cannot be exactly ascertain'd how long it is since the accident happened but it must have been at least twelve years, as these people knew nothing of their country being discovered by Cap[tn] Wallis.'[73]

Cook adds 'There were twenty in the whole men and women in the Canoes.'[74] Samwell adds 'Omai . . . knew their relations.'[75] The four survivors did not wish to return with Cook to Ra'iatea; drift Tahitians had become Cook Islanders.[76]

As already mentioned, connections amongst all of the Cook Islands were close and frequent, as the islands are not so distant from one another. The missionaries and the teachers found natives of Rarotonga on Aitutaki. Aitutakians were in contact with Atiuans. Manueans visited Mangaia. The Chief of Atiu was sovereign of both Mitiaro and Mauke. And so on.

<hr>

67 Lt George Tobin's Log, in Ida Lee 1920,135.

68 Kaeppler 1978,159.

69 *Evangelical Magazine* December 1821,529.

70 Anderson in Beaglehole 1967 3(part 2),883.

71 Ibid.,843. Ma'i (Omai) was a young man whom Captain Furneaux took aboard at Huahine on Cook's second voyage to act as translator; he was taken back to England, then returned to Polynesia.

72 Decades later, Papeiha and Vahapata met a man on Aitutaki who had drifted from Maupiti; WW Gill mentions oral traditions of driftaways from Iti (southern Tahiti) and Tonga reaching Mangaia (WW Gill 1880,27, 33, 103).

73 Nor had they ever seen a European ship; Samwell in Beaglehole 1967 3(part 2),1004.

74 Cook in Beaglehole 1967 3(part 2),86.

75 Samwell in Beaglehole 1967 3(part 2),1004.

76 Aitutakians knew of Cook as well; Bligh, in Whytootackee on the Providence in 1792: 'They named Britainee and Otaheite very distinctly and spoke of a person they called Oheedidee [Odiddy]' (Lee 1920,132; Oliver 1988,266).

News spread by way of these inter-island encounters. Williams, for example, was surprised to find upon his first arriving at Rarotonga that the islanders already knew a great deal about 'Kookees', the word deriving from Captain Cook's name, and meaning Europeans, people 'entirely white'. This knowledge was evidently conveyed by a Tahitian 'heathen woman' and 'from some natives who were drifted from Tahiti down to Rarotonga in a canoe.' According to William Gill, the connection occurred around 1780, before the arrival of the *Bounty* mutineers.[77] Williams also found that Rarotongans had already heard of missionaries, and of idol burning; the important regional chief Makea had children named Tehovah and Teeteetry (Jesus Christ); one of Makea's uncles had built an altar dedicated to Jehovah and Jesus Christ.[78]

Naturally, through the various contacts, culture spread as well, such as the cult of 'Oro. It is easy to see a resemblance between several of the Cook Island fanhandle/feather bundle gods and Tahitian, also Austral, 'Oro images. Compare for instance a Cook first-voyage 'Oro from Tahiti and what may well be an 'Oro from Rurutu (Oldman N°425) with LMS 78 from the Cooks, illustrated in figures 218–220. This resemblance is probably not coincidental. It is well documented that the cult of 'Oro had spread from Ra'iatea throughout the rest of the Society Islands before the mid-eighteenth century.[79] It had also spread to the Austral Islands. The *Bounty* mutineers found evidence of a drift voyage following a skirmish on Tahiti; 'Tumotoa', a chief on Tubua'i in 1789, was 'Great great grandson to a Chief of the Island of Ryeatea'.[80] Pomare II visited Ra'ivavai in October 1819 and mentioned in his journal 'many goings on of the arioi'.[81] An 1821 letter from Williams and Threlkeld to Burder mentions the Raiatean teachers Mahamene and Puna landing on Rurutu at a 'spot . . . sacred to Oro', and also mentions the disappearance of the 'Oro-worshipping sect, *Arioi*.[82] 'Oro was evidently present in the Cooks as well, although evidence here is scant: both Davies and Bourne mention 'Oro in Mangaia;[83] there is a cognate—*kariei* or *karioi*—for Arioi in Savage's Rarotongan dictionary; and people on Rarotonga inquired at the moment of Williams' and Bourne's very first landing about the status of 'Oro on Ra'iatea following conversion.[84] Rarotongan folklore tells of longstanding connections with Ra'iatea;[85] the great drum called Taimoana of Ra'iatea was said to be from Rarotonga.[86]

In one unusual and well-documented case, an actual transport of idols from the Australs to the Societies occurred in the eighteenth century; the vectors were the *Bounty* mutineers. The mutiny took place before sunrise 28 April 1789, two days out of Tonga. After disposing of Commanding Lieutenant Bligh and 18 of his followers into a 23-foot launch, Fletcher Christian and the 25 remaining *Bounty* crewmembers sailed to Tubua'i, in the Australs. They arrived 25 May, and decided to settle there. In addition to feuding amongst the mutineers, there was intense inter-district feuding on Tubua'i as well, in which Christian's men got involved. The mutineers had originally settled in the west district, under Tamatoa. Soon they removed to the northeast district, under Taroatohoa. Tamatoa and Taroatohoa were rivals. Tamatoa joined forces with the chief of the southeast district, Tinarou. In August, there was a dispute over the gathering of coconuts. A Tubuaian was killed. Some of Christian's men were decoyed by women into Tinarou's district and stripped. Christian sent several messengers asking for the return of the clothes. Tinarou refused. Christian burned Tinarou's house down,

> but before it was set on fire we took out some Clubs and Spears, & two Curious Carved Images of their Household Gods, which were decorated with Pearl Shells, Human Hair teeth & Nails cut in a very Curious Manner, and round them was placed a kind of Grove of red feathers from the tail of Tropic birds. As Mr. Christian supposed these Images to be of Value to

---

77 William Gill 1856,21.
78 Williams 1837 106 and 199.
79 Henry 1928,128; Orsmond (Henry 1928) states that attempts began at the time of Tamatoa I of Ra'iatea, around 1650–1700.
80 Morrison 1935,72.
81 RG White translation of Tahitian transcript of Pomare's journal in JM Orsmond's Letter Book II, ML MS A2607; Gunson 1966.
82 Williams and Threlkeld to Burder 18 October 1821, SOAS; see Appendix 3.

83 Davies 1961,322 ; Bourne journal of 30 September to 11 November 1825 visit to the Cook and Austral Islands, *Trans Miss Soc* 1827,257; conversions in Mangaia had only just begun in 1825.
84 Williams ms *Journal of a Voyage*,43; PMB35.
85 Henry 1928,121 and 127.
86 Williams ms *Journal of a Voyage*,43; PMB35.

the Owner, he ordered them secured; hoping that the return of them might help to make the Peace & the House now being in Flames He returned to the Ship.[87]

Peace did not come, and matters worsened. In a major battle on 14 September, 66 Tubuaians were killed. The mutineers left for Tahiti three days later. Christian and his eight followers, after dividing up the guns, ammunition, and provisions, departed for Pitcairn Island on the *Bounty* the night of their arrival. Morrison adds 'the Toobouai images were put into my hand as a Present for the Young King'.[88]

Two weeks later, the confiscated, imported images were presented to Pomare II—with ceremony, and along with 'red Feathers, Friendly Island [Tonga] & Toobouai Cloth, Matting and War Weapons. . . . [It was] thought a Valuable present, and produced a general exclamation of wonder when they were held up to Publick View.'[89]

Roger Rose speaks of the 'cultural amalgamation' that had become well-established in central Polynesia (Societies-Australs-Cooks) by the late eighteenth century.[90] Because of the increasingly close connections amongst the islands with time, it is not surprising the distinct island types and styles of objects became blurred. There is good reason, for instance, that Cook Island god images sometimes resemble Austral and Tahitian 'Oro images.

POLYNESIAN–EUROPEAN EXCHANGE

Polynesians also showed a rapid and keen interest in incorporating European elements into their own culture, including their sacred ensigns and their idols. There are several instances of this occurring very early in the 30-year interval between the very first contact with Europeans and the arrival of the missionaries. Wallis tells the first story—that of losing an English flag to Tahitians at Matavai Bay the night after second lieutenant Tobias Furneaux raised it on 26 June 1767. The Tahitians promptly cut it into pieces, but 'they . . . paid

the highest honor that they could have bestowed upon it by attaching it to the royal girdle of red and yellow feathers [maro ura] of the high chief, Amo, of Papara.'[91] Cook saw this maro in 1777.[92] Bligh saw it 15 years later, on the second breadfruit voyage; he was astonished to see that it incorporated not only the portion of Wallis' pennant, but also a lock of hair belonging to Richard Skinner, one of the *Bounty* mutineers, who was the ship's barber. Both the pennant and the hair were red. Bligh did not depict Skinner's hair in his watercolour of the maro (see fig. 224). It should be mentioned that hair of important people was highly valued. So were bones and skulls. Tobin, visiting 'marae point' at Pare was shown the skull, 'kept with great care', of mutineer John Thompson, killed by a Tahitian after murdering fellow mutineer Charles Churchill.[93] Bligh's watercolour of a 'travelling marae', a double-hulled canoe built for the purpose of transporting 'Oro images, shows an English flag fastened across the two sterns, and red trade cloth covering the 'Oro. The watercolour vividly illustrates European exotica taking a central place in a sacred setting (see figs. 45–47).

Another early visitor who witnessed Tahitian esteem for objects from Europe was Máximo Rodríguez. Two examples: speaking of Vehiatua, a nearby regional chief, and Rodríguez' contemporary and friend: '[He] had a great display . . . of the objects from ships that had visited . . . , looking like a stock-in-trade of shop wares . . . , [now] offerings . . . to his God named Eatua.' Another entry: 'Vehiatua was very ill, and said he had come for the chest that was in our house to offer up to [his] God Eatua, and . . . would bring it back afterwards.'[94] Tahitians placed a high value on chests; they protected their valuables against thieves, which were numerous. Tahitians requested both Cook (1777) and Vancouver (1791–92) to make plank chests for them.

Designs were appropriated as well as objects. Sydney Parkinson describes the pattern painted on a Tahitian tapa garment presented to Cook: 'bright yellow, bordered with red, in the middle many crosses, which we

87 Morrison 1935,58.
88 Pomare II, according to Davies, would have been about seven years old in 1789.
89 Morrison 1935,77; Bligh notes that Christian also brought a drum from Tubua'i; Bligh in Oliver 1988,124; Dening 1992,235.
90 Rose 1979,212.
91 Henry 1928,13; also Oliver 1974 3,1213; Rose 1978; Dening 1988,52; Dening 1992,236.
92 Beaglehole 1967 3(part 1),202.
93 Oliver 1988,126.
94 Corney 1919 3,73 and 108; see also Vancouver 1984 1,402.

apprehended were learned from the French.'[95] 'The French' of course refers to Bougainville, in Tahiti the year before.

Williams narrates a telling event regarding the *Bounty* that took place on her brief stop at Rarotonga, a few days after the mutiny:

> From this vessel was obtained a pointed piece of iron, about two feet six inches in length, which the natives immediately dedicated to the gods; and finding they could pierce the ground so much more easily with the iron than with their wooden tools, they were in the habit of borrowing it from the gods; and when the food thus planted was ripe, they invariably carried three portions to the marae, the first of which was dedicated as an expression of gratitude to the gods for causing the food to grow; the second in payment for the loan of the iron; and the third as a present, to induce the deities to conduct ships there [to Rarotonga] that they might obtain more of that valuable article.[96]

Again Williams, on Rarotonga:

> At Mr Pitman's station [Ngatangiia], I constructed a turning lathe, and the first thing I turned was the leg of a sofa, with which the chief to whom it belonged was so much delighted that he strung it round his neck, and walked up and down the settlement, exhibiting it to the admiration of the astonished inhabitants, many of whom exclaimed, that if they had possessed it prior to the renunciation of idolatry, it would certainly have been an object of worship, and have taken the precedence of all their other idols.[97]

There is an unusual god image in the British Museum LMS collection that incorporates red European cloth. It is one of the feather bundle family gods from the central Cook Islands, LMS 135. It consists of a small wood fan handle, about 12 inches long, adorned with two opposed clusters of about 20 large frigate bird feathers, bound together not with tapa but with coarse red wool trade cloth, and fastened with oronga (see fig. 72).[98] It is conceivable the red cloth came from the 'large piece of scarlet cloth' traded by Cook on his landing at Atiu, 1 April 1777.[99] Numerous letters in the LMS archives mention that the missionaries had run out of trade material by 1821, and entry N°18 on Papeiha's list lends credence to the possibility that the red wool came from Cook: 'there is an old tattered Silk handkercheif that was obtained from Captn Cooks Vessel & immediately presented to Ruanuu as the god or guide of fleets—'.

In the journal of an anonymous officer on the Peruvian frigate *Santa Rosalia* is a poignant illustration of unbridled Polynesian enthusiasm towards things new and foreign. It was the Spaniards' third day on San Carlos (Easter Island), 19 October 1770.

> We spent the evening in making ready for the succeeding day, on which we were to formally disembark and take possession of the island, and to erect upon it three crosses . . . on three hillocks . . . at the eastern end. [The next day:] We set out . . . accompanying the three crosses with colours flying and drums beating . . . accompanied by the natives, who lent a willing hand, singing and dancing in their fashion as they went. At half-past one we arrived at the place at which the crosses were to be set up, and this was concluded with full rejoicings, after the benediction and adoration of the holy images, by the whole concourse of [250 armed Spanish soldiers and seamen; the population of Easter Island was scarcely 1000], on seeing which the natives went through the same ceremony. [After] the procedure was duly witnessed with the proper formalities, . . . some of the natives present signed . . . the official document . . . in their own form of script.[100]

---

95 Parkinson 1773,32; Wallis had 'discovered' Tahiti ('King George the Third's Island') 18.6.1767; Bougainville landed ('La Nouvelle Cythère') 6.4.1768, Cook 13.4.1769.

96 Williams 1837,202. Williams ascertained the identity of this vessel from Rarotongans, who spoke of a visit from a ship described as a 'floating plantation', with a man named Makore aboard. 'Plantation' must refer to the 1015 potted breadfruit plants on the *Bounty*; Makore is probably a Rarotongan rendering of McCoy, one of the mutineers (Sharp 1960).

97 Williams 1837,166.

98 The missionaries found red cloth to be second only to red feathers as the most valuable item for gift and trade; others were iron axe blades, spades, razors, scissors, ribbon, glass beads, mirrors. Missionary William Henry brought red feathers in the form of live parrots from Port Jackson (*Trans Miss Soc* 1804,171). The fondness of Pacific Islanders for European exotica is discussed in Newell 2003 and 2005.

99 Ellis 1782 1,40.

100 Corney 1913 1,265. The Spaniards were the first Europeans to visit Easter Island after Roggeveen in 1722.

The Polynesian appetite for the exotic and the ready willingness to change no doubt facilitated their adoption of Christianity—or at least the beginnings of it. Of course there were other reasons for the success of Christianity, and the European 'civilizing' influence that came along with it: it offered relief from the unending cycles of brutal, revenge-driven conflict; it offered laws and 'justice';[101] a chance of security; it brought improved methods of agriculture and a variety of food; and also the promise of an afterlife. Polynesians appreciated the fixing of their languages through literacy and books. Oliver reminds us regarding the Christian god that '[one should not ignore] the potency of a god whose devotees were so numerous, so knowledgeable, so affluent, and so militarily unconquerable.'[102]

No doubt the missionaries braced and in ways prepared the Polynesians for the inevitabilities of the years to come.

[101] The missionaries drew up simple 'codes of Christian laws', with provisions for judges and juries, on all the islands. The laws addressed such problems as theft, damage done by dogs or hogs, 'land-eating', Sabbath-breaking, tattooing, and adultery; the missionaries balked at instituting laws and suggesting consequences for murder. They tried to bring penalties under 'the mild influence of Gospel principles' rather than employing the more sanguinary heathen methods; a thief on Rarotonga, for example, before Williams and Charles Pitman arrived, was sometimes murdered on the spot, the body cut up, and the limbs hung up in different parts of the farm; the house was broken down and the produce was destroyed (Williams 1837,127). See Ellis (1829 2,426) for an example of a code of laws.

[102] Oliver 1974 3,1339.

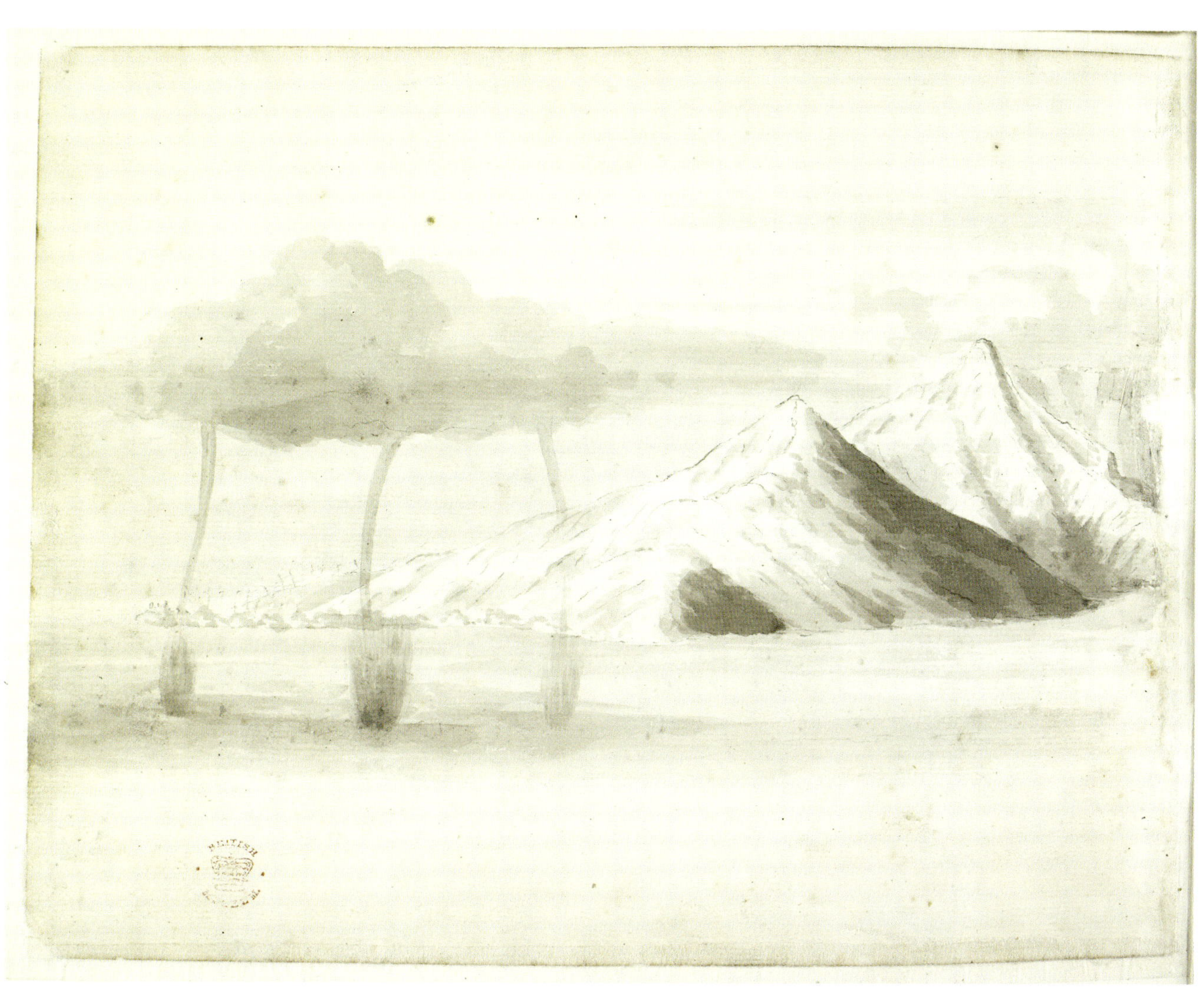

54 *Wash by Sydney Parkinson, Cook's 1st voyage.* Yooleatea, *looking south from the* Endeavour *anchorage off Opoa, Ra'iatea, 1769. Three waterspouts are in the foreground; 'Awa, the water-spout' features in Tahitian mythology (Haweis 1799,333). Ra'iatea is a prototypical Polynesian 'high island'. Barely visible at the tip of the low point (Te Po) at the far left is the Great Marae Taputapuatea, seat of the cult of 'Oro. Courtesy British Library, Add. ms 9345,51.*

Epilogue

THIS ESSAY STARTED OUT by examining the Polynesian objects strewn about Williams' feet in the Anelay watercolour in order to find out more about them. It has ended up being a diffuse and incomplete discourse on Polynesian—and missionary—culture and history. To a large extent it concerns gods and idols—what the missionaries referred to as the 'false divinities'.[1] Most of the account involves the Cook Islands, and much has ended up in the footnotes. Sources rarely agree; facts are sparse; documentation is thin; but this is all there is to go by. This book stitches together pertinent material from all primary sources that could be located, and lets the sources speak in their own words so as not to distort what little is known about the subject, and to impart some of the flavour of the times, and character and outlook of the participants.

A central finding of this investigation into the Polynesian objects depicted in the Anelay watercolour has been the rediscovery of the 47-page manuscript written by Rev John Williams entitled *More Joy for Christians*. The manuscript is largely a narrative of Papeiha to Williams, describing in intriguing detail how 'the seed of the Word' was planted on the island of Aitutaki, and took root. Accomplished by the two Raiatean teachers Papeiha and Vahapata, the process took just shy of two years, from October 1821 to July 1823. In addition to the unusually full narrative, the manuscript includes an annotated list of 31 'idols' which were surrendered to the teachers. Five of the entries on this list are fans, fan handles, and 'bundles of fans — sacred'. The annotations on this list, together with information recorded on LMS collection registration slips and in the Missionary Museum catalogues, allow the connection of these 31 'idols' with an unusual, enigmatic, and large group of objects that still exists, now housed primarily in the LMS collection in the British Museum. Five of the idols listed by Williams and Papeiha can be matched with specific objects in the British Museum LMS collection

---

1   Montgomery 1832 2,238.

and in the Oldman Collection. The others can not be identified specifically, but another unpublished manuscript provides some clues.

A 'List of [LMS Missionary Museum] Curios proposed to be transferred to the British Museum', dated 1890, consists mostly of single items, with the exception of item 10: '35 Household gods — handles &ᶜ', specifying one as 'han[dle] from Maute . . . several clusters of feathers attached', others as 'bunches of feathers . . . propitiatory offerings'. Thus, both these manuscript lists mention quantities of fans and fan handles. In all likelihood, the fans and fan handles and 'bundles of fans—sacred' on Papeiha's list include the '35 household gods' mentioned in the 1890 LMS 'List of Curios'. Some appear in the Anelay watercolour. Several were described in Charles Hercules Read's seminal article of 1892. There is evidence that all were collected not by Williams and Bourne, but by the Raiatean teachers and perhaps also by the chief of Atiu, Roma-tane, on the quick (9 to 28 July 1823) *Endeavour* trip to Aitutaki, Atiu, Mauke, and Mitiaro. The drawing by William Ellis, on Cook's third voyage, of a triangular fan from Atiu with a Janus figure handle is solid evidence confirming the connection of these objects with the central Cook Islands. The objects were brought back to Ra'iatea, and then sent on to London — some with Tyerman and Bennet, some with Captain Richard Charlton. The majority of these fans and fan handles, including the family 'feather gods' from the central Cook Islands, are in the British Museum LMS collection. As most have never been published or even mentioned, photographs of about 35 of them are shown on the plates.

Captain Cook for good reason has received much attention over the years, but less so the missionaries: they were not the first Europeans in the Pacific; their aims were dubious; their writings are often tedious and uninformative and their biases obvious; and their publications are not nearly as well illustrated. But the fact remains that although they arrived in the Pacific 30 years later, unlike Cook, they lived in Polynesia for years, associated closely with the people, and learned the language; this enabled the missionaries to learn a great deal about Polynesian cultures. Some of their writings are rich, thoughtful, complex, perceptive. They are valuable sources for several island groups and are the primary and only source for all but one of the Cook Islands; Cook never landed on the most important islands of the group that bears his name. The London missionaries didn't land on the Cook Islands, or the Austral Islands either—until conversion had already been effected, and not by the English missionaries, but by the teachers from Ra'iatea and Taha'a they trained and sent ahead to 'clear away the rubbish of idolatry'. Hence our knowledge of early Cook Islands culture is far less extensive than it is for Tahiti or Hawai'i, for example.

Missionary sources have helped fill in details of central Polynesian culture and material culture. They have enabled the delineation of the steps in the assembly of the LMS collections and the narrowing down of the places and dates of acquisition of a number of individual objects. And they have contributed to our understanding of many of the objects, for instance by further documenting important particulars concerning the sacred elements—birds, feathers, sennit, and tapa wraps. Many of the gods were equipped with sennit tails; short sections of plaited sennit could be instruments of divination. Apparently flywhisks were often family gods in the Societies and Australs, but in the Cooks, fans took their place. Missionary writings, the LMS catalogues and the British Museum LMS collection registration slips, often vague or inaccurate, have proven to be valuable sources of information nevertheless.

Although some of the LMS directors thought otherwise, the missionaries themselves started out in Polynesia reviling the idols, considering them best suited as 'food for the flames' and eager to treat them as such. It was not long before they changed their minds. Interestingly, it was first a Polynesian chief, then a Polynesian teacher, who altered the course of events and began the practice of saving the idols instead of destroying them. To both parties, the idol harvest came to be the 'ocular demonstration' of Christian conquest. By 1821, the missionaries had adopted the policy, 'if you obtain idols, burn some, but not the best.' In the sense of wanting to keep and not to destroy the idols, this time it was the missionaries who were converted by the Polynesians. Indeed, were it not for Pomare II and for Papeiha, it is unlikely there would be much of an LMS collection at all.

Many questions, of course, remain unanswered. Much of Polynesian history has been lost irrevocably, for several reasons. The explorers' recording of the cultures was spotty, and mostly inaccurate. Polynesian populations rapidly became decimated by warfare and disease, both exacerbated by European contacts, which occurred with increasing frequency. And Polynesian cultures were affected profoundly—disrupted—by the missionaries. Oliver refers to their arrival as 'the preposterous confrontation'.[2] Nowadays, the idea of missionaries is generally considered an abhorrent and alien concept. They are not blamed for the spreading of Western weaponry and diseases, but they are roundly held responsible for everything else that led to what has been called the 'cultural genocide' of Polynesia.[3] Yet, as discussed above, and seen in the plates, they have also been agents of cultural preservation—something not often acknowledged.

The following paragraph is a quote from Ellis again, who contributed to a book entitled *The Missionary's Farewell*, compiled in England on the eve of Williams' return to the South Sea in 1838. It is a good summary, written in hindsight, of how the early missionaries viewed Polynesia and Polynesians:

> But what was the state of the people? The land was full of idols, from the house of the highest chief to the hut of the lowest peasant. From one end of the group to the other there were to be found the idols of individuals, the idols of families, the idols of districts, and the idols of the nation . . . They were altogether rude, senseless, shapeless objects. The land was not only filled with idols, but with idol temples; every point of land which projected into the sea was generally surmounted by a heathen temple; every lovely valley was generally disfigured by the rude marae erected there for the purpose of idol worship. Whether you travelled across the mountain range or the deep ravine, along the sea-shore or the verdant valley, you saw the temples of the idols of the country. It was also a land of priests—but they were priests of darkness . . . If I were to select one designation by which the inhabitants of the Tahitian and Society Islands . . . might be characterised, it would be that they were a nation wholly given to idolatry. Their rites were of the most sanguinary kind. You are aware of the horrid circumstances under which human sacrifices were offered; this was the religious state of the people, a state peculiarly distinguished by barbarity, degradation, and cruelty . . . It was among this people, in the centre of all this vast expanse of degradation, superstition . . . and murder, that our brethren commenced their labours.[4]

In light of this stance, Peter Buck's remark is apt: '[We] owe a debt of gratitude to the early missionaries for sparing what they did.'[5] This statement is true; they could easily have left not a trace.

---

[2] Oliver 1974 3,1288.
[3] See for instance Lewis 1972.

[4] *The Missionary's Farewell* 1838,14, regarding Tahiti. Williams' comment on this passage: 'My beloved brother Ellis has given rather a dark picture of Tahiti' (ibid.,70).
[5] Buck 1944,310.

Idols more welcome than the Spoils of the Acropolis from Athens, are picked up, & on the Sea we wait with some impatience their arrival, by the South whaler.

55 *June 1818 entry in Rev Dr Thomas Haweis' manuscript* Autobiography 2,232. *Clearly Haweis looked forward to receiving shipments of idols. Mitchell Library.*

Artefacts

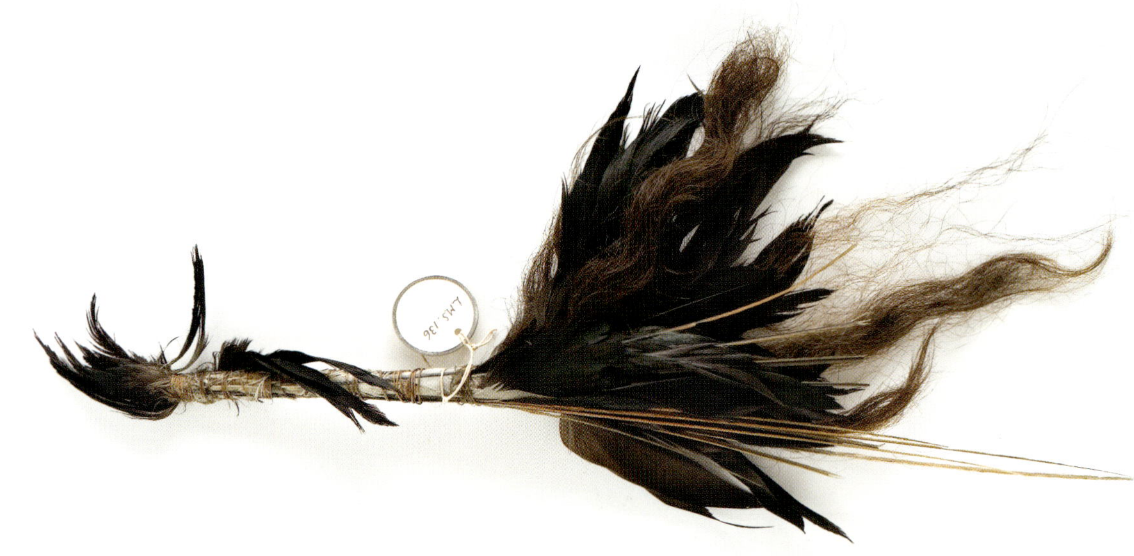

56 *Feather god: human hair, tropic bird and frigate bird feathers; central Cook Islands. 44cm. LMS 136.*

57 *God composed entirely of human hair; white tapa wrapping; central Cook Islands. 42cm. LMS 52.*

58 *Feather god: sennit bundle, opposed frigate bird feathers, white tapa wrapping; central Cook Islands. 48cm. LMS 115.*

56

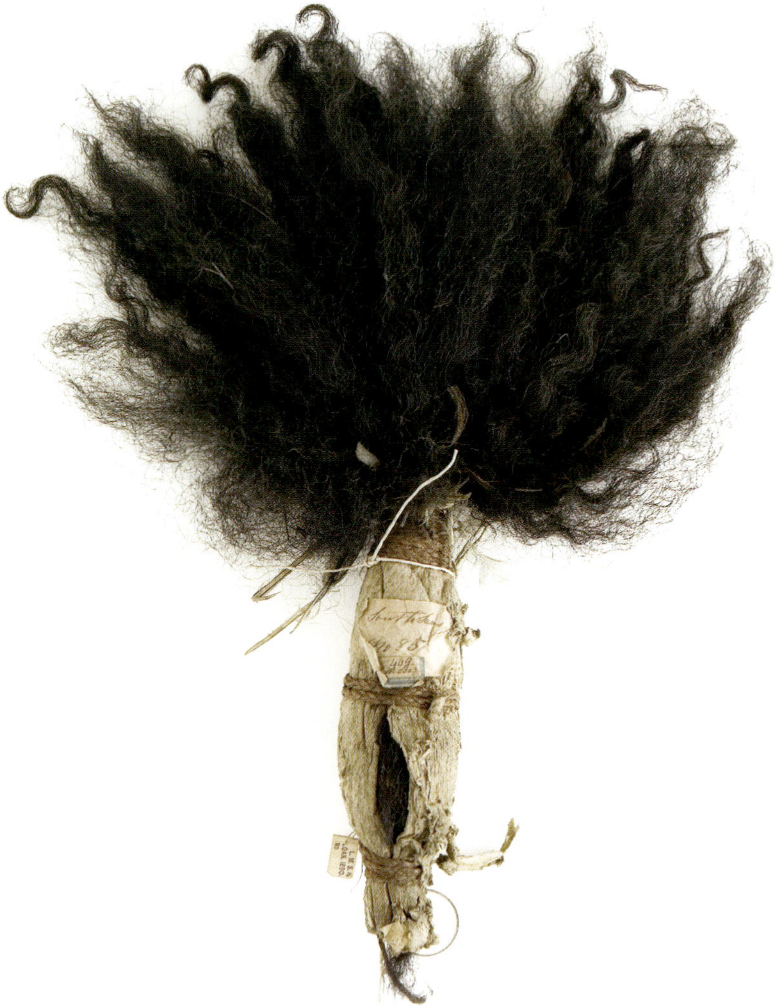

57

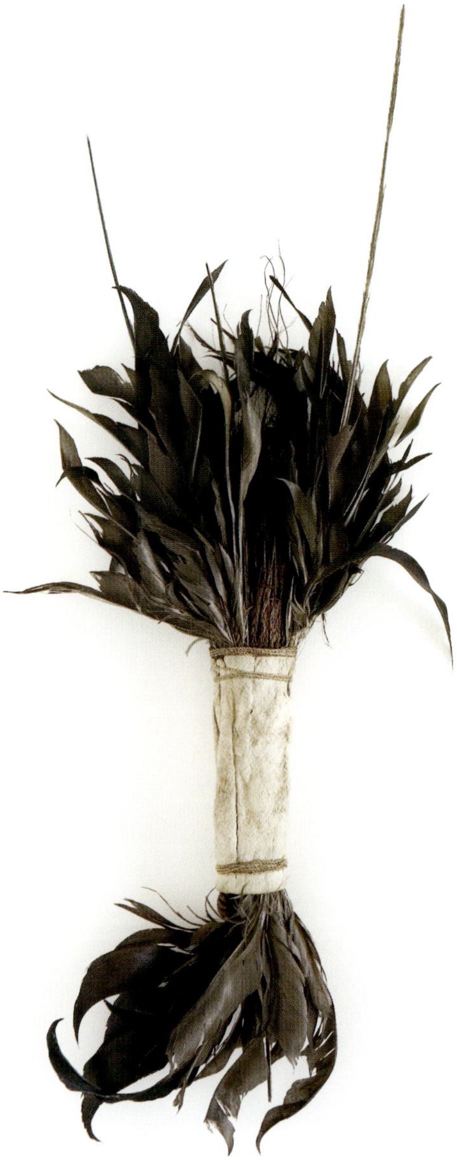

58

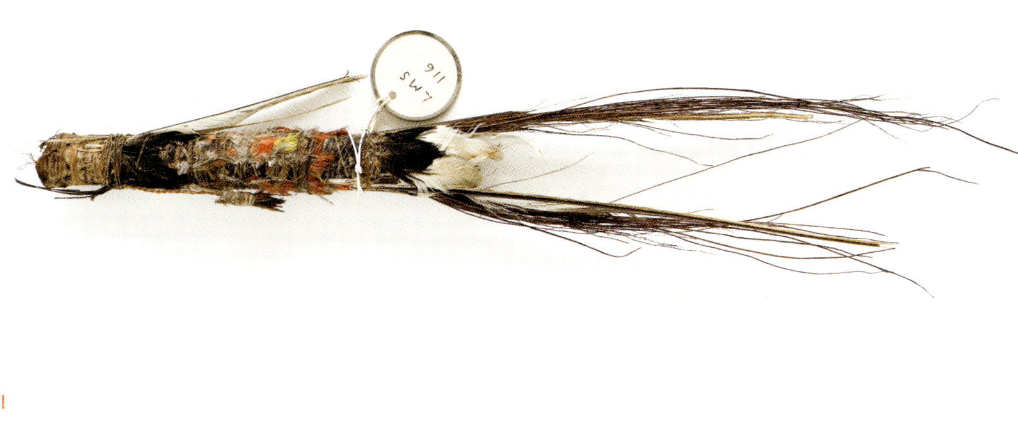

59

59   *Portion of the list of objects proposed to be transferred from the LMS Mission Museum to the British Museum, dated 11 November 1890, mentioning '35 household gods– handles &c' in a single line entry, and specifics such as 'Nº52. Han. [handle] from Maute. Several clusters of feathers attached to pieces of wood & fibre'; Nºs63 & 66 'Bunches of feathers probably portions of broken idols or propitiatory offerings.' Anthropology Library, BM.*

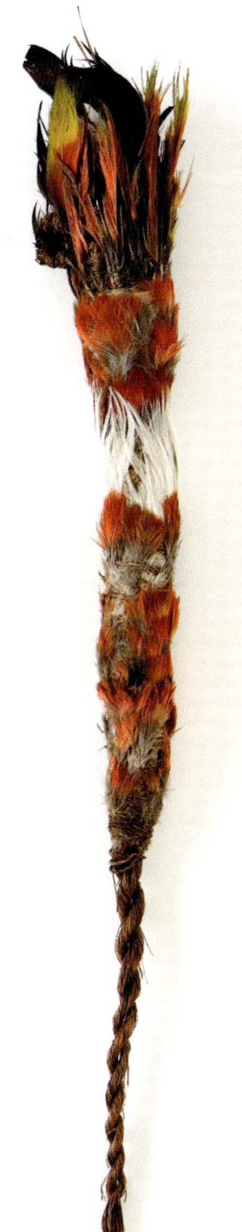

60

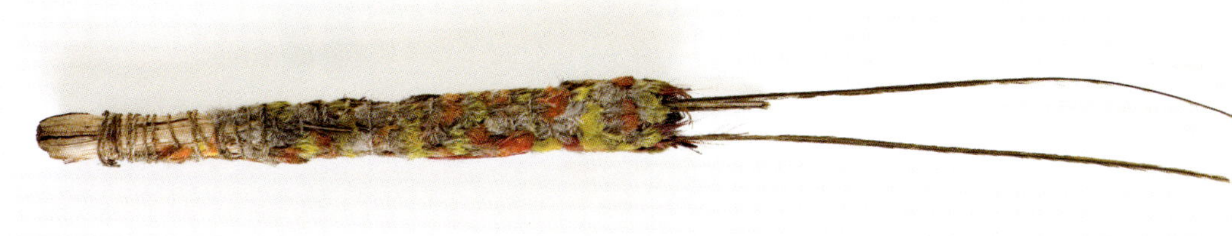

61

62

Three small feather gods: flexible sennit cores, brilliant kura (red feathers) attached, all in a remarkably good state of preservation; central Cook Islands.

60   *29cm. LMS 134.*

61   *35cm. LMS 116.*

62   *35.5cm. LMS 137.*

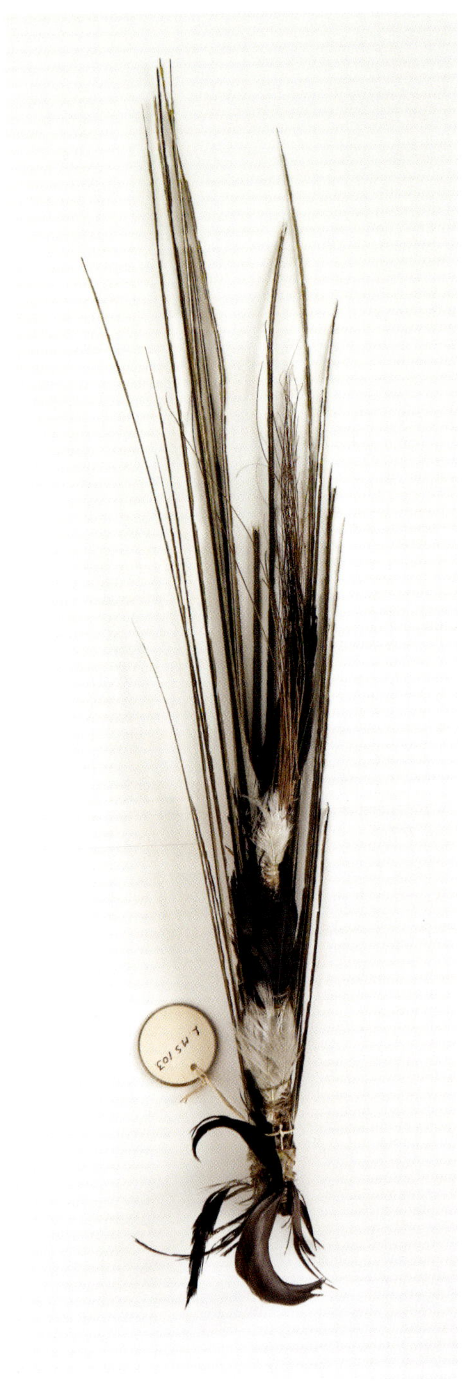
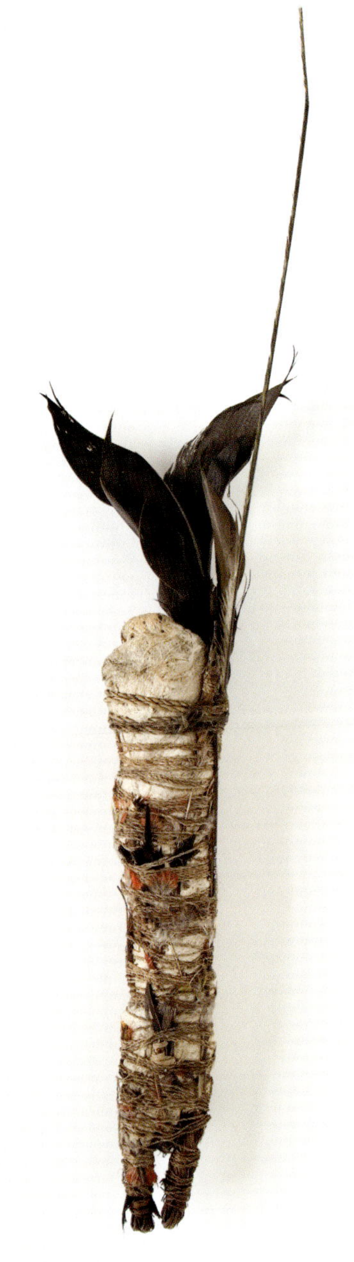
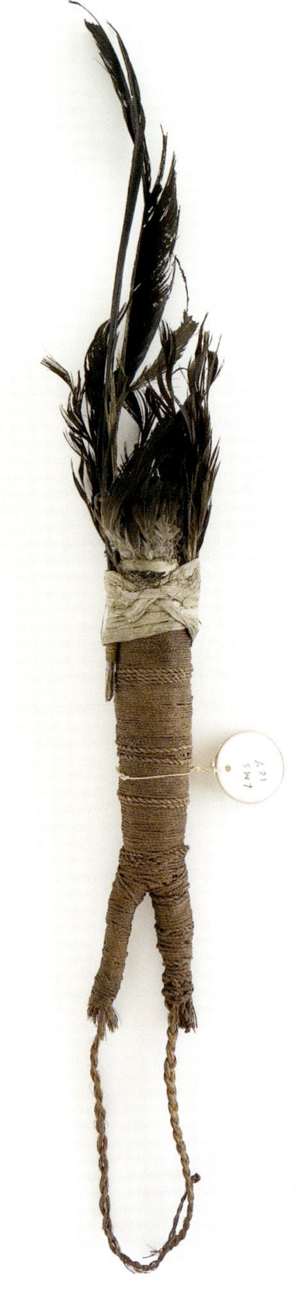

63

64

65

63 *Feather god; central Cook Islands. 52cm.
LMS 103.*

64 *Feather god with 'legs'; central Cook Islands.
38cm. LMS 104.*

65 *Feather god: 'body' and 'legs' closely wrapped
with carefully made sennit; central Cook Islands.
58cm. LMS 167.*

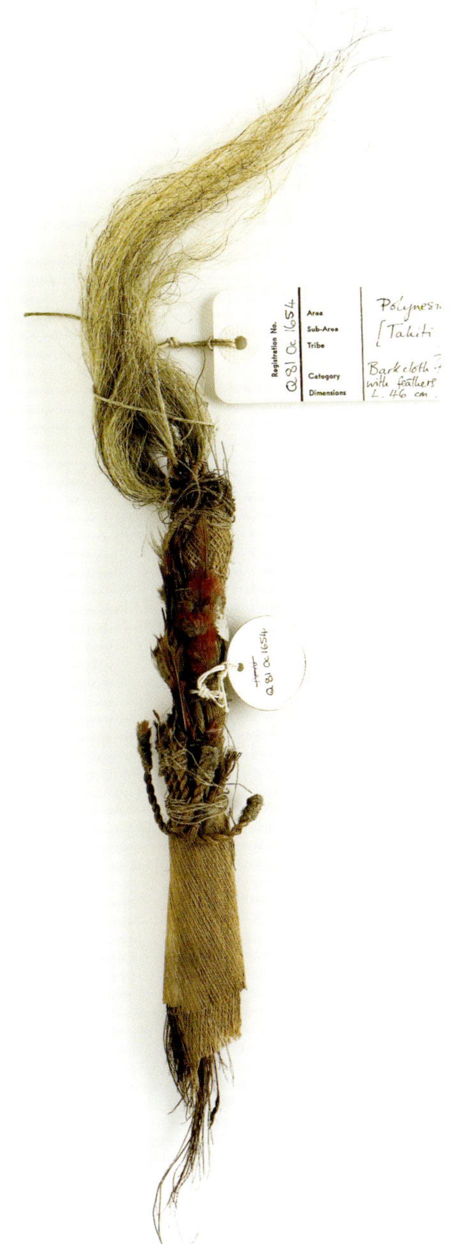

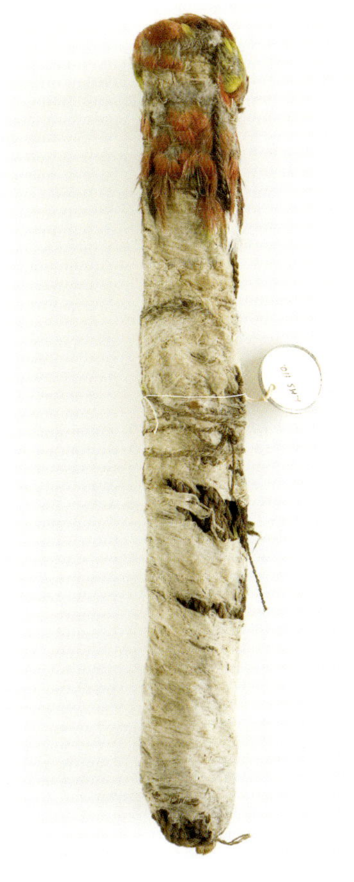

66 *Feather god with pig (?) hair, kura, cloth-like fibre from coconut leaf base; central Cook Islands. 40cm. Oc1981,Q.1654. BM (LMS).*

67 *Phallic feather god: sennit core, white tapa and kura attached; central Cook Islands. 38cm. LMS 110.*

68 *Feather god with legs and arms, white tapa wrapping. Labelled Mangaia, but probably from the central Cook Islands. 42cm. LMS. CUM Z.6094. Buck card, BPBM.*

67

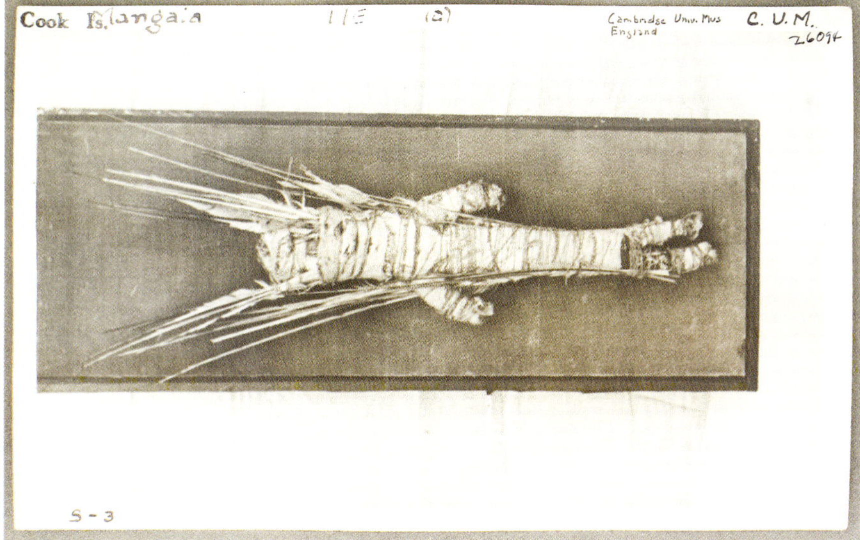

66

68

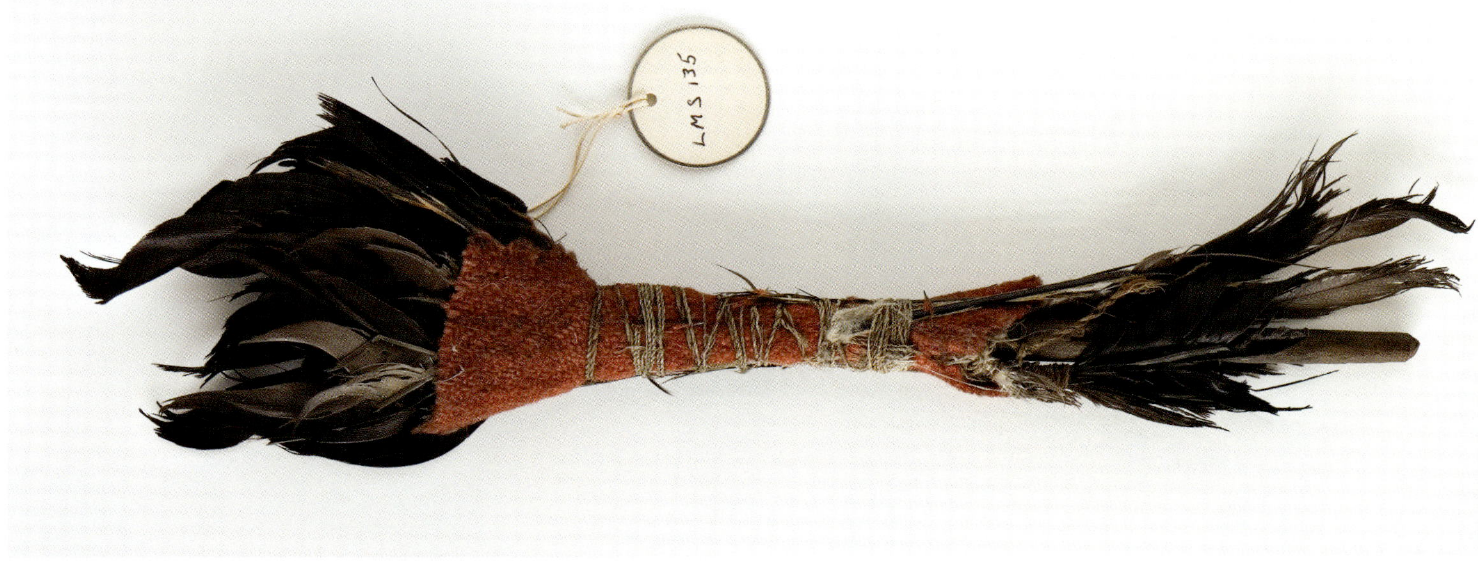

69

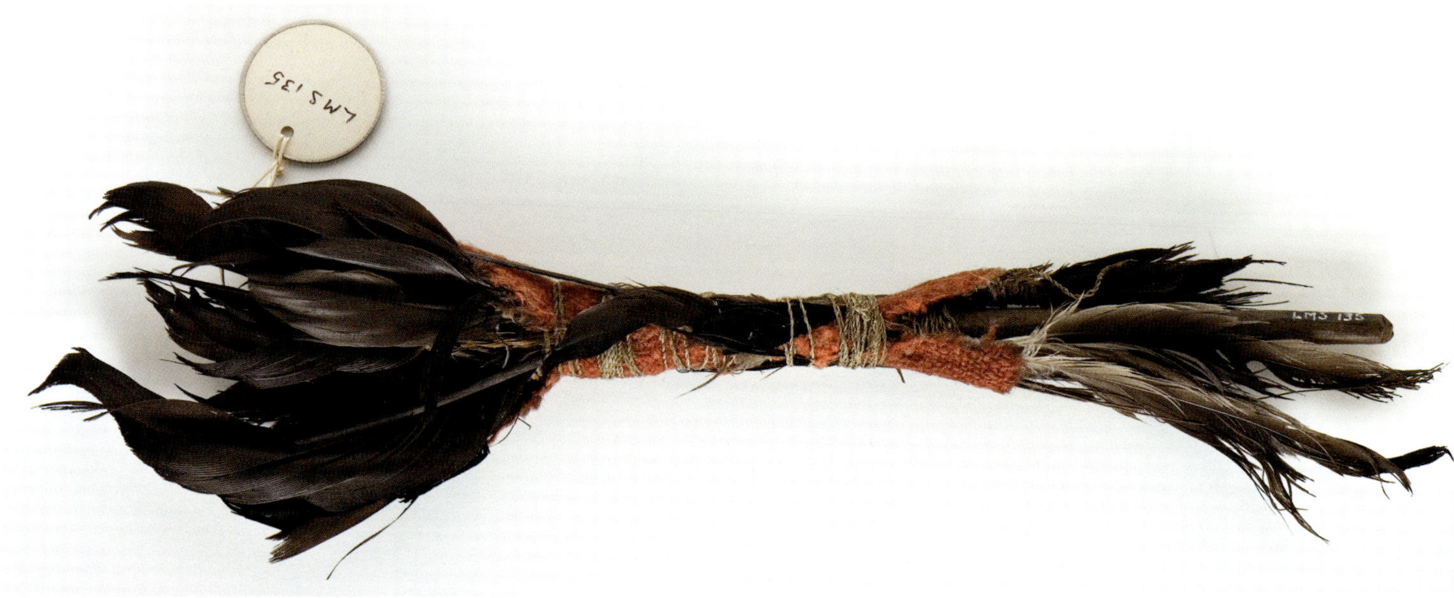

70

69 & 70 *Feather god from the central Cook Islands, showing both sides. Consists of an unusually small but complete fan handle plus tang, with opposed clusters of large frigate bird feathers bound not with tapa but with red English wool trade cloth, fastened with oronga. 31cm. LMS 135.*

71 *The fan handle, hidden from view and impossible to photograph, terminates in an open lozenge abstract Janus figure much like LMS 128. The handle is depicted on LMS 135 registration slip sketch.*

72 *The cloth appears freshly cut, and may have come from a piece traded by Cook at Atiu, 1 April 1777.*

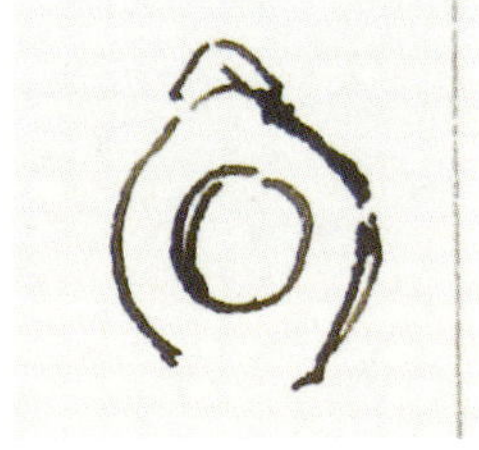

71

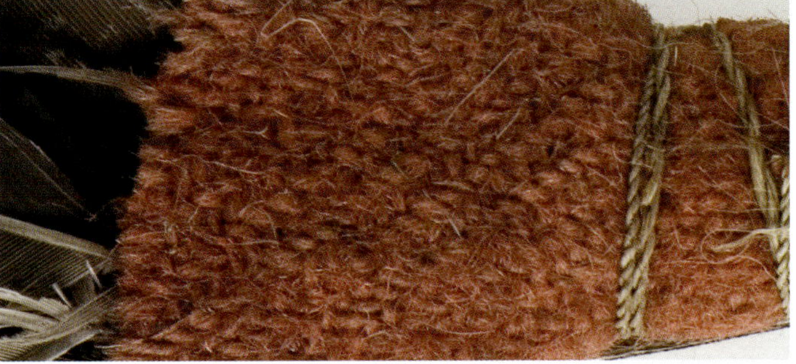

72

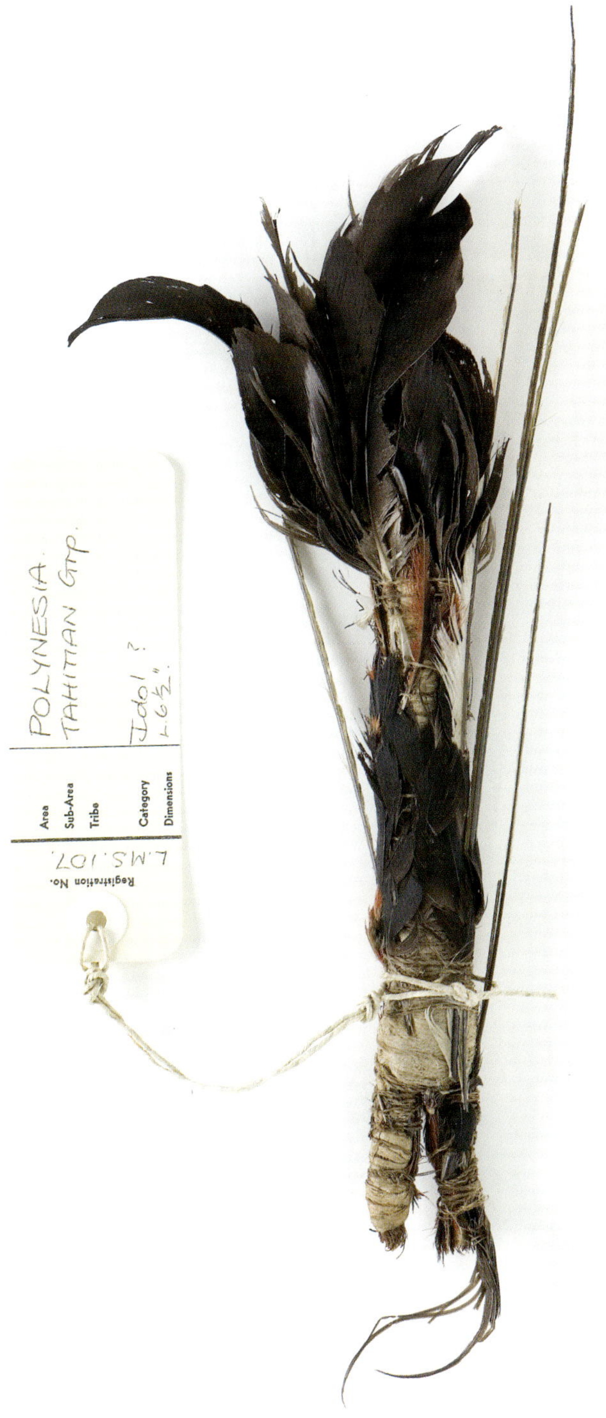

73

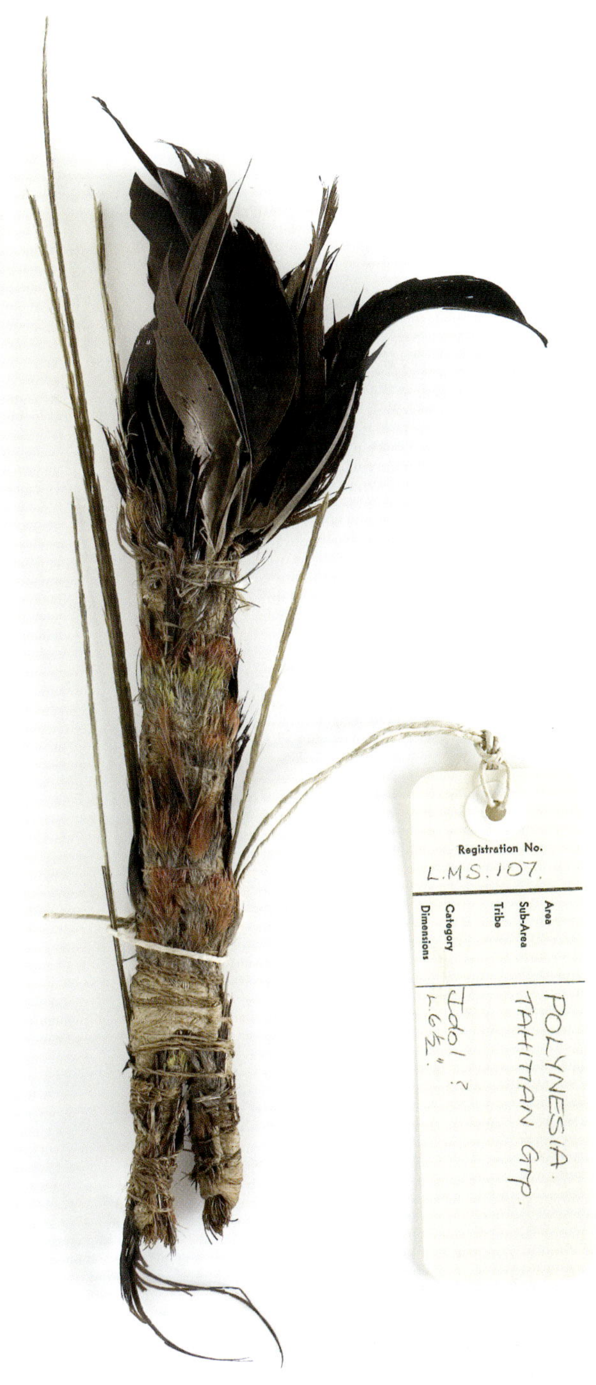

74

73 & 74 *Feather god with 'legs', both sides shown; central Cook Islands. 30.5cm. LMS 107.*

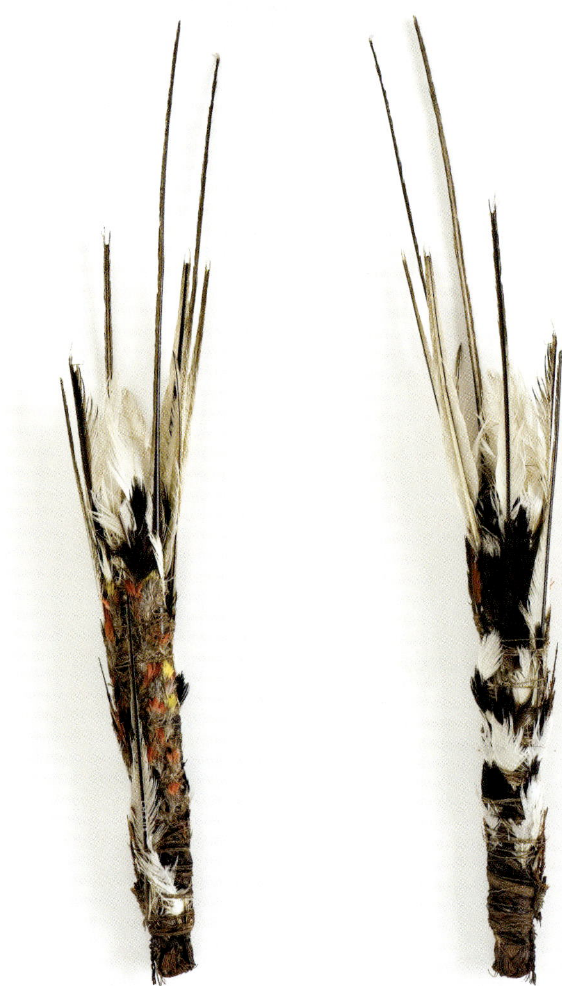

75 & 76 Small feather god; central Cook Islands. *37cm.*
LMS *112.*

77 & 78 Feather god with 'legs'; central Cook Islands.
48cm. LMS *161.*

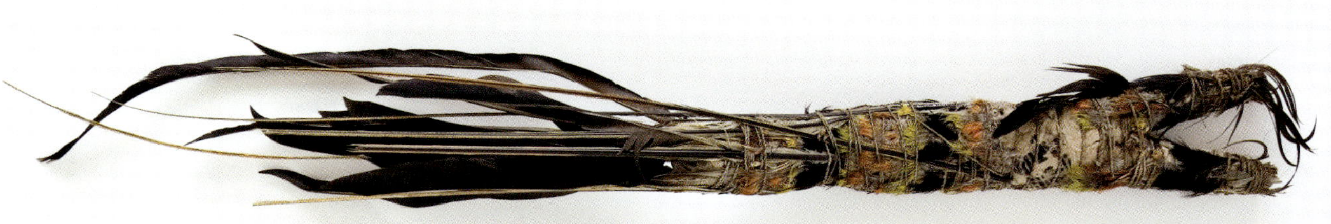

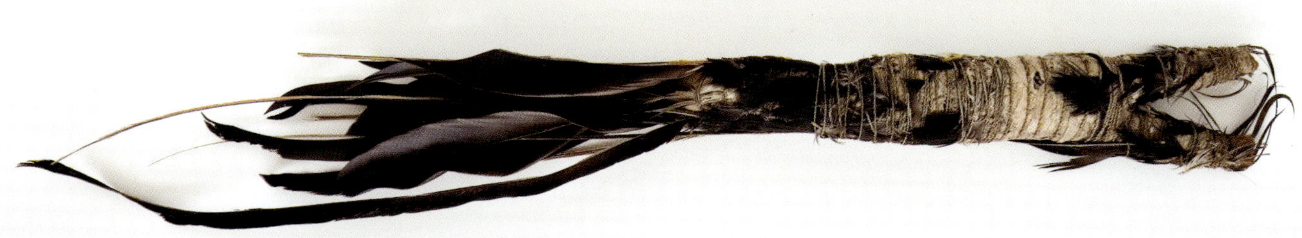

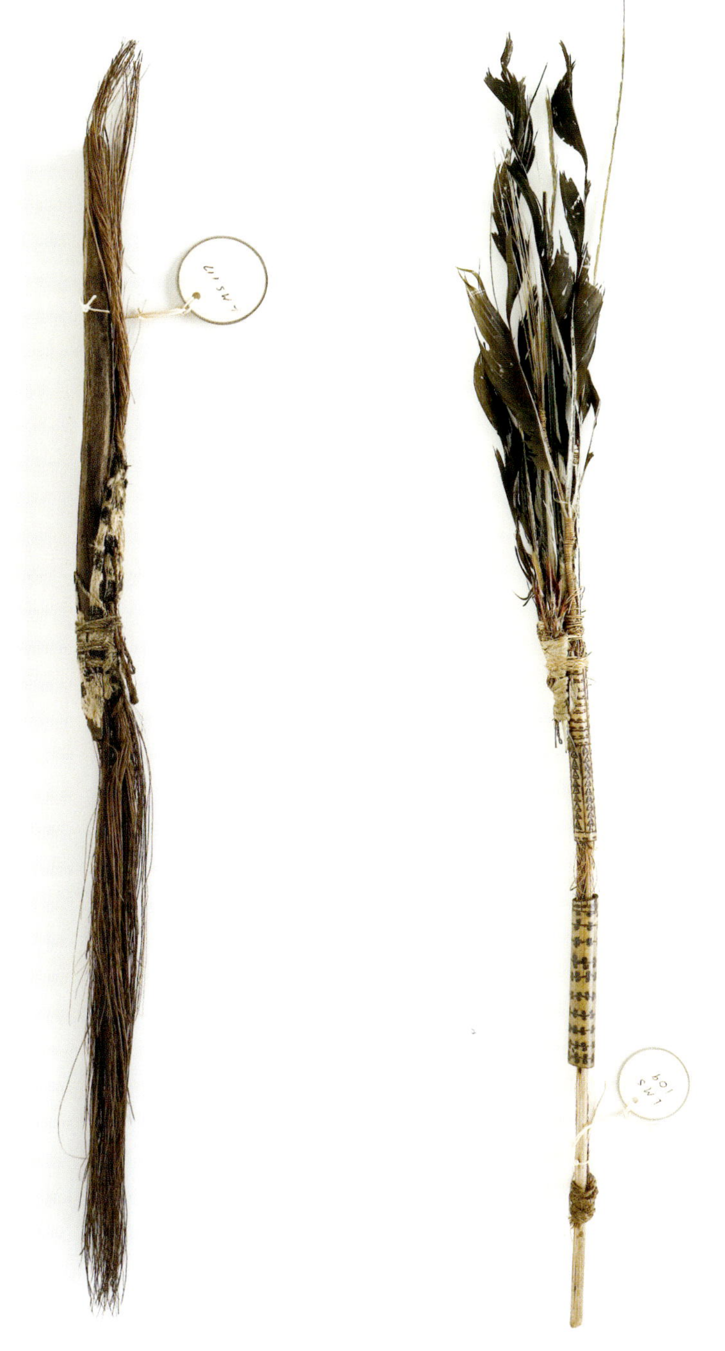

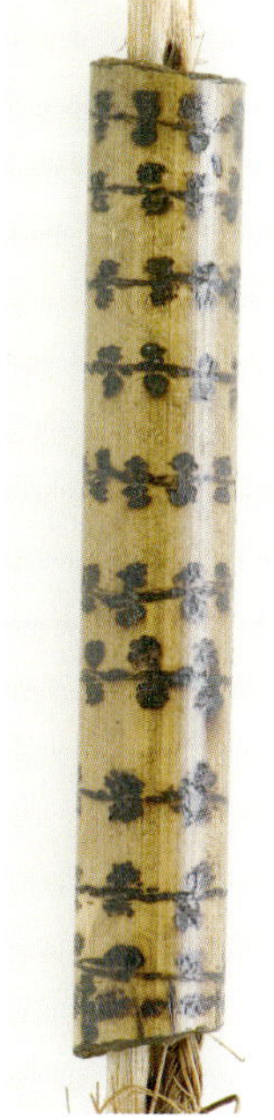

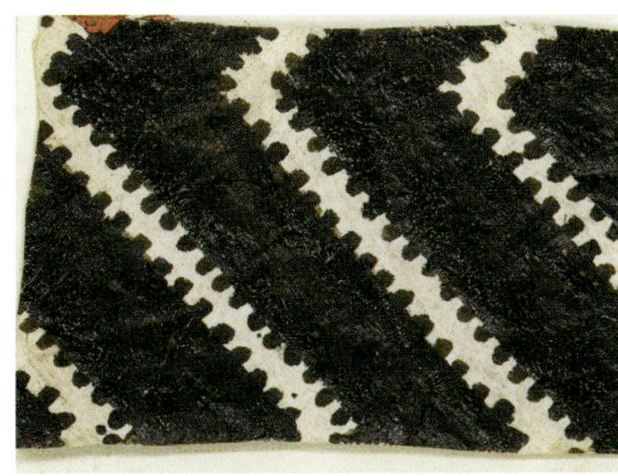

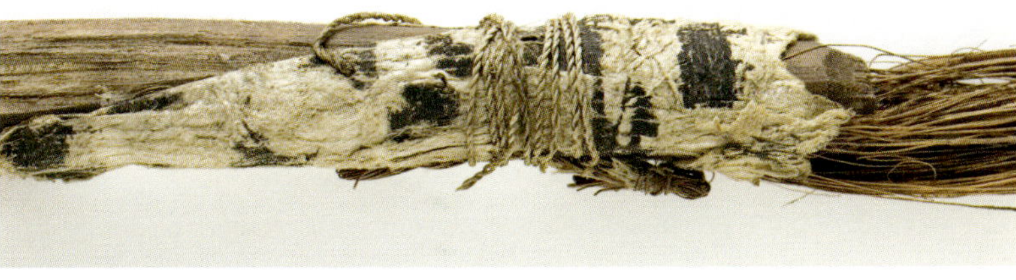

79

81

82

83

80

Two unusual family gods; central Cook Islands.

79　*Wood and sennit, incorporating decorated instead of the usual white tapa. 44cm. LMS 117.*

80　*Detail of rectangle-patterned tapa on LMS 117.*

81　*Wood, sennit, and feathers, incorporating two burn-decorated bamboo elements. 62cm. LMS 109.*

82　*Detail of bottom bamboo element of LMS 109.*

83　*Pattern on Cook Islands tapa, a gift of J Williams to one of his sisters. The pattern parallels burn pattern on LMS 109. SOAS.*

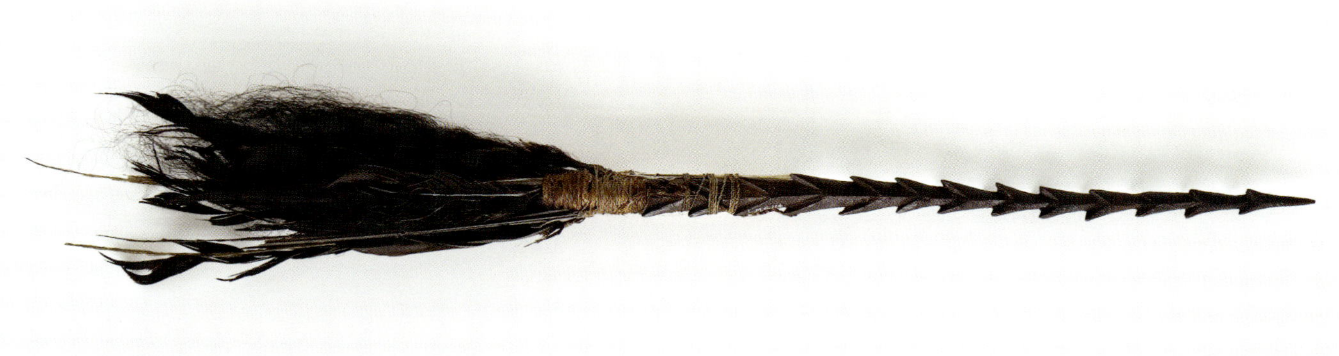

83

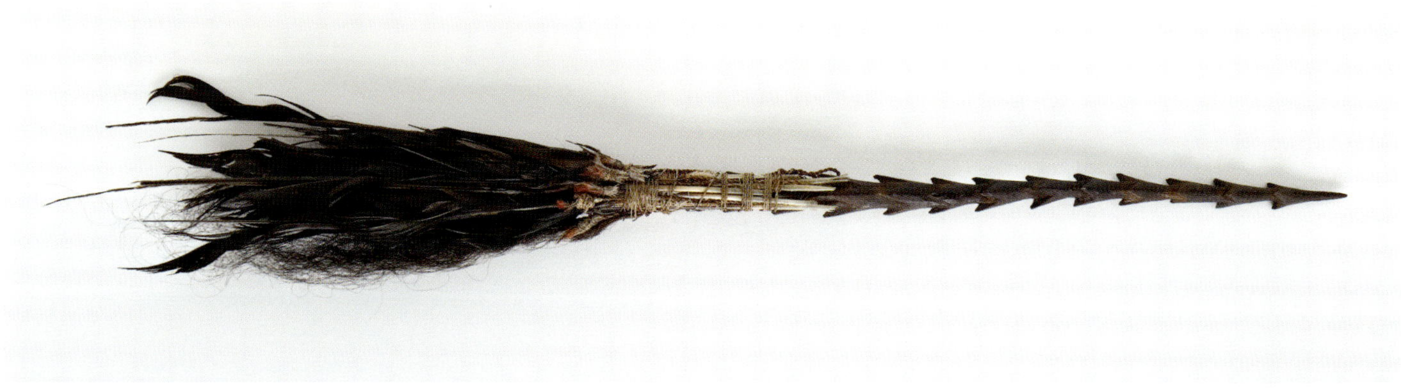

84

83 & 84 *Spear point converted into a feather god; central Cook Islands. This could be Nº6 on Papeiha's list: 'A piece of a jagged spear the point of which was broken off in a man & this was immediately presented to the God.' George Tobin's 24 July 1792 description of an Aitutaki spear head: 'the sharp point being of very dark hard wood and jagged like a turtle peg (Schreiber 2007, 137). 56cm. LMS 114.*

85 & 86 *Feather god: tapa-wrapped sennit, coconut leaf base sheath, and grooved wood composite; central Cook Islands. 34cm. LMS 105.*

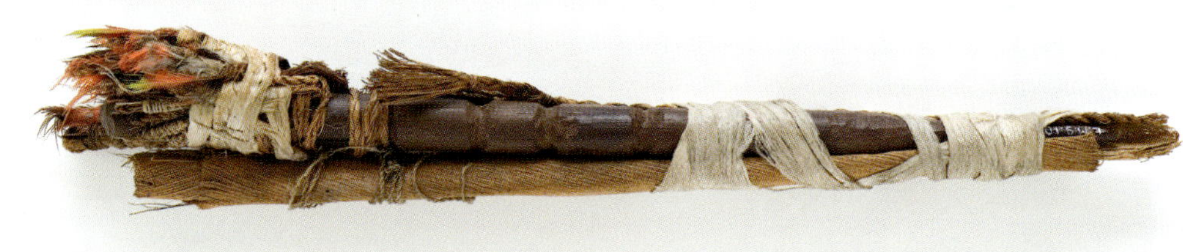

85

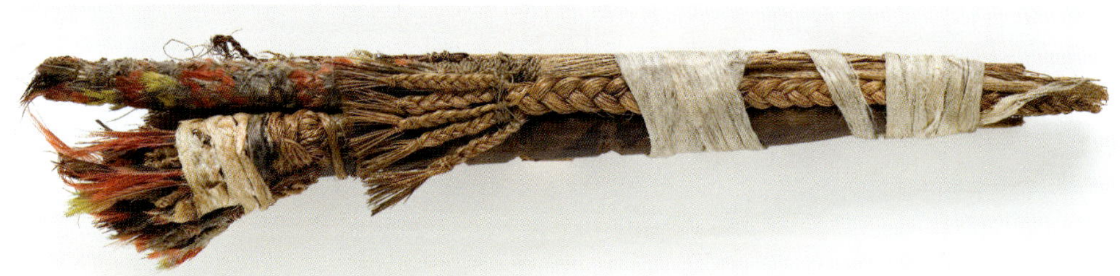

86

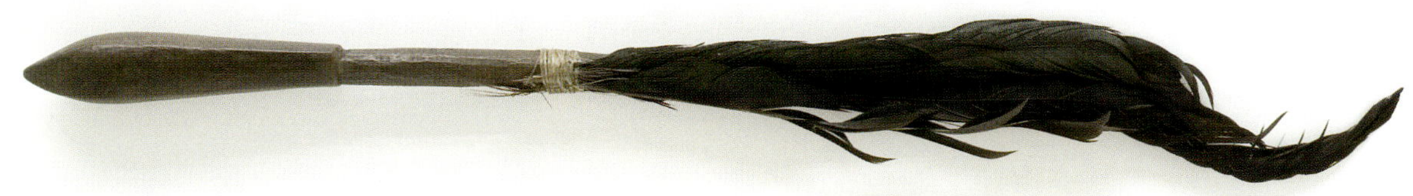

87

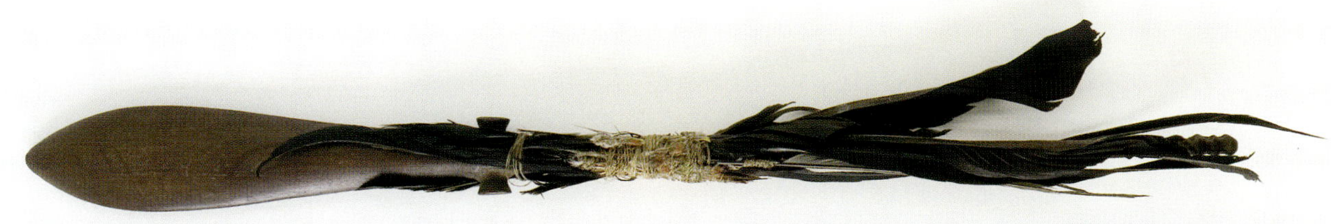

88

Fan handles converted into feather gods; central Cook Islands.

87 Handle squarish in cross section. 42cm. LMS 125.

88 Simple fusiform handles were the most abstract of all the Janus figure fan handles. 48cm. LMS 124.

89 & 90 As above. 55cm. LMS 133.

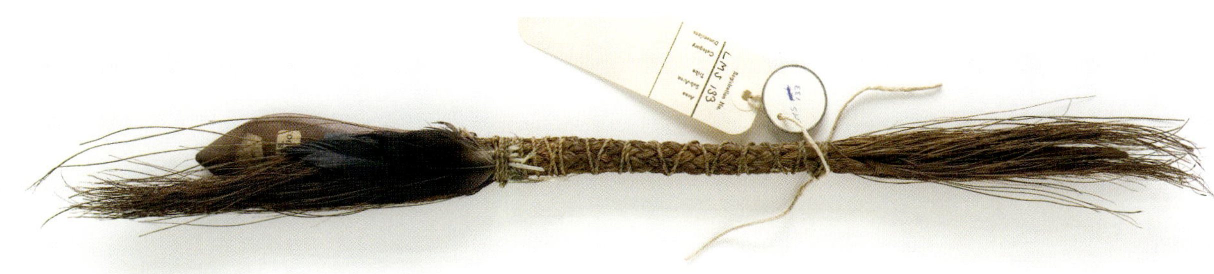

89

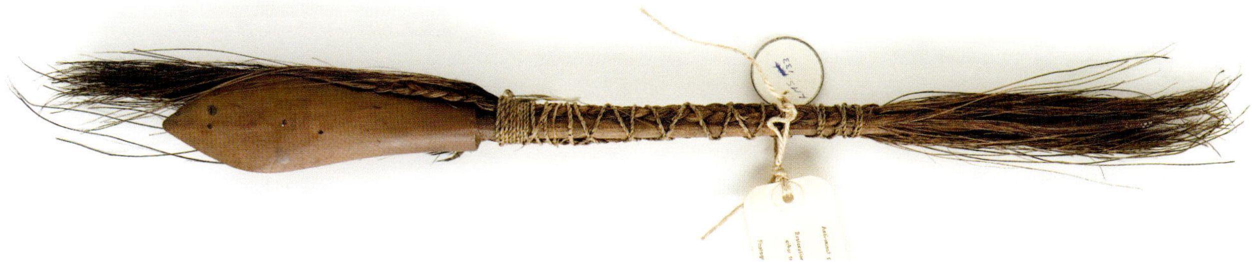

90

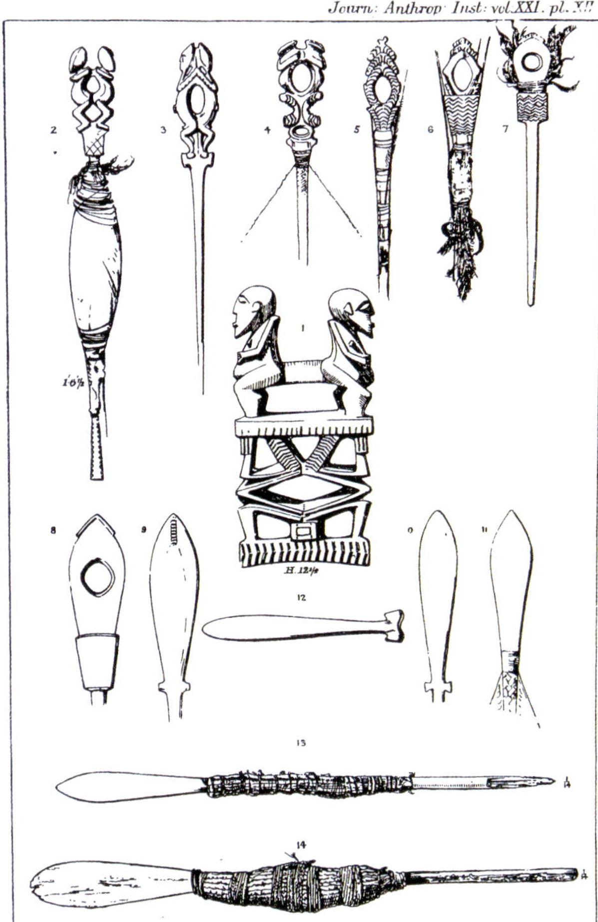

91

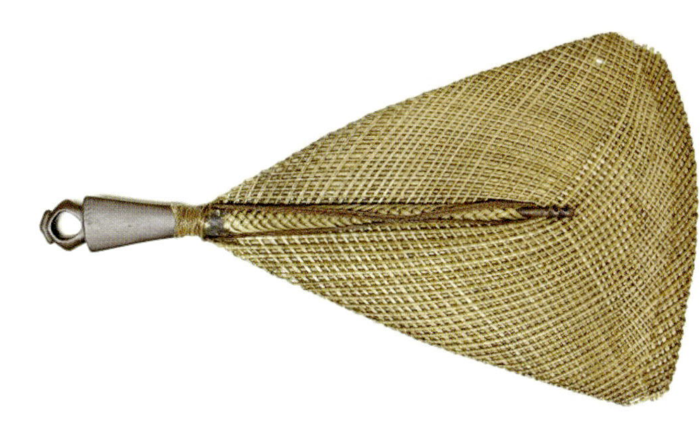

92

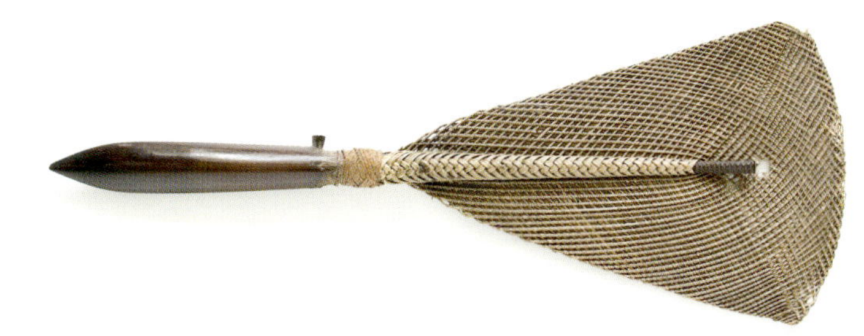

93

91 *Plate XII of Charles Hercules Read's seminal article published in* Journal of the Anthropological Institute of Great Britain and Ireland, *1892. N.os 2 to 11 are fan handles, in the BM LMS collection. They illustrate a continuum of Janus figures progressing from realistic to completely abstract. Read identifies these handles, generally adorned with feathers, tapa, and sennit, as sacred objects. N.o 2 appears in the Anelay watercolour; photographs of all of them are included in these figures.*

92 *Intact fan; central Cook Islands. 46cm. Oldman 397; no acquisition data, but likely LMS. Photo Otago Museum.*

93 *Intact fan; Central Cook Islands. 50.5cm. J Hooper 516; no documentation, but likely LMS.*

94 *Termini of the tangs were often slightly reflexed and carefully notched. LMS 51.*

95 *As above. J Hooper 516.*

96 *Simple fusiform fan handle with carved detail; central Cook Islands. 26.5cm. LMS 130.*

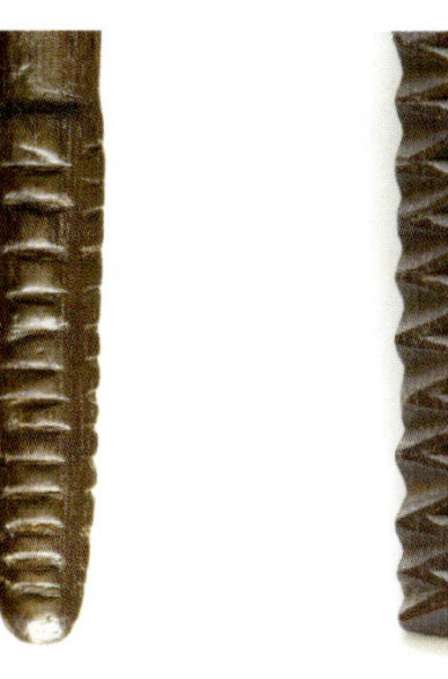

94

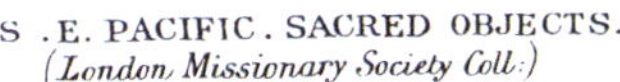

95

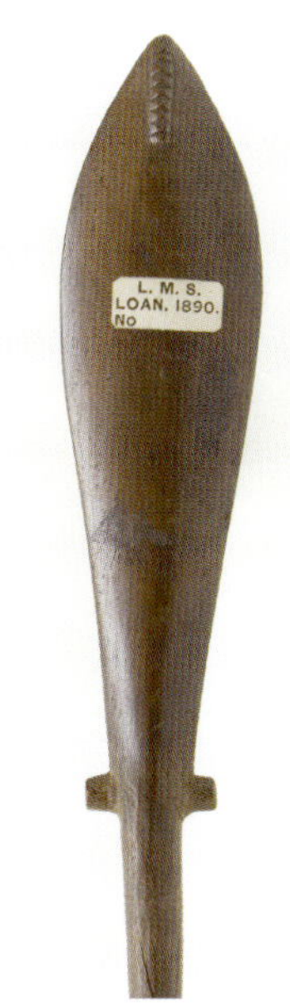

96

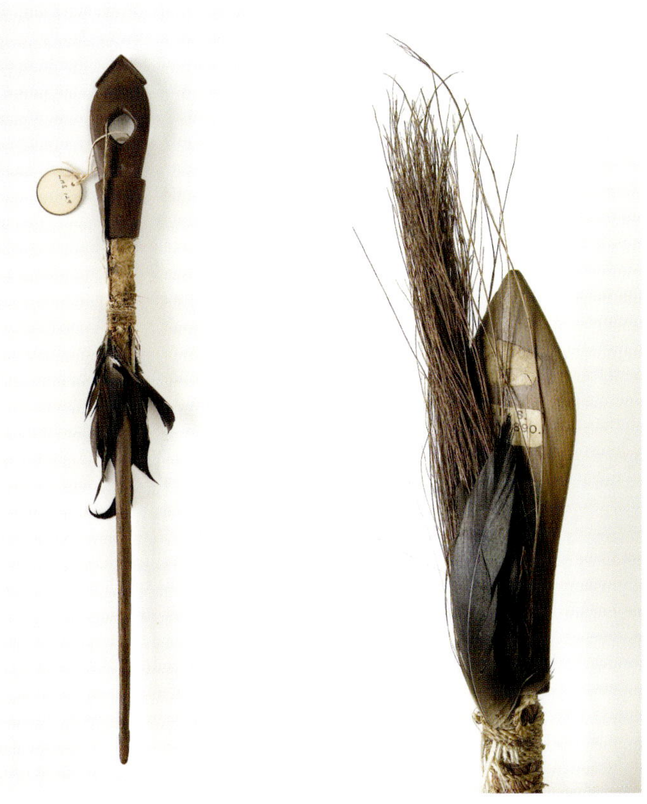

97 *Fan handle; central Cook Islands. 49cm. LMS 129.*

98 *Detail, fan handle; central Cook Islands. 55cm. LMS 133.*

99 *Plaited fan from Rarotonga. Ex-LMS. Buck card file. Courtesy BPBM.*

100 *Plaited fan from Mangaia. Ex-LMS. Buck card file. Courtesy BPBM.*

101 *Baxter colour print,* Te po, a Chief of Rarotonga. *Probably Takitumu tribe. Beautifully tattooed, he is holding a sacred fan. Frontispiece of certain editions of Williams's* Missionary Enterprises, *1837. After painting by John Williams Jr.*

101

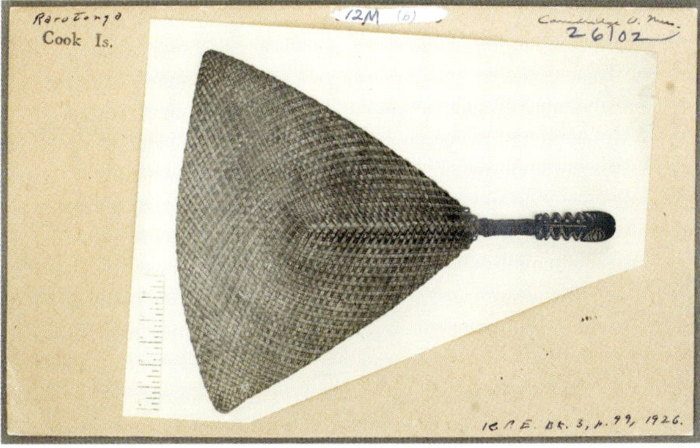

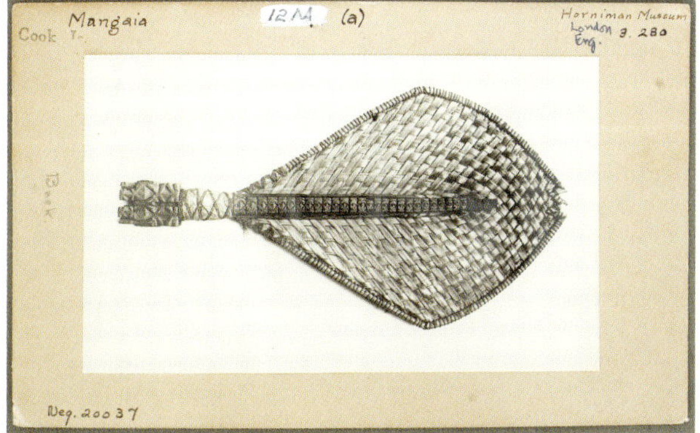

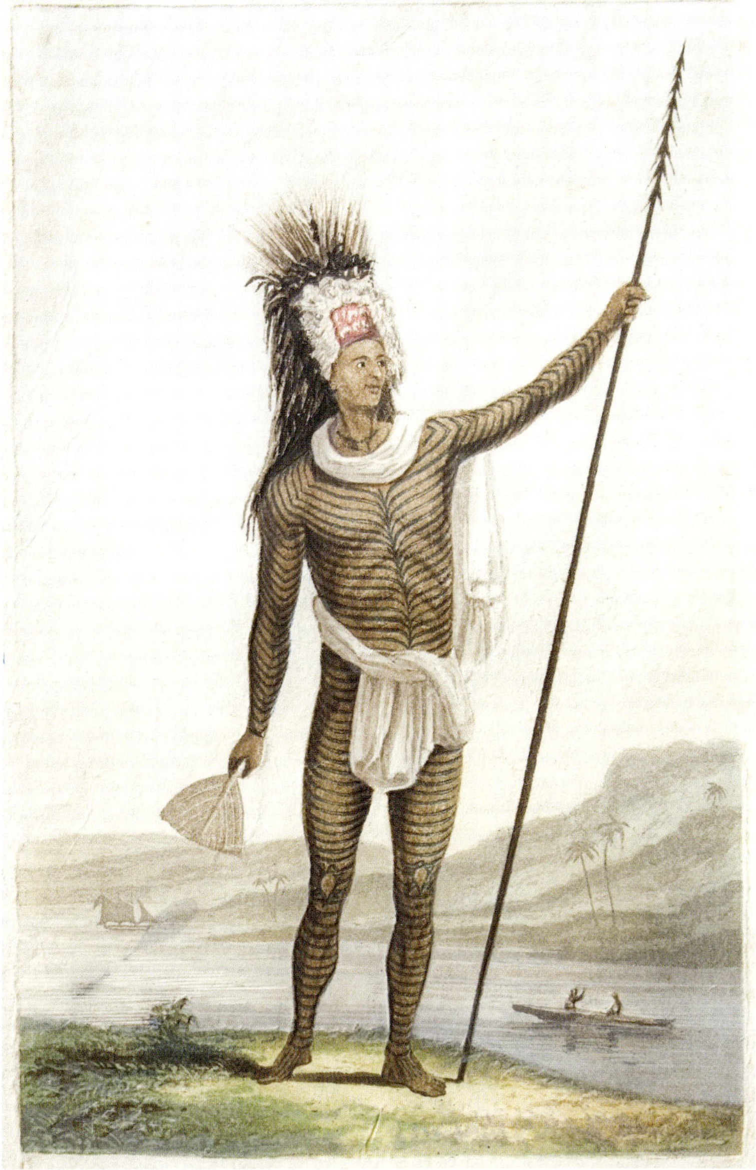

102 *Plaited fan from Rarotonga. Ex-LMS. Buck card file. Courtesy BPBM.*

103 *Plaited fan from Rarotonga. Ex-LMS. Buck card file. Courtesy BPBM.*

104 *Plaited fan from Rarotonga. Ex-LMS. Buck card file. Courtesy BPBM.*

105 *Plaited fan from Mangaia. Ex-LMS. Buck card file. Courtesy BPBM.*

106 *Janus figure handle of fan; central Cook Islands. LMS 58.*

105

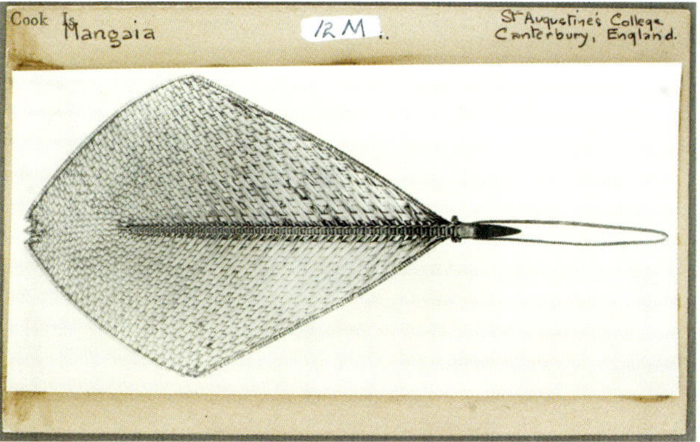

102

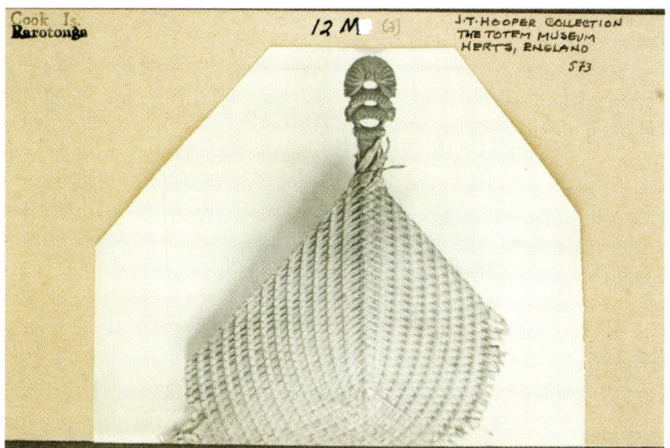

103

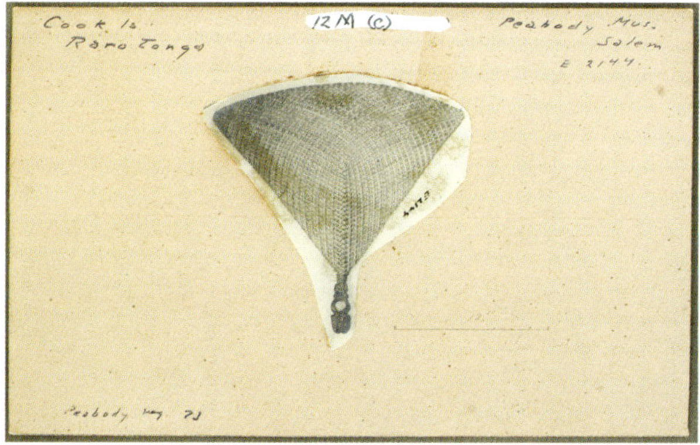

104

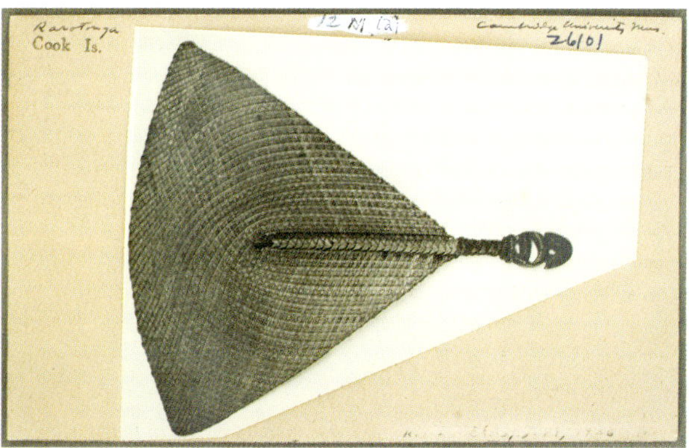

106

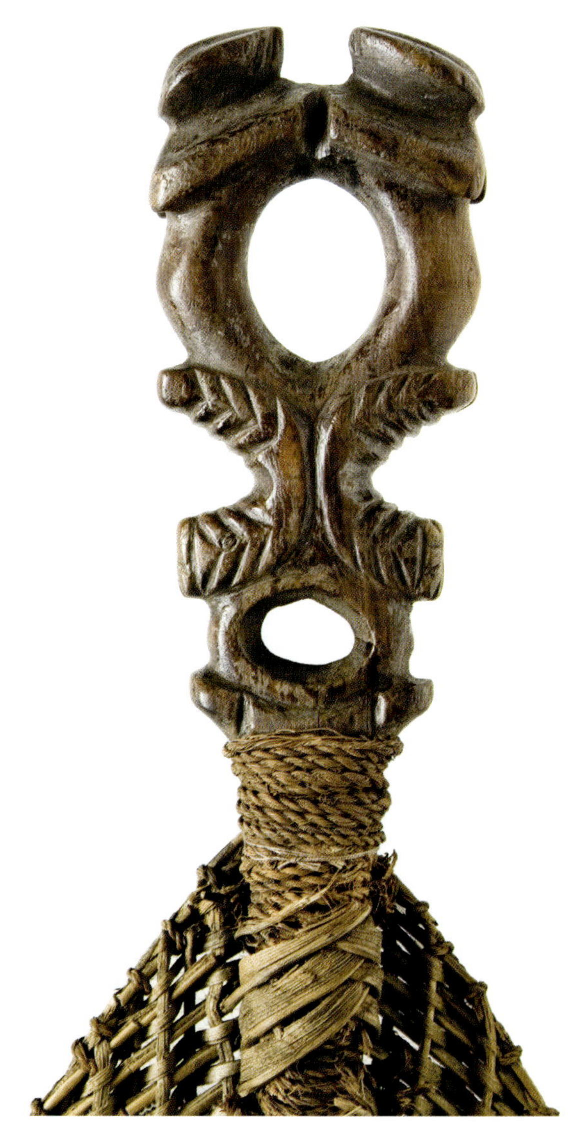

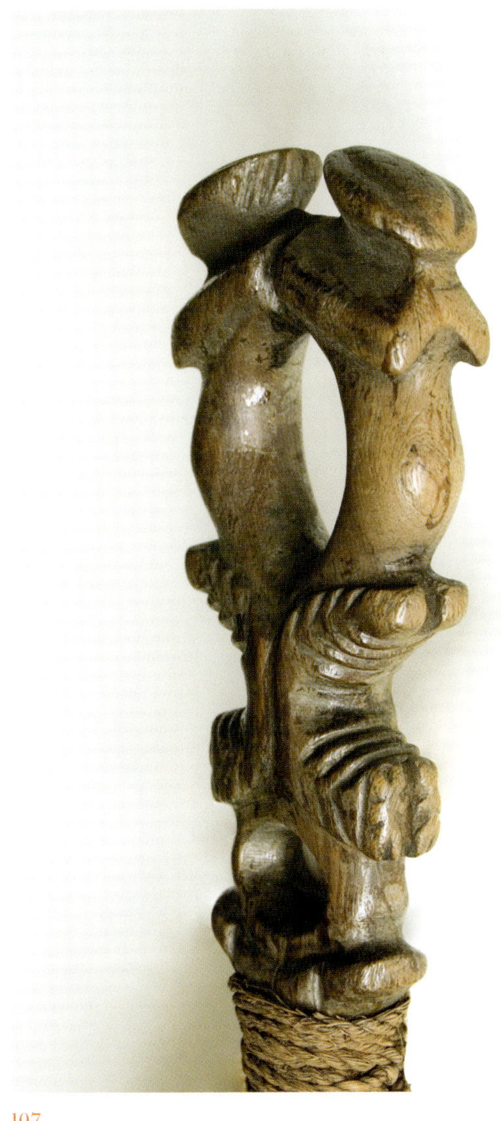

107

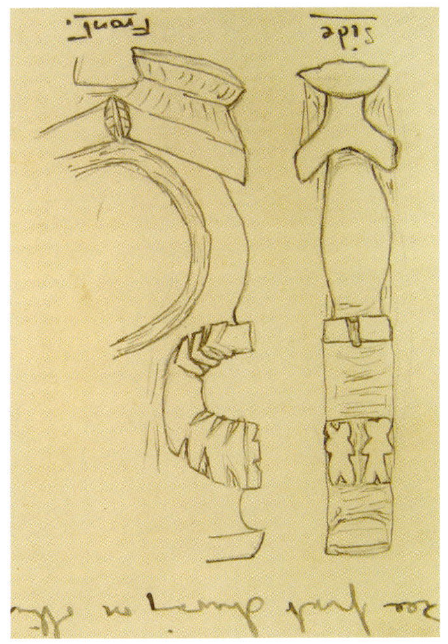

108

107 *Janus figure handle of fan. Carved portion 13cm. LMS 58.*

108 *Drawing of fan handle of LMS 58 by Peter Buck. Courtesy BPBM.*

109 *Buck card photograph from BM glass negative xxxvii/9, which was made about 1912. LMS 58. Courtesy BPBM.*

109

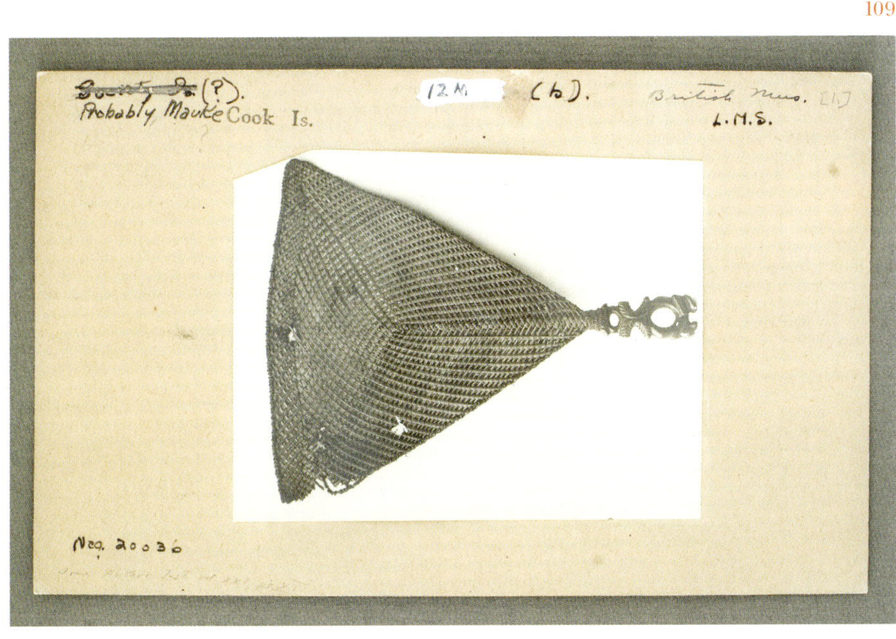

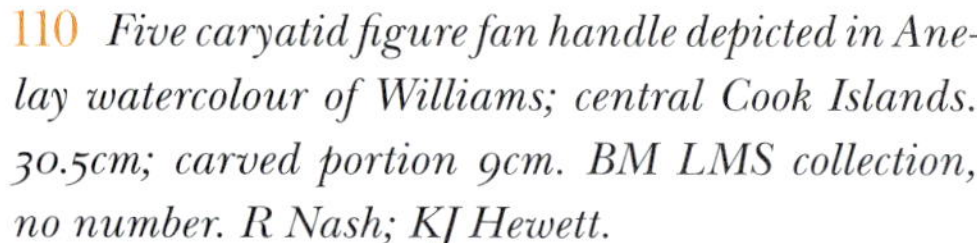

110   *Five caryatid figure fan handle depicted in Anelay watercolour of Williams; central Cook Islands. 30.5cm; carved portion 9cm. BM LMS collection, no number. R Nash; KJ Hewett.*

111   *A fan handle cut down, according to the registration slip; feathers formerly attached to tip are now largely missing. 16cm. LMS 108.*

112   *Four complete flywhisks; Rurutu. Whisks of straight- and helically-formed sennit, dyed black in the mire of a taro bug. Worked pearl oyster shell elements on lower whisk were probably imported from the Tuamotus, and rattled during oratory. Handles ~36cm. G Bennet; Sheffield Museum. CUM Z5026A-D.*

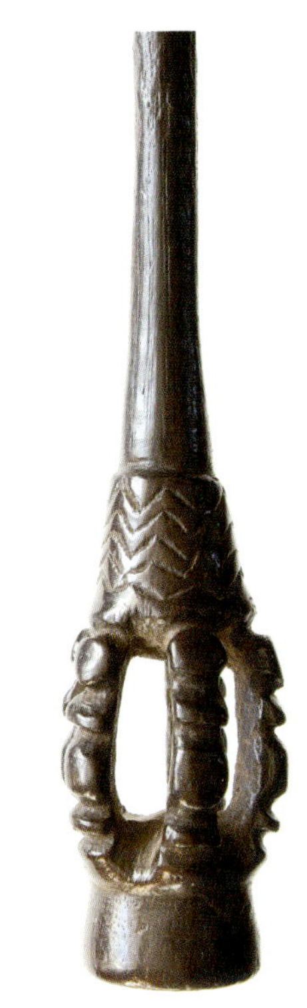

110

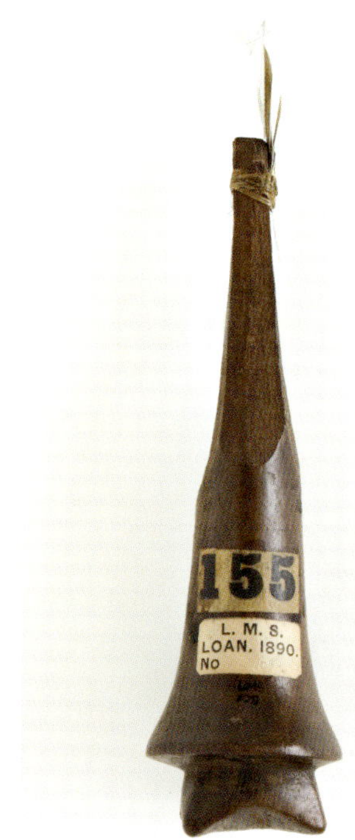

111

112

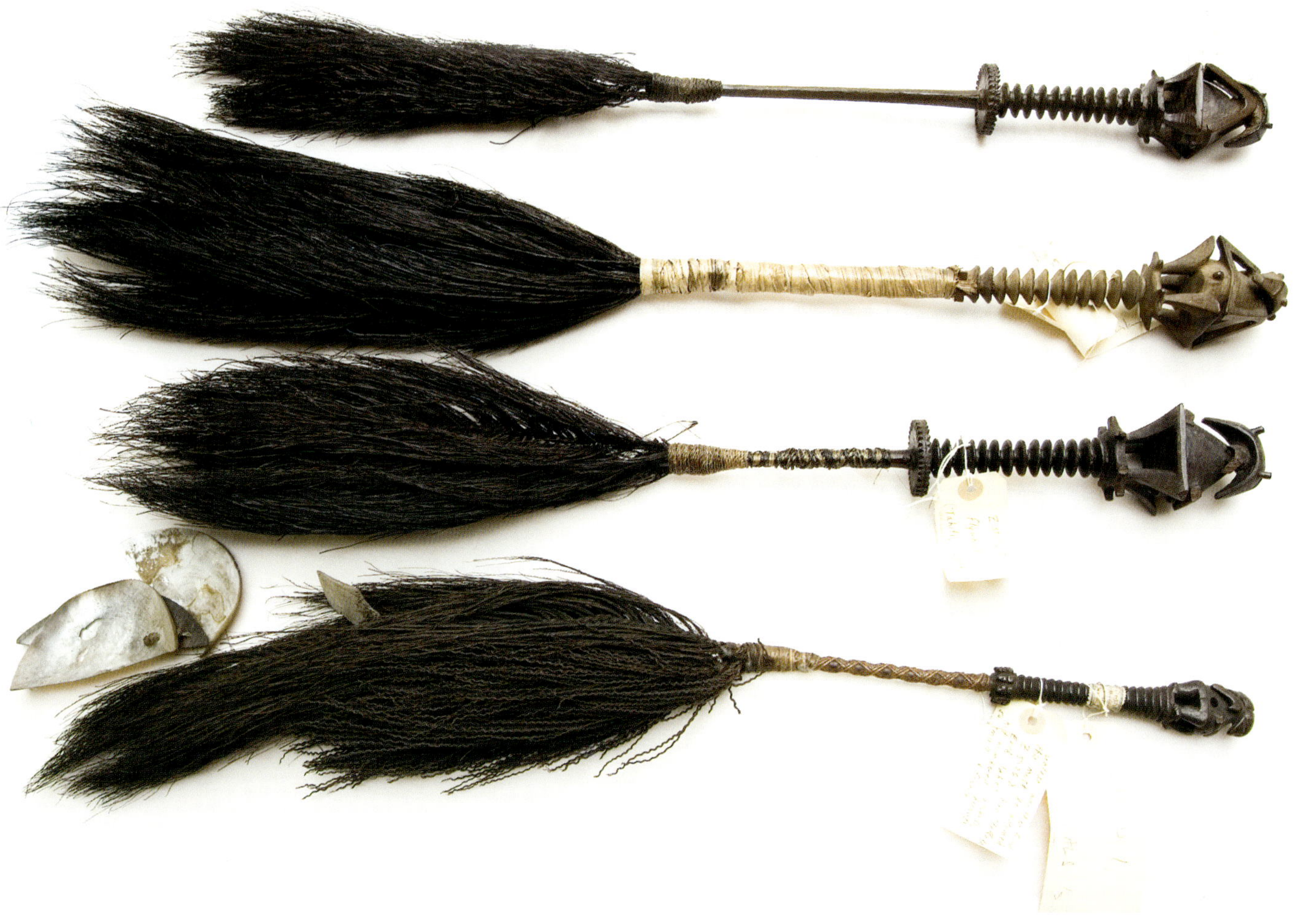

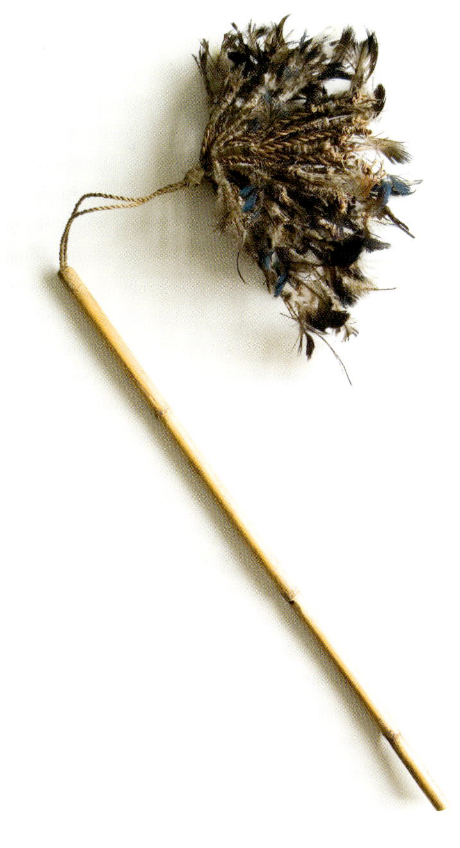

113

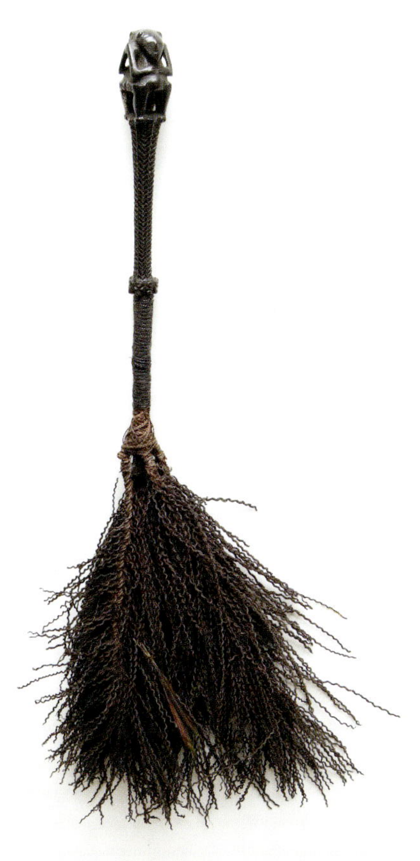

114

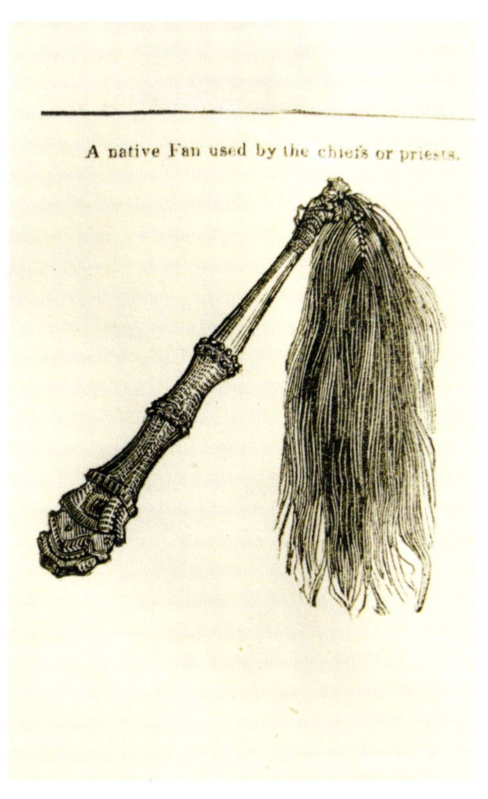

115

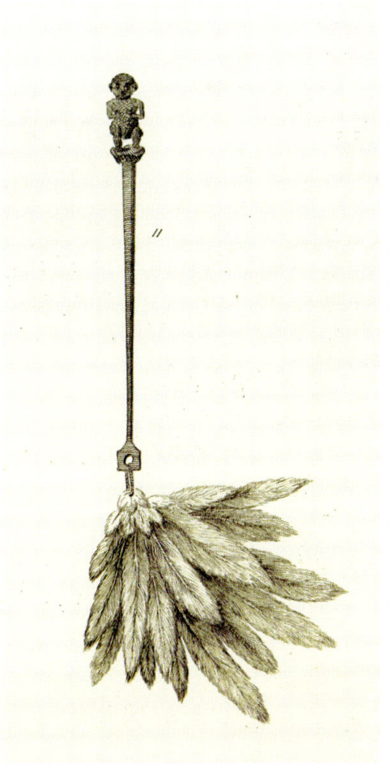

116

113 *Flywhisk with bamboo handle. Whisk is composed entirely of tufts of blue feathers bound with sennit. Feathers are probably from the small blue Tahitian lorikeet,* Vini peruviana *(a misnomer). A type often mentioned by the early explorers (see Parkinson engraving below) and the missionaries, this appears to be the only intact feather flywhisk that still exists. Handle 30.5cm. Tahiti, 1792; Vancouver collection, BM. VAN 352.*

114 *Intact flywhisk with carved wood handle, and whisk of helically formed, dyed sennit; Rurutu. Total length 50cm. BM LMS 1910-260.*

115 *Flywhisk; Rurutu. Whisk of sennit. Wood engraving from Ellis 1829, vol 2, fp181. Actual object not located. The missionaries used the terms 'flywhisk' and 'fan' interchangeably.*

116 *'A Fly-flap, the handle made of hard brown wood, is thirteen inches long.' Whisk appears to be of feathers. Cook's first voyage; Parkinson 1773, plate XII. Plate title reads 'Otaheite & the adjacent islands'.*

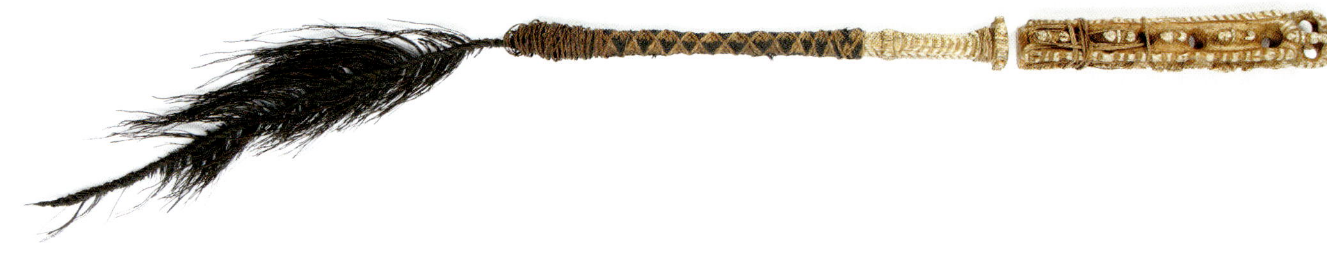

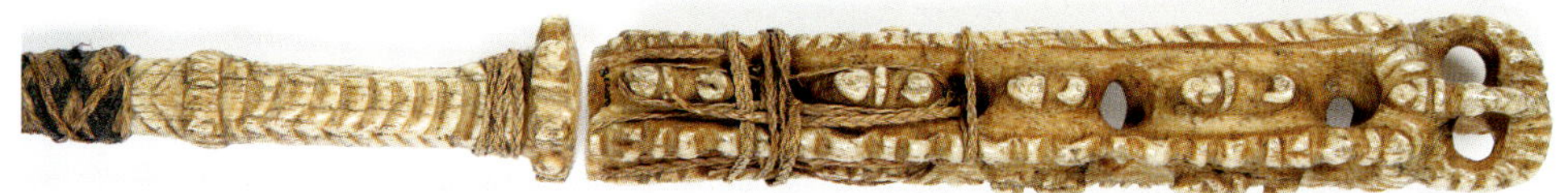

117   *Sennit flywhisk with carved whale jawbone handle. Handle 21cm. 'Given to Rev. E.S. Prout by Rev. J. Williams. Austral Group.' Ebenezer Prout was Williams' biographer. Oldman 381. Courtesy Auckland Museum.*

118   *Carved handle of Oldman 381. Courtesy Auckland Museum.*

119   *Wood engraving from* Missionary Sketches 3, *October 1818, N°9, illustrating LMS 57. This was one of Pomare II's family idols. SOAS.*

120   *Flywhisk handle of whale jawbone; probably Tahiti. 25cm. LMS 57.*

121   *Legend for N°9, cover,* Missionary Sketches 3, *October 1818. SOAS.*

No. 9.

TAHIVI ANUNAEHAU, the handle of the sacred fan with which the priest drove away the flies, while about his prayers and sacrifices. The fan is lost, the handle only remains. These sacred relics are very old and dirty; but they were reckoned no less sacred on that account.

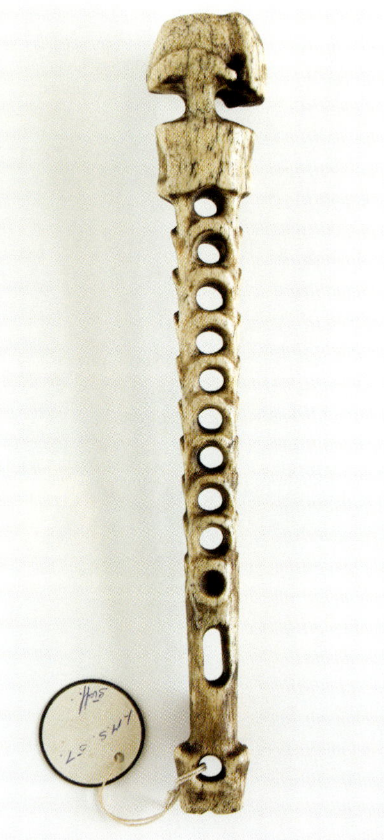

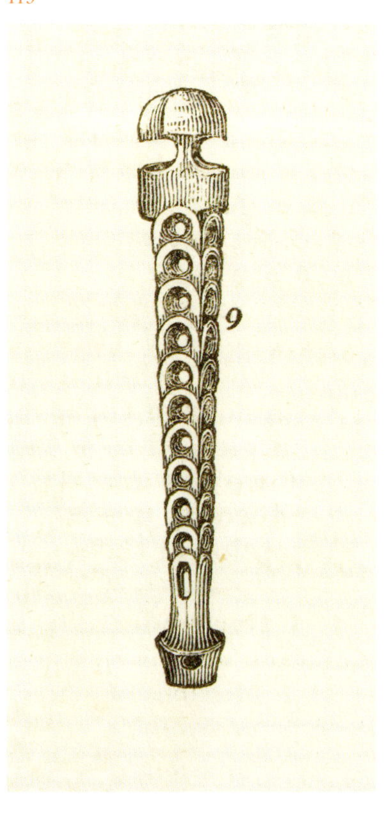

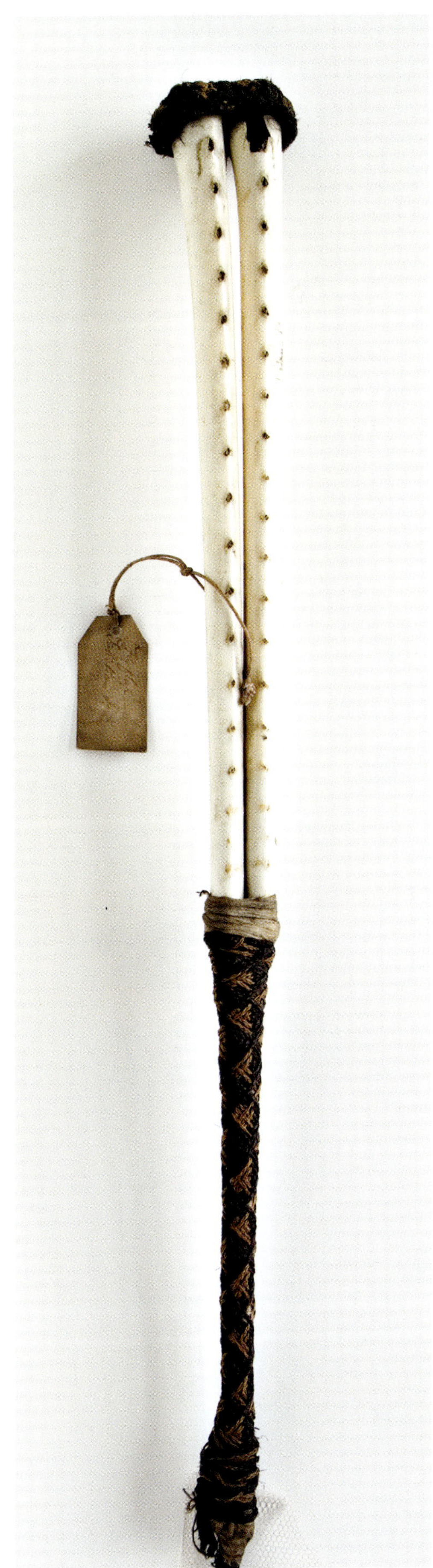

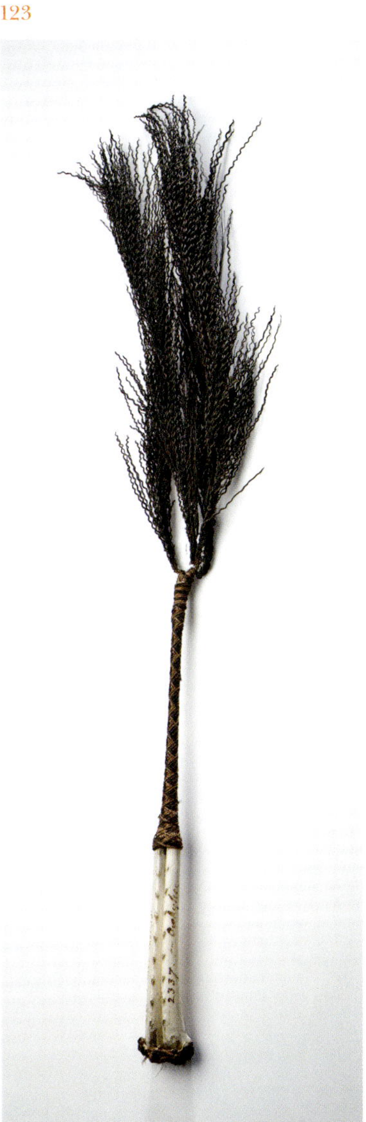

122 *Flywhisk handle of two frigate bird (Fregata) ulnae, intricate binding of human hair and fine sennit in* inaere *design (see Buck, 1944,46); Rurutu. Handle 29cm. BM LMS Oc.7051.*

123 *Intact flywhisk, with handle of two frigate bird (Fregata) ulnae; Rurutu. Inscribed 'Used to kill insects, from Owhyhee.' Handle 29cm. Acquired Dr Babbett, 1822. PEM 7122A2 (E5266); Courtesy PEM.*

124 *Intact flywhisk, with handle incorporating portions of frigate bird (Fregata) ulnae. Handle 19cm. (LMS) Oc1910,-255.*

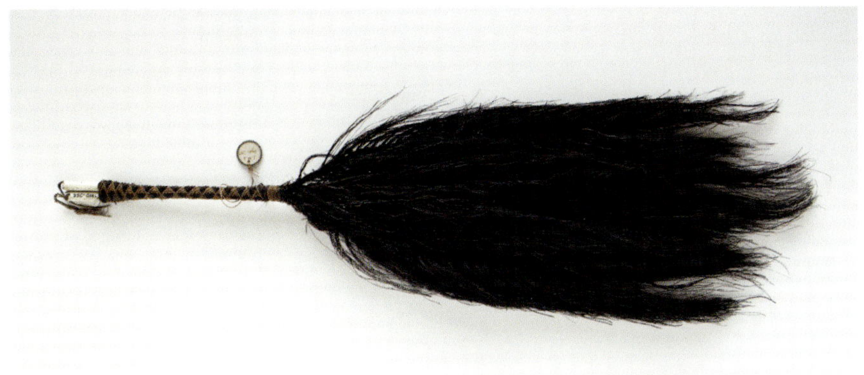

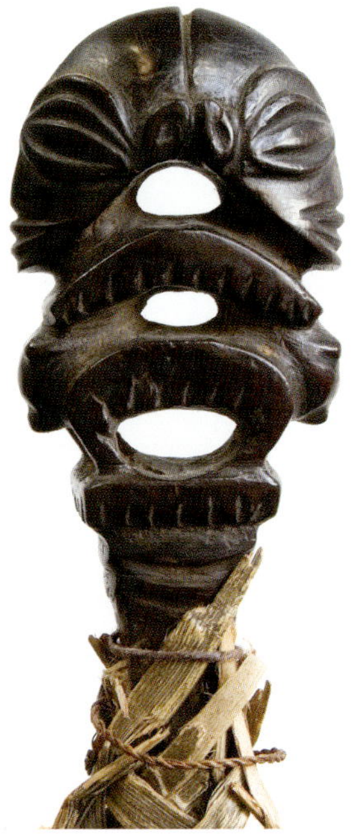

125 *Janus figure handle of fan; Rarotonga.
Carved portion 10cm. Entire fan shown in
fig. 102. J Williams; J Hooper 573.*

126 *Janus figure flywhisk handle; Rurutu.
Carved portion of handle 29cm. J Leff;
no collection data; identical to BM LMS
1910-260.*

127 *Janus figure terminus of Rurutu fly
flap handle. Figure ~9cm. G Bennet, Sheffield Museum; CUM Z5026B.*

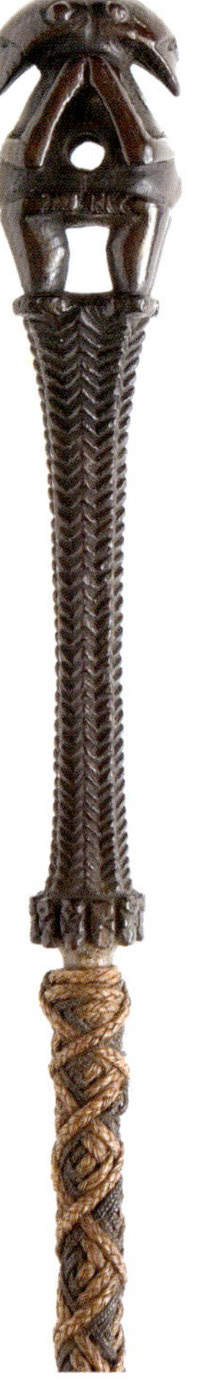

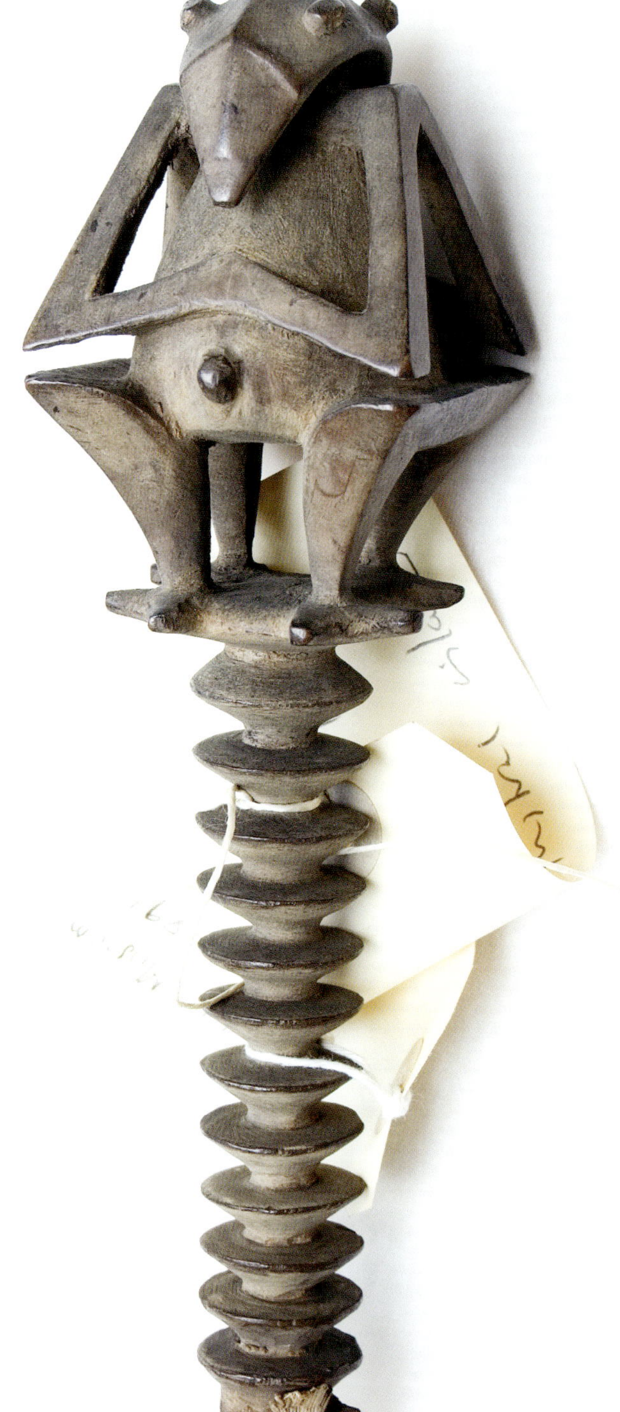

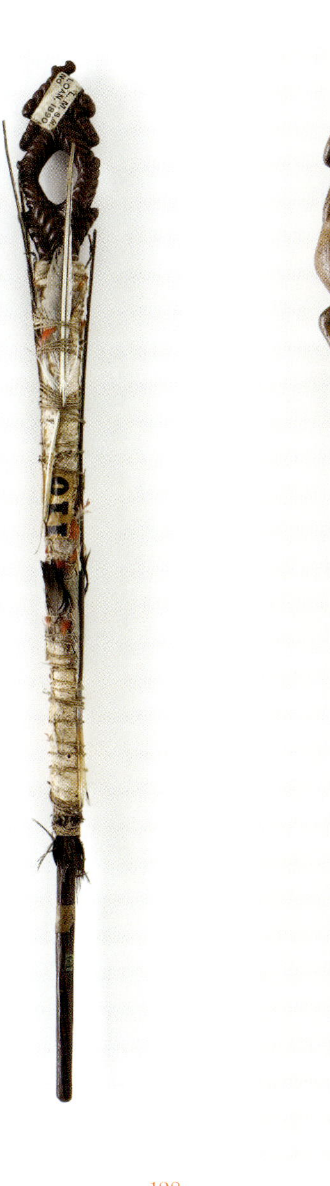

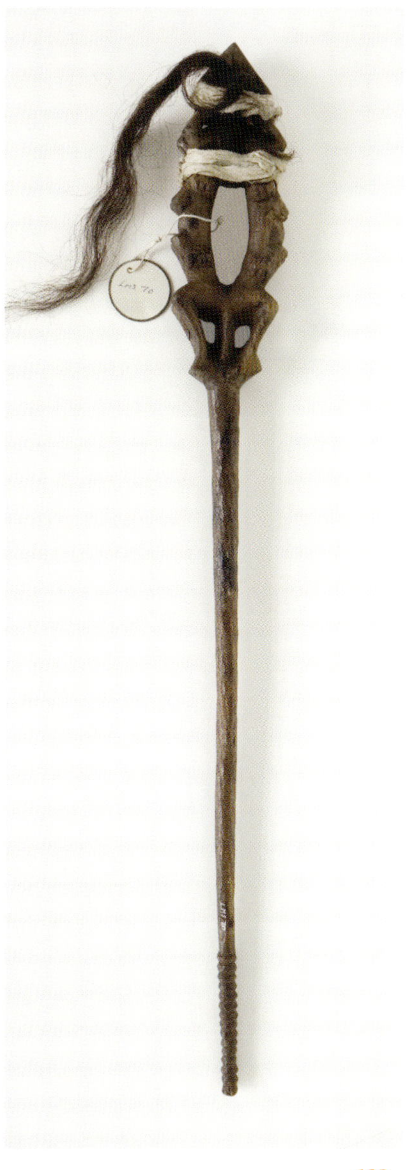

128 *Janus figure fan handle with feathers and white tapa bound with oronga. 47.5cm. LMS 131.*

129 *Detail of fan handle in figure 128.*

130 *Anelay Nº5. More realistic Janus figure fan handle; central Cook Islands. Feathers depicted in Anelay watercolour are now missing. 40.5cm. (LMS) TAH.139.*

131 *Detail of fan handle in figure 130.*

132 *Large fan handle, female Janus figure, human hair attached with white tapa; central Cook Islands. 56cm. LMS 70.*

133 *Detail of fan handle in figure 132.*

128 130 132

129 131 133

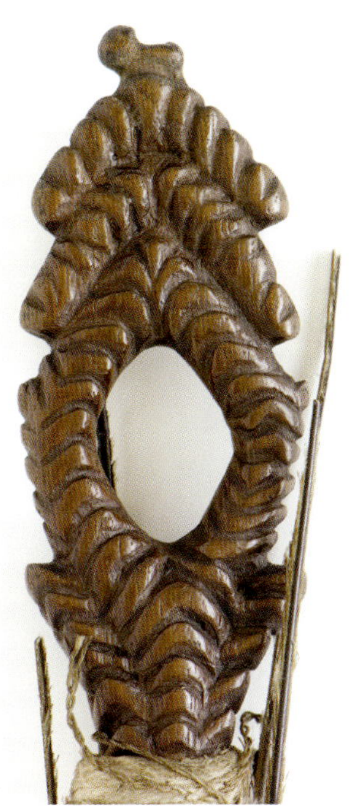

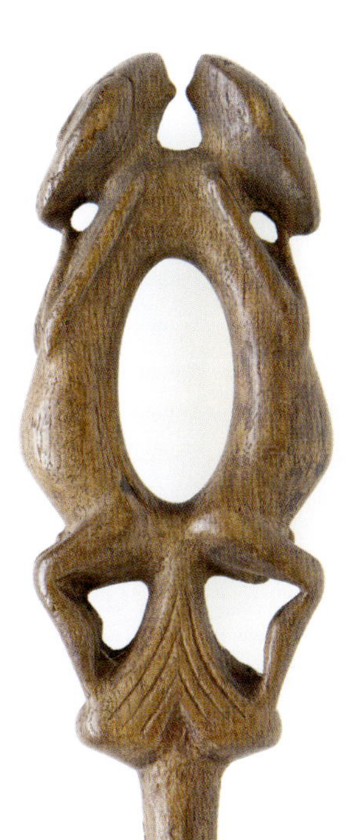

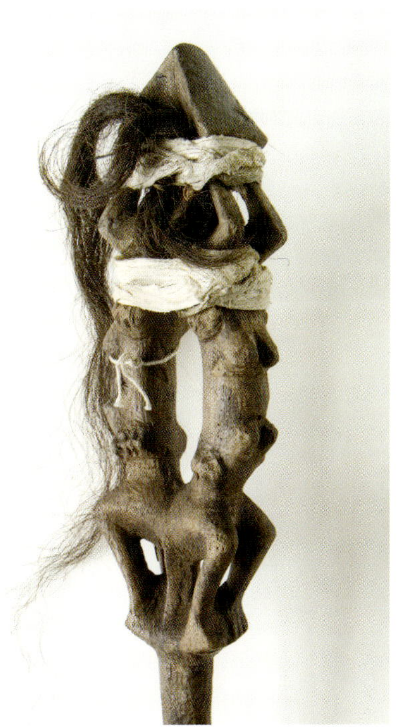

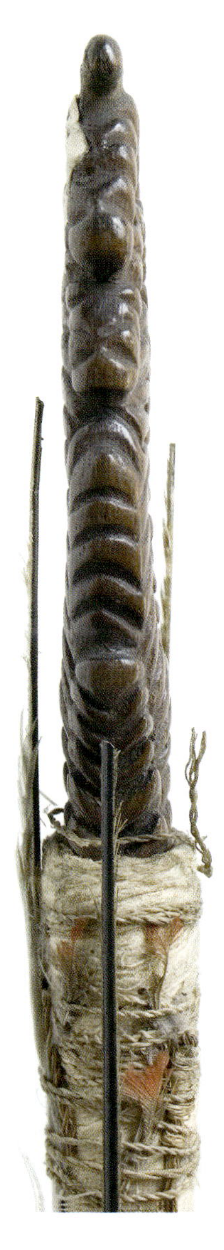

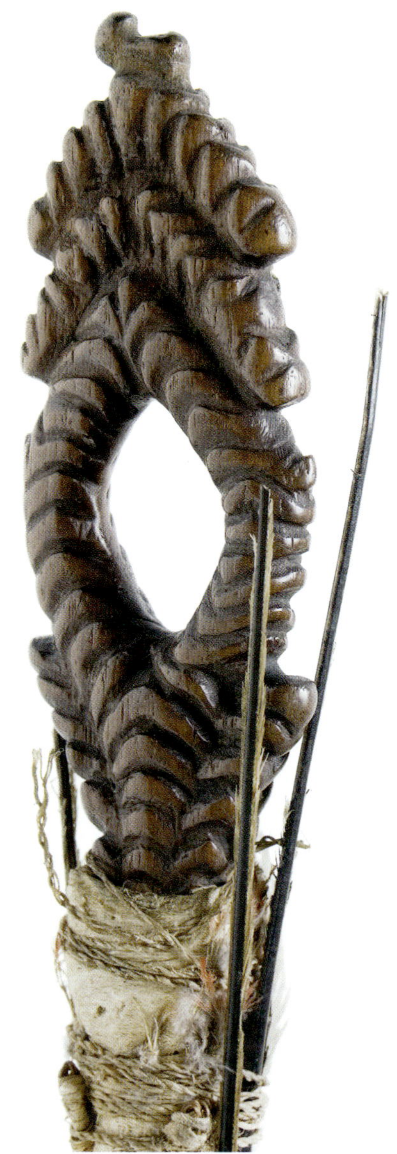

134 & 135 *Two views of fan handle with tropic bird feathers and kura bound onto the tang with white tapa and oronga; central Cook Islands. Carved portion ~9cm. (Also shown in figs. 128 & 129, preceding page.) Depicted in Read's plate XII, Nº5 (see fig. 91). LMS 131. Semi-abstract Janus figure resembles the one on handle of fan acquired on Atiu and depicted by Ellis 1777 (see figs. 142, 143).*

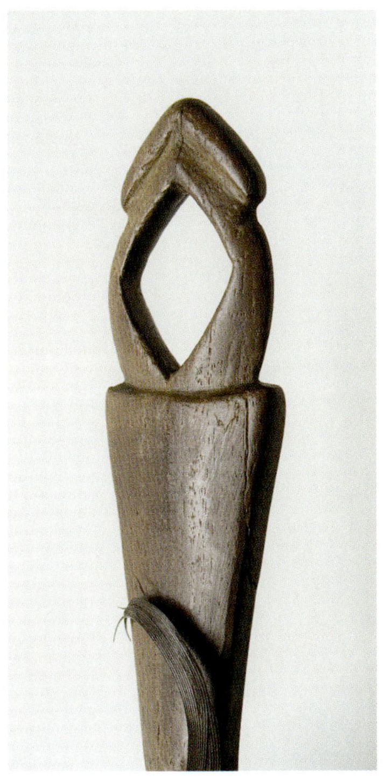

136

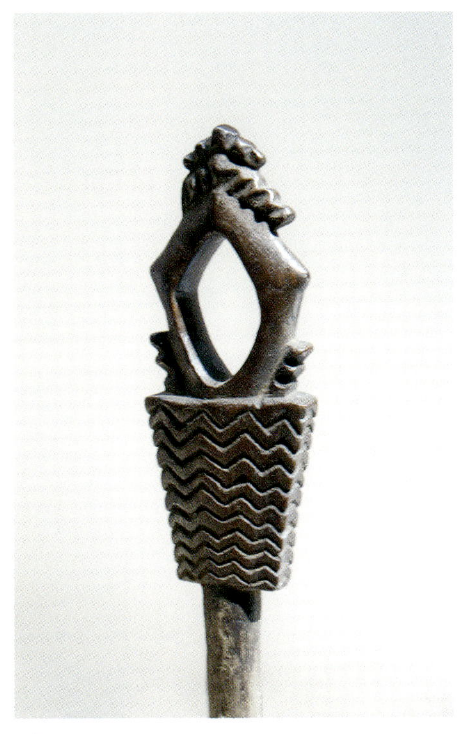

137

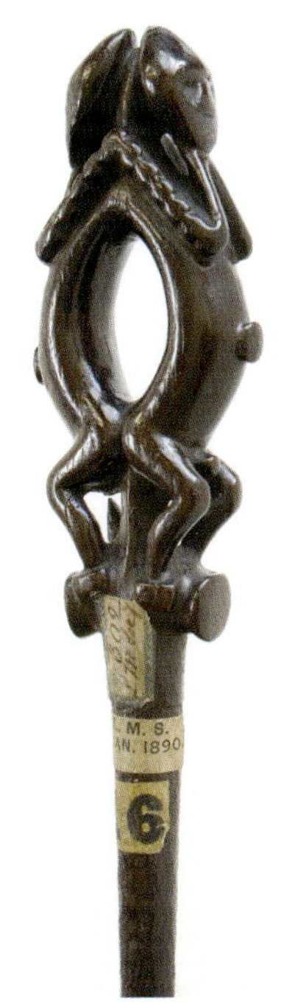

138

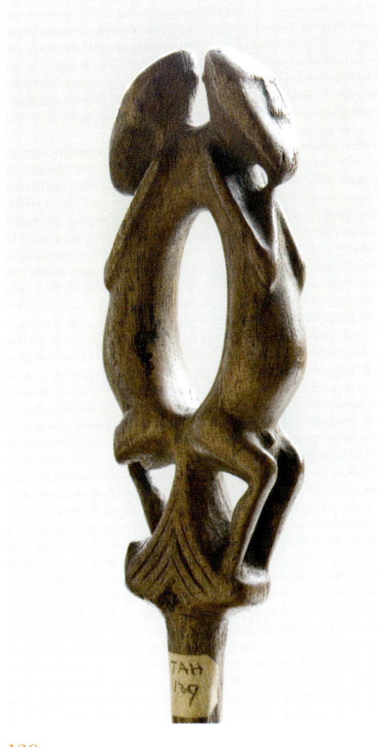

139

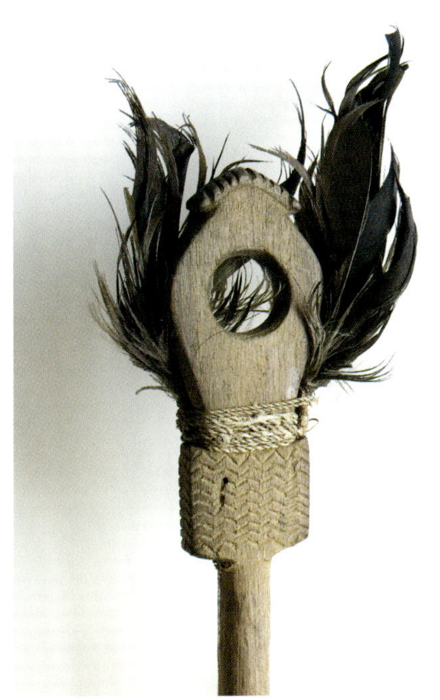

140

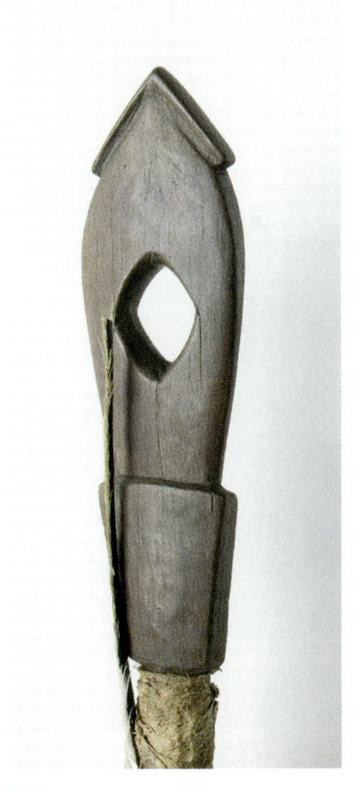

141

Janus figure fan handle feather gods, illustrating various stages in Read's continuum from the realistic to the abstract; central Cook Islands. The simple lanceolate handles (figs. 93, 96), are the most abstract.

136 *LMS 128.*

137 *LMS 132.*

138 *LMS 51.*

139 *TAH.139.*

140 *LMS 127.*

141 *LMS 129.*

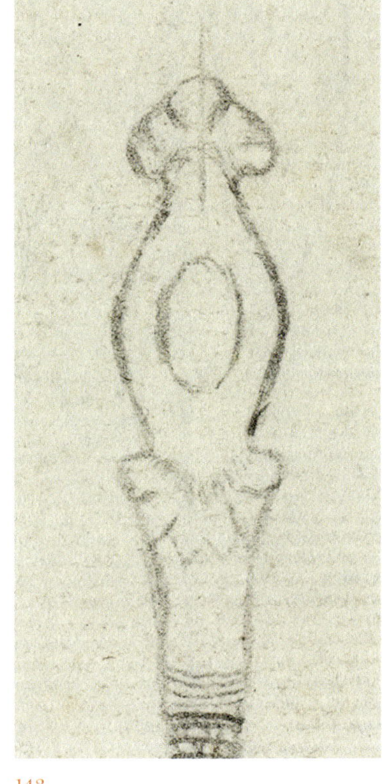

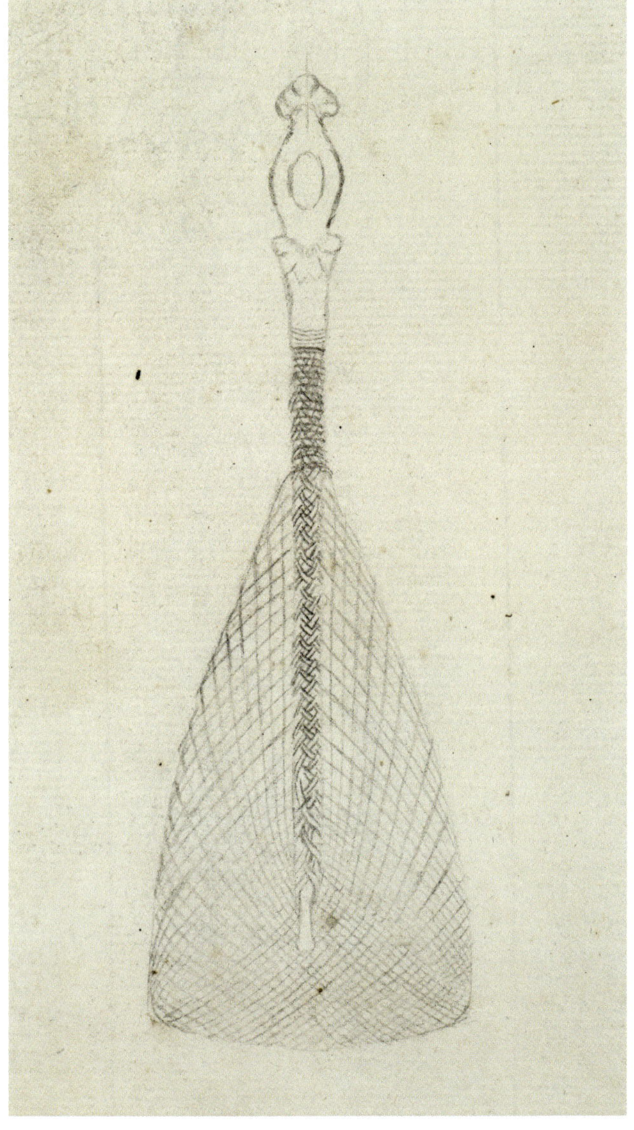

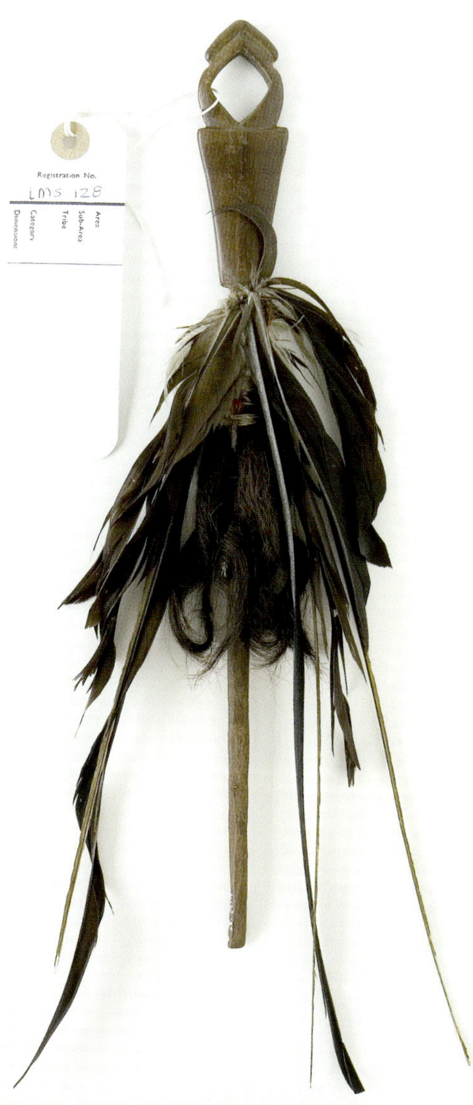

142 *Pencil drawing of a fan acquired on Atiu by William Ellis, artist and surgeon's mate on Cook's 3rd voyage, April 1777. This is the earliest known depiction of a Cook Islands object. Courtesy Alexander Turnbull Library, Wellington.*

143 *Detail of handle, an abstract Janus figure.*

144 *Abstract Janus figure fan handle converted into feather god; central Cook Islands. 33cm. LMS 128.*

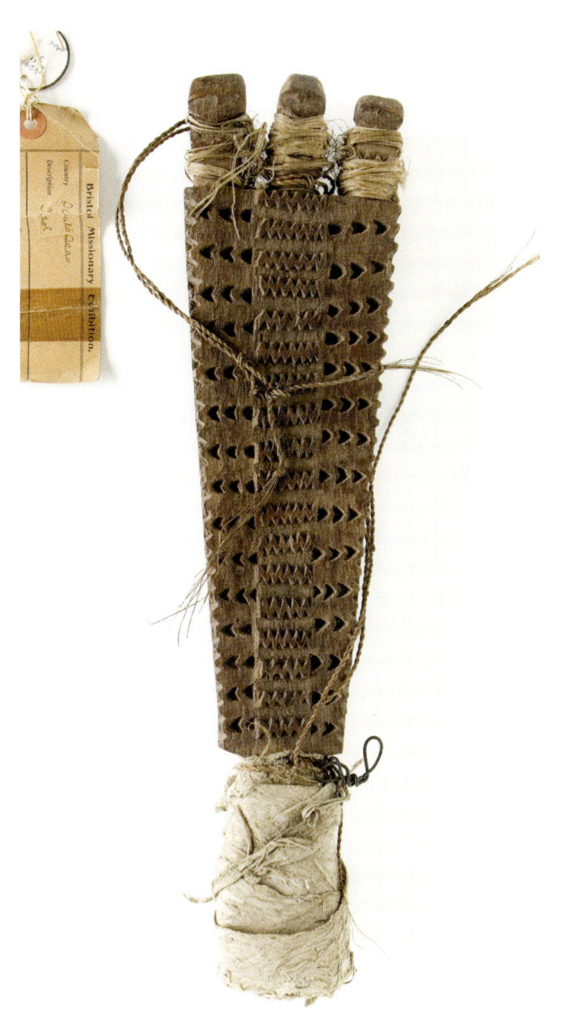

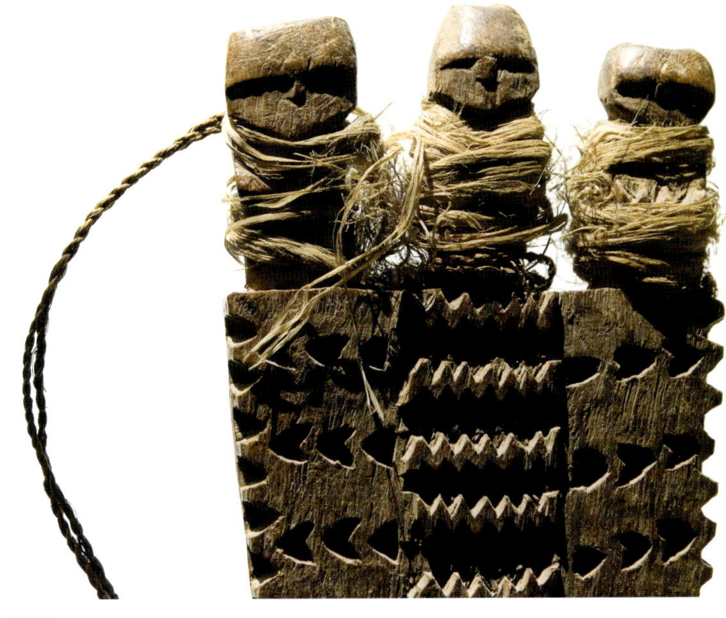

146

145 *Slab god; Aitutaki. Label indicates 'Bristol Missionary Exhibition'. 43cm. BM LMS Oc1939,11.3.*

146 *Three human figures at the top of BM LMS Oc1939,11.3.*

147 *Slab god, front; Aitutaki. 49cm. LMS 44.*

148 *Rear of slab god, with tail attached. LMS 44.*

145

147

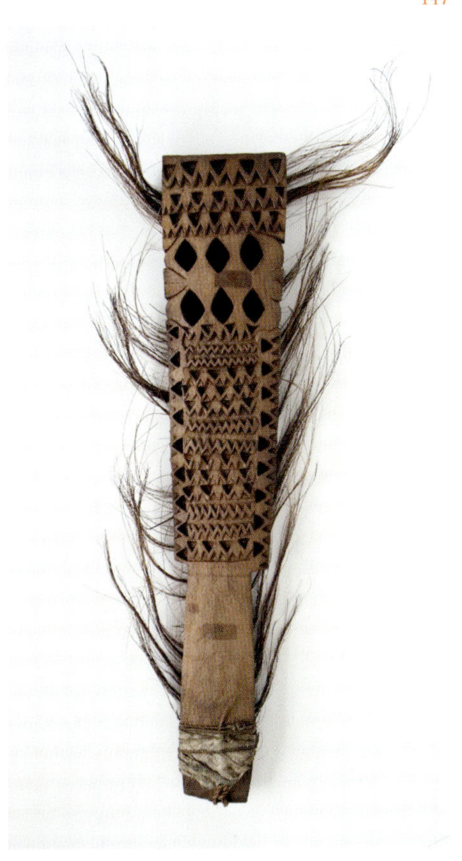

148

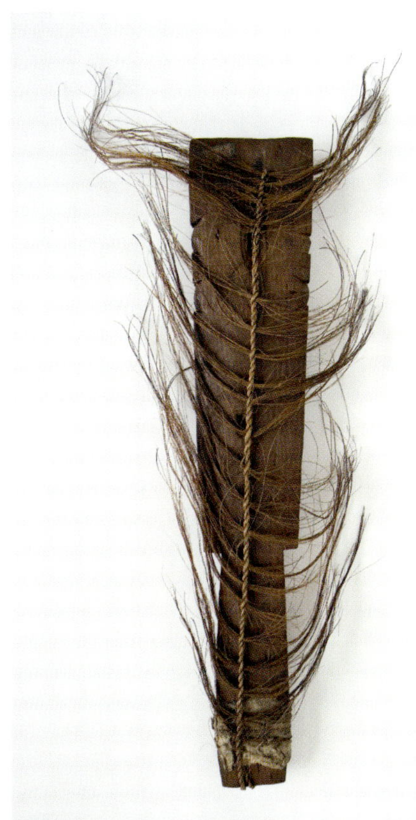

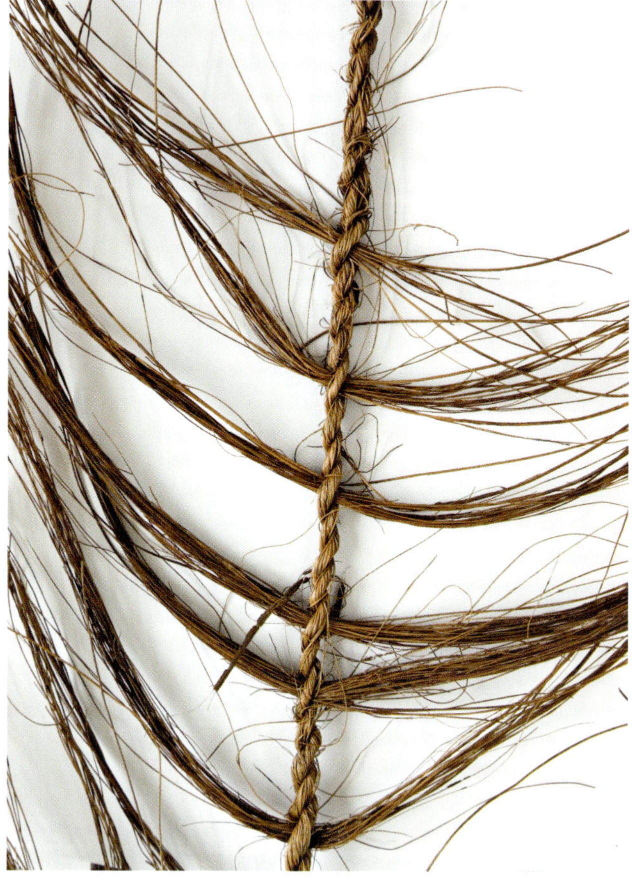

149

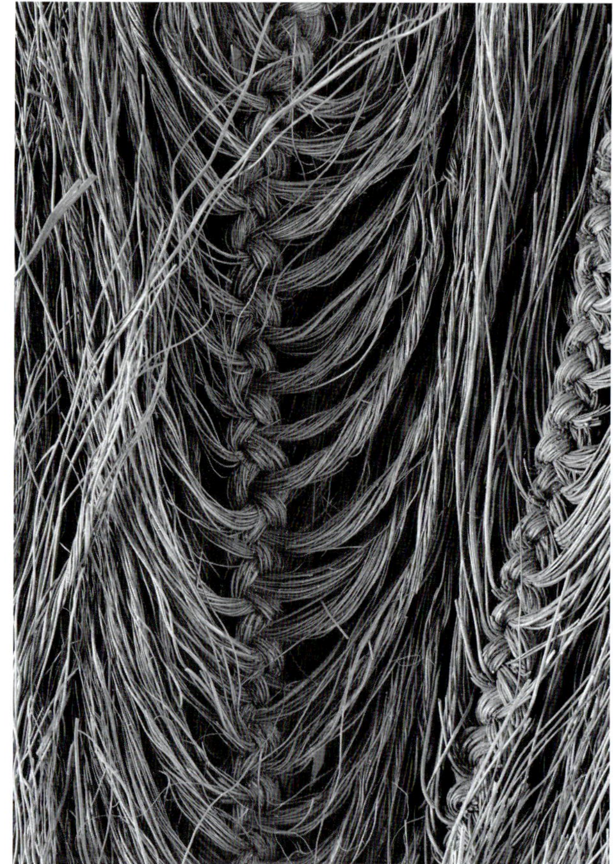

150

149 *Close-up of branched sennit tail of LMS 44, fashioned using Buck's technique a.*

150 *Close-up of branched sennit tail of LMS 46, fashioned using Buck's technique c.*

151 *Buck 1944 fig. 226, showing three techniques to produce branched sennit. Courtesy BPBM.*

152 *Elaborate branched sennit and feather tail portion of Aitutaki slab god. 53cm. LMS 46 (wood portion shown in fig. 155, opposite page). LMS registration slip notes: 'attached to it, [LMS 46] is a plaited tail of fibre bound at the end with fine cord with remains of feather plumes, now taken off as being separate object.'*

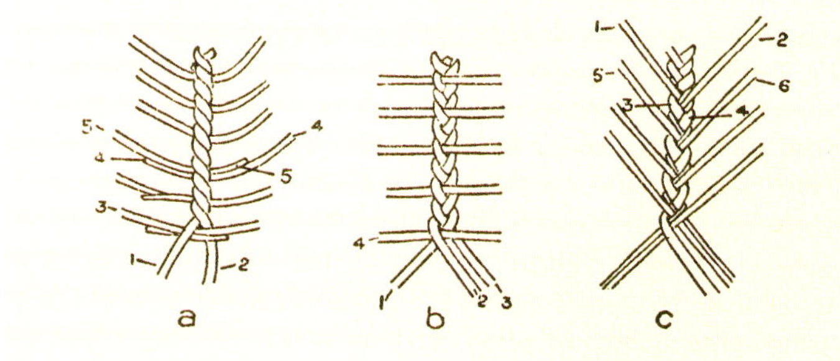

151

152

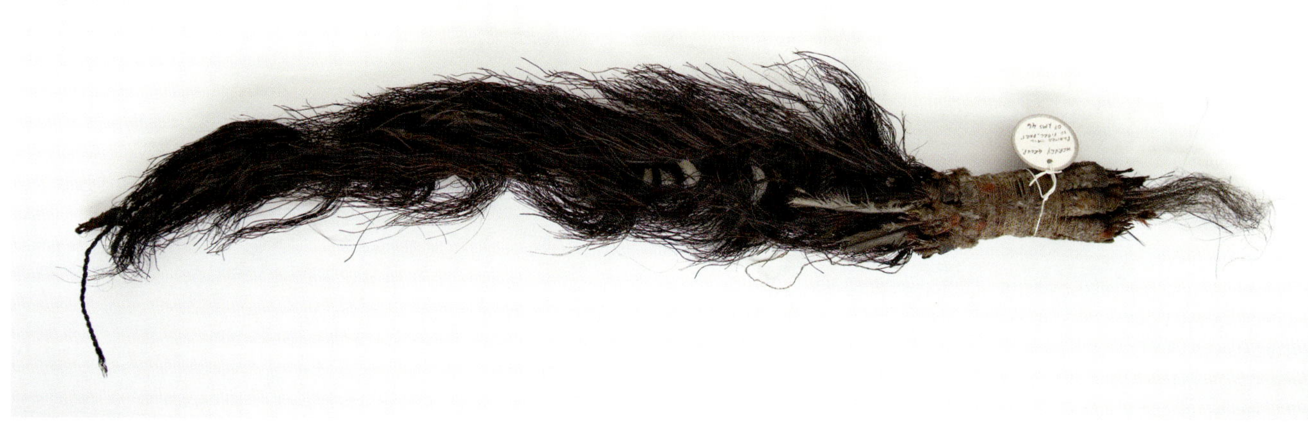

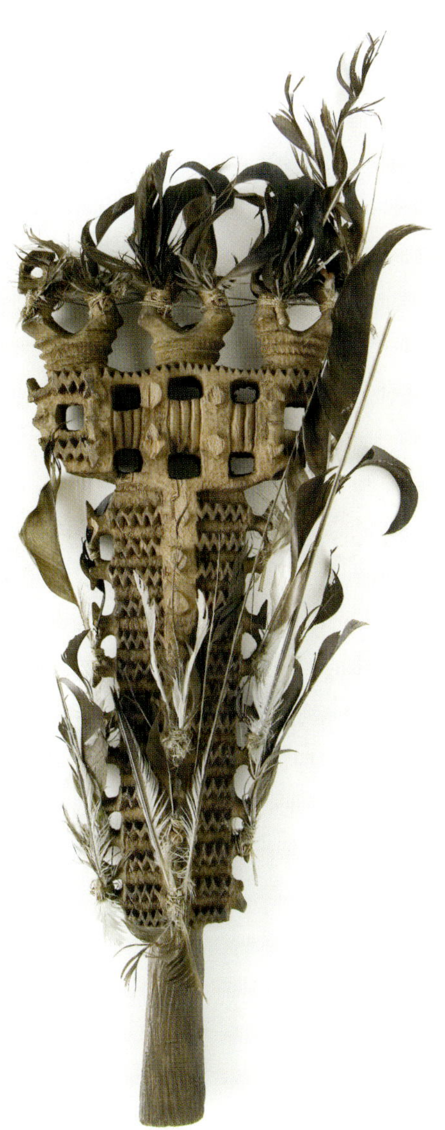

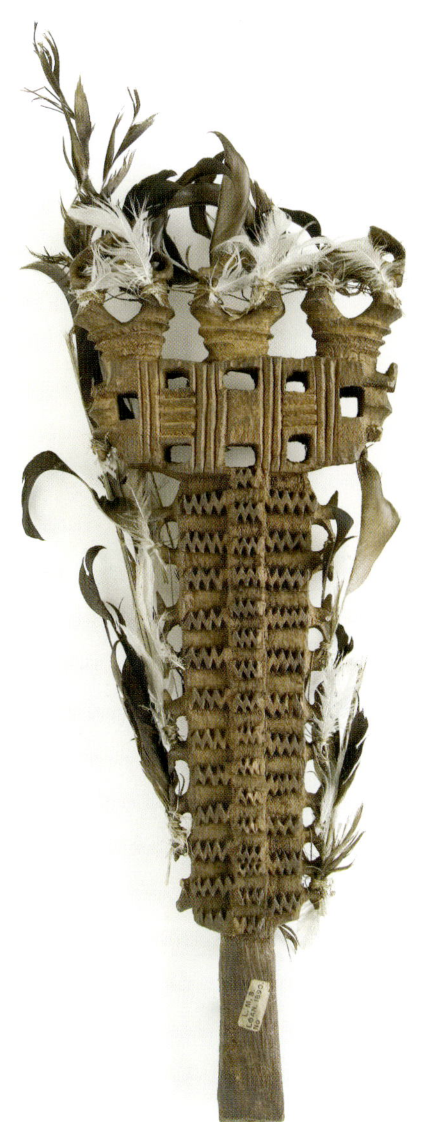

153 & 154 *Elaborate slab god with numerous feathers still attached to cleats; Aitutaki. 51cm. The cleats are identical to ones on Mitiaro godstaffs. LMS 45.*

155 *Wood portion of slab god; Aitutaki. 47.5cm. Possibly Nº12 on Papeiha's list, 'Family god called Vei with a tail which the priests take off & decorate themselves with when they wish to be inspired.' Tail shown in fig. 152. LMS 46.*

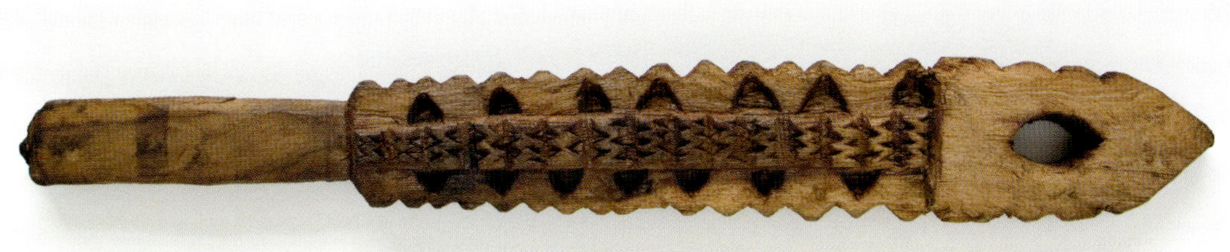

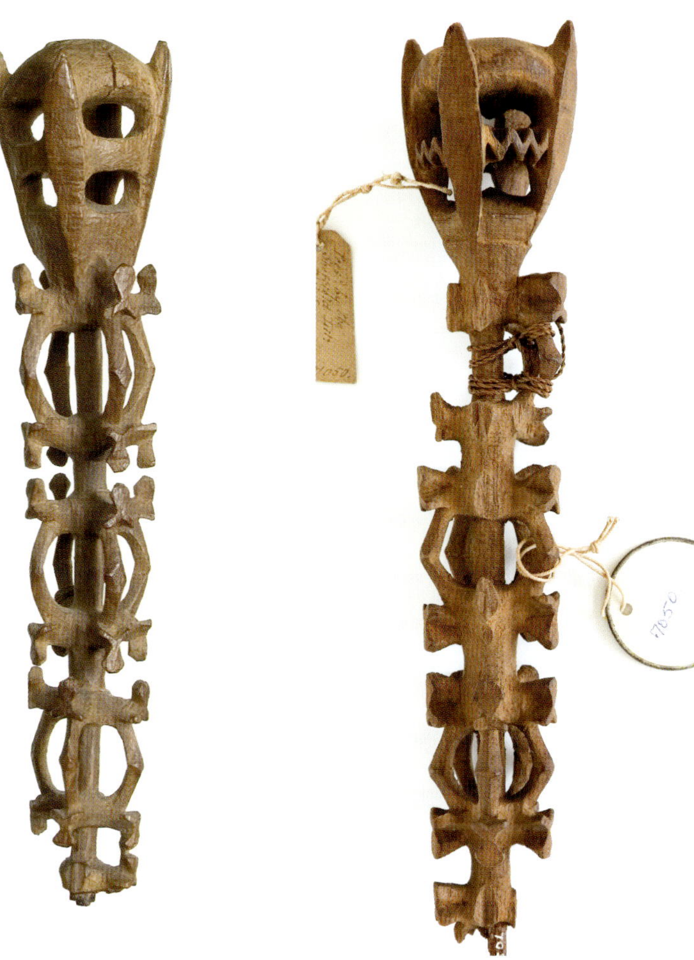

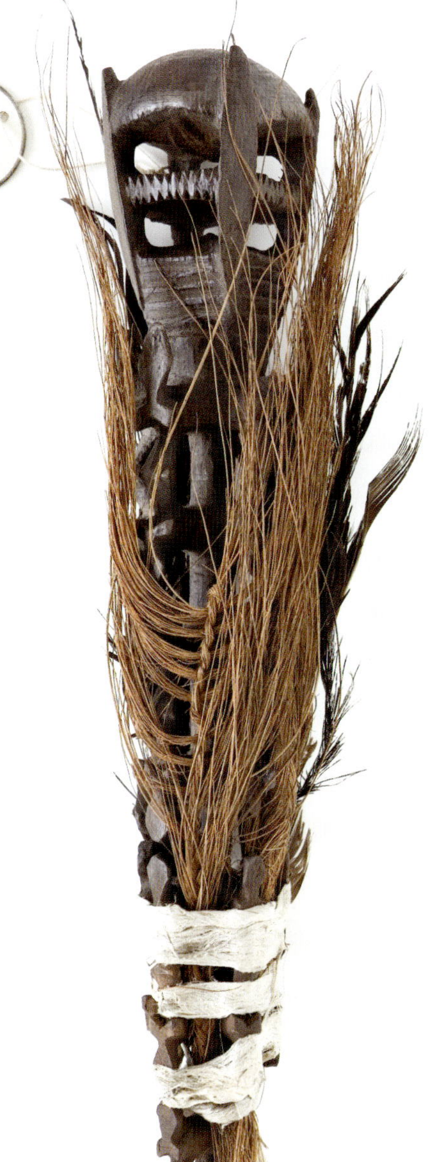

156

157

156   *Top portion of staff god; Mitiaro. 21cm. Presented to William Carey's museum at the Baptist Mission in Serampore by Tyerman and Bennet, 3 May 1826.*

157   *Top portion of staff god; Mitiaro. 24cm. Label reads 'Presd by the Sheffield Lit & Phil Soc 12.11.1871.' BM LMS Oc.7050.*

158   *Top portion of staff god; Mitiaro. 32cm. Likely Ellis frontispiece vol 2 N°4 (see fig. 161), with sennit and feather tail elements remounted upwards. LMS 48.*

159   *Intact staff god; Mitiaro. 40.5cm. Probably all of these staff gods were collected on the July 1823 LMS Endeavour voyage. BM LMS Oc1982,Q.121.*

158

159

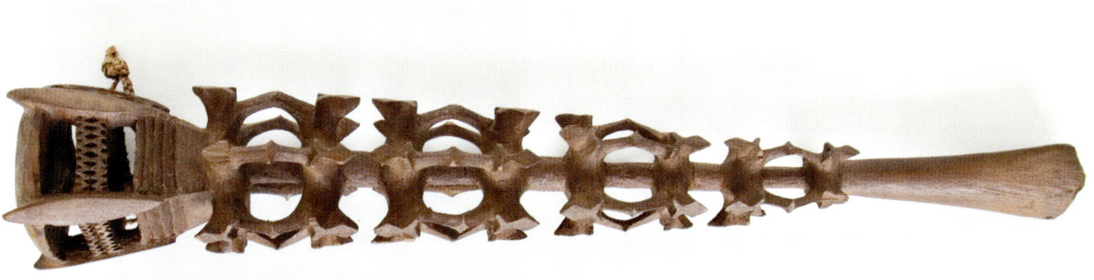

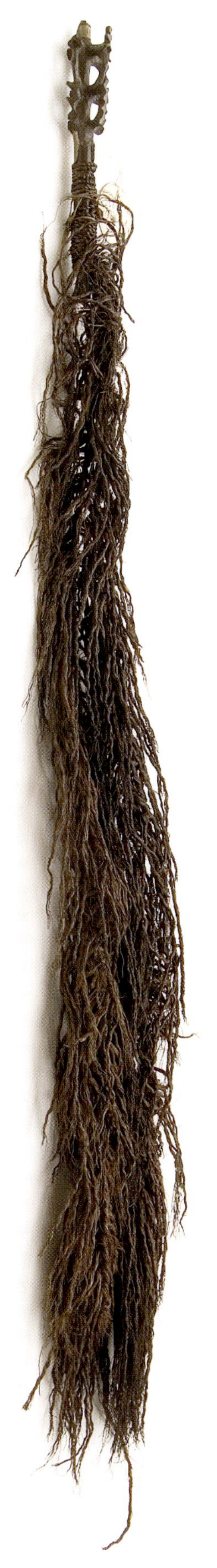

160 *Lower carved wood segment of a Mitiaro staff god with long branched sennit tail attached to the spatulate end; tail is in a remarkably good state of preservation. 75cm. G Bennet; Sheffield Museum exchange, 1890. CUM Z.6046.*

161 *Ellis 1829, frontispiece vol 2 N°4, sennit and feather tail still attached.*

162 *Detail of remaining lower wood portion of Mitiaro staff god CUM Z.6046; entire object shown at left (fig. 160). ~7cm shown here. Exceptionally delicate wood carving.*

163 *Top view of broken Mitiaro staff god, remaining lower wood portion with long sennit tail attached, similar to CUM Z.6046, showing pentamerous symmetry of carving; same provenance. CUM Z.6045A.*

161

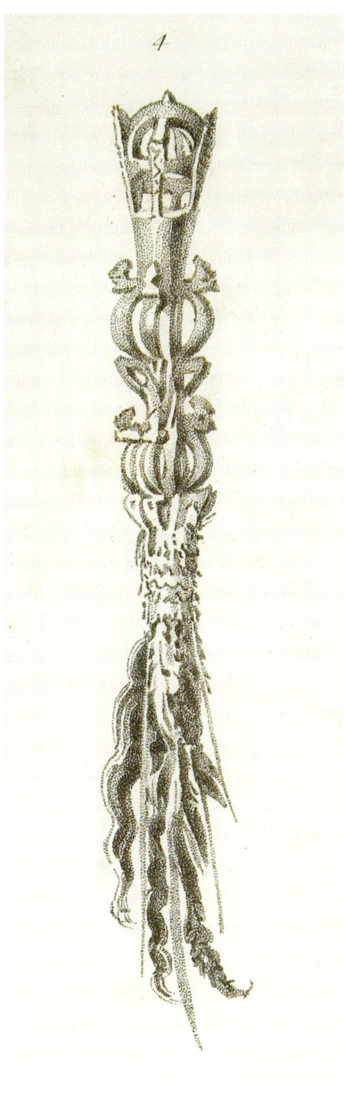

162

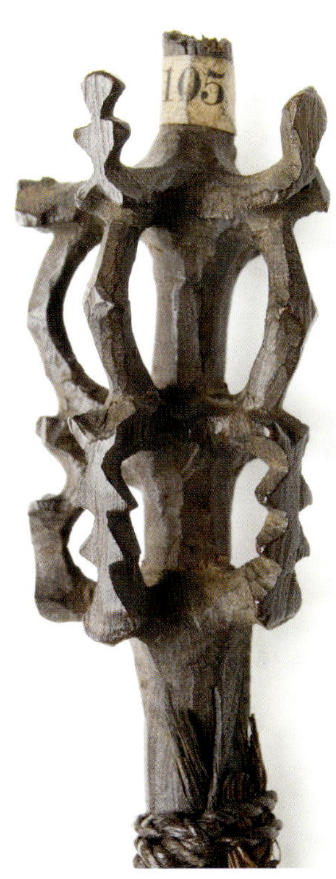

163

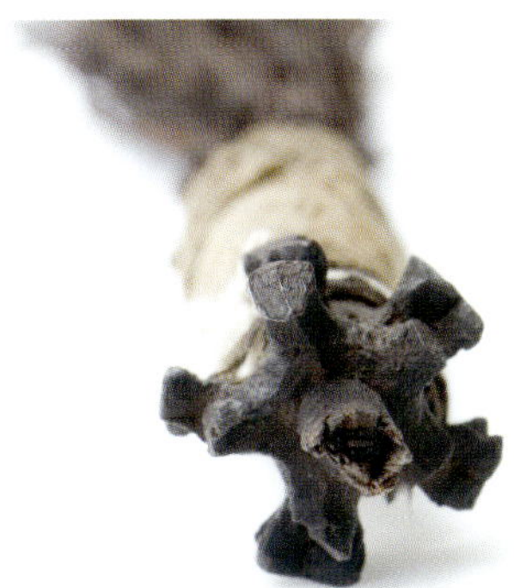

160

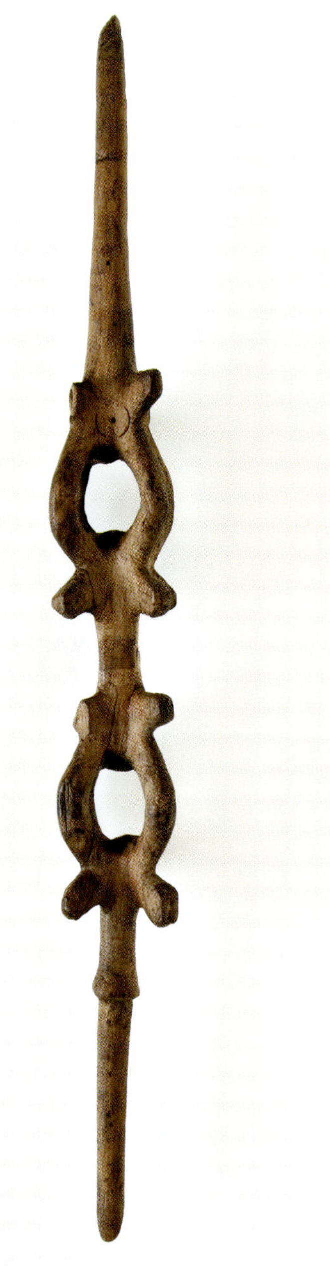

164 *A unique carved wood object, probably also a staff god from Mitiaro. 62cm. LMS 209.*

165 *Finely carved Mitiaro godstaff. 23cm. Label on top reads 'Exch Sheff Mus 18++2 AF.' AF is Augustus Franks, Keeper, Department of British and Medieval Antiquities and Ethnography, BM, 1866–96. BM LMS +2060.*

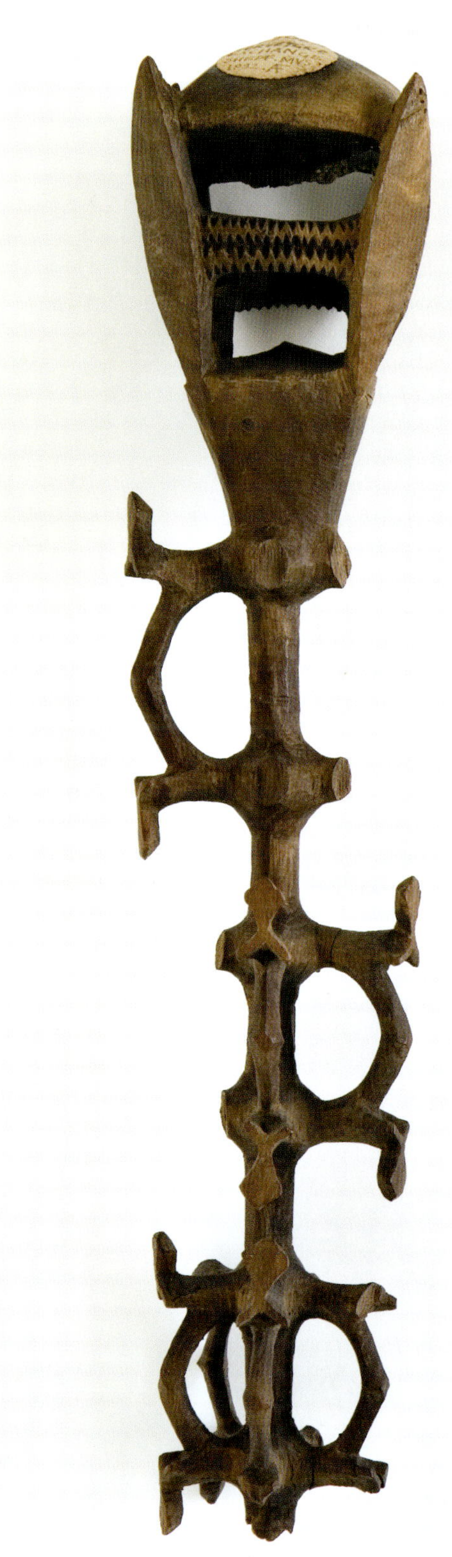

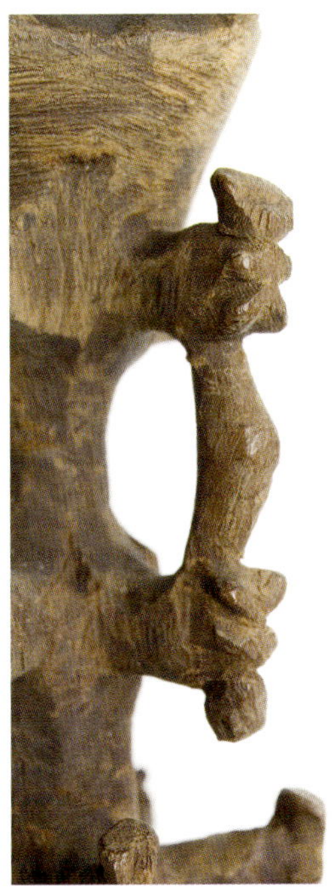

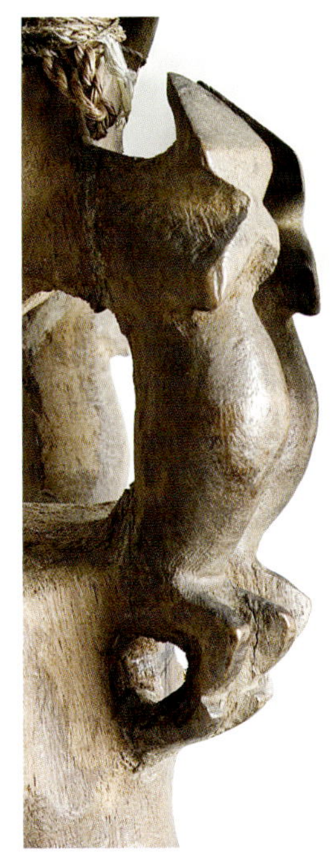

166

167

168

169

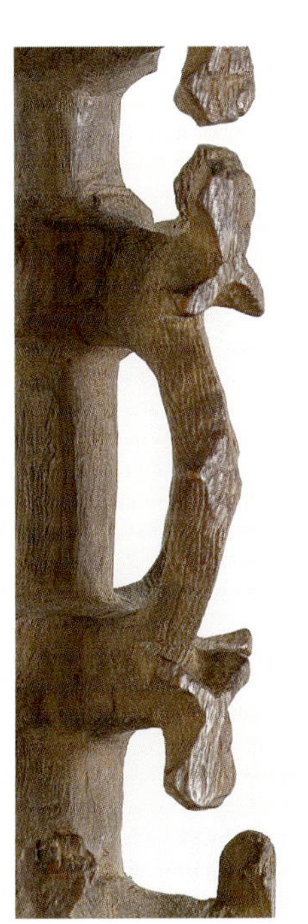

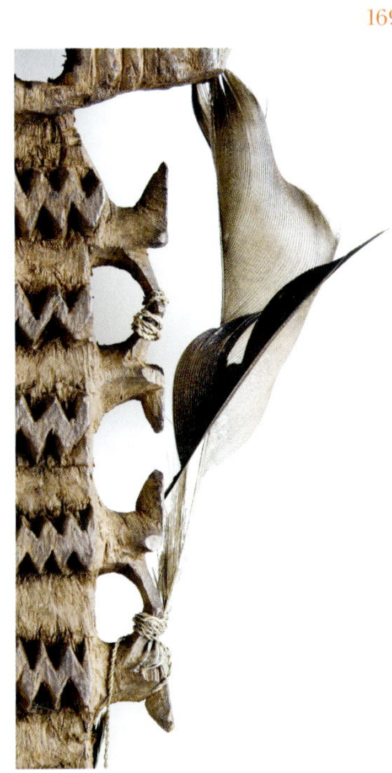

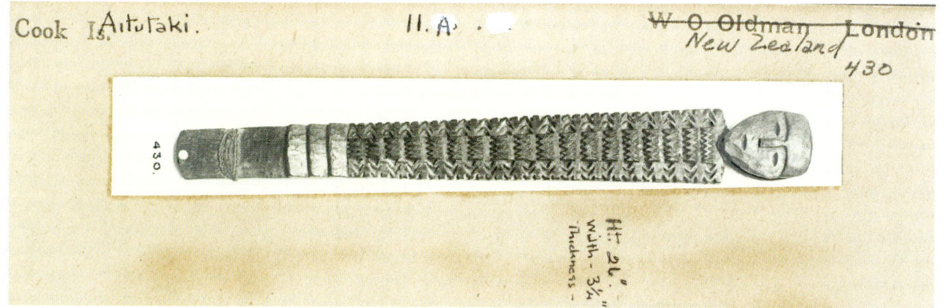

170

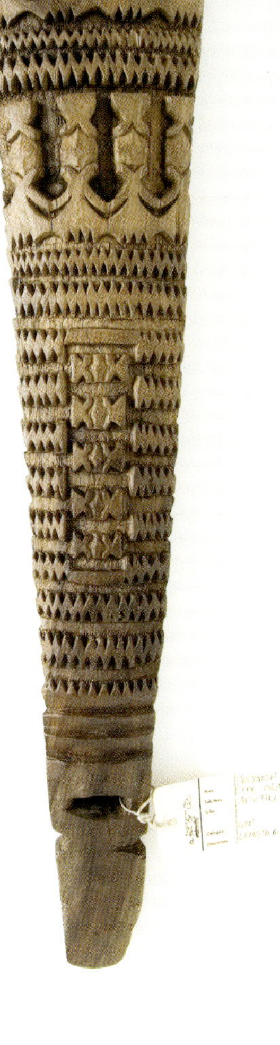

170 *Buck card of Aitutaki slab god. 66cm. 'Believed to have been brought home by Rev. John Williams. Hervey Group.' Oldman 430. Courtesy BPBM.*

171 *Slab god with tail. Ellis 1829 frontispiece vol 2, N°2; actual object not located.*

172 *Slab god; Aitutaki. 66cm. BM LMS Oc1982,Q.120.*

173 *LMS 50. ~1.5m. Entry BM LMS catalogue nd p. 7 N°35 reads: 'TARIGNARUE, the superior god of Atui; a very deeply carved idol with red feathers, also, a large piece made of cinet and feathers. These are but portions of the god; the rats, having made a nest in him, destroyed the remainder.' Evidently the rats only cut this god in two; LMS 50 is the 'body' of the god, LMS 49 the top. Courtesy BM.*

174 *Read's figure of LMS 49, depicting remnants of tail still attached.*

175 *Buck card of LMS 49. Read's figure indicates that some of the sennit and red feather strands have been remounted. Courtesy BPBM.*

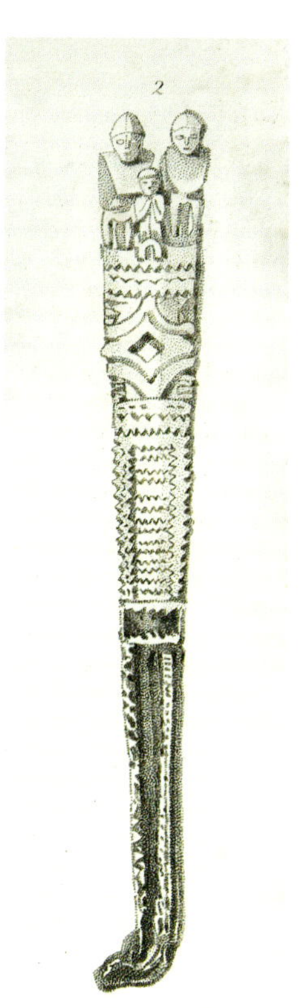

173

171

172

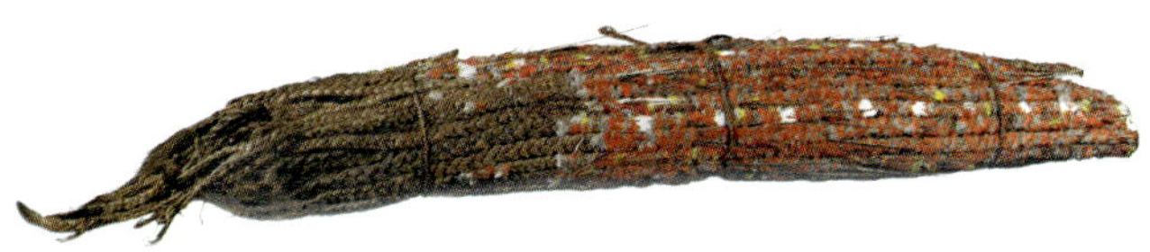

174

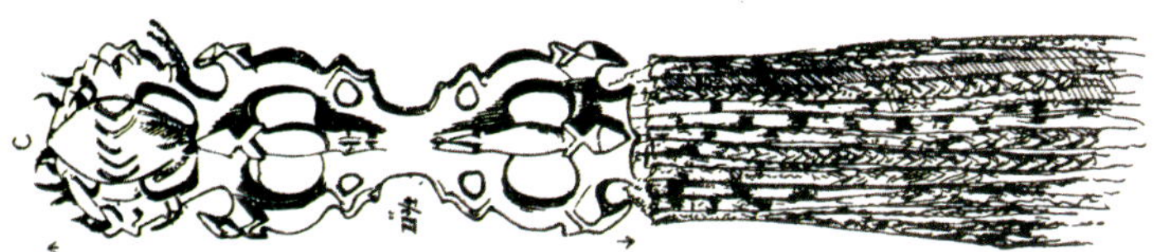

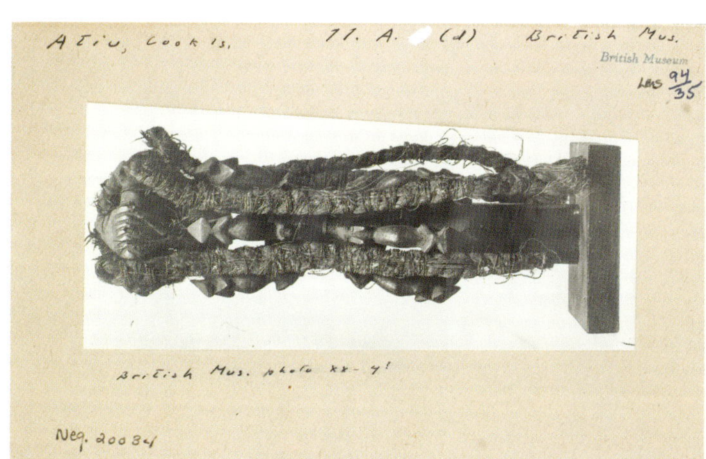

175

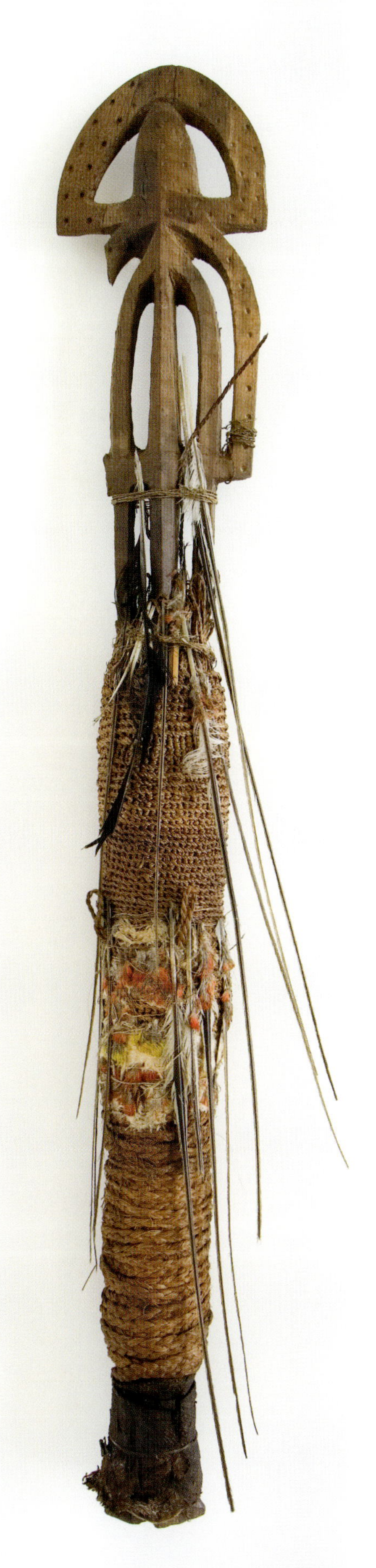

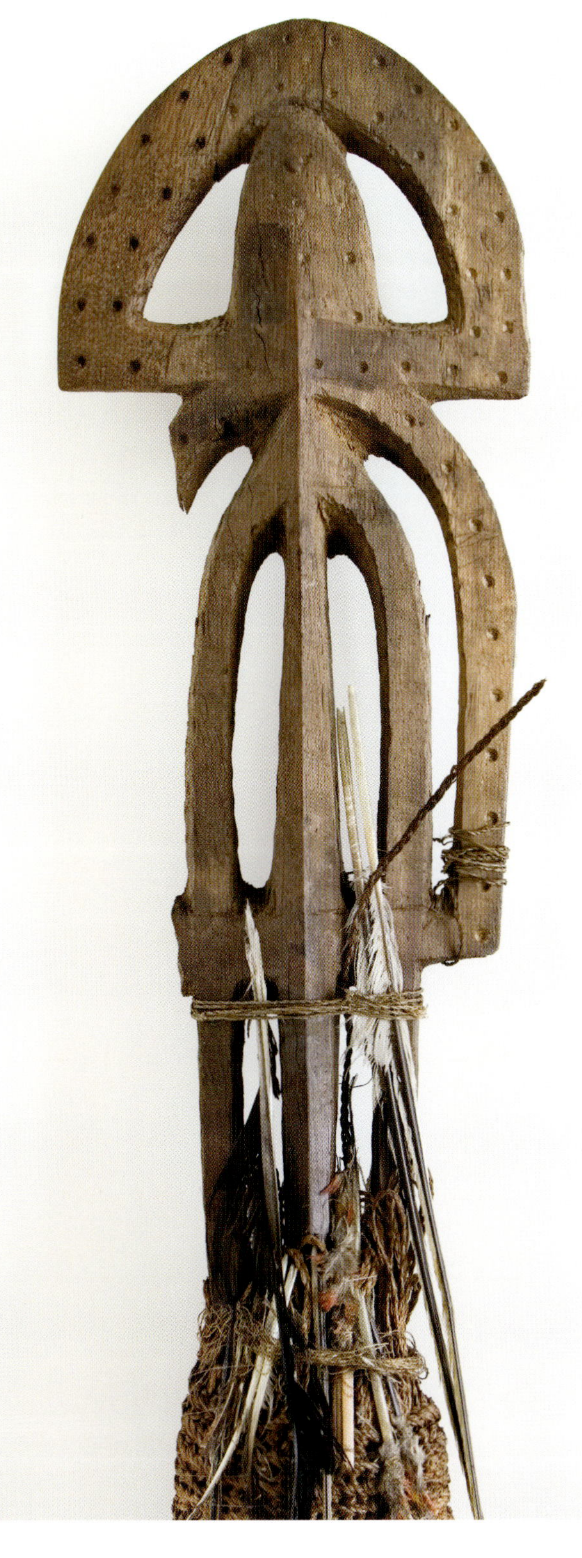

177

176 & 177 *'Oro? Central Cook Islands. 84cm. The LMS slip
and an early 20th century label, both of questionable accuracy,
assert this is 'A form of Tangaroa; Mauke.' Catalogue nd, p. 7,
No25 entry reads 'TANGAROA from Maute, with feathers and
fibre cinet appended to it.' LMS 171.*

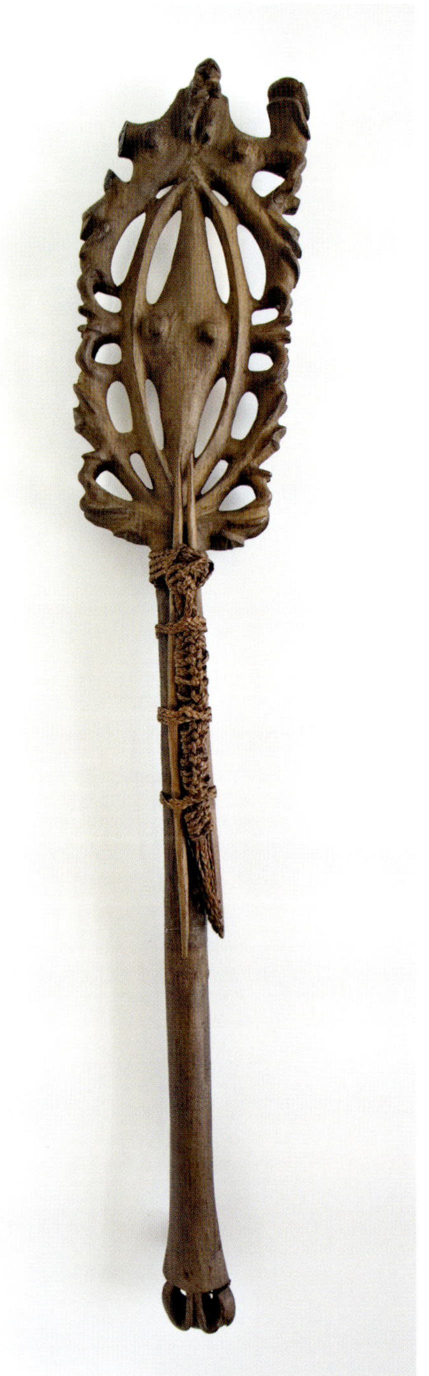

178

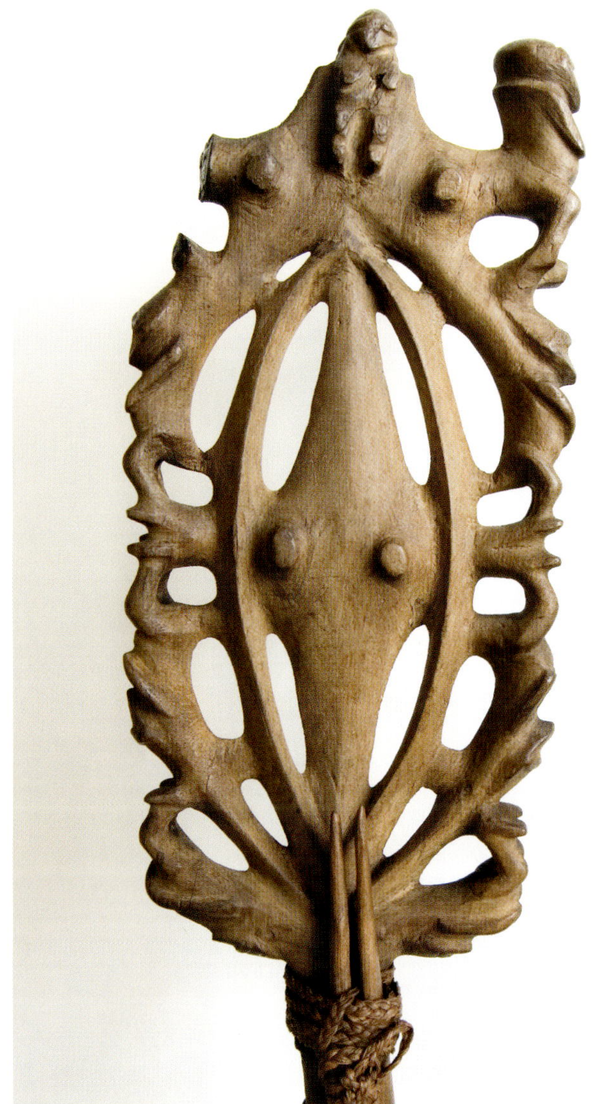

179

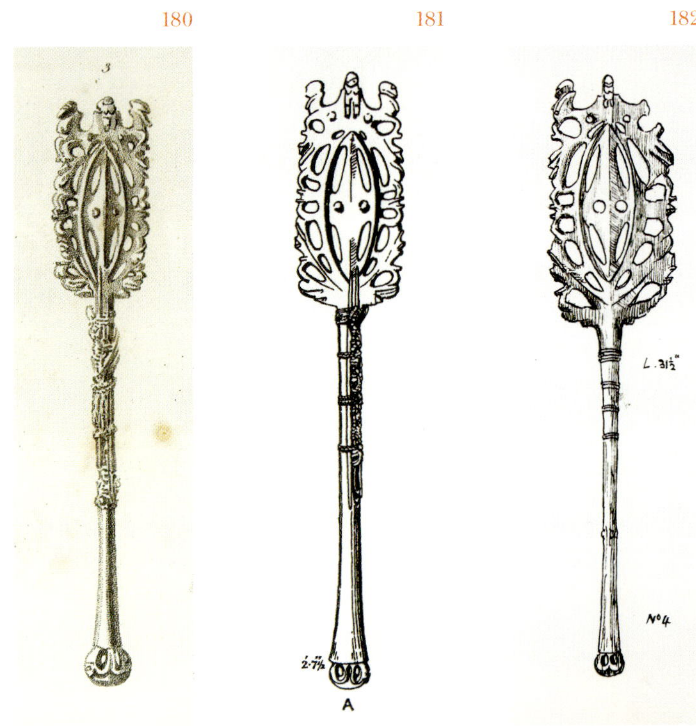

180   181   182

178 *Staff god. 82cm. Aitutaki idol Nº4 on Papeiha's list: 'The District of Natipaki's Idol of Tangaroa left at the great Marae as its representative.' LMS 168.*

179 *LMS 168, top portion.*

Three depictions of LMS 168:

180 *Ellis 1829.*

181 *Read 1892.*

182 *Edge-Partington 1890.*

122

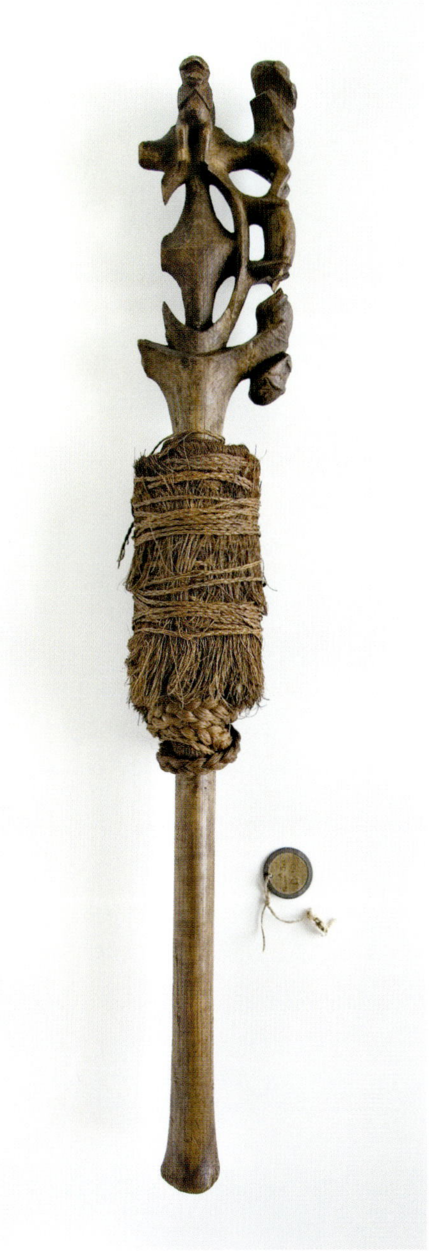

183

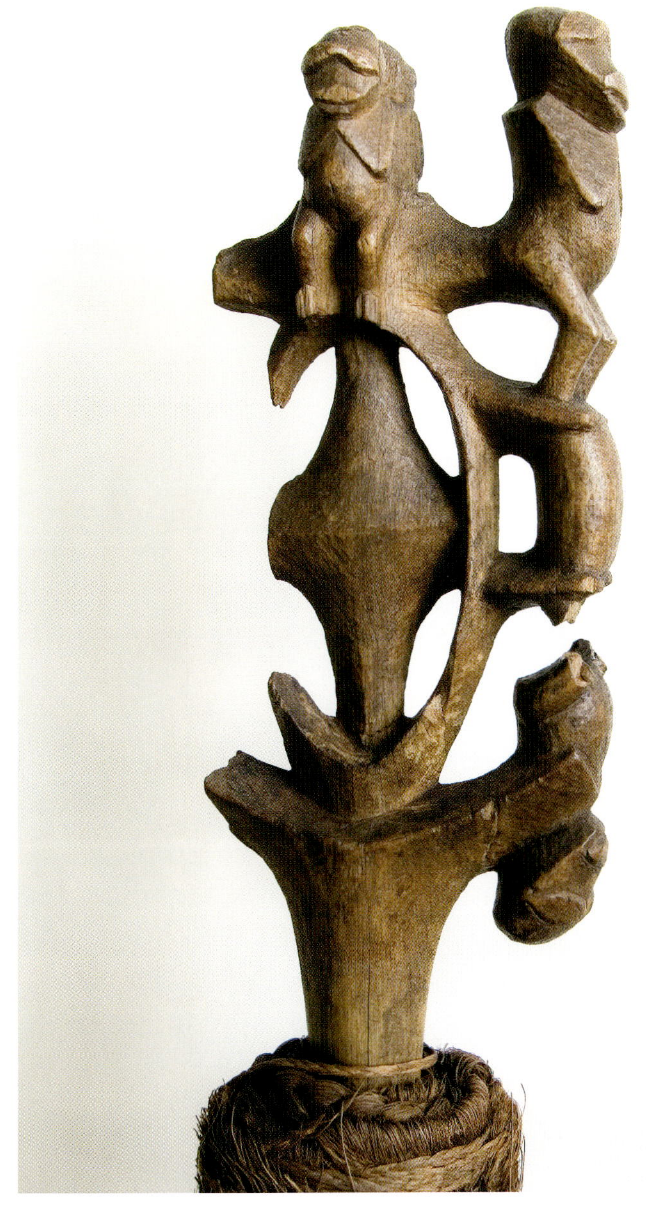

184

185

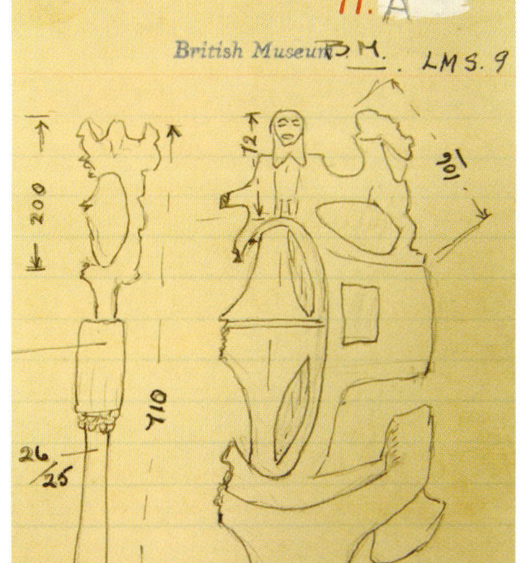

186

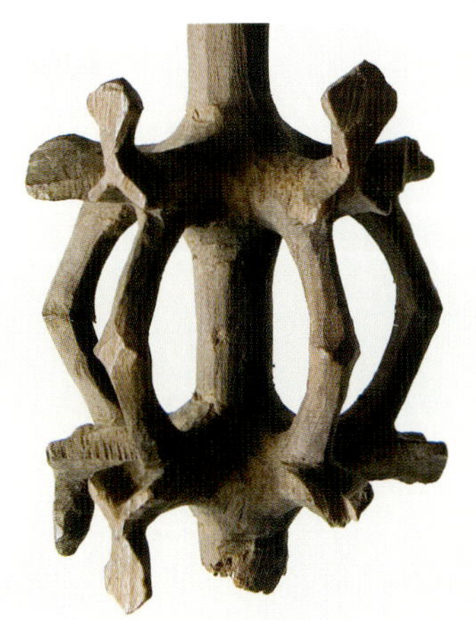

183 *Staff god; Aitutaki. 70cm. BM LMS Oc1982,Q.119.*

184 *Detail of BM LMS Oc1982,Q.119.*

185 *Buck drawing of Oc1982,Q.119. BPBM.*

186 *Bottom segment of staff god showing similar, but multi-dimensional, construction; Mitiaro. LMS +2060.*

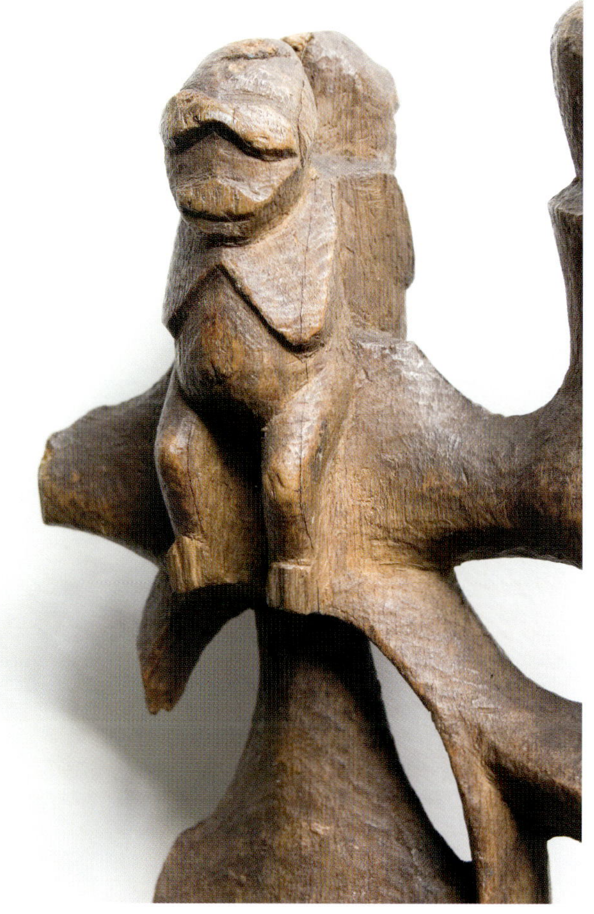

187

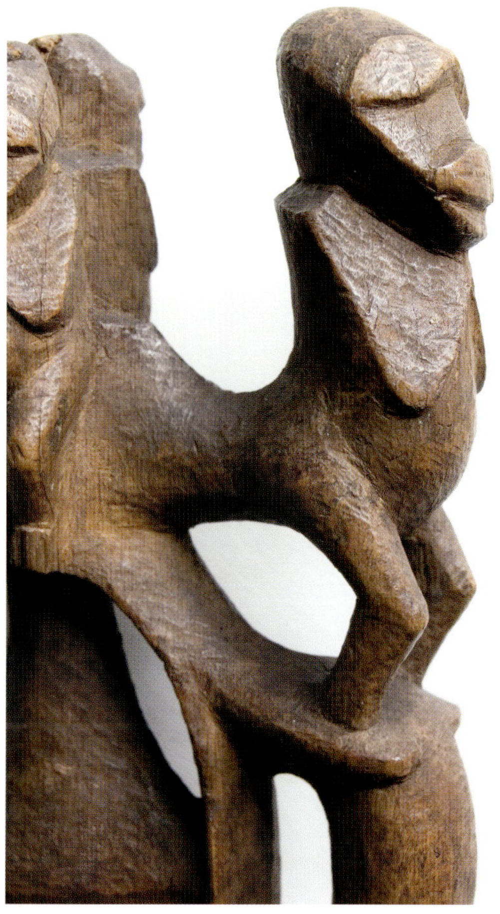

188

187 *Central figure at the top of staff god; Aitutaki. BM LMS Oc1982,Q.119.*

188 *Side figure at the top of Aitutaki staff god BM LMS Oc1982,Q.119.*

189 *& 190 Two views of Janus figure at the top of 'Oro(?) from Rurutu. 'Given to Rev. E.S. Prout of Halstead, by John Williams about 1835.' Ebenezer Prout was Williams's biographer (1843). Oldman 425. Courtesy Auckland Museum.*

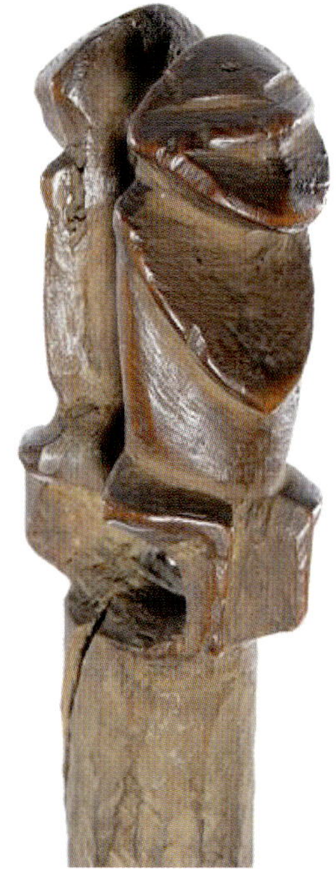

189

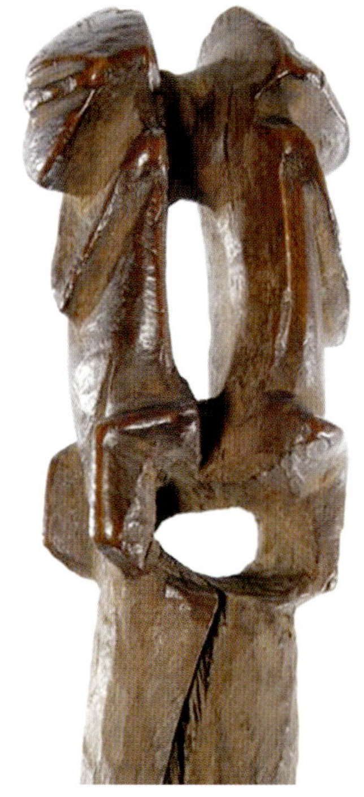

190

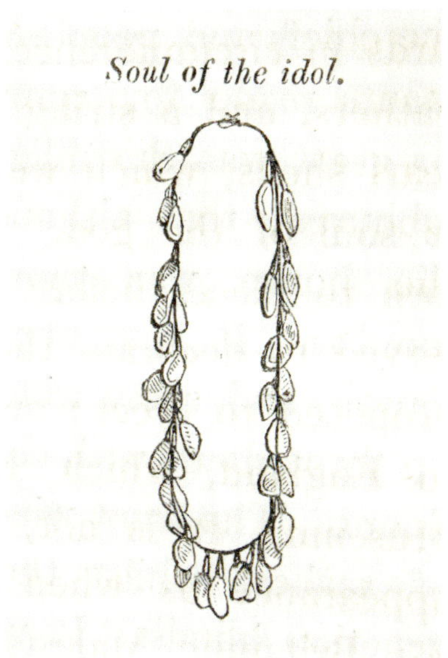

191

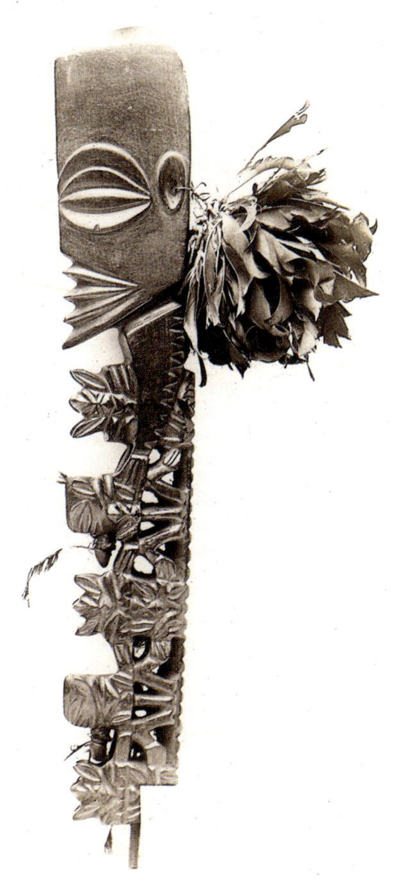

193

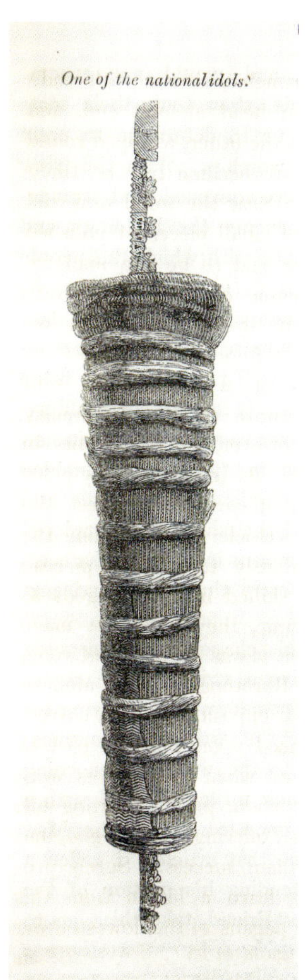

192

191 & 192 *Baxter wood engravings in Williams'* Narrative *showing large staff god, Rarotonga, probably BM LMS Oc845.Q.78. Williams states 'Near the wood were red feathers and a string of small pieces of polished pearl shells, which were said to be the manava, or soul of the god.'*

193 *Top of Rarotonga staff god, BM LMS collection. Photograph taken by BM. Gunson collection.*

194 *The Museum of the London Missionary Society from* The Illustrated London News, *Saturday 25 June 1859, showing immense Rarotonga staff god. The people to the left give an idea of the size of these idols, and of their tapa wraps.*

194

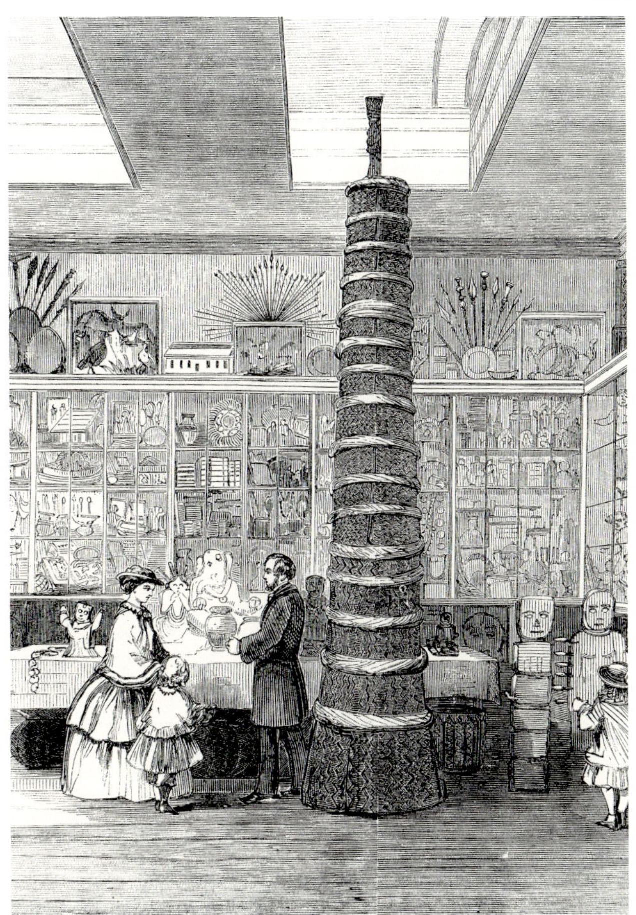

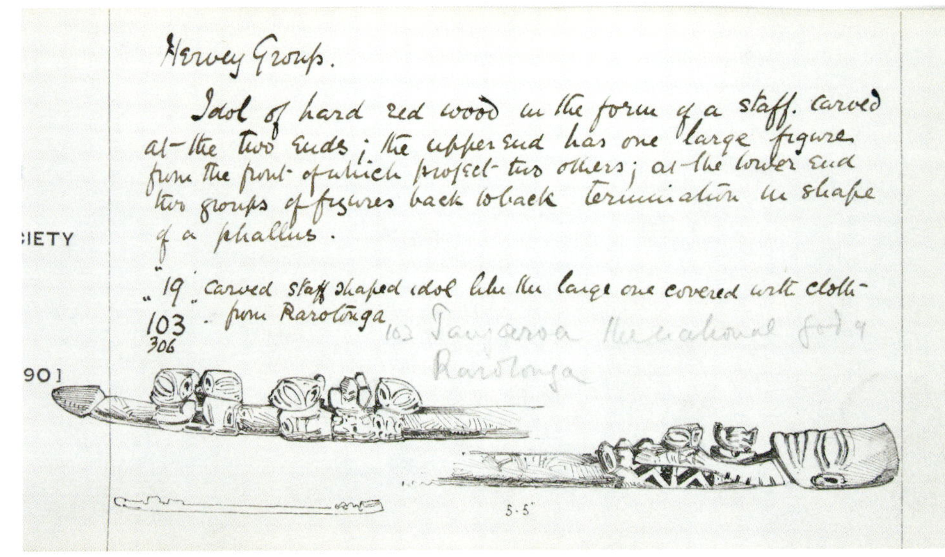

195 *Staff god; Rarotonga. Edge-Partington drawing on registration slip for LMS 39.*

196 *Watercolour poster made for Williams to illustrate the lectures he made in England, 1835-1838, to gain publicity and raise money for the South Sea Mission. The tapa wrapping appears as wooden slats. ~60 x 75cm. Nan Kivell Collection, National Library of Australia.*

197 *Three large openwork staff gods; Mangaia. LMS 42, LMS 62 (centre, 140cm; Anelay Nº8), and LMS 43. Photograph taken by BM and used by Buck (1944); ex-LMS; N Gunson. The 'handles' are abundantly decorated with sennit. LMS catalogue nd p. 7 entry for Nᵒˢ30,31 refers to these as 'district gods of Mangaia'.*

197

196

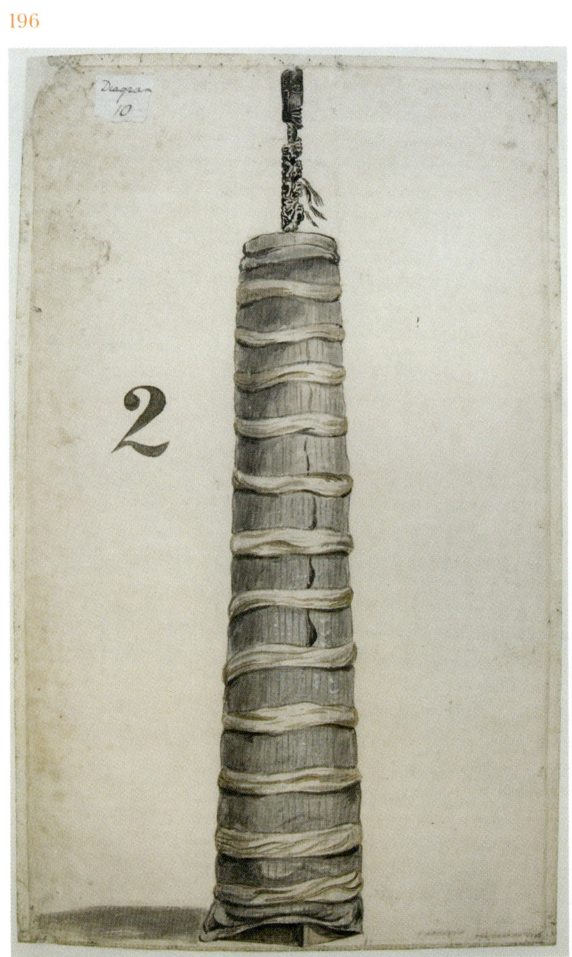

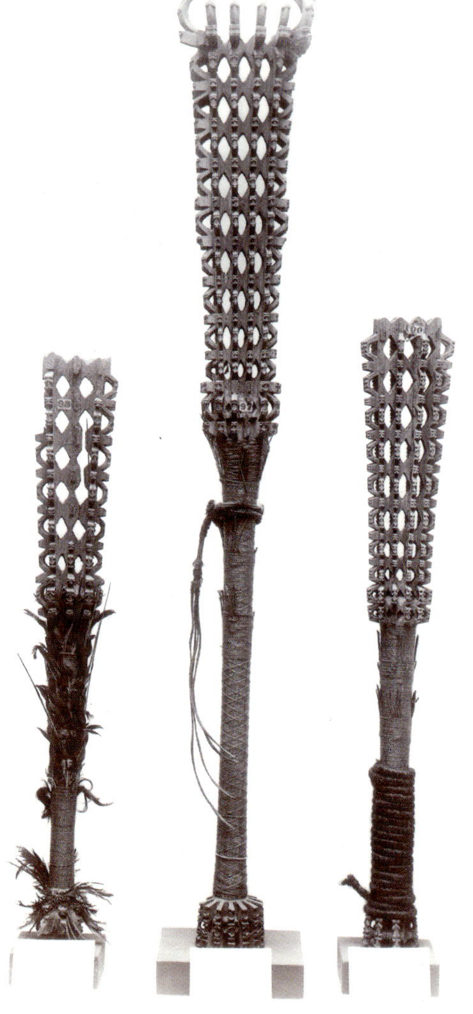

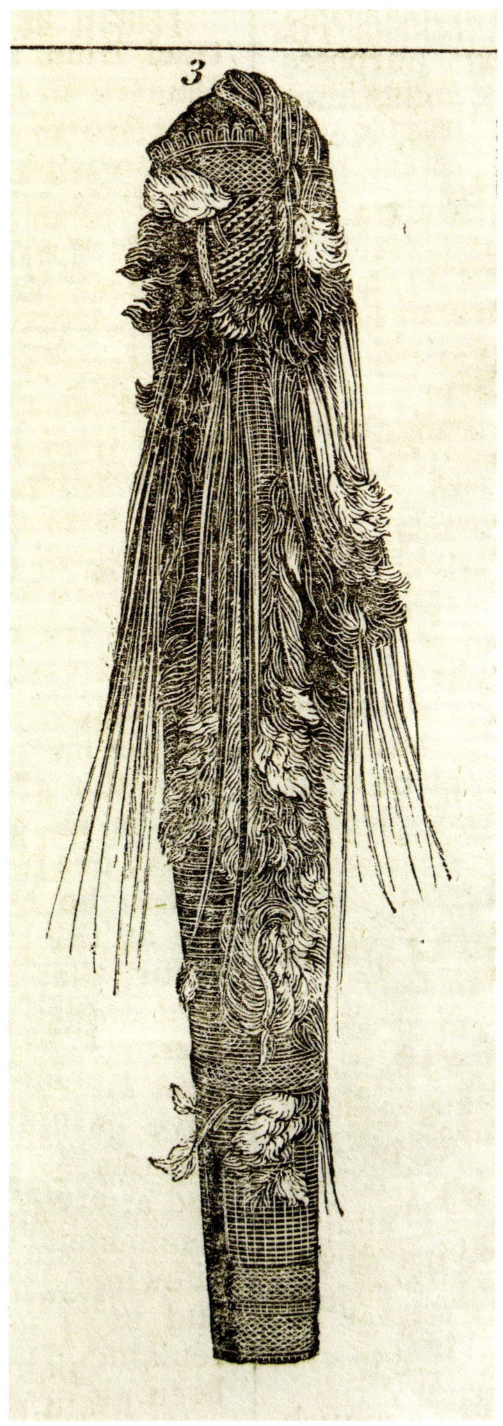

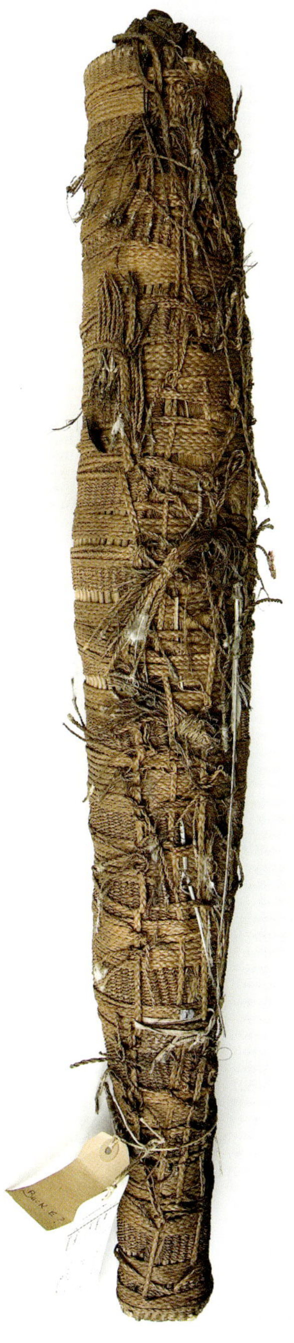

198 *Cover of* Missionary Sketches 3, *October 1818, The Family Idols of Pomare. 'No. 3 Temeharo.'*

199 *'Oro; Tahiti. Temeharo, Pomare I's own god. 84cm. Considerable information about Temeharo is in the quote below. BM LMS Oc1981,Q.1552.*

200 *Translation of Pomare II's letter (Tahiti) to the Missionaries (Ra'iatea) 19 February 1816 accompanying the presentation of his family idols, which included Temeharo, to the missionaries (Griffin 1822,180). 'Oro images perplexed the missionaries: 'The public will no doubt feel much disappointed on the view of these despicable idols . . . these convey no idea whatever of an animated being . . . we are totally at a loss to account for their form' (*Missionary Sketches 3, *October 1818, re 'Oro images).*

200

That principal idol, that has the red feathers of the Otun, is Temeharo—that is his name—look you: you may know it by the red feathers; that was Vairaatoa's own god, and those feathers were from the ship of lieutenant Watts; it was Vairaatoa that set them himself about the idol. If you think proper, you may burn them all in the fire; or if you like send them to your country, for the inspection of the people of Europe, that they may satisfy their curiosity, and know Taheiti's foolish gods.

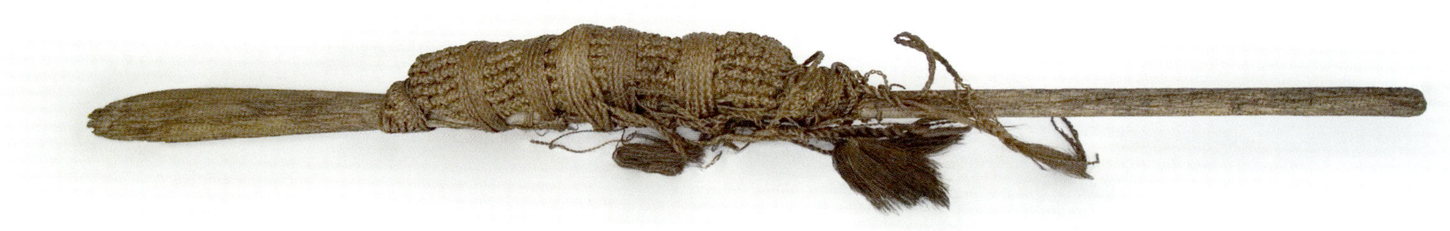

201 *Large 'Oro image; Tahiti. LMS 101—one of the two large ones in the BM LMS collection. 157cm. Presented to Tyerman & Bennet by Pomare II. See also figure 270.*

202 *LMS 101, Buck card photograph, 1933. Courtesy BPBM.*

203 *LMS 101 as depicted in Edge-Partington 1890 1,22 N°3. In 'Additional Notes–1895' he adds 'Household god of Pomare, king of Tahiti, presented to Messrs (Tyerman-Bennet) Feb:19.1821.' (The date is an error.)*

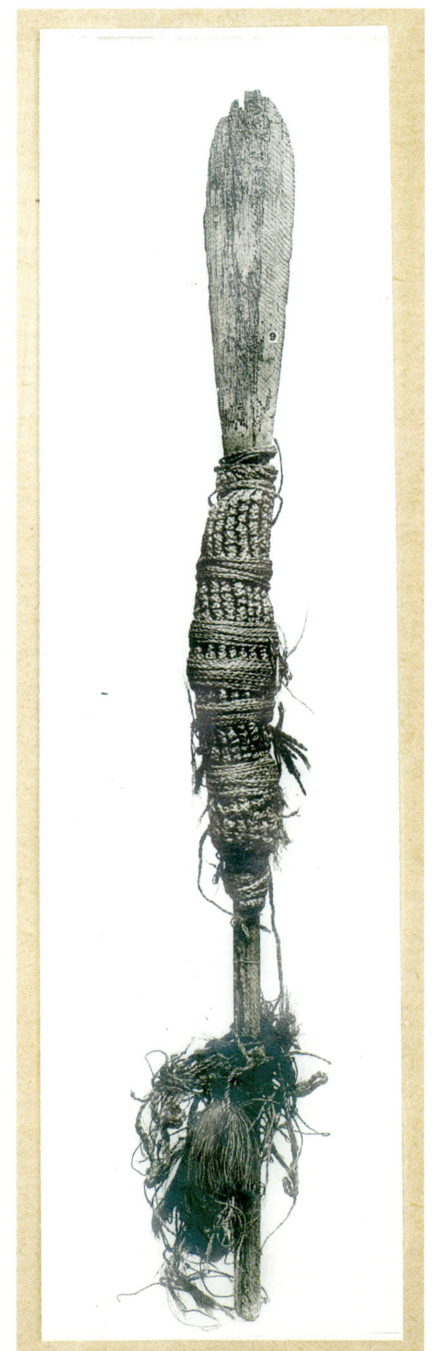

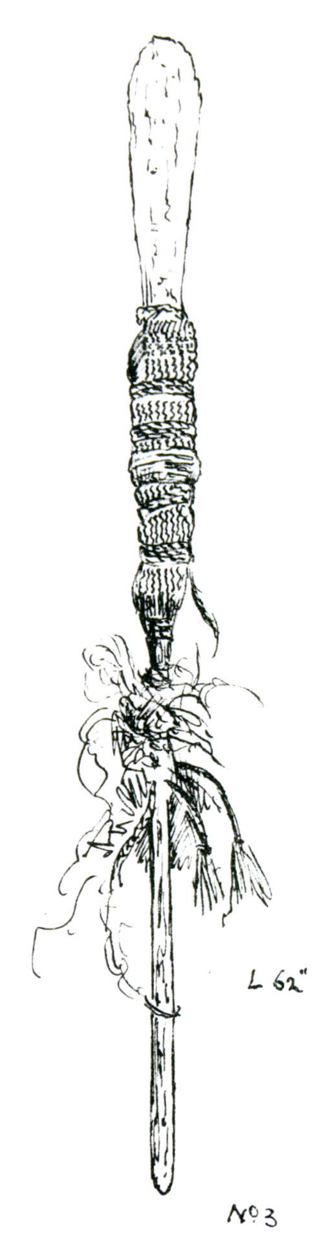

“The gods of the South Sea Islands were numerous, inhabiting the air, the earth, and the sea. The albatross, the heron-bird, the dove, and the swallow, the dog, the rat, the lizard, and the centipede, the daring shark, and the terror-striking sword-fish, with a multitude of smaller fishes, were deified by the Tahitians. But the god Oro was the chief object of their dread: and him they endeavoured to propitiate by human sacrifices.

204 *From* Missionary Sketches *77, October 1837. SOAS.*

205–208 *The second large LMS ‘Oro, LMS 100. Probably also presented by Pomare II, along with LMS 101, opposite (fig 201). 118cm. Evidently there were even larger ‘Oro: ‘The great national ones, which were of the same kind, only much larger, have been some time ago entirely destroyed.’ The fate of one of them: ‘the log of wood which formed the body of the great god Oro . . . was set up in the King’s kitchen to hang baskets of food upon’ (Missionary Sketches 13, April 1821).*

204

205

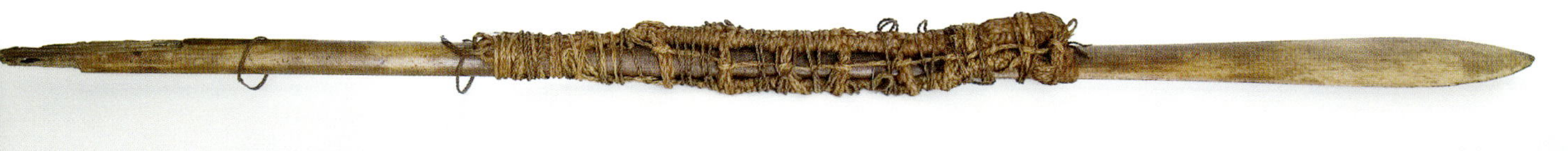

206

207

208

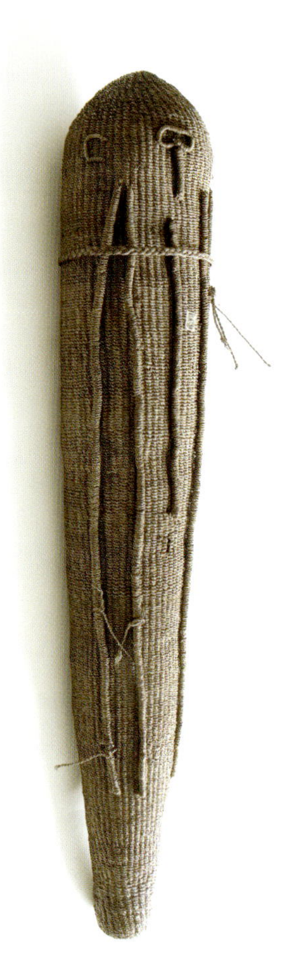

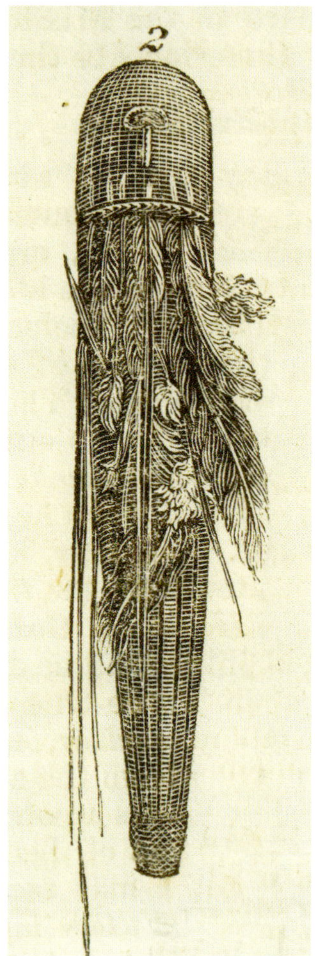

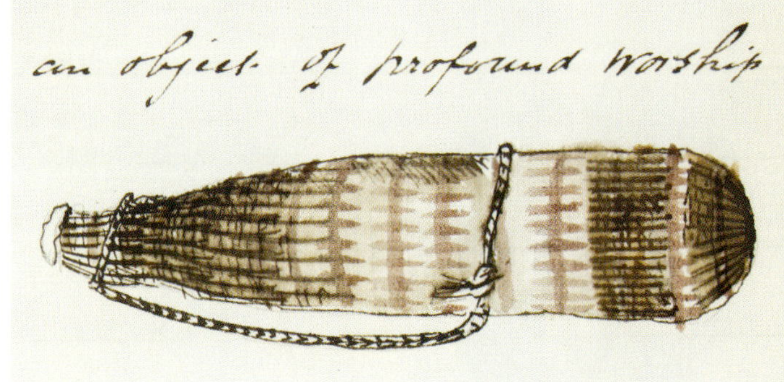

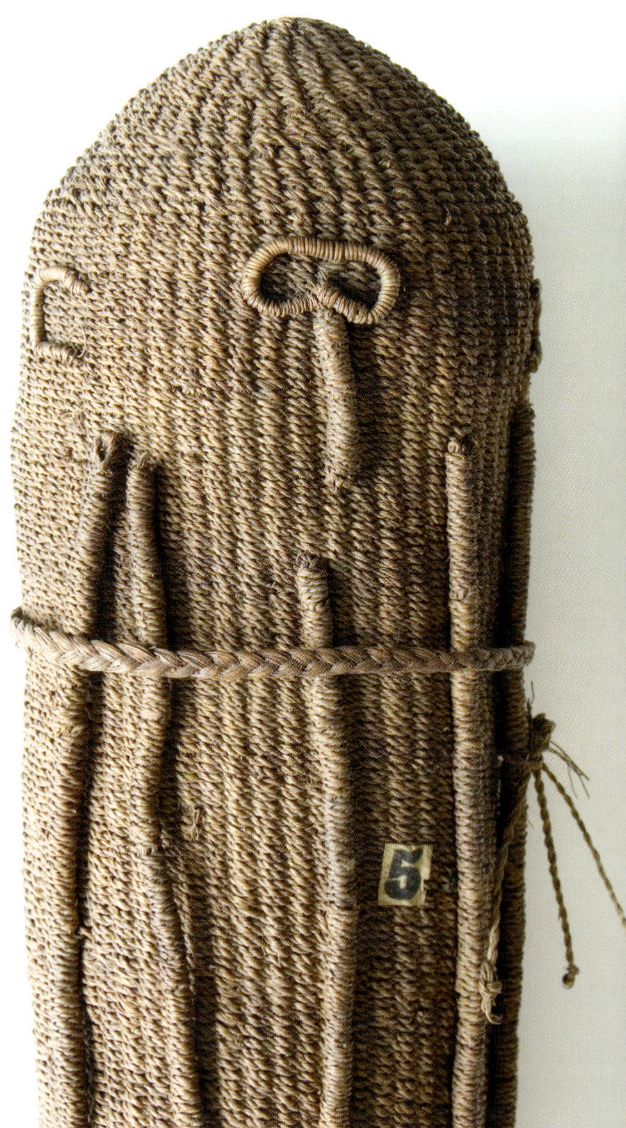

No. 2.
The Missionaries could not learn the name of this idol.

209   *Pomare II's family idol Nº2. 61cm. Cook mentioned this type of Eatua but never acquired one: 'This is a thing made of the twisted fibres of the husk of the coca-nut, shaped something like a large fid, that is roundish with one end much thicker than the other. We have very often got small ones from different people, but never knew their use before' (Cook visiting a marae at Attahouru, Paea, Tahiti, 2 September 1777). BM LMS Oc1981,Q.1551.*

210   *'Oro; Tahiti. Nº2, 'The Family Idols of Pomare', cover of* Missionary Sketches 3, *October 1818. SOAS.*

211   *Legend for Nº2,* Missionary Sketches 3, *October 1818. SOAS.*

212   *'Oro image depicted in Augustus Franks' Leeds Notebook. [Legend reads: "Varua Ino (Evil Spirit) formerly an object of profound worship in Tahiti, brought from its concealment in a hole in the Mountains and sold to George Bennet Esq, Oct. 1823, by whom it was presented" It is cylindrical, tapering towards one end—& is made up of cocoa-nut sinnet interwoven on the outer surface & painted with dark red stripes. A couple of small loops are worked at the larger end. L. 15½ D. 3½ inches.] It is more likely the sennit was dyed and woven, not painted. Present whereabouts unknown. BM Anthropology Library, LS6.*

213   *Detail of 'Oro depicted in figure 209.*

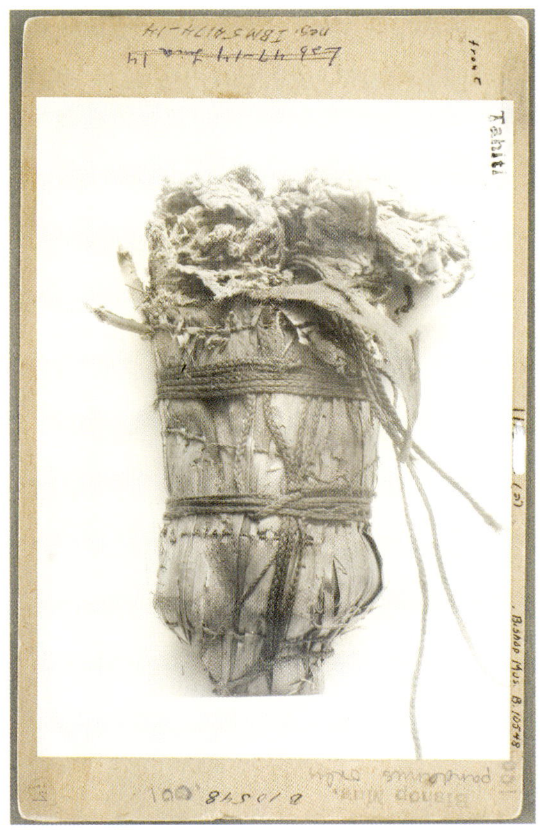

214

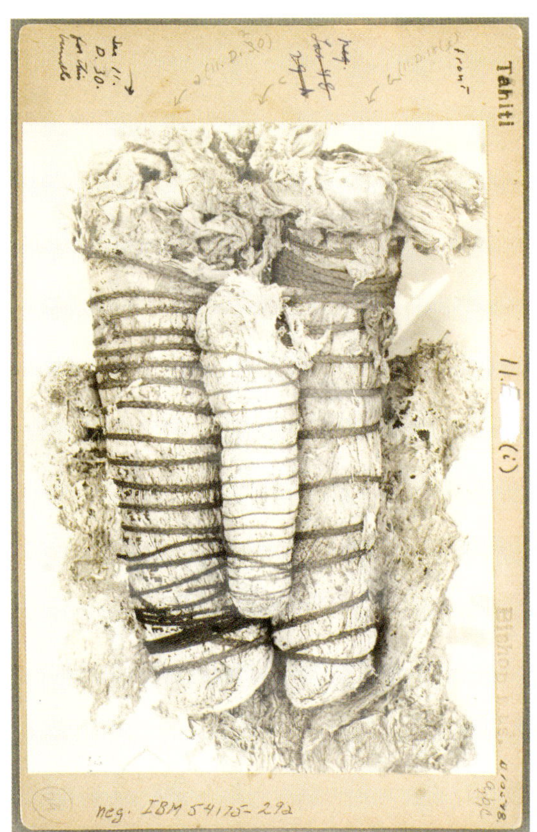

215

214–217 *Multiple elaborate layers of wrapping around three ʻOro images. The package was found intact in 1925 by a young Tahitian pig hunter in a cave; Orofere Valley, Paea district, Tahiti. Photographs Kenneth Emory. Courtesy BPBM.*

216

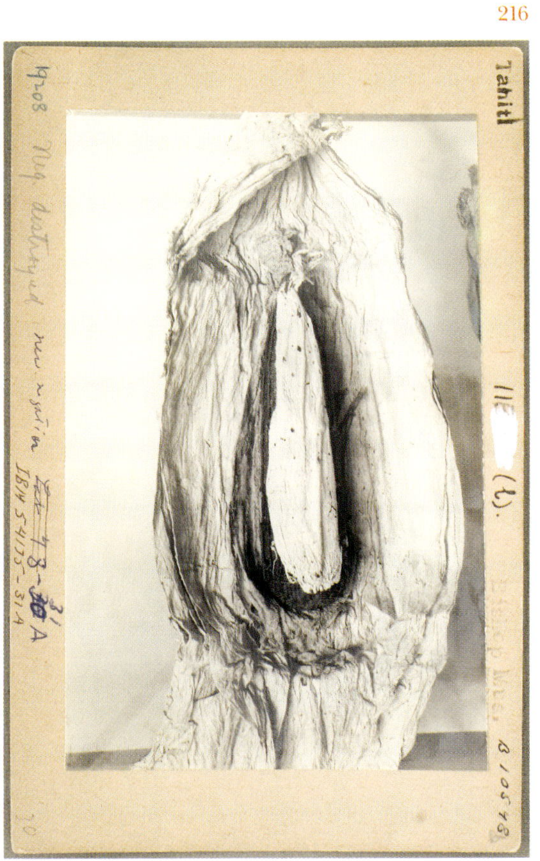

217

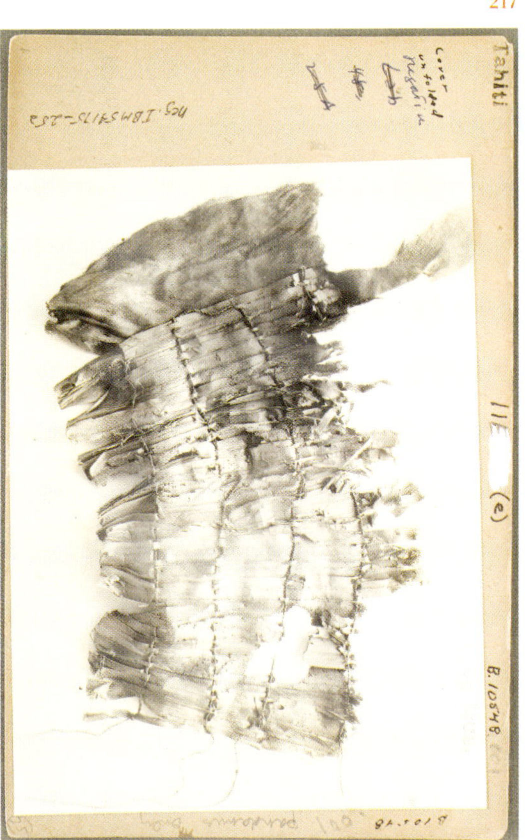

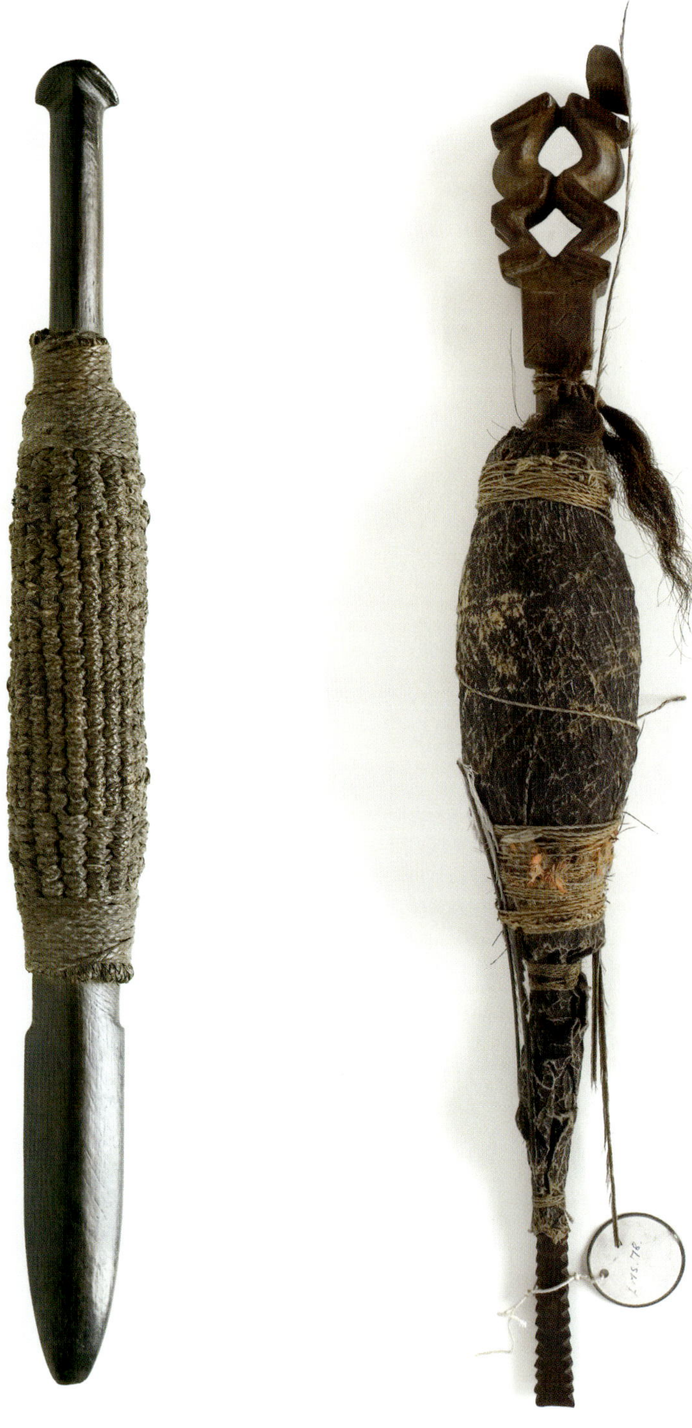

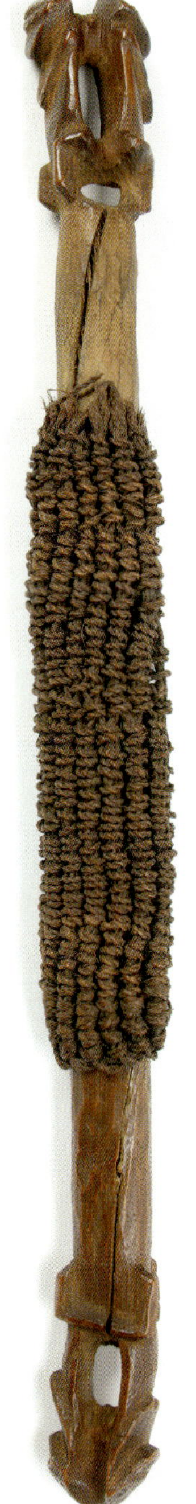

218 *'Oro; Tahiti or Ra'iatea. Cook's 1st voyage. 57cm. Earls of Warwick; KJ Hewett. Illustrated in JF Miller 1771 pen and wash drawing, BL Add Ms 15508,26.*

219 *'Oro image? Attached is bundle of sennit which is wrapped in black tapa, fastened to large wood fan handle with oronga; central Cook Islands. 47cm. LMS 78.*

220 *'Oro? Rurutu. 57cm. 'Given to Rev. E.S. Prout, of Halstead, by John Williams about 1835.' Captain Grimes' description of a Rurutu idol could apply to an 'Oro image: 'merely a small piece of wood covered with cloth in all about the size of a man's leg & thigh' (see Appendix 3). Oldman 425. Courtesy Auckland Museum.*

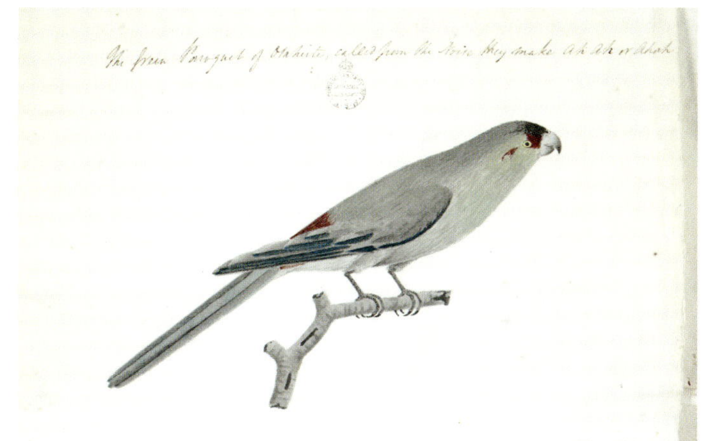

221

222

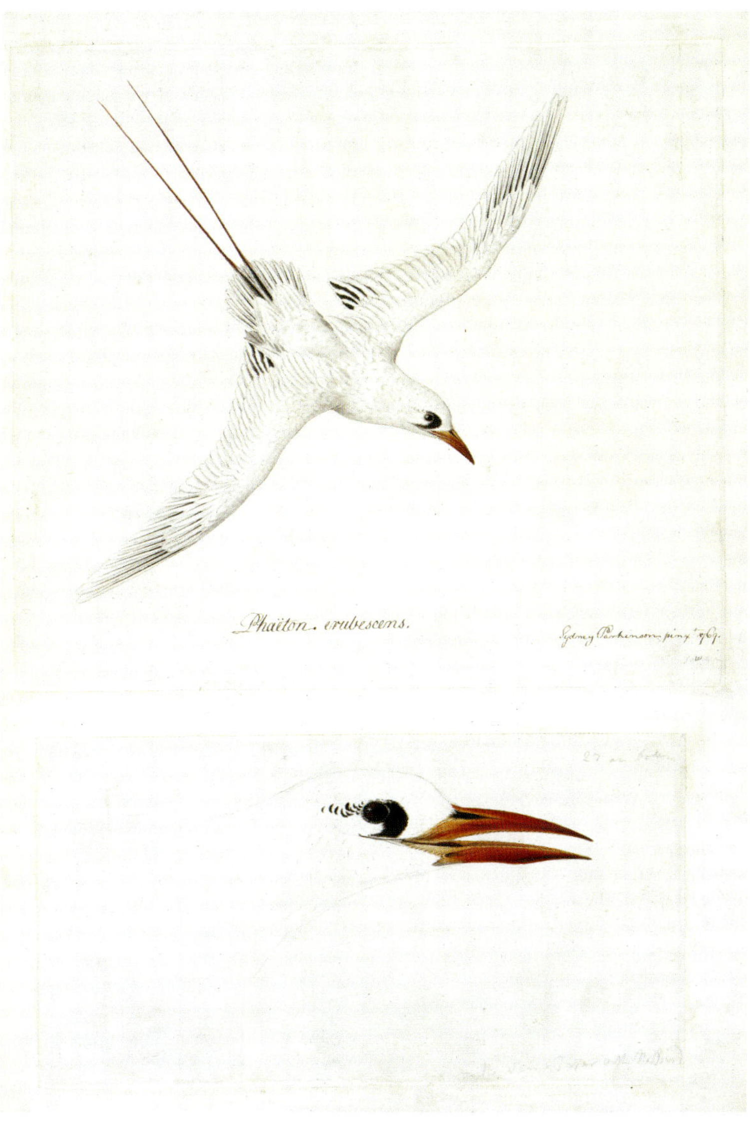

223

221   *Watercolour by Lt Bligh,* The Green Paroquet of Otaheite, called from the Noise they make Ah Ah or Ahah. *Probably the lorikeet* Vini zealandicus *(a misnomer). Now almost extinct. Small parrot species supplied the red, yellow, and green feathers for the god images. Courtesy Mitchell Library.*

222   *Watercolour by Sydney Parkinson of the same species of parrot.* Endeavour Drawings *part 3,8. Courtesy Natural History Museum, London.*

223   *Watercolour by Sydney Parkinson of the red-tailed tropic bird,* Phaethon rubricauda. *These supplied long filamentous red feathers, two per bird.* Endeavour Drawings *part 3,31 and 32. Courtesy Natural History Museum, London.*

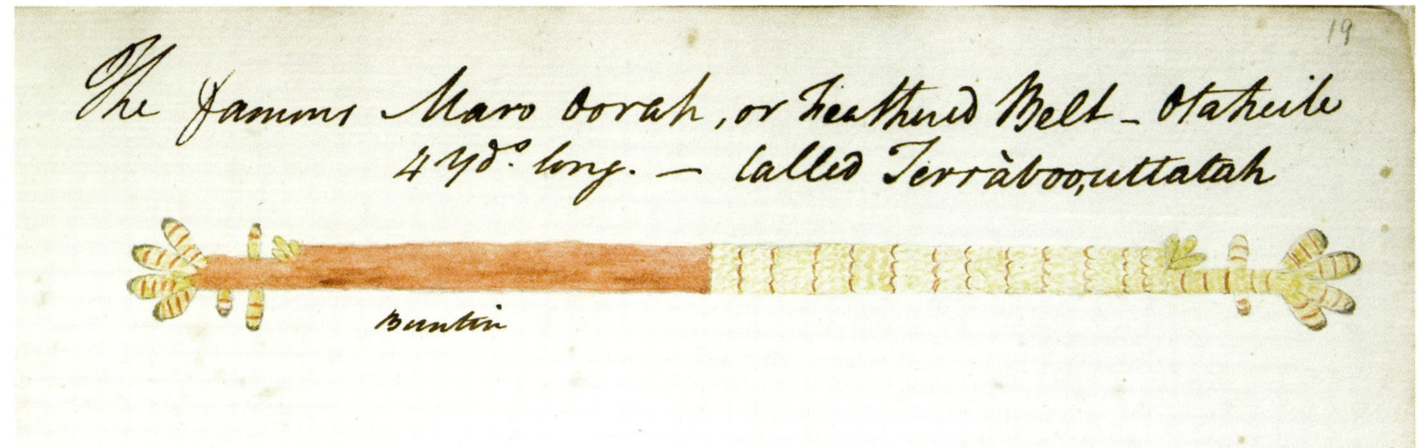

224

224   Watercolour by Lt William Bligh of the yellow and red feather girdle, maro ura, which incorporated a portion of the British ensign that Wallis raised on taking possession of Tahiti in 1767. The ensign was stolen during the night. Pomare won the sacred cincture from his enemies and brought it to his marae at Tarahoi, Pare, where Bligh drew it (see Dening 1988). Bligh denotes the pennant portion (left) 'Buntin'. He does not depict the lock of mutineer Richard Skinner's auburn hair which was also incorporated. Mitchell Library.

225   Plaited bichrome pandanus tatua (maro); Rarotonga; 8.53m or 28 feet long. Wm Wyatt Gill. BM LMS 9963. Buck card, BPBM.

226   Large chipped basalt god; Tahiti; 51cm. LMS 121.

227   Large basalt god, remarkably precise symmetry and finish; Tahiti. 51cm. LMS 122. Figured Edge-Partington 1,22 N°8.

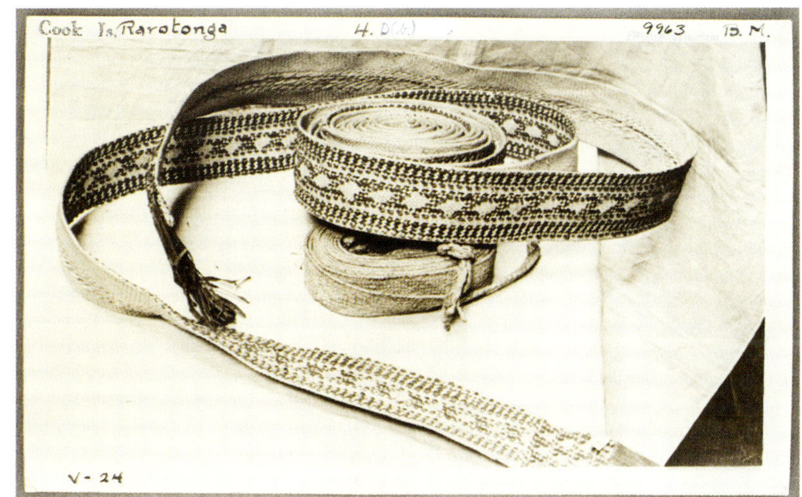

225

226

227

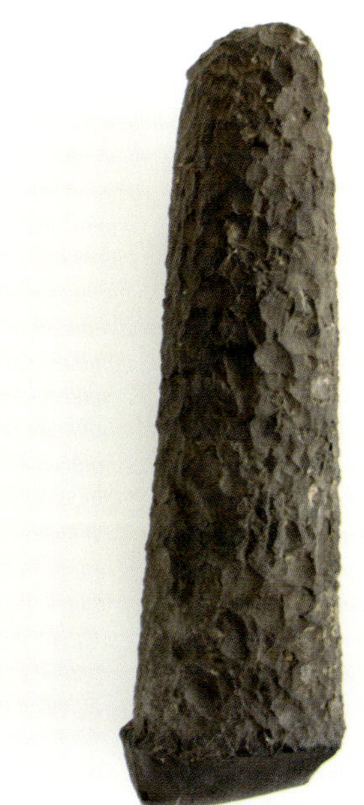

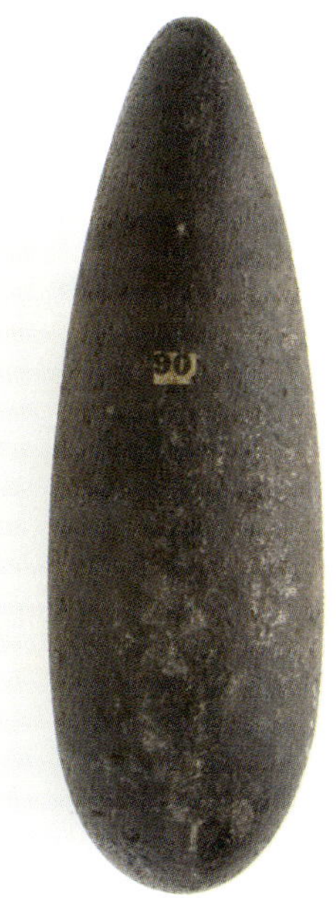

134

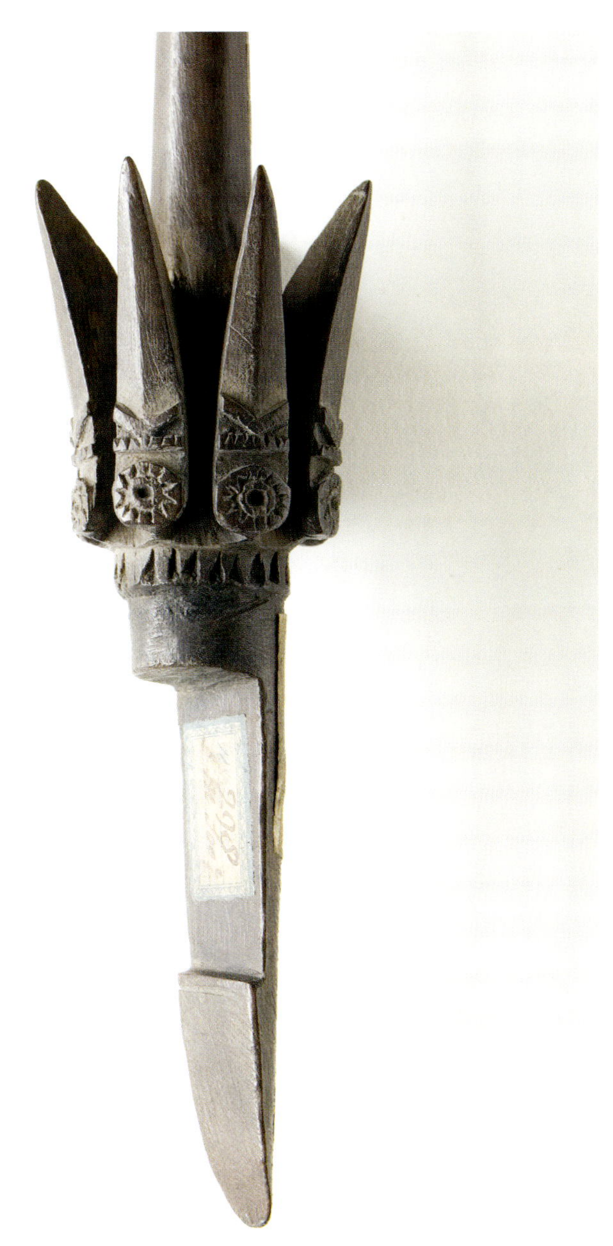

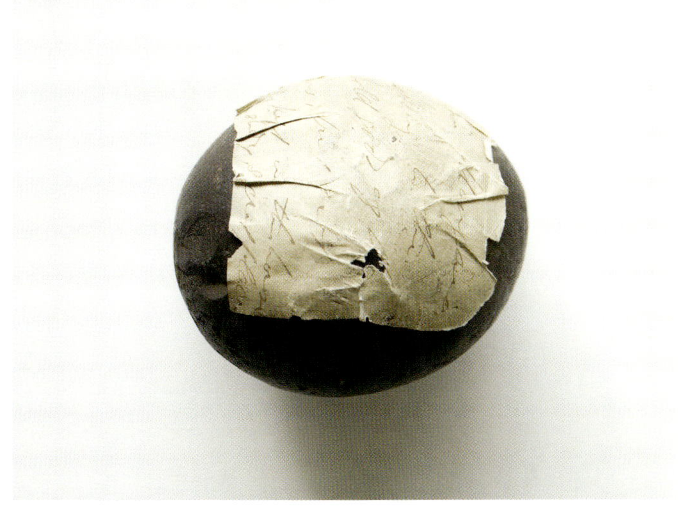

228 *Base of spear head; Austral Islands. 50cm. G Bennet. Morrison mentions Tubua'i 'fishing spears . . . pointed with Toa which evry fisherman makes for Himself' (1935,68). Hollow gods are often mentioned as containing family gods and the points of spears. LMS 28.*

229 *'Household god . . . Mangaia . . . but not usually kept in the house—in some shady secret place' (label partially illegible). 5.5cm. WW Gill. Toka-kura in Savage: 'sacred stone, talisman.' Missionary John Eyre journal entry, Tahiti, 10 January 1798, mentions a 'stone, with leaves bound round it,' held by Pomare during an oration, presented to brother Main, and then buried (Trans Miss Soc 1804 1,21). BM LMS 9939.*

230 *Sennit-tied coconut leaf god (Mokoiro) from Mangaia. 42cm. WW Gill. 'In heathenism no canoe ever ventured over the reef at Mangaia to fish without first fastening to its bows the fisherman's god. This consisted merely of the extremity of a coco-nut frond secured with fine-plaited sennit tied into a bow. I have deposited one of these charms in the British Museum' (WW Gill 1894,149). John Jefferson journal entry 3 Oct 1898, Marae Opare, Tahiti: 'At the foot of this pavement the priest worships, with his face directed towards the headstone [pou] and plank [unu], and throws his offering, consisting of a young plantain-tree root, green leaves, or the leaf of a coconut, twisted in a peculiar fashion, upon the pavement' (Trans Miss Soc 1804 1,98). BM LMS 9940.*

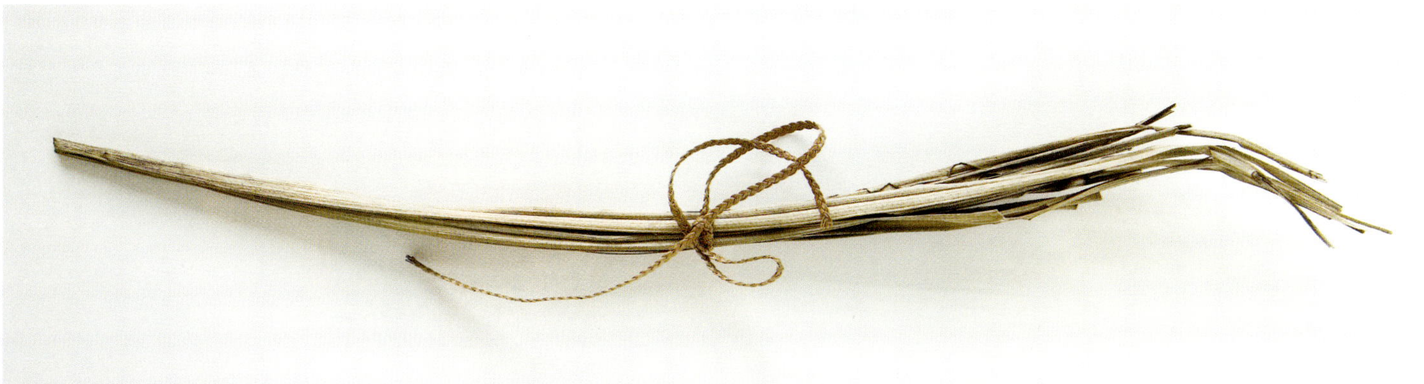

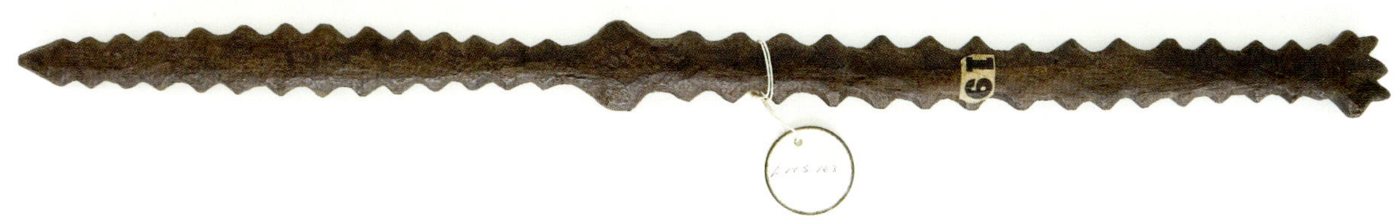

231

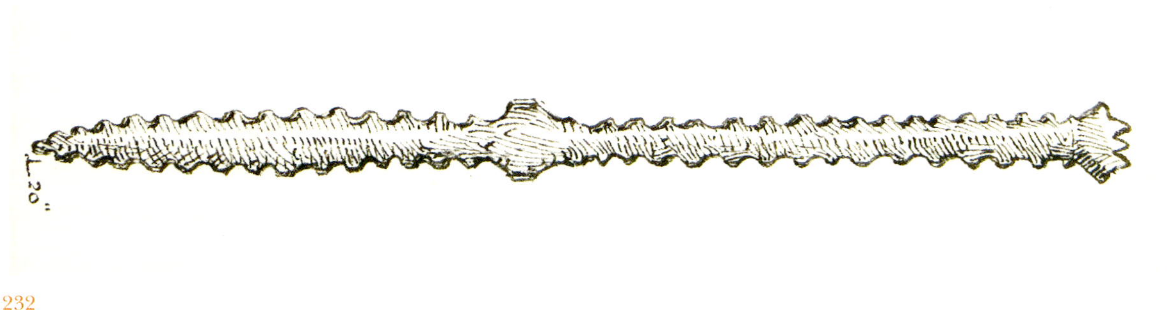

232

231 *Unique red hardwood staff with serrated edges. 52cm. LMS 163.*

232 *Edge-Partington drawing on registration slip of LMS 163. Designated 'Hervey Group'; 'Tii vahine [female spirit]—represents deified female ancestor' is added in pencil.*

233 & 234 *Two views of unique edge-notched god of prismatic basalt; Mo'orea. 32cm. Attached modern label: 'Basalt Idol worshipped by King Pomare + family, Island of Eimeo.' Tyerman and Bennet, journal entry 22 October 1821, visiting Pomare on Mo'orea: 'He told us that he had given orders for all such things to be collected for us (curiosities of the country) as we might desire to take home on our return' (Montgomery 1832 1,90). Pomare, from Tahiti, was sick at the time and had taken refuge on Mo'orea; he died 7 December. Notched edges occur frequently in tapa decoration (figs. 237 & 238) and on wood carvings in central Polynesia. G Bennet; Sheffield Museum; CUM Z32402.*

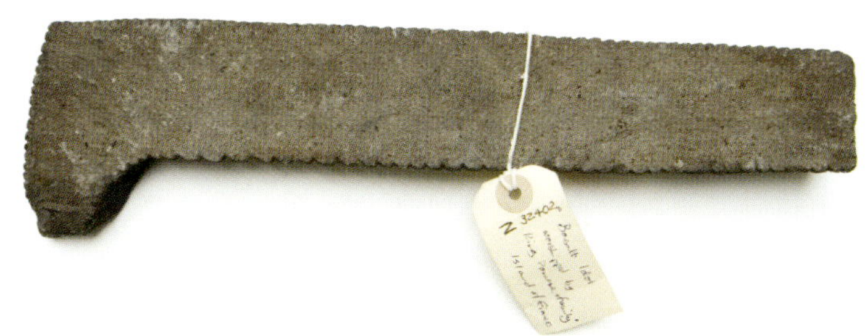

233

234

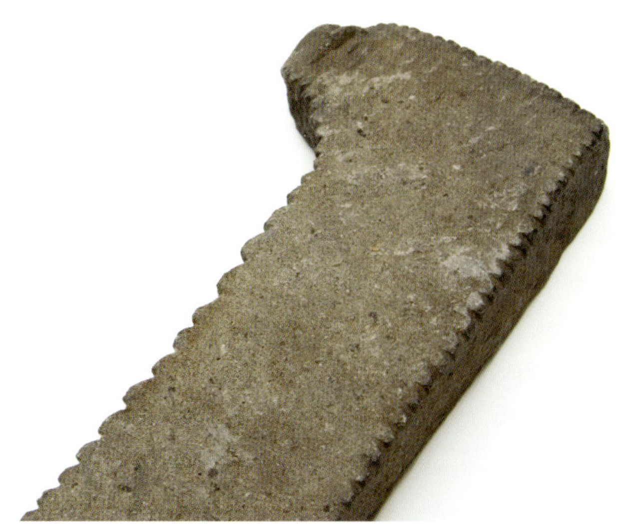

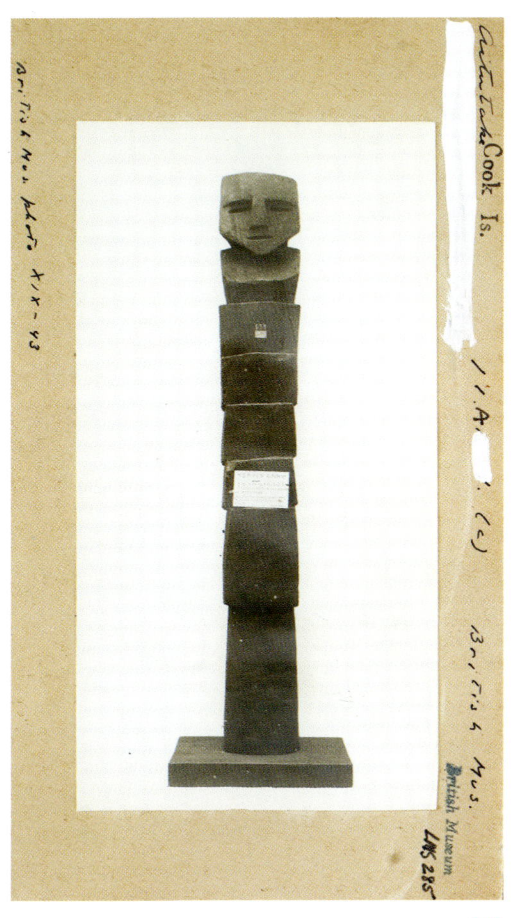

235

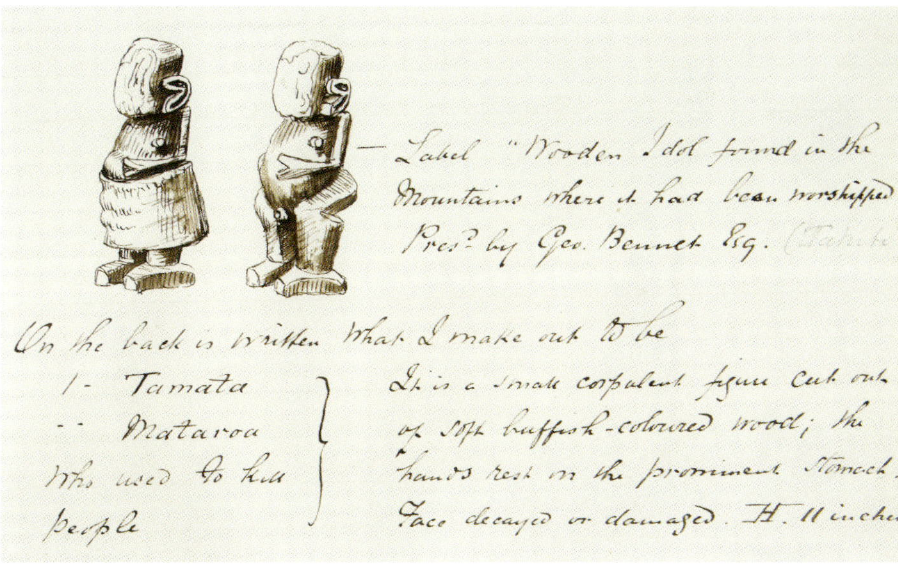

236

235   *Large wood human figure which Papeiha found being used as a post supporting the roof of a cooking shed on Aitutaki. 125cm. This is N°6 on Papeiha's list—'A great god purchased with a fish-hook. This was one hung at the yard arm on our entrance in the harbour – it is most likely a household or family God.' LMS 38; Buck card, courtesy BPBM.*

236   *Tahitian ti'i depicted in Augustus Franks' Leeds Notebook. [Legend reads: Label "Wooden Idol found in the Mountains where it had been worshipped. Pres^d by Geo. Bennet Esq. (Tahiti). On the back is written what I make out to be 1–Tamata,–Mataroa who used to kill people. It is a small corpulent figure cut out of soft buff-ish-coloured wood; the hands rest on the prominent stomach. Face decayed or damaged. H. 11 inches.] Present whereabouts unknown. BM Anthropology Library, LS6.*

237   *Sample of Cook Islands tapa with notched or serrated motif, on a sampler entitled 'Specimens of bark cloth sent by John Williams to his sister.' SOAS.*

238   *Tapa with notched or serrated motif; attached to feather head-dress; Rarotonga. Headdress figured in Buck 1944 plate 7 B. LMS 88.*

237

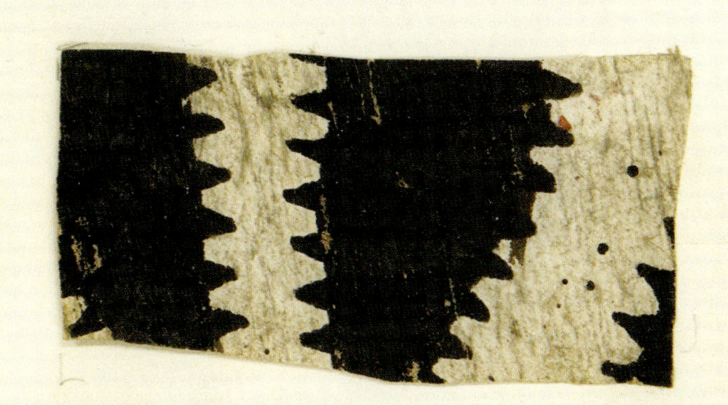

238

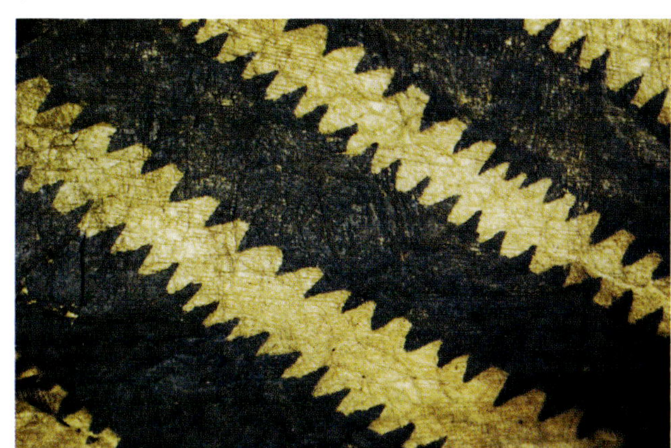

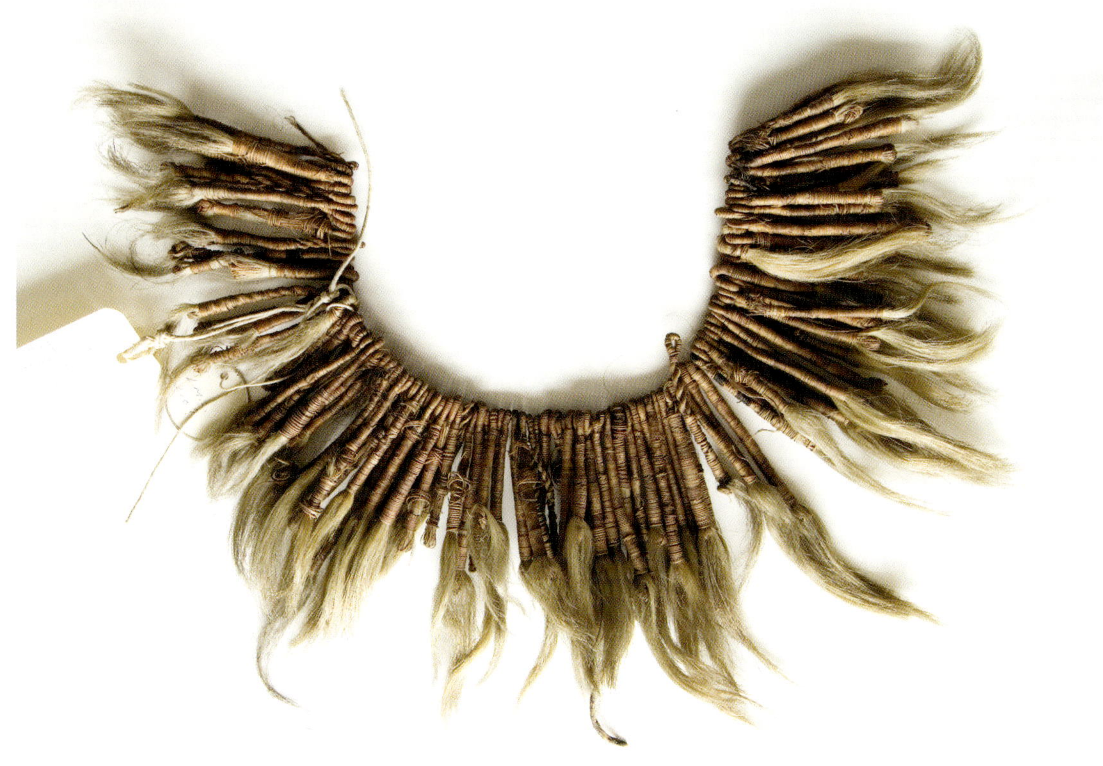

239

241

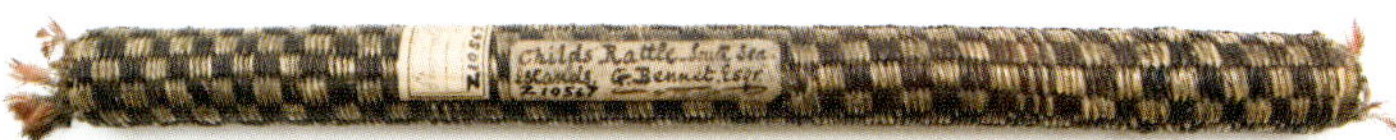

240

239 *Necklace of dog hair and plant fibre; Tuamotus. Length ~64cm. LMS 210.*

240 *Labelled 'Child's Rattle, South Sea Islands, G Bennet Esqr'; 'Sheffield'; red feathers attached. 32cm. Figure legend for a similar object in Edge-Partington 2,19 N°2, 'Tahitian group etc.' reads 'used in dancing the hara. Mus of Lit & Phil Soc: Leeds.' CUM Z10567.*

241 *CUM 6075, G Bennet; Sheffield Museum, labelled Mangaia. Length ~44cm. These necklaces are of uncertain origin. One with a reasonably certain attribution was collected by Tyerman and Bennet on Tubua'i in the Australs in 1824, now at the Saffron Walden Museum (Pole 1981,22). Anderson mentions testicular pendants on Atiu in 1777 (Beaglehole 1967 3[part 2],840). Savage mentions necklace elements in the Cook Islands: under the entry* tuaki taaroa, *he refers to carved phallic neck ornaments (rei); under the entry* rei: *'[neck] emblem . . . carved . . . to represent the testicles of the male and the other portion to represent the private parts of the female.'*

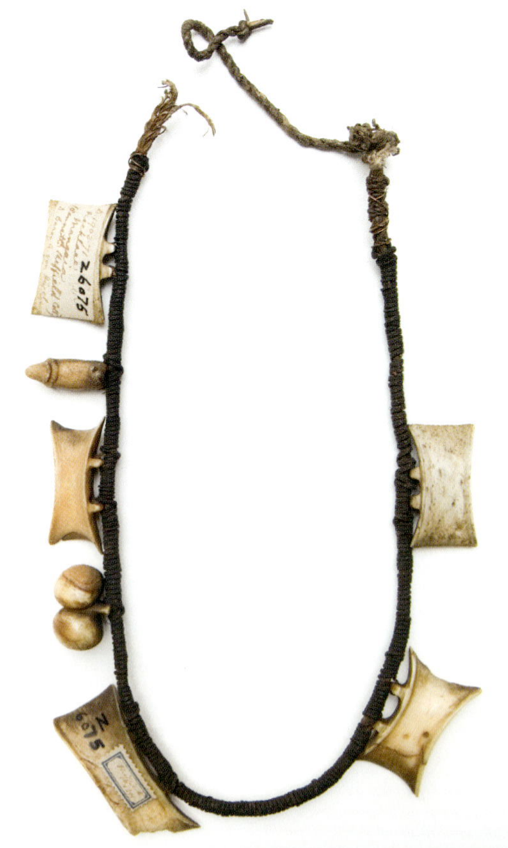

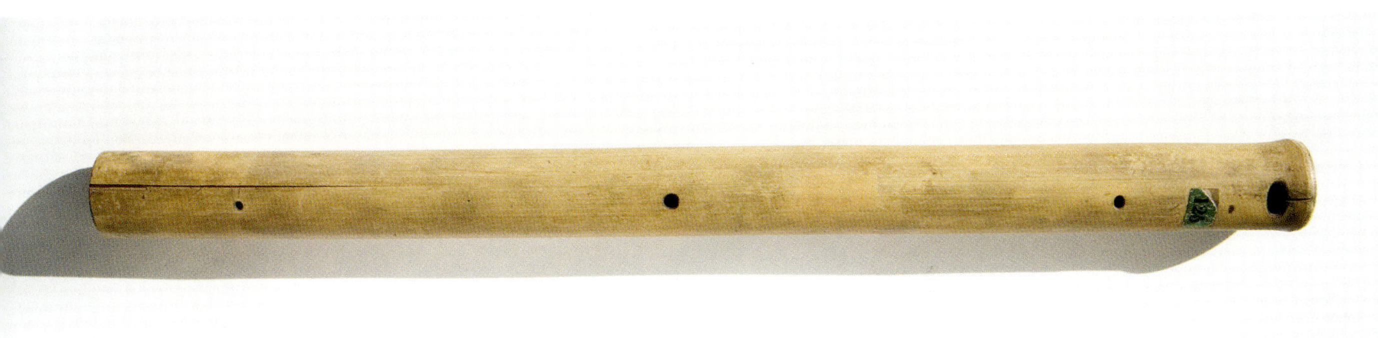

242

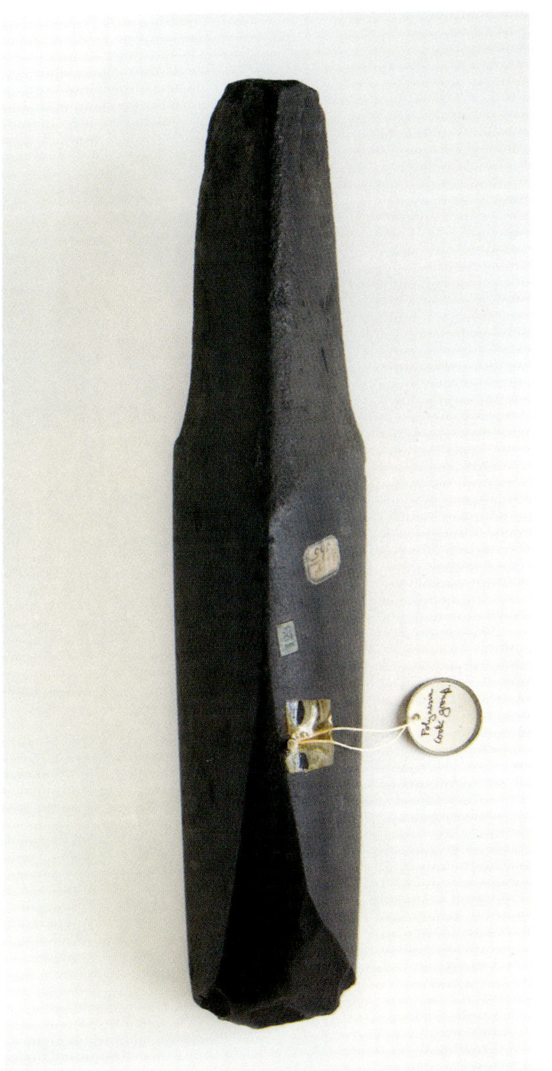

243

242 *Bamboo nose flute. 'Tahitian group.' 35cm. Some of the Cook voyage flutes are decorated with sennit bindings; the LMS examples are not. LMS 79.*

243 *Unusually large and carefully fashioned basalt adze blade. 40.5cm. Described 'Triangular in section; well finished. Hervey Group' on the BM registration slip; probably from Rarotonga. LMS 164.*

244 & 245 *Two views of rasp, made of ray skin tightly fastened around hibiscus wood core. Labelled 'Tahitian Group.' 20cm. Files of ray or shark skin, and of coral, were used to smooth the wood carvings. LMS 93.*

244

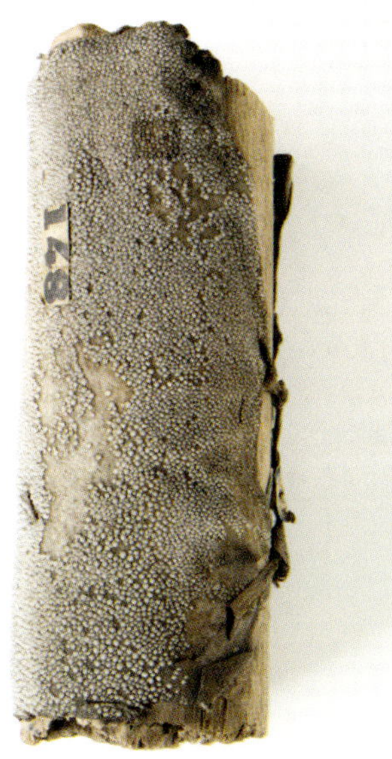

245

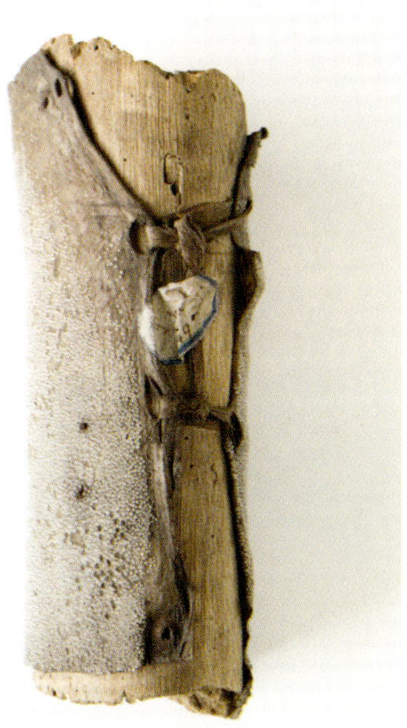

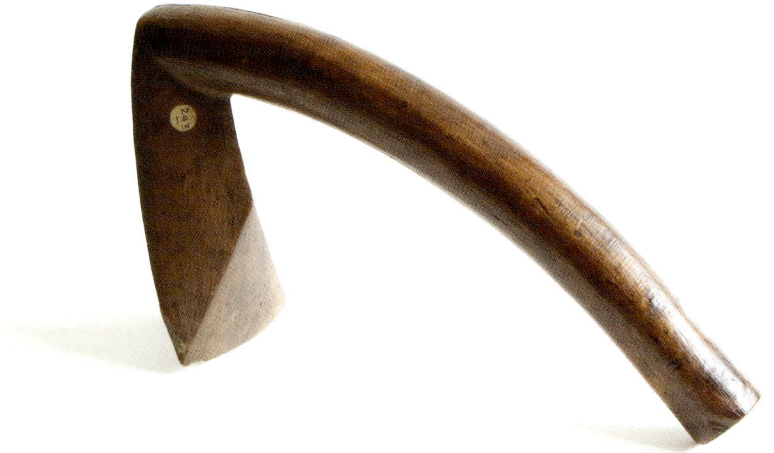

246

247

246 *Breadfruit splitter; Tahiti. Handle 30cm. Wooden blade is an accurate effigy of a basalt adze blade. 'G Bennet' is inscribed in pencil on the blade; Wm Oldman 243; J Hooper 484.*

247 *Bowl, labelled 'Tata . . . or scoop used for baleing water out of canoes in Island of Mangea . . . G Bennet July 1824.' 25cm. Evidently collected on the return of the deputation to England via Sydney, on the* Endeavour *portion of the voyage. CUM E1906.136.*

248 *Headrest, labelled 'Pillows, made of the wood of the Bread Fruit Tree, Tahite, G Bennet Esq. (Sheffield).' 11 x 23cm. CUM 1907.615.*

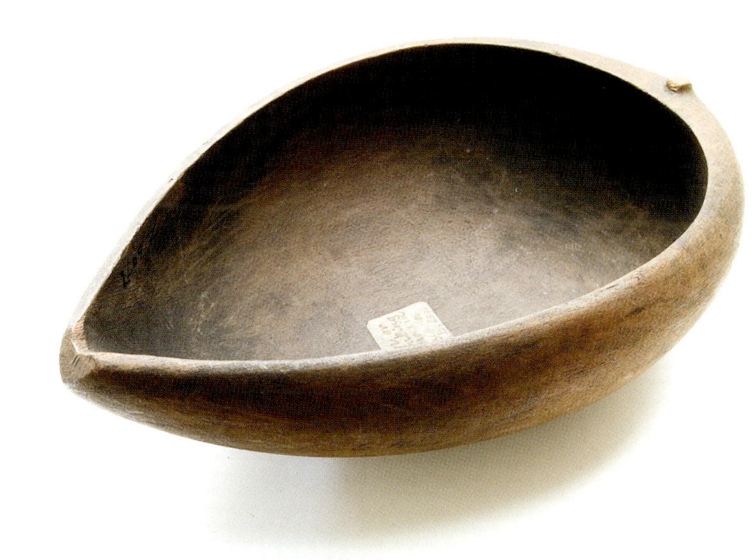

248

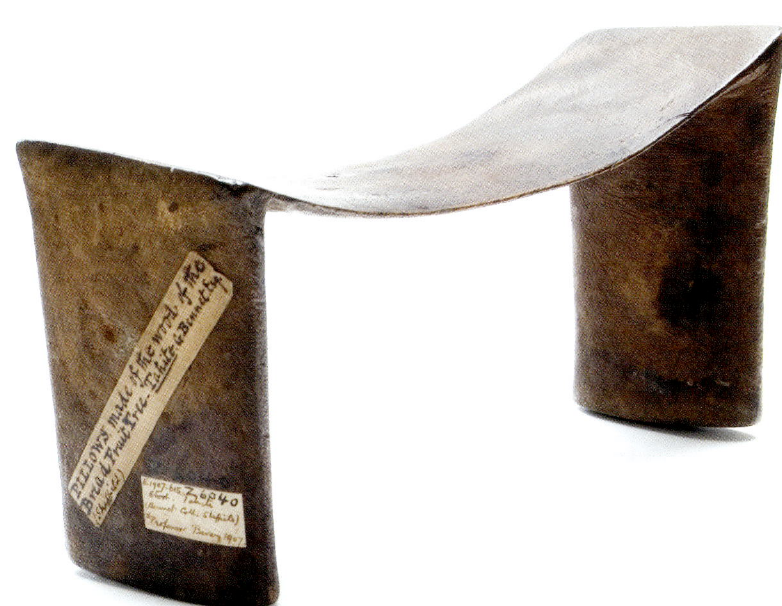

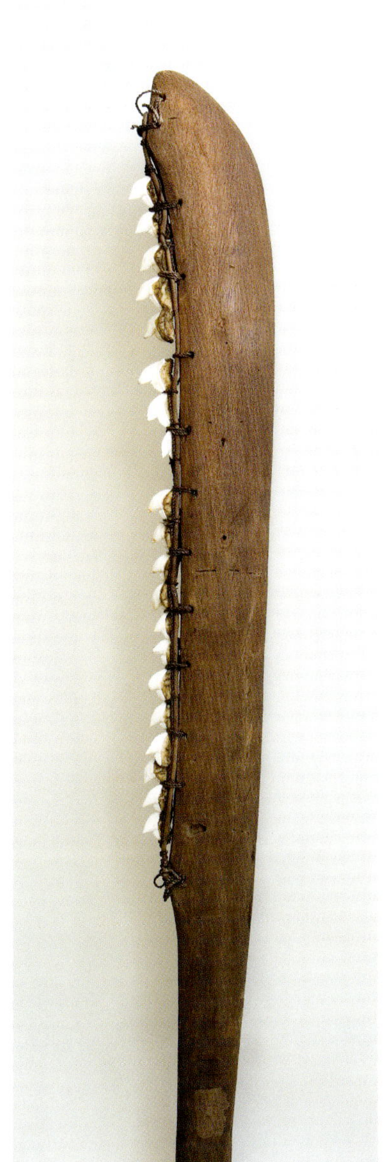

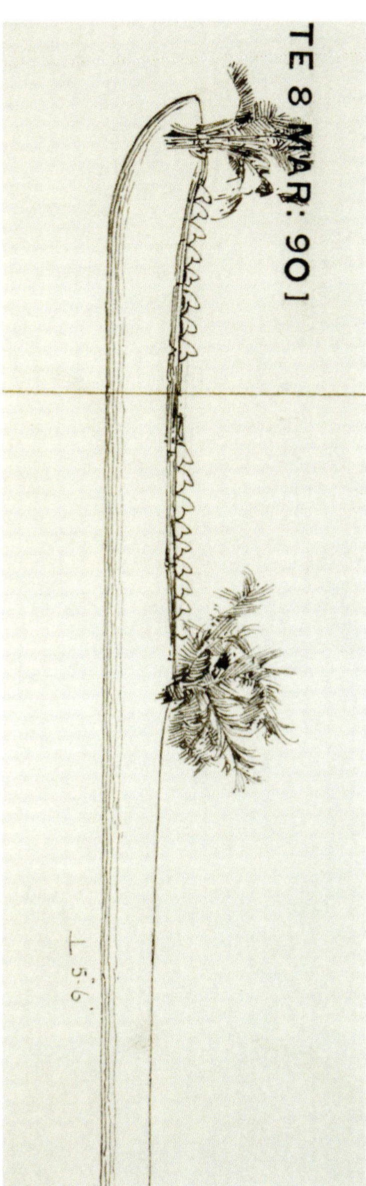

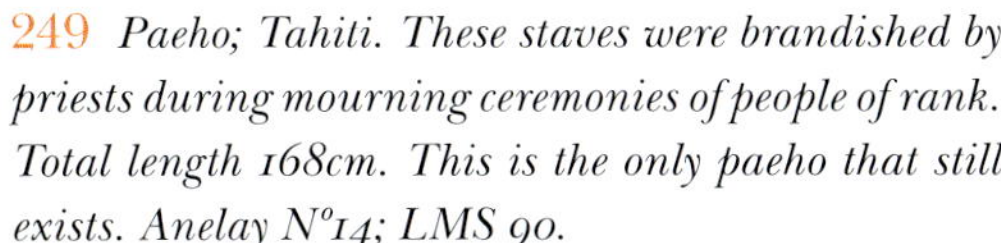

249 *Paeho; Tahiti. These staves were brandished by priests during mourning ceremonies of people of rank. Total length 168cm. This is the only paeho that still exists. Anelay N°14; LMS 90.*

250 *Paeho; Tahiti. Edge-Partington drawing on registration slip of LMS 90. Feather tufts now missing. This may have been collected or even made on Rurutu; see Ellis; 1853 1,299 footnote.*

251 *Detail of paeho in figure 249. Probably not a very effective weapon, as the shark teeth are loosely affixed.*

252 *Engraving of Tahitian priest in mourning dress, holding a paeho. From account of Cook's 3rd voyage by William Ellis,1782, op 129.*

249

250

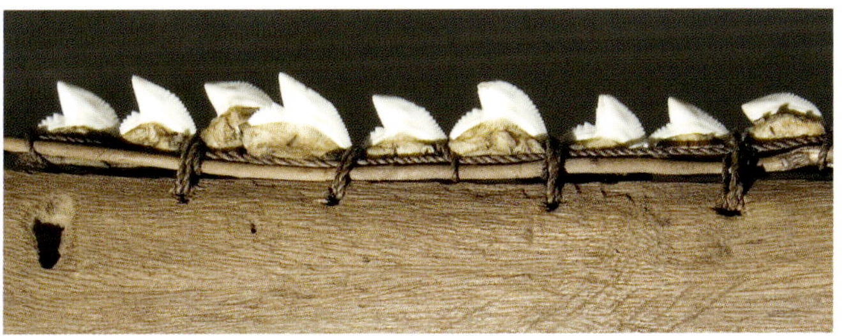

251

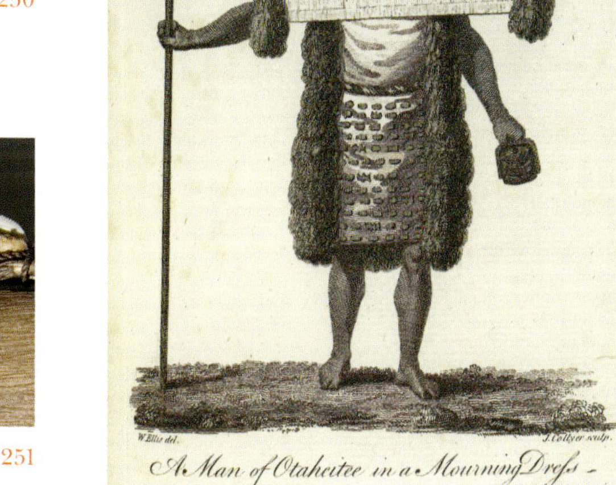

252

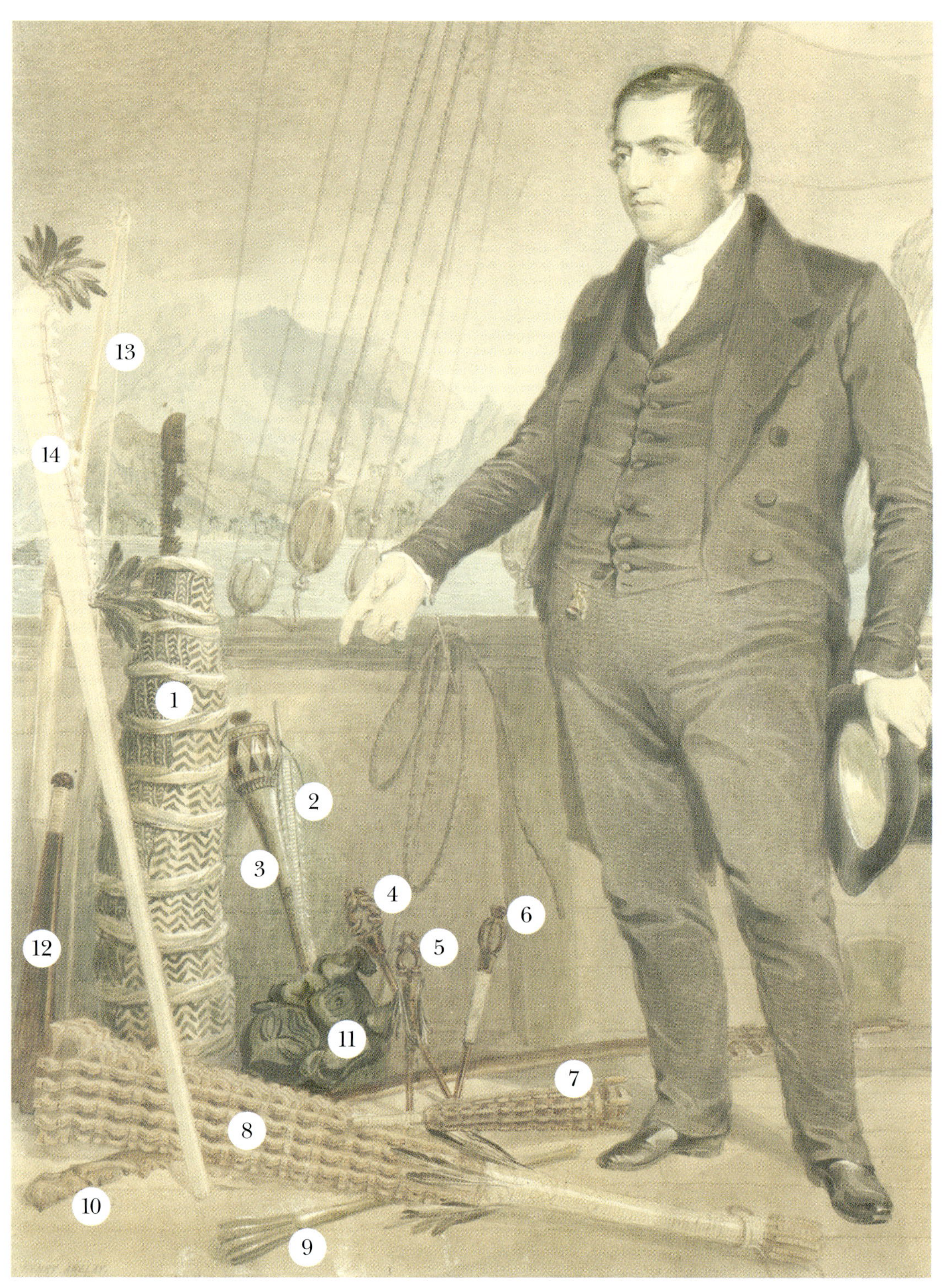

253 *Key to Polynesian items in the portrait of John Williams by Henry Anelay.*

Polynesian objects lying at Williams' feet in the Anelay watercolour

A very accurate colour lithograph of the Anelay watercolour, perhaps done by Anelay himself, is reproduced opposite the Introduction on page xii. Below is an annotated list of the objects at Williams' feet, numbered arbitrarily 1–14 in the key, shown opposite for reference.

ANELAY Nº1   Carved ironwood (casuarina) 'staff god' from Rarotonga, complete with zigzag-patterned tapa wrapping. Staff gods have been frequently illustrated and are thoroughly discussed by Buck; this one appears to be what he refers to as a 'small staff god'.[1] Ten of these, approximately this size, appear on the title page engraving of Williams' *Narrative*, lying at the feet of Williams and Pitman, who are seated in front of a missionary residence with their wives (see fig. 21).

An extraordinary Rarotongan staff god in the British Museum LMS collection is over 12 feet high and is likely one of the 'two immense idols which I [Williams] brought up from Rarotonga [on the *Messenger of Peace*]' to exhibit at the annual May meeting of the LMS in Ra'iatea, 1828.[2] Williams brought one of them back to England on the *Sir Andrew Hammond* in 1833. He explains that 'his Britannic Majesty's officers fearing lest the god should be made a vehicle for defrauding the king, very unceremoniously took it to pieces; and not being so well skilled at making gods as in protecting the revenue, they have not made it so handsome as when it was an object of veneration to the deluded Rarotongans.'[3] This may explain why the tapa wrapping appears in reversed orientation in various renderings. Williams adds 'Near the wood were red feathers and a string of small pieces of polished pearl shells, which were said to be the manava, or soul of the god.'[4] If Anelay Nº1 still exists, the wrapping has been removed. See staff god images in figures 191–196. It is astonishing that despite their obvious 'importance', the identity and meaning of these spectacular staff gods remain unknown.

---

1   Buck 1944,316.
2   Letter from Williams quoted in Prout 1843,277.
3   Williams 1837,117.
4   Ibid., 117; see wood engraving, ibid., 118. The feathers and shells are now missing.

Robert Bourne, on his visit to Rarotonga in 1825, states 'Four principal deities were formerly worshipped, viz. Taaroa, Butea, Toahiti, Motoro.'[5] It seems likely that Rarotongan staff gods represent one of these four. A letter Williams to Ellis dated 22 November 1827 mentions 'I have also prepared a very long account of the island [Rarotonga], gods, introduction of Christianity &c . . .' Unfortunately, this potentially very useful account cannot be found.[6]

ANELAY N°2   Illustrated in Williams 1837,534 'Weapons' plate, N°7, and designated 'Kingsmill Island [Gilbert Islands] dagger, with shark's teeth'. This is LMS 8.

ANELAY N°3   Illustrated in Williams 1837,534 'Weapons' plate, N°8, 'A Tongatabu hand club'. This club was given to the University of British Columbia Museum of Anthropology by Michael Williams in 2007.[7]

ANELAY N°4   This is LMS 51 (exchanged from the British Museum by London dealer Ralph Nash 23 January 1971; subsequently collections G Ortiz, C Monzino). Although figured in the catalogue of the 1972 exhibition at the Musée de l'Homme, *La Découverte de la Polynésie*, as a 'manche de chasse-mouche', from Tahiti, it is a fan handle from the central Cook Islands. It is referred to on the LMS slip as 'handle of handscreen, Hervey Group', in Read as a fan handle.[8] The fan is missing. The handle portion is a carved hardwood Janus figure. The slightly recurved tang terminus and the arms of the Janus figures are deeply notched. Janus figures appear throughout central Polynesia on such objects as Rurutu fly flaps[9] and Rarotonga fan handles (see figs. 125–127). Notches are also a common feature of central Polynesian wood carvings. The figures resemble those on LMS 49, from Atiu (figs. 174, 175),[10] which in turn appear to be related to feather cleats (figs. 166–169).

ANELAY N°5   Another Janus figure fan handle, also from the Hervey group, this is (LMS) TAH.139, figured in Archey,[11] slightly smaller but otherwise much like the above. The fan is missing. Note the clusters of dark feathers loosely attached to the tangs of both (LMS) TAH.139 and LMS 51 as depicted in the watercolour. The feathers of both are now missing.

ANELAY N°6   This unique object, probably also a fan handle, was also exchanged from the British Museum LMS collection by Ralph Nash 23 January 1971, along with LMS 51, and subsequently acquired by London dealer K J Hewett. No LMS registration slip exists. The handle is composed of five simple arched caryatid figures standing on a simple conical element. The figures with their protruding bellies resemble the Janus figures on Anelay N°4 and N°5. Above their heads is a section encircled with four rows of deeply carved zigzags. The white tapa wrapping around the tang to which the fan blade was originally fixed is now missing. The Anelay watercolour is the only known rendering of this object.

ANELAY N°7   Mitiaro staff god, also in the British Museum LMS collection, probably Oc 1982,Q.121 (see fig. 258). This is a large, complex, and finely carved staff god, with four intricate tiers of five or six arched cleats, terminating in an unusually elaborate dome. It is figured in Buck.[12] There are five panels on the 'head'. Feathers were originally attached to the cleats with fine sennit. No feathers appear in the Anelay watercolour depiction. Interestingly, the lower portion appears to be wrapped with white tapa.[13]

ANELAY N°8   Large, complex, openwork-carved wood Mangaia staff god, handle adorned with sennit and feathers, LMS 62 (see fig. 197). Mangaia staff gods are discussed and illustrated in detail by Buck.[14] Bourne, in 1825, visited Mangaia: 'Manaia has five principal deities Oro, Tane, Teahio, Toahiti, Motoro; they offer human sacrifices to Oro, but they are not frequent. They have maraes, none of the kings [have] renounced heathenism, they still remain, the gods are also still retained. . . .'[15]

---

5   *Trans Miss Soc* 1827–1832 vol (SOAS),262.
6   Prout 1843,254.
7   Mayer and Shelton 2009.
8   Read 1892 plate XII N°3; see fig. 91.
9   Rose 1979.
10   According to registration slip LMS 49 and Read 1892 plate XIV C, called 'Taringarue'.
11   Archey 1965 fig. 2.
12   Buck 1944 fig. 220f; also Hooper 2006 N°207.
13   The lower portion of Oldman N°379 is wrapped with sennit; this is where the tails were attached.
14   Buck 1944.
15   *Trans Miss Soc* 1827–1832 vol (SOAS),257.

It seems likely that Mangaia staff gods represent one of these five deities.

ANELAY Nº9   Delicate, enigmatic object, not yet identified, copied from the Weapons plate in Williams 1837,534 Nº1, where it is referred to as 'A Samoa club'. Samoa was singular in Polynesia in that it was, in Williams' words, 'godless'; 'idolatry [was] not so firm . . . the people generally have no idols to destroy'.[16] Samoan 'gods' were *aitu* or spirits, generally residing in beasts and birds, some in finely woven fibre girdles (see p. 50 re Papo). Samoa had no temples, altars, priests, sacrifices. Edge-Partington[17] figures a unique small (35cm) carved wood LMS object which he refers to as a Samoan staff god, LMS 173 on British Museum registration slip. It has six tiers of four cleats somewhat reminiscent of the feather cleats on Mitiaro staff gods; it is Nº56 in LMS catalogue nd, 'A SAMOAN GOD, a short round stick.'

ANELAY Nº10   A small, slightly curved Rarotongan staff god, this could well be LMS 40, which is figured in Edge-Partington.[18] Conspicuous arms are held downwards, the staff is curved, there are several figures above the phallic terminus, and there is no tapa wrapping.

ANELAY Nº11   A Rarotongan 'fisherman's god' with penis removed. Williams makes two comments about these images: (1) 'An idol . . . was placed on the fore part of every fishing canoe; and when the natives were going on a fishing excursion, prior to setting off, they invariably presented offerings to the god, and invoked him to grant them success';[19] (2) 'I do not recollect to have seen two precisely similar representations of the same deity, except those placed on the fishing canoes.'[20] That is all that is known about them. They are mentioned by WW Gill,[21] and are thoroughly discussed by Buck.[22] There are about a dozen known examples, and it is true—all are similar. The Anelay rendering appears to have been copied from Williams' 'Idols' plate referred to above;

peculiarly, the eyes sag somewhat downwards and three pairs of parentheses bracket the navel in both renderings. It is likely that both the Anelay and the Williams (Baxter) renderings depict the unpainted fisherman's god figured by Ellis and by Edge-Partington, which is LMS 36.[23] See figures 255–257.

ANELAY Nº12   Appears to be a club, handle wrapped with sennit.

ANELAY Nº13   Appears to be a bamboo bow.

ANELAY Nº14   Paeho, LMS 90; see fig. 249.[24] Neither idol nor standard weapon, these were brandished by priests in the mourning *heiva*—the mourning ceremony of a deceased person of high rank. Ellis describes the paeho as 'a terrific weapon, about five feet long, one end . . . a handle, the other broad and flat, and in shape not unlike a short scythe. The point was ornamented with a tuft of feathers, and the . . . concave side armed with a line of large, strong sharks' teeth, fixed in the wood by the tough fibres of ieie.'[25] It was supposedly used for cutting or 'emboweling' those who got in the way or otherwise did not show the greatest respect for the 'infuriated', 'demoniacal' chief mourner as he led a days-long procession through the region after the death.[26] The mourners, painted in charcoal and clay, tore their hair and lacerated their faces and bodies with shark teeth until they were covered with a good deal of blood. There are several published descriptions of this dramatic ritual. It was promptly outlawed by the missionaries. LMS 90 is apparently the only paeho that exists. Because paeho are depicted in so many Cook voyage illustrations of Tahiti, it is assumed this paeho is Tahitian in origin, although the mention by Ellis of a paeho (likely LMS 90) in conjunction with mention of 'A Rurutuan helmet' raises the possibility that it could have been found and even made on Rurutu.[27]

---

16   Williams 1837,436; Prout 1843,326.
17   Edge-Partington 1890 1,78, Nº4 (15¼").
18   Ibid., pl 23 Nº6 (41").
19   Williams 1837,117.
20   Ibid., 546.
21   'At Rarotonga it was customary for fishermen and voyagers to take with them in their canoes pieces of wood carved roughly into the human form, as charms' (WW Gill 1880,102).
22   Buck 1944,311.

23   Edge-Partington 1890 1,20 Nº1 (18½"); the parentheses are probably cracks in the wood; also figured Ellis 1829, frontispiece vol 2, Nº7, as annotated on the original LMS stand, visible in Buck card photo.
24   Edge-Partington 1890 1,26 Nº4 (67").
25   Ellis 1853 1,413; ieie refers to the extremely strong fibre made from aerial roots of the unusual vine-like pandanus, *Freycinetia* (the plant is called *farapepe* in Tahitian).
26   Ellis 1853 1,297 and 412; for a full discussion of the funeral heiva, see Oliver 1974 vol 1.
27   Footnote, Ellis 1829 2,498; 1853 1,299.

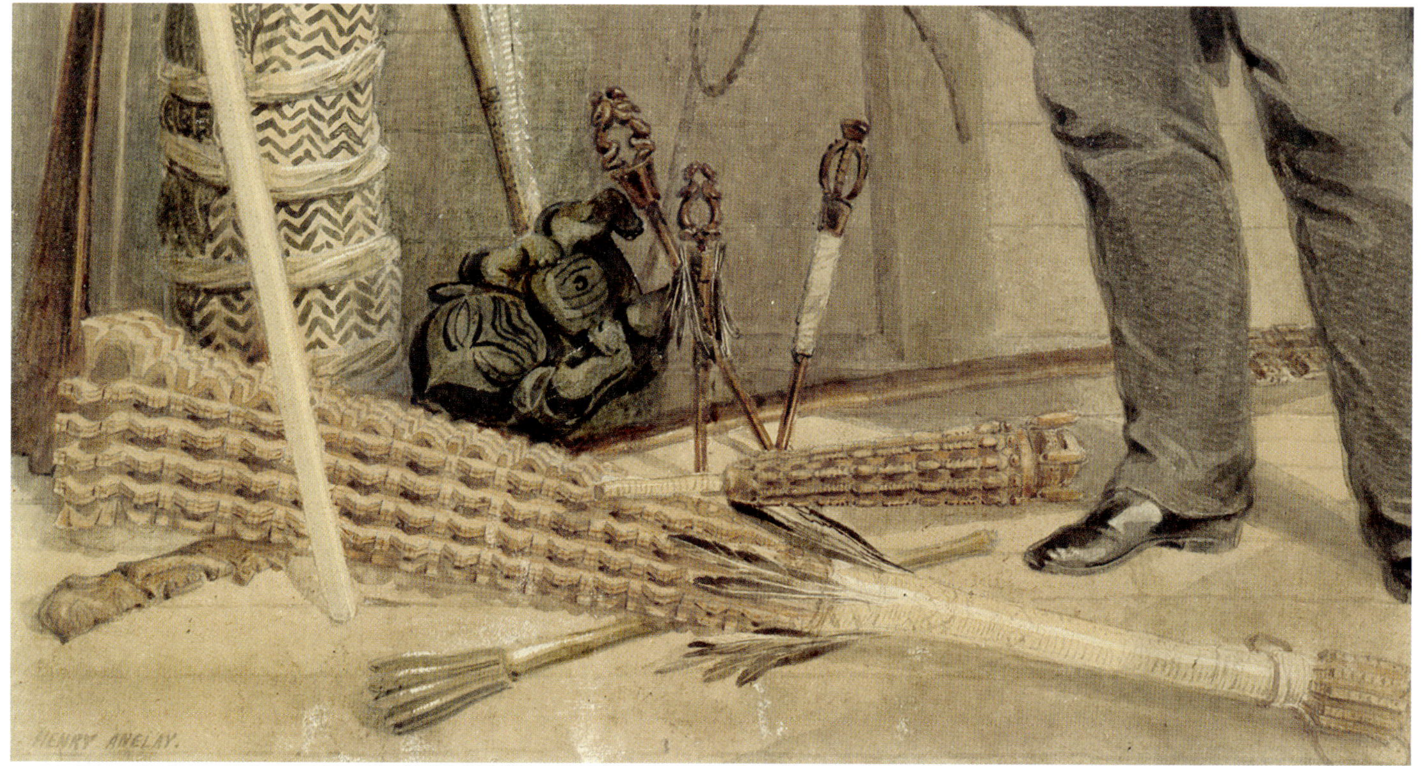

254

254   *Detail of some of the idols at Williams' feet in the Anelay watercolour;
National Library of Australia, Canberra. Engravings and photographs of
five of the actual idols depicted are shown on this spread.*

255   *Fisherman's god. LMS 36; Ellis 1829, frontispiece vol 2.*

256   *Fisherman's god. LMS 36; Baxter wood engraving in* Missionary
Enterprises *1837, 118.*

257   *Buck's card of fisherman's god, Rarotonga. LMS 36. 44cm. Courtesy
BPBM.*

255

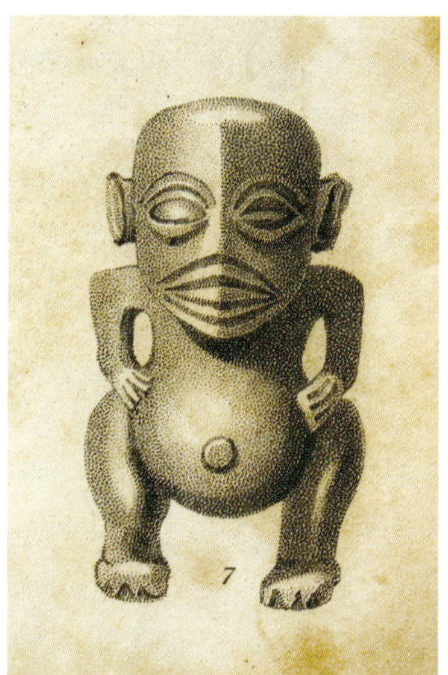

256

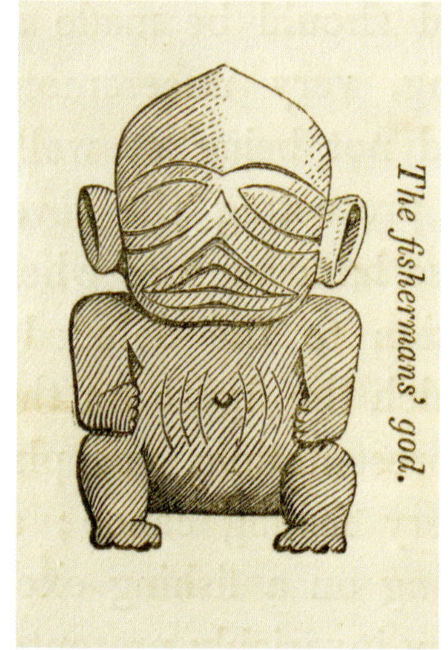

257

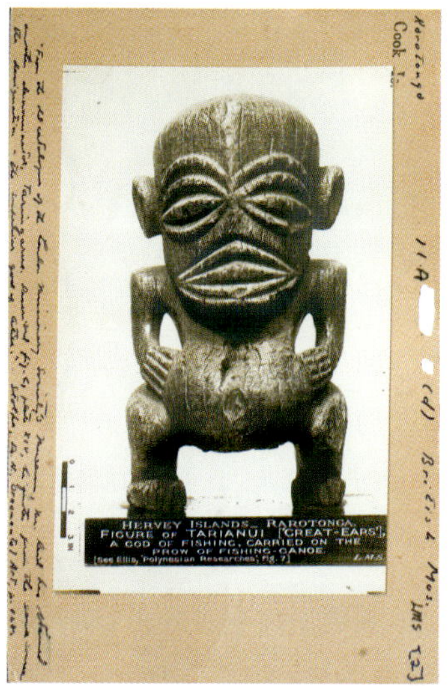

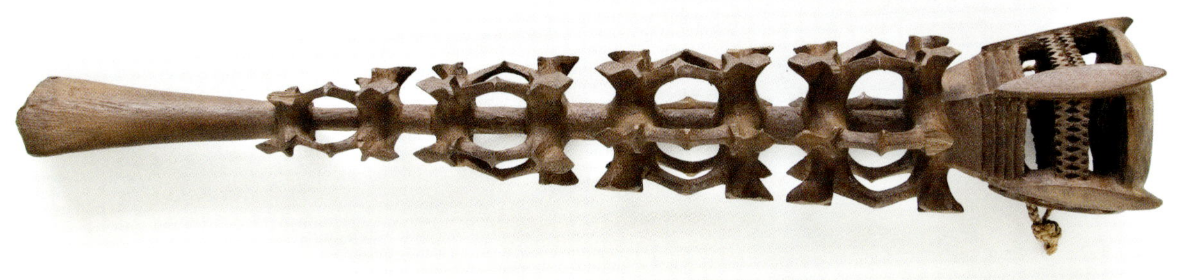

258   *Staff god, Mitiaro. 40.5cm. BM LMS Oc1982,Q.121.*

259   *Janus figure fan handle; central Cook Islands. 43.5cm. BM LMS collection; R Nash; G Ortiz. LMS 51. Feathers are now missing.*

260   *Janus figure fan handle, central Cook Islands. 40.5cm. (LMS) TAH.139. Feathers are now missing.*

261   *Caryatid fan handle, central Cook Islands. BM LMS collection, no number; R Nash; KJ Hewett. White tapa wrapping now missing. 31cm.*

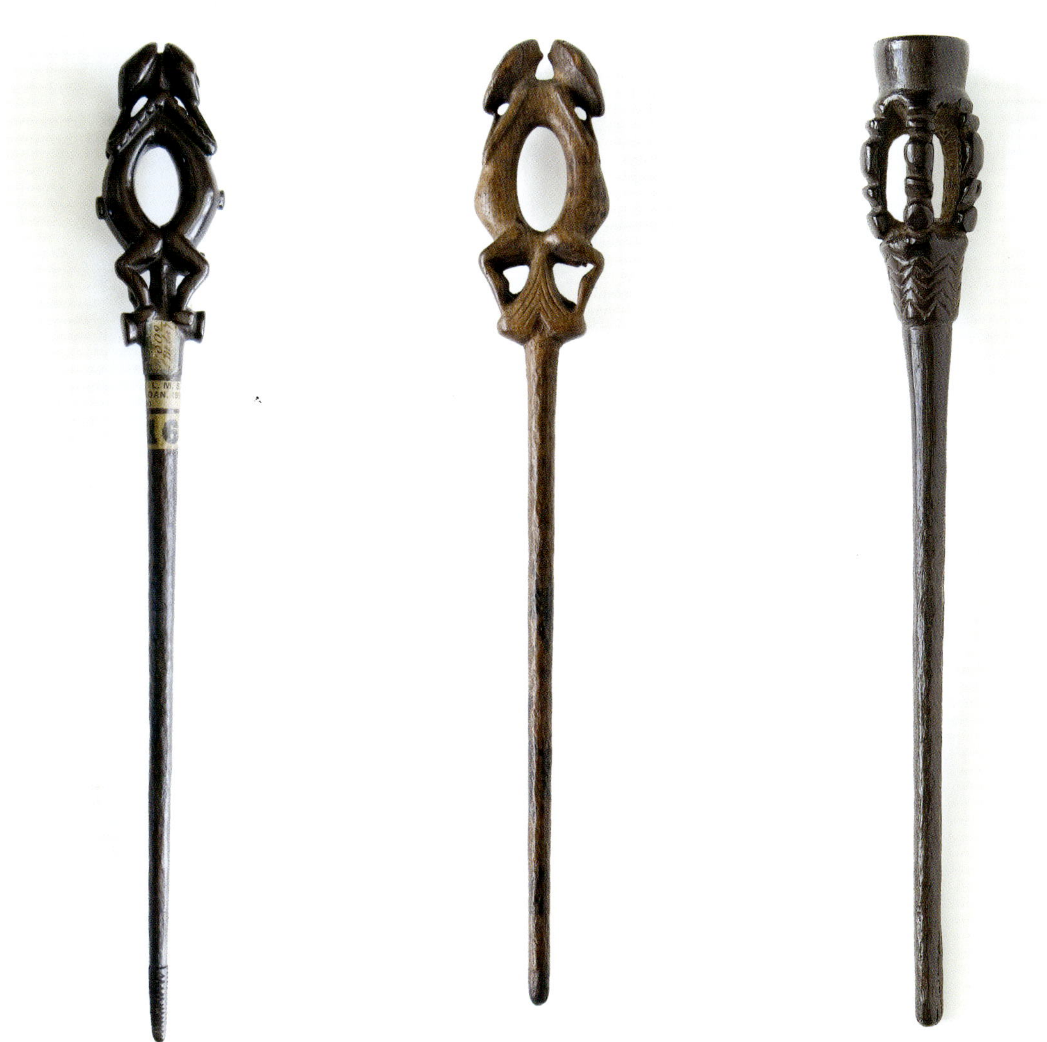

147

TRANSACTIONS

OF THE

Missionary Society.

VOL. I.

FROM ITS INSTITUTION IN THE YEAR 1795,
TO THE END OF THE YEAR 1802.

THE SECOND EDITION.

PUBLISHED FOR THE BENEFIT OF THE SOCIETY.

LONDON:

PRINTED BY BYE AND LAW, ST. JOHN'S SQUARE;

AND SOLD BY

T. WILLIAMS, No. 10, STATIONERS' COURT, LUDGATE STREET.

1804.

John Jefferson's account of his visit to a marae at Opare, Tahiti, 3 October 1798

This narrative is the first detailed account of a missionary visit to a marae and is also one of the most informative. It is the 3 October 1798 entry from the journal of John Jefferson, who was one of the four ordained ministers who came to Tahiti on the *Duff*. The entry describes his trip from Matavai Bay down the coast to Opare (Pare), to visit the principal marae of Pomare II, home of the great 'Oro image captured by Pomare from the people of Atehuru. A keen observer, Jefferson had been on Tahiti only seven months but had clearly learned considerable Tahitian. He was accompanied by a Tahitian priest. This passage contains information about marae, pou (stone uprights), unu (wood altar carvings), and Tahitian religious ceremonies that appears nowhere else. Jefferson's journal contains excellent accounts of missionary life during the difficult early years of the Tahitian Mission and offers many insights into Tahitian culture. It is a valuable but generally neglected resource. Much of it was published in *Transactions of the Missionary Society*, as was this entry (1804,98; SOAS).

use the appointed means, *his* to bless them.   We still continue
to believe we are not brought and preserved here in the manner
we have been for nought ; we look forward to a period, when
we hope to see the word of God run and be glorified.   Many
dark seasons may intervene, and many fiery darts from Satan
cause pangs unutterable before the arrival of that period ; but
the sight of *one* convert to Christ, will more than overpoise
gloomy prospects and Satan's arrows.

—————————

Brother JEFFERSON's Account of his Journey to Opare,
on October 3, &c.

" My chief intention in this journey was to see a *morai* in
" the district of Opare, where the inhabitants of the land shed
" the blood of captives taken in war, both men and women, and
" offer it up in sacrifice to their gods.   For my guide I was
" accompanied by an Otaheitean priest.   *Morai*, in the lan-
" guage of the country, signifies a place appropriated to the
" worship of Eatooa, or deity.   As the Otaheiteans have a
" plurality of deities, so they have many *morais*.   They are
" temporary or permanent. Temporary *morais* are erected
" before the corpse of the dead agreeable to the fancy of the
" erector, and (from what I have hitherto seen) are commonly
" small altars, variously decorated, with leaves and the fruit of
" palm tree, that grows in abundance, and upon which are
" placed divers offerings of food.   Permanent *morais* are nu-
" merous and diverse : they are usually enclosed spots of ground
" surrounded with trees of different kinds, and having in them
" sundry small pavements of stone : at the head of each stands
" a stone of larger size, and at the back of the stone is generally
" fixed a board five or six feet long, with a little rude carving
" on it ; the top divided into five parts, or slits, to represent the
" fingers of a hand : sometimes the board has the figure of a
" man or bird carved on its top.   At the foot of this pavement
" the priest worships, with his face directed towards the head-
" stone and plank, and throws his offering, consisting of a
" young plantain-tree root, green leaves, or the leaf of a cocoa-
" nut twisted in a peculiar form, upon the pavement.   Besides
" these kinds of oratories within the enclosure, there are altars,
" on which meat offerings are placed, and before which prayers
" are made.   Altars for the like purpose are scattered up and
" down the country where there is no *morai*.   At one perma-
" nent place of worship, there are frequently a plurality of
" *morais* dedicated to different deities : thus the one I now
" visited, had in it two others dedicated to as many false gods.
                                          " This

" This *morai* stands on a sandy point of land, that shoots a
" little out towards the sea, forming a small bay on each side :
" the easternmost exposed to the sea breeze, and indifferent
" landing for the canoes ; the westernmost sheltered from the
" east wind, and pretty good landing. The whole point is
" covered with fragments of sharp coral rock. Distant from
" point Venus by land between three and four miles, and by sea
" about three miles. Close to the *morai* grow bread-fruit,
" cocoa-nut, purrow, and its trees : the fruit of the two former
" are sacred, being only used by particular persons : the two
" latter bear no fruit for food. The name of the *morai* is
" tábboo-tábboo-wāātáā, and which is the general name of all
" the *morais* where human sacrifices are offered, and of which
" there is one in the district of Attāhoóroo, and another in
" Pāpārā, besides what are in Tiaraboo. We arrived at the
" *morai* between eleven and twelve o'clock : before we entered
" it, my guide gathered a bunch of green leaves that grew upon
" the beach ; and as soon as we came to the accustomed place
" for making offerings, he threw the leaves upon the pave-
" ment, and repeated, in a seemingly indifferent manner, a few
" words as a prayer to the supposed deity for his good-will
" towards us. The place where the priest performed this cere-
" mony, is dedicated to their principal *Eatooa*, called Oóro.
" It is a rough stone pavement about eighteen feet square : at
" the north end, which faced the sea, is a large hedge of stones
" five feet or more high, three or four feet wide, and eighteen
" feet long. Upon the top of this pile are several pieces of
" board, some of them six feet long, and a foot broad, the tops
" slit into five parts, to represent a hand with the fingers a little
" open. At the south end are set up five stones, three of them
" larger in size than the other two. These stones are for those
" who officiate as priests : the three largest for superior, and the
" two smallest for inferior ones. They sit cross-legged upon
" the pavement, and support their backs against the stones :
" and in this mode of adoration, with their faces towards the
" pile of stones and boards, they make their prayers. The middle
" space is where the human victims are slaughtered by being
" knocked on the head with a club and stones : after which a
" principal priest takes out the eyes of the murdered person,
" and holding them in his hands, he presents them to the mouth
" of the king, who opens his mouth as if to receive and eat
" them : when this ceremony is performed, the carcase is
" thrown into a pit, and covered with stones. By the number
" of pits surrounding the place, and by the expressions of my
" conductor, I apprehend there have been many hundreds of
" men and women thus sacrificed by the abominable superstition   " of

" of these idolaters. Besides the captives taken in war, the
" bodies of those slain in war, or cut off by the commandment
" of the great chief, or that are purposely killed for human
" sacrifices in any other part, under the jurisdiction of the great
" chief, or king, are brought to the tábboo-tábboo-wāātáā, and
" there prayers are made over them, and then they are buried
" as before observed. A little to the right of this pavement of
" blood, and nearer towards the point, is an altar to Oóro,
" raised upon three rows of wooden pillars, thirteen in a row,
" nearly seven feet high, and four or five feet broad: the top
" covered with cocoa-nut leaves, and the front and ends deco-
" rated with the leaf of the sugar-cane, so fixed as that they
" may hang down like long fringes. Upon this altar offerings
" of fish, hogs, bread-fruit, and mountain-plantains, are laid.
" A large hog was upon the altar, which seemed to have been
" placed there no long time. Fish and mountain-plantains are
" offered raw ; hogs and bread-fruit are baked : frequently the
" hog is smeared with its blood before offered up. A little more
" to the right was the frame of an altar going to decay, dedi-
" cated to a supposed deity named Orā-mādóoā : upon this lay
" some pieces of wood that had once formed something be-
" longing to their idolatrous rites, but I could not plainly com-
" prehend what. Proceeding towards the point a few yards,
" at the extremity of the land, a large pile of stones appeared in
" view : from our house on point Venus, where it may be
" seen, it appears like a rock : it may be ten or twelve feet high,
" and twice as much in length : it consists of a number of
" stones piled one upon another without much art, and sacred
" to an imagined sea god whose name is Teepáh. The priest
" informed me, that before this pile of stones are also offered
" human sacrifices. Tired and disgusted with this awful proof
" of man's apostacy, and the devil's power over him, I desired
" my guide to withdraw. Considerations of the importance,
" arduousness, and danger of the work in which myself and
" brethren are engaged, gradually arose in my mind : the flesh
" quaked for fear, and the god of this world was not wanting
" with his suggestions ; but I committed our cause to Christ.
" Having quitted this scene of human infamy, I proceeded with
" my conductor to the westward, purposing to see the chief of
" Hăpyāno, who was but a few miles distant. We passed the
" residences of Pomére, Owo, Otoo, and the late Orepiah,
" which all stand within the compass of a mile : at present desti-
" tute of their owners. Otoo's house is situated upon the bank
" of a tolerable good river, about an hundred yards from the
" sea ; no otherwise to be known as the habitation of the great
" chief of Otaheite, than by two posts, with the head of a man
                                                    " carved

" carved on them, placed in the main road opposite his house,
" at between seventy and eighty yards distant on each side,
" Every islander, whether chief or common person, when they
" come to either of these posts in passing the king's dwelling,
" make bare their shoulders; nor must they cover them again
" till they have passed the opposite post. In whatever part of
" the island the king has an habitation, it is dignified with such
" pillars, and the like ceremony of baring the shoulders ob-
" served, though the chief is elsewhere. These pillars are
" called Tee, which is the name of a sort of household gods,
" worshipped under the form of a man carved in wood. I do
" not understand that this action of theirs is any religious cere-
" mony paid to the image, or supposed deity, but a mark of
" respect to their king: which is shewn him wherever he goes,
" and by all who appear in his presence, his father and mother
" not excepted, the queen being the only person exempt. And
" so strictly is this custom adhered to, that a wilful breach of
" it would certainly be attended with death; and if it should so
" happen that the king passed a person unobserved, who had
" his shoulders covered, his cloth would be deemed sacred, and
" must no more be worn by that person, but given to the king,
" or torn. I saw Edéä, the king's mother, (who is exceedingly
" rigid for the honours and prerogatives of majesty) so caught
" once. She was in her dwelling, and happened not to notice
" the approach of the chief, who went by her house on his
" man-horse. He was no sooner gone by, than Edéä's attend-
" ants (who were present, and saw not the king) perceived their
" error, and gave her notice of it: she immediately took off her
" *teeāpóotā*, and rent it to pieces. To prevent such mistakes,
" it is usual for the first discoverer of the king's appearance,
" to give the alarm by calling out aloud: by which means
" people are prepared. This ceremony of uncovering the
" shoulders has never been attempted to be imposed upon us.
" We have made them understand what mark of respect is paid
" to the king of England by all who enter into his presence,
" and we pay the like to Otoo. About three in the afternoon
" reached Vitua's: the chief received me kindly, and lodged
" me courteously. Being at no great distance from the large
" house called Nānu, I purposed to see it: accordingly the next
" morning I took leave of Vitua and his wife, and with the
" priest pursued our journey. After an hour's walk we arrived
" at a point that forms the north-east extremity of a small but
" pleasant bay called Towpo. In the middle of the bay stands
" a little sand island named Motutā, and in the bottom is built
" the Nānu, but a few feet from the edge of the sea. On this
" point are a few houses belonging to Pomére and Edéä, and
" a plantation

" a plantation of fine pumpkins. Under a shed is a pair of
" large canoes, of a very different and superior construction to
" any I had seen before: they seem to have been put together
" with much labour and pains, and appear capable of carrying
" upon their platform forty or fifty men. Each canoe had upon
" its stem and stern the figure of a man, half as large as life,
" rudely cut, and one extremely obscene. These kind of ves-
" sels bear the name of Pāhée, (the same as is given to ships)
" whereas a canoe is called Vāā. Between this point and the
" Nānu, we met with three sacred canoes belonging to Eimeo:
" one of which carried what the Otaheiteans call the House of
" God. The canoes were hauled upon the beach under the
" shade of a large *purow* tree; upon the top branches of
" which, wrapped up in a basket made of cocoa-nut leaves,
" with a long pole run through it, hung a man that had been
" destroyed for a sacrifice, and which these canoes were going
" to convey to a great *morai* on Eimeo. On asking the per-
" sons belonging to the canoes who the man was, and why he
" was killed, they very quickly answered, he was one of those
" who assisted in stripping me and my three brethren on the
" 26th of March, and for which Pomére had killed him. I
" know not whether it was really so or not, but my guide
" assured me it was. The double canoe, that contained the
" house of the supposed god, was quite new, as was the house,
" and all its appurtenances. The house was upon the left hand
" canoe, on a kind of forecastle that projects beyond the stem.
" First there was a thing called the legs of God, not unlike a
" cradle that is sometimes used by surgeons to rest a broken
" limb on: the cradle was between three and four feet long:
" on the top of this was fixed a box four or five feet long, and
" one foot square: the end towards the stem of the canoe open,
" and by which the divinity was said to enter: over this was
" a thatch of palm leaves. The cradle, box, and roof, were
" about four feet high. On the right hand canoe, upon the
" fore part of it, was also a kind of cradle, but somewhat dif-
" ferent from the former. On this likewise lay a box about
" five feet long, and one foot square, open at the top and ends.
" Against this box, on each side, were placed five pieces of
" board, about a foot and an half high, and eight inches broad,
" the tops slit to represent a hand and fingers, and these were
" called the hands of God: a little scratching on some of the
" boards for ornament: between each hand was an offering of
" a bunch of green leaves; and in the box lay a stinking
" hedgehog fish. The other two canoes had each a piece of
" plank lashed athwart their forecastles, with a few hands of
" God stuck against them, and one of them a reed about five
　　　　　　　　　　　　　　　　　　　　　　　　" feet

" feet long, with a sprig of very small red feathers at the top,
" two small pieces of a stick tied across the reed in different
" places, and round which a piece of cord was twisted. No-
" thing could be more rude and barbarous than the whole work
" of this singular exhibition of South-sea superstition and ido-
" latry. I asked, as I was able, a few questions concerning
" the god to whom this house belonged, and received for
" answer, that it was Oóro's; and that when Pomére or
" Mannĕmannĕ prayed, Oóro came and entered into his house,
" and was there seen by them. I dropped a word or two sig-
" nifying they were wrong, but ignorance of the language pre-
" vented me from saying much upon so important a subject.
" Leaving the canoes, a few minutes walk brought us to the
" Nānu. As Mr. W. Wilson, the chief mate of the Duff,
" took a particular description of it while here *, I need only
" add, that the roof of the house is going to decay, and thou-
" sands of fleas have taken possession of the floor, which is
" sand covered with coarse grass. It is said, that the house is
" sufficiently large to contain *all* the inhabitants of the island.
" Whether it is so or not, I cannot pretend to say; but it is
" the general rendezvous of the chiefs, and their attendants,
" who meet here upon some occasions. The noise, disorder,
" and wantonness, that prevails at such times, among an as-
" semblage of several hundred licentious barbarians, may be
" better conceived than expressed. Having accomplished my
" desire, I returned with my conductor (who took great pains
" to instruct me in every thing I wished to know) to Vitua's.
" After taking some refreshment, we took leave of the chief
" and his wife, and returned to Matavai.

" Opare is one of the finest districts in the island, and is the
" principal residence of Pomére, &c. It is formed (like every
" other district) into a number of divisions and sub-divisions,
" of which I cannot at present speak particularly. The con-
" stant inhabitants of Opare appear to be very few in proportion
" to the extent and fertility of the land. The houses, as in
" every other part of the island, are scattered, being seldom
" more than five or six together. Bread-fruit-trees, cocoa-
" nuts, plantains, yellow apple-trees, &c. are in great plenty,
" and yield a large superfluity of food. As these grow spon-
" taneously, agriculture is but little practised. A few patches
" of ground are to be met with, cultivated with yávvā, the cloth
" plant, and a few esculents; while the rest of the country is
" covered with coarse grass, cotton-trees, shrubs of various
" kinds, &c. and which are sometimes set on fire to clear the
" ground. The roads are the sea beach, and narrow foot-

* See Missionary Voyage, page 210.

" paths

" paths inland, seldom wide enough to admit two persons to
" walk a-breast. The whole land is well watered, and with a
" little industry, capable of being rendered sufficiently fruitful
" to subsist, I think, many times the number of its present
" occupiers."

SECTION III.

Transactions of the Missionaries during the Year 1799.

JANUARY 2d.—Held a prayer-meeting about the time we
judged some of our brethren in England would be assembled on
New Years' eve, in which, with them, we endeavoured to thank
our merciful Father, through our gracious high-priest, for the
blessings of the past year, and supplicated favours for the new.
In the evening again met, and held another undisturbed prayer-
meeting. Blessed be the God and Father of our Lord Jesus
Christ for his manifold mercies towards us!

Jan. 4th.—A pleasant and peaceable day. Mr. Lewis attended
morning prayers.

Jan. 7th.—Peter visited us: he presented us with a large
baked fish. He tells us things are still in a very unsettled state
in Attāhóroo and Păpărā. He appears desirous to get off the
island if he could, but he knows not where to go. Fine
weather.

Jan. 8th.—Held our monthly prayer-meeting at the usual
time. Cloudy weather.

Jan. 11th.—Brothers Nott and Jefferson returned from an
excursion to Teáray. Nothing particular occurred to them
during their absence. The country (which presented an awful
spectacle of brutality and heathenism of the grossest kind)
appeared in peace, and no talk of war; while the poor inhabitants are pursuing their abominable practices with greediness.
The preaching of the gospel, we perceive, will be an arduous
work indeed, attended with much difficulty.

Jan. 12th.—Much time engaged at the language: the farther
we advance in the knowledge of it, the greater reason we have

8

to

Letter Williams and Threlkeld (Ra'iatea) to Burder (LMS London) 18 October 1821 concerning the introduction of Christianity to Rurutu

This informative account clearly formed the basis for 'Account of the introduction of Christianity into Rurutu' printed in *Missionary Sketches*, January 1824, as well as Ellis' account of Rurutu in *Polynesian Researches*. It describes the conversion process, and idols; it also mentions Arioi and 'Oro in Rurutu. The manuscript account is transcribed here in its entirety because it contains a good deal more information than has been published before. Lancelot Threlkeld had medical and acting experience before his ordination; he was stationed on Mo'orea, Huahine, and Ra'aitea along with Williams. (SOAS LMS SS incom corresp box3b folder6; original pagination indicated in brackets).

An account of the renunciation of Idolatry & of the reception of Christianity by the natives of the Island of Rurutu an Island in the South Seas—150,51 East Long, 22,29 S. Lat called in Charts Ohetiroa

Raiatea Oct 18 1821

The whole of the circumstances having been peculiarly interesting & encouraging to us—we desire that all who are anxious for the universal spread of divine truth & feel interested in the success of Christian Missions may be acquainted with it that they may be partaken with us of our joy.

On March the 8th last we saw a strange sail at Sea which made toward the reef & appeared to be determined to hazard the running on the reef instead of bearing up for the proper harbor, a practice resorted to by the natives when in extremity. Perceiving their imminent danger the cheifs manned our boats & went off to pilot the strangers safely into the proper harbor, where they arrived[.] [W]e found they were natives of the island of Rurutu, they had come from Maupiti Touched at their at Porapora but could not get in for the contrary wind. They had been drifted about at Sea for three weeks & latterly without both food & water excepting Sea water which they were obliged to drink, contrary winds drove them from their own Island, but the Lord to whose merciful designs winds & waves are subservient protected & guided them to these Islands—Maupiti was the first Island they could make although they attempted to make both Raiatea & Porapora.

They were exceedingly astonished at the difference of custom[:] men & women eating together; the Arioi Society, their dances, & every lascivious game completely put away[.] [W]hen they heard of the new System of Religion & saw the people worshipping the living & true God they were convinced of its propriety & superiority & immediately began to learn to read.

The cheif with his wife & a few others went onshore at Porapora—Mr Orsmond the Missionary of that Station paid every attention to them during their short stay—gave them books & began to teach them to read, but as the Cause & the greater part of the people were at Raiatea they soon followed. They were about 25 in number men & women—we set apart a certain time for their instruction supplied them all with Elementary books & gave them in charge to our Deacons who were very much pleased with & diligent in the discharge of their new office. Their language being somewhat different the Deacons could make themselves better understood than we could. Auura their cheif paid particular attention as well as his wife—the greater part of the others appeared slothful[;] he appeared to appreciate the worth of Knowledge & the value of the good tidings of Salvation, his attention was great & his questions—upon general subjects were very judicious—but his attention to & questions upon our discourses were such [2] as surprised not only the Raiateans but ourselves also. We think he possesses a very acute judgment so far as he knows we do not wish in thus speaking to be understood that we believe him to be what would be called in England a converted character, though we have now indisputable evidence that he is a true convert from Idolatry to Christianity, God hath called them out of darkness to the knowledge of his son, Christ Jesus may they soon really know ____[?] whom to know aright is eternal life—Auura was continually expressing his anxious desire to return to his own land & to carry to his poor country men the knowledge he had obtained of the true God & his son Jesus Christ—expressing his fears in an affectionate manner that when he got back he should find very few left as the Evil Spirit was killing them so fast. The Brig Hope from London Captn Grimes touched at Raiatea on July the 3d we mentioned to the Captain our wish to get these poor people to their own Island, he with a readiness which does him the highest credit offered immediately to touch at their island & to take our boat in tow, that we might have an opportunity should our boat return from this yet unknown land to open a communication with the natives. We sent for Auura Cheif & his wife who were highly delighted with the prospect of returning, but raised an objection to going to his land of darkness unless he had someone with him to instruct him & his people. We were rather at a loss how to act[—]however we immediately called the Deacons, informed them of the circumstance & desired them to enquire who would volunteer their services to go as teachers to their poor people. They assembled the church when 2 came forward we hope with the Spirit & language of the Prophet of old "Here are we send us" They were the very men we should have chosen had we thought it prudent to nominate but knowing it was at the hazard of their lives & that their wives & little ones we dared not interfere but left it to him who disposes the hearts and thoughts of men

according to his will[.]Mahamene a deacon was one with his wife no children Papa a steady & we hope a truly pious man & his wife with 2 children was the other they were both men we could ill spare on account of their steadiness & our confidence in them but such characters are the only proper persons for such a work therefore every other consideration was obliged to give way—the crew was the next consideration to bring back our boat this being settled which took up best part of the night, they had to get ready for the ship which was to sail early the next morning. The brig got under way early the 5th July & after most affectionately committing Mahamene & Puna [3] with their wives & little one to the care of our Lord & God in the presence of the congregation, we gave to each a letter in English & Tahitian recognizing them as under the patronage of the London Missionary Society with our Sanction recommending them to any Captain of Vessels that might touch there.

The Vessel laying too outside the reef for us prevented us having a regular service but though short it was both affecting & interesting. At length we conducted our new fellow laborers to the Brig—the Captain paid every attention took our boat in tow & departed, leaving us anxiously waiting to hear in due Season of their reception & success—nor were we disappointed.

The night previous to their departure was spent in supplying them as well as we could with those articles which they could find both necessary & useful—every member of the Church brought something as a testimonial of his affection—one brought a razor, another a knife, another a roll of cloth, another a few nails—some one little thing & some another[;] we gave them all the elementary books we could spare with a few of the Tahitian Gospels of Matthew. Thus we equipped them for this interesting little Mission as well as our circumstances would allow. On August 9th after a little better than a months absence we had the pleasure of seeing the boat return laden with the prisoners, the gods of the Heathen, taken in this bloodless war won by the blood of him who is the Prince of Peace. They were 6 days at sea in the open boat. On reading our letters we felt something of that holy joy & sacred pleasure that the Angelic ___[?] experience when shouting the kingdoms of this World are become the Kingdoms of our God & of his Christ[.] We received letters from Auura the Cheif of Rurutu Mahamene & Puna. Although Auura was only with us so short a time he made such progress that he had completely learned the Spelling Book part of the Catechism & could read in the Gospel[—]before he left, he could write & spell correctly. The following is a translation of a letter received by us from

Mahamene & Puna the 2 Native Teachers[.] To Messrs Williams & Threlkeld dated Rurutu Friday July ____[?] 1821 May you two have peace through God in your residence in Raiatea. We think God has heard your prayers because we received no ill treatment on board the Ship & because we are both now alive at Rurutu. Behold! They have given to us this land, not because we asked for it but because of their own hatred to the evil Spirit. Pray earnestly to God that we may have a permanent residence at Rurutu [4] whilst we are teaching them their letter & to know the name of the Son of God—& shewing them the evil of their ways On the 18th July the meeting of the Cheifs & King was held when Auura spake thus to the Cheifs & King: Friends this is my desire & therefore am I come to this land that you may know the name of the Son of God & the work of the Holy Spirit in enlightening our hearts, & the mercy of God towards us. This is my desire let the evil spirit be this instant cast into the fire[.] Is it agreeable to you Kings & cheifs, shall we burn the evil Spirit even now, shall we overthrow his Kingdom, do not any more let us worship him never more let us implore him, let him have no more reign in our hearts[.] Let him have nothing in this land that has no teachers, let the government of these little lands become Jehova's & his alone & then my heart will rejoice through you[.] Behold you thought I had been eaten up in the depths of the Sea by the evil Spirit but behold I am not destroyed by him, he is the great foundation of all deceit. I did not know that God would guide me to that land (Raiatea) where the teacher are[;] the word of God flourishes & grows & behold—God has guided me back again. Will it be agreeable to you that we should all assemble at one place & all eat together; The King & Cheifs answered thus, it is perfectly agreeable to us[—]we will receive & hold fast the word of life. We are pleased because of your saying burn the evil spirits in the fire. Yes—we will burn them Auura that our Anger against them may be appeased whilst they are totally burnt in the fire, let everything made by our hands (as a God) be charred in the fire. Behold you O Auura, say we have Spirits or Souls; we never knew man possessed a Spirit no, never. Auura then answered thus I have one word more to say to you. These two men (the teachers) are chosen by the Church at Raiatea. God caused the thought to grow in the hearts of Missionaries & behold they have sent them to teach us to read, because of their great love to us, these 2 are sent. The Missionaries think very much of them, for the Missionaries are very compassionate towards us[.] The people of Raiatea thought in their regard to these 2 Men that they would be killed in our land & that the boat would be seized by us[.] The Raiateans think our land is a barbarous land therefore do not ill use these men but behave with the greatest kindness to them, & then it will be well. The King & cheifs answered It is perfectly agreeable to us. Now lo! Upstarted two men inspired by the evil spirit, One of the evil spirits said, Its agreeable, Its agreeable we will hold the good word. The other man who was also inspired by the evil Spirit thus spoke, I have seen the foundation of the firmament—up in the sky Taaroa (the great Idol) brought me forth. Auura then answered the evil spirit thus[.] Do you leap up thus that we may see you flying up into the sky. Do so now immediately. Truly thou are even the very foundation of deceit[—]the people of Rurutu have [5] been completely destroyed through you & through you alone & now you shall not deceive us again[—]we will not be deceived again through you. We know the true God, ______[?] If the Son of God stood in our presence you would be completely ashamed. When Auura had done speaking he sat down. Mahamene then stood up & said you have agreed & your desire is to Jesus that he may save your Spirits—you are the lands for which the Missionaries—at Raiatea, Tahiti, Mo'orea, Huahine, Porapora & England have prayed—The Churches wherever there are Missionaries have compassion upon the lands that have no teachers[.] Therefore they subscribe properly that the word of God may be sent to the lands that are without teachers. The Missionaries of Raiatea haven't us two to teach you letters, & the name of the true God. May you be saved through Jesus Christ. Mahamene then sat down. Puna (the other teacher) then arose & said, Dear friends. This is my thought towards you, & my affection grows in my heart now towards you, in your living in Darkness & in the Shade of Death. Behold you are eating the food of death—the poisonous fish & drinking the bitter water. Behold we are here before you to make known to you the true God—that you may know him. This I say to you O Kings & Cheifs prepare one place where you may all eat together you & your wives & children & your king at one eating place & there the evil spirit who has just now inspired the man shall be completely ashamed—he has no refuge but cast away every disgraceful thing from among you for that is the reason he remains among you, you worship him & he is accustomed to deceive you but now be fervent in prayer to God that you may escape. Should you not listen to that word you will die & you will hear the wrath of God & you will be led by the evil spirit you have now cast away into the fire of Hell, but if you regard the word & the name of the Son of God you will in that means be saved. May you be saved through Jesus Christ

Mahamene

Puna

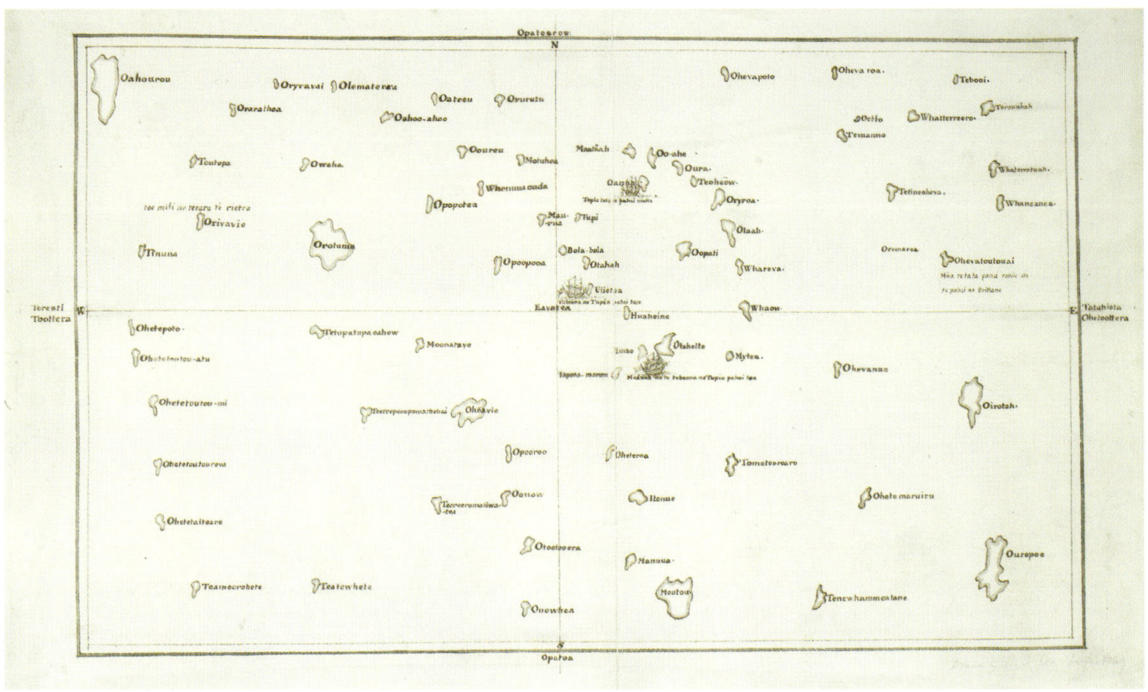

263 *Copy of Tupaia's map of Polynesia, in what appears to be Cook's hand. On it are indicated 74 islands. Most can be identified. Included are the Tuamotus, the Australs, the Cooks, the Marquesas, Tonga and Samoa. Orarathoa, for instance, is Rarotonga; Oheteroa is Rurutu. This map, drawn in 1770, vividly illustrates Tahitian awareness of islands as far away as 1500 miles. Courtesy British Library, Add. ms 21593,c.*

To Messrs Williams & Threlkeld
Raiatea
On Monday we came to the Island of Rurutu & on Tuesday we held the meeting—

Copy of a letter from Captain Grimes of the Brig *Hope* dated Rurutu July 9 1821

Dear Sirs
After sailing from Raiatea I experienced very unfavorable winds & several heavy squalls which endangered the boat[.] I did not make the Island until the 8th[—]after making the land I sent your boat on shore & in a short time the principal cheif a lad of about 15 years of age came off[.] It appears that Auura is but a petty cheif among many others but highly respected & I think in every respect the finest man on the Island. The population is very small the natives having been reduced by frequent [6] plagues from the thousands to about 200 men women & children included. I landed & found them remarkably civil & I think will be easily tamed from their abominable customs which are nearly the same as the former Tahitian except human sacrifice & infant murders; but the best of their property is occasionally offered to their Idol. The subject of changing their religion was mentioned to the cheifs & strongly urged by the Tahitians & Auura, he after many tears consented that the Idol should be secretly taken away which was done the same evening & delivered to me & was merely a small piece of wood covered with cloth in all about the size of a mans leg & thigh, they have but one Priest[—]he is a well favored Gentleman, he was much agitated when he heard the news, there also appeared a great consternation in the mind of the people but I think they will be easily reconciled. The land is fertile producing every requisite in superfluous abundance[.] Hogs are plentiful also fowls. The Island is a moderate height & about 18 miles in circuit & similar to the Society Isles with respect to appearance. The natives cultivate great quantities of Tarro—Yams are not so abundant however I got a good supply—Their houses are low but complete built upon raised pavements and roofed in the Tahitian style with reeded or matted walls. Tis customary to dry the dead bodies of relatives & suspend them in their houses there were 2 in that of the principal cheif. There is no Anchorage for a Ship at least no secure place. There is an American here but I have no great idea of his propriety of conduct[.] I think he favors their Idolatry. I spoke to him on the subject but his answers were equivocal. Should the

boat return in safety I would not advise a second attempt. If they follow my directions they will not fail in making one of the Society Islands, but to attempt making a small island at 350 miles distance would be ridiculous with only their knowledge[.] The Island bears about S by E 348 Miles of Raiatea—

Hoping that your expectations will be realized & the word of God planted with success is the fervent wish of —Yours Sincerely

John Grimes

To Messrs Threlkeld & Williams—Raiatea
It appears that the Brig sailed from the Island in the evening & it was not till after she sailed that the meeting was held. The eating together was on the day after the meeting & was to be the test of the truth of the word of God[.] If they died according to the predictions of the priests namely that any woman eating either hog or turtle would surely be eaten by the evil Spirit or anyone eating on a sacred place would surely die & be eaten also. Then they [7] would not Destroy [missing] Gods but if no one sustained any injury they would then utterly destroy all their Idols. They met according & after satisfying their appetites without sustaining any injury they arose boldly seized the Gods set fire to three houses residences of their God ___[?] & then proceded to demolish totally the Maraes which was all completely effected that day. It is worthy of remark that when the boat first reached the shore Mahamene & Puna with their party knelt down on the Spot to return thanks to God for their ___[preservation?] not knowing the spot was sacred to Oro one of their Idols—the Rurutus said immediately, this people will die. The party also ___[?] inadvertently on a sacred spot—when the Rurutus saw that they said no doubt they will die for this trespass on the sacred ground & looking earnestly expecting someone to have ___[?] or fallen down dead suddenly—but after they had looked a considerable time & had saw no harm come to them they changed their minds, & said surely theirs is the truth but perhaps the God will come in the night & kill them we will wait & see. One man went in the night to the wife of the Cheif [Auura] who also eat a part of a hog or turtle on this sacred spot, & said—Are you still alive? When the morning arrived & the Rurutus found no harm had happened—to any of them—they became exceedingly disgusted at their having been deceived so long by the Evil Spirit.

With respect to the Idol being secretly brought in the Evening to Captn Grimes we have made enquiry & it appears to have been ______[?] by Auura it being his own family God which shows his determination to cast away Idolatry even

before his countrymen had made up their minds, for the meeting was not held until the day after the Brig sailed—We add no more but hope that vessels will be more frequent in their trading visits to these Islands for our wish is next to their receiving the Gospel in truth is to see a fair & equitable trade carried on among these Islands either by means of Vessels of their own or other Vessels, trading not for old rusty Cannon & Muskets, but for clothing, tools, & even food to preserve them in health, Industry & Independency in a word that they may live the Gospel—

J Williams
L E Threlkeld

[8] P.S. On our way to the Colony [missing] least before we left Raiatea we requested Captn Potton [?] to touch at Vaitutai [probably Aitutaki] an Island about 500 Miles to the West and agreed—we therefore selected 2 Natives people—we called there & left them the natives gladly received them—will treat them kindly no doubt, I talked to them as well as I could about the folly & deceit of Idols—told them what the power of God had effected at Tahiti. They appeared pleased and did not seem to possess that deep rooted superstition some of the natives of these Seas do. Their language is more like the New Zealanders than the Tahitian. I hope & pray & expect that they will soon renounce the idols in which they trust. They have maraes but I could not ascertain whether they had human sacrifices & infant murder or not. There are several Society Islanders residing there who drifted there many years ago—I am sorry to say that Shimgee & Waikato are out upon a murder & plundering expedition have been out this 3 month have laid and call ____[?] their European manners & are killing & eating all they can lay their murderous hands upon, expected to be out 15 or 18 months more, & glutting themselves with human flesh[.] Mr Kendall & friends are very kind to us we are residing at Mr Kendalls house[—]I have been correcting and English translation he had been trying to make of out Catechism in order to translate it into New Zealand[—]he is very indefatigable in acquiring the language

There is one thing now that I have forgotten. The Cheifs in the Leeward Islands say why are such handsome presents being sent so continually to Pomare as tho he was the only Cheif[;] he continues to treat the Missionaries so unkindly & none to them[.] [W]e noted in one of the publications that you said Tamatoa (or Tapa as he was then called) was a steady industrious man but forgot the ______[?] to send the writing desk we requested for him.

Letter Bourne and Williams (Ra'iatea) to Tyerman and Bennet (Tahiti) 11 August 1823 summarizing the *Endeavour* voyage to central Polynesia

This letter is in Williams' words 'an *outline*' of the *Endeavour* voyage. In it, Bourne and Williams offer Tyerman and Bennet 'all the idols of Aitutaki—a great company of them—an excellent lot.' Information in this letter complements that in Appendices 5 and 6. This is the letter as printed in *Missionary Chronicle*, October 1824,454. SOAS.

inhabitants. Idolatry exists no longer; they profess generally the Christian religion; the women no longer come on board the vessels, and they are very reserved on all occasions. Their marriages are celebrated in the same manner as in Europe, and the King confines himself to one wife. The women are also admitted to the table with their husbands. The infamous Society of the Arreoys exists no longer; the bloody wars in which the people engaged, and human sacrifices have entirely ceased since 1816. All the natives can read and write, and have religious books translated into their language, printed either at Tahiti, Ulitea,* or Eimeo. They have built handsome churches, where they repair twice in the week, and show the greatest attention to the discourses of the preacher. It is common to see numerous individuals take notes of the most interesting passages of the sermons they hear."

Letter of Messrs. Bourne and Williams, missionaries, dated Raiatea, Aug, 11, 1823, addressed to Rev. D. Tyerman and Geo. Bennet, Esq.

Dear Brethren,—WITH this you will receive a letter, dated July 4, which we wrote jointly to you previously to our setting off on our journey. Mr. Threlkeld having had no opportunity of sending to windward since that time, this letter, informing you of our return, and the singular success that has attended our labours, will arrive as soon as those that were intended to have informed you of our undertaking. This letter is only intended to give you an *outline* of our interesting journey.

The groupe we have visited is a very important one; it consists of eight islands,† some of which are inhabited; four of them very numerously. Three of the islands are not named in any chart or book we had on board, therefore we had to seek them, and providentially we were successful in finding them all. At some of these islands they had never seen a vessel; at others they had not seen a ship since Captain Cook's.

We have settled teachers at *four* of the islands, and are under engagements to send five or six more by the return of the schooner, on her way to the colony.

---

* i. e. Raiatea.

† This groupe of islands lies to the south-west of the Society Islands, between 19 and 22 deg. S. Lat. and 158 and 160 deg. W. Long.

Reception of the Gospel at the island of Aitutake.

The first sound that saluted our ears at *Aitutake* was, "It is well with Aitutake. Aitutake has embraced the good word of God. The word of God has taken deep root at Aitutake. The maraes are all destroyed. The *varua ino* is consumed with fire." These, with similar expressions, were heard from every canoe that we passed. We being rather hard of belief, they pointed to the hats on their heads to convince us of the truth of what they said, and held up their spelling-books. Others began spelling words to induce us to let them on board. We admitted the chief, and a man who was among the first that embraced the good word, from whom we got the following information; viz. "that every marae in the island was destroyed and burned to ashes; all the remaining idols were in the possession of the teachers; the profession of Christianity was universal, even to a man; that a large plastered *Fare bure raa* (chapel) was erected, only waiting our arrival to open it." This news was as welcome as astonishing. But what, or who can resist the power of the Holy Spirit?

The teachers (natives) are both in good health, and at home in their work. They confirmed all that had been told us, and more, saying, that the sabbath was regarded by all as a sacred day. Service was attended by all, and that family prayer was attended to by nearly all.

We opened their large chapel, settled two more teachers with them, *Paumoana* and *Maraitai*, with their families; obtained all the idols; brought away with us the young king and his wife, with the grandfather of the king, and his wife; likewise *Papeiha*, one of the former teachers, in order to be able to converse more fully with the people of the other islands we were intending to visit.

Mangeea, or as the natives call it, *Ahuahu*, was the next island we visited; and, although we cannot rejoice you by a relation of the success that attended us there, yet we think our visit to that island will afford you and all our friends great interest. For the particulars we must refer you to the journal of the voyage; * suffice it to say, that from the

---

* Extracts from the Journal of Messrs. Williams and Bourne, containing the particulars referred to, have been already inserted in the Annual Report of the Society for the present year, and will appear in a future Number of the Missionary Chronicle.

very improper conduct of the natives towards the wlves of the teachers, we were obliged to bring them away again, after having every article seized from them, and their clothes literally torn off them. The church at Tahaa will send two single men by the first opportunity, and we do not doubt that success will soon attend their labours.

Gospel embraced by the islands of Maute and Mitiaro.

From *Mangeea* island we sailed for *Atui*. We found brother Orsmond's two poor people in a pitiable state.* They had had every article stolen from them; and, to use their own words, were living like pigs, without cloth to cover them either by day or night—that it was a land of very wicked people, and none would listen to them. They were very much disheartened. We encouraged them, and supplied their wants as well as we could. For an account of the singular success that attended our labours at *Atui*, and two adjacent islands, under the authority of the king of *Atui*, we must refer to our journal. We wished him much to come with us to Borabora, but he refused. We took him to sea with us for two or three days, and by preaching, praying, and conversing with him, he determined to embrace Christianity, and destroy all his maraes, erect a *Fare bure raa*, by the time you [i. e. the Deputation] visit him, and then open it. We assured him that you would be much rejoiced. We prevailed upon him to go with us to *Mante* and *Mitiaro*, two islands adjacent, of which he also is king, and use his influence in settling *Haavi* and *Tauaa* on these two islands. He agreed, and his influence was invaluable; for by it our desires and wishes were effectually accomplished, and the gospel of Jesus embraced by the natives of Mitiaro and Mante. He came on board the vessel a bigoted idolater; he was induced to embrace the true word; to use his influence in overthrowing the adoration of ages at two islands, and returns to his own with a full determination to do the same there. We were constrained to say, " It is the Lord's doing, and is marvellous in our eyes."

Means taken for introducing Christianity into the island of Rarotonga.

From thence we sailed for *Rarotonga*, a large fine island. The inhabitants very numerous. Our people intended for this island, received similar treatment with those who were landed at *Mangeea* island,

* These two pious men had been left there a few months before.

therefore we would not leave them. But Papeiha, the teacher we took with us from *Aitutake*, was agreeable to stay by himself until the next opportunity of conveying one or two more to his assistance. He had a small company of professors to begin with. We took two men and four women belonging to *Rarotonga* from *Aitutake*, one of whom was a chief of considerable influence, and who, with all the others, promised steadfastly to adhere to the profession they had made for some time at Aitutake.

Not being able to leave married teachers at Rarotonga, it afforded us great joy that we had *Papeiha* with us, whose worth had been tried and proved at Aitutake. Our visit to this island is by no means destitute of interest. The Lord works in a way most conducive to his own glory.

We have made mention of you wherever we have been; and at three of the islands your presence is anticipated with much pleasure. We fully expect that a place of worship at each will be erected, and we gave them reason to expect that you would be present at the opening of them.

At Aitutake they expect to enjoy your company when the first candidates are baptized. We tried to get chiefs from every island we visited, but only succeeded at Aitutake.

We have in our possession all the idols from Aitutake—a great company of them —an excellent lot. Should you wish to take them with you to India, &c. we will not send them to England by Captain Charleton. If it were possible for you to see them, and propose questions to *Tamatoa* of Aitutake upon them, and get information yourselves from him respecting them, previously to his return to his own island, it would add much to the interest with which you would show them to your different friends in your journey, and at England.

The whole account will afford you, we hope, much gratification, and be interesting to yourselves and the numerous friends that you may yet see in the course of your journey.

Letter of Messrs. Threlkeld and Williams, dated Raiatea, Nov. 20, 1823 ; addressed to the Directors.

Dear Brethren in Christ,—THE following account of a visit to the islands of Rurutu and Rimatara, though short, will interest you, as it shows that the gospel of Christ in these islands is like the leaven in the parable of our Lord, diffusing with amaz-

2 T 2

Extract from the Journal of Williams and Bourne describing the introduction of Christianity to the central Cook Islands in 1823

An abbreviated narrative of the middle days of the *Endeavour* voyage, with information regarding Atiu, Mitiaro, and Mauke, as printed in *Missionary Chronicle*, March 1825,119. SOAS. This account was evidently extracted from the original unedited journal of Williams and Bourne, which is now lost.

SOUTH SEAS.

Particulars of the Introduction of Christianity into Mitiaro and Maute, Islands belonging to the King of Atui, extracted from the Journal of Messrs. Williams and Bourne. (See Missionary Chronicle for Oct. 1824, p. 455, and note on page 454.)

WE had now time to converse with the King of Atui (*i. e.* after he came on board the Endeavour,) and found him a very interesting, sensible, and inquisitive young man. We spent the whole afternoon in conversation with him. Towards evening his mind began to waver. He desired Maratai,* of whom he seemed very fond, to ask us if he should be obliged to cut off his hair, in case he embraced the Gospel. We immediately set his mind at rest on that subject. He then expressed his determination to destroy his maraes, and embrace Christianity, saying, that he would not go with us now, (*i. e.* to the Society Islands,) as he could not go under the same favourable circumstances as those under which Tamotoa, King of Aitutake, would go, who had already destroyed his maraes, and burnt his idols, and erected and opened his chapel; but that when he had done the same, then he would visit us.

We now retired to rest, but the old chief from Aitutake, and the native teachers from Atui, kept up a conversation the whole night, on the expected destruction of idolatry, and the erection of a chapel, in the island of Mitiaro, to which we were going.

A few weeks ago, Roma a tane, the King of Atui, sent orders to Mitiaro to erect a large house for him, as he intended celebrating a great feast there. " Now (said the king) the posts collected for that *sacred house* intended for the *Evil Spirit* will do well for the *Fare bure raa*, (praying-house,) the building of which we will desire them to commence immediately." He further said, that on his return to Atui he would call a meeting of all his chiefs and people, to make known to them his determination to become a Christian, and to propose the general destruction of idolatry. Vahineino † said to him, " Will you never return to the worship of idols?" " No, (replied he,) I never will." There were three or four very large idols in the vessel. Tamotoa, the King of Aitutake, said, " Behold the things which have killed us, logs of wood!" " Yes, (replied the King of Atui,) they are only wood that we have decorated, and called gods." The next morning the King of Atui expressed a wish to purchase an axe to cut down posts for a chapel. We promised to present him with one. His heart seemed fully bent on the accomplishment of his purpose. It being the Sabbath, Mr. Williams preached from Mark xvi. 15 and 16. The King of Atui paid great attention during the whole of the service. He afterwards conversed on what he had heard, and appeared to have understood it very well, and particularly remarked on the truth of the last clause of the text, and some quotations from the Psalms and Isaiah respecting idols. " Eyes, it is true, (said he,) thay have, but wood cannot see: ears they have, but wood cannot hear." He proposed various questions on different parts of the sermon, which we answered, and he appeared greatly pleased on finding that he understood so much. Mr. Williams showed him the Bible, and explained to him that it was the gift of God to man, to teach him the way of salvation, through his Son Jesus Christ, asking him if his gods, Oro, Fane, or Tangarva, had given him a Bible. " No," (replied he,) adding, " is it in the power of wood to give a book?" It was proposed to him that we should visit Maute, (another island belonging to him,) as well as Mitiaro, to which he consented.

Reception of the Gospel at the Island of Mitiaro.

When we made Mitiaro, the king landed, accompanied by the teacher, Maratai. He immediately sent for the chief of the island, and explained his object to him, and observed, that he would leave a teacher, who would instruct him and his people in the word of the true God; that they must burn all their maraes, cast off all their evil customs; and that the house they were putting up for him, they must convert into a house of prayer, under the direction of the teacher. The people listened with astonishment, and inquired, saying, shall we not all be strangled? " No, (replied the king,) it is not in the power of wood, that we have adorned and called a god, to kill us." They asked, if Atui had received the Good Word that he had brought? He replied, that he had embraced it himself; upon which the chiefs of Mitiaro and all the people agreed to do the same; but, said one, must we destroy Taria Nui? ‡ (or Great Ears,)

---

* One of the native teachers from Borabora, sent by Mr. Orsmond to Atui.

† One of the teachers from Raitea, who accompanied Messrs. Williams and Bourne, in the *Endeavour*.

‡ The name of the god of which the king himself was the priest.

N 2

" Yes, (replied the king,) he and all the *evil spirits* with him." He then charged them to behave kindly to the teacher, and to listen to his instructions. They asked him, if he would not come to the celebration of the great feast which he had ordered them to prepare. He said, " No, but I will come on a different business ; I will come to behold your steadfastness in the Good Word brought to us, and your kindness towards the teacher you have received."

Reception of the Gospel at the Island of Maute.

When we approached the island Maute, the chiefs and a number of the people were collected on the beach to welcome their king. The first words the king said were, " I am come to advise you to receive the word of Jehovah, the true God, and to leave with you a teacher and his wife, who will remain with you and instruct you." They replied, " That is good." The king then resumed, " Let us burn all our maraes, and all our *evil spirits*, with fire. Never let us worship them again. They are wood, that we have carved and decorated, and called gods. Here is the true God, and his word, with a teacher to instruct you. The true God is Jehovah, and the true sacrifice is his Son Jesus Christ." He said further, " Erect a house in which to worship the true God, and be diligent in learning the Good Word of God." They replied, " We will do it ; we will receive the Good Word that we may be saved." The king then exhorted the principal chief, Tararo, and his wife, to attend family worship that same evening, to which they immediately consented ; " and on Wednesday (added he) let every person, man, woman, and child, attend the worship of the true God, and make a public profession." He then exhorted them to leave off drinking ava, to discontinue all their games and feasts, not to steal, and not to commit fornication ; but, with the *evil spirits*, to cast off all evil customs. They asked the king, whether he would not come to the great feast they were preparing for him, and to another ceremony, at which the most disgraceful actions were practised. The king replied, that these and every other bad custom of the *evil spirit* would now fall, but that he would visit them again to behold their steadfastness in the Good Word. He then exhorted them to behave kindly to their teacher and his wife, whom he now called to him, shook hands with them, and gave them a new house on the island, which had been erected for himself. After this we departed.

" Were ever (continue the brethren) three islands converted from idolatry in so short a time—so unexpectedly—islands, almost unknown, and some never visited by any vessel, in one day induced to consent to the destruction of what has been the adoration of ages. As to the natives of the latter island, Maute, the very first vessel that ever visited them brought them the glad tidings of salvation. How remarkably are the words of David fulfilled in this people—" *As soon as they hear of me, they shall obey me ; the strangers shall submit themselves unto me !*"

Extract of a Letter from Mr. Thomas Jones, Missionary at Papara, Otaheite ; dated Jan. 29, 1824 ; addressed to the Treasurer and Secretary.

Honoured Sirs,—I HAVE had the pleasure yesterday of receiving your kind letter, under date March 29, 1823. It gives me pleasure to find that you both were then in the enjoyment of health, and I hope you still enjoy the same blessing. Mrs. Jones's illness has lasted now more than twelve months, and still continues, though not quite so violent as it once was. She is very weak and very low, and great have been my trials on that head. Pray for me. Her illness has retarded my progress in the language ; but I have at last commenced preaching in the Tahitian tongue ; and I find, by conversation afterwards, that the people understand the subjects I wish to explain to them.

Since I have commenced preaching, I am much engaged with the people in answering their various questions and hearing their little *talk* and *thoughts* on things, as they call them, and explaining different passages of Scripture to them. Thus, of late, I have been generally employed from five o'clock in the morning till ten at night. A short time since, at our evening family prayer, I told some of our neighbours I should be glad if they would tell those who live near them to come and join us ; since that time our house has been found too small to contain the people who come, and we have been obliged to go to a large native house just at hand. Our method of conducting the worship is as follows:—First, sing a hymn ; then read a portion of Scripture ; then question those present on what is read, as for instance, Matt. vii. 13—*Enter ye in at the strait gate*, &c. What is to be understood by the " strait gate ?" Why is such a command given ? What makes the gate strait ? &c. &c. Many of the people are very ready in their answers.

More joy for Christians - or the power of
Christ displayed in effecting mighty things
by weak instruments, in the complete overthrow of Idolatry in the Island of Aitutake written by Mr Williams from the mouth
of Papeiha one of the Native Teachers
sent to that Island by the Church of
Christ at Raiatea - - - - - -

In the month of October 1821 I with my
family took a Voyage to the Colony of New
South Wales principally for the benefit of my
own health & of Mrs Williams'. The Captain
of the Vessel in which we were to go obligingly
said he would permit us to send two native
Teachers & leave them at Aitutake an Island
by which we were to pass. Mr Threlkeld &
myself thought it a favorable opportunity of
attempting to introduce the Gospel in to that
Island & were desirous of embracing it. We
therefore proposed it to the Church. they selected
two from among them. Papeiha & Vahapata
whom we set apart to their office. in an in-
-teresting service held on the day of our depar-
-ture from Raiatea. We preferred two single
men, as we knew little of the Island & did
not know but that I might be obliged to
take them on with me to New South Wales
Aitutake is situated in 18-58 S Latitude &
159. 48 W Long'. We made it on the 26 Oct'
we were soon surrounded by Canoes the
Natives were excessively noisy & as wild as

264 *Page one of Williams' 47-page manuscript 'More Joy for Christians', an account of the one month*
Endeavour *voyage he took with Robert Bourne, 4 July to 7 August 1823, to the central Cook Islands.*
Included is Papeiha's narrative of the two years he spent Christianizing Aitutaki. Several versions of
this account were prepared; this is probably the pencil copy sent to George Burder—clear and intended
for duplication, as mentioned in letter Williams (Ra'iatea) to Burder 20 September 1823. SOAS.

APPENDIX 6

'More Joy for Christians': Williams' account of the July 1823 *Endeavour* Voyage to the central Cook Islands, consisting mainly of Papeiha's narrative of the conversion of Aitutaki

This remarkable manuscript pamphlet is probably the most personal, immediate, and detailed account which describes an actual conversion in the South Sea. It also contains specific information about 31 idols. Largely a narrative of the Raiatean teacher Papeiha to Williams recorded during the *Endeavour* voyage of July–August 1823, following Papeiha and Vahapata's highly successful conversion of Aitutaki,[1] it documents exactly how native teachers were more effective missionaries than the English ones; recall Williams' words, in a 21 August 1823 letter (Ra'iatea) to Tyerman (in Tahiti): 'Beside native teachers know how to [go] about clearing away the rubbish of idolatry & superstition far better than newly arrived or even Old Missionaries.'[2] Williams knew the best teacher of all was Papeiha, who was, as Williams himself was, energetic and purposeful. Ernest Beaglehole speaks of Papeiha as 'a shrewd, conscientious, capable, determined and courageous person. What more could have been expected from a native servant of the Lord at this time is hard to know.'[3]

The SOAS manuscript in pencil, in Williams' hand, is evidently a copy prepared for George Burder, LMS secretary in London. It was written with a manifold writer, as explained in a letter from Williams (Ra'iatea) to Burder 30 September 1823[4] transcribed here on page 170; the letter also establishes that the pamphlet was written during September and October the same year. Tyerman and Bennet probably received a copy of it as well; a letter 21 August 1823 Williams (Ra'iatea) to Tyerman (Tahiti) reads: 'The journal of our voyage is long. . . . I will draw up in the shape or form of a pamphlet & present to you before you leave us.'[5]

---

1   Williams 1837,171.
2   SOAS LMS SS incom corresp box8 folder1 jacketB.
3   E Beaglehole 1957,23.
4   SOAS LMS SS incom corresp box4 folder2.
5   SOAS LMS SS incom corresp box4 folder1 folioA jacketB.

Williams was pleased with the Aitutaki Mission. Following is a quote taken perhaps from his unedited journal, written as he was leaving Aitutaki:

At Aitutaki, we spent two most gratifying days, and witnessed the most joyful scenes that could present themselves to the eye of a Christian missionary. When I first saw this people, they were stealing everything they could—ends of rope, iron, and even some fish which we had purchased from them just before; and nothing could have been more wild and savage than their appearance. Some of their faces were painted white, red, yellow, or black. Both men and women were dancing and shouting like mad people. But now, nothing of this kind is to be seen, and nothing was stolen but one small piece of iron.

After taking an affectionate leave of the teachers, and commending them to God, we departed. What solid satisfaction it affords, what peace of mind is enjoyed, in leaving the work of God in the hands of those who are well qualified to conduct it; and whose only aim is the temporal and eternal welfare of the people among whom they labour. But while well pleased with the prospect of usefulness before them, as we went towards the beach, we were much disgusted at seeing some females, who had cut themselves shockingly. The blood was streaming from their heads, faces, breasts, arms, and legs, while their cries and shrieks and howling were dreadful. On asking them why they did this, they replied, they were grieving at the departure of their friends. We endeavoured to make them understand that such conduct was exceedingly disgusting, and quite inconsistent with a profession of Christianity; but it has been so common, that there is probably not a woman in the island whose breasts and arms are not scarred from this barbarous custom. The old chief who accompanied us behaved very well. Every friend he met he embraced; and, after giving his friend's nose a hearty rub with his own, he walked on, quite unconcerned at the hideous cries they set up. The people loaded us with all the kinds of food which their island produces.[6]

Thus were the labours of two comparatively weak instruments rendered 'mighty through god' in effecting the utter overthrow of an idolatry, dark, debasing, and sanguinary, which had shrouded the by-gone generations of this verdant little island, and held them bound in its fetters.[7]

LETTER WILLIAMS (RA'IATEA) TO GEORGE BURDER (LMS LONDON) 30 SEPTEMBER 1823

This letter contains interesting background information regarding Papeiha and Williams' narrative pamphlet *More Joy for Christians. (SOAS LMS SS incom corresp box 4 folder 2; punctuation in brackets added.)*

Rev[d] & dear Sir/

We have not sent you an account of our own proceedings at our Station in Raiatea by this conveyance as my Brother Threlkeld is much engaged owing to Mrs T's confinement & I have been busily engaged in writing the account of our Missionary excursion & the History of the Mission at Aitutake [—] we will therefore send our joint letters by next conveyance which will be in a few months[.] I wrote the account with a Manifold writer therefore have sent the Pencil copies to you thinking that they will be the plainest & most to be depended on[.] I have not had time to read them since I wrote them therefore you must correct what wants correcting & transpose what wants transposing. Should the pencil copy fail I have sent one to Rev[d] Mr East of Birmingham—one to Mr Stokes of ___[?] yard—& to my friends from ___[?] of whom you can obtain the Copy which will perhaps be intelligible in parts of yours that may be obliterated.

I hope & trust that the work auspiciously began will be carried on by the great head of the Church[.] I fully intended to have drawn a chart of our Journey but time forbids[.] I must simply give you the latitudes & longitudes of the various Islands we visited—3 of which are not laid down in any Charts—

Harvey's Island   19–17 S 158–56 W

Aitutake   18–58 159–48

Atiu   20–1 158–14

These were all visited by Capt[n] Cook & laid down in charts—so was Mangeea 21-56 158-3

---

6   As transcribed in Prout 1843,180. The original unedited journal of Williams and Bourne is evidently lost. A 44-page manuscript copy of another pamphlet version of the *Endeavour* voyage, different from the SOAS manuscript and also in Williams' hand, is in the possession of Williams' family, and is available from Pacific Manuscripts Bureau, Australian National University, PMB35.

7   Williams 1837,575.

Mitiaro

Maute

Rarotonga—I cannot find the latitudes & longitudes of the islands now but Mitiaro bears from Atiu—N 73 Ea 28 Miles Maute bears from Mitiaro S 65 Ea 25 Miles—Rarotonga bears from Atiu—S 53 W—119 Miles[.] [T]here are several other Islands about there[.] [S]hould I be spared to visit them again I hope we shall find them[.]

The Cheif of Aitutake is now with me & requests me to say he wishes very much for 2 Sugar pans—I have promised to make him a mill & Paumoana knows well how to boil Sugar. Poor people they have no means of procuring the smallest article of European Manufacture—they have few Coca Nutts—no arrow root—no pigs—I cannot say that they will pay for them as they have no means at present—but I say that if you will send out 4 or 6 pans [—] 3 for Aitutake & 3 for Rarotonga I will make a large Sugar mill for each & if you will send a few turning tools I will make them a lathe each as both the Native Teachers know the turning business—

You must excuse my enlarging as the ship has gone over to T____ [probably Taha‘a] & is to sail to day.

I remain Dear Sir
Yours very affect^{ly}
J Williams

WILLIAMS' AND PAPEIHA'S NARRATIVE

(SOAS LMS SSJ box4 folder59; original pagination indicated in red; puncuation in brackets added.)

More joy for Christians—or the power of Christ displayed in the effecting of mighty things by weak instruments, in the complete overthrow of Idolatry in the Island of Aitutake written by Mr Williams, from the mouth of Papeiha one of the Native Teachers sent to that Island by the Church of Christ at Raiatea———————

In the month of October 1821 I with my family took a voyage to the colony of New South Wales principally for the benefit of my own health & of Mrs Williams'. The captain of the Vessel in which we were to go obligingly said he would permit us to send two native Teachers & leave them at Aitutake an Island by which we were to pass. Mr Threlkeld & myself thought it a favourable opportunity of attempting to introduce the Gospel in to that Island & were desirous of embracing it. We therefore proposed it to the Church—they selected two from among them, Papeiha & Vahapata whom we set apart to their office in an interesting service held on the day of our departure from Raiatea. We preferred two single men, as we knew little of the Island & did not know but that I might be obliged to take them on with me to New South Wales[.] Aitutake is situated in 18-58 S Latitude & 159-48 W Long. We made it on the 26 Oct^r[.] [W]e were soon surrounded by Canoes[.] [T]he natives were exceptionally noisy & as wild as [2] possible both in their appearance & manners[.] [S]ome were tatooed from head to foot, some painted various colours, others smeared with Charcoal, dancing—singing & jumping. We invited the cheif on board whose name I found to be Tamatoa[.] I immediately began to converse with him by telling him what had taken place at the Society & other Islands with respect to the destruction of Maraes—burning their Idols & he asked me very significantly where the great National god—Tangaroa was[.] I told him that he was consumed with fire—he then asked where the other great god Koro was[.] I told him that he also was consumed, that I had brought him two teachers to instruct him & his people in the word of the true God that they might be induced to destroy the false ones as other had been. As soon as I pointed them out to him he said will they go on shore with me, yes I replied[.] [H]e seized them immediately & rubbed their noses very heartily with his & continued his salutation some time. I told him that I gave them into his charge that he must take them to his own house—prevent any person from taking away their property, to provide them with food & treat them kindly all which he promised to do[.] [H]e took them & their little property in his large Canoe & paddled off to the shore apparently greatly delighted[.] I then learned that there were several other Islands numerously inhabited not very far distant which much increased in my estimation both the importance & interest of the Aitutake [3] Mission. Papeiha says, "Immediately we landed crowds came down to the Sea beach to see us, we were instantly given into the possession of two priests who led us before the great Marae & delivered us up formally to the god—we told [them] it was both useless & wicked to take us before the Marae—after this they led us to the house of Tamatoa—in the evening we made our little presents to the Cheif. Crowds were still about the house—we separated a corner of the house off with cloth lighted some candle Nutts read in the Gospel & had prayer after which we convened with Tamatoa the Cheif & the people around us [and] pointed out the advantages of receiving the Gospel but they paid very little attention. Several women came by us by night [—] we scolded them away saying we would not commit sin. In the day time they were welcome but not by night[.] [T]he next morning was Saturday [—] we after prayer went in search of food, obtained it & cooked it for Sabbath day. The following was Sabbath day on which happened a great feast before the marae, which is when a woman is pregnant—the husband & all his district (if he is a Cheif) prepares a great quantity of food & cloth & makes an offering to his wife[.] [T]he wife with her friends & district (if she is a cheif) prepare the same on the other side & present to the husband[.] [G]eneral incantations are said & offerings made before the marae for the child with which the woman is pregnant that it may become of great fame & be a great warrior which appears to be the summit of all their hopes & source of all their joy. They presented us says Papeiha to this feast before the [4] Marae we went. They wished us to sit among the priests but we refused, very many were inspired Men, women & children—both priests & common people. It being Sabbath day I retired into a secret place to read the Scriptures & pray with each other for the people among whom we were residing—Immediately we were missed there was a general search after us but they could not find us—when we returned the feast was finished.

As soon as we arrived in our residence we were fetched by the people of a neighboring district as they wished to see us & salute us. We replied that the day was sacred & we would [not] come to maraes[.] [T]hey would not be satisfied so we were obliged to go [—] when we arrived they brought us great quantities of cloth & covered us up with it—we told them we would have nothing to do with it, it being Sabbath day. We went into their house & sat down—they talked much to us but we could not understand them well. We told them what our object was—to teach them the word of the true God, that we had but one desire viz that the good word of God might take root in their land—they took little notice of us & continued talking [—] talking to us about their Heathenist customs[,] offering us their wives & daughters to commit sin[.] [W]e endeavoured to convince them of the wickedness of their conduct & told them to inform them of the evil of such practices & teach them the true way was, the reason why we came to their land[.] [W]e returned home that evening—Nothing of particular importance occurred for about a month except that we embraced every opportunity of telling the people the object we had in view & persuading them to listen to the truths of the Gospel[.] [A]t the end of [5] about a month- a great feast took place before the Marae called bure Arii, which is a general assembly of all the people of the island before the Marae[.] [T]he kings or rather all the family of the kings take their seats in separate situation from the common people [—] they cover themselves completely with cloth except a small part of their faces. [T]hey remain for a month sometimes longer before the Marae eating & drinking certain to us unmeaning ceremonies[.] [A]fter this the Priests & many of the people smear themselves with charcoal[,] the people clothe with the finest of their cloth & make a tour round the Island previously to which they go to the Marae & cover the Kings with Cloth in great abundance[.] [T]he following morning they all leave the Marae every one with a large piece of wood on his shoulder which they use in the separation of their wrestlers—for when they leave the Marae they make a tour of the Island wrestling at every district—sometimes there are two or three in every district—this finishes the ceremony of the bure Arii[.] [T]hey fetched Papeiha & Vahapata to go & remain with them before the Marae, which they refused but says Papeiha it was a favorable opportunity of speaking to them about the Gospel of Jesus—so many persons being assembled from the different parts of the island—although they treated us kindly they would not regard the truths we spoke to them. About this time while we were gone one day in search of food some person broke open our Box & stole all the little property [—] fish hooks, scissors, & knives—we thought it prudent not to say any thing about it. Another day shortly after when we were seeking food our box was again broken open & our Axes [6] were stolen[.] [W]e were much grieved at the loss of our Axes but did not say any thing at the time, but prepared to leave Tamatoa (the Cheif into whose care I gave them) & place ourselves in the protection of his Uncle the grandfather of the present King, but Tamatoa would not suffer us to leave him & got our Axes back for us. A man from Maupiti one of the Society Islands who drifted to Aitutake many years ago informed us that it was Tamatoa himself who had taken our Axes[.] Tamatoa was very angry seized his spear & was about to spear the Maupiti man[.] [H]e in his own defence seized his spear & they would have speared each other had not Papeiha have held one of them & Vahapata the other & made peace between them[.] [S]hortly after some person stole a piece of dungarie [?] from us but we obtained it again. As the little property we had was continually being stolen from us we determined to accept the old grandfather offer to take our Box & place it in his possession[.] [A]ccordingly we arose in the night & took it to his house & remained there during the night. In the morning when Tamatoa found we were not at his house searched for us

& found our Box at his Uncles[.] [H]e took it away by force & replaced it in his own house. We had early in the morning set off for the other side of the Island to see the old Maupiti man who had retired to his own district for fear of being killed for informing us who had stole his property[.] We were fetched the same day—by a Messenger from Tamatoa[.] [W]hen we returned we found that our bedsteads & Box were taken again to Tamatoa's house w[h]ere we again took up our residence & remained a considerable time[,] the Natives observing our Worship morning & evening & our [7] retiring for worship on the Sabbath day. They asked us what we were doing [—] we told them we were praying—they said—Praying that we all die? We informed them that we were praying that they might live & be saved—that they might hear & receive the word of Salvation that we had brought[.]

About this time a War broke out, in consequence of one Cheif's finishing a Sacred house before others erected by Tamatoa & other Cheifs were finished- They were erected before the Marae[.]

The former mentioned cheif having finished his two—he would not wait the finishing of the others but had his dancings & games in his Sacred houses without regarding the others—which appears was the origin of the War[.] Tamatoa & his party immediately took the *pa* which is a grove of trees planted regularly & forms a kind of palisading—behind which each party remains in a defended state & prepared at a moments notice to engage the enemy. When Vai rua Rangi—the Cheif of the opposite party who in Tamatoa's estimation was the aggressor heard that Tamatoa had taken the *pa*[,] he immediately took another *pa*—each party remained in a state for war with their respective Prophets[.] After a day or two—on the third morning the two parties met—two or three Cheifs from the opposite party came over & requested us not to fight—both parties therefore returned into the *pa*[.] Papeiha says "The old grandfather took us with him—the parties met two or three times without coming to blows—at length they commenced clearing away the brush [illegible] that they might have room to engage. The teachers were continually exhorting them not to War but the reply was War is a good thing. The whole [8] of the time they were employed in clearing away they were exhorting each other the word of exhortation was—Clear away well that we may Kill & eat & have a good feast this day. In the evening each party returned to their respective *pa* & impatiently waited the morning light. Early in the morning the War commenced but the opposite party that is of Vai rua rangi did not make a very stout resistance their numbers being far inferior—a few spears were thrown by each party when that of Vai rua rangi took their Canoes & fled to a Small Island about ½ mile distant from the main land—They remained there three days—A messenger was sent to fetch them back they replied they would not return as they were sure to be Killed & eaten if they did. The Messenger assured them that they should not upon which they returned to the Shore & were made captives—but after four or five days the greater part were liberated. Papeiha says "We were not at all afraid or discouraged at the War [—] we thought that it was in the hand of God & he would make it a means of overthrowing Idolatry in this land. We continued every talking with them & endeavouring to teach them but they would not regard us—About this time we commenced our house—cut down the posts & had some of the thatch prepared when another War broke out between the conquered & the conquering party[.] All the captives of a former & the late War joined & formed a large party [—] they betook themselves to the *pa*, so did Tamatoa's party but when Tamatoa's the conquering party saw the superiority of the enemies numbers by the union of all the Captives—they fled without coming to an engagement & remained nearly [9] a month. A messenger was sent by the conquering party for their return. They refused saying they would be killed & eaten[.] [U]pon assurance to the contrary they returned. These two skirmished as the teachers though turned out to advantage for during the interim they had began to erect their house in the district of the party formerly conquered & did not go with Tamatoa & his party as before but remained at home working at their house[.] [T]he party in whose district their house was erected being conquerors tended greatly to exalt them in the estimation of the people—who full of superstition immediately ascribed great power to them Saying "which ever party they join are sure to conquer"[.] As soon as peace was established says Papeiha we made a tour of the Island for the purpose of teaching & conversing with the people of every district. The first district at which we stopped—all the people came to prayer[.] [W]e taught many the Alphabet & some the Lords prayer which was the course we observed all round the Island during our journey[.] [T]he King sent for us but we determined to proceed on our journey[.] The next district at which we arrived was Tautu[.] Here we held an argument with an old Priest[.] [H]e began by saying that Te erui made all the lands [—] he made Aitutake & after he had made it he formed it by clasping it in his hands. We told him it was not so. That God alone had the power to create

[—] he made this & every other land. The Priest continued saying that Te erui was the first man[.] [W]e asked him who was the parent. He replied O te tareva—we asked him from whence Tareva was—he replied from Havai—we asked Where is Havai—It is beneath. Ta neva climbed up from beneath & because he arrived at the top he was called Ta neva—We said to him perhaps this land was made before this [10] Man arrived—Yes replied the priest—then said we how can Te erui be the maker of a land which you say was made before even Ta reva his Parent arrived. We then spoke to them upon the existence of God before anything was made[,] that he only existed & was without beginning and without end—We then spoke of the Creation of Angels & of one part [?] falling from their state[.] We then spoke of the creation of the world & all things therein—every person was silent & when the least noise was made there was a general cry of "Be still & let us hear[.]" We proceeded to The Creation of Adam and Eve [—] of their being placed in the Garden of Eden[,] of their Sinning against God[,] of Gods giving his Son to die a Sacrifice for us. When they heard these things they said with one accord—Surely that is the truth ours is all deceit. From that time many began to listen attentively & believe what we said[.]

We passed on to another district called Vaipai [—] the Cheif received us kindly & asked us our business[.] [W]e told them we had but one that was to teach them the word of God. He asked us various questions [and] requested us to take up our lodging all night with him & in the morning go & burn his Marae[.] [W]e replied we would stay with him but he must burn his own Marae. The house of the cheif being full we proposed prayer and conversation to which he agreed—when we kneeled down to prayer the whole company present did the same. After which he repeated his wish that we should burn the Marae not liking to do it himself—We told him however much he prized his Marae that the time would speedily arrive when it would be burned to [11] ashes. In the morning early we found him worshipping at the Marae he had requested us to burn on the preceeding evening. It was doubtless prudent in them not to burn the marae as in all probability it was a snare laid for them. They say however had the Man have burned his Marae as they expected he would have done[,] they would have taken up their residence with him. The prudence of the Teachers in this as well as in other instances is highly commendable. We went from district to district & from house to house & spoke to all that would listen to us. As we were returning home we met a company of Prophets & Priests to the number of 50 or 60—all smeared with charcoal & all inspired going to a Canoe launch—which was occasioned by a number of Canoes small & large being finished[,] over which the priests must perform some ceremony & have a large feast before they are launched—however as they took no notice of us we did not of them—but their appearance was frightful as nothing but the whites of their eyes were to be seen shining through their Charcoal smeared faces. We remained at home some time working on the New house we had commenced[.] [S]ome time since when several persons said to us—You will surely be strangled—we enquired Why. They replied because you are working[.] [W]e enquired Who would strangle us—they told us the great gods Tangaroa & Koro would. For continued they[,] there was a Man here from Raiatea many years ago who began to make an *Umete*—a large bowl & he was killed by the God & so should we be if we continued to work at our house. Cast it away said they[,] do no more at it, we replied it is out of the power of your gods to kill us [—] he himself Oro & Tangaroa will become food for the fire [12] [L]et him remain never so long he will be sure to [perish?] burned at last. We continued working at our house without experiencing any interruption from Koro. About this time four lads came to us & expressed a wish to be instructed[.] Their names are Bua Berea (?) Toare & Aarona[.] [T]hese were the first[.] [T]hey took up their residence in our house & we taught them every evening. Shortly after three others came & united themselves [—] their names are Tebati KoreKore & Te Arataia. These persons heard our debates & conversations on the other side of the Island which induced them to come & seek instruction in the "New Word"[.] [O]ur number was now increased to 8 [—] we therefore untied our bundle of spelling books & gave one to each[.] Te bati took up his residence with us[,] the other two being captives were threatened with death if they came [—] therefore they only came a little while of an evening when they could avoid being seen. Every evening all were diligent in learning. When the Sabbath day arrived we all united together for prayer in a small house adjacent to our own[.] [W]hile we were at worship a number of persons came to disturb us[.] [T]hey broke down the sides of the House—threw out every article that was in the House[,] raked up the grass with which our house was laid [X] (footnote [X]: all native houses have dried grass spread upon the ground which forms a floor) & endeavoured by every means in their power to vex & interrupt us. We took no notice of them but continued our worship & when ended

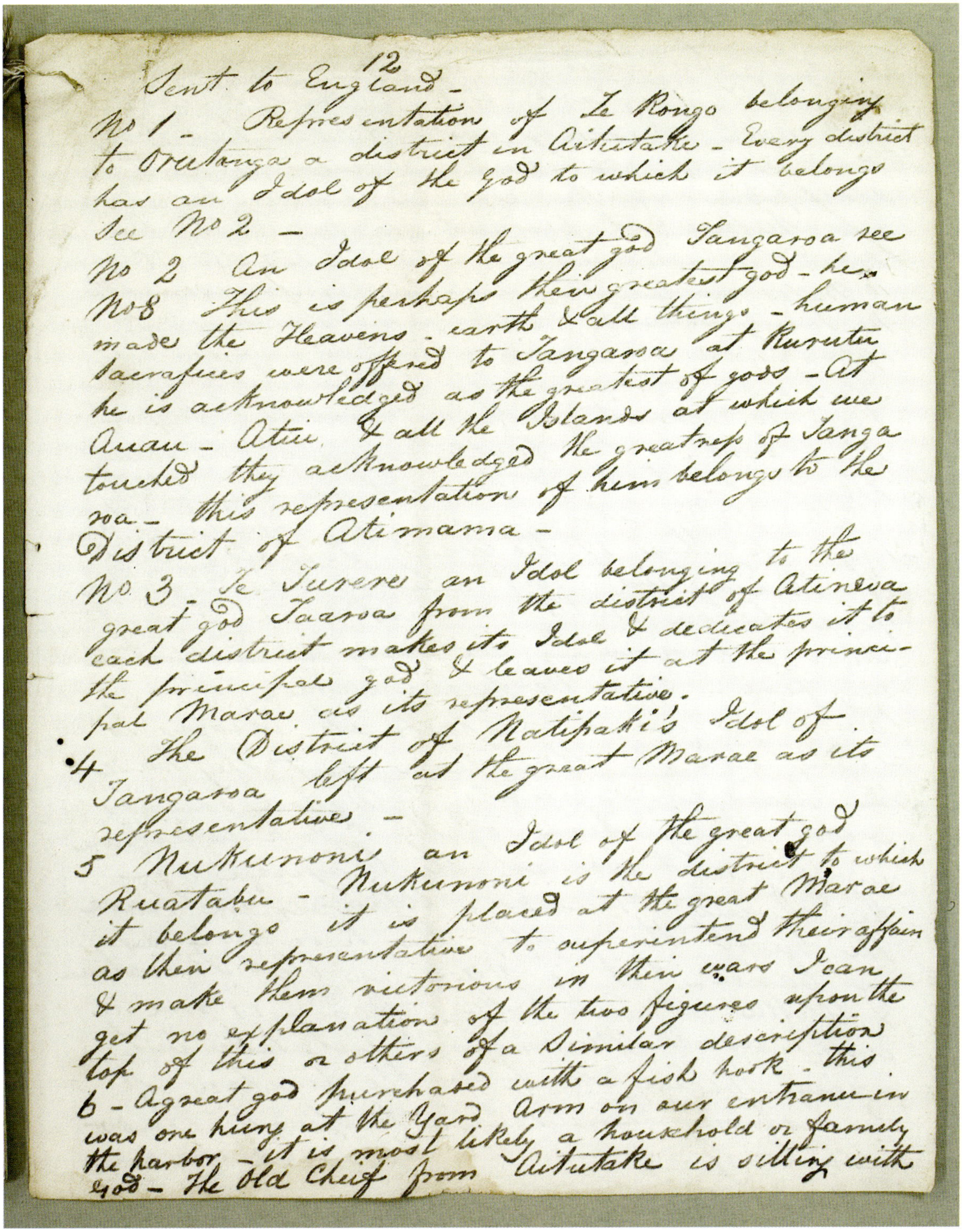

Sent to England —
No 1 — Representation of Te Rongo belonging
to Oretanga a district in Aitutake — Every district
has an Idol of the god to which it belongs
See No 2 —
No 2 An Idol of the great god Tangaroa see
No 8 This is perhaps their greatest god — he
made the Heavens — earth & all things — human
sacrifices were offered to Tangaroa at Rurutu
he is acknowledged as the greatest of gods — At
Auau — Atiu, & all the Islands at which we
touched they acknowledged the greatness of Tanga
roa — this representation of him belongs to the
District of Atimama —
No 3 — Te Turere an Idol belonging to the
great god Taaroa from the district of Atineva
each district makes its Idol & dedicates it to
the principal god & leaves it at the principal Marae as its representative.
4 The District of Natipaki's Idol of
Tangaroa left at the great Marae as its
representative. —
5 Nukunoni an Idol of the great god
Ruatabu — Nukunoni is the district to which
it belongs it is placed at the great Marae
as their representative to superintend their affair
& make them victorious in their wars I can
get no explanation of the two figures upon the
top of this or others of a similar description
6 — A great god purchased with a fish hook — this
was one hung at the Yard Arm on our entrance in
the harbor — it is most likely a household or family
god — The old Chief from Aitutake is sitting with

265 More Joy for Christians *includes an annotated list of 31 idols collected. Shown here is page 45 of the manuscript, which lists the first six idols which were 'Sent to England'. SOAS.*

we left them in the house & returned to our own dwelling. This was early on Sabbath Morning[.] [S]oon after our Arrival at home, a man came to KoreKore & Te arataia & told them to make their escape with all possible speed for they are to be sought after & killed. They informed us says Papeiha of the circumstance & asked our advice[.] [W]e told them we thought it advisable [13] for them to return to their own district as it was out of our power to afford them protection. We with little company determined to go with them to their own district lest they should be killed by the way—on our way thither we passed a small house unoccupied in which we held our morning worship after which we spoke comfortably to KoreKore & Arataia exhorting them not to fear, God would protect them & not to return to the worship of Idols[.] [W]e accompanied them a little farther & then returned. Desiring Te bati to see them safe home. In about 5 days after they came to us again by night & remained with us learning very diligently[.] [A]s soon as it was known that they had come again[,] the Cheifs & people with one accord determined to put them to death[.] [A] person came & told us of it [—] they therefore made their escape by night. Te bati continued to come & learn & would carry what he had learned to KoreKore & Arataia who in consequence of being Captives were afraid to come[.] [T]hey remained away about 20 days[.] They came again to us by night—but as soon as it was known another plan was laid to kill them[,] a relation came & told them[.] [T]hey again made their escape by night & did not return again to us. About this time Tamatoa the King of Island a lad about 15 Years of Age noticed the progress his playmates were making reading & spelling & that several of them could say the Lords prayer. He came to us & expressed his wish to be instructed but said he was afraid of Satan & asked us if there was not a fear of his being strangled by Satan if he [14] received this word[.] We told him that if he received & held fast the good word[,] Satan would have no power over him to hurt him. He then determined to take up his residence with us & be instructed—we were much rejoiced at this important accession—we gave him a spelling book & spent our evenings very pleasantly in teaching our scholars who were now 6 in number KoreKore & Arataia being afraid to come.

About this time another feast took place called a Faatia raa Fata or Erection of Altars on which a quantity of food is placed—After certain portions are put upon the Altars before the marae where it is left to rot. The remainder is eaten by the priests & a certain class of people only in consequence of its being sacred & if eaten by others they will be strangled by the Varua ino—Evil Spirit. We thought it a favourable opportunity of shewing the folly of their superstitious fears[.] We went therefore to various Altars[,] took food from off them & eat it in the presence of the people. They assured us we should be strangled as the food was Satan's (a name they had learned from the teachers)[.] We told them that Satan was not the Lord of any food [—] that God was Creator of all food & it was to be eaten by all & everyone with thankfulness. We took some home with us & divided it amongst our little company who were afraid to eat of it lest they should be strangled. We told them they had nothing to fear for Satan had no such power. They eat secretly for fearing the incurring the anger if the Priest & people who were continually saying that they were inspired with madness for listening [15] to two fools who had come on purpose to deceive them. About a month after[,] another feast occurred called Fata Tarono which is a general erection of Altars of a large size on which great quantities of food is placed & which none dare eat except the Priests only & those who are inspired [—] therefore the greater part rots & spoils. The old Cheif Tamatoa brought his altar & erected close to our door & placed great quantities of food on it[.] [W]e told him that if it was placed there we would surely eat from it & so should all who were residing with us[.] [H]e replied that we might eat of it but if those who were residing with us did they would surely die. We told him that it was out of the power of Satan to kill them [—] what he had placed on the Altar was food & they should eat of it—but our little company eat of it with great fear & trembling. A circumstance of this kind might have crushed the whole of their prophets. [W]hen natives get a good supply of food they eat very heartily [such] that generally some are laid up afterwards. [I]f such had been the case in the present instance it would have confirmed their superstitious ideas with respect to the sacredness of food. Upon such slender threads sometimes depend concerns of the greatest moment. Therefore who can deny or even doubt a superintending providence over incident[s] in themselves the most insignificant but in connexion of infinite importance—When they found no harm come to them from eating this food they took courage & said they believed it was all deceit & that Satan had no power[.] [I]n this feast the whole of the inhabitants of the Island go a fishing & if they catch a Shark they bring it on Shore cut it up in small pieces divide it out [16] to the different Idols of the Island of which they make a tour, leaving portions with the Priests of every district[.] [A]s they pass they clothe themselves in their best [—] smear themselves with Charcoal others with Red oker—others with pipe clay & after they have gone round the Island they return to their houses. We were all this time at work at our houses & met with no interruption except on Sabbath days[.] [W]hen we went to worship we were therefore obliged to go into the bush one at a time one one way another another & appoint a place where to meet[.] [T]his we were obliged to do a considerable time. We were continually exhorting our disciples not to be afraid—God would preserve both us & them & his word would ultimately triumph.

About this time the young King Tamatoa who was making great progress in learning said to us I will go & break down my Altar on which my sacred food is placed. We said to him go [—] he went immediately & broke it down & brought away the baskets of food to our house[.] [W]e took out the food & threw away the baskets—The grandfather & others collected them with great care & placed upon their own altars. The people said to the young King you'll surely be Strangled—You have cast away this Altar. I do not fear said he neither do I regard the Altar. This was the first outward attack upon the ensigns of

Idolatry in this Island. We about this time all set off to go & see KoreKore & Arataia[.] When we arrived at their district there was a fishing party who were carrying quantities of food as offerings & presenting their Ubu's (prayers) before the Marae before they set out. This surely affords a lesson to some professing Christians [—] here are Pagans of the lowest order [—] Cannibals [—] presenting offerings to their God & imploring his blessing upon them before they set out on a fishing expedition [17][—] to return to our subject. Papeiha says, "We found KoreKore & Arataia well, they were very glad indeed to see us. They informed us that they had continued to learn—that [they] had had family prayer & had observed the Sabbath day ever since they had left us. Arataia said I'll go & burn my marae[.] We replied—go—burn it—burn it directly—he left us & went to his Marae & set fire to it. The fame soon spread that Arataia had burned his marae—Upon hearing which A great Cheif by the name of Te ui collected a number of Men armed them with barbed spears & other of their war instruments & set off immediately with his gang for the residence of Arataia when they arrived they immediately encircled the house in which Arataia, KoreKore, Te bati & a brother of KoreKore's were sitting—Te Ui said to Arataia, Why did you burn my God. Tangaroa-Koro Te ihi tabu & Tangaroa the great God is scorched with the

fire & fled to the Skies. I am come to be revenged to you to put you to death to cut you to pieces & to eat you. You shall be food for me[.] [T]he poor Man sat in silence encircled by the ruffians all armed with their frightful spears ready in a moment to execute the orders of their bigoted Chief[.] Te bati then spoke to Te ui saying what has Arataia done that you should talk of killing & eating him. With this Te ui began to quarrel with Te bati saying you have destroyed us all. Through you my god is burned. Te bati replied—I have destroyed you all but saved you all when you were beaten in the war & driven down into the Sea[.] [W]ho was it fetched you & brought you to your lands again. Was it thought that you would ever become Men[?] [W]ere you not all regarded as food & behold your mouth is Speaking to me. You shall not kill or hurt Arataia[.] [W]ith this [18] Te ui & his party set off to the Teachers house[,] Aarona one of the Scholars being his own Son & another lad his Nephew[.] [H]e desired them all to disperse immediately & not to come to our house again[.] [T]hat was the cause of his god being burned[.] [I]f he caught them at our house again he told them he would kill them all & place them upon his altar. Upon this all our Scholars left us except Tamatoa the Young King. A Message was also sent to him from his grandfather saying that if he continued at our house he also should be killed & placed upon the Altar before the Marae[.] [T]he lad took no notice of it but remained with us. The Cheifs were so jealous that the next morning a few lads were playing about the house[.] [A]n old Cheif came up & drove them away[.] [T]he young king also was afraid & ran away but returned soon after. We were now reduced to three in number our two selves & the Young King [—] he was with us continually. On Sabbath days he always went with us to worship—& was very diligent in learning saying he would never cast away the good word of God[.] We remained for about a month when three more joined us[,] Te bati & his wife & a lad whose name was Tena. [S]oon after 4 others joined us—Te ina & his brother with their wives—they were all very diligent in learning[.] [W]e spent our evenings in teaching them. Our number now amounted to 10. These persons had observed KoreKore Arataia & Te bati who although they were obliged to separate us were diligent in the observance of all they knew—they were diligent in learning to read—had family prayer Morning & evening—& worshipped regularly 3 times every Sabbath day. This was the occasion of this new accession[.] About this time there was another great feast. When all the people assemble [19] before the Marae with their faces smeared with

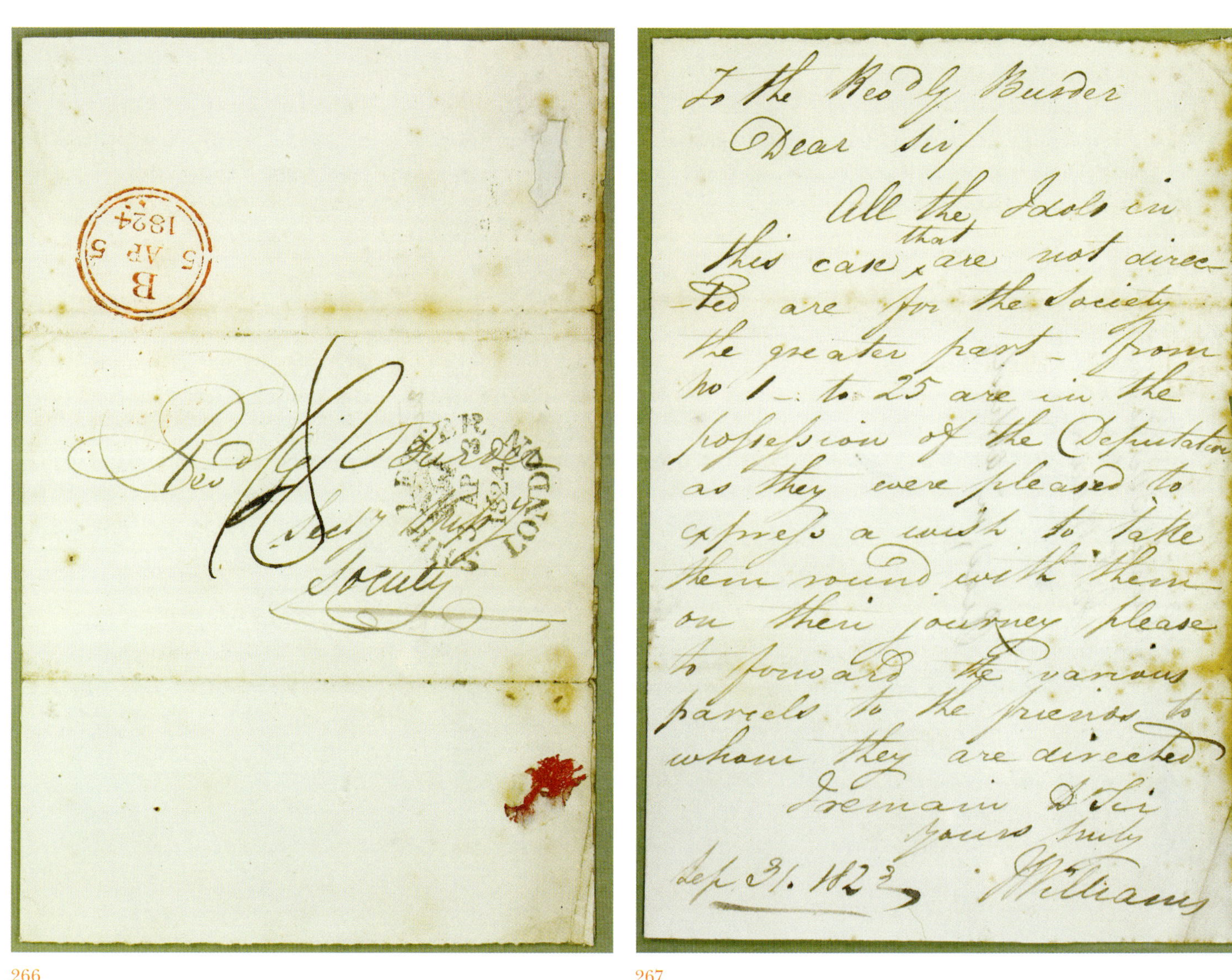

266

267

266 & 267 *Letter Williams (Ra'iatea) to Burder 31 September 1823 which accompanied the case dispatched to London with Captain Charlton, containing the six central Cook Island idols 'Sent to England' listed on page 45 of* More Joy for Christians; *this page is shown in figure 265. The remaining 25 idols accompanied Tyerman and Bennet. SOAS.*

charcoal as usual & with the best of their cloth on. The god was inspiring many. We determined with our little company to go & see them. We sat ourselves down by the side of the pathway which they were to pass by in leaving the Marae. The people saw us[.] [T]hey were filled with rage & turned away their faces[.] [E]nquiries were immediately made who were the persons that were with us & had forsaken them. They found that it was Te bati Te ina & the others[.] [T]here was then a division among the whole of the Idolators. One party was extolling the word of God deceit & calling those that regarded it fools. Some said they would come join us directly the feast was over [—] others said they would not [—] all was lies[.] [A]s soon as the feast was over three accordingly joined us Tu paea Tarabu & Ota—these from among the Idolators. Our number was now 13[.] [W]e gave our New Scholars a Spelling Book each which was our custom when any one came & expressed their wish to be instructed—They were all very diligent in learning—observed family worship & regarded the Sabbath day. About this time the whole of the people of the district to which Te ina belonged came & demanded him & desired that he should not [____?] the word of God as their district was threatened with War & death by a neighboring one[.] [I]f Te ina was obstinate we thought it advisable to let him & his wife & Brother go. They remained a short time away from us but continued to attend to family prayer & worship on Sabbath day & diligent in learning to read. There were only them three selves among all the people of their district who had embraced the Gospel. The people of their district made great game of them calling them fools & mad people—however they bore [20] all with patience. We exhorted them when they left us on such occasions—not to fear God would protect them & bear patiently all the unkind treatment with which they might meet. & to continue steadfast in their attention to family prayer & the Sabbath day[.] [A]fter three or four weeks elapsed they returned again & took up their residence with us. About this time another war broke out a War in which all the people of the Island were engaged. The origin of this war was a desire on the part of Tamatoa & his party to resume authority over the other party which he had in a great measure lost in his late defeat. However Vai rua rangi & his party seeing the determined & desperate preparations making by Tamatoa resigned rather than come to blows which Terminated this affray. After this was over another man & his wife joined us named Tuava which increased our numbers to 15. Our former Scholars the lads who were driven away from us began to take

courage & pay us occasional visits & not being threatened again they came & took up their abode with us. Bringing with them three other lads which made our number 25. To the honor of these lads be it said—That during the whole time of their separation from their teachers they attended morning & evening to family prayer—cooked all their food on the Saturday & worshipped 3 times every Sabbath day in the bush or any secret place where they could worship without molestation[.] [T]hey submitted patiently to all the insulting & threatening language of their cheifs & the People of their districts to which they belonged[.] The Brother of one of the lads with his wife observing the diligence & steadfastness of the lads determined to come & join us which brought our number to 27[.] About the same time 3 Brothers of Te ina who was fetched away by the whole [21] of the district to which he belonged returned & brought 3 Brothers with him made 30. Gods ways are indeed higher than our ways—He is wonderful in counsel and excellent in working. Those who united them selves to the teachers are permitted to be driven away into their different districts by the persecuting hands of their own friends so that in a very short time family prayer & a regard to the Sabbath is observed more or less in every district round the Island—so that like the scattered disciples of old they went every where / in effect / preaching the word. The wrath of man in this instance is made to praise Him. & the remainder of that wrath when likely to terminate in War & bloodshed he wonderfully restrains as the following anxious times will show[.] Another War broke out. [A]ll Tamatoa's party were assembled[.] [H]e was walking up & down haranguing his people and exhorting them to bravery. While he was thus engaged we took our little company about 30 in number & walked up to the party[.] [E]very one of us had a hat on & a piece of white cloth. Immediately he saw us he changed the subject of his discourse & said pointing to us Behold this company—they are not in perplexity as we are—they have no War weapons in their hands—they are all clad in white cloth & have hats on their heads—Theirs is good—Ours is bad—Theirs is truth, ours is deceit. Let us all receive the good word lest we should all be consumed in War. Upon hearing which the general reply from the whole assembly was Yes—Let us all receive the good word that we may be saved. They instantly determined not to go to war & everyone returned in peace to his own habitation[.] As soon as we returned from witnessing the wonder just related we were joined by three more which brought our number to 33. Shortly after Taeta his wife & two Children joined us he was a [22] Priest of the Evil Spirit—he was the first Priest that joined us—he came to us saying—I wish to embrace the good word—& to be instructed but as I am a Priest I shall perhaps be killed by Satan. We assured him that if he embraced the good & true word & did not turn back[,] Satan nor any one else would have power over him to hurt him but if he turned back to Satan, Satan would turn back again to him. He determined to embrace & was diligent in learning. About this time Obura the great Uncle of the King & Father of the Tamatoa to whose care I committed. Papeiha & Vahapata began to unite with them, Papeiha says. [H]e would frequently come & talk with us[.] [O]n Sabbath days he would come in at times to Worship with us[.] [H]is Son also would at times attend worship. As soon as it was known that the old Cheif Obura had united with us in worship[,] the general outcry was that he would certainly be strangled for he is a prophet of the Gods, & when he was strangled that they would dry him & hang him up in the Teachers house. Ever since which Papeiha says that the old man has been very kind to them & active in suppressing all kinds of evil. After which our numbers increased rapidly & all wives of the men who had cast them away on embracing the word returned to their husbands & embraced also. About this time a great wind arose which blew down the houses, bananas etc. The Idolators all assembled before the Marae to offer their prayers that it might soon die away. [T]hey observed all their foolish rites [—] blacking their faces—carrying their spears etc as on some occasions a great wind is the cause of a War[.] We convened with them upon the folly of such a practice [—] told them that God made the wind as well as every other thing & all their incantations & offerings would [23] not cause it to cease till it had blown Gods time[.]

They were continually upon the outlook expecting that some who had joined us would die but not one was even ill [—] while numbers were both ill & dying of the Idolatrous party. They said among themselves why are not these people ill or dying as we are[.] They have burned the Gods & we are dying. There is nothing remarkable in this for out of a population of at least 1500 people it is natural to suppose that more would die out of 1400 than out of 40 or 50 but if even one of their number had been sick they would have immediately ascribed it to the Anger of their god upon them. Although Papeiha says they were continually telling the people that the bodies of the Worshippers of the true God were as liable to disease & death as those of others. Many said that if the

body would not die of those who believed then it would be a Good Word indeed. We told them that God had declared that Man was from the Earth & to the earth he should return.

After this a ceremony concerning the Kings took place a ceremony with them of great pomp [—] the installation of the king. They fetched our people [—] Taeta the priest & all of authority—but as we had finished our house & plastered it we shut them in & they all refused to go. The King the lad who had been with us from the first was fetched by his grandfather—he would not go. [A] large company then left the Marae & came with a determination to carry him away by force before the Marae. He told them resolutely he would not go & they should not make him. His grandfather came again & forced his way into the house & desired the lad to go with him—he still persisted in refusing—The old man left—we met him at the door—I said to him—What is your business. He told us he had come to fetch his grandson upon which we requested him not [24] to force him to go against his will[.] [T]he old cheif at length consented to leave him. A great party left a second time with a full determination to take the Priest & people of authority from us by force but the house being fastened they could not get at them & returned without them—others came & grieved over them because they would not come—cut & scratched themselves & smeared themselves with blood & howled over them a considerable time[.] One of our party joined them & did not return to us for some time afterward.

About this time we made a Nett & went out a fishing[.] We were told that we should not catch any for we had not said our prayers at the Marae before we went. However we had great success & among other fish caught a Shark which is a very sacred fish[.] [W]hen they saw it they were astonished & said Behold they have caught fish as well as ourselves[.] The Shark was brought before the Young King before being first offered before the Marae which made the other party very angry as the shark is the most sacred fish & those that are not used at Sacred feasts must be cut up at the Marae. & certain parts presented to the god. The Idolators now expected the destruction of our party as they had not eaten a Shark [—] they were however disappointed in their expectations. We had frequently told them that our Ship would visit us soon which they threatened to seize as we & our party had eaten a Shark without previously having presented it to the god. The grandfather of the King said Let them alone let us see which will grow[.] [W]e are now worshipping before the

Marae regarding their word [—] if ours prevails we will all
be steadfast [25] to it [—] if theirs prevails we will all unite
with them. Some said we were two paltry deceivers turned
on shore like two persons drifted to Sea & that their great
gods Te Rongo & Koro kept it back with foul Winds & it
could not get here. We remained a considerable time without
any thing particular occurring except that we had great &
continued additions to our numbers [—] so much that our
small house for Worship would not contain the people that
assembled on Sabbath days. The Idolatrous party were living
around the King's Marae attending the various ceremonies
of their Worship[.] [O]ur house being very near the Marae
where the people were assembled[,] we were daily gaining
some of them until our party became nearly as numerous
as the party assembled before the Marae [—] they ceased
then to threaten & abuse us. This month the Vessel arrived.
[I]mmediately she hove in sight[,] there was a general outcry—Theirs is the true Word. Here is the Vessel of which
they have been speaking. The Canoes of the opposite party
according to their threat when the shark was eaten put off to
seize the Vessel[.] [W]hen they got near the Vessel the captain enquired for the Teachers [and] shewed the Cheif of the
party the bundle of Spelling Books etc that we had sent—upon
which the party immediately returned on Shore[.] Papeiha
& Vahapata asked them where the Vessel was they went off to
take [—] they replied it runs too fast we cannot overtake it.
As soon says Papeiha we knew what Vessel it was—Vahapata
with some of our party went off. & I remained on Shore with
the rest[.] Faaori a native of Raiatea[,] a Sailor[,] was sent
up Shore by the Captain with the Books & presents he had
from Raiatea for us[.] [U]pon his landing Papeiha led him
[26] to their own house. They passed by the Marae before
which the people were assembled Worshipping.

The Idolators crowded around Faaori seized him and led
him before the Marae [and] delivered him up formally to
the god as they had previously done to Papeiha & Vahapata.
Faaori looked up at the immense high Idol struck it & said
to the Idolators Why don't you burn this Evil Spirit & this
Marae. It is Satans why do you leave it[.] Its all deceit that
you are now regarding[.] If he is a god tell him to shew himself as such [—] fly on board our Ship & we'll believe him,
they replied—we are all ignorant [—] we have been kept in
darkness by Satan a long time & we do not know the truth[.]
Faaori replied this is the truth that your teachers have brought
[—] receive it & be saved. They replied—When you return

Tell Mr Williams if he will come down we will burn all our
Idols destroy our Maraes & receive the Word. Papeiha went
on board ship & took with him the old grandfather thinking
he says to conquer him with kindness as although he behaved
kindly to us yet was a most zealous & bigoted Idolator. The
Captain treated the Cheifs with great kindness & sent his
boat on Shore with us. We received the Pigs goats etc sent to
us by our friends from Raiatea. [W]e gave him our letters
for Raiatea & he set sail—In the Morning the grandfather
divided the Goats & Pigs we received to his different
Cheifs—The She goat he gave to a Cheif by the name of Te
uru—The He Goat & Boar he gave to Vai rua rangi the Sow
he kept himself. As soon as the ship left at least a few days
after there was a general wish to embrace Christianity[.] The
old Cheif the grandfather was obstinate & would continue
before the Marae[.] [27] [A] week or two elapsed & he came
to us & expressed his determination to receive the word of
God—We told him that was very good[.] [H]e wished to finish his Worship at the Marae first[.] [W]e told him it would
be well to embrace immediately[.] [H]e determined to finish his Worship[.] Soon after one of his daughters was taken
ill[.] [T]he Priests were at the Marae from Morning till
evening presenting their offerings [and] using their Encan-
tation [but] the daughter died in the night[.] He did not
shave his head & cut & hack himself as is their custom. Early
the next morning he sent his Son & set fire to his Marae[.]
[T]wo other Maraes being very near they also caught the fire
& were destroyed. The Son then went to the Marae before
which they were all assembled worshipping & endeavored to
set fire to that but they seized him & dragged him away. This
was on Sabbath day in the Month of December 1822 In which
Month the reception of Christianity became general. Whole
districts Men Women & Children with their Cheif at their
head came & expressed their desire to be instructed & their
determination to embrace Christianity[.] [B]efore the next
Sabbath day every district had come in the above mentioned
manner viz the whole people of the district headed by their
Cheif & expressed themselves worshippers of the true God.
Not one professed Idolator remained in the Island. On the
Sabbath day following the whole inhabitants of the Island
assembled for the first time to Worship the living & true God
under a grove of large Shady trees[.] After the evening worship we told the people that we would hold a general meeting
with them in the morning[.] [O]n Monday Morning early
the Cheifs & the whole of the people of the Island

assembled[.] [28] Papeiha addressed the meeting viz—Kings Cheifs & people—You have received the word of God. Hold it fast. Hold it firm—it is truth. Recollect your strength in worshipping Satan [—] building up great stone walls[,] fetching immense stones & erecting as gods to worship—your cutting down large trees[,] carving them & making gods of them. Recollect that your time—your strength—your property & all that you have were devoted to the Evil Spirit- & Behold what is it—is it not all worthless & deceitful—Now let your strength—activity & steadfastness in the true word[,] in the good word[,] far exceed. Behold Satans reign in this land is at end [—] Jesus is your Lord—he is your King [—] the reign is his—We have two propositions to make to you [—] The first is that all the Maraes in the Island be burned. & that you bring to us all the remaining idols that we may send them to our Brethren & friends at Raiatea that they with us may rejoice in the triumph of Gods word. The second is that we immediately commence the building of the House for Jehovah the true God—they cheerfully agreed to both our propositions. The meeting broke up when a general conflagration of the Maraes ensued—many were consumed & destroyed on that day—& on the next the whole were completely despoiled so that not one remained on the whole Island. The Priests & Cheifs of the different districts brought their Idols & gave them to us in return for which we divided out our remaining stock of Spelling Books to the various districts which only amounted to 3 & four each district—they all immediately began to work at the fare bure raal [—] [29] a Chapel[.] [W]e had to instruct them in every fact of it as their houses are very different to those of the Society Islands[.] [W]e worked a piece of the ridge Pole & one of the outside posts & gave to them as patterns[,] when every man made his to the pattern given[.] While we were at work at the Chapel a large turtle was caught[.] [T]hey came & asked us what was to be done with it—we told them to bake it & eat it & let the Women eat of it also—they bake it & the men eat it but no Woman dare touch it for fear of being strangled by the gods as the turtle & shark are Sacred fish. Shortly after they caught another large turtle & brought it to us—we had it baked [—] we sent to many of our Neighbors to come to our house with their wives[.] [W]e seated them all in a circle then sent for all the Prophets & Priests near us & seated them also—had the oven of food opened & the turtles brought & placed in the midst of the circle before they were aware of why they were sent for. We asked a Blessing & then divided out portions of the turtle to the Women & Priests & desired

them all to eat heartily & without fear which they did & when they found that no harm came to them—the people said Behold the deceit of all these Priests making us believe that there was power in a turtle to kill us & our wives & see there is no truth in all that they have said. A third turtle was caught & taken to the grandfathers[.] [H]e sent for us to come & partake of it—We sent word that we would come if Women were allowed to eat of it also [—] if not we would not touch it—[30] We went to his house & told him the terms on which we would become his guests—he said Let not Women partake of it. It is a Sacred fish [—] we told him that there was no sacred fish [—]God made all to be eaten by all with thankfulness—he had given them for food for Women as well as Men therefore let all the fish that you call sacred be common to all [—] to Women as well as Men—he agreed to what we said & sent for his own wife— [and] a few neighbors with their wives[.] [T]hey in a very short time consumed the Turtle & from that time all such things have fallen[.] Women unite in eating with Men what God hath given & drinking also out of one Cup which a Woman dare not do on any account formerly. All this time we were getting on fast with the Chapel but their houses being so very different we had some difficulty to make them understand—their houses have no sides or Walls but the thatching & rafters reach from the ridge pole down to the ground. Therefore we had to attend & direct them in every part[.] [W]e marked out the semicircular ends[,] the distances of the posts & formed a piece of the Wall plate for them all of which they followed—we then took a rafter each & fitted it on[,] from which every man took pattern & each fitted on his rafter[.] [T]he thatching was the next thing about which they were at a loss—we each took a reeds length of thatch & thatched up to the ridge Pole. They saw how it was done and in two days had the whole building thatched in. The burning of the lime excited their astonishment much[.] [E]very one was crowding to see it & were all much delighted with it—astonished at its softness & whiteness—some whitened their cloth [31] with it[,] others white washed their hats & walked about thinking themselves very fine. As soon as a part was wattled & plastered they came & examined it [—] particularly they felt it—knocked it with stones & expressed their astonishment in the following words "The very stones in the sea & the sand on the shore become good property in the hands of those who worship the true God & regard his good Word[.]" [W]e told them says Papeiha That we were formerly like them & equally ignorant—our houses were formerly like theirs but this as well as many other

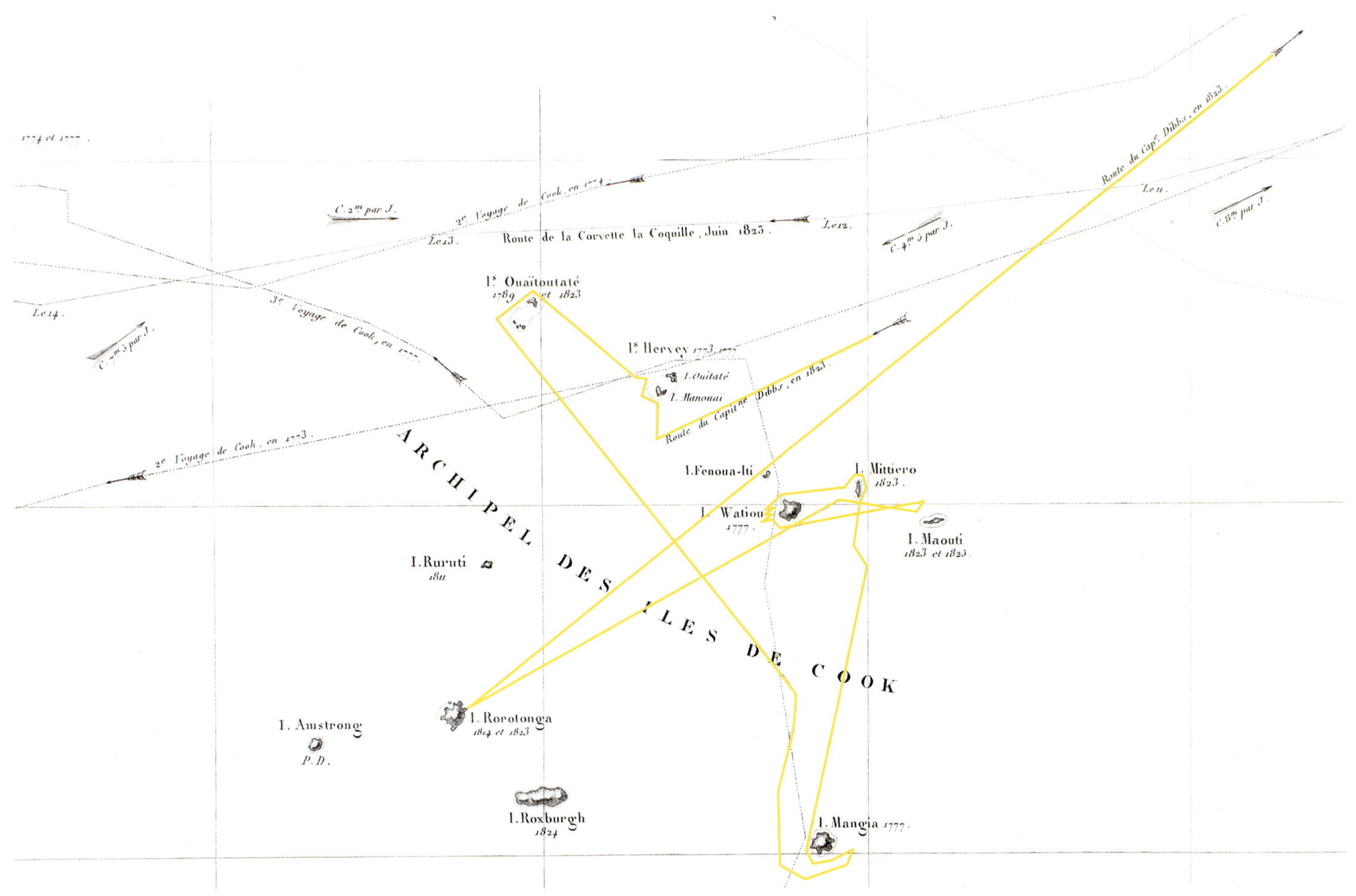

268 *A portion of Duperrey's 'Carte des Isles situées au Sud et a l'Ouest des Isles de la Société', dated 1823, from the atlas of* Voyage autour du monde, *the account of the voyage of* La Coquille. *Interestingly, it shows the route (yellow line) taken by Master John Dibbs on the 4 July to 7 August 1823 voyage of the* Endeavour. *Iles Armstrong and Roxburgh are both Rarotonga, renamed and incorrectly plotted by subsequent traders; Ruruti does not exist (see Findlay 1877,494).*

Good things were brought to us by the good word of God[.] [A]s soon as the chapel was finished many persons began to erect dwelling houses after the pattern of ours[.] [O]thers were diligent in making bedsteads & all who had books were diligent in learning[.] [F]amily prayer became general & attention to the Sabbath day became universal. Thus were all the labors of two comparatively weak instruments crowned with abundant success. This is the conclusion of the account of Papeiha—

In the month of April 1823 the vessel returned from the colony of New South Wales when we received the letters Papeiha & Vahapata wrote to us Stating the various dangers to which they had been exposed[,] the partial success that had attended their labors[,] & requested that two more laborers might be sent to join them[.] Faaori the Native Sailor delivered his Message—viz That if Mr Williams would visit them they would destroy their Maraes—& embrace Christianity—we likewise received other important information viz that that there were several Natives from an adjacent Island called Raratoa at Aitutake who had embraced the truth & were desirous of returning to their own Island [32] with teachers[.] [T]hese circumstances appeared to us very promising openings for the permanent introduction of the gospel to this important group of islands[,] several of which I was informed when I visited it in 1822. We therefore determined to embrace the first opportunity[.] [A]ccordingly we employed the Vessel belonging to the Cheifs of the Society Islands. Mr Bourne took two teachers from Tahaa.

We selected four with their wives from Raiatea two of whom were intended for Aitutake viz Paumoana & Mataitai. *July 2ⁿᵈ 1823* They with Vahineino & Fanauara for Rarotonga were set apart to these important office[.] [I]n a very interesting Service Mr Threlkeld addressed them from Luke 14.28 etc. He exhorted them to count the cost & he told them plainly & faithfully of the dangers & difficulties with which they might & ought to expect to meet. He warned them against expecting that all conquests would be obtained so easily as that of Rurutu & exhorted them to be faithful unto death—After which I addressed them from the words of the eminent Missionary Paul Acts 20.24—I exhorted them notwithstanding & in face of all the difficulties & dangers of which they had just heard to exditate [?] the devoted Apostle & say "None of these things move me"—The church provided & equipped them without any expense to the Society for their Voyage & Stations—after taking an Affectionate leave we set sail for Aitutake on the *4ᵗʰ July*. On the *9ᵗʰ* early in the Morning we made the land[.] [T]o our astonishment we found that the great Work was done before we arrived—We had a grateful salutation from every Canoe that passed us[.] Some cried out—Good is the [33] word of God—& It is now well with Aitutake. The good word has taken root at Aitutake. Some pointed to their hats[,] others held up a Spelling book to convince us of the truth of which they said—As soon as Cheifs canoe came alongside we learnt from Te Bati one of the first who embraced the Gospel that all the Maraes were destroyed & burned not one remained whole—That all the idols that had escaped the general conflagration were in the possession of the teachers—that the profession of Christianity was general—so much so that not an Idolator remained. That a large chapel was erected nearly 200 feet long plastered & waiting my arrival to open it—we rejoiced at hearing this good & unexpected News—As soon as we saw the Teachers they confirmed all the good news that we had heard—We immediately went on shore & held a meeting with the Cheifs & people. I expressed to them the great joy of our hearts in hearing & seeing that they had cast down their Maraes & embraced the Gospel of Jesus Christ & that they had erected so fine & so large a House for Jehovah the true God. We would open it tomorrow morning if agreeable to them—that they must lay aside their Heathenish ornaments—wash themselves clean & cloth themselves decently to all of which they assented—I told them that the Church at Raiatea had sent two more good men to instruct them more fully in the word of God whom I would leave with their wives at Aitutake—they expressed

themselves much delighted[.] [34] After the meeting was closed we went to see the Chapel[.] [I]t is a fine Large building from 180 to 200 feet long about 30 feet wide—wattled & plastered in imitation of our Chapel at Raiatea[.] [A]fter this we walked in land to see the teachers house etc[.] [I]t is a neat well-built house—plastered & divided into 5 small rooms—I commended them for the good example they had set the people[.] [P]osts for houses on a similar plan are collected in every direction[.] [M]any are erected & many more are in hand[.] Bedsteads are in many of the houses[,] encircled with white cloth in imitation of those of their teachers[.] [M]y heart rejoiced much at witnessing such a scene-little did I expect to behold such things in such short a time when I landed the two teachers about 18 months ago among the wildest people I had ever witnessed. But Christ must be exalted—the heathen must be saved—Satans empire must totter nay it must fall & be rooted out from its very foundations[.] We held various interesting conversations with the people in the course of the day. The next day also we had much conversation with them on subjects which are of infinite importance to all—See Journal of Voyage July 9 & 10 [this journal is evidently lost.]

While conversing in the chapel with the people already assembled our attention was arrested by the sound of an Axe being struck with a Stone which substitutes a bell—the Ringer or rather striker was followed by a number of persons decently dressed in white cloth both Men & Women—As soon [35] as the people were all assembled Mr Bourne commenced the Service with reading singing & prayer[.] I addressed the people with Gospel of St John 3 Ch 16—God so loved the world etc—I spoke as plainly & simply to them as I possibly could [—] I was happy to find that they understood the principal part of what we said. As soon as Service was ended we went in land to take leave of the teachers[.] I endeavored to impress upon their minds the necessity of maintaining the Strictest unity among themselves—& gave them instruction in addition to the written ones—1ˢᵗ to behave with kindness to Vahapata & not to lessen him in the estimation of the people. 2 If he wished to marry not to object to it. 3—Never to accustom themselves in the slightest degree to the Aitutake language. But at all times speak themselves & accustom The people to speak the Raiatean language. 4—As soon as they knew the people, their state, the different influences in the Island to make their arrangements accordingly & if for the sake of peace it is necessary to separate & one join one party, the other, another, by all means do so[.] [L]ose sight of every private wish & feeling for the promotion of the great object they had in view. 5—to select as soon as prudent those whom they thought sincere in their profession & were acting consistently therewith & prepare to Baptize them when Messrs Tyerman & Bennet should visit them—After this we took an affectionate leave of them committing them to God & the power of his grace & left them well pleased with the prospect [36] of usefulness before them. I hope for great things—pray for great things—& confidently expect great things to result from the labors of the Teachers & their wives in the Island of Aitutake.

What solid satisfaction it affords[,] what peace of mind is enjoyed in leaving the work of God in the hands of those well qualified for their work & whose only aim will be the temporal & eternal welfare of the people among whom they labor[.] [S]uch I trust is the case with Paumoana & Mataitai[.] After visiting the other Islands which our Mission to this gave rise we returned to Raiatea on the *7th of August* [1823 and] entered the harbor early in the Morning with our vessel decorated with the trophies of Victory. On the Friday Evening following there was a public exhibition of all the Idols in our large Chapel[.] [I]t was lighted up & presented a brilliant appearance[.] Mr Threlkeld commenced the Service with "blow ye the trumpet blow etc—& prayer—After which I gave a part of the Account of our interesting journey—The Numerous Idols were hung in various parts of the Chapel but especially about the pulpit desk etc[.] Many very interesting addresses were delivered on the occasion from which the following are selected—Te maure Arose & said—To the people of Raiatea do I address myself—My thoughts have been growing all day upon the great power of God & his great compassion to the [37] laws of darkness. Surely the prayer of Raiatea has been heard—We have prayed that the good word of Jesus might reach the abodes of ignorance[,] That Savages might be tamed by the power of the Gospel & behold (says he pointing to the two Aitutake cheifs & their wives) we see them here this evening—Rejoice O Raiatea in doing the good work of God—We sent two teachers to Rurutu formerly & we saw what the power of God effected by them. Their idols were set up in this place of worship & our hearts rejoiced[.] We have this morning another exhibition of evil spirits—We did not expect this so soon. Our thoughts were heavy, very heavy, but Gods thoughts were not our thoughts. With himself his own word is irresistible. I have been thinking of what Mr Williams has told us this evening about Aitutake [—] that it will outstrip us if we are not diligent—they have bedsteads—many are erecting decent houses all over their Settlement. Let us Beware lest the Branch should outgrow the trunk. Lest we should be last & they first. Pointing to the idols he said The Teeth of these Monsters are blunted by the word of Jesus[.] [T]hey will devour no more men or Children in the Island of Aitutake—he concluded by addressing the Cheifs & their wives from Aitutaki in a very pathetic manner & saluting them in the name of our common Lord & Saviour[.]

Atihuta—then arose & said—This dear friends is not the first day of my joy—The man Varua ino (the Evil Spirits) were seen thro' the telescope hanging to the yard Arms of the Vessel as she entered the harbour[.] True indeed is the word that says All the gods that did [38] shall be destroyed. Behold we see them hanging here this evening—There are some things we term the poisons of the Seas—These Idols hanging here are the poison of the land for both body & soul are poisoned by them. But let us rejoice their reign is over[.] [D]id we know that they would be obtained so soon—did we think of being gratified by beholding them so speedily[.] He then addressed himself to unbelievers in saying behold these are still your gods although you do not acknowledge them—he exhorted them earnestly to turn to Jesus by whose power alone these Idols were conquered. & how says he can you resist his power[.] [G]ods of wood are food for the fire but the god without form his head cannot be reached. These gods are conquered & destroyed but the invisible God will remain for ever. We have become like a fountain let us therefore be diligent—for if the fountain is good its goodness will extend to the end of every stream that flows from it, if the trunk is good its goodness will extend to the end of every branch. These Idols hanging here we[re] formerly unconquerable but the power of God is gone forth long since men become Men & savages Brethren in Christ—

Mataute arose & said We have been praying that God would exert his power & cause his word to grow—That his kingdom might come with power. & now behold every man with his own eyes the effects of that power[.] [T]hese Idols are not obtained by means of spears clotted with human blood as formerly—No Guns—No Spears—No spikes No other weapon but the powerful [39] Gospel of our Lord Jesus Christ. Formerly all was theirs—pigs—fish—food. Men—Women Children & everything we possessed & Now behold them hanging in degradation before us—This evening is now the commencement of saying—We saw the Idols hanging about the Vessels & joy sprang in our hearts. They called our ship a Ship of God & true it is—It has carried the Gospel to distant

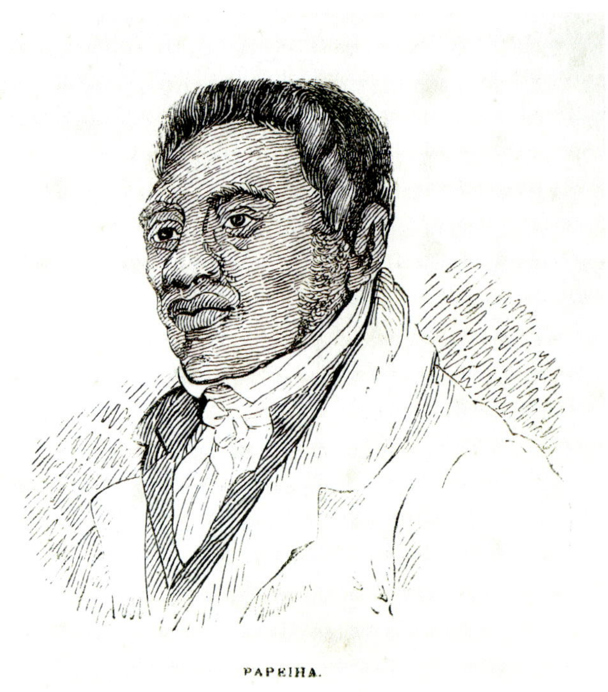

269 *Papeiha, the most effective LMS teacher and the best LMS collector. Baxter wood engraving in* Missionary Enterprises, *1837; from a camera obscura projection by Rev Aaron Buzacott on Rarotonga.*

Islands & brought back the trophies of its Victory—does praise grow in every heart—is joy felt by all—let us not only rejoice that d_____[illegible] are subject to us—but that our names are written in the book of life—

Paremo addressed as follows—Mr Williams told us when he took leave of us to pray[,] for prayer was mighty with God & truly we now behold the effects of its might[.] Alluding to the Cheifs of Aitutake—he said These people we never beheld before—they are Kings—& are now seated among our Kings the goodness of the Word of God. Let every King pray for other Kings[,] thinking within himself I am a King—Let every Cheif pray for other Cheifs saying within himself I am a Cheif [—] Let every common man pray for common people thinking within himself I am a common man—Let every Woman pray for other Women thinking I am a Woman—Pointing to the Idols he said Behold these great these powerful Gods—once adored by us—how foolish how contemptible in our sight they now appear—this is the second Manifestation we have had of the great power of God[.]

It being late we determined to finish Narration[.] [O]n Sabbath Morning Vahine ino who returned from Rarotoa concluded the [40] whole interesting Service in a sensible & excellent prayer[.] [O]n the Sabbath morning following I finished the narrative of our journey—Fanauara & Vaheineino gave an account of what passed Between them & the people of Rarotonga[,] related in pages 20 & 22 of our Journal[.]

Mr Threlkeld concluded with a short exhortation singing & prayer[.] Instead of Catechising as is our custom on Sabbath Noon we devoted this our third meeting to the exhibition of the Idols when many persons addressed the meeting with propriety & energy.

Descriptions of the Aitutaki Idols in possession of the Rev D Tyerman & G Bennet Esq—Deputation from MS [Missionary Society]

No1 'Kau[8]—A principal & powerful god [—] his name is taken by a fish of that name which pierces with its nose & by which the priests of Kau are inspired. Sacrafices were not offered to it but it was famous for Strangling & Inspiring-

No2 Te Rongo. The priests of this god were inspired by the shark. This is one of the great gods & Kai tangata Man eater -

No3 A fan belonging to the great god Tangaroa—This is also an object of adoration as it is decorated with red feathers.

No4 A bundle Sacred fans used by the priests at worship before the Marae [41]

5 An offering to the god or rather the first piece obtained from a large log of Aito[9] which they were splitting & of which

---

8   Probably Ka'ukura, a celebrated ancestor; see Savage 1962,93.
9   Ironwood, *Casuarina equisetifolia*; also called toa, which also means weapon; weapons were made of ironwood. Omnipresent in the tropics, the wood is indeed nearly 'hard as iron', and is so dense it sinks in seawater.

were making Spears [—] this being the first piece obtained was deified & presented to the god.

6 A piece of a jagged spear the point of which was broken off in a man & this was immediately presented to the God.[10]

7 Tongaiti (or Toahiti inKaiatea [?]) The god of the mountains. The priests of this god are inspired by a lizard.

8 Tangaroa the great National God of Aitutaki & of all most all the Islands in the South Seas. He has his nett with which he catches men & the spirits of men as they fly from their bodies & his spear with which he kills them—& a piece of Aito an offering to him as N°5—

9 An image of the powerful god Rongo belonging to a celebrated Cheif & Warrior called Ruabu—

10 The handles of 2 sacred fans—& 2 pieces of platted Cocoa Nutt husk—by the Cocoanutt husk the priest prognosticates the fate of Canoes & when gone whether they have arrived at the place to which they were going[—] the Priest places the Cocoa nut husk in a certain position in the house of the god [—] if it remains a certain time in that position he assures the friends that the Canoe has arrived [—] if it be moved in the least—it is lost—[42]

11 Te Rongo & his three sons the name of the first is Te bua Kina—the second tu Ka rere—the third Tino Kura. They are gods of the Sea [—] to them prayers are offered for the Safety of Canoes—at sea—[11]

12 Family god called Vei with a tail which the priests take off & decorate themselves with when they wish to be inspired.[12]

14 The handle of a Sacred fan & part of a Cocoa Nutt leaf that has been brought from an opposite party & presented to their enemies as a prediction that they will be conquered in War—when they receive it they take it before the marae & say—We have received this Niau poke no tatou—leaf of death for us—

15 A rod with snares at the end which the priest uses in catching the Spirit of the god (Observe the snares at the ends of the strings.) It is used in cases of pregnancy. The woman is taken before the Mgr & the Priest uses this snare to catch the spirit of the god. Only cheifs had the honor of the ceremony—it was of importance both in Raiatea & Aitutaki & becomes an occasion of boast in succeeding years to all that

had it performed for them. At Aitutaki it was used for catching the god by his leg in War to Secure his influence on the side of the party who performed this Ceremony[13]

16 O te Ao aka Maru—a great God to whom they applied in all cases of difficulty & perplexity in going to Sea—overtaken [43] with Storms—in War—in Sickness & to this great god also sacrifices of various kinds were offered & to him all persons killed in War were presented [—] he was considered very powerful in killing men—

17 Te I ma te tabu. A man from Raiatea ages ago who drifted to Aitutaki[,] distinguished himself in their Wars & was afterwards deified

18 Ruanuu[14]—a Cheif from Raiatea ages past. He sailed from Raiatea in his Canoe & settled at Aitutaki[.] [F]rom him a genealogy is dated—he is termed—Te Atua taitai tere or a leader of fleets. He was drifted to Aitutaki & was a powerful & great God. To this God is ascribed the preservation of Rairai a cheif of Raiatea[—] he was sailing a fleet to Tahiti[, was] overtaken with a foul wind[, and] drifted to Leeward[.] Rairai offered prayers to Ruanuu—Tah nia a Shark by that name came up to eat them, but Ruanuu in answer to Rairai's prayer appeared in the shape of a Crane & settled upon the Canoe. Rairai said to the evil spirits that appeared in the shape of a shark—No do not hurt this canoe [—] it has been settled on by the crane [—] we are disciples of Ruanuu & out of your power- thus he & his fleet were saved & taken to shore[.] [O]n Ruanuu there is an old tattered Silk handkercheif that was obtained from Captn Cooks Vessel & immediately presented to Ruanuu as the god or guide of fleets—-

19 Bundle of fans—Sacred [44]

20 Koke an inferior order of their [gods?] that have no sacrifices—no disciples [or?] offerings & are referred to in a degrading manner—as treating a man with courtesy they say He is a man. Is he not a Koke? That is—is he not a man without family—without house without food—without friends as the koke—so is he without honor

21 The remains of a garment in which a Warrior had been victorious & on his return presented to the god as a covering—the one with feathers is a girdle in which the King blows a conch shell at some of their large Feasts

---

10 This could well be LMS 114; George Tobin's 24 July 1792 description of an Aitutaki spear head certainly fits: 'the sharp point being of very dark hard wood and jagged like a turtle peg' (Schreiber 2007,137); see figs. 83, 84.

11 This is Oldman 437; see p. 72.

12 This could be the small Aitutaki slab god with detachable tail, LMS 46; see figs. 152, 155.

13 Perhaps the 'snare for catching a god' illustrated in Williams 1837,65; not located in British Museum LMS collection, nor mentioned in either LMS catalogue; see page 223.

14 Tahitian spelling of Ruanuku, the name of a god; see Buck 1944,331.

22   A Sling & part of a spear by both of which men (perhaps many) have been Killed [—] they are therefore presented to Rua tabu the great god of War [—] his fan & other things are also in the bundle

23   Other representations of the great god Te Rongo—N°2 inspired by the shark with the garment used by the Priests—

24   Tangi ia [—] A man formerly known from Opoa in Raiatea—drifted to Aitutaki—distinguished himself in war & deified—He is the god of War belonging to the district of Aipai[15] in Aitutaki

25   Ta'—with his fan & the God of Thunder [—] when the thunder claps—they say that this god is flying —[16]

13   Skipped—A Priests dress— [45]

Sent to England—

N°1   Representation of Te Rongo belonging to Orutanga a district in Aitutaki—Every district has an idol of the God to which it belongs See N°2[17]

N°2   An Idol of the great god Tangaroa see N°8 This is perhaps their greatest god—he made the Heavens earth & all things—human sacrifices were offered to Tangaroa at Rurutu he is acknowledged as the greatest of gods—At Auau—Atiu & all the Islands at which we touched they acknowledged the greatness of Tanga roa—this representation of him belongs to the district of Atimama—

N°3   Te Turere an idol belonging to the great god Taaroa[18] from the district of Atineva [—] each district makes its Idol & dedicates it to the principle god & leaves it at the principal Marae as its representative—

N°4   The District of Natipaki's Idol of Tangaroa left at the great Marae as its representative—[19]

N°5   Nukunoni an idol of the great god Ruatabu—Nukunoni is the district to which it belongs [—] it is placed at the great Marae as their representative to superintend their affairs & make them victorious in their wars [—] I can get no explanation of the two figures upon this or others of a Similar description[20]

N°6   A great god purchased with a fishhook. This was one hung at the yard arm on our entrance in the harbour—it is most likely a household or family God[21]—the Old Cheif from Aitutaki is sitting with [46] me & wishes that the idols may not be sent to England but burned to cook food with as they will expose his folly.

I intended to have given a short description of the Island, people, language etc[.] [S]uffice at present to say that the Island is situated 18–58 S[,] 48 W about 10 miles in length[,] low in comparison with the Society Islands but presents a very fertile appearance—there is a small reef on the West side & a narrow entrance sufficiently large to admit with the greatest safety a large boat. The people resemble the Society Islanders—but at present are very filthy.

The productions are in all respects similar to those of the Society Islands but the Breadfruit not near so abundant or fine. Cocoa Nutts are not so abundant[.] Taro and Bananas are very abundant & very fine—so is the Sugar cane- The language as it respects its idiom is exactly like Raiatean but they have the hard consonants & Nasal sounds with the rejection of the l & h which are in frequent use in the Language of the Society Islands—Wherever we have the break they supply the k or ng—as in Canoe—it is va-a in the Raiatean & waka at Aitutake—food is ma-a with us & Maanga at Aitutake but I gave special charge to the teachers to accustom themselves to speak their own language to the people & I am [47] in great hopes that the difficulty will not be great as the Aitutake Cheifs at Raiatea have attained the Raiatean language very quickly—I conclude this account hoping it will afford you & all our Christian friends joy—& encourage them in their works & labor of love for the thousands that are still destitute of the knowledge of our Lord Jesus Christ—thus you see my dear brothers & sisters I have written a long account[.] I don't know how you will be able to make it out [—] it is written with a Manifold writer[.] [Y]ou must excuse all blindness—as I have not time to read it over again[.]

I remain Very dear
Father Brothers & Sisters
Yours very affecty
J Williams

I have no need to say that it is intended for you all _____

---

[15]   Vaipae, east Aitutaki; see map in Buck 1927.

[16]   LMS cat nd N°46, 'The god of thunder, of carved wood, adorned with feathers. From Rarotonga' could well be Papeiha's N°25, but the actual object remains unidentified.

[17]   This is the large sennit and feather figure LMS 170; see p. 71.

[18]   Ta'aroa is Tahitian spelling of Tangaroa.

[19]   This is the 24cm openwork staff god, LMS 168; see p. 71 and figs. 178–182.

[20]   Possibly Oldman 430; see below; Nukunoni is not on Buck's map of Aitutaki.

[21]   This is LMS 38, figured Williams 1837,65 (Williams describes it as 'grim-looking'); Buck 1944,337 fig. 209 (h 1.28m); Edge-Partington 1890 1,21 N°4; LMS cat nd p. 14 N°3: 'Another rude idol of wood, with a human head, from Aitutaki, figured by Mr. Williams p. 65'; LMS ms cat [95]437[692]: 'A god from Aitutaki which on the introduction of Christianity was deposed and used as a post in a cook-house and afterwards given for a few fish-hooks to Mr Williams'; see fig. 235.

The LMS Collection:

Catalogue of The Missionary Museum;
British Museum LMS
Collection registration slips;
Some particulars
of the Missionary Museum

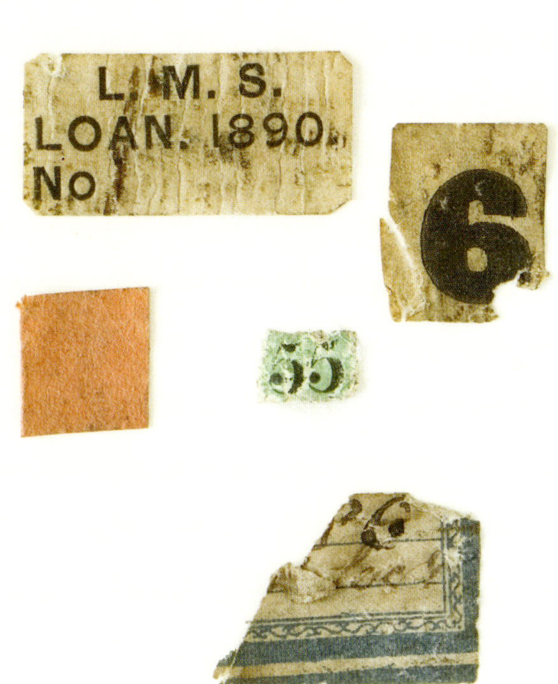

270 *Various labels from Pomare's large 'Oro, LMS 101. Over the years, objects in the British Museum LMS collection have been subject to a number of cataloguing and labelling systems. Green label '55' corresponds with N° 55 in the green page (South Sea) section of the LMS (nd) catalogue; see figure 198.*

The LMS Collection:

Polynesian Section,
Catalogue of the Missionary Museum,
Blomfield Street, Finsbury, (nd)

The Missionary Museum opened in early 1815. The first known *Catalogue* was printed in 1826. This is the second known *Catalogue*; it is undated. An internal clue as to the date appears in an annotation on page 14, 'N°4 Tahitian idol chest [LMS 120], presented by the late Mr. Bennet'; George Bennet died 13 November 1841. This particular copy belonged to Captain AWF Fuller. Courtesy BPBM.

CATALOGUE

OF

THE MISSIONARY MUSEUM,

BLOMFIELD STREET, FINSBURY;

INCLUDING

SPECIMENS IN NATURAL HISTORY,

VARIOUS IDOLS OF HEATHEN NATIONS,

DRESSES, MANUFACTURES, DOMESTIC UTENSILS,

INSTRUMENTS OF WAR,

&c. &c. &c.

———

Admission by Tickets, for a limited number of Persons, signed by a
Director or Officer of the Society.

———

OPEN TUESDAY, THURSDAY, AND SATURDAY.

———

*From Lady Day to Michaelmas, from 10 to 4 o'clock ; and from
Michaelmas to Lady Day, from 10 to 3 o'clock.*

THERE are two divisions, in the arrangement of the Museum;—
HISTORY AND NATURAL HISTORY. The specimens, illustrating the former, are subdivided according to the Missionary Stations from whence they have been received,
and are distinguished by the colour of the paper on
which the number is printed, as under.

GREEN.—South Sea Islands. *In Cases A and C.*

YELLOW.—China and Ultra Ganges. *Ditto D E M and I.*

BLUE.—India, including the three Presidencies. *Ditto F and G.*

RED.—Africa and Madagascar. *Ditto G H and N.*

PINK.—America, North and South. *Ditto O.*

WHITE.—The Miscellaneous Articles, and Natural History.
Ditto B and Lobby.

ADVERTISEMENT.

THE articles which compose this Museum were supplied chiefly by the Missionaries employed by the London Missionary Society; a few others are donations from benevolent travellers, or friendly officers of mercantile vessels. The Missionaries rightly judged that the natural productions of the distant countries in which they reside would be acceptable at home, especially to their juvenile friends, and to others who may not have opportunity of viewing larger Collections. The efforts also of natural genius, especially in countries rude and uncivilized, afford another class of interesting curiosities; whilst they prove how capable even the most uncivilized of mankind are of receiving that instruction, which it is the study of the Missionaries to communicate.

But the most valuable and impressive objects in this Collection, are the numerous, and (in some instances) *horrible*, IDOLS, which have been imported from the South Sea Islands, from India, China, and Africa; and among these, those especially which were given up by their former worshippers, from *a full conviction of the folly and sin of idolatry* —a conviction derived from the ministry of the Gospel by the Missionaries.

A 2

It is hoped that a view of these "trophies of Christianity" will inspire the spectators with gratitude to God for his great goodness to our native land, in favouring us so abundantly with the means of grace, and the knowledge of his salvation; and at the same time, with thankfulness that these blessings have, in some happy degree, been communicated, and by our means, to the distant isles of the Southern Ocean. Many of the articles in this Collection are calculated to excite, in the pious mind, feelings of deep commiseration for the hundreds of millions of the human race, still the vassals of ignorance and superstition; whilst the success with which God has already crowned our labours, should act as a powerful stimulus to efforts, far more zealous and extended, for the conversion of the heathen.

MISSIONARY MUSEUM.

IDOLS, AND OBJECTS OF SUPERSTITIOUS REGARD, FROM ISLANDS IN THE PACIFIC OCEAN.

THE mission to the South Sea Islands was the earliest undertaken by this Society. The first party of missionaries, about thirty in number, arrived by the ship *Duff* at Tahiti on the 6th of March, 1797.

On the 18th of July, 1812, Pomare, the late king of Tahiti, who had always behaved in a friendly manner, declared to the missionaries his full conviction of the truth of the gospel, and his determination to worship Jehovah, as the only living and true God.

His example was soon followed by the principal chiefs, who, convinced of their idolatry, burnt their idols, destroyed their maraes, *abandoned human sacrifices and infant murders,* forsook their abominable impurities, and strictly observed the Lord's day.

Pomare, in a letter to the missionaries, dated Feb. 19th, 1816, when he sent his family or household idols to them, says, " I wish you to send those idols to *Britain,* for the Missionary Society, that they may know the likeness of the gods that Tahiti worshipped." The original letter, with the idols alluded to, and numerous others from different Islands, will be found in

Case A.

1 TEMEHARO, the principal idol of Pomare's family, one of the chief deities of Tahiti and also the protector of Mateo.

2 TERIAPATURA, son of the great God Oro, and national protector of Tahiti, Raiatea, Huahine, Tahaa, Borabora, and Marua.

3 Name unknown.

4 TIIPA, very powerful, and said to preside over the winds.

5—7 ORAMATUAS, spirits of deceased relations, to whom prayers were offered for the recovery of sick persons, &c.

8 VARUA INO, Evil Spirit. A name by which idols are now generally designated.

9—11 Idols, which, like all the preceding, are made of cinet or braided cord, formed of fibres of the husk of the cocoanut ; the first, having rude features, is TANGAROA.—*Presented by the late Mr. Bennet.*

12 ORO, the god of war. A rude uncarved staff of hard casuarina wood, said by Mr. Ellis* to have been decorated with feathers. It was the cause of many battles ; and human sacrifices were offered to it.—*Presented by the late Mr. Bennet.*

13 A small column of basalt, worshipped by the royal family of Tahiti, when staying at the southern part of Eimeo.—*Presented by the late Mr. Bennet.*

14 Another from the same place.

15 Another stone idol, to which this silly legend was attached : that the priest could throw it into the sea, and make it swim back again.

16 A long carved wooden idol, beset with curved spines, and having six small heads at top ; large spider-shells are also suspended from it. Hervey, or Navigators' Islands.

17 Sacred ornament from a canoe ; the two heads at top were worshipped by fishermen at Huahine. (See Ellis, fig. 6.)

18—20 Three carved staff-shaped idols, like the large one covered with cloth from Rarotonga.

21 Another, shorter, with a head at each end, and ornamented with a few feathers, from Rarotonga.

22 TAAROA UPAO VAHU, from Rurutu, the supreme deity of Polynesia. In addition to the demi-gods that stud the outside, designed to show the many that had proceeded from him, a number of small idols were found in the interior of this deity, deposited there probably to imbibe his

* Polynesian Researches, vol. ii. p. 220.

supernatural powers, prior to their dispersion as his representatives.　(Ellis, vol. ii. page 220.)

23 Another form of TAAROA, left as his representative at the great marae, in the district of Natipaki.　(See Ellis, fig. 3.)

24 Like the last.

25 TANGAROA from Maute, with feathers and fibre cinet appended to it.

26 A carved flat club-formed idol, with an appendage of plaited cocoa-nut fibre.

27, 28 Two, resembling the last, with feather appendages.

29 A ditto of RUATABU, with two heads and two cinet appendages.　Nukunoni was the district to which it belonged, and it was placed at the marae, to superintend their affairs and make them victorious in war.

30, 31 Two elaborately carved club-formed idols, whose names are now lost; they were district gods of Mangaia, one of the Hervey Islands.

32 A larger ditto.

33 TE BUA KINA, three sons of the great RONGA, gods of the sea, to whom prayers were offered for the safety of canoes.

34 RONGA, a rude human figure, covered with feathers, belonging to Orutanga, a district of Aitutaki.

35 TARIGNARUE, the superior god of Atui; a very deeply carved idol with red feathers, also, a large piece made of cinet and feathers.　These are but portions of the god; the rats, having made a nest in him, destroyed the remainder.

36 A rope idol, with limbs covered with red feathers.

37, 38 Two narrow flat idols, covered with red feathers, and a profusion of the tail feathers of the Tropic bird.

39 TII VAHINE.　A Tahitian goddess.

40 Ditto ditto.　They are rudely carved human figures.

41 Another Tahitian idol, with numerous black figures painted on it.　(See Ellis, vol. i. page 24.)—*Presented by the late Rev. Rowland Hill.*

42 A large well-finished figure, cut out of hard wood, with three demi-gods attached to the breast.　From Rarotonga.

43 TARIA NUI, or great ears, a fishing god. (See Ellis, fig. 7.)

44 An idol made of a compact species of coral.

45 A large wooden idol, with very prominent grotesque features, from the Sandwich Islands. Taken, with permission of the governor, Kuakene, from the walls of an ancient marae at Kairua, Hawaii, by the Deputation.

46 The god of thunder, of carved wood, adorned with feathers. From Rarotonga.

47 Another resembling it.

48 A ditto, without feathers.

49 Idols from Metiaro : one resembles the last.

50 ROMATANE, from Maute, adorned with a long tail of cock's feathers, and tufts of human hair.

51 KAU, an idol of stone.

52 HAU, from Maute. Several clusters of feathers attached to pieces of wood and fibre rope.

53 An idol of two figures, one on the head of the other, with black markings and feathers.

54 TIKIHE ATUA, a rude sitting figure, with a tuft of cock's feathers on the head, taken from a canoe.

55 Two large paddle-shaped idols, with fibre rope attached.

56—60 A SAMOAN GOD, a short round stick; and numerous small variously shaped idols, some decorated with feathers.

61, 62 Propitiatory offerings to RONGA and TAGNAROA, to appease them when removed to new habitations: Hervey Islands.

63—66 Numerous bunches of feathers, probably portions of broken idols or propitiatory offerings.

67—70 Four amulets of green Jade stone. New Zealand.

71 A tabooing rod, or else a rod carried before royalty at the Sandwich Isles.

72 Handle of the sacred fan, TAHIVI ANUNACHAUS. (See No 3, Missionary Sketches.)

73, 74 Two sacred fans, with which the priests drove away flies at the human sacrifices. The first is from the Marquesan Islands.

75 A whip, or fly-flap, made of cocoa-nut fibre. (See Ellis, vol. ii. page 54.)

76—80 Various whips; one of the handles is of carved bone, the others wood.

On the Floor under the north Skylight.

A GIGANTIC IDOL, twelve feet high, covered with bark cloth, ornamented with black zigzag lines, brought from RAROTONGA, by the lamented Missionary, the Rev. JOHN WILLIAMS. (See his Missionary Enterprises, chap. vii.)

(*For Case B, see page 46.*)

Case C.

ARTICLES OF DRESS, DOMESTIC UTENSILS, IMPLEMENTS OF WAR, MUSIC, &c., FROM ISLANDS IN THE PACIFIC OCEAN.

SOCIETY AND FRIENDLY ISLES.

81 Cap, or head-dress, of feathers, worn by a chief mourner. Tahiti.—*Presented by the late Rev. John Williams.*

82 Ditto, worn formerly by the master of the ceremonies of the native dances, but latterly by the chief judge of the Island of Aitutaki.—*Presented by the late Rev. John Williams* (See Missionary Enterprises, chap. xxx.)

83, 84 Two other dancer's caps, also richly ornamented with feathers, and rattles of pearl shells.

85 A lofty cap of red and black feathers, the back, like all the above, covered with a profusion of human hair.

86, 87 Cloth made of bark of the paper mulberry tree, (*Broussonetia papyrifera.*) The devices are cut out of dark cloth and stuck on.

88—98 Various specimens of bark cloth, plain, printed, and varnished. For an interesting account of the whole art of this manufacture, see Ellis, vol ii. page 173.

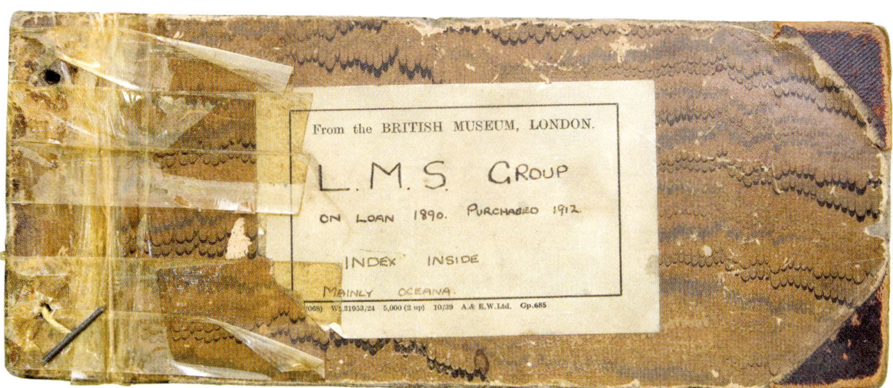

The LMS Collection:

The British Museum LMS collection registration slips by James Edge-Partington

A selection of 12 British Museum LMS Polynesian collection registration slips. The descriptions and accurate drawings in ink are by James Edge-Partington. There are approximately 350 LMS objects from Polynesia in the BM LMS collection; 220 have registration slips; 130 of these pertain to central Polynesia. Many of the fan handle and feather gods discussed in this book are depicted. The original slips cannot be located, but a set of photographic reproductions, made early in the twentieth century, is in the BM Anthropology Library.

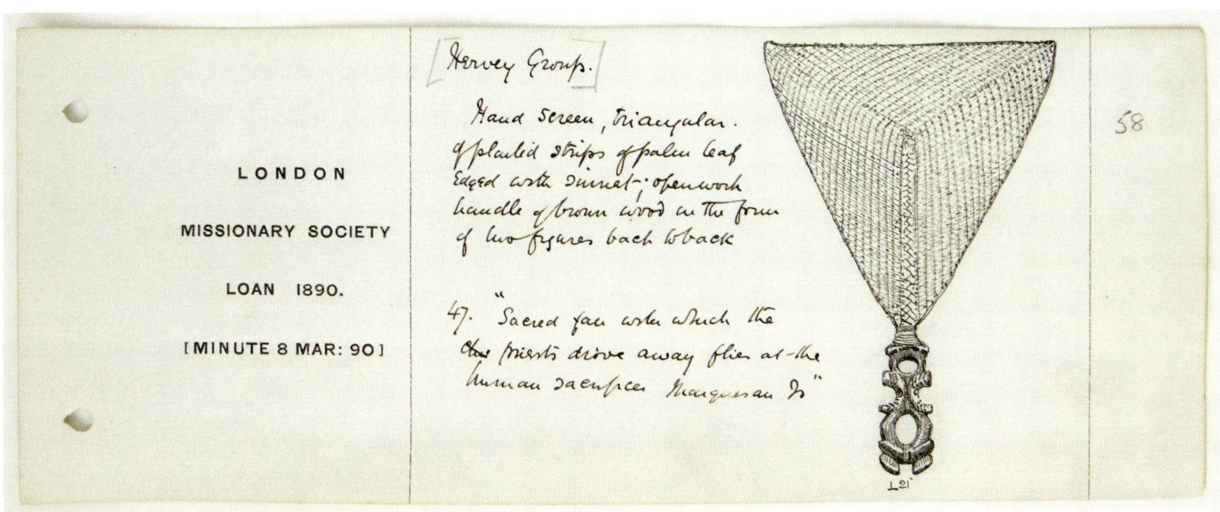

272 *LMS 58*

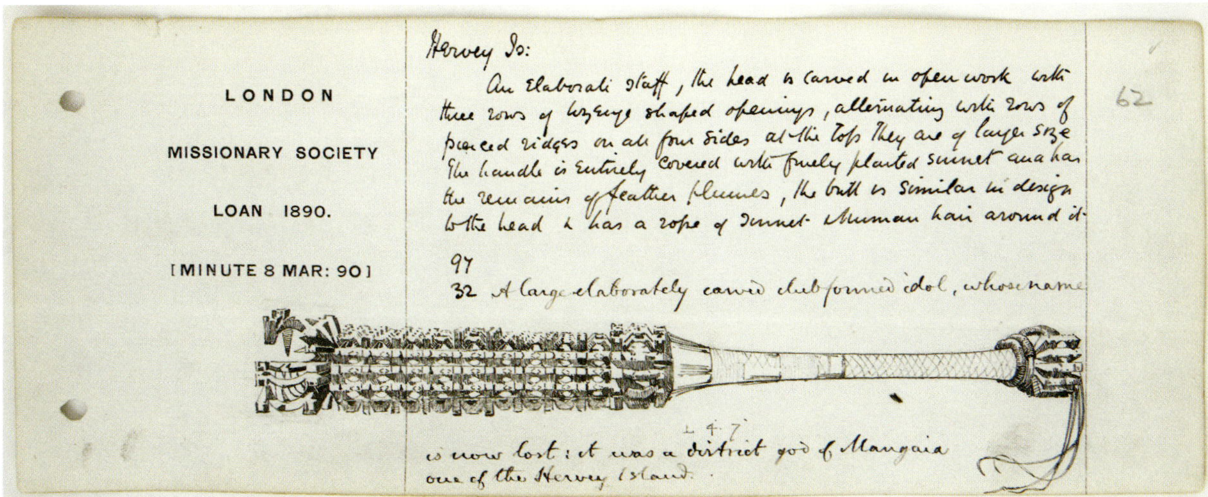

273 *LMS 62*

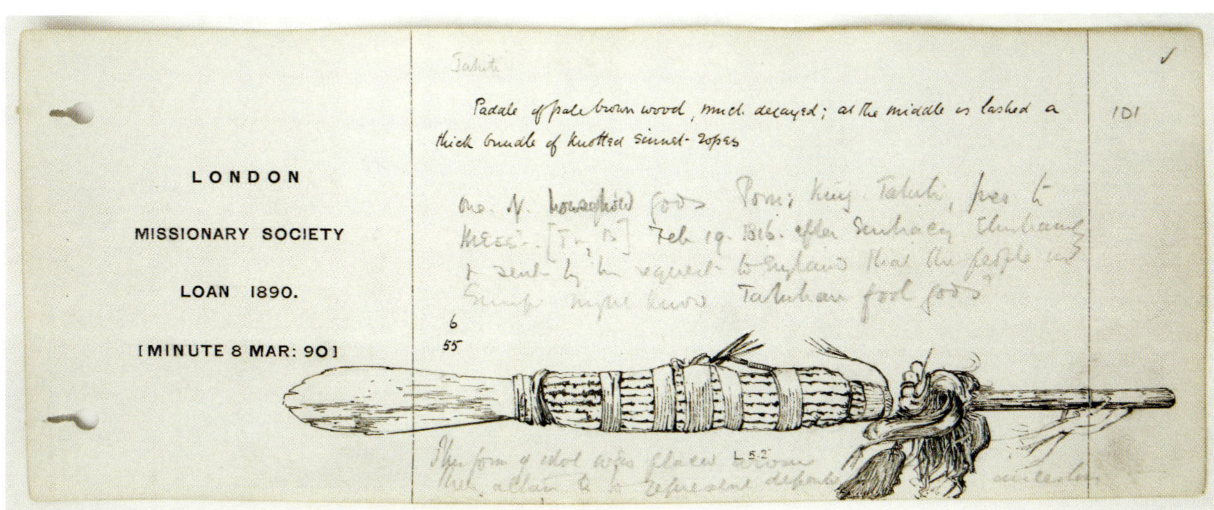

274 *LMS 101*

275 LMS 135

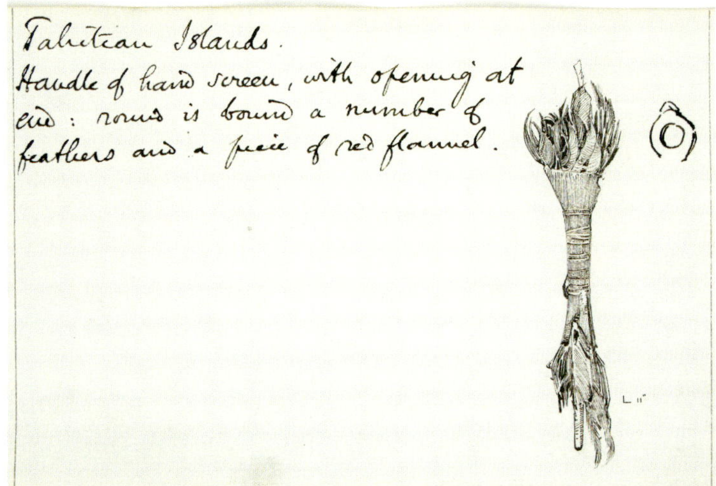

Tahitian Islands.
Handle of hand screen, with opening at
end: round is bound a number of
feathers and a piece of red flannel.

276 LMS 136

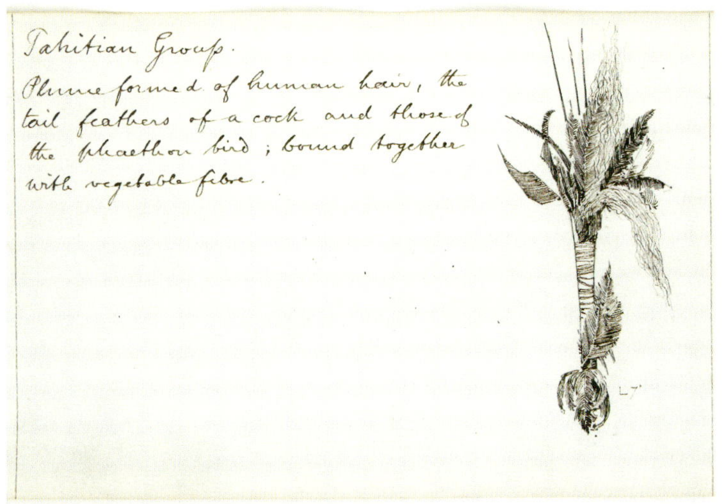

Tahitian Group.
Plume formed of human hair, the
tail feathers of a cock and those of
the phaethon bird ; bound together
with vegetable fibre.

277 LMS 52

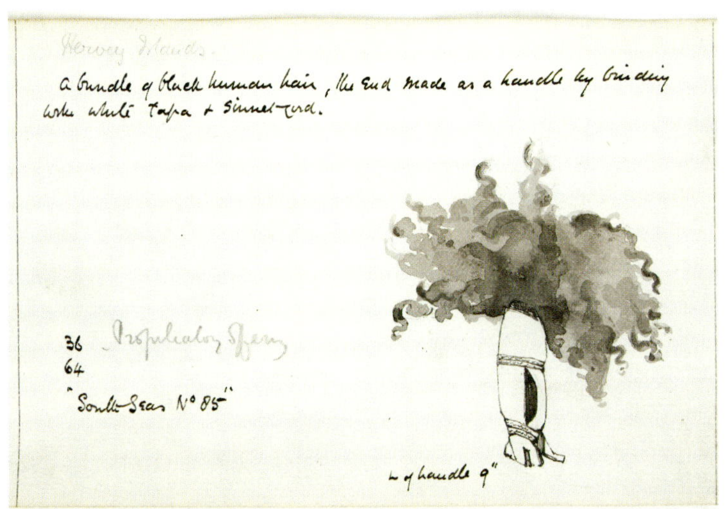

Norway Islands.
A bundle of black human hair, the end made as a handle by binding
with white Tapa & Sinnet-cord.

36 Propitiatory Offering
64
"South Seas Nº 85"

L of handle 9"

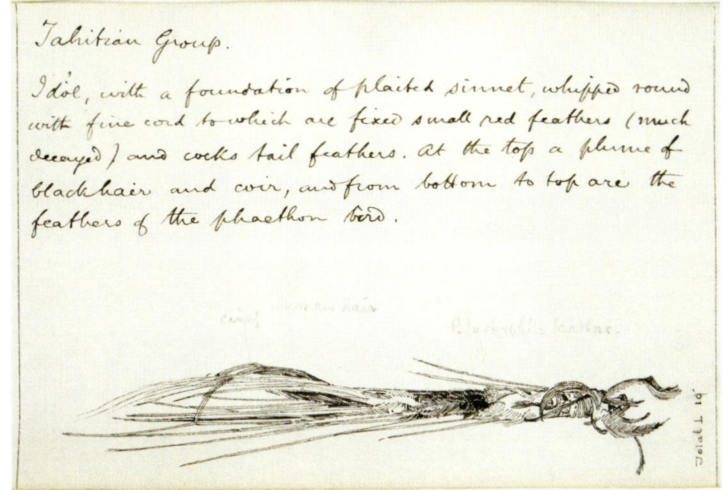

Tahitian Group.

Idol, with a foundation of plaited sinnet, whipped round with fine cord to which are fixed small red feathers (much decayed) and cocks tail feathers. At the top a plume of black hair and coir, and from bottom to top are the feathers of the phaethon bird.

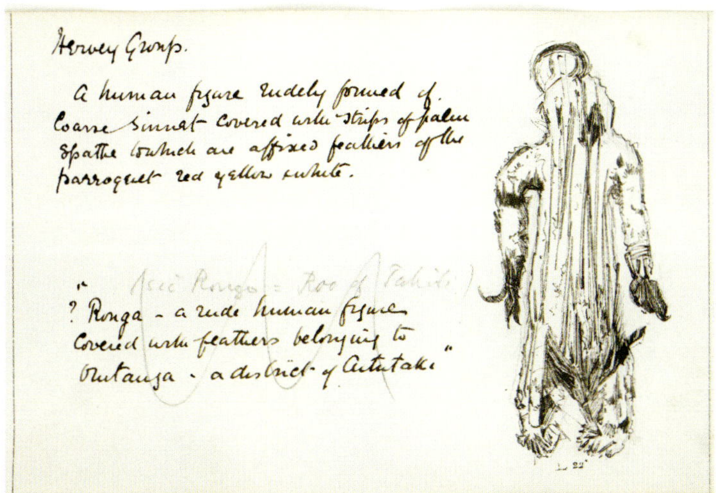

Tahitian Group.

Handle of a hand screen, spatulate, with two projections at sides of stem; plume of phaeton and cock feathers bound with cord and red parrot feathers

22
LMS. 292.

Hervey Group.

A human figure rudely formed of coarse sinnet covered with strips of palm spathe to which are affixed feathers of the parroquet red yellow & white.

"(see Ronga = Roo of Tahiti)
? Ronga - a rude human figure covered with feathers belonging to Outanga - a district of Aitutaki."

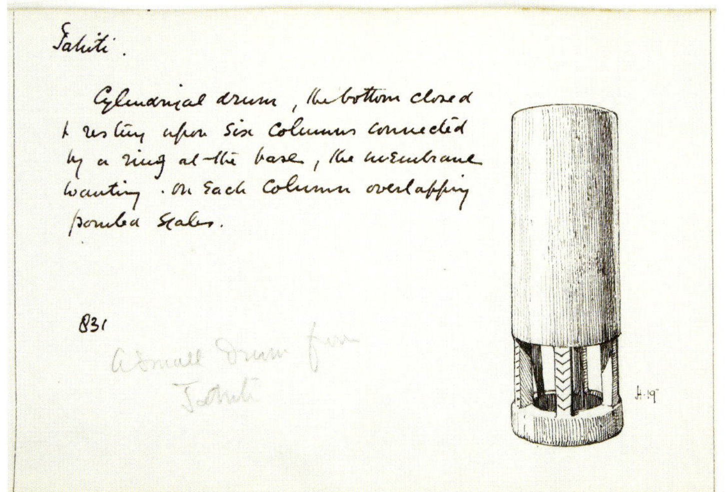

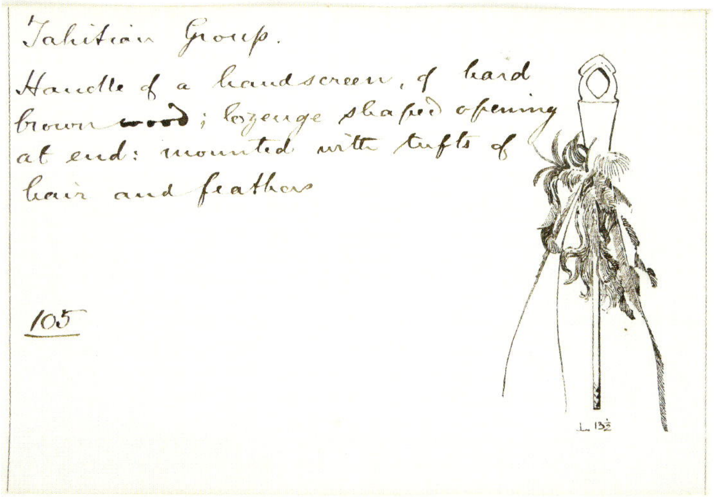

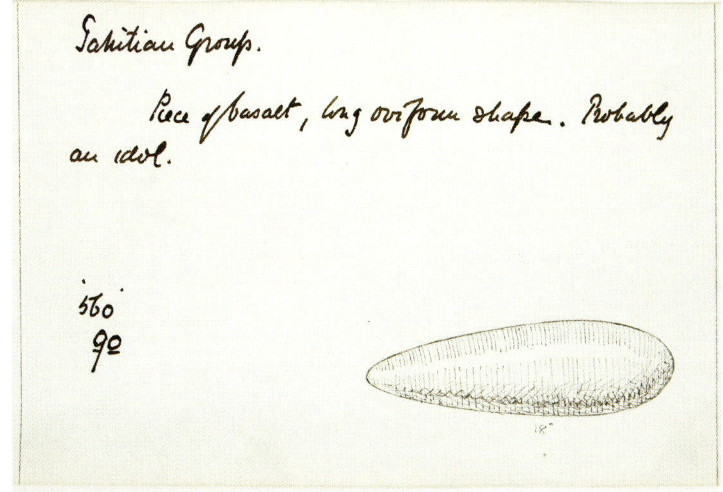

The LMS Collection:

Some particulars regarding the
LMS Missionary Museum

Mission House, a spacious, commodious, substantial, plain building. On entering the hallowed edifice, you find yourself in a large hall; on your left is the messenger's room, through which is a door that leads into the warehouse; the little room, on your right, is the waiting room, and the door on the left of its fire-place opens into the office of the Home Secretary, the Rev. John Arundel, which is in front of the building, while the room behind his forms the accountants' office. That double glass door you see at the further end of the hall, admits you to the Missionary Museum, an awful yet glorious place ! There is not such another, connected with Protestant missions, in England, in Europe, or in the world. The numerous idols and articles of heathenism which you behold, were supplied chiefly by the missionaries of the London Missionary Society; a few other interesting objects are donations from benevolent travellers, or friendly officers of mercantile vessels.

Let us now glance at these horrid idols. The cases marked A and C, comprise considerably upwards of *three hundred* gods and objects of superstitious regard, from islands in the Pacific Ocean. There is TEMEHARO, the principal idol of Pomare's family, and one of the chief deities of Tahiti; there is TERIAPATURA, the son of the great god Oro, and national protector of Tahiti, Raiatea, Huahine, Tahaa, Borabora, and Manua. There are two sacred fans with which the priests of idolatry drove away flies from human sacrifices ! That gigantic idol was brought from Rarotonga, by Mr. Williams; you will find the history of it in the seventh chapter of his Enterprises. You observe that arrow ? Ah ! that suggests a sorrowful event. It was brought from Erromanga by a sailor who witnessed the murder of the devoted and honoured missionary ! It was shot at the men who manned the boat of the Camden, and, sticking in her side, was secured and brought home. That bow, and these ten arrows, as also these two clubs, are likewise from the same fatal island. That bow and this bundle of arrows are from Tanna, which likewise stands so affectingly associated with the close of the martyr's career.

 A portion of Rev John Campbell's description of Mission House, Blomfield Street, Finsbury, published in Moffat's Farewell Services, *1843,134; this appears to be the first description of the Missionary Museum.*

MISSIONARY MUSEUM.

As the Museum of the Society is an object in which the Religious Public take a lively interest, while it tends to promote amongst the numerous persons who visit it, and especially the rising generation, a zeal for the Missionary cause, the Directors have judged it expedient to make suitable provision for its reception, in the premises taken by them in Austin Friars. An additional room is building in the yard of the house, to which access will be prepared without inconvenience to the Officers. A contract has been made for the erection, which, with the necessary expenses of fitting up, will amount to £ 500.

285 *Announcement of the installation of the Missionary Museum at Austin Friars, printed in* Missionary Chronicle, *April 1823.*

286 *Visitor 'regulations' for viewing the Missionary Museum, printed in* Missionary Chronicle, *August 1824. 'The CATALOGUE which is being prepared' implies that the first Missionary Museum catalogue was printed before August 1824, and that the 1826* Catalogue *may be the second one.*

MISSIONARY MUSEUM.

THE Members and Friends of the London Missionary Society are respectfully informed, that the articles contained in their Museum being now arranged, and a Descriptive Catalogue printed, the Museum will be opened on *Wednesday the 4th of August,* and on every succeeding Wednesday, under the following

REGULATIONS.

1. Admission can only be by Tickets.

2. Tickets may be obtained (gratis) of any of the Directors or Officers of the Society.

3. A Ticket, which is not transferrable, will admit only the person whose name is written upon it, and such a number of other persons as is stated in figures upon it. (Children excepted).

4. WEDNESDAY is the only day of the week on which the Museum will be open. From Lady Day to Michaelmas from Ten o'clock to Four; and from Michaelmas to Lady Day from Ten to Three.

5. It has been the hope of the Directors in preparing the Museum for the gratification of the Public, that the expenses thereby incurred should not fall on the funds devoted to the support of the Missions: a box therefore is placed in the Museum, for the reception of any donations which visiters may please to give towards that object.

The CATALOGUE which has been prepared, will, it is hoped, be purchased by visiters—the price will be left to their own liberality.

The attendants are not allowed to receive any gratuity from visiters.

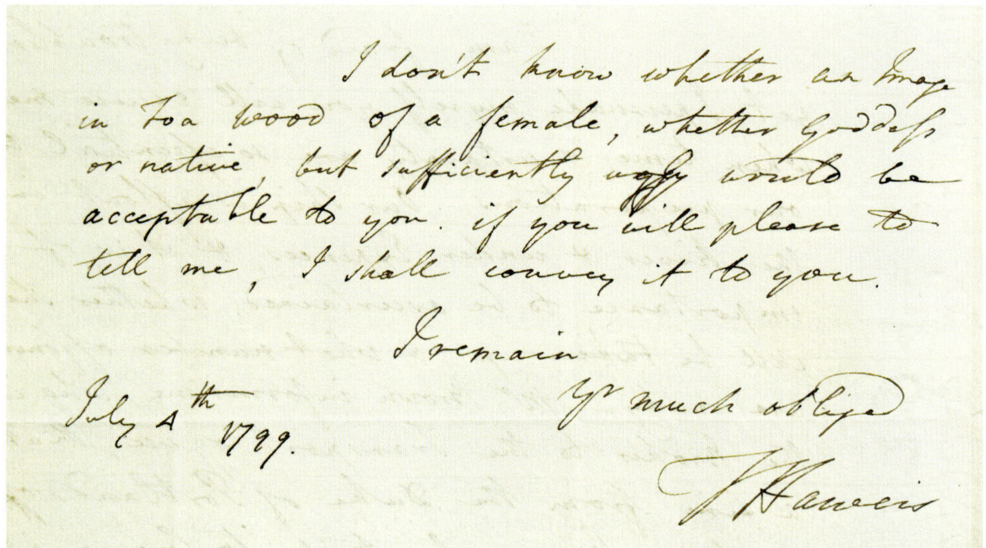

287 *Portion of letter from LMS director Thomas Haweis, 'father of the South Sea mission', offering Joseph Banks an idol of toa (ironwood or casuarina). This letter, written in 1799, documents that at least one Polynesian idol, probably from Tahiti, was brought back on the* Duff, *19 years before Pomare II's idols reached London. Sutro Library, LMS 1:33.*

Such was the ship 'Duff' and her crew—thirty souls all told. She was, as has been related, fitted out by my grandfather, the Rev. Dr. Haweis, and a body of gentlemen in the last century, who founded the London Missionary Society. She was the first purely missionary vessel that ever sailed the seas. Her trophies may still be seen in the collection of idols and South Sea curiosities preserved at the Society's rooms in Blomfield Street, but some of the best have been transferred to the British Museum; most of them were presented by Dr. Haweis to the society before he died. The best preserved idol, made of beautiful yellow, green, and red feathers, and woven with cocoa-nut fibre, is now in my possession. It was sent by the King of Tahiti to Dr. Haweis, after the conversion of the island. I also have the oil cruse which anointed in heathen fashion the kings of Tahiti for one hundred years; the sacred fan handles, made out of carved human bones, which were laid up in the temple at Tahiti, and used only at coronations; letters from King Pomare, written to Dr. Haweis, with tomato juice, in European characters, but in the Tahitian language.

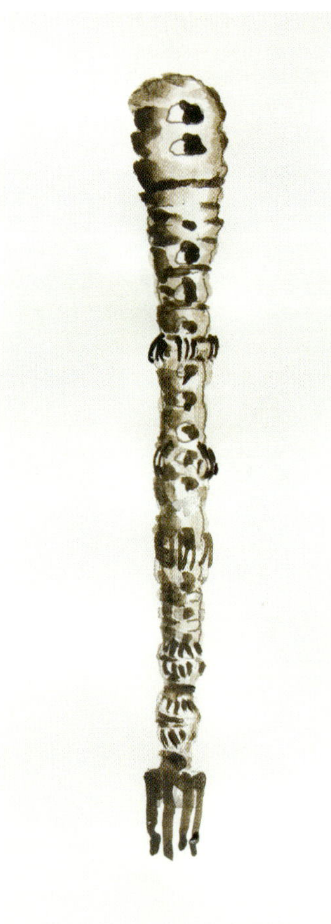

288 *From* Travel and Talk *written by Hugh Reginald Haweis (1896 2,224). HR Haweis was Rev Dr T Haweis' grandson. The 'sacred fanhandles' were likely the whale ivory, wood, and sennit flywhisk handles now in the Wielgus collection (figured at right) and the Metropolitan Museum (65.80). This passage suggests that T Haweis himself retained a number of Tahitian objects and gave them to the Missionary Museum before he died in 1820.*

289 *Whale ivory, wood, sennit flywhisk handle. 31cm. 'Haweis coll.', KJ Hewett, Wielgus collection, University of Indiana (65-271). (See figure at left.) Wash by author.*

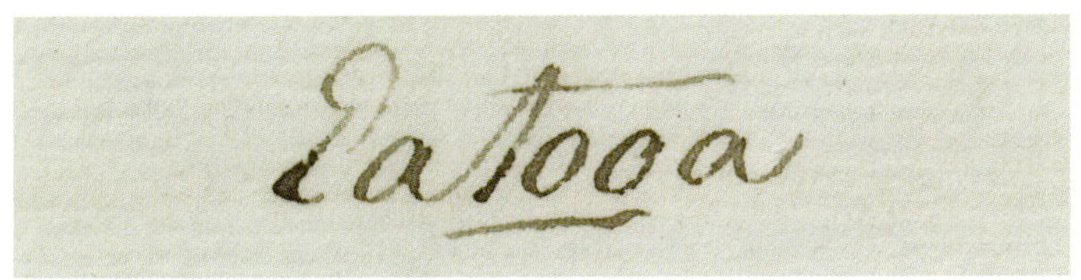

THE WORD ATUA IN JAMES MORRISON'S OWN HAND, FROM HIS
MANUSCRIPT *JOURNAL* 1792,269; MITCHELL LIBRARY.

APPENDIX 8

Polynesian terms pertaining to gods and god images

Multiple Polynesian words are associated with gods, spirits, and idols or god images; they are not often used consistently. The aim of this Appendix is to bring together the earliest definitions of these various terms as rendered by the most reliable primary sources—the *Bounty* 'mutineers' and the early missionaries.

The first term to be considered is *atua*. Atua is Morrison's Eatooa, which he defines 'the general name for deity, in all its ramifications'.[1] Heywood's definition of atua is also 'deity'. Jefferson, 1798: 'Atóoā is used to express the object of worship'.[2] Atua is also 'god, deity' in Davies and in Savage. Atua seems to be the only term about which there is general agreement.

The first specific information on the subject of Polynesian gods was recorded by *Bounty* 'mutineers' James Morrison and Peter Heywood in 1792. Both were intelligent and educated, and young enough to learn to speak and understand Tahitian. Morrison's account of Tahiti, including his discussion of deity, has been published. To condense what he wrote on Eatooa: 'Their religion is without form or regularity. . . . They have images but they offer them no kind of Adoration. Their Deitys are three which are calld by the General name of Eatooa but worshipd as three distinct persons . . . , Tāanè the first or Father of Gods . . . , maker of the World . . . and the Cause of all things . . . , Ōrōmăttōwtōoă the son who presides over War and peace . . . , Tēepāhōoămănnŏo the Friend of both and is their Messenger to Earth.'[3]

The following is Heywood's discussion of the word *Eatooa*, evidently the sole surviving entry from his *Vocabulary of the Otaheitian Language*. It was included in a letter submitted in 1797 to *Evangelical Magazine* by Rev Dr Thomas Haweis;[4] as this periodical is not easily found, the letter is shown below. Heywood distinguishes the great deities from the household gods. His and Morrison's

---

1   In Haweis 1799,333; see also Vancouver 1984 1,412.
2   *Trans Miss Soc* 1804 1,121.
3   Morrison 1935,176 and manuscript Journal MS2 1792,269 (ML).
4   *Evangelical Magazine* 1797,23.

words deeply impressed Haweis regarding the intensity of Tahitian religiousness—something the missionaries were soon to discover on their own. The letter:

CURIOUS TRADITION,

AMONG THE INHABITANTS OF OTAHEITE.

MR. EDITOR,

Among other singular instances of Divine Providence, leading to encourage us in the work we have been attempting of a mission to the South-Seas, I cannot but reckon some manuscript communications and particularly a vocabulary, in which, under the word *Deity*, in the Otaheitan Language, we have such an account of the traditionary knowledge of the true God, preserved amongst the South Sea Islanders, as is scarcely to be met with in any part of the heathen world beside. The authenticity of the information is indubitable, and the more striking, as the persons from whom the knowledge is derived* (*The mutineers of the Bounty. See our article of Intelligence last October.), never had an idea of the use thus eventually drawn from it. As I have the fullest evidence myself that no imposition was intended, and that the fact is exactly as represented, I shall transcribe the words relative to this subject from the vocabulary.

TAHEITAN NAMES.

Deity.—Eātōōǎ.

The names of the three superior Deities of Taheite are,

1. Tāānè te Medōōǎ,—*The father.*

2. Ōrōmǎttǒw. 'Tōōǎ tě tē Mydě.—(*Literally God in the Son.*)

3. Teēpāhōōǎ.

Mǎnnǒo tè Hōa.—(*Literally the bird, the friend.*)

These three, call them either *Persons* or *Gods*, are the great Deities of the Taheitans, and in their idea *Supreme*, and entitled to the highest worship. These they style,

Eātōōǎ Fwhānōw Pō.

God born of night or darkness.

Besides these, they have inferior Deities, a kind of household gods, the *Diipenates*, and each man and woman is supposed to have such a tutelary deity, as their guardian or good genius. He is one of their departed relatives, whose spirit hath received deification from the Eātōōǎ for their goodness and excellencies in this life. These guardian divinities are regarded by them as endued with power by them to inflict sickness, or remove it, and to counteract all the evils which a wicked spirit, whom they call Tēe, is endeavouring to bring upon them. To these, therefore, they address their prayer, when afflicted by disease or distress of any kind, and never

to the *Sacred Three*; for they esteem them so transcendently great and glorious, as to be above being troubled with the trivial concerns of inferior persons. It is only on occasion of war, or national calamity, or the illness of the king or chiefs, or storms, and the like, that the supreme Eātōōǎ are to be addressed.

Respecting the third person here mentioned, it is still more singular, that though under the name deity he is tè Hōǎ (the friend), yet in another place, under the word *inspired*, he is called tè Hōōǎ (or *the Spirit.*)

[Heywood then gives a few examples of blessings offered, for example, on sneezing.]

There is something in the whole of this very singular, and I hope our missionaries will, in time, give us fuller information on the subject.

I remain your's,
T. HAWEIS
Spa Fields, Nov. 28, 1796.

Regarding central Polynesian terms other than atua that are connected with gods and god images, definitions differ. A Tahitian term that appears in missionary literature in reference to god images is *to'o*; Ellis defines to'o as 'image',[5] and also as 'national or family gods',[6] but Davies, in his *Dictionary*, is more specific: 'Too, a piece of wood forming the body of an idol.' To'o does not appear in Morrison, Heywood or Haweis. A Tahitian term connected with spirit images is *ti'i*. Both Haweis (rewriting Morrison)[7] and Davies define ti'i (*tii*) as 'an image; a demon or wicked spirit'; Davies adds 'a class of beings supposed to be different from men and gods.' Ellis defines tii similarly.[8] Neither to'o nor ti'i appears in Savage (in Rarotongan spelling); *tiki* is simply carving. Another relevant term in Davies is 'Toounuhi, the decayed too of a god taken out'; yet another is 'Apaa, an idol made of sacred cloth and birds feathers.' Orsmond (T Henry) describes ti'i as magicians' images, also called 'fetchers', in which resided malevolent spirits. Orsmond states that ti'i were fashioned of wood, stone, or coral, 'in caricature form of human beings, which were dressed as little men and women in various kinds of tapa fastened on with fine sennit. . . . The marae or

---

5   Ellis 1829 2,191.
6   Ibid.,203.
7   Haweis 1799,333.
8   Ellis 1829 2,201

inclosures of the ti'i were distinguished from all others by a little house called fare ti'i (fetchers-house) set upon high pillars, in which the images were systematically placed upon shelves. . . .'[9] Orsmond again: 'The great tutelar god was represented by an image of wood, called a *to'o*, or of fine wickerwork covered with feathers, called a *huamanu*.'[10] Davies on huamanu: 'bunch of red feathers taken to an artificer when a canoe was to be built' (*manu* is 'bird' in Tahitian).

An informative passage explaining ti'i appears in the journal of missionaries James Elder and Charles Wilson describing their trip from Matavai down the coast to Papara (Tahiti) in June 1804. In a discussion of sorcery, they state:

> It is [through] the influence of something that the natives call tii, that they kill people. They make out of wood an image of human form; this they call a tee; but the real tee is in the Arooe, or other world, and are spirits, but not the spirits which they call their gods. When the sorcerer practices on any person, he prays to the Tee in the Arooe, and they enter into the wooden image, and then he tells them to go and kill such an one. The person is accordingly possessed and dies in about a fortnight, or a month or two after. The natives are much afraid of these tee, and say they are very powerful. They say also, that when children of sorcerers die, their spirits become tee.[11]

Buck redefines *to'o* as an image in nonhuman form, *ti'i* as an image in human form.[12] Terms for god and for casuarina (ironwood)—the extremely dense wood from which many of the god images were fashioned—are close: *aitu* is defined as 'a god or goddess; see atua' in Davies, 'a god, a deity, a spirit' in Savage; *aito* is casuarina in Davies; *toa* is casuarina in both. The term *oromatua* referred to skulls, as well as to 'the ghosts of the dead, who were supposed to be transformed into a sort of inferior gods, but of a malevolent disposition, and therefore prayers were addressed to them to coax them from doing mischief.'[13]

One early missionary journal entry is of particular interest in that it describes the portable nature of the god images, and also separates the use of the terms *Oro* and *to'o*:

> The god Oro, that was brought up yesterday [from Pare to Teaarabu by Pomare], has five other gods to accompany him, and then Oro is to be left there, and the others to be returned to Eimeo. Oro is in his house in a second canoe; in the same house is also the Too, or image representing Ohero one of the Gods. The Too of each of the other gods is wrapt up in cloth, and placed on separate canoes, covered with thatch of fara [pandanus] leaves; their names are Tane, Temeharo, Ruahadu, and Huae-maa—the two last men offered to Oro are hanging up in long baskets in the branches of the fara trees, about the Marae. . . .[14]

As stated in the text, at this point, one can only speculate on what these terms actually meant to Polynesians 200 years ago.

9   Henry 1928,203.
10 Ibid., 153.
11 *Trans Miss Soc* 1806,351.
12 Buck 1944,469.

13 Davies 1851.
14 *Trans Miss Soc* 1807,171. Identity of missionary not specified.

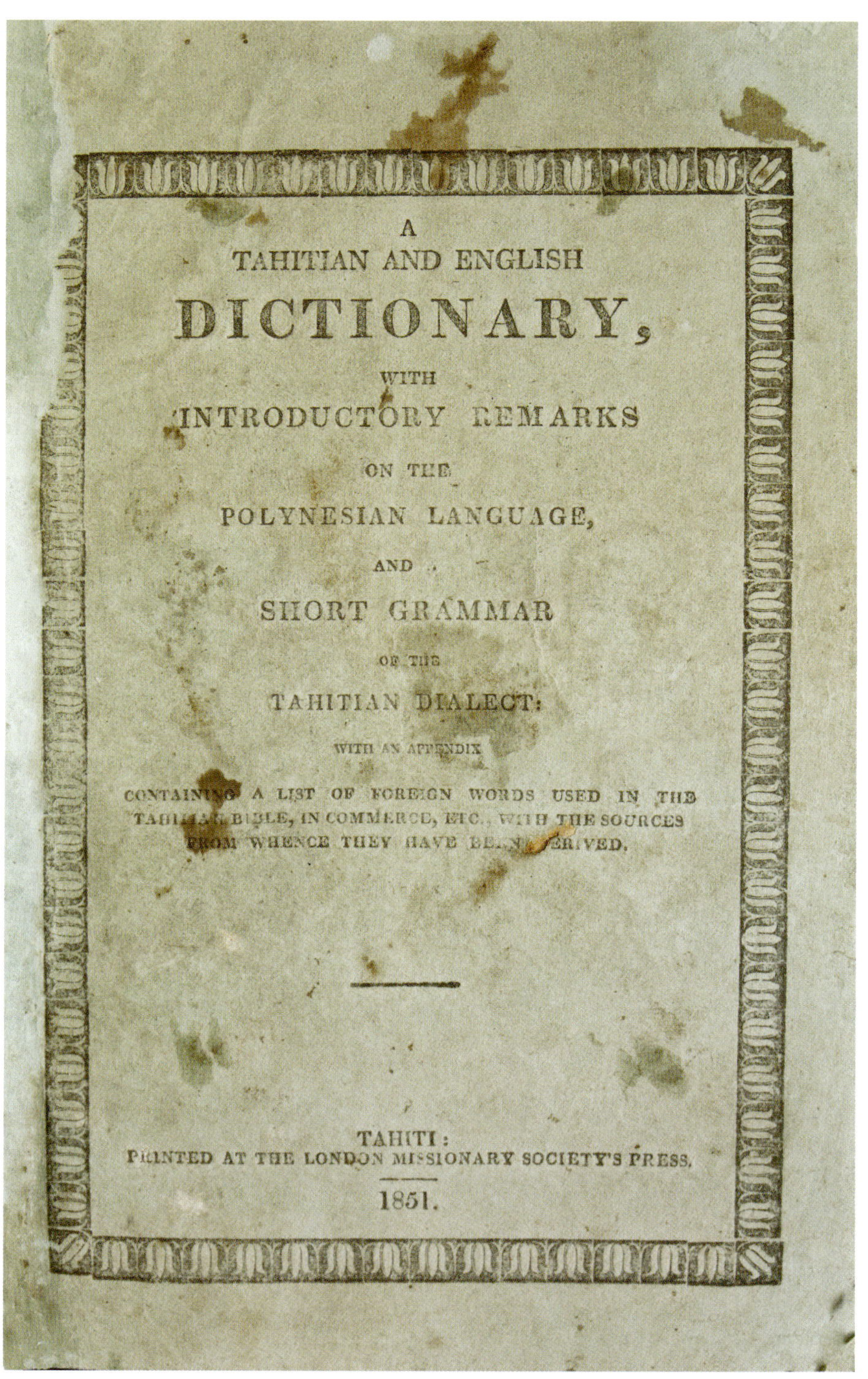

290 *Cover of Davies'* Tahitian and English Dictionary, *printed by the LMS press on Tahiti; it was compiled over a period of 38 years through the combined labour of probably all the missionaries. Although finished in 1838, it was not published until 1851 (see page 3).*

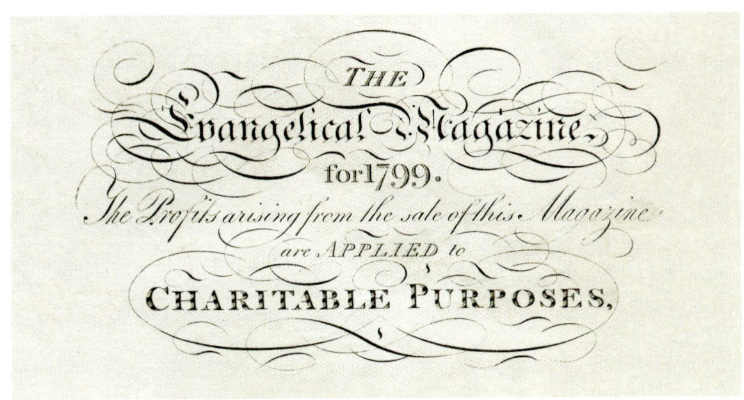

Bibliography

Adams Henry. 1901. *Memoirs of Arii Taimai E, Marama of Eimeo, Teriirere of Tooarai, Teriinui of Tahiti, Tauraatua I Amo.* Paris.

Allon Rev Henry. 1852. *Euthanasia: a funeral sermon for Mrs. Williams, (widow of the Rev. John Williams, missionary to the South Sea Islands,) preached in Union Chapel, Islington, on Sunday morning, June 27th, 1852, with a memoir by her son.* John Snow, London.

Anonymous. 1805. *First Missionary Voyage to the South-Sea Islands* and *Second Missionary Voyage*, in *The Universal Navigator and Modern Tourist.* Albion Press, London. (See note under Haweis 1799.)

Anonymous (Jonathan Seymour?). 1820. *The South Sea Islander; containing many interesting facts relative to the former and present state of Society in the Island of Otaheite: with some Remarks on the Best Mode of Civilizing the Heathen.* W Gilley, New York.

Anonymous. 1826. *Catalogue of the Missionary Museum, Austin Friars; including Specimens in Natural History, Various Idols of Heathen Nations, Dresses, Manufactures, Domestic Utensils, Instruments of War, &c &c &c.* W Phillips, London. (Photocopy in Anthropology Library, British Museum.)

Anonymous. 1839. *Missionary Records. Tahiti and Society Islands.* Religious Tract Society, London.

Anonymous. nd. *Catalogue of the Missionary Museum, Blomfield Street, Finsbury; including Specimens in Natural History, Various Idols of Heathen Nations, Dresses, Manufactures, Domestic Utensils, Instruments of War, &c &c &c.* (A clue as to the date is in annotation p. 14 Nº4, Tahitian idol chest, 'Presented by the late Mr. Bennet;' Bennet died 13 November 1841; original in BPBM Library.)

Anonymous. nd; ca 1900. *Adventures in the South Pacific by one who was born there.* Religious Tract Society, London. (According to Irene Fletcher, this was written by the youngest son of missionary Robert Bourne and was probably edited by Richard Lovett; the last chapters contain material from Henry Nott.)

Archey Gilbert. 1965. *The Art Forms of Polynesia. Bulletin* 4, Auckland Institute and Museum.

Babadzan Alain. 1981. 'Les Dépouilles des Dieux: Essai sur la Symbolique de certaines Effigies Polynésiennes.' *Res* 1,8-39.

Baessler Arthur. 1900. *Neue Südsee-Bilder.* G Reimer, Berlin.

Beaglehole Ernest. 1957. *Social Change in the South Pacific.* George Allen & Unwin, Aberdeen.

Beaglehole J[ohn] C[awte]. 1963 (2nd edition). *The Endeavour Journal of Joseph Banks.* 2 Vols. Angus & Robertson, Sydney.

Beaglehole J[ohn] C[awte]. 1967–68. *The Journals of Captain James Cook on his Voyages of Discovery.* 4 Vols. Cambridge University Press, Cambridge.

Belcher Lady. 1870. *The Mutineers of the Bounty and their descendants in Pitcairn and Norfolk Islands.* Harper & Brothers, New York.

Bellwood Peter. 1978. *Archaeological Research in the Cook Islands. Pacific Anthropological Records*, N°27. Bishop Museum Press.

Bellwood Peter. 1978. *The Polynesians: Prehistory of an Island People*. Thames & Hudson.

Bellwood Peter. 1979. *Man's Conquest of the Pacific*. Oxford University Press, New York.

Bovis Edmond de. 1976. *Tahitian Society before the Arrival of the Europeans*. (Written 1850-55.) Translation by Robert D Craig 1976. The Institute for Polynesian Studies, Brigham Young University, Hawaii.

Braunholtz HJ. 1953. 'History of ethnography in the museum after 1753 (Pt. I).' *The British Museum Quarterly*, 18,90.

Brown William. 1820. *The History of Missions; or, of the Propagation of Christianity among the Heathens, since the Reformation.* McCarty & Davis, Philadelphia.

Buck Peter Henry (Te Rangi Hiroa). 1939. *Anthropology and Religion*. Yale University Press, New Haven.

Buck Peter. 1944. *Arts and Crafts of the Cook Islands. Bulletin* 179, BP Bishop Museum, Honolulu.

Buck Peter. 1993. *Mangaia and the Mission*. R Dixon and T Parima (eds). IPS, USP in assoc with BPBM (press not indicated).

Burder George. *1821. Missionary Anecdotes; in two parts: exhibiting I. The Idolatry, Superstition, and Cruelty of the Heathen in all ages, and II. The Efficacy of the Gospel in their Conversion, in the successive ages of the Christian Era.* Francis Wesley, London.

Burder Henry Foster. 1833. *Memoir of the Rev George Burder, author of "Village Sermons" and Secretary to the London Missionary Society.* F Westley & AH Davis, London.

Campbell John. nd; ca 1816. *The Comprehensive Hymn Book: One Thousand Hymns, Original and Selected.* John Snow, London

Campbell John (ed). 1838. *The Missionary's Farewell; Valedictory Services of the Rev John Williams, Previous to his Departure for the South Seas.* John Snow, London. (This interesting small book records the service held on the eve of Williams' return to the Pacific on the *Camden*, April 1838; it includes sections by Ellis and Williams.)

Campbell John. 1840. *Maritime Discovery and Christian Missions, considered in their Mutual Relations.* John Snow, London (includes short biographies of Burder, Haweis, Hardcastle, Eyre, Bogue and many others).

Campbell John. 1842. *The Martyr of Erromanga, or, the Philosophy of Missions, Illustrated from the Labours, Death, and Character of the late Rev John Williams.* John Snow, London.

Campbell John (ed). 1843. *The Farewell Services of Robert Moffat, in Edinburgh, Manchester, and London.* John Snow (Moffat was an LMS missionary in South Africa, as was Campbell.)

Carey William. 1792. *An Enquiry into the Obligations of Christians to use Means for the Conversion of the Heathens in which the Religious State of the Different Nations of the World, the Success of the Former Undertakings, and the Practicability of further Undertakings, are considered.* Ann Ireland, Leicester.

Carr DJ (ed). 1983. *Sydney Parkinson, Artist of Cook's Endeavour Voyage.* British Museum Natural History and Australian National University Press, Canberra.

Cathcart Michael, Tom Griffiths, Lee Watts, Vivian Anceschi, Greg Houghton, David Goodman. 1990. *Mission to the South Seas: The Voyage of the Duff, 1796-1799.* University of Melbourne. (A thoughtful history; all authors were students of Greg Dening.)

Caygill M and J Cherry (eds). 1997. *A.W. Franks, Nineteenth Century Collecting and the British Museum.* BMP, London.

Colquhoun Kate. 2006. *The busiest man in England: A life of Joseph Paxton, Gardener, Architect, and Victorian Visionary.* D Godine, Boston.

Condliffe JB. 1971. *Te Rangi Hiroa: The Life of Sir Peter Buck.* Whitcombe & Tombs, Christchurch.

Corney Bolton Glanvill. 1908. *The Voyage of Captain Don Felipe Gonzalez in the Ship of the Line San Lorenzo, with the Frigate Santa Rosalia in Company, to Easter Island in 1770-1.* Translated and compiled by Corney, Hakluyt Society, Cambridge. (See notes on Corney in Langdon 2009.)

Corney Bolton Glanvill. 1913-19. *The Quest and Occupation of Tahiti by Emissaries of Spain during the years 1772–1776.* Translated and compiled by Corney. 3 Vols. Hakluyt Society, London.

Cumming C[onstance] F[rederica] Gordon-. 1882. *A Lady's Cruise in a French Man-of-War.* Wm Blackwood & Sons, Edinburgh, London.

Dalrymple Alexander. 1797. *An Account of the Discoveries made in the South Pacifick Ocean.* London. (Facsimile issued by Australian National Maritime Museum and Hordern House, 1996.)

Danielsson B. 1967. *'Kia ora Keneti.'* In *Polynesian Culture History: Essays in Honor of KP Emory.* GA Highland & RW Force, A Howard, M Kelly Y Sinoto (eds). Bishop Museum Press.

Darlow TH and HF Moule. 1903-1911. *Historical Catalogue of the Printed Editions of Holy Scripture in the Library of the British and Foreign Bible Society.* London. (The B&FBS donated hundreds of reams of paper for the printing of the Scripture in the Tahitian language.)

Darwin Charles. 1842. *The Structure and Distribution of Coral Reefs. Being the first part of the Geology of the Voyage of the Beagle, under the Command of Capt. Fitzroy, R.N., during the years 1832 to 1836.* Smith, Elder & Co, London.

Davies John. 1851. *A Tahitian and English Dictionary.* London Missionary Society's Press, Tahiti. (See notes in Sources.)

Davies John. 1961. *The History of the Tahitian Mission 1799-1830, written by John Davies, Missionary to the South Sea Islands, with Supplementary Papers from the Correspondence of the Missionaries.* CW Newbury (ed). University Press, Cambridge. (Written 1827-1831; never published by the LMS. Quoted extensively by Robert Thomson [missionary in Tahiti and the Marquesas 1835-1851], whose *History of Tahiti* [unfinished ms, SOAS] remains unpublished. It is unfortunate that Davies' 'Account of the government, religion, and customs of the natives' which he promised to send to Rev William Orme was never written.)

Dening Greg. 1988. *The Bounty: An Ethnographic History.* University of Melbourne.

Dening Greg. 1992. *Mr Bligh's Bad Language.* Cambridge University Press.

Duke of Devonshire (William Spencer Cavendish). 1845. *Handbook of Chatsworth and Hardwick.* Privately printed, London.

Dunmore John (transl and ed). 2002. *The Pacific Journal of Louis-Antoine de Bougainville 1767-1768.* Hakluyt Society, London. (In this volume, young volunteer CPE Fesche provides the fullest account of Tahiti.)

Du Rietz Rolf. 1969. *Bibliotheca Polynesiana: a catalogue of some of the books in the Polynesiana collection formed by the late Bjarne Kroepelien and now in the Oslo University Library.* Almqvist & Wiksell, Stockholm.

Du Rietz Rolf. 1986. *Peter Heywood's Tahitian vocabulary and the narratives by James Morrison: some notes on their origin and history. Banksia* 3. Dahlia Books, Uppsala.

Dodd Edward. 1967. *The Ring of Fire: Polynesian Art.* Dodd, Mead, New York.

Duff Roger. 1974. *Prehistory of the Southern Cook Islands. Bulletin* 6, Canterbury Museum, Christchurch.

Elder John Rawson (ed). 1932. *The Letters and Journals of Samuel Marsden, 1765-1838, Senior Chaplain in the Colony of New South Wales and Superintendent of the Mission of the Church Missionary Society in New Zealand.* Coulls Somerville Wilkie Ltd & AH Reed, Dunedin.

Ellis James. nd, ca 1889-1890. *John Williams: The Martyr Missionary of Erromonga.* SW Partridge, London.

Ellis John Eimeo. 1873. *Life of William Ellis, Missionary to the South Seas and to Madagascar.* (Supplementary chapter by Henry Allon.) John Murray, London.

Ellis William. 1782. *An authentic narrative of a voyage performed by Captain Cook and Captain Clerke on his majesty's ships Resolution and Discovery during the years 1776, 1777, 1778, 1779, and 1780.* 2 Vols. Robinson, London.

Ellis William. 1829. *Polynesian Researches during a Residence of nearly six years in the South Sea Islands* (1ˢᵗ edition; 2 Vols). Fisher, Son & Jackson, London. (Pagination and arrangement vary in subsequent editions; references to Ellis 1853 are to 'a new edition, enlarged and improved', 4 Vols, Henry Bohn, London.)

Ellis William (ed). *The Christian Keepsake 1835.* 1834. Fisher, Son, & Co., London. (Includes 'Missionary Perils' by Rev John Williams.)

Ellis William. 1836. *Memoir of Mrs Mary Mercy Ellis, Wife of Rev William Ellis, Missionary in the South Seas, and Foreign Secretary of the London Missionary Society.* Crocker & Brewster, Boston.

Ellis William. 1844. *The History of the London Missionary Society.* John Snow, London.

Emory Kenneth P. 1933. *Stone Remains in the Society Islands. Bulletin* 116, BP Bishop Museum, Honolulu.

Findlay AG. 1877 (4ᵗʰ ed). *A directory for the navigation of the South Pacific Ocean.* RH Laurie, London.

FitzRoy R and CR Darwin. 1836. 'A letter, containing remarks on the moral state of Tahiti, New Zealand, &c.' *South African Christian Recorder* 2(4),221-238. (Darwin on Tahiti: 'A more orderly, quiet, inoffensive community I have not seen in any other part of the world.')

Fletcher Irene. 1963. 'The fundamental principle of the London Missionary Society.' *Transactions Congregational Historical Society.* In three parts: 19,138; 19,192; 19,222.

Forster Johann Reinhold. 1996. *Observations made during a voyage round the world.* N Thomas, H Guest, and M Dettelbach (eds). University of Hawaii Press.

Gill William. 1856. *Gems from the Coral Islands, or incidents of contrast between Savage and Christian Life of the South Sea Islanders.* Presbyterian Board of Publication, Philadelphia. (Not to be confused with William Wyatt Gill.)

Gill William. 1880. *Selections from the Autobiography of the Rev William Gill in the South Sea Islands, being chiefly a Record of his Life as a Missionary.* Yates & Alexander, London.

Gill William Wyatt. 1880. *Historical Sketches of Savage Life in Polynesia with Illustrative Clan Songs.* Didsbury, Wellington.

Gill William Wyatt. 1876. *Myths and Songs from the South Pacific.* HS King, London.

Gill William Wyatt. 1885. *Jottings from the Pacific.* The Religious Tract Society, London.

Gill William Wyatt. 1894. *From Darkness to Light in Polynesia.* The Religious Tract Society, London.

Gosset RWG. 1940. 'Notes on the Discovery of Rarotonga.' *Australian Geographer* 3,4.

Green Roger and Kaye Green. 1968. 'Religious Structures of the Society Islands.' *The New Zealand Journal of History,* 2,66.

Griffin John. 1822. *Memoirs of Captain James Wilson, containing an account of his enterprises and sufferings in India, his conversion to Christianity, his missionary voyage to the South Seas, and his peaceful and triumphant death.* 1ˢᵗ American edition Armstrong, Crocker & Brewster New York. (1ˢᵗ English edition published 1815.)

Gunson Niel. 1963. 'A note on the difficulties of ethnohistorical writing, with special reference to Tahiti.' *Journal Polynesian Society* 72,415.

Gunson Niel. 1965. 'Patronage, the Missionary Society, and Joseph Banks.' *Historical Studies Australia and New Zealand* 11,513.

Gunson Niel. 1966. 'Journal of a visit to Raivavae in October 1819 by Pomare II, king of Tahiti.' *Journal of Pacific History* 1,199.

Gunson Niel. 1972. 'John Williams and his ship.' In *Questioning the past: a selection of papers in history and government.* DP Crook (ed). University of Queensland Press.

Gunson Niel. 1978. *Messengers of Grace: Evangelical Missionaries in the South Seas 1797-1860.* Oxford University Press,

Melbourne. (Useful particulars of both English and Polynesian missionaries are included in appendices.)

Gunson Niel. 1980. 'Cover's notes on the Tahitians, 1802.' *Journal of Pacific History* 15,217.

Gunson Niel. 1990. 'The Tonga-Samoa connection 1777-1845.' *Journal of Pacific History* 25,176.

Gunson Niel. 1992. 'Missionaries and the unmentionable: Christian propriety and the expanded Tahitian dictionary.' In *The language game: papers in memory of Donald C. Laycock.* T Dutton, M Ross, and D Tryon (eds). Canberra.

Gunson Niel. 1994. 'British missionaries and their contribution to science in the Pacific Islands' in *Evolutionary Theory and Natural History in the Pacific: Darwin's Laboratory.* R MacLeod and P Rehbock (eds). University of Hawaii Press.

Gunson Niel. 1995. 'Ecumenism and denominational rivalry in the background of the London Missionary Society.' *Proceedings of the Uniting Church Historical Society (Victoria)* 2,12.

Gutch John. 1974. *Beyond the Reefs: the life of John Williams, Missionary.* Macdonald, London.

Handy ESC. 1931. *History and Culture in the Society Islands. Bulletin* 90, BP Bishop Museum.

Harding George L. 1941. 'Tahitian imprints, 1817-1833.' *Papers of the Bibliographical Society of America* 35,1.

Harding George L and Bjarne Kroepelien. 1950. *The Tahitian Imprints of the London Missionary Society, 1810-1834.* La Coquille qui Chante, Oslo.

Harding Julian. 1994. 'A Polynesian god and the missionaries.' *Tribal Arts* 1,27-32.

Haweis, Hugh Reginald. 1896. *Travel and talk 1885-93-95; my hundred thousand miles of travel.* 2 Vols. Chatto & Windus, London. (Author is Thomas Haweis' grandson, a musician; book includes T Haweis correspondence.)

Haweis Thomas. 1795. *Sermons preached in London at the formation of the Missionary Society, September 22,23,24, 1795.* T Chapman, London.

[Haweis Rev Dr Thomas, anonymous compiler and editor; Samuel Greatheed wrote much of the Preliminary Discourse, James Morrison the Appendix]. 1799. *A Missionary Voyage to the Southern Pacific Ocean, Performed in the Years 1796, 1797, 1798, in the Ship Duff, Commanded by Captain James Wilson. Compiled from the Journals of the Officers and the Missionaries.* Printed by T Gillet for T Chapman, London. (A deluxe edition was printed simultaneously on large wove paper by S Gosnell for T Chapman, which differs in pagination and in the list of subscribers. It was also issued in 20 weekly numbers, with all engravings. The section *Missionary Instructions* was issued separately as a 44-page octavo, T Chapman, 1796.)

Hawkesworth John. 1773. *An account of the voyages undertaken by the order of his present majesty for making discoveries in the southern hemisphere, and successively performed by Commodore Byron, Captain Wallis, Captain Carteret, and Captain Cook, in the Dolphin, the Swallow, and the Endeavour.* 3 Vols, Strahan & Cadell, London.

Hayes Ernest H. 1922. *Wiliamu, Mariner-Missionary; the Story of John Williams.* The Religious Education Press Ltd, Wallington, Surrey.

Henry Teuira. 1928. *Ancient Tahiti. Bulletin* 48, BP Bishop Museum, Honolulu.

Hill Kenneth. 2004. *The Hill Collection of Pacific Voyages.* William Reese & Hordern House.

Hooper Steven. 2001. 'Double-figure Fly Whisk Handles from the Austral Islands.' *Arts & Cultures,* 2,178-92.

Hooper Steven. 2006. *Pacific Encounters: Art & Divinity in Polynesia 1760-1860.* British Museum Press, London.

Hooper Steven. 2007. 'Embodying Divinity: The Life of A'a.' *Journal Polynesian Society* 116,131-179.

Horne C Silvester. 1894. *The Story of the L.M.S., 1795-1895.* John Snow, London.

Horne Melville. 1794. *Letters on Missions, addressed to the Protestant Ministers of the British Churches.* Bulgin & Rosser, Bristol. (Multiple English and American editions; name spelled also Melvill.)

Howell William. 1809. *Some interesting particulars of the Second Voyage of the Missionary Ship, The Duff, which was captured by The Buonaparte Privateer, in the year 1800* [corrected to 1799 in *Erratum*]. Hargrove & Son, Knaresborough.

Idiens Dale. 1997. 'Les dieux bâtons des Îles Cook.' In *La découverte du paradis Océanie: Curieux, Navigateurs et Savants.* Somogy, Paris.

Jessop Leslie. 2003. 'The exotic artefacts from George Allan's Museum, and other 18th century ethnographic collections surviving in the Hancock Museum, Newcastle upon Tyne.' *Transactions Natural History Society of Northumbria* 63,89.

Joppien Rüdiger and Bernard Smith. 1985. *The Art of Captain Cook's Voyages.* 3 Vols. Yale University Press, New Haven.

Kaeppler Adrienne L. 1978. *Artificial Curiosities. Special Publication* 65, BP Bishop Museum.

Kaeppler Adrienne L. 2007. 'Containers of Divinity.' *Journal Polynesian Society* 116,97-130.

King Joseph. 1895. *Ten decades: the Australian centenary story of the London Missionary Society.* John Snow, London.

Kirch Patrick Vinton and Roger C Green. 2001. *Hawaiki, Ancestral Polynesia.* Cambridge University Press, Cambridge.

Kooijman Simon. 1964. 'Ancient Tahitian god-figures.' *Journal Polynesian Society* 73,110-125.

Kooijman Simon. 1972. *Tapa in Polynesia. Bulletin* 234, BP Bishop Museum.

Krauss Bob. 1988. *Keneti: South Seas Adventures of Kenneth Emory.* University of Hawaii Press.

Lamb Jonathan, Vanessa Smith, Nicholas Thomas. 2000. *Exploration & Exchange: a South Seas Anthology.* University of Chicago Press.

Lang John Dunmore. 1877. *Origin and migrations of the Polynesian nation; demonstrating their original discovery and progressive settlement of the continent of America.* Sampson Low, Marston, Low, & Searle, London.

Langdon Robert. 2009. *Kon-Tiki Revisited.* Australian Scholarly Publishing, Melbourne.

Lange Raeburn. 2005. *Island Ministers: Indigenous Leadership in Nineteenth Century Pacific Islands Christianity*. Macmillan Brown, Canterbury, and Pandanus Books, Canberra.

Lee Ida. 1920. *Captain Bligh's 2nd Voyage to the South Sea*. Longmans, Green, London.

Lewis CT Courtney. 1908. *George Baxter (Colour Printer) His Life and Work*. Sampson Low, Marston, London.

Lewis David. 1972. *We, the Navigators, the Ancient Art of Landfinding in the Pacific*. University Press Hawaii, Honolulu.

Lincoln Margarette (ed). 1998. *Science and Exploration in the Pacific*. Boydell Press. Woodbridge, Suffolk.

Lingenfelter Richard E. 1967. *Presses of the Pacific Islands*. The Plantin Press, Los Angeles.

Love John. nd; ca late 1790s. *Addresses to the people of Otaheite designed to assist the labour of missionaries and other instructors of the ignorant*. T Gillet, London.

Lovett Richard. 1899. *The History of the London Missionary Society, 1795-1845*. 2 Vols. Oxford University Press, London.

[Lucett Edward] 'A Merchant'. 1851. *Rovings in the Pacific from 1837 to 1849, with a glance at California*. 2 Vols. Longman, Brown, Green, Longmans, London.

Mackaness George. 1931. *The Life of Vice-Admiral William Bligh*. Farrar & Rinehart, New York.

Marsden Rev JB. 1858. *Memoirs of the Life and Labours of the Rev Samuel Marsden, of Paramatta, Senior Chaplain of New South Wales; and his early connexion with the Missions to New Zealand and Tahiti*. W Clowes & Sons, London.

Martin John. 1827. *An Account of the Natives of the Tonga Islands in the South Pacific Ocean with an Original Grammar and Vocabulary of their Language Compiled and Arranged from the Extensive Communications of Mr William Mariner, Several Years Resident in those Islands*. 2 Vols. Constable, Edinburgh. (An excellent, early account of life on Tonga: William Mariner at age 15 was the lone survivor of the wreck of the English whaler *Port au Prince* in 1806. Mariner was adopted by the 'king', lived in Tonga for four years, returned to England, and became a stockbroker. His account was compiled by Dr John Martin and published in 1817.)

Mayer Carol E and Anthony Shelton (eds). 2009. *The Museum of Anthropology of the University of British Columbia*. Douglas & McIntyre, Vancouver.

Miller Edward. 1974. *That Noble Cabinet: A History of the British Museum*. Ohio University Press.

Mitzman Max. 1978. *George Baxter and the Baxter Prints*. David & Charles, Newton Abbott.

Montgomery James. 1832. *Journal of Voyages and Travels by the Rev. Daniel Tyerman and George Bennet, Esq. deputed from the London Missionary Society, to visit their various Stations in the South Sea Islands, China, India &c. between the years 1821 and 1829*. 1st American Edition, 3 Vols. Crocker & Brewster, Boston. (1st London edition 2 Vols. Westley & Davies 1831; 2nd 'corrected' edition with the title *Voyages and travels round the world . . .* , 1 Vol. 1841. John Snow, London.)

Morrell WP. 1960. *Britain in the Pacific Islands*. Oxford.

Morison John. 1814. (New edition 1844.) *The Fathers and Founders of the London Missionary Society: A Jubilee Memorial including a sketch of the Origin and Progress of the Institution*. Fisher, Son, & Co., London. (An account of the formation of the LMS; includes 36 biographical sketches and 21 portraits of the principal founders.)

Morrison James. Owen Rutter (ed). 1935. *The Journal of James Morrison, boatswain's mate of The Bounty, describing the mutiny & subsequent misfortunes of the mutineers together with an account of the Island of Tahiti*. Golden Cockerel Press, London. (See p. 2, f8; this journal has recently been republished, edited by D Maxton.)

Morrison James. Donald Maxton (ed). 2010. *After the Bounty. A sailor's account of the mutiny and life in the South Seas*. Potomac Books, Washington.

[Mortimer Mrs Thomas.] 1838. *The Night of Toil; or a familiar account of the labours of the first missionaries in the South Sea Islands*. J Hatchard, London. (Written for youths.)

Murray Archibald Wright. 1888. *The Bible in the Pacific*. J Nisbet & Co, London.

Musée de l'Homme. 1972. *La Découverte de la Polynésie*. Paris.

Neich Roger. 2007. 'Tongan figures: from Goddesses to Missionary Trophies to Masterpieces.' *Journal Polynesian Society* 116,213-268.

Neich Roger. 2009. 'James Edge-Partington (1854-1930): An ethnologist of independent means.' *Records of the Auckland Museum* 46,57-110.

Neich Roger and Mike Pendergrast. 1997. *Traditional Tapa Textiles of the Pacific*. Thames & Hudson, New York.

Newbury Colin. 1980. *Tahiti Nui; Change and Survival in French Polynesia 1767-1945*. University Press of Hawaii.

Newell Jennifer. 2003. 'Irresistible Objects: Collecting in the Pacific and Australia in the Reign of George III' in *Enlightenment*. K Sloan (ed). Smithsonian Books, Washington.

Newell Jenny. 2005. 'Exotic possessions: Polynesians and their Eighteenth-Century collecting.' *Journal of Museum Ethnography* 17,75-88.

O'Reilly Patrick and Édouard Reitman. 1967. *Bibliographie de Tahiti et de la Polynésie Française*. Publications de la Société des Océanistes N°14, Musée de l'Homme.

Orsmond John, see Teuira Henry.

Oldman William. 1953. *Polynesian Artifacts. Memoirs Polynesian Society*, vol 15.

Oliver Douglas L. 1974. *Ancient Tahitian Society*. 3 Vols. University of Hawaii Press.

Oliver Douglas. 1988. *Return to Tahiti: Bligh's Second Breadfruit Voyage*. University of Hawaii Press.

Parkinson Sydney. 1773. *A Journal of a Voyage to the South Seas, in His Majesty's Ship, the Endeavour*. Printed for Stanfield Parkinson, London.

Partington James Edge-. 1890, 1895, 1898. *An Album of the Weapons, Tools, and Ornaments Articles of Dress, &c of the Natives of the Pacific Islands Drawn and Described from Examples in Public & Private Collections in England*. 3 Vols. Private printing, J Edge-Partington & C Heape, Manchester.

Payne Ernest A. 1942. *The Church Awakes: The Story of the Modern Missionary Movement*. Edinburgh House Press, London.

Phillip Arthur. 1789. *The Voyage of Governor Phillip to Botany Bay with an Account of the Establishment of the Colonies of Port Jackson and Norfolk Island*. John Stockdale, London.

Pole Len. 1981. 'The Bennet collection in the Saffron Walden Museum'. *Museum Ethnographers Group, Newsletter N°11*. Ipswich.

Pole Len. 1987. *Worlds of man*. Saffron Walden Museum, Essex.

Porter William Smith. 1922. *Sheffield Literary and Philosophical Society. A centenary retrospect. 1822-1922*. JW Northend, Sheffield.

Pritchard George. 1844. *The Missionary's Reward; or, the Success of the Gospel in the Pacific*. John Snow, London.

Prout Ebenezer. 1843. *Memoirs of the Life of the Rev John Williams, Missionary to Polynesia*. John Snow, London.

Read Charles Hercules. 1892. 'On the Origin and Sacred Character of Certain Ornaments of the S.E. Pacific.' *J Roy Anthro Inst Gt Britain and Ireland* 21,139-159.

Rennie Neil. 1995. *Far-fetched Facts: The Literature of Travel and the Idea of the South Seas*. Clarendon Press, Oxford.

Richards Rhys and Robert Langdon. 2008. *Tahiti and the Society Islands. Shipping arrivals and departures 1767 to 1852*. Pacific Manuscripts Bureau and J-L Boglio Maritime Books. Australian National University Printing Service.

Robertson George. 1948. *The Discovery of Tahiti: A Journal of the Second Voyage of HMS Dolphin round the World, under the Command of Captain Wallis, RN, in the Years 1766, 1767, and 1768 written by her master George Robertson*. Hugh Carrington (ed). Hakluyt Society, London. (Robertson was first mate on the *Dolphin*; this is the fullest account of Wallis's voyage.)

Robertson George. 1955. *An Account of the Discovery of Tahiti, from the Journal of George Robertson, Master of the HMS Dolphin*. Oliver Warner (ed). The Bath Press, Avon.

Rose Roger. 1978. *Symbols of Sovereignty: Feather Girdles of Tahiti and Hawaii. Pacific Anthropological Records*, N°28. Bishop Museum Press.

Rose Roger. 1979. 'On the Origin and Diversity of "Tahitian" Janiform Fly Whisks.' In *Exploring the Visual Art of Oceania*. Sidney Mead (ed). University Press of Hawaii, Honolulu.

Routledge S & K. 1921. 'Notes on some archaeological remains in the Society and Austral Islands'. *J Roy Anthro Inst Gt Britain and Ireland* 51,438-455.

Rutter Owen, see Morrison 1935.

Ryskamp Charles and Frederick Pottle (eds). 1963. *Boswell: The Ominous Years, 1774-1776*. McGraw-Hill, New York.

Salmond Anne. 2003. *The Trial of the Cannibal Dog*. Yale, New Haven.

Savage Stephen. 1962. *A Dictionary of the Maori Language of Rarotonga*. Government Printing Office, Rarotonga. (Savage lived in Rarotonga 1894-1941.)

Schreiber Roy (ed). 2007. *Captain Bligh's second chance: an eyewitness account of his return to the South Seas By Lt George Tobin*. Chatham Publishing, London.

Seton Rosemary. 2011. 'Reconstructing the museum of the London Missionary Society.' *Material Religion*, in press.

Sharp Andrew. 1960. *The Discovery of the Pacific Islands*. Oxford University Press.

Sharp WD, JG Kahn, CM Polito and PV Kirch. 2010. 'Rapid evolution of ritual architecture in central Polynesia indicated by precise ^{230}Th/U coral dating.' *Proc Nat Acad Sci US* 107, 13234.

Shevill Ian. 1949. *"Pacific Conquest:" The History of 150 years of Missionary Progress in the South Pacific*. Robert Day, Son & Co., Sydney.

Sidney Edwin. 1834 (2nd edition). *The life of the Rev. Rowland Hill, A.M.* Baldwin & Craddock, London. (5 editions, 1834-61.)

Sinoto YH. 1966. 'Polynesia, 1963-4.' *Asian Perspectives* 9,48-61

Sivasundaram Sujit. 2005. *Nature and the Godly Empire: Science and Evangelical Mission in the Pacific 1795-1850*. Cambridge University Press.

Smith Bernard. 1985 (2nd edition). *European Vision and the South Pacific*. Yale University Press, New Haven.

Smith Keith Vincent. 2005. 'Tupaia's Sketchbook.' *eBritish Library Journal* 2005, article 10.

Smith Thomas. 1824. *The History and Origin of the Missionary Societies, containing faithful accounts of the voyages, travels, labours and successes of the various missionaries who have been sent out for the purpose of evangelizing the heathen and other unenlightened nations in different parts of the habitable globe compiled and arranged from authentic documents including the latest discoveries and embracing many valuable and curious facts connected with the spread of the gospel the whole forming a new and complete missionary repository*. 2 Vols. T Kelly & R Evans, London.

Smith Thomas and John Choules. 1837 (4th edition). *The Origin and History of Missions*. 2 Vols. Gould Kendall & Lincoln, Boston. (1st edition 1832.)

Smith William. 1813. *Journal of a voyage on the Missionary Ship Duff, to the Pacific Ocean in the years 1796,7,8,9,1800,1,2 &c. . . .* Collins & Co., New York.

Sparrman Anders. 1953. *A Voyage round the World with Captain James Cook in H.M.S. Resolution*. Robert Hale, London. (Originally published by Golden Cockerel Press 1944.)

Stanley Brian (ed). 2001. *Christian Missions and the Enlightenment*. Curzon Press, Richmond, Surrey.

Steadman David W. 2006. *Extinction and Biogeography of Tropical Pacific Birds*. University of Chicago Press.

Stimson J Frank with Donald Stanley Marshall. 1964. *A Dictionary of some Tuamotuan Dialects of the Polynesian Language*. Martinus Nijhoff, The Hague.

Stoddard A. 1841. *History of the Establishment and Progress of the Christian Religion in the Islands of the South Sea*. Tappan & Dennet, Boston. (Despite 1841 publication date, book primarily covers the *Duff* voyages and the early years of the Tahitian Mission; copy in Phillips Library PEM, 990 S8 681.)

Stolpe Hjalmar. 1890-1. 'Utvecklings-företeelser i naturfolkens ornamentik' *Ymer* 1890 193-250 and 1891 198-229. First English translation: 'On evolution in the ornamental art of savage peoples.' 1891-2. *Transactions of the Rochedale Literary and Scientific Society* 3. Reissued 1927 with preface by Henry Balfour.

Summers Catherine C. 1990. *Hawaiian Cordage. Pacific Anthropological Records*, N°39. Bishop Museum Press.

Sunderland JP & A[aron] Buzacott (eds). 1866. *Mission Life in the Islands of the South Pacific, being A Narrative of the Life and Labours of the Rev A Buzacott, Missionary of Rarotonga, for some time Co-worker with the Rev John Williams, Martyr of Erromanga.* John Snow, London.

Swan William. 1831. *Letters on Missions.* Perkins & Marvin, Boston, and Thames & Hudson, London.

Tewsley U and Johannes Andersen. 1926. *Zimmerman's account of the third voyage of Captain Cook, 1776-1780. Alexander Turnbull Library Bulletin* 2.

Thomson Robert. nd. *History of Tahiti.* See note under Davies' *History.*

Tregear Edward. 1891. *The Maori-Polynesian Comparative Dictionary.* Lyon & Blair, Wellington.

Trotter MM (ed). 1974. 'Prehistory of the Southern Cook Islands'. *Canterbury Museum Bulletin* 6.

Twells Alison. 1999. 'A Christian and Civilised Land: the British middle class and the civilising mission, 1820-1842.'

In *Gender, Civic Culture and Consumerism.* A Kidd and D Nicholls (eds). Manchester University Press.

Twells Alison. 2009. *The Civilising Mission and the English Middle Class, 1792-1850.* Palgrave Macmillan.

Tyerman Daniel & George Bennet, see Montgomery 1832.

Vancouver George. 1984. *A Voyage of Discovery to the North Pacific Ocean and Round the World 1791–1795.* WK Lamb (ed). 4 Vols. Hakluyt Society, London.

Waldegrave William. 1833. 'Extracts from the journal of William Waldegrave.' *J Roy Geogr Soc London* 3,168. (Captain Waldegrave RN, of the *Seringapatam*; Marquesas 1830, Raiatea 1833.)

Waldegrave William. 1836. 'Notices of Tahiti and Eimeo.' *The Christian Keepsake 1836.* Fisher Son & Co London.

Wallis Samuel. nd. *Extracts from Captain Wallis Journal*; manuscript, ca 1780-1800, British Library.

Williams John. 1837. *A Narrative of Missionary Enterprises in the South Sea Islands.* John Snow, 26 Paternoster Row, London. (Pagination differs among the many editions; text references here are to the 'sixth thousand' edition, 1838.)

Williamson Robert W. *1937. Religion and Social Organization in Central Polynesia.* Cambridge University Press, London.

Wood Arthur Skevington. 1957. *Thomas Haweis, 1734-1820.* S.P.C.K. London.

Woroncow Barbara. 1981. 'George Bennet: 1775-1841'. *Museum Ethnographers Group, Newsletter N°12.* Ipswich.

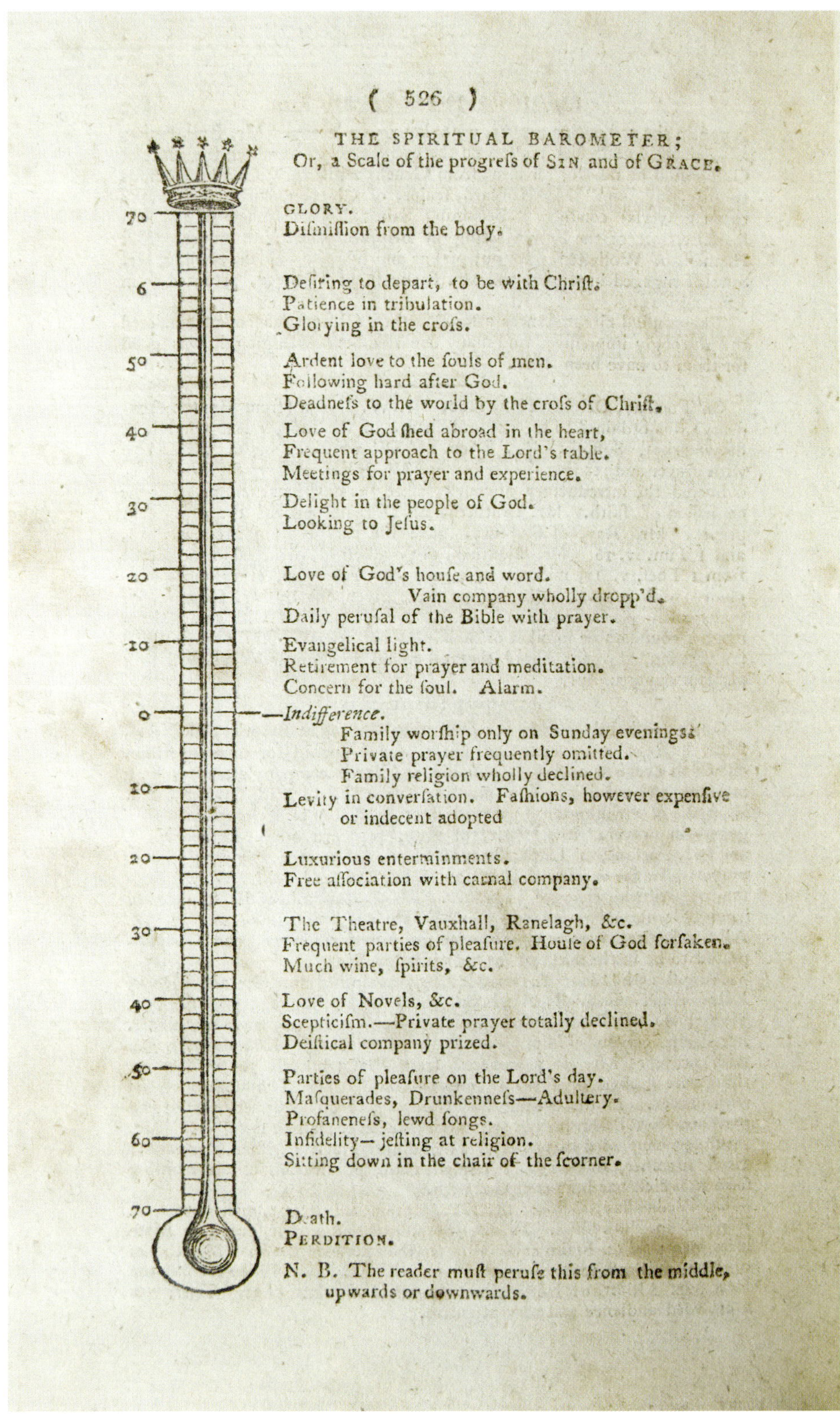

The Spiritual Barometer *from* Missionary Chronicle,
August 1824,526.

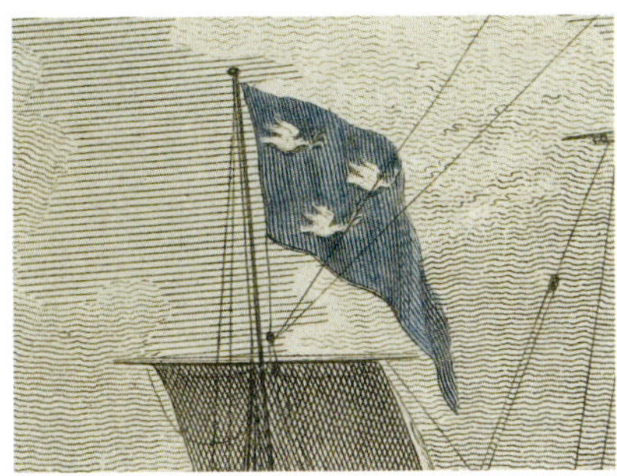

Index

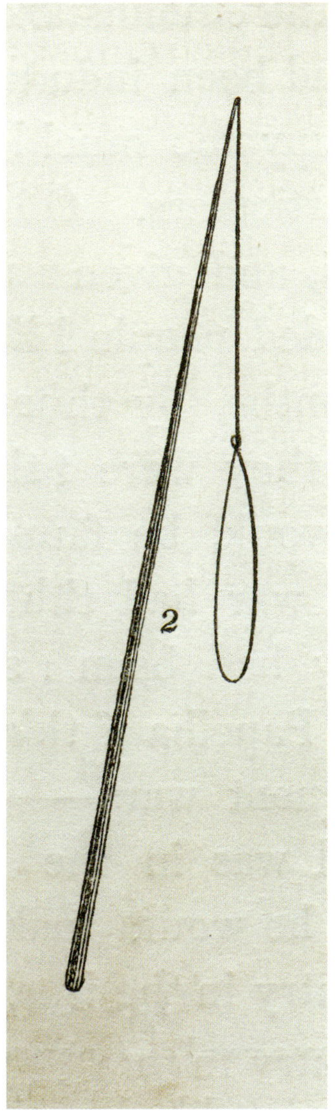

the snare for catching a god

The snare for catching a god, *Baxter wood engraving from Williams' Missionary Enterprises, 1837,65. See Appendix 6, page 187, Nº15 on Papeiha's list.*